IKE

IKE

His Life and Times

PIERS BRENDON

1817

HARPER & ROW, PUBLISHERS, New York
Cambridge, Philadelphia, San Francisco, Washington,
London, Mexico City, São Paulo, Singapore, Sydney

FIRST EDITION

Designer: C. Linda Dingler
Copy editor: Abigail Bok
Index by S. W. Cohen and Associates
Maps by David Charles, Kirkham Studios

Library of Congress Cataloging-in-Publication Data

Brendon, Piers.
  Ike: his life and times

  Bibliography: p.
  Includes index.
  1. Eisenhower, Dwight D. (Dwight David), 1890–1969.
2. Presidents—United States—Biography. 3. Generals—
United States—Biography. 4. United States. Army—
Biography. I. Title.
E836.B74   1986   973.921′092′4 [B]   85–45183
ISBN 0–06–015508–6

---

86 87 88 89 90 HC 10 9 8 7 6 5 4 3 2 1

To
Rupert *and* Sophia
with love

Contents

viii   CONTENTS

Maps and Illustrations

ILLUSTRATIONS

With the exceptions noted below, all photographs are courtesy of the Dwight D. Eisenhower Library, Abilene, Kansas.
Following page 112

The first known photo of Ike.

The Eisenhower brothers, 1895.

Abilene, Kansas, c. 1900. *Courtesy of the Dickinson County Historical Society.*

Belle Springs Creamery, Abilene, 1902.

The Eisenhower family, 1902.

Ike on a camping trip, c. 1907.

West Point football player, 1912.

Howitzer portrait.

Ike and Mamie—the wedding portrait.

Major Eisenhower with a "coffin on wheels."

Mamie, Icky, and Ike, 1919.

Acknowledgments

I would like to express my warmest gratitude to all who have helped with this book. I have received assistance from a great number of librarians and archivists on both sides of the Atlantic. In particular I must mention Elizabeth B. Mason of the Butler Library at Columbia University, James H. Hutson of the Library of Congress, and John E. Wickman, Martin M. Teasley, and Rod Soubers of the Dwight D. Eisenhower Library. The last of these, Rod Soubers, was particularly generous with his time and spent many weeks patiently guiding me through the vast collection at Abilene. I am also grateful to the staff of the British Library, the British Newspaper Library at Colindale, the Churchill College, the Seeley Library, and the Cambridge University Library, where much of my work was done.

In the United States I received help and hospitality from many people. The welcome afforded by Abilene (largely through the mediation of Tom Sharpe) was especially warm. I am grateful to Jim Collins, Lynda and Tom Cummings, Henry Jameson (who shared his memories of Ike with me), and Connie Duggan and her family, with whom I spent some idyllic hours, riding Tonya's horses over the Kansas prairie. I am also grateful to Bob and Hannah Kaiser and their children, who made me feel at home in Washington, and to Mae Berger, who performed the same office in New York.

In addition I owe thanks to Barley Alison, Kathy Banks, Field Marshal Lord Carver, Don Cook, Richard Cohen, the late Professor Stephen Koss, Sally Quinn, Dr. Hew Strachan, and Dr. Jay Winter. Andrew Best cast his practiced eye over my manuscript and made countless valuable suggestions. Michael Beschloss took time off from writing his excellent study of the U-2 crisis, *Mayday* (Harper & Row, 1986), which he was kind enough to let me see before publication, to go through my own work with meticulous care and outstanding expertise. He has saved me from many errors, though, needless to say, I alone am responsible for any that remain.

I also thank Joseph Alsop for permission to publish extracts from his and his brother's papers in the Library of Congress.

This book could not have been completed without the word-processing skills of Avril Symonds, who cheerfully and accurately produced a coherent typescript from a jumble of handwritten drafts.

Finally, I must once more acknowledge the aid and comfort of my wife, Vyvyen, and my sons, George and Oliver. Their forbearance during the long periods I have spent closeted with Ike has been beyond praise and thanks.

Glossary of World War II Code Names

ANVIL	Invasion of southern France in 1944—renamed DRAGOON
BOLERO	Transport of American forces to Britain before the continental invasion
COBRA	American operation that led to the breakout in Normandy, 1944
DRAGOON	Invasion of southern France in 1944
GOODWOOD	Attempted British breakthrough in Normandy, 1944
HUSKY	Invasion of Sicily in 1943
MARKET GARDEN	Airborne assault on Arnhem, 1944
MULBERRY	Artificial harbor used during the Normandy invasion
OMAHA	The St. Laurent beach for the OVERLORD assault
OVERLORD	Invasion of northern France in 1944
PLUTO	Underwater oil pipeline used for the Normandy invasion
RED BALL	One-way express traffic route between the Normandy beaches and the front line in France
ROUNDUP	Projected invasion of France in 1943—renamed OVERLORD
SLEDGEHAMMER	Limited assault on Cotentin Peninsula projected for 1942
TORCH	Invasion of North Africa in 1942
TRIDENT	Washington conference between Roosevelt and Churchill, May 1943

TUBE ALLOYS	Anglo-American atomic bomb project
ULTRA	British decrypts of German codes
UTAH	The Varreville beach for the OVERLORD assault landings

Introduction

Anyone who lived, as I did, through the war years in Britain is likely to be fascinated by the character and career of Dwight D. Eisenhower: for Ike became the symbol of the Atlantic Alliance which crushed Nazi Germany, something that had seemed impossibly remote in 1940. Eisenhower even confessed, much to the disgust of General Patton, that he no longer thought like an American but like an Ally. The strains on Anglo-American unity during the war were intense, ranging as they did from atavistic national antipathies to divisions caused by the common language, from disagreements about grand strategy to personal rivalries between the leading figures on both sides. "There is only one thing worse than fighting with Allies," Churchill observed memorably, "and that is fighting without them."[1] Naturally most Britons welcomed the arrival of huge numbers of American troops in 1944 because it signified the imminent invasion of Europe. But there were serious tensions, and many repeated the familiar jibe that the Yanks were overpaid, oversexed, and over here —to which the stock response was that the Limeys were undersexed, underpaid, and under Eisenhower. This retort lost much of its sting simply because almost everyone in both nations, from public person-ages to private soldiers, really did like Ike. He had become the most persuasive advocate of harmony between the United Kingdom and the United States and the personification of the Allied will to win.

A small boy growing up in Cornwall, I was scarcely aware of the global struggle, let alone of the tensions between the Allies. As an infant I had spent some time in and around London during the Blitz. This was before my father was posted abroad, where he devoted several years, as he put it, to running away from the Japanese. (He was notably modest about his military achievements, once remarking that the bravest thing he did in the war was to push me through Hyde Park in my pram, accompanied by a long-haired, green-toenailed Quentin Crisp.) But the barrage balloons, the air-raid sirens, and the bombs quickly faded from my memory when we moved to the West Country, though I do recall sitting under the stairs of a rented house near Aldershot and asking my mother why she was shivering when it wasn't cold. Having known nothing else, I was hardly even conscious of the grim circumstances of the Home Front in the little Edwardian seaside resort of Bude. The blackout, gas masks, double summer time, ration books, lines, barbed wire on the beaches, pillboxes on the cliffs, tank traps on the commons, spy and submarine scares, evacuees both rough and smooth, tea leaves to clean the carpets, carrot flan which made you able to see in the dark, sinister varieties of fish which tasted of cod-liver oil, sausages so full of bread that it was a question whether they should be served with mustard or marmalade—these formed the accepted pattern of our existence. Then the Americans came.

They arrived in trucks and jeeps, parking in long khaki lines behind our terraced house. They changed the atmosphere literally as well as metaphorically, driving everywhere and overlaying the smell of horse dung with the stench of gas fumes, blotting out the clang of the canalside smithy with the roar of internal combustion engines. They were tough, rangy men with twanging accents familiar from the movies and weird Western expletives never heard before. They were open, amiable, gregarious, and above all generous. "Got any gum, chum?" became the first slogan my lips uttered and, like thousands of contemporaries, my jaws soon ached with chewing. From their fantastic abundance the Americans lavished a cornucopia of coffee, candy, Camels, corned beef (not to mention contraceptives) on the pinched people of northern Cornwall. It was as though a dozen Liberty ships, like the one that was wrecked at Bude in May 1944, had spilled their cargoes on the shore. I was introduced to bananas for the first time; oranges, rare and delicious luxury, were tossed to grasping youngsters from the backs of speeding jeeps. We got to know Ruddle's Rangers[2] best—the heroic commandos who stormed the cliffs at Pointe du Hoq on D-Day. Unlike other soldiers, they were actually billeted on the civilian population and became part of local families—a great boon for homesick young men. And they established friendships that have lasted for forty years, as the D-Day reunion, celebrated in 1984, affectingly demonstrated. They practiced climbing up and abseiling down the cliffs at Bude, and when they fired a huge gun from Compass Point half the ceilings in Breakwater Road fell down. One or two could sometimes be seen in the streets doing punishment duty by threading cigarette butts onto a piece of string. They hated the English food and sent home for more Hershey bars to distribute to us children at Christmas.

Perhaps the Americans first captured our imaginations through our stomachs. But their exploits during the last year of the war—the assault on Hitler's fortress Europe, the breakout in Normandy, the pursuit through France, the bitter battles on the German border, and the final destruction of the Third Reich—all this confirmed our feelings of affection and affinity. As supreme commander, Eisenhower was, of course, the chief focus and beneficiary of these emotions. He seemed a typical American and it was appropriate that he should be invested with the glamor of his countrymen. Apart from his looks, which were made for the role (always an important consideration with the military), he was in fact an odd sort of general, being modest, tolerant, candid, peace-loving, suggestible, and conciliatory to the point of weakness. He was an astonishing contrast to the flamboyant egotists, prima donnas to a man, who dominated the contemporary stage—Churchill, Roosevelt, de Gaulle, Montgomery, MacArthur, Patton. Yet in this people's war it was his qualities that appealed to the people. He had the charisma of a film star yet he exuded self-effacing moderation and natural good sense. Ike was the epitome of the common man. And he managed to convey his ordinariness in an extraordinary manner, not articulately—though he had the courage of his clichés—but by the projection of human warmth. On occasions Ike was also capable of something approaching eloquence. His famous speech at London's Guildhall in June 1945 (which included the words, "humility must always be the portion of any man who receives acclaim earned in blood of his followers and sacrifices of his friends")[3] was compared by British newspapers to the Gettysburg Address. It hit exactly the right note and generated hero worship amounting almost to ecstasy. The prevailing national mood when I attended the Victory Parade soon afterward was one of exhaustion rather than elation, of determination to build the future rather than to conjure with the past. There was even a revulsion against Churchill's leadership. Only the esteem felt for Eisenhower remained, in the glow of victory, undimmed. As his backer for the presidency, Cliff Roberts, wrote in a secret Republican report, Ike was "America's untarnished hero. No man in our lifetime ever achieved such an exalted place in the hearts and minds of the people."[4]

So we too liked Ike, and as a conservative youth I was as delighted as most Britons to see him winning his way to the White House in 1952. But disillusionment gradually set in and was all the more bitter when it came. There was Eisenhower's adoption of Richard M. Nixon as his vice-president—I was just old enough to recognize the Checkers speech for the Hollywood hokum it was. There were the shaming compromises with Senator Joseph McCarthy (in Britain, as in the United States, compared to Hitler) and with cold warriors among the Republicans. There was the nuclear brinkmanship of John Foster Dulles. There was Ike's incessant golfing with millionaires and the growing suspicion that he was doing a part-time job. "Ben Hogan for President," said one bumper sticker, "(If We've Got to Have a Golfer in the White House, Let's Have a Good One)."⁵ Then came the Suez crisis, Britain's epilogue of empire. At the time it divided the nation deeply and I sided with my mother against my father in supporting Eden's final, doomed essay in gunboat diplomacy. We were correspondingly hostile to Eisenhower's administration. Soon afterward, thoroughly ashamed of myself, I became a teenage radical; but by then I had other counts against Ike. The scandal of Little Rock reverberated throughout the world and to my dismay the president failed, despite much high-minded rhetoric, to take a stand on the issue of civil rights. His government's obsession with Communism led it to interfere openly or clandestinely all over the world—in Iran, Guatemala, Formosa, Cuba, Lebanon, the Congo—despite the danger of sparking an atomic war. Nothing seemed to convict Eisenhower's administration of mental and moral obliquity more devastatingly than the U-2 fiasco. Nothing seemed to sum up the achievements of his presidency more succinctly than the joke about the Eisenhower doll—you wind it up and it does nothing for eight years.

Worse still, however, televised press conferences mercilessly exposed the former idol's feet of clay. Eisenhower was the first television president, and his wartime glamor melted away under the glare of the klieg lights. The crisp, uniformed figure disappeared and in his place was an ailing, incoherent senior citizen, forever, as journalists liked to say, uttering "five-star generalities"⁶ and "crossing the thirty-eighth platitude."⁷ I remember in particular a ludicrously stilted television discussion, full of unctuous uplift, staged between Eisenhower and Harold Macmillan as though for an audience of imbeciles. Military intelligence, as we well knew in Britain, was a contradiction in terms and it was increasingly difficult to quell the suspicion that the brilliant commander who had won the war was a figment of the Allied propagandists' imaginations. Now Ike's compromising moderation looked like infirmity of purpose, his "statesmanlike" equivocations smacked at best of intellectual ineptitude and at worst of moral cowardice. Was not the president, like the general, adept at leading from behind? With his passion for sport and his addiction to pulp literature, Ike had long been recognized as a refreshingly simple man. But now his lack of culture seemed philistinism and his lack of sophistication seemed naïveté. His tortured syntax and garbled verbiage ("in these troubulous times," "in this nucular age")[8] appeared now to betoken not so much sincerity as stupidity. It seemed amusing in 1957 to greet Eisenhower's attack of aphasia by echoing Dorothy Parker's comment on the death of Calvin Coolidge: "How could they tell?" It was diverting to chortle with other undergraduates over Dwight MacDonald's anthology of *Parodies* (1960), which included Oliver Jensen's "Gettysburg Address in Eisenhowese" ("I haven't checked these figures but 87 years ago, I think it was, a number of individuals organised a governmental set-up here in this country, I believe it covered certain Eastern areas, with this idea they were following up based on a sort of national independence arrangement . . .") and then capped it with a real presidential speech which was more grotesque than the parody ("It is indeed, difficult, in the circumstances in which I find myself, to discover words that seem applicable to this situation . . .").[9] By the end of his second term Eisenhower had become for me, as for many, a figure of fun.

At a more serious level, Eisenhower's negative and unimaginative presidency seemed an altogether apt reflection of the tawdry decade of the 1950s. Seen from the restricted vantage point of their immediate aftermath, these were years of cold-war intransigence spent under the shadow of McCarthyism, years of inertia and stagnation when major problems such as racial injustice, pollution, and urban decay were ignored or postponed. They were years of rampant materialism, timid conformity, and reactionary cant. They were suburban, adolescent years, with *I Love Lucy* on the television, rock-'n'-roll on the record player, *The Power of Positive Thinking* on the bookshelf, tinned pet food in the refrigerator, and finned automobiles in the garage. They were years of Davy Crockett hats and crew-cut hair, of hula hoops and 3-D movies, of flying saucers and Sputniks. The Eisenhower age began with "Rudolph the Red-nosed Reindeer" on the valve radio and ended with Elvis Presley's "Blue Suede Shoes" on the transistor. No wonder that Norman Mailer called it "one of the worst decades in the history of man."[10] No wonder, after the pieties and velleities of Eisenhower, after what the Democrats unkindly called "the eight long years of golfing and goofing, of puttering and putting,"[11] of "the bland leading the bland," that we became entranced by his young, bold, smart successor, John F. Kennedy, who promised to get America moving again and who gave promise of a brave new world.

Needless to say, the promises were not fulfilled. Kennedy was assassinated, but not before he had become embroiled in the Bay of Pigs invasion and the Cuban missile crisis and had permitted the United States to move dangerously close to the vortex of Vietnam. Lyndon Johnson allowed the country to be sucked in completely, thus frustrating his ambition to build the great society. From his retirement Eisenhower publicly favored the war, though before his death in 1969 he was expressing private reservations about it: "open conflict is something that should be brought to an end as soon as possible . . . our people inevitably get tired of supporting involvements of this kind which go on and on for a long time, with no end in sight."[12] Ike barely survived to witness the trauma Vietnam inflicted on the psyche of America. And though in 1968 he endorsed the presidential candidacy of Richard Nixon—perhaps on the principle enunciated by a Republic hierarch during the "slush fund" imbroglio in 1952: "He may be a sonofabitch but he's *our* sonofabitch"[13]—Ike did not live to see Nixon's apotheosis at the climax of the Watergate scandal. Yet these two events, Vietnam and Watergate, had such a momentous impact on America that they affected not only the present and the future, but the past. Seen from the perspective of 1974, the prosperous, peaceful fifties seemed something of a golden age. And Eisenhower's administration appeared moderate, honorable, and wise. His reputation benefited from the simple fact that he was not Johnson or Nixon, or even General Alexander Haig, whose mode of speech made Ike sound like Pericles.

As a distant but sympathetic observer of the American scene I was somewhat skeptical about this changing interpretation. At the same time, in the recession-ridden seventies I was not immune to wistful yearning for the fifties, when, in the slogan that Harold Macmillan borrowed from George Meany, we had "never had it so good." However, I was now a professional historian. I appreciated the truth in the axiom that all history is contemporary history, that current preoccupations determine retrospective judgments. Was there any real reason to alter one's view of Ike, a view confirmed by the critical consensus of contemporary journalists, of whose work I had made a study? Certainly the revelations of Senator Church's committee in 1975 about CIA "dirty tricks" under Eisenhower—secret surveillance of and experiments on unsuspecting citizens at home, subversion and assassination abroad—hardly constituted an unequivocal tribute to his presidency. Again, it was easy to trace the roots of the Iranian crisis, in which President Carter's administration culminated so disastrously, back to the covert intervention in 1953 by which Eisenhower had placed the shah on the Peacock Throne. Finally, by the 1980s, did not the revised version of Eisenhower, his portrayal as a strong, active, and successful leader, owe more to political calculation than to historical reinterpretation? Those who now eulogize Eisenhower as a great statesman, a brilliant politician, and "a genius of the first order"[14] must be aware that they are thereby also assisting the cause of Ronald Reagan.

Of course, the similarities between the two gerontocrats are legion. Ike read nothing but Westerns and Reagan, who appeared in so many, is still apt to confuse cinema with vérité. Like Eisenhower, Reagan is a committed cold warrior who hankers to "roll back" Communism, preferring to do so by clandestine means rather than through open warfare. Like Eisenhower, Reagan achieves a magisterial detachment from contentious domestic issues, preferring to deal in religiose rhetoric. Yet there is no escaping the adamantine conservatism of both men. To accuse either of being illiberal is beside the point—it is (to paraphrase George Orwell) like accusing the pope of being a bad Protestant. Eisenhower's contemporaries were astonished that he somehow managed to remain "above criticism." One of them wrote, "As far as I know, no other President in our history was ever able to put over the idea that it is a disloyal action to say anything against him."[15] Reagan is jokingly known as "the Teflon president" because nothing sticks to him; his reputation remains untarnished by his shady entourage, by his personal gaffes, by the failure of his initiatives international and domestic.

Indeed, like Ike, Reagan seems to grow in stature with everything he does not do. Largely on the strength of personal charm, of sheer likability, Reagan has established himself securely, as Ike did, in the affections of middle-class, middle-brow, middle-of-the-road Middle America. He is the first president since Eisenhower to have transcended his role as party leader and enshrined himself as head of state. In view of these palpable resemblances, the recent revaluation of Ike is bound to send up Reagan's stock. To suggest, for example, that Ike's amiable amateurism was a better qualification for the presidency than the slick professionalism of "machine" politicians like Johnson, Nixon, or . . . Mondale, is clearly to promote Reagan. And, paradoxically, to assert that Eisenhower's avuncular manner and apparent shallowness masked a cool Machiavellianism is to imply that Reagan too has hidden depths.

On the other hand, like the most cursory student of the case, I could
not but realize that much of the reassessment of Eisenhower, even his
restoration to the war-hero's plinth of honor, owed as little to propaganda as it did to nostalgia. For one thing the process of revision has
been going on continuously since 1961, and even before that. As early
as 1956, for example, Samuel Lubell said that, contrary to the "widely
held image of Eisenhower as a five-star babe in the political woods,"
he was "a highly skilled professional, as compleat a political angler as
ever fished the White House."[16] Newspapermen like Arthur Krock
and Richard Rovere by no means shared their colleagues' low opinion
of Ike at the time, regarding him as a powerful and active leader.[17]
In the later sixties others, such as Murray Kempton, extolled Ike's
"marvelous intelligence" and concluded that he had been grossly
underestimated.[18] There followed a spate of articles and books, most
of which maintained that Ike was not the dull incompetent of myth
but a shrewd and vigorous chief executive, though there was more
accord about the man than about his achievement.[19]

This favorable verdict was largely sustained by the many scholars
who burrowed into the vast collection of original documents made
available for inspection at the Eisenhower Library in Ike's home town,
Abilene, Kansas, during the 1970s.[20] Former critics such as Arthur M.
Schlesinger, Jr., acknowledged that Eisenhower was a much abler man
than they had reckoned twenty years before.[21] Historians who had
placed Ike near the bottom in the pantheon of American presidents
now promoted him almost to the top, thus fulfilling the prophecy of
his special counsel Bernard Shanley: "Some day when all is known,
Eisenhower will rank with Washington and Lincoln, and not where he
has been presently relegated."[22] In particular, historians asserted what
has perhaps become the new orthodoxy about Eisenhower—that he
was a master of disguise, concealing his political adroitness beneath
a cloak of geniality, vagueness, and even ineptitude.[23]

There are, of course, several objections to this thesis. It places
Eisenhower in a moral vacuum, appraising him on the basis of crafty
means rather than worthy ends. It fails to reconcile the dexterity
claimed for his methods with the frustration of so many of his intentions. And it explains either too little or too much: too little in that
it does not show why a bright Ike should willingly have discredited
himself by pretending to dimness; too much in that it gives no clear
indication of where illusion ends and reality begins. This dialectical
technique, of representing something as the opposite of what it seems,
is capable of infinite extension and productive of infinite confusion.
Certainly I became confused when trying to pin Eisenhower down

while doing research for my recent biography of Winston Churchill. I also became intrigued, which is why I leaped at the chance of following that book with this life of Ike.

For an Englishman to undertake such a task in a field already crowded with American experts may be deemed rash, if not foolish. Yet even American academics find it hard to survey and assimilate the mass of books, monographs, dissertations, and articles about Eisenhower, let alone the documents on miles of shelves at Abilene. I have benefited from all these sources and I have done my best to distill the essential Eisenhower from the accumulation of print and manuscript. But I could not have attempted to pen a vital portrait of the man, set in the context of his age, without standing on the shoulders of eminent American scholars. In particular, like every future writer on Ike, I am deeply indebted to Stephen Ambrose, whose magisterial study enshrines a sophisticated version of the new orthodoxy. I am uneasily aware that in finding his interpretation not only too flattering but also insufficiently complex, I am taking issue with a great authority on the subject. But I hope that by examining Eisenhower from an unusual angle I may cast new light on a character that was at once as simple as skittles and as complicated as a conundrum.

That paradox, and indeed the paradoxical nature of almost everything about Eisenhower, explains, and I trust excuses, the insistent obtrusion of what he used to call "the vertical pronoun" into this introduction. For in my fluctuating attitude toward Ike I am nothing more than a fairly typical representative of my age—and in matters of historical testimony egotism is true modesty. Moreover, my various conversions—from admiration, through disdain, to critical regard—do not just reflect new perspectives afforded by the advance of years. Nor are they simply the product of historiographical reappraisals percolating down from academe. They mirror the real paradoxes of the president, the ambiguities of his career, and the countless barely reconcilable facets of his personality, all twinkling like the light from a cut-glass chandelier.

There is scarcely a single aspect of Ike's life or character about which the evidence is not conflicting or contradictory. Eisenhower was brought up in an atmosphere of intense piety and professed to be the most religious man he knew. Yet when chided by General MacArthur for never attending a place of worship Ike replied that he had "gone to the West Point Chapel so g.d. often," he was never going inside a church again.[24] As president, of course, he formally joined the Presbyterians and behaved in public as if God were honorary chairman of the Republican party. His private exclamations, however, remained a curious combination of the sacred and the profane—in the Cabinet, for example, he was liable to blurt out, "Goddamnit, we forgot the silent prayer."[25] Ike was a Midwesterner whose energies at high school and military academy were devoted almost exclusively to sport—so little did he aspire to be a member of the intelligentsia that he never learned to spell the word. Yet he was to be quite at home in cosmopolitan company and could hold his own in historical arguments with Winston Churchill. He could also correct his highbrow speech writer, Arthur Larson, for saying Alcibiades when he meant Aristides the Just. Ike graduated first out of 275 officers at the Command and General Staff School at Fort Leavenworth in 1926, and during the 1930s General MacArthur described him as the best officer in the army. Yet he spent sixteen years as a major, much of that time engaged in coaching football teams.

Assessments of Eisenhower's performance commanding Allied armies in battle ranged from the reverential to the contemptuous. Sir Frederick Morgan, who drew up the original plans for the Normandy landings, liked to intone, "There was a man sent from God and his name was Ike."[26] Field Marshal Montgomery stated flatly that Ike's "ignorance as to how to run a war is absolute and complete."[27] As a general Eisenhower changed his mind over every major military issue and many minor ones. Yet on 5 June 1944 he made the most momentous decision of the war and after the invasion of France he imposed a strategy that led to victory. As a civilian Ike was so irresolute that he sometimes found it difficult to choose which dinner jacket or tie to wear,[28] and one aide thought he resembled "a debate come to life."[29] Yet many who knew him well were impressed by his strength and firmness, and he certainly showed no hesitation in breaking off his romance with Kay Summersby immediately after the war. Eisenhower himself was indecisive about whether he was decisive, one minute confessing he was "a weak, vacillating and easily swayed individual,"[30] the next asserting that he was "a stubborn, stubborn Dutchman."[31]

Ike would never even acknowledge that he had resolved to seek the presidency of the United States. He had less trouble than most in being elected. But opinions differed about whether he was well equipped to hold the office, or even whether he could be classed as a politician at all. Sherman Adams, his chief of staff, said that the president never learned the art of politics. By contrast, Bernard Shanley declared that, despite Ike's protestations, "he was the best damn politician I ever saw or ever will see."[32] In the White House Eisenhower was, depending on whose view one accepts, either capable, well informed, and energetic or incompetent, ignorant, and idle. He either had a retentive memory, or conveniently selective powers of recall—or he was abysmally forgetful.

Nor was there agreement over whether Ike had the requisite intelligence to do the top job. David Lilienthal had reckoned him "one of the least profound men, I might say one of the most pleasantly superficial men of great reputation and achievement, I think, I have ever listened to."[33] But George Kennan, hearing the president sum up the conclusions of the "Solarium" study of American policy toward Russia, said that he "showed his intellectual ascendancy" over every one of the hundred or so experts in the room.[34] Even Ike's capacity for expressing ideas articulately, however—something about which the evidence might seem all too plain—was subject to controversy. Colleagues in government tended to claim that he was the master of spare and lucid prose, though he often indulged in deliberate obfuscation to conceal his purposes or simplified his words and adopted a pedestrian style in order to get across to the man digging a ditch in Kansas. Political opponents agreed with the press in thinking that his incoherence was entirely authentic—when Adlai Stevenson went to see Eisenhower in the White House before setting off on his Asian tour in 1953, he emerged muttering, "The man is a Jabberwock."[35]

Similarly the more nebulous qualities that contributed to Eisenhower's success are matters of dispute. Some found him bland and bonhomous, while others noted that there was substance in his jest, "I've got the most even disposition in the world—it's always bad."[36] They were also amazed by Ike's occasional "fiercely physical" rages, during which his voice would rise to a shout, his teeth grind, his cheeks flame like a Bessemer furnace, and "his arms wave threateningly."[37] Such apoplectic outbursts were as fleeting as summer storms, and Ike's charm was supposed to lie chiefly in the human warmth he radiated, a natural warmth that "could not be caught by headlines."[38] On the other hand, President Kennedy regarded him as "a terribly cold man,"[39] a view supported by veteran reporter Robert J. Donovan. Ike himself glowed in response to cheering crowds which he would afterward coolly dismiss as "yowling mobs."[40] Eisenhower's ponderous invocations to a sense of humor suggest that he did not possess one. Yet his frequent laughter reminded Henry Cabot Lodge of Thomas Jefferson's dictum that the first requirement of worldly success is good humor,[41] and Ike's infectious grin was his best campaigning asset.

Modesty was another attribute that was always eulogized in Eisenhower, who frequently alluded to his own "horror of self-praise."[42]

But, like MacArthur, Eisenhower hankered to design a distinctive general's uniform for himself and, according to the diplomat Robert D. Murphy, he only possessed the "externals of modesty; I think at times ego was evident."[43] Ike's admirers always commended his transparent honesty, but now they do so while simultaneously harping on his unrivaled capacity for dissimulation. In this artfully artless president, it seems, candor coexisted with casuistry, openness with concealment, sincerity with duplicity. Richard Nixon perhaps summed up this state of affairs best in his singularly revealing comment that, contrary to received opinion, Ike had been much more "complex" and "devious" than most people realized—but "in the best sense of those words."[44] Certainly Eisenhower's application of high ethical standards to the business of government was thought by many, not least himself, to be his political raison d'être. About Ike, as one of his staff put it, "the towering fact was integrity."[45] Yet one of Nelson Rockefeller's aides could affirm that Eisenhower was "the most immoral man I have ever known."[46]

Eisenhower's achievements were scarcely less paradoxical than his personality. He was a victorious general who was also a crusader for peace. He ended the war in Korea yet did much to set the scene for the war in Vietnam. He took a hard line against Communism but was reckoned soft by Nikita Khrushchev. He was haunted by fears of an atomic holocaust but sacrificed conventional forces to build up a massive nuclear arsenal. He proclaimed the need for restraint in the conduct of international affairs but turned the CIA into a secret army to impose his government's will throughout the world. He appeased Senator McCarthy but expressed satisfaction when during his first administration McCarthyism became "McCarthywasm." He passed the first civil rights bill in eighty years but had little enthusiasm for accomplishing equality between the races. He sympathized with the South but sent troops into Little Rock. He deplored state intervention but initiated the greatest interstate road-building program in history. He paid elaborate homage to the prerogatives of Congress but asserted the doctrine of executive privilege and strengthened the "imperial presidency." He championed the small man but was the associate of big business. He presided over lost opportunities during wasted years, but in the fifties the United States prospered as never before. He was a military man in a Cabinet full of industrial tycoons but issued the celebrated warning against "the military–industrial complex." He tried to recreate the Republican party in his own moderate image but found himself endorsing Goldwater, Nixon, and Reagan.

The task of tracing Eisenhower's voyage through life is complicated by a further puzzle. How far did he deliberately steer a middle course between dangerous extremes and how far did he simply drift with the tide of events or swing with the wind of public opinion? Ike liked to be liked and could inspire something close to idolatry in his acolytes. He enjoyed exerting his magnetic charm, and even if he was denied adulation he was accustomed to respect. Dulles was scarcely exaggerating when he told the president in 1956 that he (Ike) had "greater prestige throughout the world than any single man had ever had before."[47] While professing indifference to criticism, Eisenhower was acutely sensitive to it. His entire career can be seen as a selfish effort to do nothing that might jeopardize his popularity.

On the other hand, West Point had imbued Ike with devotion to duty, honor, and country, and he always aspired to serve a great united state rather than a Grand Old Party. He believed that common sense lay in consensus and he had an immoderate faith in moderation. He thought "extremes are crazy."[48] He refused to demean the office of the presidency by getting (as he put it) into "a pissing contest with a skunk" like Joe McCarthy,[49] or to degrade the "respectable image of American life before the world"[50] by tub thumping and name calling in the manner of President Truman. The role of the Allied commander, he thought, was to implement a joint strategy. The part of a democratic statesman was to execute the general will. Ike's whole existence can be represented as a selfless endeavor to realize his vision of the golden mean.

Eisenhower was a palimpsest of conflicting views on which the latest impression was the clearest. Yet he was also ambitious to make his own orthodox mark on the tablets of history. By exploring and resolving these paradoxes, not least by setting them in their proper historical context, I have endeavored to depict one of the most enigmatic characters ever to occupy the White House.

I

★

President of the Roughnecks

David Dwight Eisenhower was born on 14 October 1890 in Denison, Texas, during a fierce thunderstorm. He took his first name from his father, who was prone to read occult significance into worldly events, and perhaps wondered if the elements had contributed to his third son's tempestuous nature. Certainly Dwight (as he came to be called, in a reversal of Christian names designed to avoid domestic confusion) loved thunderstorms as a boy. And his behavior was correspondingly wild. His rages were so violent that he once threw a brick at the head of his eldest brother, and when frustrated he was capable of beating his fists to a bloody pulp against the trunk of a tree. His parents imposed severe discipline, his father with a maple switch, his mother by means of oft-repeated religious and moral precepts: "He who conquers his temper is greater than he who taketh the city."[1] Dwight —he was so named after the famous evangelist Dwight L. Moody— eventually learned a measure of self-control, which he always attributed to the excellence of his mother's instruction. Those who later witnessed his fiery outbursts of wrath, often snuffed out with the same sudden force with which they were ignited, sometimes reflected that his mother had done a much poorer job than he thought.

A century and a half before Dwight's birth his ancestors had emigrated from Europe in search of the freedom to practice their strict Protestant faith and the opportunity to cultivate a rich New World. The name Eisenhower means "iron hewer" in German (or perhaps more simply "smith"), and it was in Germany that the family originated. But its persecuted members had moved first to Switzerland, then to the Netherlands, and by the time Hans Nicol Eisenhauer (as it was then spelled) reached America in 1741 they were farmers. Hans's great-grandson Jacob (Dwight's grandfather) was born in

1826 and became a preacher as well as a tiller of the soil. In fact he was a leader of a sect known as the River Brethren, one of many Puritan or Mennonite splinter groups flourishing among the Pennsylvania Dutch. They were so called because of their practice of baptizing adult converts in the Susquehanna River. The Brethren were an exclusive congregation but one so loosely knit that during the Civil War the federal authorities doubted whether they were a true denomination and they had to adopt a formal title—the Brethren in Christ—to enable members to gain exemption from military service on conscientious grounds.[2] They set less store by outward forms and dogmas than by personal conviction and belief in the salvation of their souls. Yet, according to the familiar paradox, while believing themselves to be members of the elect by faith, they felt that they must prove it by works.

So they abstained from "all appearance of evil."[3] They lived lives of primitive simplicity, prohibiting tobacco, alcohol, cards, and the theater. They wore plain, old-fashioned clothes, the men adopting shallow-bowled black felt hats and the women clad in long dark dresses and bonnets. They studied the Scripture, convinced that it was the literal word of God. They held "inspirational services"[4] and love feasts, during which foot washing, testifying, and speaking in tongues took place. They were pacifists and refused to hold public office or (in many cases) to vote; instead they dedicated themselves to private enterprise, industry, piety, charity, and thrift. Like many of his fellows, Jacob Eisenhower was a skilled, progressive farmer, and he prospered. With his long hair, shaved upper lip, and bushy underbeard; with his austere mien and flashing eye; with his capacity to deliver eloquent sermons both in German (which he spoke at home) and in guttural English, Jacob was a formidable patriarch. He combined the intrepid independence of a pioneer, bent on taming the wilderness here below, with the ferocious self-restraint of a pilgrim anxious to cleave to the straight and narrow way leading to the celestial city.

Both these impulses led Jacob Eisenhower and a large company of the River Brethren to go west in 1879. By the late 1870s, Pennsylvania was crowded with settlers, often uncongenial ones. Kansas not only promised land but might become the Promised Land. The Indian menace had virtually disappeared—some Cheyennes had jumped the reservation in 1878, but this was the last Indian raid on Kansas. The buffalo had also gone—so many had been slaughtered in 1872 that literally acres of prairie had been covered with their drying hides. Similarly, the West was less wild now that the cattle kingdom was in decline, thanks to the spread of railroads and the adoption of new meat-processing techniques such as refrigeration. Barbed wire and improved agricultural methods meant that farmers on the plains could cultivate a larger acreage in safety.[5] The legislative and financial climates (land grants and easy credit) were as favorable as the weather itself—Kansas, though it suffered from ferocious extremes of temperature, enjoyed a beneficial wet cycle between 1878 and 1886. Of course, the exodus was not without its risks. In 1874, for example, Kansas had endured a plague of grasshoppers, which destroyed all vegetation and sometimes even halted trains, whose wheels could get no purchase on rails smothered in the oily mess of their squashed bodies. Nevertheless, the attractions of Dickinson County seemed to outweigh any such dangers.

The River Brethren carefully surveyed the area in advance, finding excellent alluvial soil, plenty of fresh water in streams bordered by cottonwood, oak, ash, elm, and walnut trees, not to mention flourishing orchards and rich grass. In 1879 Jacob Eisenhower, accompanied by his large family and several hundred of the Brethren, arrived in Kansas. Their move, including the selling of old property and the buying of new, was organized with remarkable efficiency. They brought with them fifteen carloads of household and farming equipment and half a million dollars in cash. Jacob and his wife, Rebecca, trusted in God, though not to the extent of some of the Brethren, who refused to insure their property; but they were determined to make the land flow with milk and honey. By taking great pains and indulging in few pleasures, they quickly made a success of the 160-acre farm which Jacob bought. It was situated close to the Smoky Hill River and not far from the sleepy little town of Abilene, which is itself only a few miles from the geographical center of the United States.

Abilene had passed through the most turbulent phase of its history a few years before the Eisenhowers arrived. Contrary to popular myth, the town had not been blown together by a Wizard-of-Oz-style tornado. It had grown up slowly during the late 1850s and early 1860s, though it remained "a small, dead place . . . of about one dozen log huts."[6] Then, between 1867 and 1871, the town boomed; it became the junction of the Chisholm Trail and the Kansas–Pacific railroad. For those four years Abilene was "the cow capital of the world."[7] Huge herds of Texas steers were driven there for transit to the East, the first major drive being led by Joseph McCoy, the real McCoy. Soon the town attracted hordes of saloon keepers, gamblers, thieves, whores, and desperadoes, who preyed on cowboys, buyers, and citizens alike. The effect of this influx can be gauged from a report in the *Western News* of 11 February 1870:

In the last three years there have been murdered in Abilene seventeen men; seven of these were murdered through the influence of fancy women and six were slaughtered through intemperance and drunken rows, the remaining four being murdered outright in cool hand-to-hand fights. Murder, lust, highway robbery and prostitutes run the town day and night. Decent women dare not walk the streets, and men who made the town dare not appear on her sidewalks.

At one time it was estimated that there were no fewer than one hundred prostitutes in Abilene, segregated in a stockade inside the red-light district just south of the tracks. One writer lamented that "youth and beauty, womanhood and manhood, were wrecked in this valley of perdition."[8]

But if, as it was said, Texas Street led straight from the open range to the delights of hell, another Abilene, north of the tracks, had its eyes firmly fixed on heaven, or at least on its secular substitute—respectability. The Topeka *Record* of 5 August 1871 drew attention to the contrast:

The north side is literary, religious, and commercial, . . . the south side . . . possesses the large hotels, the saloons, and the places where the "dealers in card board, bone and ivory" most do congregate. When you are on the north side of the track you are in Kansas, and hear sober and profitable conversation; . . . when you cross to the south side you are in Texas.[9]

That the north side of Abilene triumphed over the south was due not to the employment of Wild Bill Hickok as town marshal, but to the extension of the railroad, which moved the cattle terminus farther west. By the late seventies Abilene had settled into sedate and prudish middle age. But for those inclined to romance it never quite lost the glamor of its lawless youth.

David Eisenhower, one of Jacob's thirteen children, certainly appreciated Abilene's lurid past. He enjoyed recalling the excitements of the old West for his own sons, Dwight included, varying his Bible punching with tales of cow punching, cattle rustling and saloon-bar shootouts. No doubt this was innocent escapism: for David, who had been born in the year of Gettysburg and who was sixteen when the family made the great trek to Kansas, was raised according to the strict code of the Brethren. And he adhered to it all his life. But he did permit his fancy to stray into remote realms of mysticism: as a young man he possessed a huge chart showing how the dimensions and positions of the Egyptian pyramids prophesied events recorded in Scripture. Later in life he was more "concerned with the millennium" than with worldly affairs.[10] David soon demonstrated that he had an inquiring mind and that he was dissatisfied with the tedium of farming. With some difficulty he obtained his father's aid and consent to acquire further education at Lane University. This was a small Nonconformist college at Lecompton, imposingly named after Lincoln's friend Jim Lane, the demonic demagogue who was the first senator for Kansas. David was enrolled, aged twenty, and studied an incongruous assortment of subjects—rhetoric, penmanship, Greek, and mechanics. More important than the curriculum, however, was the fact that at Lane he met and fell in love with his future wife.

Ida Elizabeth Stover was a lively and attractive sister, so to speak, of the River Brethren. Born in Virginia in 1862, Ida also came from German-Swiss farming stock. Although she did not remember the horrors of the Civil War, the Stover family, like other peaceable Mennonites in the Shenandoah Valley, had suffered at the hands of both the Confederates and the Union Army as Sheridan pursued Grant's scorched-earth policy—an experience that may have contributed to the premature death of her mother. At any rate, pacifism for Ida became a passion: she later endured unpopularity and risked arrest because of her outspoken opposition (courageous in one with a German name) to the First World War. At Lane she was receiving tuition in English, history, and music, the last being the love of her life after religion. Hymn tunes were seldom off her lips, and she preserved her ebony piano through all vicissitudes. Ida complemented David, being vivacious where he was moody, dynamic where he was imaginative, gregarious where he was shy, extroverted where he was introspective, submissive where he was dominating, incorrigibly cheerful where he was prone to rages. They also complemented one another physically. He was large, dark, and stern; she was slim, brown-haired, and smiling. It was a smile of such radiance that it seemed to light up her soul and all her children, including Dwight, inherited it. Ike himself would say that his mother was "the happiest person he ever knew, in spite of great discouragements."[11]

David married Ida on his twenty-second birthday, 25 September 1885, and the couple never afterward, as far as anyone knew, exchanged a cross word. Jacob Eisenhower gave them the usual wedding present he reserved for his children, a sixty-acre farm and two thousand dollars. But David was determined not to work on the land—though his father insisted that it was peculiarly God's work—and he mortgaged the farm. The proceeds were invested in a general store which he opened, with a partner named Milton Good, in a village just south of Abilene called Hope. Unfortunately, as he must often have bitterly reflected, Hope did him no good, and neither did Good.

Within three years his store was bankrupt, his partner had absconded, and David's young family—their first child, Arthur, had arrived in 1886 and Ida was again pregnant—faced destitution.

What had caused the disaster it is now impossible to say. Perhaps David had spent more time above the store, luxuriating in his new-found domesticity, than in it. But more probably, since he was the embodiment of the Puritan work ethic, David had extended too much credit and simply become yet another victim of the slump which afflicted Kansas in 1888 with the ending of the wet weather cycle. As crops withered in the scorched earth, farmers could not pay their bills and mortgages were foreclosed. Even the bank at Hope, in which Jacob Eisenhower had an interest, crashed. Now many of the once-hopeful emigrants headed back east, often in covered wagons bearing the forlorn legend: "In God we trusted, in Kansas we busted."[12]

David Eisenhower also fled from Kansas, but he traveled south to Texas, where he obtained a job in the machine shop of the Cotton Belt Railroad at Denison, earning ten dollars a week. It is not clear whether he went primarily in search of employment or because he was so ashamed of his failure that he could not face the folks at home. What is certain is that the crash permanently blighted his life. This was true in the pecuniary sense, for he was always to remain relatively poor and anyway, as Ike later wrote, "having beaten back from this terrible reverse to a respectable position of retirement and financial holdings in 1929, he again found everything he owned went up in smoke."[13] But David was also a ruined man in the psychological sense. He now became even more repressed, severe, aloof, and mel-ancholic. He studied his Bible more intently and made work his sole recreation, as though to search out the causes and wipe out the effects of the disaster.

In fact Ida was left in Hope to pick up the pieces and to give birth to their second son, Edgar, who arrived in January 1889. After paying creditors and their grasping lawyer, she managed to save little from the wreck except her ebony piano. Then she joined David in Denison, where they eked out a frugal existence in a gabled frame house on the outskirts of the town. Inside this tiny refuge the atmosphere was doleful: David visibly bore the stigma of adversity, while even the buoyant Ida was disillusioned by the rapacity of lawyers and others which had attended their downfall. The view outside was equally cheerless: bales of cotton were stacked beside the railroad tracks in front of their house and herds of goats browsed on the meager vegeta-tion in the flat, dusty fields. These were the dour circumstances which surrounded the birth of Ida's third son, Dwight.

However, rescue was at hand. In the summer of 1890, shortly before Dwight's birth, his paternal grandmother, Rebecca, had died. Jacob, doubtless requiring his family's support, recalled the prodigal son. A job was found for David as a mechanic at the Belle Springs Creamery in Abilene, set up by the River Brethren to deal with their surplus of milk. So, early in 1891, David and Ida Eisenhower, with their two young sons and the infant Dwight, returned to Kansas. (Always proud of being a Kansan and not a Texan, Ike would later assert: "A chicken may hatch her eggs in the oven, but they're still not biscuits").[14] The Eisenhowers rented a tiny one-story shack, bare of any conveniences, on South East Second Street, Abilene. It was close to the creamery but on the wrong side of the tracks, in what had once been the most notorious part of the town, known variously as "Hell's Half-acre" and "the Devil's Addition."

There they stayed for the next seven years, while the family expanded apace. Roy was born in 1892, Paul in 1894 (he died of diphtheria in infancy), Earl in 1898, and finally Milton in 1899—Ida was so disappointed to have had another boy that she let Milton's hair grow, until he was four, in ringlets. However, the year before his appearance David and Ida, their home bursting at the seams, made their last move. They first rented and later bought the small, but substantial and attractive, two-story gabled house owned by his brother Abraham. He was going west to preach the Gospel and he wanted David to look after their ailing father. This they did until Jacob's death in 1906, themselves remaining in the house, now beautifully preserved on the site of the Eisenhower Library and Museum, for the rest of their lives.

There were hollyhocks in the yard of 201 South East Fourth Street and the property included an orchard full of cherry, apple, and pear trees, and three acres of land which enabled the family to be almost self-sufficient in food. There was also a large Dutch barn, scene of many mock and real adventures for the growing boys. But although it was a vast improvement on their previous dwelling, Abraham's house was still fairly primitive. There was no running water and no inside lavatory: baths were taken in a large tin washtub full of well water heated on the pot-bellied stove. There was no electricity until Dwight was fifteen; his childhood was illuminated by kerosene lamps and candles. Moreover, the accommodation was still cramped, and when a maid (who was paid two dollars a week) came to live in, the boys had to sleep four to a bedroom. With patriarchal vehemence David insisted that the household should be run on well-ordered lines. Ida, described by one of her relations as "a fine genteel woman,"[15] kept it prim and proper. Her parlor, in which the ebony piano took pride of place, was a shrine to social propriety.

During the Second World War reporters and biographers became eager to portray Ike as a prodigy. He responded by urging a friend to draft a heroic account of his life "starting from the time when I was a very brilliant and precocious baby."[16] There was, of course, nothing remarkable about Dwight's infancy. He was similarly ironical at the expense of those who tried to romanticize his childhood, though he did admit to his brother Edgar that it would not be difficult, given time, to "make you and me look like Tom Sawyer and Huckleberry Finn."[17] There were indeed similarities between Mark Twain's fictional urchins and the two Eisenhower brothers, nicknamed Big Ike and Little Ike. Edgar and Dwight often went barefoot and wore ragged, hand-me-down clothes. Almost from the cradle they were saddled with onerous chores. They were always short of toys, candy, and cash, and they tried to fill their pockets by a variety of juvenile expedients, including the humiliating one of peddling their vegetables to the richer citizens of Abilene north of the tracks. They played hooky, practical jokes, and games of all sorts. They roamed far and wide, loved fishing and hunting, got into scraps and scrapes. They read pulp magazines—on 27 December 1902 Dwight won second prize in the Picture Lesson Puzzle Competition organized by *The Boys' World,* perhaps the first time his name appeared in print.

The young Eisenhowers also filled their heads with tales of the Woolly West, some of them told by an old-timer who claimed to have been deputy to Wild Bill Hickok. The boys once even searched Abilene cemetery, without success, for traces of the six men said to have been killed by the famous marshal. In short the two Ikes, like most healthy small-town boys at the time, had all the instincts of Mark Twain's heroes, especially the violent ones. Edgar and Dwight were always coming to blows. Of course, the older brother invariably won, as he did in all their competitions except shooting—Ike later acknowledged, "I was just the tail to your kite."[18] But the younger would never admit defeat. Their parents seldom intervened, presumably on the grounds that it was natural for boys to fight and that anyway they had to learn to stand up for themselves. When Edgar became a lawyer and Dwight a soldier (both professions were anathema to their parents, though, again, they did not interfere), the martial younger brother sought revenge for all his childhood defeats and the judicious older one offered to meet him "with boxing gloves at forty paces."[19]

But if Dwight was permitted considerable freedom as a boy it was clearly limited by the authority of his devout parents and by the narrow circumstances of his upbringing. Ike later described his father as "breadwinner, Supreme Court, and Lord High Executioner."[20] David worked twelve hours a day at the creamery, imposed a rigid discipline on the household, and punished miscreants without mercy. Ike himself was often beaten for climbing onto the roof of the barn. The boys usually took their "lickings" like men, and as men believed that such treatment had been good for them as boys. But Dwight did once try to restrain his father physically from thrashing Edgar, exclaiming: "I don't think anyone ought to be whipped like that, not even a dog."[21] Their father was then, as Ike said, "the czar" as far as the conduct and training of the family was concerned; whereas their mother "talked more of standards, aspirations and opportunities."[22] Or, as Edgar put it, "Dad was the anchor" while "mother had the fire."[23]

Ida was, in Ike's words, the "tutor and manager."[24] She taught them the Bible with the unquestioning faith of one who had learned much of it by rote. She expected her sons to do likewise and gave Dwight a gold watch for reading the Good Book from start to finish. She also distributed the chores—cooking, cleaning, washing, wood chopping, feeding pigs and poultry, milking the cows, tending the crops, storing the produce, curing meat in the smokehouse—and she rotated the tasks among her sons in order to reduce their boredom. Dwight most hated rising at five o'clock to light the stove, and he devised a lazy way of minding the baby, rocking it with his foot while he lay reading. Ida fed the children, who might sometimes have gone hungry but for their large plot of land. Dwight evidently acquired his lifelong habit of bolting his food as a result of treating the end of grace as the signal for the eating race to start. Ida also clothed her boys, though in such motley and threadbare garb that the younger ones especially were little better than ragamuffins. Both Edgar and Dwight had to wear their mother's old button-top shoes to school, which made them a laughing-stock. Derision in turn, said Edgar, "made us scrappers."[25]

Certainly there was little other stimulus to be found in Abilene during the 1890s. By then the first-generation descendants of the frontiersmen who had hacked a town out of the hostile wilderness, and preserved it against cowboys as well as Indians, seem largely to have abandoned their sturdy individualism. The citizens of Abilene, like those on Sinclair Lewis's Midwestern *Main Street,* apparently allowed themselves to be "ironed into glossy mediocrity." The rule of orthodoxy became absolute. And the litany that Lewis recorded could be heard whenever boys like Dwight gathered around the crackerbarrel to nibble dried prunes and imbibe vernacular wisdom: all Socialists should be hanged; Europeans are wicked; it is not respectable to be too rich . . . or too poor; virgins are not as virginal as they used to be; wine bibbing leads to the gutter in this life and damnation in the next; the Republican party is the secular agent of the Almighty and of the Baptist church. The Nonconformist churches imposed a numbing conformity on Abilene, as to some extent they still do. When Ike was a boy the influence of religion was paramount in every sphere. It extended from family prayers and communal Bible study, via school and Sunday school (the Sabbath being strictly observed), to the evangelists in their pulpits. They mightily endorsed the status quo and unabashedly proselytized for secular conservatism, one reason why Kansas was a "dry" state. The churches also provided most of the social life, including the picnics which Dwight so enjoyed, not least because they enabled him to indulge his taste for fried chicken, potato salad, and apple pie.

Abilene could offer few headier excitements. It was a hard-working, law-abiding, tightly knit community of about four thousand people, none of whom was liable to surprise any of the others. There were distinctions of wealth but no class divisions. There was no conspicuous consumption—the Abilene stores offered little of note to consume— and social pretensions were anathema. Anyone who imported effete airs to Abilene would have been scorned. Ike was later to compare the antecedents of General MacArthur, whom he called an aristocrat, with his own: "I'm just folks. I come from the people, the ordinary people."[26] The outside world was doubtless full of snobbery and sin, but it was remote from Ike's straitlaced, inward-looking home town, and there was little awareness of it save as a vague menace.

For, by a strange paradox, to live at the center of a great continent bred a defensive, ghetto-like insularity. At its most reactionary, Midwestern conservatism became a kind of communal paranoia. This was epitomized by Colonel Robert R. McCormick's wildly bigoted newspaper, the Chicago *Tribune,* which felt itself to be surrounded by enemies—the British Empire to the north and east (New York was a suburb of London), Democrats and racists to the south, "nuts" and "freaks" to the west. Abilene was quieter and, they insisted, more tolerant. Seldom was heard a discouraging word, unless it was directed against Populist troublemakers or long-haired pinkoes. Instead there were expressions of intense local patriotism. Abilene may have had wooden sidewalks and unpaved streets (full of horses and buggies, and a few bicycles) but it was God's own town in God's own country. Its citizens saw nothing incongruous when General Eisenhower, in his famous Guildhall speech after the war, mentioned Abilene in the same breath as London.

Young Dwight was a typical product of this environment. All the accounts of his childhood confirm his essential ordinariness. All the more or less familiar anecdotes sustain the view that he was just another noisy, mischievous, inquisitive, good-hearted, grinning boy. The fact that he carried a torch for McKinley in 1896 did not mean that he was a fledgling Republican (though he later claimed never to have met a Democrat in his youth), but that he enjoyed the thrill of going on a torchlight parade. His juvenile fondness for guns—he had a muzzle-loader first, then a single-shot rifle, and finally a Winchester pump-action shotgun—did not betoken soldierly aspirations but a passion for hunting. His dangerous voyage on a homemade raft during the flood of 1903 was no symbolic anticipation of his taking the ship of state to the brink; it was simply a boyish adventure. His epic seventh-grade battle with Wesley Merrifield, when Little Ike would not yield to his larger opponent despite having taken terrible punishment, was no embryonic feat of arms but an adolescent fistfight. Everything was just what it seemed—his schoolboy interest in Hannibal and history, his taking part in debates, boxing matches, and poker games at the Tip-Top Restaurant, his preference for dying rather than having a poisoned leg amputated and never being able to play football again. Although, in the light of Ike's future career, all sorts of significance can easily be read into his early exploits, they should be taken at face value.

Nevertheless, they do reveal something of Ike's stubbornly combative nature. They point to his hail-fellow-well-met sociability, his life-long need to be part of a gang, one of a team. Obviously Dwight was a "regular guy" from his youth up. He always sought popularity with his peers. Being good-looking, self-confident, outgoing, and gregarious as only one raised in a large family can be, he always found it. He was intensely competitive and profoundly conventional. He took the standard part-time jobs—aged seven he was earning a nickel a day for delivering newspapers. He enjoyed the same recreations as his friends, played the same practical jokes they did, first shyly eschewed and later boldly pursued girls as they did. It is clear, too, that the young Dwight was, as he remained, more involved in backwoodsmanship than in bookishness. He learned more from an illiterate old hunter named Bob Davis (who taught him the arts of fishing and hunting and winning at poker) than from an inept physics teacher, whom he persecuted. Indeed, his education—first at Lincoln Elementary School, just across the road from his house, then at high school

—was meager. He was ever a mixture of active curiosity about practical matters and passive indifference to abstract ones. He never had much interest in, or sympathy for, culture, and out of the line of duty he invariably read not for intellectual stimulation but to avoid thinking altogether. He regarded grinds as "sissy" in youth, and as an adult he sneered at "short-haired women and long-haired men."[27] His presidential remark that "You have got to get the American people to understand that a football player is no more important than a person who does well in mathematics, or a good well-balanced student,"[28] was a comically backhanded tribute to the worth of scholarship.

It is true that in the classroom Dwight was taught how to write a decent theme. He also enjoyed spelling bees, learned some poetry by heart (including Kipling's "If"), and proved outstanding at mathematics and history. In fact he so excelled in the last subject—at any rate he displayed such a mastery of facts and dates—that his teachers commended him, and his classmates predicted that he would become a professor of history at Yale (whereas Edgar would serve two terms as president of the United States). So Dwight became a competent, if not an especially diligent, student. His logical mind and retentive memory enabled him to score the maximum grades with the minimum effort. But if he acquired some knowledge he made little attempt at a genuine understanding of anything apart from games. He was a keen, clean player of both baseball and football, though his considerable ability did not quite match the fanatical energy which he invested in these pursuits. Still, with his large, hamlike hands (all the Eisenhower brothers, said Edgar, had hands "like elephants' feet"),[29] his quick eye and his lithe, tough body (he was 5 feet 10 1/2 inches tall and weighed 150 pounds) Dwight could be an intimidating performer on the field. He was also a noisy one, encouraging his own side with constant shouts. Sport was so much the raison d'être of school for him that he actually returned there, aged twenty, not only to cram for the West Point entrance examination but to take part in a last season of football.

Dwight's choice of West Point was quite fortuitous and had nothing to do with any military ambitions, though he was later to claim that the newspaper reports of troops leaving to fight in the Spanish–American war had made him burn to be a soldier. In fact he was not principally concerned to equip himself for a career but to complete his education—which really meant playing football at college. In 1909 Edgar had gone off to study law at Michigan University; because his father would not support him while he qualified for such a reprobate profession, Dwight agreed to assist him instead. The understanding was that this help would be reciprocated the following year, when

Edgar would earn money and Dwight would enter Michigan. So Dwight took a job in the creamery, rising from iceman to stoker and then to night foreman. This was a task which gave him the leisure to play poker with his friends (he invariably won), to devour quantities of purloined ice cream, and to fry eggs on a shovel over the furnace. He also had time on wet afternoons to broaden his mind by reading big-city daily papers at the office of his friend Jim Howe's Abilene weekly *News,* and he was later to confess that "from boyhood days, newspaper work has always seemed to me to be clothed in an atmosphere of romance and adventure."[30] Much of Dwight's ninety dollars a month went to Edgar. But there was enough left over for him to buy the shotgun shells he needed for hunting. He was always accompanied on these expeditions by his adored, circus-trained fox-terrier bitch Flip, and sometimes by his younger brother Earl—Dwight would forge notes to enable him to play truant from school. Dwight could also afford to change his scruffy clothes for natty ones. This important and permanent transformation was precipitated by his acquiring (after a fleeting variety of other dates) a steady girlfriend.

She was attractive, red-haired and violet-eyed, and her name was Ruby Norman. To judge from the few extant letters which Dwight sent her from West Point, their relationship was an innocent, roguish affair. It was physical only in the sense that Dwight kept threatening to beat her black and blue and to pound her head off if she did not root for his football team. It was romantic only in a determinedly facetious way. Ike wrote to her,

I believe it would be great sport to play the leading role in one of these present day five cent (selling for a dollar and a half) novels—don't you? I'm not tall and graceful enough to be a Robert Chambers hero—nor big enough to be one of Jack London's. But just for an ordinary author, who is not too darn particular about his leading man—I might fill the place right nicely. All of which shows that if the price of aeroplanes doesn't come down, I'm going to have to quit business. (Perfectly harmless, ladies and gentlemen, he'll even eat out of your hand).[31]

Dwight called Ruby "dear," insisted that they were friends, and loved to hear her play the violin. She admired his "wonderful personality," "powerful physique," and "splendid intellect."[32] Perhaps she had a civilizing effect on him, though as late as 1913 he was still describing himself to her, in a phrase which aptly sums up Little Ike, as "the president of the roughnecks."[33]

Certainly after a year's work at the creamery, by the summer of 1910, Dwight was aspiring to higher things. But probably Ruby had less influence on him than a new friend, Everett "Swede" Hazlett. He was a local doctor's son whose uncritical affection and admiration for Ike lasted all his life. Actually after Abilene Hazlett pursued a naval career that was blighted by ill health, and they seldom met. But as president, Eisenhower was to write some of his longest and most intimate letters to Hazlett, explaining his actions, justifying his policies, trying out his ideas, and generally using "Swede" as a sort of ruminative wastepaper basket. The first fruit of their friendship was that Hazlett persuaded Little Ike to abandon his plan to follow Big Ike to Michigan—their arrangement for mutual support had in any case somehow collapsed. Instead Dwight should apply for a free place at Annapolis, where Swede himself was intending to train for the navy. But for an accident of history General Eisenhower might have been Admiral Eisenhower.

He obtained letters of recommendation from the leading citizens of Abilene to Republican Senator Joseph Bristow of Kansas soliciting his patronage. But although these doubtless contained enthusiastic tributes to his own qualities, not to mention his father's scrupulous promptness in paying his bills, they were ignored. Instead Bristow held an examination in Topeka to determine the best candidates on merit. This Dwight took in October 1910 and, despite having studied hard, he only managed to gain second place. The winner having plumped for the naval college, Bristow appointed Dwight to the military academy. Swede, disconsolate at the prospect of their separation, urged Dwight to ask Bristow for a transfer to Annapolis. But Dwight found that, at twenty, he was actually too old to be accepted there. Although he had claimed to be a year younger than he was in a letter to the senator, he would not (as Swede suggested) lie about his age to the naval academy. So Dwight accepted Bristow's appointment gratefully and applied himself to the scientific courses at Abilene High School. In January 1911 he went to Saint Louis, the farthest he had ever journeyed from home, and passed the West Point entrance exam with flying colors.

Ike's fate was thus determined, and he prepared to quit his happy home and the familiar environment of youth for the outside world and the challenges of man's estate. Despite a background of poverty and a jejune education he was surprisingly well equipped, partly because his character had been agreeably shaped by creative tensions and ambivalent circumstances. These had helped to make him what his country—and, as it turned out, what the American people—wanted, namely, a conventional individualist.

The paradox is crucial. From infancy upward Ike had been imbued

by his parents both with a respect for authority and with a reverence
for the worth of independent judgment. David and Ida, in their strict
adherence to the tenets of revealed religion, were true Nonconfor-
mists. They so valued their children's right to self-determination that,
despite their pacifism, they never protested about Dwight's choice of
career. Indeed, they regarded self-discipline and private devotion as
so much more important than formal affiliation to the church that in
due course they left the River Brethren. Ida eventually became a
Jehovah's Witness and David, taking the schismatic impulse of the
Brethren to its logical conclusion, ultimately refused to commit himself to any congregation of dogmatists. Ike obviously sympathized
with his father because, when urged by a Republican friend to join
a church in July 1952, he replied that he and his brothers had always
been "a little bit 'nonconformist' in the business of actual membership
of a particular sect or denomination [though] we were all very earnestly and seriously religious, we could not help being so considering
our upbringing." Ike had no real objections to belonging but said, "I
have always sort of treasured my independence."[34] The early signs of
that independence were his, and his brothers', progressive drift away
from the puritanical standards of their parents and toward the secular
mores of the professional class, particularly toward smoking, drinking,
gambling, and swearing. Indeed, nothing better illustrates how far Ike
had traveled from home than (what he was to call) his "frequently
fluent flow of Western Kansas profanity,"[35] especially (what an aide
called) his "familiar battle-cry . . . 'Jee-ss-uss Che-ee-rr-is-t.' "[36]

Similarly, the young Ike had been affected by the tension between
the zestful individualism of the old frontier cow town and the solid
Babbittry of the new, well-ordered commercial community. Of
course, as a boy Dwight had not experienced at first hand life as it had
been lived by the Stetsoned and chapped six-gun toters of the Wild
West. But the myth about these picturesque heroes, born even as they
were dying, was far more potent than the reality. Dwight not only
steeped his imagination in the romance of the frontier, he personally
engaged in many pioneering pursuits and aspired to embody the
backwoods virtues, especially resourcefulness and true grit. Competitive games were a kind of surrogate frontier for Dwight, a tamed and
domesticated adventure which called for the same qualities of courage
and initiative. They also gave the same reward in terms of excitement,
though they exacted less dire penalties for failure. Nothing ex-
hilarated Ike like sport. All his life he yearned to escape into the
artificial world of green turf or green baize, the moral equivalent of

the Western, there to engage in mock contention with golf clubs, footballs, playing cards, fishing rods or shotguns.

No doubt Ike's choice of a military career partly reflected a desire to recapture the piquant thrills of the frontier and to conjure up again opportunities for individual enterprise and bravery in the face of danger. At the same time the army provided a firm framework of traditional authority like that of Dwight's home life. This was imposed not only by the pervasive force of hierarchy and discipline but by an accepted code of custom. Officers adhered to the same set of standards, manners, and beliefs, as did the citizens of Abilene. And they all lived in what Dwight, despite his frontier fantasies, acknowledged to be the real world, the world of his seed time, the world epitomized by Abilene. It was a friendly, respectable, tradition-bound world, remote from the more brutal manifestations of emergent industrialism; a moderate, balanced, homogeneous world, which paid lip service and more to ethical and egalitarian ideals; a narrow, mealy-mouthed, hypocritical world, which preferred ancient prejudices to novel ideas and banished plain speaking along with abrasiveness; but a world of conciliation, compromise, simple verities, and common decency. So although Dwight's imagination rode the range, his intellect was suffused with the conservative values of Midwestern, small-town America. Carl Becker summed up the paradox in a seminal essay which concluded that "the fundamental characteristic of Kansas individualism is the tendency to conform."[37]

If the army gave more scope for individual initiative it also imposed more conformity than the safe, orthodox professions pursued by Dwight's brothers. Arthur, who briefly rented a room in the same boardinghouse as Harry Truman, worked himself up to be a successful Kansas City banker. Edgar became an industrious and highly paid lawyer in Tacoma, one whose views were so right-wing that they often led him into fierce disputes with Ike. Roy remained closest to home, in Junction City, Kansas, where he set up as a pharmacist and established himself as a pillar of the community, a Republican, a mason, a member of the local chamber of commerce, a golfer, and a bridge player. Earl qualified as an electrical engineer and later got a job at La Grange, Illinois, as general manager of a biweekly newspaper, *Suburban Life*. Milton served as a government official, one sufficiently capable (and flexible) to earn, despite his Republican sympathies, the approval of New Dealers from Roosevelt and Henry Wallace downward. In 1943 he returned to academic life, becoming president first of Kansas State College and then of Pennsylvania State University.

When Ike entered the White House, Milton acted as his most trusted adviser and confidant. Thus all the Eisenhower boys adopted conventionally reputable and remunerative occupations and were suitably grateful to their industrious parents for enabling them to do so. Clearly respectable affluence was the earthly goal of the entire Eisenhower clan.

Dwight too aspired to raise himself in both status and standard of living, and he shared his brothers' admiration for solid commercial success. Indeed he was so set in the Midwestern mold that it was not unreasonable for later critics to assume that he would have reached his full potential as a charismatic president of the Abilene Elks. But this was to ignore the steely independence concealed behind Ike's hearty manner. It was to discount the calculating dexterity with which he promoted himself while retaining the protective coloring of good fellowship. It was to overlook the intrepid idealism which he camouflaged with stock sentiments. It was to miss the remarkable individual in the conformist group. Ida Eisenhower must have recognized that the handsomest of her sons was also the most adventurous, and she could do no other than foster his independence of spirit. But she was saddened both as a pacifist and as a mother when Dwight departed for West Point in June 1911. After he had left the house she went to her room and—for the first time in her youngest son Milton's experience —she wept.

2

⭐

Duty, Honor, Country

Dwight was on the best of terms with himself and with the rest of the world as he boarded the train at Abilene. He had striking looks, being an inch or so short of six feet tall and having a powerful body trained to a high pitch of fitness by athletics. His features were regular and his face was expressive almost to the point of elasticity. His light brown hair was thick, his blue-green eyes were large, and they lit up when he grinned with full lips the crooked grin that was to become famous. He had succeeded at school in both work and sport, had earned his own living for a year, had won his right to a free education, and had achieved a good measure of popularity in his home town, not least with members of the opposite sex. He had, it is true, no interest in culture or ideas, but there were few in Abilene to criticize him for that. Indeed, he was content to live on a superficial plane. Ike liked others and liked to be liked himself; and others found much about him to like—his charm, enthusiasm, modesty, and simplicity. Yet even at this stage he looked—in his overlarge, rustic clothes and rakishly angled cap—more simple than he was.

En route to West Point he stopped in Chicago to visit Ruby Norman, who was there studying the violin. He was evidently fond of her, but not fond enough to involve himself in any commitment. And the cautious words of his letters to her from West Point indicate an early capacity for equivocation, the political art of which he was to become as much a master in his way as that "Byzantine logothete" Woodrow Wilson:[1] "I'm not going to open up and tell you all I'd really like to this evening. No thank you—I want to hear from you. Although at one time I would have told it all—this business of being *friends* is different and I have to watch myself."[2] Moreover, when he again broke his journey, at Ann Arbor to see Edgar, Dwight did not allow himself to be diverted from his ambitious course by the attractions of the University of Michigan. The brothers hired a canoe and spent a romantic evening paddling on the Huron with a couple of female students. Not without a pang, Dwight left these voluptuous delights for the spartan rigors of Beast Barracks at the Military Academy, where upperclassmen concentrated on depriving their charges of any taint of civilian self-esteem.

The rationale behind the savage induction of the Beasts, as fledgling "plebes" (or freshmen) were called in their first three weeks, was that it was necessary to instill the foundations of discipline and military knowledge into them immediately. Thus Ike and the 264 other new cadets were "shouted at all day long by self-important upperclassmen" and kept "running, running, running."[3] But they were at the same time indoctrinated with high notions of tradition, ceremony, service, and the key concepts of duty, honor, country. They could not fail to be captivated by the imposing beauty of West Point, overlooking the Hudson River and itself overlooked by the ruins of Fort Putnam— which Ike loved to explore in his rare hours of leisure, working out tactical problems in his head and ruminating on what George Washington had considered to be the most important military position in America. The recruits proudly donned their gray uniforms. They watched the Cadet Corps march past while the band played martial music. They took the oath of allegiance, thus formally joining the United States Army. Ike was profoundly moved by this ritual: "Suddenly the flag itself meant something."[4] And his devotion to the Stars and Stripes was reinforced when he became color sergeant. During the Second World War he was to tell his son John, "I was very proud of it. No man can carry the national flag through a West Point year and not experience within him the growth of a certain patriotism that stays with him always."[5]

However, Eisenhower and his fellow Beasts—all white and nearly all Anglo-Saxon Protestants like himself, many from rural backgrounds in the South and Midwest, and very few gentlemen according to George C. Patton—were given little time to dwell on the more elevated purposes of their military apprenticeship. They were pushed from pillar to post at the double. They were taught the elements of drill to a cacophony of curses, inspected constantly, and subjected to a merciless hazing. This practice continued throughout the boiling summer camp, where they were obliged to perform humiliating chores for their seniors, and for the rest of the plebe year. It was actually an index of the decadence of West Point, unreformed and unreconstructed as it was during Ike's time there. For although there had always been more or less severe teasing, hazing in systematic form had been gradually introduced by the cadets themselves. Its function was to alleviate the boredom they suffered at an institution that was living almost entirely on the credit of its past prestige. The Military Academy was stagnant with tradition, and brutality had become a substitute for creativity. Senior cadets argued that hazing made soldierly men out of slovenly boys (and perhaps Ike did acquire his lifelong prejudice against slouchers as a Beast). But actually the practice amounted to deliberate bullying, sometimes even to torture, and in a number of notorious instances plebes suffered injury or death as a result.

Ike arrived at West Point when the system had reached what one authority calls "a fine flower of sadistic ingenuity."[6] Favored forms of torment were making plebes "brace" (stand exaggeratedly at attention for long periods), obliging them to eat unpalatable things such as soap, Tabasco, or prunes by the hundred, and ordering them to perform many exhausting, degrading, and dangerous exercises like "sitting on the bayonet" (George C. Marshall was nearly emasculated while doing this at the Virginia Military Institute). If fourth-class men resisted this treatment their seniors were liable to force them into bare-knuckle fights, an effective final sanction barely distinguished by Queensberry Rules from outright thuggery. Needless to say, quite a number of plebes, including Ike's first roommate, who came from Kansas and cried every night, could not endure this treatment and left. Ike himself, being older, sturdier, and more mature than most, was philosophical about it. He reflected simply that there was nowhere else he could get a free education.

He took the harsh conditions at West Point—designed by the father of the academy, Sylvanus Thayer, to form the characters of officers and gentlemen—in his stride. But he often eased his lot by bending or breaking the rules. Thus, for example, he rebelled against the disgusting food, smuggling in forbidden tidbits which he "enjoyed in the barracks after taps."[7] He also led raids by members of his own F Company, which included the tallest and most athletic recruits, on the "boodle," or secret food hoards, of "runt" companies. And, like other cadets, he deliberately flouted the prohibition against tobacco. Inevitably he earned demerits but, venerating the honor system as he was to do all his life, Ike often reported himself, taking his punishment like a man. In fact, as a contemporary said, he was a "happy go lucky . . . frontier kid,"[8] and he despised milksops who slavishly toed the line. They lacked drive and initiative, whereas he actually courted the wrath of his superiors. On one occasion, as he was fond of telling, he and another plebe took literally an order to report in "full-dress coat," the shorthand expression for full uniform. They presented themselves naked, apart from their coats, and though retribution was swift Ike reckoned the jest (an old one) was worth it.

He summed up his mutinous impulses in a semisatirical letter to Ruby Norman: "Fact is, I feel right devilish tonight, you know, just like I could smoke a cigarette, and swear and do all the other mean things like drinking pop and oh—I just know I'm awfully tough."[9] He was tough enough, at least, to endure the long tedium of his minutely regulated existence in that great neo-Gothic barracks. It was an existence passed under continual scrutiny and assessment, unbroken by any vacation during the first two years, and unalleviated by spending money or even basic comforts. The onerous daily routine had remained virtually unchanged since Grant was a cadet, as H. H. Arnold remarked. However, there was one major difference—which put the point in West Point as far as Ike was concerned—and that was the introduction of the football season and the primacy given, since the 1890s, to physical culture.

In part this reflected the growing national interest in sport, itself a result of increasing wealth and leisure, and of the determination, best expressed by Theodore Roosevelt, that in a competitive world America must be fit not only to survive but to progress. In part it was an attempt by the authorities to domesticate the animal spirits of the cadets in a way that would advertise the academy to the nation. The aim was to sublimate energies that had manifested themselves in sword fighting (sometimes lethal) or naked bathing (which shocked the susceptibilities of vigilant ladies across the river) and to transform horseplay into ballplay. The importance of athletic pursuits was symbolized by the new gymnasium, built in 1910, which superseded the first one erected only eighteen years earlier. Dwight thrived in this atmosphere and did well at all the most important sports, boxing, baseball, running, and gymnastics—he was so strong that he could pull himself up to a bar five times with his right hand, three times with his left. But he chiefly distinguished himself, in an institution obsessed by football, as a football fanatic. He worked, talked, thought, dreamed, and played football. He even ate football, stuffing himself with food to increase his weight. On the field he used his size, strength, speed, and stamina to impressive effect. He was also the embodiment of pugnacity and believed in getting in his retaliation first. "Watch that man!" shouted one opponent, pointing at Ike. "Why?" asked the referee, "Has he slugged you or roughed you up?" "No!" came the reply, "But he's *going* to!"[10]

In his plebe year Ike earned a place in the junior squad and in the autumn of 1912 his cup of happiness overflowed when he was promoted to West Point's varsity team. Within a few weeks the *New York Times* was hailing him as "one of the most promising backs in Eastern football." Unfortunately, before he could fulfill that promise Ike twisted his left knee in the same year's game against Tufts—an injury for which dozens of mature men were later to claim responsibility. Subsequent premature exercise at cavalry drill permanently damaged the tendons and the doctors told him that he would never play football again.

It was one of the worst blows he ever suffered and for a while it deprived his life of meaning. He several times came close to resigning from the army because he had lost the desire to excel. His "game pin" transformed "Sunny Jim," as Ike told Ruby Norman, into "Gloomy Face." As much as a year later he would write, "I never had such a protracted case of the blue devils in my life."[11] His work and behavior naturally suffered in consequence. He slipped from 57th out of 212 in his plebe year to 81st out of 177 as a yearling, and he was to graduate 125th in conduct. His misdemeanors included "late at 9:30 gym formation; shoes under bed dirty; failed to execute 'right into line' properly; alcove not in order; in room in improper uniform." He also swore a lot and talked interminably, especially after taps. Classmates described him as being good at "Mexican athletics," in other words "slinging the bull."[12] Nevertheless, Ike put on a brave front. When he returned to Abilene for a month in the summer of 1913, for his first furlough, he behaved like the conquering hero. He swaggered through town in his uniform, knocked out a black opponent in a boxing match, and pawned his gold watch to Earl in order to raise enough money to date a girl called Gladys Harding.

Evidently female company assuaged to some extent his miserable lot. Ike told Ruby Norman that he longed "to start one of those 'chance acquaintance romances.'" He also apparently invited a student from Vassar to West Point, "so Ike gets out his full dress-coat and plays the devoted swain for a day or so."[13] But his ardor was dampened by the punctilio of West Point. For when, despite one admonition, he whirled his partner around the floor so enthusiastically that she exposed her ankles, perhaps even her knees, he was "busted" from sergeant to private. He consoled himself by playing more poker, in defiance of the rules, and by singing (unmelodiously) songs like "Calamity Jane" and "Bury Me Not on the Lone Prairie." And he formed a Misogynists' Club with some classmates, vowing to remain indifferent to the charms of fair outsiders who attended the West

Point "hops." This did not stop him corresponding with female friends, especially on the subject of football, though he acknowledged to one, Natalie Brush, that he would be kidded "for a week for writing to a girl."[14]

Although he could not play football, Ike found some satisfaction in becoming a rousing cheerleader. He took a prominent part in all the pageantry of the sport, the processions, rallies, bonfires, chants, and shouts—it was regarded as a disgrace for cadets to be able to speak the day after a big match and Ike expected them to be hoarse for the following week. He designed black-and-gold cheesecloth capes which cadets could wear over their uniforms to spell out the word ARMY. And as a senior he coached the plebe football team, thus beginning a long career and providing the earliest instance of his inimitable brand of rhetoric: "Now fellers, it's just like this. I've been asked to say a few words this evening about this business. Now, me and Walter Camp we think. . . ."[15] But although Ike reveled in the vertiginous excitement of the contests, exhortation from the sidelines was no real substitute for participation on the field. He chafed inwardly, telling Ruby: *"Believe me,* if I was knocking around a little instead of being here—oh golly! Some *doin's!"* There was indeed one bright spot in that "trouble with Mexico seems imminent. We might stir up a little excitement yet. Let's hope so." But as it was, he complained, "I lead the darndest quietest humdrum existence you ever heard of—I can't even get sick."[16]

Certainly Ike received little or no stimulus from the academic curriculum at West Point, which seemed designed, as Douglas MacArthur remarked, to prepare cadets for the War of 1812.[17] The teaching methods—textbook recitation not far elevated above pure parrotry—had remained unchanged since Thayer's day. And the instructors, themselves complacent and often unthinking products of the system, were loath to improve on it. The course of study, with its heavy stress on mathematics and technical subjects such as engineering, was also old-fashioned, a relic of the time that West Point had been the foremost scientific school in the country. Cadets suffered accordingly. "Hap" Arnold, commander of the Army Air Force in the Second World War, never heard mention at the Military Academy of the Wright Brothers or their achievement. George Patton, who criticized some of his contemporaries for speaking ungrammatically, himself emerged from West Point barely literate—"I have trouble with the A, B, and—what do you call that other letter?"[18] The First World War taught the academy no new lessons during Ike's time—except that, contrary to what he had been told in lectures, it *was* possible for

European countries to carry on a war for more than thirty days. While soldiers were chewing barbed wire in the trenches of Flanders Ike and his classmates visited Gettysburg and learned cavalry tactics. No one was sent to Europe to study French or Spanish *because* of the war. In fact cadets were not educated beside the Hudson, they were trained according to narrow, antique modes to become patriotic Christian gentlemen. (The fortresslike chapel, built in 1910, symbolized the Church Militant.) As the secretary of war, Newton D. Baker, said firmly, "In the final analysis of the West Point product, character is the most precious component."[19] Character training produced sound subalterns capable of leading spit-and-polish regulars (though not a huge force of conscripts) into battle. It also produced generals who could look with stern and fearless gaze at any prospect, even that of Armageddon itself—and fail to see it. The United States Army was less well prepared for the First World War than for any conflict in the nation's history.

Yet paradoxically, in West Point song and story, Ike and his fellow graduates of 1915 became "the class the stars fell on." Altogether they won 111 stars, as 59 cadets out of the 164 who gained degrees eventually reached the rank of general. Of course, this was partly an accident of history. The class of 1915 was precisely the right age to benefit from the promotion explosion caused by the vast growth of the armed forces during the Second World War. However, those stars also reflected genuine military distinction, often earned in combat. At the very least West Point instilled moral qualities into its charges, challenged the livelier ones to seek their own professional salvation, and, within a rigid framework of conformity, gave scope to noncon-formists. Ike was such a one. When he produced a simple solution of his own to a mathematical problem, instead of the complex answer prescribed by the textbook, he only escaped rebuke through the inter-vention of a senior officer. After one unhappy experience of hazing —Ike mockingly suggested that one plebe looked like a barber, only to discover that he had been one—he abandoned the practice in disgust, though he never ceased to approve of it in theory. He never learned to wear his hat straight or to suppress his air of jauntiness. He yearned to march to the sound of guns, but he was placed in the awkward squad because he was so unmusical that he could not march in time with the band. In the satirical opinion of *The Howitzer* (1915) Ike was "the terrible Swedish Jew, as big as life and twice as natural," who excelled at "tea, tiddlywinks and talk."

Yet he accepted fundamentally and uncritically the code which West Point taught. At the time he called it a "Hell Hole"[20] and later said that if he and his fellows had had the leisure to think they would have left on the first train. But this was just soldierly grousing—a habit he never lost—and at the end of his life Ike concluded that the Military Academy "did more for me than any other institution."[21] This was surely because West Point confirmed the lessons he had learned in Abilene. Thus Ike was an individualist who extolled teamwork, a dissident disciplinarian, an average soldier with a gift for command. Perhaps they spoke with hindsight, but many of his contemporaries claimed that they "knew he was going to go places."[22] At the time Ike was prophesying greatness for his fellow member of the "jock" F Company, Omar Bradley (nicknamed Darwin for his supposed resemblance to an ape), though it would have seemed inconceivable to anyone that they would both eventually wear five stars.

In fact there was some doubt, in view of his knee injury, whether Ike would receive his commission at all. This did not especially concern him because he had formed "a curious ambition to go to the Argentine." He had become interested in gauchos, doubtless because of their resemblance to his cowboy heroes, and the country sounded "a little like the Old West."[23] He was drawn equally by the excitement of the frontier and by the allure of the army, but the latter offered him a secure and honorable profession as well as the prospect of danger and glory. In the end, therefore, having graduated a comfortable but undistinguished 61st out of 164, Ike was perhaps glad to accept his commission, which was given with the proviso that he join the infantry and not the cavalry. This was a curious stipulation, for presumably he would find riding easier than walking. But it was characteristic of a military bureaucracy which, for the first twenty-five years of his military career, seemed bent on thwarting him.

Its next stroke was to deprive him of a tour of duty in the Philippines. Ike had volunteered for this unpopular assignment because it promised more in the way of adventure than the routine life in one of the army posts scattered throughout the United States. And he was so confident that he would be sent abroad that he purchased cheap tropical kit and spent the rest of his uniform allowance in postgraduation celebrations while on leave in Abilene. He hunted, watched football, strutted around town, drank bootleg whiskey, played poker, and sang improper songs. Then, in September 1915, he received orders to report to Fort Sam Houston in San Antonio, Texas. So he had to borrow money from his father and go into debt with his tailor to acquire the correct outfit for a home posting.

As it turned out, Ike told Ruby Norman, his life at Fort Houston "is, in the main, uninteresting—nothing much doing—and I grind sometimes." With his debts and an income of only about 150 dollars a month, he was sadly short of cash with which to buy himself "a good time," and "toward the end of each month I have to hibernate and wait for pay day—Awful!"[24] However, there were compensations. Although he took his military duties seriously they were not heavy. He had plenty of leisure for shooting and riding and was able to supplement his pay by playing poker. He also acquired his "best friend," Leonard Gerow, a graduate of the Virginia Military Institute. Ike later described him as "intensely loyal—painstaking, energetic and possessed of a sound analytical mind . . . and a splendid personality." Actually Gerow lacked the warm and ingratiating personality of an Eisenhower, being simply the model of a meticulous staff officer. But it took Ike to recognize that he was also a fighter and, thanks to his friend's patronage, Gerow got the chance to distinguish himself as a combat commander in World War II. Ike thought that the neat, handsome, courteous Gerow possessed only one real fault: he was "a little too respectful of rank."[25] Eisenhower himself was less respectful. But he did defer to General Funston, who asked him to accept the invitation of a local military school to coach their football team. Ike did so with characteristic vigor and obtained successful results. He told Ruby (in handwriting still wayward but an improvement on the immature scrawl of his West Point letters) that the school "gave a dance not long ago at a big hotel, and I attended. When I entered the ballroom everybody stopped and started clapping and cheering. I blushed like a baby—Gee! surely was embarassed [sic]."[26] (Ike later professed to be a martinet on the subject of orthography, but his own spelling remained wayward.)

San Antonio was a rough city even at the beginning of the century, as Ike discovered while commanding patrols in its red-light district, where he several times came under fire. But it also had a delectably romantic aspect and was known as "the mother-in-law of the army" because so many of its daughters married into the service.[27] San Antonio was also, on account of its dry winter climate, something of a health resort, and among its pretty seasonal visitors no one was more eagerly awaited by young officers than Mamie (really Mary) Geneva Doud. The second of four daughters, she had been born in Boone, Iowa, on 14 November 1896, and was therefore six years younger than Ike. But when they met, in October 1915, there was an immediate mutual attraction. Mamie was drawn to Ike because he struck her as "a bruiser" at a distance, and on closer inspection she thought him "just about the handsomest male I have ever seen."[28] Ike was seduced by Mamie's dainty looks and saucy ways. She had rich brown hair, bright blue eyes, a pleasant oval face, and a slender, delicate figure. She breathed gaiety and vivacity, being by turns ebullient, demure, frivolous, and shy.

Like Ike, she was a thorough extrovert and loved being surrounded by admirers. Her education was even sketchier than his. Her father, a prosperous retired meat packer who doted on his "Puddin' " (as he called Mamie, after Puddn'head Wilson), had valued ladylike accomplishments above book learning. So Mamie had been "finished" at Miss Wolcott's fashionable school—its motto was "Noblesse Oblige" —near their substantial summer home on Lafayette Street in Denver. There she was instructed in the more decorative of the domestic arts. She learned to play the piano and sing. She also learned to flirt. Ike pressed his suit energetically and, with Mamie's compliance, soon elbowed all her other beaux out of the way. He persuaded not only Mamie (who disliked all sports except ice skating) but also her parents and sisters to support his football team. Together they made other expeditions, driving and fishing; and he took Mamie to cheap vaudeville shows and cheaper restaurants. He established an easy rapport with the whole family, including Mamie's large and forbidding father, aptly nicknamed Pooh-Bah. Fun bridged the evident social and financial gap between Ike and the Douds. As he wrote to Ruby in January 1916: "The girl I run around with is named Miss Doud, from Denver. Winters here. Pretty nice—but awful strong for Society—which often bores me. But we get along well together—and I'm at her house whenever I'm off duty—whether it's morning, noon, night. Her mother and sisters are fine—and we have lots of fun together."[29]

Ike was being somewhat disingenuous with his old flame about the passion he felt for his new one. At Christmas he had given Mamie a heart-shaped silver jewel case engraved with her initials, a present so lavish that it clearly signified the seriousness of his intentions. On Valentine's Day, after she had accepted his proposal of marriage, he gave her his West Point ring. The Douds were not altogether happy about the match. Mamie was only nineteen and immature for her age. Indeed, she never really did grow up: her mother still called her "Baby" and Ike always treated her like a baby doll. Mamie possessed no useful domestic skills, having been used to a full staff of servants, including a personal maid. She had no idea what life would be like on a first lieutenant's pay in the married quarters of an army barracks. John Doud was subsequently to give her an allowance of one hundred dollars a month, but at the time he promised nothing and counseled delay. However, Mamie was impatient and after about a month she announced their engagement during a party held in the "Garden of Allah" at an old theater on Alamo Plaza.

The announcement coincided with further troubles on the Mexican border and increasing fears that the United States would be drawn into the European conflict. Consequently, the army was expanding and President Wilson was, as the *New York Times* noted, changing his tune to "Johnny Get Your Gun." Ike volunteered to go on Brigadier John J. Pershing's punitive expedition against Pancho Villa but was ordered instead to train new recruits. He accomplished this task so efficiently that, ironically enough, the War Department decreed that he must stick to it, causing him to miss the battle experience he craved. However, in the spring of 1916 it seemed as if he might be off to war at any moment, so Ike and Mamie resolved to marry without delay. The wedding took place on 1 July 1916 in the gladioli-filled music room of the Douds' Denver house. Both bride and groom wore white, Mamie a gown of Chantilly lace, Ike his tropical dress uniform —he refused to sit down until after the ceremony in order not to spoil the razor-sharp crease in his trousers.

They spent two days of their honeymoon at Eldorado Springs, Colorado, and then went by train to Abilene, arriving at four o'clock in the morning. Mamie immediately endeared herself to David and Ida by saying how glad she was to have brothers at last. They welcomed her as their first daughter. It is not clear whether Ike and Mamie had their first quarrel at Abilene. She remembered being furious because, despite her remonstrations, he sat up half the night with friends in town playing poker. But when Ike read the story in Kenneth Davis's excellent account of his life he said that it destroyed his faith in biographies, because the incident had really occurred several years later. Whatever the truth, the couple were soon back at Fort Sam, where Mamie did her best to turn their two cramped, insect-infested rooms, bare of anything but a few sticks of miserable furniture, into a home. She smartened things up, bought flowers, and put up a plaque saying "Bless This House" (which was proudly displayed in every one of their future residences). She acquired bric-a-brac, rented a piano for five dollars a month, and made their quarters a lively center of evening entertainment for their many friends. Beer, cards, song, and good fellowship made this the first "Club Eisenhower" (as visitors named it) of many. Mamie, who possessed wit as well as grace and charm, called this time of newly wedded happiness her "potato salad days."

Mamie disliked slaving over a hot stove. Indeed, her culinary accomplishments were limited to making mayonnaise and fudge, so either Ike cooked or they ate in the officers' mess. Opening a doomed campaign that lasted all her life, Mamie did try to prevent Ike from eating his food like a starving bear. She had slightly more success in her efforts to instill a few other social graces into him, but he was always inclined to despise artificial refinement. Still, both accepted the patriarchal canons of the day whereby women minded domestic matters and manners while men concentrated on their work. The trouble was that Mamie was such a delicately nurtured Southern belle that she could scarcely cope with the practical side of home life. She could not even make a bed properly, let alone sew. Thus, despite his ideas about the woman's role, Ike took charge where necessary. For example, he let out her dresses when she became pregnant—despite his large hands Ike wielded a deft needle. Occasionally he was irritated by Mamie's helplessness and urged her to "grow up"—in due course she did learn to "squeeze a dollar until the eagle screamed."[30] But in general Ike seemed content to be the masterful male. He seldom talked shop at home and apparently found the very idea of his wife's venturing out alone in the automobile which John Doud had given them faintly comical. Mamie wanted the whole road as a driver, he noted, "and I must say she needed it."[31] Unfortunately Mamie in some respects lived up to the contemporary stereotype of femininity. According to an oft-repeated story, she once had to ask her husband to jump aboard the car because she did not know how to stop it.

Perhaps Ike would have had some sympathy with George Patton, who told his sweetheart that for a woman to like the army she must be "narrow minded, not over bright and half educated."[32] Like other army wives, Mamie was fated to endure long periods of monotony punctuated by sudden domestic upheavals. There is no doubt that in due course alcohol helped to alleviate her boredom, but the frequent moves—one a year on average until Ike settled into the White House and bought his farm at Gettysburg—proved a struggle. She found them particularly exhausting because, like her sisters, two of whom died young, Mamie had a weak constitution; and like her parents, who lived to a ripe old age and worried about their health all the time, she was inclined to valetudinarianism. She suffered from claustrophobia but could not walk any distance in the open. She hated the seaside, disliked going abroad, was afraid of flying, was prostrated by heat and cold, was terrified of insects, and became the victim of a host of complaints, physical and psychological. In 1954 Ike wrote that his wife "used to suffer very greatly from indigestion and heart flutter, which would make her extremely nervous and fearful, and the results were sometimes almost alarming."[33] Nevertheless, Mamie was tougher than she seemed and she outlived Ike by nearly a decade.

Mamie was evicted from her first married quarters in September 1917 when Ike was posted to Fort Oglethorpe in Georgia. Instead of getting the army to store or transport the nine hundred dollars worth of furniture they had acquired Mamie made the mistake of selling it —for ninety dollars. She then traveled to her parents' home in Denver to have her first baby. He was born on the twenty-fourth of the month and christened Doud Dwight, but was always known as Icky. Ike was bitterly disappointed not to be going to Europe with the expeditionary force which General Pershing had been organizing ever since America entered the war on 6 April. In fact, Eisenhower applied for an overseas posting so often that he received an official reprimand from the War Department. Gritting his teeth, he engaged in training recruits to fight in battles that he would never see. But his ideas of how to conduct them were probably no more unrealistic than those of Pershing, who was still demanding cavalry regiments as late as August 1918.[34]

It is clear that Ike was just too good at his job to be used as cannon fodder. He was a stern disciplinarian who meted out severe punishments—he once ordered an offending soldier to dig a grave-sized hole in the ground and then fill it up again. But he also knew how to inspire his men. One wrote in January 1918,

Our new Captain, Eisenhower by name, is, I believe, one of the most efficient and best Army officers in the country. He is a . . . corker and has put more into us in three days than we got in all the previous times we were here. He is a giant for build and at West Point was a noted football and physical culture fiend. He knows his job, is enthusiastic, can tell us what he wants us to do and is pretty human, though wickedly harsh and abrupt. . . . He has given us wonderful bayonet drills. He gets fellows' imaginations worked up and hollers and yells and makes us shout and stomp until we go tearing into the air as if we mean business.[35]

Consequently Ike kept being praised, promoted, and transferred to new locations to train the vast citizen army that was being created. The task was made more difficult by a disastrous shortage of arms: at Fort Riley, for example, General Leonard Wood, the chief apostle of military preparedness, was reduced to ordering the men of the Eighty-ninth Division to whittle rifles out of sticks.[36] In December 1917 Ike was sent to Fort Leavenworth in Kansas as instructor in the Army Service School. In February 1918 he went to Camp Meade, Maryland, to take part in forming one of the first tank battalions. This was largely a theoretical exercise, since there was an embarrassing absence of tanks—the United States had possessed none at the beginning of the war and no American tank ever reached the front.

Ike hoped to do so himself in the spring of 1918. Instead he was sent to Camp Colt in Gettysburg, Pennsylvania, to found a separate armored unit known as the Tank Corps. And as if to compensate for the fact that he and his ten thousand men lacked not only tanks but other basic equipment and supplies, including accommodation, fuel, and food, he was advanced in June to the brevet rank of major. At Camp Colt Ike scrounged, wheedled, and improvised brilliantly, using for the first time political arts to achieve military ends. Soon he had a smart, well-organized force, high in morale and trained to the limit of its logistical capacity. He even managed by the summer of 1918 to obtain a few tanks, two-man French Renaults. These minia- ture mechanical dinosaurs lumbered over the fields where once Union and Confederate troops had clashed so bloodily, where now Ike loved to roam with Mamie (who preferred to stay indoors), appraising the familiar ground with expert eye, and where they were finally to settle into the first home of their own.

Ike's achievement was recognized at once by his promotion, in October 1918, to the rank of temporary lieutenant-colonel and—after a decade's delay—by the award of the Distinguished Service Medal. The citation read: "he displayed unusual zeal, foresight and marked administrative ability in the organization and preparation for overseas service of technical troops of the Tank Corps." Ike himself was thrilled to receive orders to embark for overseas service in November. But at the eleventh hour—of the eleventh day, of the eleventh month of 1918—the armistice destroyed his hopes. Instead he faced the task of dealing with the impact on Camp Colt of the epidemic of Spanish flu, so virulent that it killed more people throughout the world than the war itself. Then he had to dismantle the camp altogether and play his part in the rapid demobilization of the millions of men under arms. America was desperate to return to "normalcy," which chiefly meant isolation—a return complicated first by Prohibition and then by the Depression. In any case the watchword, in a nation which had seen its debt rise during the war from just over one billion dollars to just under twenty-four billion, was economy. The army shrank to a peace- time complement that varied between 100,000 and 150,000 men, and no one heeded Cassandras like General Peyton C. Marsh, who warned that in the military sphere America had voluntarily made herself weaker than Germany, whose forces were limited by the Treaty of Versailles.

What concerned Ike was that the shrinkage of the service narrowed his field of action and restricted his opportunities to excel. There was no scope for valor and little for initiative. The top brass restored the conventions which had prevailed before the war, when, as George Marshall said, "It wasn't as if brains didn't exist in the Army . . . it was just hazardous to use them. You followed the book."[37] Moreover, as the army contracted in size Ike was reduced in rank. He became a captain once again in July 1920, and although he at once attained his majority there was no prospect of further promotion in the foreseeable future. In fact, thanks to the war and to his own endeavors, Ike's advancement had been relatively swift—it took Marshall, hailed by his superiors as a military genius, fourteen years to attain the rank of captain. What is more, in the tiny interwar establishment it was no small thing to be a major. As president, Eisenhower liked to say that the Defense Department could never deceive him because he knew the location of "every bald-headed major in the army."[38] Contained in this remark was a sardonic reflection on the sixteen years during which he lost most of his hair while pegged at this rank. What he never lost throughout this discouraging period was his spirit. In fact the disappointments of the First World War spurred him on to greater efforts and made him even more determined to shine. When he heard the news that hostilities had ceased Ike exclaimed vehemently, "I suppose we'll spend the rest of our lives explaining why we didn't get into this war. By God, from now on I am cutting myself a swath and will make up for this."[39]

3

★

Bald-Headed Major

Ike first hoped, after the war, to compensate for his lack of combat experience by helping to perfect a revolutionary form of warfare. Having completed short spells of duty at Camp Dix and Fort Benning, he returned in the spring of 1919 to Camp Meade. There he commanded a battalion and tried to explore, and to persuade the army to exploit, the possibilities of the tank. He was shortly joined in this endeavor by Major George C. Patton, Jr., who was said to have assaulted the Hindenburg Line during the Argonne offensive sitting astride a tank and waving a sword. Although Patton had been wounded in this battle—"missing half my bottom but otherwise all right"—he nevertheless concluded that the tank was not, as he had first thought, a "coffin on wheels."[1] On the contrary, properly developed and skillfully deployed en masse, it was capable of overrunning barbed wire, trenches, and machine guns. It could thus end the murderous defensive deadlock and restore mobility to warfare. Eisenhower and Patton shared the same vision, essentially a romantic one, of creating a mechanized cavalry. They thus looked simultaneously forward to the Blitzkrieg and back to a conflict in which mounted soldiers gave tone to what might otherwise have been a vulgar brawl. In an article written in the *Infantry Journal* (1920) Ike noted that the charge of a German cavalry brigade at Vionville in 1870 against the flank of the advancing French columns "saved an army corps from certain annihilation. . . . There is no doubt that in similar circumstances in the future tanks will be called upon to use their ability of swift movement and great firepower in this way."[2]

In view of the relative failure of tanks during the First World War —they had proved too slow, cumbersome, and unreliable—it was difficult to visualize their future potential. But Ike and Patton worked

hard with the few tanks at their disposal, light and heavy ones mod-
eled on the British Mark VII and the French Renault, respectively.
They drove the former to their screeching limit of fourteen miles per
hour, stripped one down and reassembled it, tested towing mech-
anisms—once a snapping cable nearly cut them off in their prime,
scaring them both (as they later ruefully acknowledged to each other)
half to death. Together the two majors evolved ideas about armored
warfare. They rejected the old concept of using tanks as mobile artillery platforms intended to support infantry. They published propaganda extolling the offensive capacity of full-grown versions of the
grotesque and premature war babies (as Patton called them) of 1918.
Ike wrote, "The tank is in its infancy and the great strides already
made in its mechanical improvement only point to greater ones still
to come. The clumsy, awkward, snail-like pace of the old tanks must
be forgotten, and in their place we must picture a speedy, reliable, and
efficient engine of war."[3]

All this, in the eyes of his military masters, was so much science
fiction. It is true that Ike and Patton had come to the same conclusions
(independently) as European experts such as J. F. C. Fuller and Basil
Liddell Hart, not to mention early and late champions of the tank like
Winston Churchill and Charles de Gaulle. But this seemed no reason
for the hidebound American War Department to abandon its aversion
to expense, its infatuation with cavalry, and its (somewhat inconsistent) preference for static slugging matches rather than rapid maneuver. In any case, the First World War had been fought to end war and
few yet realized that a peace had been made at Versailles to end peace.
Consequently no funds were spared for dubious experiments with
mechanized armor. By 1934 the U.S. Army had only a dozen tanks
in service which had been built since the war. And despite Patton's
advocacy, it had failed to invest in the potent prototype designed by
J. Walter Christie, who only saved himself from bankruptcy by selling
it to Russia where it was developed into the T-34, a better heavy tank
than anything available to American forces in World War II. Moreover, the two pioneers at Camp Meade were warned by their superiors
not to persist with their novel and dangerous heresies. It was said that
Patton in defiance ordered his own tanks from Sears Roebuck, but this
was a canard. As for Ike, he was actually threatened with court-martial
if he did not conform. He wrote, "With George's temper and my own
capacity for something more than mild irritation, there was surely
more steam around the Officers' Quarters than at the Post Laundry."[4]

However, out of this frustrated enthusiasm was forged a crucial and
lasting friendship. Patton had a mystical faith that he was destined to

be one of the great captains of history, indeed that he was somehow the reincarnation of the great captains of history. As a boy he had informed his father, "I would like to get killed in a great victory."[5] When told as a general (by Sir Harold Alexander) that he would have made a great marshal for Napoleon if he had lived at that time, Patton replied, "But I did."[6] Yet Patton recognized that Ike was, like himself, "a profound military student" who had devoted "years of thought and study" to the mastery of his craft.[7] And the older man was soon receiving premonitions that he would serve under Eisenhower in a global war. "Ike, you will be the Lee of the next war, and I will be your Jackson."[8]

Ike himself was less intuitive and less vainglorious. He was also less temperamental than Patton, less flamboyant, profane, impulsive, brutal, prejudiced, poetical, egotistical. And he was less rich. Patton had been brought up liberally in comfortable surroundings and had moved in high society. He played polo, had distinguished himself in the pentathlon during the Olympic Games of 1912, had taken épée lessons in France, and had married a wealthy woman in whom he inspired (despite his compulsive infidelities) a passionate hero worship. She wrote to him in 1919 for example, "George you are the fulfilment of all the ideals of manliness and high courage and bravery I have always held of you since I have known you."[9] Given to self-deprecation and averse to bombast, Ike was the antithesis of Patton.

Certainly he blended into the military scene better. Patton attracted attention wherever he went by his immaculate tailor-made uniforms and his swaggering, bullying, martinet manner—an especially smart salute was known as a Georgepatton. In any case, no one could ignore a man capable of shooting out chandeliers with the ivory-handled revolvers which, in defiance of decorum, he wore on his hips. Patton was notorious for his quicksilver moods, for his rapid shifts from charm to rudeness, violence to contrition, anger to flattery. With his boasts and self-doubts, his extreme right-wing bluster and his coarse oaths, all uttered in an incongruously high-pitched voice, Patton missed, as Ike was fond of telling him, countless opportunities to keep his mouth shut. Patton himself acknowledged that Ike was "probably right" when he informed people that he (Patton) was "crazy like a fox."[10] During the war Ike's task, a tricky one—he complained that it deprived him of his remaining hair—was to contain Patton's manic fury until such time as it could be unleashed on the enemy. Eisenhower advised him that "a certain sphinx-like quality upon occasion will do one hell of a lot toward enhancing one's reputation."[11]

Ike himself was, of course, living proof of the wisdom of this counsel. His entire relationship with the awkward, mercurial, talented Patton illustrates his infinite capacity to seem, if not to be, all things to all men. Tact became a way of life to Ike, whereas Patton (to paraphrase Winston Churchill on John Foster Dulles) was a bull who always carried his own china shop around. Or as Patton admitted in a rustic metaphor of his own, "I have no more gift for politics than a cow has for fox-hunting."[12] Naturally Ike and Patton were united by a common ambition to succeed in the profession of arms. But this did not preclude an element of rivalry and jealousy, which was to fester in Patton's soul and cause him privately to rail against Eisenhower during the war. For Patton was devoured by what he called a "self-sacrificing love of fame,"[13] while Ike's mode of self-promotion was subtle and elliptical.

By discouraging Ike's enthusiasm for tanks the authorities merely added to his already abundant leisure. The army provided many agreeable ways to fill it. In the summer of 1919, for example, Ike accompanied a military truck convoy on a journey right across the continent, which was designed to test the efficiency of both vehicles and roads. Neither showed to advantage, for the expedition proceeded, on average, at little more than a brisk walking pace; but the seed was sown which grew to fruition in President Eisenhower's ambitious interstate highway program. Ike relished the camping, the open-air cooking, and the constant horseplay en route. But Camp Meade also had much to offer in the way of enjoyable recreation and good company. Ike coached the post's football team and engaged in outdoor sports such as shooting and riding. He was a popular member of the Officers' Club and the Club Eisenhower was not less favored on account of the bootleg gin he brewed in the bathtub. Ike liked gardening and spent many quiet hours with Burpee's seed catalog in his lap. And when he and Patton wanted some real excitement they would arm themselves to the teeth and drive slowly down a dark road which was notorious for holdups—much to their disappointment they never met any bandits.

Altogether the army provided a most congenial way of life. It is true that (to paraphrase the popular song) the money did not roll in, but Mamie did not have to take in washing and they enjoyed complete security. There were also important fringe benefits, such as medical care, which Ike always valued highly. It was, moreover, a pleasantly cloistered existence. Ike was sheltered from the worst tensions and dislocations which accompanied the peace, from the police strike and the rum rebellion, the Klan revival and the Red scare. In fact, the external affair which seemed to concern him most immediately after the war was the World Series baseball scandal. Eight players for the Chicago White Sox were accused of having "thrown" the game against the Cincinnati Reds, and Ike, in an indignant hyperbole, denounced the corruption (never proved) as "an all-time low for disloyalty and sellout of integrity."[14]

In the army Ike was also insulated from the sharper effects of civilian disillusionment with war and the isolationist revulsion against Europe. It was widely rumored in the United States that the French had charged rent for the land on which the doughboys had dug their trenches. And American resentment toward the British, whose empire actually expanded as a result of Versailles yet who would not pay their war debts, was scarcely less pronounced. America had by no means lost sight of her manifest destiny, but never had foreign entanglements been viewed with greater suspicion than during the 1920s. Never had there been such emphasis on the horror, as opposed to the glamor, of war; never such aversion to militarism; never such willingness to embrace pacifism. Of course Eisenhower was aware of these developments and even, to some extent, sympathetic to them—he always felt that no military glory was worth the blood it cost. But he did not believe in disarmament, in negotiation from a position of weakness, or in turning the other cheek. And his views were confirmed by one of the most brilliant officers in the army, Major General Fox Conner, whom he met through George Patton.

Conner had been chief of operations at Pershing's headquarters in France. Together with George C. Marshall and one or two others, he had been responsible for the greatest achievement of American staff work during the First World War, the sudden shift of attack westward from the Saint-Mihiel salient to the Meuse–Argonne region. Conner was not only a profound student of warfare, he was an enormously influential figure in the stunted postwar army. Indeed, he has been described as a military gray eminence whose power was as extensive as it was well concealed. Ike impressed Conner (as he was to impress the other outstanding senior officers with whom he came in contact, notably Pershing himself, MacArthur, and Marshall) initially by his enthusiasm for tanks. Soon the amiable general was being charmed by Ike's relaxed "joshing" manner, which indicated his refusal to be unduly awed by rank. In due course Conner became for Ike not only a patron and teacher, but also something of a father figure. A decade or so later he wrote that Conner "has held a place in my affections for many years that no other, not even a relative, could obtain." Ike added that Conner was a "wonderful officer and leader with a splendid analytical mind. He is as loyal to subordinates as to superiors, and

. . . is quick to give credit to juniors."[15] Conner also liked to instruct his juniors, and the main lesson he taught Ike was that the pursuit of professional excellence was not just an end in itself. It was a means to help win the next war, which was inevitable, Conner asserted, within Ike's lifetime.

Nothing seemed more remote at the beginning of the 1920s. Far from contemplating further belligerency, the people of the United States were turning in on themselves and grappling with the domestic problems resulting from the war: unemployment, depression, labor disputes, race riots. But while trying to get back to business, America (or at any rate, booming urban America) was also hell-bent on pleasure. Bobbed hair and lipstick, short skirts and silk stockings, coonskin coats and hip flasks, cigarettes in public, psychoanalysis in private, cheek-to-cheek dancing in speakeasies, tin lizzies in the streets, skin-tight bathing suits on the beach, jazz on the radio, vamps in the movies, flappers in the polling booth, the departure of chaperones and the arrival of contraceptives—all seemed to signify a heedless hedonism. The most popular number of the day was a hymn to frivolity: "Yes, We Have No Bananas." And Ike's favorite song, "Abdul Abulbul Emir," was scarcely more serious, which did not stop him from singing it at length—he knew over fifty verses by heart.

The main factor in Ike's own happiness at this time was his small son Icky. Ike adored him, had bathed and fed him as a baby and loved to dandle the infant on his knee. Later Ike took him to watch football matches and ride in tanks, and played riotous games with him. With shocking suddenness, however, Icky's life was cut off. He caught scarlet fever from their maid and, after a fortnight's struggle against the disease, during which Ike could only watch helplessly, he died. This blow, which fell on 2 January 1921, was the most crushing Ike ever suffered and he mourned long and loud and bitterly. Mamie, who was equally (though silently) grief-stricken, later said that "it was as if a shining light had gone out of Ike's life. Throughout all the years that followed, the memory of those bleak days was a deep inner pain, that never seemed to diminish much."[16] Inevitably, Ike and Mamie blamed themselves and each other for the tragedy, and their own relationship deteriorated as a result. It seems that Ike never really communicated with Mamie on anything other than a superficial level, but now his reticence turned almost into coldness. The strain on their marriage did not lessen until after the arrival of their next child. Even then Ike was apparently not able to give his second son quite the unconditional love, let alone the indulgence, he had lavished on his first. Perhaps he had been too devastated by Icky's death to risk

engaging his affections so deeply again. One might even speculate that
the loss helped to harden Ike's character and blunt his emotional
responses, to lessen his dependence on others and make him more
ruthlessly self-regarding. At any rate, nothing could alleviate the pain
caused by Icky's death. Each year on the anniversary of his birthday
Ike would send Mamie flowers, and today Icky lies with his parents
at the Eisenhower chapel of rest in Abilene.

Anxious to get away from Camp Meade and its melancholy associa-
tions, Eisenhower was delighted to accept Fox Conner's invitation to
serve in Panama as executive officer in his brigade of infantry. Having
done his job with the football team, Ike packed up and took ship. He
was accompanied by Mamie, who was soon to find herself pregnant
again, and by their Model T Ford, which broke loose in a storm and
"raced round the deck to the eternal detriment of its finish and
shape."[17] However, in January 1922 they arrived safely at Camp
Gaillard, a jungle post overlooking the Panama Canal, where their
quarters consisted of a verminous shanty on stilts. Even worse than the
cockroaches, Mamie found, were the bats. Ike had to murder at least
one of these flying intruders with his dress sword, something of a
struggle as it was not a weapon with which he was particularly adept.

Ike's official task was to ensure that his section of the canal, the
Culebra Cut, was properly defended in the event of attack. This was
a remote contingency, but, as usual, Ike took his duties seriously. He
kept open the jungle trails, often exploring the difficult terrain on his
much-loved horse Blackie, which was so well trained that once, when
it fell into a swamp, Ike was able to stop its struggling and effect a
rescue. Ike instructed his men in the use of the Browning automatic
rifle and insisted that discipline and efficiency be maintained. Inevitably some of his colleagues felt that parade-ground smartness was not
appropriate to the tropics, and Ike's popularity suffered because "he
handled his job categorically, without kid gloves."[18]

For her part Mamie, who loathed the climate, the insects, and the
lack of social amenities, felt that the tropics were no place to have a
baby. So, with her hair now bobbed and banged, on account of the
heat rather than the fashion, she returned to Denver. There, on 3
August 1922, she gave birth to her second son, christened John Shel-
don Doud Eisenhower. Referring to the fact that his father's military
strictness extended into the home, John would later say that he was
born "standing at attention" and remained, figuratively, in that posture for many years. Indeed, John continued, perhaps he had not been
born at all but, like a top sergeant, issued. As he grew up John found
his father a "terrifying figure."[19] Partly this was on account of those

fierce paternal rages, though precisely because Ike feared his own temper, he never laid a hand on John. Partly the Eisenhowers' only child (as he remained) was intimidated by the passion which his parents, still grieving for Icky, now invested in him. Mamie smothered him with protective love, and Ike, compensating for this concern and in a sense complementing it, duplicated the paternal discipline which had helped to strengthen his own character.

Certainly in Panama Ike was demonstrating that the fruit of discipline was self-discipline. Whereas other officers amused themselves as best they could and tried to keep cool, he treated his three-year tour of duty as a course in military higher education, with Fox Conner as his willing tutor. Conner encouraged him to set aside his Westerns and make a serious and advanced study of the profession of arms. Ike converted part of the upper verandah of their house into a workroom and immersed himself in Clausewitz. He read biographies of generals like Napoleon and Grant, refought their old campaigns, and discussed their strategy with Conner. The two men were marvelously congenial, and they found time to go off on long fishing expeditions as well as to make an agreeable social life for themselves. But they talked soldiering interminably. Ike became intrigued by all aspects of war. When his old friend Swede Hazlett turned up at Panama in command of a submarine, nothing would satisfy Ike's curiosity but a detailed inspection of the vessel and a dive. Still, as Hazlett observed, Ike had not changed his nature, given up poker, or lost his ebullient sense of fun. He had by no means turned suddenly into a military intellectual. But, as Conner assured him, Ike was better equipped than anyone he knew to fulfill his ambition to attend the Command and General Staff School at Fort Leavenworth, Kansas.

This was the army's graduate college, and an officer who did well there would be singled out for promotion to the highest ranks. Ike, having blotted his copybook on the tank question and stereotyped himself neatly in the mind of the War Department as a football coach, experienced great difficulty in gaining entry to Leavenworth. He returned from Panama in September 1924, glad to leave the enervating climate and suffering from loss of weight and from the first twinges of the internal disorder which, he said, "seems to border on dyssentery [sic]."[20] The doctors attributed it to nervousness and lack of exercise but, to be on the safe side, Ike had his appendix taken out in August 1925 (without Mamie's knowledge). Not until Ike had his ileitis operation as president was the real malady, which plagued him intermittently for thirty years, discovered and cured. The appendectomy was a clearing of the decks for Leavenworth once Fox Conner had exerted his influence on Ike's behalf. The War Department, as Ike wrote, "moves in mysterious ways its blunders to perform."[21] It was not until he had completed two brief assignments, first as a football coach, then as a recruiting officer, that he was actually appointed to the Command School. On hearing the news he felt exultant: "ready to fly—and needed no airplane."[22]

Leavenworth was much more progressive than West Point: it was concerned not to win the war of 1812 but to prepare for that of 1914–1918. The rigid military philosophy of the Command School could be summed up in the famous (and mythical) pronouncement of Marshal Foch: "My right is driven in; my center is giving way; the situation is excellent, I attack."[23] In other words, constant aggression was the key to victory. Ike himself was influenced by this maxim. But he was unusual in foreseeing a war of movement, though he was quite willing to turn out model answers on approved lines. He certainly agreed with the orthodox view at Leavenworth that teamwork, especially among efficient and dedicated staff officers, was a surer method of winning wars than reliance on military genius. In fact, he was altogether skeptical of the notion of military genius, writing soon afterward, "There are no 'great men' as we understood that expression when we were shavers. The man whose brain is so all-embracing in its grasp of events, so infallible in its logic, and so swift in its formulation of perfect decisions, is only a figment of the imagination. Yet as kids we were taught to believe in the shibboleth of the 'superman.' "[24] Yet with this attitude, to which he adhered throughout life, Ike strove mightily for personal distinction during the punishing year he spent at Fort Leavenworth. Apart from discovering the delights of golf for the first time, Ike permitted no interruptions. With his friend Leonard Gerow, he labored day and night in a study at the top of his quarters. The pair were duly rewarded, Gerow coming in second out of the 275 officers in their class, while Ike, one-fifth of a mark ahead of him, was first.

Congratulations poured in and Ike celebrated with a large party at a hotel in Kansas City, which was enlivened by plenty of bootleg liquor and renderings of "Casey Jones" and "Steamboat Bill" from the principal. There followed a full family reunion at Abilene, in June 1926. Ike was a dutiful son who sent his parents gifts and returned home at least once a year when he was in the United States. And he made himself useful when he came, painting the barn, building a sidewalk, erecting a rose arbor, laying concrete foundations for the porch. But this was the only time that all the brothers, who were joined in what Edgar called "an unbreakable ring" of affection,[25] met

as adults. Together they indulged in their usual joking, teasing, rois-
tering, and arguing. The flavor of their relationship was well evoked
by Ike when, as supreme commander in Europe, he responded to
some knockabout fraternal criticism: "I am quite sure that all my
brothers reserve the right to point out my mistakes verbally and in
written form, possibly even by singing."[26] The Eisenhower brothers
swaggered through the streets of Abilene lined up abreast with arms
linked and played golf at the country club. They were entirely at ease
in their world. Edgar managed to avoid fighting Ike, but David Eisenhower, claiming to be "as good a man as ever he was," issued his own
challenge, and his soldier son had some difficulty in wrestling him to
the ground.[27]

Ike must have been mortified, after his triumph at Leavenworth,
when the War Department offered him nothing better than an assignment at Fort Benning, Georgia, to serve as executive officer to the
Twenty-fourth Infantry and . . . to coach another football team. But
once again Fox Conner used his influence, and in January 1927 Ike
was transferred to Washington to work for the formidable Black Jack
Pershing, who was head of the Battle Monuments Commission. Since
the tragic death of his wife and three of his four children in a fire in
1915, Pershing had become icily withdrawn. He invited no intimacy
with his subordinates, only requiring of them complete dedication to
their duties. Even the charm of an Eisenhower could not melt Pershing's taciturn frigidity. But Ike did earn the general's respect by the
efficiency with which he fulfilled his task of compiling a guidebook to
the U.S. battlefields of Europe.

In this he was ably assisted by his brother Milton, who had been a
journalist and a consul, and was now an official in the Department of
Agriculture. Milton also introduced him to many friends in both
government and the press, always asserting that he was a coming man
—though Milton's own career seemed much more promising at the
time. Among these new acquaintances was the handsome and sociable
Harry C. Butcher, then editor of the *Fertilizer Review* but shortly to
become an executive of the Columbia Broadcasting System. Butcher,
who was to accompany Ike to Europe as his "naval aide," had a vivid
memory of their first meeting. They were all performing parlor tricks,
and Ike did one that nobody else could imitate: standing to attention
he toppled stiffly forward until his face was about to hit the floor, when
he broke his fall by suddenly shooting out his large, strong hands.

Pershing was so pleased with the guidebook that he commended
Ike's "superior ability . . . unusual intelligence and constant devotion
to duty."[28] He also recommended him for a place at the army's War

College, Fort McNair, Washington. There Ike spent one of the most relaxed years of his career, for the course was not competitive and no final grading was given. So Ike merely attended lectures and seminars and studied in a desultory fashion. He did write one interesting research paper, annotated by Fox Conner, who became commandant of the War College while he was there. In it he argued that Congress should create a Regular Army Reserve because the service's active strength was now "at least 75,000 less than that essential to carry out its vital missions in an emergency."[29] Otherwise Ike had plenty of time for playing golf and entertaining his friends at the new Club Eisenhower, in Wyoming Apartments on Connecticut Avenue near Rock Creek Park.

Having set the seal on his military education by graduating in June 1928, he returned to the Battle Monuments Commission in order to produce a revised version of his guidebook, one based on a personal inspection of the battlefields. Actually Ike protested at this assignment, "I'm an Army officer, not a doggone Baedeker. I want to be with troops." But Mamie, who was never allowed by her frugal, even parsimonious, husband to forget their relatively straitened circumstances, thought it would be a wonderful opportunity to see Europe at the army's expense. They did, indeed, travel quite widely. And Ike traipsed over and appraised the still-ravaged killing grounds of the First World War, which provoked the exclamation, "Fox Conner must be wrong. Men can't be that crazy so soon again."[30]

But although they lived in Paris for over a year (in an apartment on the Quai d'Auteuil which they found unsatisfactory because its plumbing was antiquated, its heating insufficient, and it had no icebox) the Eisenhowers never aspired to be anything other than tourists. They mixed almost exclusively with Americans and took no interest in anything French—except the shops, which Mamie loved. It is true that Ike did try to learn the language, attending daily classes. But he could never get his tongue around it and he ended by speaking French with a wholly Kansan accent and a largely Kansan vocabulary. As one wartime journalist concluded, Ike had "absolutely no sophistication in the European sense."[31] Nevertheless, he found his time in Europe "very interesting" as well as enjoyable, "in spite of the old maidish attitude of my immediate superior." Ike was referring to the secretary of the commission, and his diary comment on how he handled their difficult relationship provides an early insight into his capacity as a military diplomatist: "I was not so successful as I should have been in concealing my impatience with some of his impossible ideas and methods. However, we are good friends . . . [though] I was not sufficiently suave and flattering."[32]

The Eisenhowers returned home on the eve of what John Maynard Keynes likened to a new Dark Age—the Great Depression. Doubtless to Ike's untutored eye everything seemed much as usual when their liner, the *Leviathan,* docked in New York, its skyline more rampant than ever, on 23 September 1929. Babe Ruth had hit over forty home runs that season. Miniature golf was about to become a fleeting craze, taking over from mah-jongg and crossword puzzles. Women's dresses were even flatter than before. *All Quiet on the Western Front* was at the top of the best-seller list. Rudy Vallee was the crooner of the moment. Bobby Jones was the golfer. Mickey Mouse had just arrived. Amos 'n' Andy were about to take the country by storm. But there were no thunderclouds on the horizon.

True, the orgy of stock-market speculation was continuing and, in the view of a few alarmists, Wall Street was "devouring all the money of the entire world."[33] Moreover, for a few weeks the New Era boom had been faltering. But this had happened before. Most people agreed with Calvin Coolidge, who with his genius for "alert inactivity"[34] had presided over the (admittedly patchy) prosperity of the mid-twenties, that the country was sound. Henry Ford certainly agreed, and the state of the automobile industry appeared to bear him out: in 1929 about 5.36 million cars were manufactured, which compares favorably with the figure of 5.7 million in the first full year of Eisenhower's presidency. With his new Model A, Ford seemed set to fulfill Herbert Hoover's election promise of "two cars in every garage"—Harry Truman's cynical comment that he meant "two families in every garage" was far in the future.[35] Yet within a month confidence gave way to panic. Share prices slumped disastrously and, unlike earlier financial crises, this one proved not to be temporary. Indeed, the Depression had such profound and lasting effects—cutting industrial production by half, putting thirteen million people out of work, causing many farmers to burn their underpriced corn to keep warm—that it was likened by a sober committee of the Social Science Research Council to the explosion of a bomb dropped in the midst of society. It was ironic that at the moment that the nation's peacetime economy was collapsing, Ike's new job was to make a study of how it could be mobilized in case of war.

Although Ike did "not like to live in a city," he looked forward "to the opportunity of learning something about the economic and industrial conditions that will probably prevail in this country in the event of a major war.''[36] So he embarked on a survey of the military–industrial potential of the United States. Clad in mufti he made extensive journeys, staying in cheap hotels and finding little by way of entertainment even in the movies—"Punk as usual" was his comment on one film, "Lord, but they are banal.''[37] Ike inspected factories, assessed priorities, explored ways to convert industry to a war footing and to procure synthetic substitutes for raw materials. He also met business leaders, among them Bernard Baruch. Accepting the need for financial incentives, Ike endorsed their opposition to a Congressional commission that was trying to banish war by minimizing its profits. All told, however, it would have been difficult to find an exercise more academic than the one on which Ike was engaged.

The irrelevance of his report was demonstrated by its reception. As Ike recalled years later, one of Herbert Hoover's staff sent him a note saying that the president was "far too busy to read such dribble as this —'that the Government is not thinking of a future war and has no intention of doing so'—and that was that." On the other hand, when the war did finally materialize, Bernard Baruch apparently told Ike that he had unearthed his "old study" and, while one recommendation (about rubber) was unhelpful, its "analysis of what would happen was quite valid and was very valuable.''[38]

If Ike was ignored by the White House, he was now winning golden opinions in the War Department. His boss in the office of the assistant secretary of war, Major General George Van Horn Moseley, paid him this glowing tribute: "You possess one of those exceptional minds which enables you to assemble and analyze a set of facts, always drawing sound conclusions and, equally important, you have the ability to express those conclusions in clear and convincing form.''[39] Moseley himself was thought by Secretary of War Patrick J. Hurley to have "the most brilliant mind in the entire Army,''[40] and Ike served him in a confidential capacity for three years, observing his views and translating them into directives. He reckoned that the thin, wiry, alert Moseley, who had been Pershing's chief of supply, would be "a peach" in the role of chief of staff. For Moseley worked "personally," not "organizationally," and was an enemy of ritual. He was also "likable" and "generous to a fault," especially to his juniors. Moreover, Moseley was "essentially honest and straightforward—very sensitive, but not unduly avid for self-advancement." Ike regarded him as "a splendid gentleman and a true friend.''[41]

The fact that Moseley's political creed was indistinguishable from Fascism apparently did not at all interfere with this friendship. Ike could scarcely have sympathized with the general's diatribes against

Jews, radicals, and unemployed veterans who, Moseley thought, should be placed in concentration camps on a desert island in the Hawaiian group where they could "stew in their own filth."[42] Perhaps Ike was able to interpret such nonsense as a maverick form of patriotism. More likely he was exhibiting premonitory signs of the moral tolerance—or indifference, or cowardice—which comported so uneasily with his moral professions, but which also enabled him to avoid clashing with the likes of Joseph McCarthy. Certainly Ike was able to gloss over any unpleasantness (his invariable tactic) and at least to appear sympathetic—Moseley extolled not only his brain but "that big heart of yours."[43] Moreover, if Ike was a consummate diplomatist on the personal level, Moseley recognized that he himself was an embarrassing extremist. During the war he advised Ike to avoid mentioning his name because to do so would be "a liability" to "your brilliant career."[44] During the grim years of the Depression, however, Moseley did much to promote that career, forecasting that Ike would go far and recommending that no limit should be placed on his progress.

4
★

Best Officer
in the Army

Ike acquired a new and even more powerful patron in the early 1930s, no less a person than the flamboyant chief of staff, General Douglas A. MacArthur. He quickly came to appreciate the worth of Moseley's assistant and quite soon was employing Major Eisenhower as an additional aide to draft his own speeches, reports, and letters. Several times Ike tried to escape this kind of staff work in Washington. At least once, when he unofficially applied to return to San Antonio in December 1931, this was as a result of "insistent" family pressure. "I hate the heat [of Texas]," he wrote, but "Mamie is concerned chiefly with getting a post where servants are good—cheap—plentiful." In any event, the job went to someone else. "What a break!!" exclaimed Ike, but his family continued to press for a move and he grumbled, "just another thing for me to worry about."[1] Usually, however, Ike made efforts of his own to obtain service with troops; but on each occasion MacArthur declined to release him. Ike was simultaneously frustrated and flattered. MacArthur was "very nice to me," he wrote in February 1932, "and after all I know of no greater compliment the bosses can give you than to want you to stay around."[2]

So although MacArthur "emphatically refused" to let him take at least one "marvelous opportunity" in 1933, Ike concluded, "I'm glad I'm staying with the general."[3] MacArthur assured Ike that "as long as he stays in the Army I am one of the people earmarked for his gang." He was also "very appreciative of good work" and extremely generous with praise for the "masterly and magnificent" job Ike did.[4] In one letter MacArthur congratulated Ike on being "an outstanding soldier" and continued,

Your unusual experience in the Department will be of no less future value to you as a Commander than as a staff officer, since all the problems presented to you were necessarily solved from the viewpoint of the High Command. . . . You have never sought to employ staff authority in lieu of a proper application of leadership methods, but to the contrary, have invariably demonstrated an ability to organize complicated tasks quickly and efficiently, to secure cheerful cooperation from all concerned and to carry group efforts to successful conclusion.[5]

Another letter of commendation, Ike recorded, was so "splendid" that "Mamie had it framed!!!"[6] In Ike's efficiency report, his official file at the War Department, MacArthur stated flatly, "This is the best officer in the Army. When the next war comes, he should go right to the top."[7]

Ike's initial impressions of MacArthur, also favorable, were expressed in a character sketch which he penned in June 1932. Ike found his boss "magnetic and extremely likable." He was "impulsive—able, even brilliant—quick—tenacious of his views and extremely self-confident." He was also "a genius at giving concise and clear instructions." Though averse to social duties and possessing "a reserved dignity," MacArthur "is most animated in conversation on subjects interesting [to] him." (The general shared with the major a passion for both Westerns and football.) Surprisingly, Ike reckoned MacArthur hostile to favoritism and lacking in political ambition. But although he thought that MacArthur "does not seek the limelight except in things connected with the Army," he recognized that the chief of staff was "essentially a romantic figure."[8] This was a sound, if unoriginal, conclusion but it did reveal an awareness that, in spite of superficial similarities, MacArthur was the antithesis of Eisenhower himself. With his paunch carried (as one correspondent noted) like a military secret, with his gorgeous uniforms and jeweled cigarette holder, with his tendency to refer to himself in the third person and his fondness for sentimental histrionics, MacArthur was not so much an anachronism as a figure out of some chivalric myth.

Over the next few years Ike often witnessed his capacity to indulge in florid rhetoric, to adopt a heroic pose, and to dramatize his life in messianic terms. Their offices in the War Department building (opposite the White House—the Pentagon had yet to be built) were only separated by a slatted door. So Ike could overhear the grandiloquent monologues in which MacArthur, his image magnified by the fifteen-foot-high mirror behind his desk, would finally profess himself delighted by the fascinating conversation of his visitor, who had remained silent throughout their interview. Ike also had a ringside seat at the epic performance MacArthur gave when, in July 1932, he forcibly dispersed the army of destitute veterans (the "Bonus Expeditionary Force" or BEF) who had marched on Washington to demand immediate payment of their promised compensation for war service. The "bonus," amounting to an average of some one thousand dollars, did not fall due until 1945, but Congress had already passed a bill paying half of it, and the members of this army of unemployed desperately needed the other half. About twenty thousand of them demonstrated their plight, and their brutal reception was one of the most shameful episodes in American history. If MacArthur unequivocally played the villain, Ike's own small part in the affair reveals him in a characteristically ambiguous light.

Actually, by 28 July, thanks to the liberal and firm conduct of Washington's unorthodox police chief, Brigadier General Pelham D. Glassford, the BEF was already dispersing of its own accord. There were now perhaps only ten thousand veterans left, most of them camping in the tarpaper shacks of a makeshift "Hooverville" on Anacostia Flats. However, the army's top brass, notably MacArthur and Moseley, chose to interpret their waning protest not as a desperate expression of helplessness by once-proud soldiers but as a determined act of insurrection on the part of criminal subversives. In fact, the BEF, whose watchword was "Eyes front, not left,"[9] loathed the few Communists within their ranks and had their own vigilante groups to hound them. But military intelligence (evidently staffed not only by the stupid but by the credulous) insisted that the BEF was riddled with Reds—one report said that Bolshevik elements were controlled by the wholly Jewish motion picture company Metro-Goldwyn-Mayer, itself supported by the USSR. Thus when federal troops were called in after an outbreak of violence, MacArthur told Glassford, "We are going to break the back of the BEF."[10] In deference to prevailing anti-militarist feelings, including those of the Quaker President Hoover, officers in the War Department wore civilian clothes, but MacArthur was delighted to don his general's uniform, with its five rows of ribbons, and he sent his unwilling aide home to change. Ike apparently protested that it was no business of the chief of staff to take part in such an operation. He was also cross because, despite much pulling and pushing, as well as generous applications of talcum powder, getting his boots on was hell!

Although not directly in command, MacArthur supervised the troops, supported by six tanks and machine gunners, as they drove the veterans from the center of Washington. The cavalry used the flats of their sabers (though Patton later claimed to have sliced off a veteran's ear) while the infantry threw tear-gas bombs. They employed a quite unnecessary degree of force, especially as there was no organized resistance. By the evening the veterans had retreated to their encampment on Anacostia Flats. President Hoover sent MacArthur two direct orders not to pursue them, but the general, who was "very much annoyed [at] having his plans interfered with in any way until they were executed completely," disobeyed.[11] Soldiers crossed the Anacostia Bridge, cleared the BEF from the Flats, and, it seems, set fire to their pathetic shanties. In his egotistical press conference (held against Ike's advice) after this triumph, MacArthur claimed that the veterans had burned down their own dwellings. And he asserted that it was vital to deal severely with the BEF because it was "animated by the essence of revolution." To this the Baltimore *Sun,* summing up with admirable succinctness the opinion of a generally hostile press, responded simply: "Horsefeathers."[12]

There were more horsefeathers in MacArthur's official report of the incident, drafted by Ike, which vainly strove to justify the army's tactics by representing the BEF as the riotous advance guard of a Communist uprising. Thus despite the sound counsel which he claimed to have given MacArthur, Ike played the loyal team member and championed, albeit uneasily, his chief. At the time he privately dismissed the public outrage—"a lot of furor has been stirred up but mostly to make political capital." Moreover, because of the rigors of the Depression his own bent was then markedly authoritarian. He did not go as far as other members of the military establishment, who were pleased that Hitler had restored discipline in Germany.[13] But in February 1933 he did write, "For two years I have been called 'Dictator Ike' because I believe that virtual dictatorship must be exercised by our President."[14] And years later, when he had become more critical of MacArthur, Ike would not openly condemn him. In fact the account of the Bonus March in Ike's informal memoir *At Ease* might be described as a somewhat apologetic apologia for MacArthur. The chief of staff, Ike relates evasively, "did not hear" the orders forbidding him to cross the Anacostia Bridge. At the same time he was not acting as anything other than an agent of the civil power. Similarly, Ike is sympathetic toward the "ragged, ill-fed" veterans but refuses to commit himself on the question of "whether or not they were mistaken in marching on Washington."[15] His entire account is purged of awkward details. It is bland, inaccurate, euphemistic, at once ingenuous and disingenuous. It is also charitable. Ike was ever ready to sacrifice plain-speaking on the altar of benevolence.

He certainly learned the value of discretion after being appointed to the post of MacArthur's senior aide, "military secretary—working on confidential or special missions for the General,"[16] toward the end of February 1933. The Depression was then plunging to its nadir. It was almost as if the 1930s were a punishment for the previous "decade of debauch," as Roosevelt called it.[17] One wage earner in four was out of work and only a quarter of those unemployed were receiving any kind of assistance. Breadlines were lengthening and city streets were haunted by women selling apples and panhandlers begging buddies to spare them a dime. People were starving, and one-fifth of the nation's schoolchildren were suffering from malnutrition. Agriculture and industry were devastated. One percent of the population owned fifty-nine percent of the wealth, but so many banks had failed that others were threatening to close their doors. In the words of the catchy Depression hit that kept running through Edmund Wilson's mind as he contemplated "the American Earthquake," there was "No more money in the bank."[18] The nation was close to collapse and despair.

Even in Washington, that "drowsy sun parlor" as John Dos Passos called it, which was protected by the federal government from the worst effects of the Depression and threatened to take over from Wall Street as the financial center of the country, Ike feared that "if things should get as bad as some predict" cash itself would be worthless, for "A socialistic or communistic regime would be forced to confiscate money."[19] He therefore supported the employment of the strongest powers by President Roosevelt, whose election he had welcomed (something he later preferred to forget) in spite of having "no definite leanings toward any political party."

I believe that unity of action is essential to success in the current struggle. I believe that individual right should be subordinated to public good, and that public good can be served only by unanimous adherence to an authoritative plan. We *must* conform to the President's program regardless of consequences. Otherwise dissension, confusion and partisan politics will ruin us.[20]

Unfortunately these sentiments came into conflict with Ike's loyalty to the service. The army reached what he called its most "extreme" state of "skeletonization" in the first two years of Roosevelt's presidency,[21] falling to seventeenth in rank among the armed forces of the world. In April 1933 Ike was worrying about proposed cuts in an already meager appropriation, and he forecast that "we will have left only a shell of a military establishment." In June he noted that although the service to some extent benefited from its involvement with the New Deal's Civilian Conservation Corps, the consequent reorganization in its own ranks "vitally and adversely affects the Army." And he now protested that Congress had given the president "almost autocratic power in this matter. . . . My God, but we have a lot of theorists and academicians in this administration."[22]

Ike's own efforts seemed somewhat academic as he struggled to help MacArthur resist further reductions in America's military strength: for he still argued in favor of mobile strategy based on the employment of tanks and airplanes, despite the almost complete absence of these vehicles of Blitzkrieg. In the annual reports, which he drafted for the chief of staff, Ike complained not only about shortages of manpower but about the army's hopelessly obsolete equipment—most of it was left over from the First World War and troops were still armed with 1903 Springfield rifles. Such appeals were doomed. Pacifism was in the air, much to Ike's disgust—the pacific beliefs of David and Ida Eisenhower had evidently made no impression on their soldier son, save perhaps in giving him a realistic understanding of the horrors of war—but he did not go as far as MacArthur, who described pacifism as the bedfellow of Communism. Economies were so stringent that Ike had to indent for his streetcar fare from the War Department building to the Capitol and back.

Although Ike facetiously denied, in a letter to his army friend Everett Hughes, that "an aide is only a tail to a cow,"[23] his dissatisfaction with the service could not have been lessened by the fact that he had to do the chief of staff's unofficial dirty work. Two Hearst journalists, Drew Pearson and Robert Allen, mounted a series of attacks on MacArthur after his harsh treatment of the Bonus Marchers. Ike wondered if these "scandalmongers" were acting at the behest of Steve Early, the president's press secretary, "one of the small fry suffering from illusions of grandeur," or if they were "giving expression to an inferiority complex by ceaseless attempts to belittle a man recognized as courageous, if nothing else."[24] Anyway, when MacArthur filed a suit for $1.75 million against Pearson and Allen they threatened to produce his discarded Eurasian mistress in court to testify against him. Major Eisenhower was sent to find and dissuade her, a mission which he singularly failed to accomplish. So MacArthur, who was terrified that his formidable mother would learn of his liaison, dropped the suit.

Ike was understandably tempted to quit the army in 1935 when he himself was offered a job as a journalist (writing on military affairs) at more than five times his annual salary of three thousand dollars. But although his immediate prospects of promotion looked poor, he perhaps sensed that Fox Conner's prophecy about another war would soon be fulfilled. Anyway, nothing could for long undermine Ike's constitutional confidence, though as he told Hughes, Doubting Thomas's "progeny plague us and insult us—they laughed at Fulton; they imprisoned Bunyan; they burned Joan d'Arc, and they invented the Bronx cheer."[25] He still enjoyed the security of service life, especially the company and the recreation. On Saturday afternoons, for example, he would listen to the army football games on the radio, plotting the plays on a sketch pad. Like MacArthur, he enjoyed prize-fights. He was passionate about golf, and bridge had superseded poker as his favorite card game, though he played bridge as he played poker —with an admixture of pugilism. He not only tried to read his opponents' minds, but he banged the cards down on the table violently. He even took up tennis, knocking balls against a wall for hours and sometimes, when the shots went wrong, getting so "mad" (Mamie said) that he "butted his head against a tree."[26]

Yet to remain in the army was for Ike to remain in MacArthur's thrall. And when the general finished his term as chief of staff, in the autumn of 1935, he insisted that his aide should accompany him to the Philippines. The colony had been acquired by the United States after the war with Spain, when, according to Mr. Dooley, the average American did not know whether the Philippines were "islands or canned goods." Before long, however, the United States became all too aware of the embarrassment of being an imperialist power, and by the 1930s Washington was trying to slough off its responsibilities. Thus the Philippines were now passing through a transitional state, prior to the attainment of complete independence, promised for 1946. And America was reluctantly assisting Manuel Quezon's Nacionalista government to prepare for its own defense.

MacArthur was appointed military adviser and charged with creating a Filipino army. Ike was to act as assistant military adviser, much against his will. He had been hoping for service with troops or for one of the plum jobs which MacArthur had dangled in front of him. The Philippines were remote and backward—in the mountains around Manila native warriors untouched by colonialism still hunted with bows and arrows. As Marshall later observed, MacArthur did not have a staff but a court; and being a courtier, even for someone as flexible as Ike, was an increasing strain. The climate would not agree with Mamie, whose state of health was frail—she increasingly took to her bed. John's schooling would be interrupted. Admittedly there would be generous extra pay and allowances, as well as comfortable quarters underneath MacArthur's palatial penthouse in the Manila Hotel, overlooking the bay. As it turned out, Ike's final billet was an opulent suite in its air-conditioned wing, full of brocade and gilt furniture. The walls were lined with damask, a huge crystal chandelier hung from the ceiling, and the marquetry floors were covered with oriental rugs (which Ike loved and had begun to collect)—but he pronounced it all "too danged fancy to suit me."[27]

Ike had little faith in the capacity of the Philippines to govern themselves, let alone to defend themselves. As recently as 1932 he had drawn up a report which must have delighted the secretary of war and other conservatives, for it denied "the ability of [the] Filipino masses to express intelligent opinion on the many questions involved until they shall have reached a substantially higher cultural plane."[28] After his arrival Ike found that the defense budget was impossibly small. Political considerations, such as Quezon's fear of antagonizing Japan and Roosevelt's reluctance to supply arms to the Philippines, placed a fatal bar on military progress. Moreover, the Filipinos themselves were adept in the arts of obstruction and procrastination. Having struggled with these intractable circumstances for eighteen months, Ike poured out his frustration to Moseley:

The two great obstacles to success in the military effort in which we are engaged are insufficient finances and the difficulty of developing an efficient officer corps. Although I have been here for a year and a half I am not one of those who attempt to ascribe to the Filipino any racial defect which would make it impossible for him to become a good officer. Genghis Khan produced one of the finest military machines the world has ever seen. . . . In spite of these comforting reflections, however, I must say that I have been disappointed in the result of our efforts to galvanize the officer corps now available to us into intelligent and efficient action. The other day I read a comment by an eminent Chinese educator. He said that the Oriental is satisfied with things that are good, but that the American is always striving for the best, with resultant bad effects upon his blood pressure, happiness and longevity.[29]

Ike's blood pressure must also have been adversely affected by MacArthur, who with age was becoming, if possible, even more self-intoxicated. As they traveled to the Philippines the general learned that, no longer being chief of staff, he had been demoted by two stars. He let fly, Ike later recalled, "an explosive denunciation of arrogance, unconstitutionality, insensitivity, and the way the world had gone to hell."[30] In the Philippines MacArthur, now the most highly paid professional soldier in the world, did little work. He only appeared in the office for about a couple of hours each morning, immaculate in a gray checked tropical suit, white and tan shoes, a bow tie and a silk shirt which (although it was said that he did not sweat) he changed three times a day. But the general seemed increasingly dissatisfied with Ike's performance. He wanted his industrious junior, advanced to lieutenant colonel in 1936, to be more enthusiastic (and less realistic) about the prospects of the Philippine army. He also urged him to form a closer liaison with the mercurial Quezon, though the two men were already on excellent terms and often played bridge together on weekends aboard the presidential yacht.

MacArthur regularly subjected Ike and his close friend (from West Point days) and assistant, Major James B. Ord, to "shouting tirades."[31] He was "particularly bitter" toward Ike, who claimed that he stood up to him. And he was especially furious over Ike's response to his promotion to field marshal in the Filipino army. This title MacArthur had secretly solicited from Quezon, though he pretended that it had been offered spontaneously. He was "tickled pink" with the new rank,[32] especially as it gave him the chance to strut about in a sharkskin uniform he had personally designed, consisting of black trousers, a white tunic festooned with red ribbon, gold braid, medals and stars, and a cap amply decorated with scrambled egg. Ike protested that MacArthur had achieved the rare and proud distinction of being a four-star general in the United States Army, and he demanded, "Why in the *hell* do you want a *banana* country giving you a field-marshalship?" MacArthur was incensed. "Oh, Jesus!" Ike recorded. "He just gave me hell!"[33]

He also gave Ike hell when he forecast that Alf Landon would be defeated in the presidential contest of 1936. Ike probably supported the conservative Kansan, but he recognized the immense popular appeal of Roosevelt as well as the political mastery epitomized by his devastating jibe at Landon's sunflower symbol—it was yellow, had a black heart, was useful only for parrot food, and always died before November. But MacArthur condemned Ike and Ord almost hysterically as "fearful and small-minded people who are afraid to express judgements that are obvious from the evidence at hand." Yet, having been proved humiliatingly wrong, MacArthur was not gracious enough to apologize for this "awful bawling out."[34] Nevertheless, in spite of MacArthur's temperamental behavior, life in the Philippines had its compensations.

Ike learned to fly and enjoyed the experience so much (despite two nearly fatal accidents) that he would demonstrate his prowess at the dining table, using a knife as the joy stick. John loved his time in the Orient. Mamie, though literally prostrated for much of the time by the humidity and her own ill health, at least had the pleasure of going on shopping expeditions with Jean MacArthur—followed by drinks at the Army and Navy Club. There were minor domestic upsets. Mamie had been horrified to find Ike bald when she first arrived, some time after him, at Manila—he had shaved off what remained of his hair because of the heat. When John acquired one exotic pet, a cockatoo, and planned to get another, Ike roared, "There's nothing I hate worse than parrots and monkeys!"[35] As John had good cause to know, his father's constant affability was a myth: "Sure, he's good-natured at home as long as everything goes his way, but if someone musses up the paper, for instance, before he's had a chance to read it he has a fit. Mother makes the house revolve around him, and he just sits back and lets it revolve."[36]

Although friends would flatter Mamie that she was the "power behind the throne,"[37] Ike's will almost invariably prevailed at home. But at work his chief became steadily more overbearing. Various stories are told about what caused the final rift between these two outstanding leaders of the Second World War. According to one authoritative account, a group of Filipino legislators decided that Eisenhower was bearing most of the burden while MacArthur was receiving most of the credit. They proposed to introduce a bill that would abolish the top job and put Ike in charge. He heard of the scheme and said that he would return to the United States if it were implemented. But MacArthur also heard of it, or heard a different version of it, and became convinced that Ike had conspired to supersede him. As Eisenhower himself explained, "He thought I was stealing his publicity."[38] "From that moment," one officer recorded, "he had no more use for Eisenhower."[39] Apparently he told Ike and Ord (whom he believed to be in the plot): "I would relieve you both if it weren't for the fact that it would ruin your careers. But although you'll stay, I'll never trust you again."[40]

Ike himself might have said the same of MacArthur after what he considered to be the real occasion of their break. This occurred early in 1938, when the general ordered Ike to hold a big military parade in Manila. Quezon was not consulted and when he learned of the plan he canceled it on grounds of expense. MacArthur then claimed that he had only instructed his subordinate to investigate the possibility of holding a parade, not to make actual preparations for it. Ike was livid and protested that MacArthur was calling him a liar: "I am *not* a liar, and so I'd like to go back to the United States." MacArthur put his arm around Eisenhower's shoulder and replied, "Ike, it's just fun to see that damn Dutch temper . . . take you over. . . . It's just a misunderstanding, and let's let it go at that."[41]

Their relationship was never the same again, and it deteriorated still further when Ike rose first to military and then to political preeminence. MacArthur became bitterly jealous of his former aide and roundly disparaged him in private, describing him as the apotheosis of mediocrity, the best clerk he had ever had, and a man sadly lacking in guts. Ike too made acerbic comments behind the back of his former chief, saying that for seven years he had studied dramatics under MacArthur, and that he would not trade one Marshall for fifty MacArthurs. In his diary Ike was even more scathing: he described MacArthur as a big baby who liked "boot lickers," was subject to jitters, and would probably be ruined by his "love of the limelight."[42] More revealing, Ike once exclaimed to a member of his White House staff: "I certainly don't want to be put in the same class with MacArthur. What makes anyone think MacArthur is a great man?"[43]

However, neither officer openly criticized the other, except by implication. And their private correspondence was full of ringingly insincere expressions of mutual regard. After the war, for example, Ike denounced scurrilous gossip about their rivalry and "hoped that you treasured our old friendship as much as I do."[44] MacArthur replied, "I pay absolutely no attention to scuttlebuts . . . my warm esteem and cordial regard for you, born of our many years of intimate association, are well known and understood by everyone."[45] Ostensibly, too, MacArthur, who did everything to keep his aide in Manila, parted from him on good terms. He forecast a brilliant career for Ike and emerged from his habitual seclusion to see the Eisenhowers off on the boat in December 1939.

They were delighted to leave the Far East. Mamie looked forward to living in a more temperate climate, and there was John's education to consider. Ike felt that there was nothing more that he could do to help Quezon, who so appreciated his efforts that he offered him first a medal (which was accepted) and later $100,000 (which was refused). Moreover, Ike had now lost his great friend and supporter against MacArthur, Jimmy Ord, who had been tragically killed in a flying accident. Ike was so anxious to go home that he was not even tempted by a curious job which had recently been proposed to him by a committee of Jews in Manila. They had offered him $60,000 a year to search for a haven in Southeast Asia for Jewish refugees from Nazi Germany. Ike had made no secret of his hostility to Hitler's Fascism, but as a matter of fact he was never comfortable with Jews and had none among his intimate friends. However, as Ike said, he turned down this rewarding proposal because he was wedded to his profession. And he was "convinced that we [would] eventually be in" the war which had just broken out in Europe.[46]

Indeed, on his return to the United States he soon became known as "Alarmist Ike," a title that he later recalled with "a certain amount of smug and mean satisfaction."[47] No doubt his alarm was stimulated by the way in which, en route for home, he was befriended by a Japanese who quizzed him on the state of the Philippines. And he believed that Hitler was a "power-drunk egocentric" who intended to smash civilization. To prevent him America would have to fight and, eventually, to dismember Germany.[48] True, he had now changed his mind about the correct response to the Third Reich, having at first favored appeasement on the grounds that anything was better than the "ultimate calamity" of war.[49] Moreover, in the autumn of 1939 Ike was "completely bewildered" by the "phoney war." He wondered if the Allied navies could blockade the Axis, economically as well as militarily, and whether fixed fortifications and modern weapons had turned the clock back to "the defensive form of combat." "If we assume that no violations of the flanking neutrals occur, and further that in the air, as on the ground, virtual stagnation is to occur, what," he asked Gerow, "will you tell me, is the answer?"[50] Despite his theoretical espousal of mobile warfare, Ike had yet, like the French and the British, to learn the lessons of the Blitzkrieg.

However, Ike reckoned that his "alarmism" paid off in the successful conduct of his men during maneuvers in March 1940.[51] By then he was executive officer and a battalion commander in the Fifteenth Infantry, stationed first in California and then at Fort Lewis in the state of Washington. He rejoiced at being engaged in the "fascinating work of handling soldiers" and exclaimed, "Nothing can kill my own enthusiasm for the job in hand."[52] Quickly recovering his health after the rigors of the tropics, he enjoyed the endurance test of taking his troops on battle exercises through country that "would have made a good stage-setting for a play in Hades. Stumps, slashings, fallen logs, tangled brush, holes, hummocks, and hills!"[53] Once again, Ike proved to be an excessively hard-working officer, though at their second meeting he had to reassure Marshall, who was well aware of the way in which Filipino servants coddled their American masters, that he still knew how to tie his own shoelaces.

Certainly Ike did not coddle his men. He denied them leave, for example, if their reasons were inadequate: "Moral[e] that is purchased with favors will be less steadfast in adversity than would a light o' love after she found out you didn't have two bucks."[54] Nevertheless, he was popular with his troops, who regarded him as tough but tolerant, efficient but humane. They marveled at his capacity to eat a raw onion accompanied by uncooked beef. They laughed at his solution to a feud between two soldiers—he made them clean opposite sides of the barracks windows, so that they had to face each other through the glass. Soon they would only march to the strains of his favorite song of the moment, "The Beer Barrel Polka." As for the officers, most of them were preoccupied with athletics, recreation, and entertainment, to the detriment of serious training, which they conducted (he noted severely) in a "soothing-syrup style calculated to rouse the least resentment from the soldiers themselves and from their families at home."[55] But the Club Eisenhower was in full swing once again and Ike enjoyed his usual hearty relations with his fellows.

With the collapse of France and the Battle of Britain in 1940—the British stood up to the Blitz better than Ike expected—America herself became infected by alarmism. As he put it, "During the summer and early fall, the United States at last began to awaken to their own peril."[56] Public opinion actually outran a cautious War Department and a president who still felt threatened by pacifist and isolationist pressures. Thus in September Congress was able to pass the first peacetime conscription bill in American history. Yet even then, despite all his rhetoric about the United States being the arsenal of democracy and the need to turn from economic recovery to national defense, Roosevelt made haste slowly. He was eager to find money for ships but not for tanks, referring to the Navy as "us" (Marshall complained) and to the Army as "them."[57] Far from going all out to mobilize industry in order to manufacture modern equipment for the draftees who were being trained, the president was, until Pearl Harbor, actually proposing to demobilize some of the men.

The Depression had anyway such a traumatic effect on the national psyche that as late as 1941 many industries were reluctant to take large military orders which required the construction of new plants. It was, of course, the vast munitions contracts which brought an end to mass unemployment and hard-core poverty, not the New Deal, so vociferously condemned (not least by Ike himself) as a form of creeping socialism. But in the crucial years before Pearl Harbor the past governed the present and ideas outlived reality. Roosevelt was still so hated that some army officers would not drink a toast to the president of the United States. The grapes of wrath were being trampled out at home and abroad, but Americans were reluctant to permit state action to erode their cherished individualism. Free enterprise resisted big government. In 1941 new cars poured from the production lines when there was a desperate need for armored vehicles. During the Louisiana maneuvers in September 1941 (which gained Ike his first national publicity), many of the troops were equipped with mock weapons and one cavalry division had to rent its horses—while the department stores bulged with Christmas goods. Lend Lease and the creation of new divisions after 7 December 1941 made supply shortages even more acute. Patton's Third Division was at sea in both senses of the word when, en route for the invasion of North Africa in the fall of 1942, it opened its crates of bazookas and tried to work out what to do with the contraptions.[58]

Patton was one of the many senior officers who tried to secure Ike's services in advance of what he (Patton) hoped would be "a long and BLOODY war."[59] Ike implied that he himself was above "petty jealousies" and personal ambition, saying that "long and bitter wars" bring "to the top the fellow who thinks more of his job than of his own promotion prospects."[60] But in fact he pulled every string he could to remain with troops, and he tried to obtain a regiment in one of the new armored divisions that Patton was expecting to command. Unfortunately, however, his reputation was such that he was more in demand as a staff officer. He found himself in such a quandary when Gerow, now a brigadier general in charge of the War Plans Division, offered him a post, that at first he tried to get Gerow to make the decision for him—and at the same time developed a painful attack of shingles. In the end he remained at Fort Lewis, first as chief of staff to the Third Division and then, in March 1941, promoted (much to his delight) to full colonel, as chief of staff to the Ninth Army Corps. Technically he remained "with troops," and his work involved the organization and training of huge numbers of new recruits. Ike labored fourteen hours a day and was soon transferred to an even bigger job.

He became chief of staff to the Third Army based at Fort Sam Houston, which the Eisenhowers reached on their twenty-fifth wedding anniversary, 1 July 1941. Here Ike acquired the earliest members of his "official family," "Tex" Lee, a bluff former Chevrolet salesman, as his aide, and "Mickey" McKeogh, until recently a bellboy at New York's Plaza Hotel, as his orderly. Here Ike also displayed exactly the qualities which the Third Army's commander, General Walter Krueger, had expected of him—vision, initiative, progressive thinking, and a grasp of the complex problems involved in running an enormous organization. "Luckily," Ike told Moseley, with a characteristic blend of modesty and self-esteem, "I've spent most of my life in large headquarters, so am not overpowered by the mass of details."[61]

Ike proved not only his grasp of detail but his command of strategy during maneuvers held in Louisiana. These involved over 400,000 men and were the largest yet to be conducted in the United States.

Ike, who, as much as Marshall, valued realistic battle exercises, relished the prospect: "All the old-timers here say that we are going to
a god-awful spot, to live with mud, malaria, mosquitoes and misery.
But I like to go to the field so I'm not much concerned about it."[62]
Ike's enjoyment was enhanced by the fact that, thanks in large measure
to his work and planning, General Krueger's Third Army roundly
defeated General Lear's Second. Admittedly Patton, in an operation
that astonished Ike and foreshadowed daring feats to come, almost
snatched victory for the Second Army; but the umpires ruled that his
long night drive, in tanks fueled by gasoline he had paid for out of
his own pocket, was a foul. So Ike's more orthodox tactics prevailed,
especially as none of Patton's men managed to collect the fifty-dollar
reward he offered for capturing "a certain s.o.b. called Eisenhower."[63] No one was more adept at backing shyly into the limelight
than Ike, and it was the chief of staff, not the general, who got credit
for the triumph. But the journalists recognized that Ike's military
virtues matched his publicity value: Eric Sevareid was told, "Be sure
you see Colonel Eisenhower—he makes more sense than the rest of
them."[64] The War Department seemed to agree: Ike was promoted
to brigadier general in September 1941. And General Marshall,
whose memory was so good that he could recollect telephone numbers he had used during the First World War, made what were surely
superfluous additions to the famous black book in which he recorded
details about promising officers.

For all his alarmism, Ike was literally, just as Marshall was meta-
phorically, caught napping when the Japanese bombed Pearl Harbor.
But for the next five days he worked almost around the clock. So did
Marshall, and on 11 December Secretary of War Henry L. Stimson
talked to him about the need to recruit additional help at the War
Department so that he could delegate some of his onerous duties.
Marshall asked General Mark Clark for a list of ten names from which
he could select someone to fill the vacant post of deputy chief of the
War Plans Division. Clark replied, "I'll give you one name and nine
dittos—Dwight D. Eisenhower."[65] So, on 12 December 1941, Ike
received a telephone call from the secretary of the general staff in the
War Department, Colonel Walter Bedell Smith. "The Chief says for
you to hop a plane and get up here right away."[66] Never has a
summons to destiny been expressed in more prosaic terms.

Commanding the Whole Shebang

George C. Marshall was a terrifying figure. He was almost inhumanly aloof and self-contained. He had few friends and no confidants. He so hated sycophancy that he would not laugh at Roosevelt's jokes and avoided going to the White House. And he was so formal that he never allowed Roosevelt to call him George. On the only occasion he slipped into the familiar "Ike," Marshall compensated for it by addressing his junior as Eisenhower five times in the next sentence. Marshall was widely hailed as a military genius, not least by Fox Conner, who likened him to Ike. During the war General Omar Bradley, among others, said that although Arlington Cemetery was filled with indispensable men Marshall really was the indispensable man. Certainly the chief of staff possessed a transcendent ability to match his fierce integrity. He lived for his job, abhorred inefficiency, and insisted on the highest standards of conduct and dedication. When officers fell short of them he was ruthless, consigning men to outer darkness for minor misdemeanors and seldom giving them a second chance. In the normal course of affairs he was brusque to the point of rudeness. If he actually intended to be offensive the effect was devastating: when MacArthur's chief of staff insistently staked his military reputation on the soundness of his case for a Pacific strategy, Marshall invited him to say just "what his military reputation is."[1]

Parsimonious with his time and abstemious in his habits, the chief of staff seemed to be as unbending as an automaton. Actually he did have a human side—he was fond of women, children, and horses. But his warmth and charm were carefully camouflaged, and few subordinates established any degree of intimacy with him. Bedell Smith, who himself rejoiced in being a Prussian-style officer, once exclaimed that Marshall was "as cold as a fish."[2] Others were more impressed by

Marshall's incandescent outbursts of rage which, though rare and short-lived, were said to take the paint off the walls. (Ike was convinced that Marshall's anger was put on for effect, in this respect being different from his own—"I blaze for an hour.")[3] The chief of staff was particularly brutal toward officers who failed to express themselves clearly and concisely. Many who came into his austere, taciturn presence and gazed into his glacial blue eyes were reduced to tongue-tied incoherence. Ike, who arrived at the War Department Building on 14 December 1941, was impressed but not intimidated by him.

For Ike's benefit and to test his military reflexes, Marshall at once outlined the disastrous position in the Pacific, the naval losses at Pearl Harbor, MacArthur's inexplicable failure to protect Clark Field where so many of his aircraft were destroyed on the ground, and Japan's imminent threat to the isolated and unprotected Philippines. What policy, he asked, should the United States pursue? Ike requested a few hours' grace in which to consider his answer. He returned later to say that the situation in the Philippines seemed hopeless and that it was impossible to supply MacArthur with effective assistance. But, he concluded, the Philippines could not be abandoned without fatal damage to American prestige in the Far East. Marshall agreed and he told Ike to do what he could to save the islands. In fact nothing could be done because there were not enough ships, airplanes, or supplies to enable MacArthur to hold out and what there were could not reach him. As Patrick J. Hurley wrote, "We were out-shipped, out-planed, out-manned, and out-gunned by the Japanese from the beginning."[4]

For three months Ike struggled to solve this insoluble problem. He worked such long hours that, though staying with his brother Milton, he never saw the house in daylight. He normally ate lunch, consisting of a hot dog and a glass of milk, at his desk, but he was not above drinking a couple of old-fashioneds in the evenings even though they made him sleepy. To General Krueger he professed himself "bitterly disappointed" that he was no longer serving in the field with troops.[5] But, of course, the issues which he faced at the hub of events were more important. They were also more intractable. Now it was that Ike first manifested on the national stage the remarkable capacity for ambivalence which was to be his hallmark both as a general and as a politician. He did everything possible to help MacArthur short of giving him significant aid. Janus-faced, he simultaneously looked toward the Pacific and toward the Atlantic, perceiving that while the Japanese posed more immediate problems the Germans posed more dangerous ones. Yet while he vacillated, he showed a grim determination to cut through the red tape which bound the War Department to outmoded protocol, and to secure victory at all costs.

Thus, on 17 January 1942, he favored dropping all other priorities, scraping up "everything everywhere" and sending it to the crucial Far Eastern theater. On 22 January, reversing this strategy completely, he announced: "We've got to go to Europe and fight, and we've got to quit wasting resources all over the world, and still worse, wasting time." Eight days later, as the Allied position in Asia disintegrated still further before the Japanese onslaught, Ike noted: "We're going to regret every damn boat we sent to Ireland. . . . Damn 'em. I tried, but I don't wear 45s. So the hotshots can sneer at me. Anyway I got the Ireland movement largely postponed."[6] On 9 February Ike drafted a message to MacArthur saying that he should keep the flag flying as long as there was any chance of resistance—something the embattled general hardly needed telling and resented being told. And, on 22 February, Ike drew up the order for MacArthur to leave for Australia—and then derided him for playing the hero during his retreat. Of course, some of these inconsistencies were attributable to the shifting circumstances of the war. But there is no doubt that Ike was also something of a weathercock. He tended to reflect the views of the strong men to whom he was drawn or of the last persuasive person he had seen. He resembled the former secretary of war, George H. Dern, who would never (Ike wrote) "be a warm advocate of a lost cause."[7]

MacArthur never forgave Ike for finally espousing the Anglo-American strategy of defeating Germany first and for failing to blast through the Japanese cordon and send reinforcements to Bataan. But Marshall, though he loathed obvious "yes-men," was not immune to the subtle flattery of finding his ideas echoed by a subordinate whose independent-mindedness seemed more in evidence than his willingness to surrender to the prevailing climate of opinion. For Ike *was* prepared to stand up to tough characters. He even earned the respect of hard-drinking, short-tempered, protocol-conscious Admiral Ernest J. King by answering back, though for a time he thought it would help to win the war if someone shot King. Ike's eagerness to fight was not in doubt. And he was prepared, unobtrusively, to shoulder the responsibility of taking hard decisions. By mid-February Marshall made Ike head of the War Plans Department. As Gerow walked out to take command of troops he remarked to his successor, "Well, I got Pearl Harbor on the book; lost the Philippine Islands, Singapore, Sumatra and all the Netherlands East Indies north of the barrier. Let's see what you can do."[8]

Ike could do very little of a positive nature because of the great gulf fixed between America's ambitious military aims and her limited military means. He was now desperately keen to establish a Second Front in Europe, with the purpose not only of going for Germany's vitals but of employing the major portion of British combat power offensively and keeping Russia in the war. But, like Marshall himself, Ike advocated this intrinsically sound strategy in what amounted to a logistical vacuum. As Ike recognized when he examined the practical possibilities, there were simply not enough trained and equipped divisions to mount an invasion of the Continent. Nor were there enough ships to transport them, though he was urging a tardy navy to build modern landing craft. (This was a prescient move considering that before the war Marshall had never heard of any landing craft except a rubber boat, and the British navy's landing craft were rowboats similar to those used by Wolfe at the storming of Quebec in 1759.) Patton wrote to Ike on 20 February forecasting that "We will eventually beat the hell out of those bastards—You name them; I'll shoot them!" Ike had to reply, "I don't have the slightest trouble naming the hellions I'd like to have you shoot; my problem is getting you to the place you can do it."9

Nevertheless, Ike showed a remarkable ability to cope with situations where theory was at odds with practice. In the interest of team solidarity he was always prepared to forgo intellectual coherence, just as his brother Milton was prepared to sacrifice moral scruples. (From March to June 1942 the unhappy Milton acted, at the president's behest, as head of the War Relocation Board, which moved West Coast Japanese to internment camps in response to the wave of chauvinism which swamped the country after Pearl Harbor. This unconstitutional act was one of the greatest violations of civil rights in American history.) Anyway, Marshall valued Ike's support in steering the impulsive Roosevelt and the wayward Churchill away from irrelevant operations in peripheral theaters of war. He first expressed his appreciation in a typically cool fashion, telling Ike that he was going to continue to do staff work in Washington while all the top promotions would be awarded (as they had not been during the First World War) to field officers. Ike shot back angrily, "General, I don't give a damn about your promotion."10 He told Marshall that he was doing his duty as best he could and would continue to do whatever was necessary to help win the war. Then he stalked out of Marshall's office, characteristically mitigating the effect of his outburst by turning to his chief by the door and grinning. Marshall seemed to respond in kind and Ike afterward wondered if this exchange had determined his entire future. A few days later, at the end of March 1942, Ike was promoted to major general. And at the beginning of April he was made assistant chief of staff and head of an expanded War Plans

Department, known as the Operations Division. Patton was not being particularly farsighted in prophesying to Ike that he would be "the 'Black Jack' of the damn war."[11]

Ike's commitment to a hard slog in what he recognized as the "grisly, dirty, tough business" of war deserved its reward. He was working so strenuously that when his father died on 10 March, Ike had "no time to indulge even in the deepest and most sacred emotions." He could not go to the funeral but he did shut his office door for half an hour and write a brief, sad, but curiously formal tribute to David Eisenhower,

a just man, well liked, well educated, a thinker. He was undemonstrative, quiet, modest and of exemplary habits. . . . He was an uncomplaining person in the face of adversity, and such plaudits as were accorded him did not inflate his ego. . . . I'm proud he was my father. My only regret is that it was always so difficult to let him know the great depth of my affection for him.[12]

Ike labored so diligently that he had little time even for Mamie, who had come to Washington in February (they were staying temporarily at the Wardman Park Hotel, Washington being so crowded). Nor did he see much of John, who was now a cadet at West Point anyway (and whose bearing convinced his father that the place had *not* gone to hell).

Instead Ike struggled to implement the plans to which Marshall and Harry Hopkins had secured British agreement in April. These were known by the code names BOLERO (the transportation of American men and munitions to Britain), ROUNDUP (the invasion of France in 1943), and SLEDGEHAMMER (a preliminary to that invasion, to be executed in 1942 if Russian defeat seemed imminent, consisting of the capture of a bridgehead on the Cotentin Peninsula in Normandy). Despite their agreement and massive popular support for the move, the British remained half-hearted about opening a Second Front prematurely. The volatile Churchill was excited by the prospect of an audacious landing but he was haunted not only by the specter of Dunkirk but by the ghost of Gallipoli and other Great War bloodbaths. The chief of the Imperial General Staff (CIGS), General Sir Alan Brooke, thought Marshall's plans "fantastic" at a time when "we were hanging on by our eye-lids"[13] and members of the Home Guard were still equipped with pikes.

British doubts hardened into certainties when they contemplated Marshall's embarrassed admission that the United States could only contribute two and half divisions by 15 September, which meant that the brunt of an immediate continental attack would be borne by

British troops. Nevertheless, Ike pressed on loyally with his preparations. Everywhere there were shortages and everywhere he strove to overcome them. Marshall was so impressed by his performance that he sent Ike to Britain for a week at the end of May. His task was to ensure that the Second Front would not be delayed by any American failure in London to cooperate fully with the British military chiefs.

To his surprise Ike found that there was little sense of urgency on the part of American officers in blitzed Britain. They were still wearing civilian clothes and working a five-day week. As for members of the British high command whom he met, Ike became convinced that they were intent on backing out of SLEDGEHAMMER. He formed such a low initial opinion of Brooke that in his memoirs he violated his oft-repeated rule not to criticize others by name. He described Brooke as "adroit rather than deep, and shrewd rather than wise."[14] Brooke, it must be said, was even more disparaging about Eisenhower, filling his diary with hostile remarks. But although he did not consider Ike to be a capable commander, Brooke did think him an amiable coordinator, and one blessed with great luck and wonderful charm. Perhaps Brooke suspected Ike of having deliberately staged his recommendation that Admiral Lord Louis Mountbatten, a friend of Marshall's, should lead the SLEDGEHAMMER assault. At a large meeting Ike said that he had heard Mountbatten was "vigorous, intelligent and courageous." Brooke retorted, "General, possibly you have not met Admiral Mountbatten. This is he sitting directly across the table from you."[15] If this was a maneuver rather than a gaffe it was one which would have appealed to Mountbatten, who was such an intriguer that he once provoked Field Marshal Templer to exclaim, "Dickie, you're so crooked that if you swallowed a nail you'd shit a corkscrew!"[16]

Another contretemps occurred when Ike, so addicted to tobacco that he would not attend social functions where he could not freely indulge, lit a cigarette at one of General Bernard Montgomery's briefings. The ascetic Monty sniffed the air with his thin, pointed nose and enquired brusquely, "Who's smoking?" "I am," replied Ike. "I don't permit smoking in my office." Ike dutifully extinguished his cigarette. It was the first of many snubs by which Monty tested to the breaking point Ike's capacity for genial dissimulation. In the car afterward Ike was "really steaming mad"—his face flaming red and veins standing out on his forehead like worms—at Monty.[17] Yet Ike initially described this puritanical prima donna as "a decisive type who appears to be extremely energetic and professionally able."[18] Ike finished his visit as he had begun it, sightseeing under the gushing guidance of the pretty Irish driver who had been allocated to him by the Motor

Transport Corps. Her name was Kay Summersby and, like others whom Ike encountered on this trip, she was to play an important role in his wartime life.

Ike returned home at the beginning of June having proved, as Marshall had hoped, acceptable to the British. His combination of soft answers and steely devotion to the Atlantic Alliance convinced them that Ike was at once malleable and resolute. Actually in his diàry Ike was quite vituperative about Allies in general and the British in particular. But in a wartime alliance, he had concluded, the "high command invariably involves a President, a Prime Minister, six Chiefs of Staff and a horde of lesser 'planners' . . . [so] no one person can be a Napoleon or a Caesar."[19] Now, however, he temporarily rebelled against warfare by committee. Instead he recommended that, in order to progress toward the Second Front with all possible speed, a new and more vigorous commander should be appointed with absolute control over all three American services in Britain. Marshall concurred and on 11 June appointed Eisenhower to the post. Ike realized that it was probably the biggest job of the war and told Mamie, "I'm going to command the whole shebang!"[20]

With him was to come the ruthlessly ambitious General Mark Wayne Clark as his corps commander. General Walter Bedell Smith, strong-willed but evil-tempered as only one afflicted with ulcers can be and once described as "Eisenhower's executioner,"[21] was eventually to be his chief of staff. And Eisenhower was accompanied by Commander Harry C. Butcher, who as a friend and confidant would, Ike hoped, assuage his loneliness and stop him from going crazy. Butcher, a naval officer who could not tell latitude from longitude and whose knowledge of the sea, someone rightly remarked, did not extend much beyond "Anchors Aweigh," was nominally Ike's "naval aide," a new position created with the connivance of Admiral King. In fact he was invaluable as a public relations officer and keeper of the quasi-official diary which, when published after the war (though Ike claimed to be embarrassed by it), did so much to enhance his popularity. The tone of the book is well expressed by Butcher himself, who told Mamie in 1945 that he was "compiling a second Bible and creating a second Jesus."[22]

Having said goodbye to John and waved to Mamie from the airplane as she stood, a solitary, weeping figure, by the Fort Myer flagpole, Ike reached Britain on 24 June 1942. Almost for the first time in his life he was alone, separated from his family in alien surroundings. He was at once disorientated and homesick. According to Mickey McKeogh, he complained that the suite at Claridges, with its black and gold sitting room and pink bedroom, looked "exactly like a funeral parlor"—he also compared it to a "whorehouse," and he told Butcher that it made him feel that he was living in sin.[23] After a week he moved into the less ostentatious Dorchester Hotel, where he shared quarters with his naval aide. But he soon developed "a complex" against these rooms too—they were "no home," he could not forget work in them and felt as though he were on display all the time. Ike loathed being wined and dined and having to make polite conversation until late at night. He reckoned that these occasions explained why the British did not start business until nine-thirty in the morning and he determined to close down the Social Front at once by refusing all invitations that were not strictly official. It was a rule he sometimes broke. But he did tend to eat his meals hurriedly and erratically. Sometimes he dined or supped off peanuts or candy in his Grosvenor Square office, which was anyway pervaded by the familiar wartime smell of boiled cabbage or brussels sprouts. Ike avoided these vegetables as much as possible, exclaiming disgustedly to Clark that "this must be the fartingest war in history."[24]

He told Mamie that he missed her terribly and sat looking at her picture. "Everything here is strange to me,"[25] he added, which was only too true. When he stayed at Lord Mountbatten's country house, Broadlands, for example, the servants turned up their noses at his meager luggage—so to compensate he left a handsome tip. Naturally he felt most relaxed in the company of Americans. He particularly relished meeting the jolly, fat, rich social and political climber George Allen, who, Ike said, seemed to enjoy his (Eisenhower's) rank (lieutenant general from 7 July) more than he did. Allen did not scruple to offer advice on how to win the war, which prompted Ike's classic retort that "there were only two occupations in which the amateur excels the professional, one military strategy and, two, prostitution."[26] Ike was also delighted when Patton telephoned early in August: "Ike. Goddamnit, I've just arrived in this blasted town. I'm holed up in Claridge's and don't know what to do with myself." "Georgie! Oh, boy am I glad to hear your voice! Come right over and have some Godawful dehydrated chicken soup with me."[27]

Ike's immediate task was to galvanize the American forces into a state of readiness for battle. He began by giving his staff a pep talk in which he said that pessimism and defeatism would not be tolerated. He planned to uproot their headquarters from Grosvenor Square, or Eisenhowerplatz as it came to be called, so that everyone involved in directing the war could work and "live together like a football team"[28]—in due course they moved to Bushey Park, just outside

London. And he insisted that their efforts should not be impeded by red tape or formality. When Tex Lee, overawed by Ike's third star, began to knock at his office door, the general bellowed, "If you have something, bring it in. This is no boudoir!"[29] Omar Bradley recorded that Ike was "ordinarily impersonal, sometimes severe with his official staff."[30] But this was not the general view. By September people were expressing their "astonishment at the closeness of the relationship between Ike and his immediate staff."[31]

Ike did everything he could to establish a similarly close relationship with the press and he treated journalists as "quasi-members of my staff."[32] This proved an excellent way to gain their cooperation. For newsmen in Britain, where unimaginative wartime censorship reinforced the perennial convention that public information is the private property of the government, were used to being treated (more or less) as social outcasts. Ike was astoundingly frank and friendly, though he turned out to be more confiding in manner than in matter (being almost as obsessive about security as Churchill) and he made it plain that he would deal severely with reporters who violated his orders.[33] Wars were won by public opinion, Ike maintained, and he did his best to turn newspapermen into propagandists. Most journalists were soon eating out of his hand—after one press conference McKeogh overheard two of them talking about Ike's "brilliant mind." Ed Murrow was less easily impressed and said in one broadcast that he did not know whether Eisenhower was a good general or not, a comment that made Ike chuckle.

Good public relations were particularly important at this time, when, prior to conducting their first joint military operations, American forces were landing in increasing numbers on British shores. Despite the fundamental solidity of Anglo-American friendship, which was manifested in countless ways and should always be borne in mind, their arrival inevitably created tensions. Many Americans could not conceal their instant aversion for this land of upper-class snobs and working-class slobs. Many Britishers were appalled by the racial discrimination practiced by the U.S. Army—the Red Cross even segregated black and white blood. The Americans found it hard to conceal their contempt for British military failures and their suspicion of British imperialist ambitions. The British resented the Americans' past reluctance to enter the war and their present assumption that they could win it speedily, contrasting easy U.S. words with the gallant deeds of the U.S.S.R.

Other sources of friction were less serious but equally pervasive. There were linguistic difficulties—men at Patton's headquarters thought that one English officer with a particularly aristocratic drawl was speaking French. There were conflicting conventions—American military maps indicated friendly forces in blue and enemies in red, whereas British ones did precisely the opposite. There were financial inequalities—American staff sergeants were paid as much as British captains. This sort of discrepancy exacerbated sexual jealousy, a state of affairs summed up in the old wartime joke about "utility knickers" —"One Yank and they're off." The Americans disliked the cold houses and the warm beer—their standard advice was to "pour it back into the horse." They loathed the tasteless food, sometimes horrified the British by committing gastronomic solecisms like sweetening their porridge with marmalade, and often, like Ike, they longed for delicacies such as hominy grits or U.S. Army beans. They marveled at the plumbing, which was apparently intended to promote dirt and constipation. They raged at the telephones, which seemed designed to impede communications. They could not understand the money—like most of his countrymen Mickey McKeogh just held out a handful of change and "never knew whether I was paying for just a couple of beers or helping them out with the war debt."[34] Nor could Americans accustom themselves to using the left-hand side of the road: on one of the few occasions that Ike drove himself he reached a characteristic compromise—wobbling unsteadily down the middle.

Ike recognized that "all the ingredients for a profound pessimism and mutual recrimination existed" during 1942.[35] He thus made a fetish, or as he liked to call any cause about which he felt strongly, a "crusade," of Allied unity.[36] He did everything possible to overcome division and to promote harmony. On his many tours of inspection he urged courtesy, consideration, and cooperation. He mounted education programs and sent newly arrived troops on tours of the blitzed cities. He was furious when he heard of one American boasting that the GIs would teach the Tommies to fight, and of another who first juggled with, and then ate, two grapefruit in a hotel dining room, when Britons had almost forgotten that such luxuries existed. He threatened to send miscreants like that "home by slow boat preferably unescorted."[37] And in one celebrated instance he ordered an officer back to the States for qualifying the term "son-of-a-bitch" with the adjective "British."[38] His response to the issue of a Jim Crow army was, typically, much more ambivalent: he said that black troops were equal to white and even lifted restrictions on the reporting of outbreaks of racial violence; but he decreed that segregation would continue where facilities permitted.

As for the whole question of linguistic differences, Ike treated it as a running joke. He teased British officers about their illogical pronunciation—gas mawsk—and swore that he would teach them to speak proper English. And he fined Americans a penny each time they let slip native terms like "cheerio," though he himself took to using distinctly un-American words like "flak," "petrol," even "tiffin" (lunch). Worse still, and in Patton's eyes the mark of his having "sold his soul to the devil" in the matter of Allied "cooperation," Ike adopted the decadent British habit of wearing suede shoes.[39] The benevolent sincerity of his endeavors to make the alliance work had an immediate impact in Britain. One GI spoke for many when he said that Ike was "the man of the century, a man of men, who could blend these forces into one happy and united team, where national rivalry was not so much ignored as unthinkable."[40]

Ike also made it his business to construct a good working relationship with the British leaders. At first he found it hard to obtain access to them, largely because of differences of opinion over strategy. But Ike built on his friendship with Mountbatten, who arranged to have the loyal toast drunk immediately after the soup so that his guest could smoke at mealtimes. And Ike soon managed to charm and impress other service chiefs, notably that "Nelsonian sea dog,"[41] Admiral Sir Andrew B. Cunningham, known as ABC. The outstanding figure with whom Ike had to establish a rapport was, of course, Winston Churchill. This he was able to do because of his genuine admiration and affection for the prime minister, which was alloyed with an often amused, though sometimes weary, tolerance of the great man's foibles. Before long he was on informal terms with Churchill, though, as Bedell Smith told Marshall,

This happy state of affairs carried with it the obligation of a weekly dinner at No. 10 Downing Street which is usually terminated about 2:00 A.M. Since I retain my sense of humor I must confess that I derive some comfort from the look of patient resignation on the faces of [General Sir Hastings] Ismay and the C.I.G.S. [Brooke] as they brace themselves for hours in straight backed dining chairs and listen to Mr. Churchill's flights into the stratosphere which they have heard over and over again.[42]

Being, as Butcher said, "a neurotic with an aching ulcer,"[43] Smith endured these feasts less comfortably than Ike, and in the autumn of 1942 he actually spent five days in hospital after undue indulgence in the prime minister's onion soup and game pie.

Ike himself was fascinated by Churchill's dinnertime performances, especially the battle he had with his soup, on which he vented the fury he felt for his own generals. The prime minister crouched over his plate, wielding his spoon rapidly, and the soup disappeared with "raucous gurglings" which, when Ike tried to imitate them for Butcher's benefit, "almost made him choke."[44] Still, the late nights exhausted Ike. So did the relentless pertinacity with which Churchill pressed home his arguments—in order to convince Ike, he drew on everything from the Greek classics to Donald Duck. As the prime minister courteously ushered them out after his marathons into the small hours, Ike and Smith would almost run for the door, fearful of a valedictory harangue, which could last thirty minutes or more. Staying at the prime minister's country house, Chequers, was even more of an ordeal because Ike was a captive audience in what he called a "damned icebox."[45] On one occasion when he did finally get off to sleep, in the huge oaken four-poster bed in a room said to have been occupied by Cromwell, Ike was awakened by a terrible dream in which he was being strangled. McKeogh had forgotten to pack his pajamas and Ike was wearing one of the prime minister's capacious night shirts which had worked itself into a noose around his neck.

Ike and Churchill disagreed at length over the question of SLEDGE-HAMMER. Churchill hankered for an amphibious assault on northern Norway (what Ismay called "an Arctic Gallipoli")[46] or on North Africa (which Marshall rated so irrelevant that, probably as a bluff, he recommended concentrating American resources on the Pacific). Ike did not actually think that a cross-channel operation had much chance of success, but, as he told Fox Conner, the first priority was "to relieve pressure on Russia. When that is done the fate of the Paperhanger is sealed."[47] President Roosevelt's first priority was that American troops should go into action against German forces somewhere in 1942. After fruitless negotiation, it became apparent in July that the British, whose desert stronghold, Tobruk, had fallen to Rommel the previous month, would not consent to SLEDGEHAMMER. Marshall therefore agreed to the autumn invasion of French North Africa, code-named TORCH, as the "least harmful diversion."[48] Ike himself considered that this operation was "strategically unsound" because it did nothing to assist Russia in the short term and it detracted from the long-term effort to open the Second Front in France.[49] And he prophesied that 22 July, the date that SLEDGEHAMMER was finally abandoned, might go down as one of the blackest days in history. With hindsight he completely reversed this opinion, reckoning that without proper air cover the cost of a Cotentin assault would have been great, and without strong ground forces the results would have been meager. Marshall, perhaps contemplating the disastrous failure of the Dieppe raid, went even farther than this: he acknowledged in 1943

that SLEDGEHAMMER might have been "suicidal."[50] Military historians tend to agree. Professor Michael Howard, for example, judged
the plan to be "naïve" and reckoned that the "opportunistic" Mediterranean strategy paid handsome dividends.[51]

It was a measure of Ike's palpable inexperience, or perhaps of his
willingness to defer to Marshall, that he should have supposed that
SLEDGEHAMMER might produce even a hairline crack in such a tough
nut as Hitler's Fortress Europe. It was a measure of his dutiful flexibility, or perhaps of his well-concealed ambition to make his military
mark, that he should so readily have carried TORCH once it was
handed over to him. This happened on 26 July and was officially
confirmed in August, during a nerve-wracking Anglo-American argument about exactly where in French North Africa the landings should
take place. The Americans, fearful that Spain would enter the war and
trap the Allied forces in the Mediterranean, wanted the assault to be
concentrated in the west. The British, anxious to assist their Eighth
Army in Egypt and attack Rommel from the rear, preferred a more
easterly emphasis. Ike himself tended to agree with Churchill that the
early occupation of Tunisia, which would cut the Germans off from
Italy, was "the milk of the whole coconut."[52]

As was so often the case, Ike's military instincts were sound, but he
did not act on them. He made no firm recommendations to Marshall.
And when the chief of staff outspokenly criticized Ike's choice of
subordinate commanders ("tragic error . . . decidedly mediocre"),[53]
Ike accepted instead the likes of General Lloyd R. Fredendall, a
jut-jawed bantam cock of a man about whom he had reservations
which were to prove only too justified. Ike confined himself to the
opinion that TORCH was an "ultra-risky" gamble the outcome of
which was dependent on many factors. These were the efficiency of
carrier-borne aircraft; the efficiency of the only solid airfield, Gibraltar; the weather (Ike proposed to recruit a well-qualified chaplain); the
reception which the Vichy French forces would give to the Allies; the
attitude of Spain; the German response, which might be an invasion
of Spain; and convoy losses. He concluded that "the chances of effect-
ing initial landings were better than even, but that the chances of
overall success in the operation, including the capture of Tunis before
it could be reinforced by the Axis, are considerably less than 50 per
cent."[54]

By the beginning of September the Allies agreed on a compromise
—simultaneous landings at Casablanca, Oran, and Algiers. Ike had
now less than six weeks in which to mount the invasion. He had never
been under such different kinds of pressure, having to be, as he told

Mamie, "a diplomat—lawyer—promotor—salesman—social hound
—*liar* (at least to get out of social affairs)—mountebank—actor—
Simon Legree—humanitarian—orator—and incidentally . . . a soldier."[55] British and Americans came together on his staff, he said, like
a bulldog meeting a cat, and Ike had to work overtime at his unity
crusade, encouraging the Americans to join in afternoon tea breaks
and the British to join in morning coffee breaks. He struggled with
logistical difficulties, increased by the length of supply lines. He inspected troops, watched exercises, held briefings, checked plans, coordinated services, and attended conferences until the sound of the
word "conference" almost drove him mad.

Ike's most intractable problem, however, was a political one, and
it was posed by the French—like Churchill he found that the heaviest
wartime cross he had to bear was the cross of Lorraine. The crux of
the problem was that General Charles de Gaulle, leader of the Free
French, was anathema to President Roosevelt, who put his faith in the
leaders of Vichy France, some of whom, he was convinced, could be
persuaded to oppose the Nazis. Roosevelt's policy, though influenced
by his personal antipathy to a man who saw himself (the president
believed) as the reincarnation of Joan of Arc, was understandable. De
Gaulle's *folie de grandeur* made him almost impossible to cooperate
with—he had nothing to sustain him but pride and intransigence. On
the other hand, Vichy had collaborated with the Germans and there
was every hope that it would do so with the Americans. Leaders like
Admiral Darlan were, admittedly, tainted with Fascism. But so, in the
opinion of Roosevelt, was de Gaulle—though, as Harold Macmillan
said, he was really an old-fashioned authoritarian like Louis XIV, who
believed that he should command and everyone else should obey.[56]
Moreover, the Vichy government was the actual power in North
Africa and would have to be either squashed or squared.

The chief mistake that the Americans made was in placing exaggerated trust in the assurances of the president's diplomatic representative in North Africa, Robert Murphy. He was a red-haired giant
whose main professional qualification was an infectious, but also an
undiscriminating, affability. Murphy was a Midwesterner, rather in
the mold of Eisenhower himself, who loved golf and poker and had
become a diplomat because he found the social life agreeable. He
spoke French fluently and, though inclined to identify with his friends
among the Vichy leaders, he was to become Ike's adviser on civil
affairs in the French colonies. Murphy paid a clandestine visit to Ike
in mid-September in order to explain the bewildering political situation, an account which Ike listened to with "horrified intentness."

Murphy's most important and most erroneous prediction was that Vichy forces in North Africa would rally to the standard of the anti-Nazi general Henri Giraud if he arrived with the American troops. Despite expressing complete confidence in Murphy's honesty and objectivity, Ike evidently had reservations about his assertions. He hoped for the best, and was even ready, as Churchill urged, to "kiss Darlan's arse" if he could thereby secure the French fleet. But he prepared for the worst in the way of Vichyite opposition. And in October he sent Clark on a mission, by submarine, to establish his own contacts with the Vichy resistance. This was a risky, unprofitable, and somewhat farcical undertaking, during the course of which Clark had to hide in a wine cellar (an empty one, he insisted) and lost his trousers in the surf.

Churchill found the adventure thoroughly entertaining, but Ike was not in the mood for humor. Toward the end of October he had worked himself into a "state of jitters."[57] He was tired and bothered, could not concentrate, and "wondered if he was going crazy." He told Marshall, "If a man permitted himself to do so, he could go absolutely frantic about questions of weather, politics, personalities in France and Morocco and so on."[58] However, since September Ike had had a suburban retreat where he could relax and be himself. Butcher had rented a quiet, three-bedroom house called Telegraph Cottage just outside London, and Ike found it "a godsend"—what its new inhabitants did not know was that only a quarter of a mile away there was an air-raid decoy station, where fires were lit to induce German planes to drop their bombs before reaching the capital. The large, wooded garden of Telegraph Cottage adjoined Kingston golf course, and in his rare moments of leisure Ike could hit a golf ball around a hole or two. Otherwise he threw a baseball with Butcher and McKeogh, knocked a shuttlecock about, shot pistols, read Westerns by the score, enjoyed a "sundown highball"[59] and played bridge with his "official family," once again augmented by Kay Summersby.

Theirs was now an equivocal relationship, one that even Ike's closest friends and associates could not fathom. Kay was a flighty and impulsive Irish divorcée who found Ike's easy amiability a charming contrast to the stuffy remoteness of most senior British officers. She was (until commissioned as a WAC in October 1944) the only civilian on Ike's staff and, like the rest of them, she admired Ike to the point of hero worship. Kay was a coquettish creature and, though engaged to marry another American officer, she found it easy to fall in love with her handsome middle-aged boss. Ike himself enjoyed Kay's company. She was a diversion. She stimulated him but he could relax with her.

She was fun and they laughed a lot together. He liked to show her off and he himself became (according to Patton) "show-offish" in her presence.[60] They shared a taste for the same recreations. They both doted on dogs, for example, and a great bond between them was the black Scottie of leaky disposition and uncertain temper which Ike bought for her, but kept himself until 1945. The puppy was called Telek, a name Ike refused to explain on the grounds that it was a military secret. In fact it was a telescoped version of Telegraph Cottage and Kay, "two parts of my life that make me very happy."[61]

Ike was not insensible to Kay's youthful good looks, found excuses for touching her hand or brushing her knee, and he gradually slipped into a flirtation with her. How far his emotions were engaged it is impossible to say. Ike never discussed such interior matters except to tell Kay, "I'm so used to concealing my feelings that there are times when I don't know what I feel—only what I think I ought to feel."[62] It was a singularly revealing confession. Although lonely, Ike was deprived of privacy, so despite being attracted to her he had little opportunity to express any passion he felt. However, his handling of their incipient romance was clumsy, and gossip soon inflated it into a *grand amour.* Ike had to assure Mamie that she was the only person he loved and that he did not want any other wife.

By the beginning of November Ike had done everything possible to ensure that TORCH, once lit, would burn brightly. The invasion fleets, with their total complement of 110,000 men, were sailing in convoy to their various destinations. Patton, despite a blasphemous row with the navy, commanded the western task force, bound for Casablanca. Fredendall led U.S. Second Corps, which was to attack Oran. And General Kenneth A. N. Anderson was in charge of the British First Army, which aimed to capture Algiers, though for the assault its nominal chief was an American. This was part of a stratagem designed to convince Vichy that TORCH was not an Allied invasion but a liberation being effected exclusively by the United States. It was, in fact, a paradoxical venture, as Ike recognized—an attack on a neutral in order to create an ally. However, he could no longer worry about such contradictions. The time for action had come, and after a delay imposed by the weather Ike took flight on 5 November 1942 for his new headquarters at Gibraltar. He rather relished taking operational command of this ancient fortress, "the symbol of the solidity of the British Empire."[63] And he was further gratified by Churchill, who expressed full confidence that the Rock would be safe in Ike's hands.

6

★

From TORCH to Tunis

Actually the few days Ike spent in Gibraltar were packed with the most acute anxiety he experienced throughout the war. At that time he had no famous achievements to his credit and his entire career depended on the outcome of circumstances over which he had little or no control. Sitting in the bowels of the Rock, Ike and his deputy Mark Clark discussed their situation at length and sagely concluded that they would soon be lions or lice. Meanwhile Murphy was evidently in a panic: his amateur fifth column, which was supposed to assist the Americans, was so far from being ready that he had urged the postponement of the invasion for two weeks—a fantastic request which was at once refused. Now he was sending messages in a code to which no one in Gibraltar had the key—they had to be deciphered by analytical methods and turned out to be "slightly hysterical" in tone.[1] In fact, Gibraltar proved to be altogether unsatisfactory as a communications center and Ike found it almost impossible to obtain up-to-date information about the fate of his forces. This blind waiting in the stagnant, dripping, ill-lit cave which was his headquarters tested his spirit and his temper to breaking point. Ike even took to worrying about Telek—on the day of the invasion he sought reassurance from Bedell Smith that all was well with "the black imp."[2]

The most frustrating part of Ike's ordeal was his attempt to bend the proud and stubborn General Henri Giraud to his will. Giraud had been brought from France by submarine and flying boat and he landed at Gibraltar on 7 November, on the eve of the invasion. Although Ike later denied that he had any right to impose a government on French North Africa, at the time he wanted Giraud to be the Allies' puppet governor. But the general insisted on being his own man, and unfortunately Murphy had given him the impression that he would command the Allied forces after the landings had taken place. He demanded nothing less as the price of his cooperation and even refused Ike's request to broadcast a proclamation urging Vichy forces to side with the Americans. A gaunt, unshaven figure in a rumpled civilian suit, Giraud was nevertheless every inch a five-star general. His bearing was martial, his mustache bristled, and he referred to himself (like MacArthur and de Gaulle) in the third person. He reminded Patton of Vercingetorix. And he even tried to pull rank on Eisenhower.

Giraud was a bold, adventurous soldier who had twice escaped from internment in Germany. He even had a sense of humor—diplomats got up late to do nothing all day, he once said, and generals got up early to do the same. But he was also a grotesque anachronism, the sort of oak-leafed donkey who had led lions to the slaughter in the Great War. Giraud was stately, stupid, unimaginative, reactionary, and inflexible. In an argument lasting for eight hours he remained unmoved by Ike's appeals, bribes, and threats. Instead he actually required that the invasion target be changed from North Africa to southern France, and when his impossible demands were refused he announced, "Giraud will be a spectator in this affair."[3] Though preserving a diplomatic exterior, Ike raged internally and talked of having Giraud assassinated. To Bedell Smith he angrily complained that Giraud had procrastinated for fear of alienating any Frenchmen and wanted to arrive as "a knight in white armor and be the big hero to lead France to VICTORY."[4] Actually, Ike himself had procrastinated, delaying the transmission of Giraud's cautious messages to French North Africa and ensuring that his own proclamation was broadcast in Giraud's name. Ironically, it had no effect whatsoever. Giraud was a military as well as a political cipher.

Nevertheless the invasion was a triumphant success, partly because it achieved complete surprise but mainly because French resistance proved so half-hearted. At Casablanca, it is true, General Auguste Noguès did oppose the Americans with some determination at first, but as Patton told Ike, "I am forced to believe that either my proverbial luck or probably the direct intervention of the Lord was responsible . . . because every operation went exactly as we planned."[5] There was also some fierce fighting at Oran, where the Americans performed splendidly and achieved their objectives by force of arms. However, at Algiers opposition crumbled swiftly, despite a series of mistakes which exposed Allied inexperience at the hazardous art of carrying out amphibious operations. Ships lost themselves in the dark; troops were landed higgledy-piggledy on the wrong beaches and mustered pell-mell in view of the French; equipment and supplies were late in arriving; an unnecessary frontal assault on the harbor was bloodily repulsed; coordination with resistance groups was chaotic. In short, TORCH showed that SLEDGEHAMMER would almost certainly have missed its mark, though it did become the first of several invaluable rehearsals for the invasion of France in 1944.

Still, the Allies suffered only a tenth of the expected casualties, eighteen hundred instead of eighteen thousand, though Ike understandably fumed at the "stupid Frogs" for causing these and thus delaying his vital drive toward Tunisia.[6] Moreover, apparently by a stroke of luck, Admiral Darlan happened to be in Algiers. As Pétain's deputy, he really did carry weight with French forces and when he agreed to a local cease-fire on 8 November his orders were obeyed. Meanwhile Giraud had been won round, Ike having exaggerated the extent of the Allied victory and Clark having threatened that unless the "old gentleman" at once cooperated "your ass is out in the snow."[7] So on 9 November, backed by enthusiastic American endorsements, Giraud flew to Algiers. But, still dressed in civilian clothes and wearing a bowler hat, he felt unable to put himself at the head of the French forces and soon he had to go into hiding for fear of arrest by the Vichy police.

However, on the same day Ike sent Clark to negotiate a complete armistice with Darlan. The tall, beak-nosed general treated the little bald admiral like a "lieutenant junior grade."[8] He banged the table, shouted at him, threatened him with prison and even execution, so intimidating him that Darlan soon capitulated. However, because of his sworn allegiance to Pétain and his atavistic Anglophobia, he did so with much hedging. He ordered a cease-fire in Casablanca and Oran, where Patton was almost, and Fredendall was already, victorious. But he only "invited" the Toulon fleet to join the Allies, an invitation to which Admiral De La Borde responded simply, "Merde,"[9] his equivalent of General McAuliffe's celebrated "Nuts." Even when Darlan gained complete freedom of action after the Nazi invasion of Vichy France—it was presumed that Pétain was now acting under duress—he failed to make the paralyzed Vichy leadership in Tunisia resist the German forces which were at once rushed there. So Ike was denied both the prizes which the deal with Darlan was supposed to bring him, the French fleet and the conquest of Tunisia.

This was not entirely apparent, however, on 13 November, when Ike flew to Algiers and signed the agreement with Darlan, who became in consequence high commissioner of North Africa. Indeed there seemed much to be said for a deal that secured Ike's rear, kept the colonial lid on the Arab kettle, made Giraud commander in chief

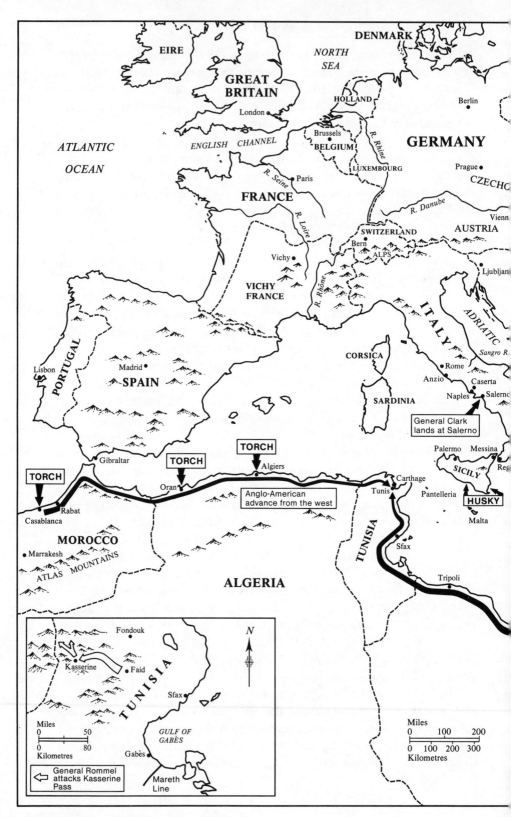

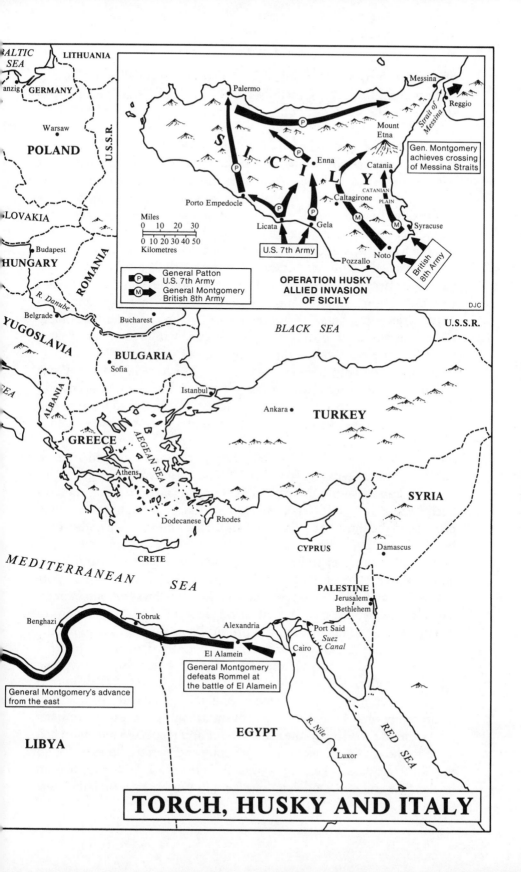

**OPERATION HUSKY
ALLIED INVASION
OF SICILY**

Gen. Montgomery achieves crossing of Messina Straits

U.S. 7th Army

Miles
0 10 20 30
0 10 20 30 40 50
Kilometres

General Patton
U.S. 7th Army
General Montgomery
British 8th Army

British 8th Army

DJC

General Montgomery defeats Rommel at the battle of El Alamein

General Montgomery's advance from the east

TORCH, HUSKY AND ITALY

of all French forces in North Africa, and transformed part of Vichy from neutral into ally. Certainly Ike thought the Darlan deal corresponded to the wishes of both Roosevelt (whose distrust of de Gaulle was such that the Secret Service protected their president with concealed machine guns when they met in North Africa) and Churchill (who in some moods thought de Gaulle worse than Darlan and was anyway prepared to hold hands with the devil in order to win the war). And it seemed to leave Ike free to concentrate on military matters. So he was, despite subsequent denials, quite unprepared for the outcry about his having treated with a Nazi collaborator. He had thus, it was said, sullied the purity of the Allied cause and brought, as *Time* magazine put it, "sickness" to the world, "disillusion" to the people of occupied Europe, and "shame" to the United States and Britain.[10] He might have anticipated de Gaulle's own condemnation of this "sickening saga."[11] But Ike had no inkling of the international storm that would be provoked by this accord with a member of what Churchill had once called the "filthy race of quislings."[12]

Ike was strangely oblivious to the Fascist character of the Vichy regime and it was indicative of his political innocence that even after the war he pronounced the word "Fatchist"[13] when complaining that this was what newspapers had called him in 1942. Yet the evidence of Fascism in Algeria, anti-Semitic statutes and concentration camps, stared him in the face. However, despite promises, he did little to eradicate these evils. This was the most serious count against his political stewardship in North Africa. For the Darlan deal might have been justifiable in military terms, as a necessary though hateful compromise in the interest of ultimate victory, like the alliance with Stalin; but Ike gave few indications of finding the Vichy government objectionable, let alone of trying to purge its most repulsive features. As late as March 1943, John J. McCloy, assistant secretary of war, wrote to him: "I can find no good reason why the Nazi laws still obtain here. Their repeal would have no effect on 'le Problème Mussulman' of which we hear so much; it would produce a profound change for the better in American public opinion"—especially if accomplished before the arrival of de Gaulle, who would otherwise receive the credit.[14] As always Ike was insensitive to civil liberties. He preferred the pragmatic approach to the moral one, though he had a compulsion to dress up what he took to be realism as righteousness. Like many Americans he worshiped the success ethic and respected men who had gone to the top in any field. Like Murphy and Patton, he even found the Vichy leaders personally agreeable. He thought Noguès had an honest face and expected that "our gang in Washington took the view of 'Oh well, he may be a son-of-a-bitch, but he's OUR son-of-a-bitch *now.*' "[15]

Actually both president and prime minister were pushed onto the defensive by the tornado of protest stirred up by the Darlan deal. But they were impressed by Ike's argument based on military necessity— so impressed, indeed, that as Roosevelt declaimed it aloud, "with the same superb distribution of emphasis that he used in his public speeches, he sounded as if he were making an eloquent plea for Eisenhower before the bar of history."[16] Ike's justification was so persuasive that Churchill's friend, the South African premier, General J. C. Smuts, who was visiting North Africa, endorsed it. He told the prime minister, and through him the president, that "Darlan was not Eisenhower's choice but that of other French leaders, some of whom were his enemies and our strong supporters and who all agreed that his leadership in cooperation was essential for our operation."[17] So Roosevelt and Churchill approved the Darlan deal as a temporary emergency measure, though the prime minister implied in a secret session of Parliament that it was really the fault of the United States. Churchill assured Ike that he would act as strong fortification covering his rear but was quick to appoint Harold Macmillan as his cabinet minister resident in North Africa to advise on future political matters.

Macmillan found Ike, who had briefly imposed censorship on political views, bewildered and hurt by the adverse publicity. "I can't understand why these long-haired, starry-eyed guys keep gunning for me," he exclaimed; "I'm no reactionary. Christ on the mountain! I'm as idealistic as Hell."[18] Butcher's complaint doubtless echoed Ike's:

In England we were harassed by those liberty loving provocateurs who thought we should develop a great social experiment of handling the negroes so they would have complete social equality. We apparently are supposed by these same busybodies [including "the louse" Ed Murrow, to whose "idealist fulminations" Butcher took particular exception] to have a general election of Arabs, Jews and French to elect a Congress and President and then go on with the war.[19]

Though "terribly proud of the firm, clear way [Ike] is handling the job,"[20] Milton Eisenhower was so worried about the public response to the Darlan deal that he flew over to help disseminate counter-propaganda, which involved him in having rows with Bedell Smith and telling Murphy that heads must roll. Actually, Ike himself was quite lucky not to have been cut off in his prime. The politicians might easily have made him their scapegoat. As ever, the chief of staff's support was crucial: he even took the unprecedented step of appealing to broadcasters and journalists not to criticize the Darlan deal. But later Eisenhower was "more-or-less bawled out by General Marshall because his presentation of the North African campaign, especially the reasons for Darlan, had not been explained by Ike as 'dramatically' as it had been done to Marshall by General Clark."[21]

Ike moved his permanent headquarters to Algiers on 23 November. He found the bleached city beautiful and picturesque, but also filthy and squalid. He told the "gang" from Telegraph Cottage, whose company he missed, "If you have any romantic anticipations involving an Arab sheik of the Rudolph Valentino type, I advise you to come prepared with half a dozen scrubbing brushes and at least a barrel of strong washing powder." However, Ike added, he had been ill (with a bout of "walking pneumonia" that lasted two months) so he would "probably have a caustic word or two to say about Cleopatra."[22] He certainly had caustic words about the villa overlooking the harbor which Butcher had requisitioned for him: it was "gloomy" and all its facilities were "typically French and you know what that means." Ike was only warm when in bed. His rest was disturbed by air raids. The food, mainly mutton, was indifferent. He lacked feminine companionship. His semi-armored Cadillac kept breaking down and it guzzled gas so fast, according to Ike, that they had to switch off the engine while filling up "or it gets ahead of the hose."[23] He was surrounded by armed guards "which makes me feel like——,"* and his work was back-breaking because of the constant switch between low intrigue and high strategy—"I don't know whether I'm a rhinoserous (guess I'm not because I can't spell it) or a house fly."[24] Ike complained so about incidental matters because by the end of November it was becoming clear that his strategy was on the point of failure. Tunisia was now firmly in the hands of the Germans.

According to Butcher, Ike resembled "a caged tiger, snarling and clawing to get things done."[25] Yet Ike bore the ultimate responsibility for the slowness of the eastward advance, and his impatience was more apparent in words than in deeds. He took to saying that anyone could have his job and that what he really wanted was to rush to the front, grab a rifle, and start killing Germans himself. He also insisted that his operations were bold and unorthodox. Churchill himself was sufficiently impressed by them to tell Ike on 7 December: "I am filled with admiration by the brilliant advance you have made and not repeat not

---

*Ike had the orthodox army officer's attitude toward swear words. He used them frequently to give added emphasis to his remarks, especially in all-male company, where his conversation was colorful rather than obscene. But on paper he deleted even the mildest expletives, preferring blanks to damns. I quote him exactly in each case.

at all disappointed by the check our vanguards have received in their audacious attempt to seize the maximum territory possible before enemy resistance solidified. You were absolutely right to run all risks."[26] In fact Ike was unduly cautious. Although he was apparently convinced that Spain would not enter the war, Ike left his best commander, Patton, in Morocco. There "Old Blood and Guts" was entertained with displays of Arab horsemanship, with falcon and boar hunts, with French and native ceremonial, and with exotic meals—including ten-course breakfasts ending in couscous and ice cream. He soon became "great buddies" with Noguès who easily persuaded him that this land, which was "half-Hollywood and half-Bible,"[27] could be a complete paradise without the Jews. Patton also hobnobbed with the sultan, telling Ike that "I was in such a rush I forgot to button my fly. Keys noted it and we closed the gap—it might have looked as if I was prepared to go all out in the harem to produce allies. . . . You may presently discover I have become a Mohammedan."[28]

If Ike had channeled Patton's drive into the attack he might have won the race for Tunisia. Instead he confronted the Germans with a poorly reinforced Anderson, whose sluggishness he privately decried. And by ordering Fredendall to secure his position, he encouraged the defensive inclinations of a general who, for all his tough talk, kept two hundred engineers busy for three weeks building him an underground command post in an almost inaccessible canyon. By 16 December Churchill had changed his tune, telling Ike: "It is wise to keep the enemy bleeding and burning up his strength even if we sustain equal losses. Thus a larger animal crushes the life out of a weaker and never gives him the chance to gather strength for a spring."[29] There were, it is true, reasons remote from Ike's leadership why progress was so slow—long and poor lines of communication, lack of transport, inadequate weapons, and muddles such as the equipping of American M-3 tanks (no match, in any case, for German Mark IV Specials) with feeble training ammunition instead of new armor-piercing shells. Finally, of course, there was the weather: when the rains reduced the ground to mud in December the advance came to a full stop.

Ike allowed himself to become bogged down in the political quagmire four hundred miles west of the front. From Algiers he was not able to exert a grip on the battle, but he also failed to forge an effective chain of command. This was not altogether his fault, as the French stubbornly refused to serve under the British. So Ike was eventually forced to appoint an American intermediary, General Lucian K. Truscott, Jr., to coordinate the operations of the three national forces. But exactly how the role of Truscott, himself stationed at a command post halfway between Algiers and the fighting, fitted with that of Anderson, Ike's "adviser" for the entire Tunisian front, was unclear.[30] Furthermore, Fredendall, whose control of American forces was remote and arbitrary enough and who disliked both British and French, did little to assist inter-Allied cooperation. It was ironic that Ike, the great apostle of coalition warfare, could not achieve unified direction of his first major military enterprise.

To overcome this serious disadvantage Ike did make a couple of exhausting journeys over bad roads to the front. But the first accomplished little and the second was interrupted by the news, delivered on Christmas Eve, that Darlan had been assassinated. His murderer, a young royalist named Bonnier de la Chapelle, had been recruited by the British Secret Operations Executive and used one of their weapons to do the killing. But he seems to have been acting out of loyalty to the French pretender, the comte de Paris. Nevertheless, there is no doubt that Darlan's death was a most welcome Christmas present for the Allies. They were, as Darlan himself surmised, planning to drop him like a squeezed lemon when he had served his purpose. Now Ike could put Giraud in his place without the risk of antagonizing Vichy forces. Unfortunately, though, Giraud was as recalcitrant as ever and Ike's energies were drained because he constantly had to resolve Allied squabbles.

He did so by an almost superhuman display of friendliness, frankness, and honesty. As Ike told Ismay, he cultivated a reputation for bluntness, particularly with the French, representing himself as "a man too simple-minded to indulge in circumlocution."[31] Actually Ike handled all the Allies with consummate tact. He really tried to conjure a single force out of the disparate nationalities. He even insisted that his command could not be properly integrated unless proper respect were paid to the rights of the relatively few serving women (though he was later to make a brief and ludicrous attempt to purge their ranks of lesbians). Ike liked to exercise his charm rather than his authority, to issue congratulatory notes rather than reprimands. He often allowed himself to be diverted from the path of strict military duty by the need to achieve compromise and to preserve unity. This is not to say that Ike was unduly weak, merely that he preferred persuasion to coercion as a means of leadership. In fact he acquired a reputation for brutal ruthlessness when it came to sending home American officers who fell short of his expectations. And he was quite capable of rebuking the disruptively ambitious Clark, though he seems also to have succumbed to pressure from Clark to give him command of the Fifth Army, which was activated in January.

Ike did not impress the Allied leaders who gathered for the Casablanca Conference, which was held in the middle of that month in an atmosphere of extreme Allied goodwill (assisted by frequent highballs, games of bezique, and community singing led by president and prime minister) to discuss future strategy. Roosevelt thought Ike jittery, though his state was perhaps attributable to a terrifying flight over the Atlas Mountains during which two of the airplane engines conked out. Still, Ike did give the president, who was in bed, such a smart salute that Macmillan whispered to Murphy, "Isn't he just like a Roman centurion?"[32] Macmillan's colleagues would have found it a suitable simile, for they considered that Ike's military expertise was roughly on a par with that of a Roman centurion. Nevertheless, they acknowledged his magical skill at leading an armed coalition in which, as Ike himself shrewdly remarked, the partners were liable to consider each other, and not the Germans, the principal enemy. So despite Ike's lack of success in Tunisia, he was designated the future commander of all Allied forces in North Africa, including Montgomery's Eighth Army. The hope of Churchill and Brooke was that Ike's British deputies, such as the genial General Sir Harold Alexander and the outspoken Air Marshal Arthur Tedder, would fight Rommel, while Eisenhower would be the Allied figurehead.

Ike himself rejected this role, insisting that he must exercise real power if he was to bear final responsibility. At the same time he availed himself freely of the advice and experience of his subordinates. For example, he abandoned his plan to advance toward the Tunisian port of Sfax in response to Alexander's criticism that the move was not coordinated with Montgomery's operations. Moreover, Ike carried to extremes the American custom of allowing his juniors to exercise a large measure of tactical initiative free of control from above. The practice was to prove its worth once the officers in question had been tried and tested in battle. But initially Ike would have done well to have kept them on a tighter rein, especially as he noticed deficiencies in his forces on his two January tours of the front—as did the Germans in their successful probes. Ike was particularly unwilling to intervene in Fredendall's dispositions. After the success at Oran Ike had told Marshall, "I bless the day you urged Fredendall upon me and cheerfully acknowledge that my earlier doubts about him were completely unfounded."[33] Although his doubts returned, especially when he saw Fredendall's underground headquarters, Ike would only proceed by hints. He suggested to Fredendall, "One of the things that gives me most concern is the habit of some of our generals in staying too close to their command posts."[34]

On 13 February, two days after receiving his fourth star, Ike visited
the front again, anxious about Rommel's imminent attack. Once
again, unfortunately, he failed to give Fredendall a clear lead. He
seemed to agree both with Truscott, who wanted to hold certain
forward regions, and with Anderson, who proposed to abandon them.
And apart from asking why so few minefields had been laid (a satisfactory answer was not forthcoming), he volunteered no criticism of the
defensive dispositions. Indeed, at the time he reported that these were
"as good as could be made pending the development of an actual
attack and in view of the great value of holding the forward regions,
if it could possibly be done,"[35] though in his war memoirs he professed to have been disturbed by what he saw. Only a few hours
before it was launched on 14 February, Ike was actually walking in
the desert at the exact point where the Germans were aiming their
attack. It caught him by surprise, largely because he placed excessive
faith in his paunchy British intelligence officer. This was Brigadier
Eric Mockler-Ferryman, who in turn put total trust in the British code
breakers. Their decrypts of German radio signals, known as ULTRA,
indicated that the assault was coming through the Fondouk Pass to the
north. Actually the German high command was itself in a state of
confusion, and Rommel was determined to break through the Faid
Pass to the south, as was suggested by other intelligence sources.
Rommel intended that his veteran troops should instill in the raw
Americans "from the outset an inferiority complex of no mean
order."[36]

Thanks to poor command coordination, interrupted communications, inferior tanks, inexperience, lack of discipline, frequent errors,
and intermittent panic on the American side, he managed to do just
that. There were factors to compensate for the reverse—individual
acts of heroism, a superb performance by the artillery, the "blooding"
of an army corps, the emergence of excellent battle commanders like
General Ernest N. Harmon, and the detection of indifferent ones like
Fredendall. Moreover, Rommel's withdrawal after taking the Kasserine Pass encouraged the notion, which was good for morale, that
U.S. forces had not been beaten and that the enemy was not invincible. The statistics did not support this optimistic view: the Germans
had lost under 1,000 men, 14 guns and 20 tanks, compared to 7,000
casualties on the American side and the destruction of 208 guns, 183
tanks, and much other materiel. Butcher concluded ruefully, "The
outstanding fact to me is that the proud and cocky Americans to-day
stand humiliated by one of the greatest defeats in our history."[37]

Moreover, at the crucial moment of the battle Ike had failed to play a sound hunch. On 22 February he sensed that Rommel had run out of steam and that now was the time to launch a counterattack. "I was so certain of this evaluation," he later wrote, "that I told the Corps Commander that I would assume full responsibility for any disadvantage that might result from vigorous action on his part." But Fredendall felt that the enemy had "one more shot in his locker" and wanted twenty-four hours to perfect his defenses. "No one," Ike concluded, with that bewildering air of detachment which he so often adopted in order to shuffle off personal responsibility, "could quarrel violently with this decision."[38] Yet it was precisely during those twenty-four hours that the Desert Fox slipped away from a field of battle on which he might have been caught.

In defense of the Americans at Kasserine it must be said that from general to private they were wholly lacking in experience—some GIs found themselves facing the best troops in the world, led by one of the best commanders, without ever having fired a rifle. Ike himself did not blink at valid criticism of certain divisions (notably the First Armored and the Thirty-fourth Infantry) but, as he told General Omar Bradley, "the experience of the British Army in its early days in the desert was, in some instances, far more unfortunate than has been our own."[39] Moreover American soldiers, though they never became as good combat fodder as the Germans, learned fast; whereas in 1944 Montgomery had doubts about the competence of some British units that had been fighting for five years. But Alexander, who took over as Ike's deputy in the middle of the Kasserine battle and helped to stiffen resistance, was right in his disparaging conclusion that the American forces had only reached the "territorial," or amateur, stage.[40]

Ike acknowledged this by asking Alexander to second some experienced British officers in order to give U.S. troops further training. Naturally this rubbed salt in the wounds, and on 4 March the journalist Drew Middleton told Butcher of "the existence of bitter feeling of Americans against British because of the recent American defeat. He thinks the cause of such feeling comes from a desired alibi of the defeat."[41] The animosity was increased by the British themselves, some of whom referred to the Americans as "our Italians" and sang "How Green Was My Ally." Ike, who was not unduly perturbed because he realized that the seeds of this discord had been sown long ago in history, had to exercise his conciliatory powers to the utmost.

Having dismissed his British intelligence officer, Mockler-Ferryman, he now determined to replace Fredendall, who had not only failed to inspire loyalty in his officers and fighting spirit in his troops, but had "permitted, if not promoted, anti-British feeling" throughout his command.[42] Ike did so partly, it seems, at Alexander's instigation, and only after characteristic velleities. Acknowledging that he should earlier have appointed Patton to Fredendall's job, Ike said that he did not now want to "let a commander down when his chin is drooping."[43] On 2 March he even assured Fredendall, "I am always perfectly frank and tell you what is in my mind. . . . I would not leave you in command of that Corps one second if you did not have my confidence." Yet on 5 March Ike fired Fredendall, disguising the fact by asserting that he would be invaluably employed training troops in the United States. Ike urged his successor, Patton (who told Butcher that he had a strong desire personally to shoot Rommel), to be cold-blooded about relieving incompetent officers—but, typically, he did not take his own advice. Indeed, he admitted to Patton that he ought to sack Anderson but did not want to hurt his feelings—even though, as McCloy reported in March, Anderson had "lost the confidence of the American commanders" and men. Once again, perhaps, Ike's visceral commitment to the Alliance stayed his hand. At any rate McCloy was "deeply impressed with the way you have welded this joint effort together. It was not easy to do with all the traditions of separation which have grown up in our Army."[44]

Ike told his son John that he sometimes felt guilty when contemplating the contrast between "the mud and slime of the Tunisian battlefields" and his comfortable house in Algiers with native rugs on the floor and "a group of darkies that take gorgeous care of me."[45] Ike was indeed cosseted. Marshall had ordered him a masseur (whom he dismissed after one session). Ike had acquired a Ping-Pong table, on which he played evenly matched games with Admiral Cunningham. Telek had been flown over from England and since Ike had not the heart to house-train him he left puddles everywhere, on one occasion, before the astonished gaze of Eisenhower and Marshall, relieving himself twice on the maroon silk cover of the bed the chief of staff was about to occupy. McKeogh shined Ike's brass, ironed his shoelaces, changed his razor blades, put paste on his toothbrush, kept him supplied with chocolate bars, chewing gum, and Westerns, helped him to dress and undress—and no man was ever more a hero to his valet.

Tex Lee looked after all his boss's other needs, though Ike joked that "one of the chief problems of a general officer is the care and feeding of his aide."[46] With his "marvelously sunny disposition,"[47] Butcher did his best to buoy up Ike's spirits and, obeying Marshall's order to "keep Eisenhower on a pedestal," he managed his chief's public relations adeptly, censoring "numerous hells, godawfuls, and frequent damns" from his pronouncements.[48] Kay Summersby was also in close attendance and in January 1943 she was even recommended for the Legion of Merit, a recommendation that Marshall turned down. In addition to her other duties Kay went horseback riding with Ike—and when a GI hooted at them the general could only glare. Eisenhower discussed Kay with his old friend Everett Hughes, who wrote in his diary: "I don't know whether Ike is alibi-ing or not. Says he wants to hold her hand, accompanies her to house, doesn't sleep with her. He doth protest too much, especially in view of the gal's reputation in London."[49]

Ike protested a good deal more to Mamie, who frequently saw Kay in the background of newspaper photographs of America's "brilliant" commander in North Africa and became understandably suspicious. He told her to ignore stories, gossip, and lies, admitted that he had been "intrigued momentarily" in the past, but asserted that he had never been in love with anyone but her. He assured her that he was too busy and lived too much in public to have "emotional involvements" and that, apart from her, he was too old for romance.[50] Mamie's jealousy was sharpened by loneliness. She was almost a prisoner in the Wardman Park Hotel, because she did not like to take a pleasure ride in a cab for fear of setting a horrible example, thereby bringing disgrace on Ike, and, as he said, "she hates walking like the devil hates holy water."[51] She had only the solitary and drunken Ruth Butcher for companionship, and Ike himself increasingly seemed to her "a dream out of the past." Her stake in him was diminishing as his fame grew and she even worried that others would see her letters to him. Clumsily confirming her fear that he had become public property, Ike assured Mamie that no one would dare to peek at his private correspondence because, "After all, here in Africa, I'm not an ignored nonentity."[52]

This was undeniable. But during the couple of months after Kasserine Ike did not actually take quite the prominent part in political and military affairs that he was entitled to, in view of his position. His morale was already dampened by the further press criticism caused by his innocent appointment of the viciously Vichyite Marcel Peyrouton as governor general of Algeria under Giraud. Later Ike admitted that this was a mistake, but at the time he was indignant about the "howls of anguish" in the newspapers. He asserted that Peyrouton was a good administrator (true enough—he had implemented anti-Semitic decrees in France) and felt that the liberals were crucifying him.[53] Ike's frame of mind was not improved when he heard that Roosevelt, who brought de Gaulle and Giraud together in his famous shotgun wedding (never consummated) at Casablanca, thought that he had not been firm enough with the French. However, when Ike did firmly refuse to allow de Gaulle to visit Algiers in April he was outmaneuvered by the Frenchman, who published the prohibition and established himself as an injured innocent. Ike was furious and doubtless inspired Butcher's fulminations against "the louse" who employed "racketeers" and permitted them to use "third degree methods" to force his countrymen into his camp.[54]

Ike could not extricate himself from the dire complexities of French politics, but he did take a back seat in military affairs for a time. Although he concealed the fact carefully, he was dejected by his own performance and embarrassed by that of the American troops. Patton said that Ike was as low as "whale tracks on the bottom of the sea,"[55] and in a strange diary entry covering the events between 19 January and 25 February Ike entirely omitted to mention the Kasserine defeat. After it he appeared to let the amiable Alexander handle strategic matters while he himself came to resemble, according to Macmillan, "the chairman of a company."[56] Ike confined himself largely to making up the losses in materiel. It was America's industrial might (Rommel had been amazed by the excellence of the equipment he captured) which spelled doom for Germany in North Africa. Nearly all Hitler's energy and attention was focused on the titanic struggle in Russia, while his army in Tunisia, enfeebled by lack of support, was squeezed to death between the Allied pincers.

Even so the crushing process was by no means easy. Montgomery himself, suffering from an excess of overconfidence, received a severe setback when he tried to penetrate the Germans' defensive Mareth Line on too narrow a front. Ike was to hear how Monty became "a complete 'wreck'—lost control of himself, etc."[57] in front of his convivial chief of staff, Francis de Guignand, and asked how the situation could be retrieved. At the time Ike concluded that Monty was unquestionably able, but, though wilfully cocksure, he was also fearful of tarnishing his success at El Alamein. Ike's complaints that Monty was too slow and cautious, while being desperate to grab glory, were to be frequently repeated. Monty's opinion of him was summed up in a letter written to Alexander shortly after Ike (who "brought no bedding!!") visited his headquarters. He liked the American. "But," he continued, in his usual tone of lofty disparagement, "I could not stand him about the place for long; his high-pitched accent, and loud talking, would drive me mad. I should say he was good probably on the political line; but he obviously knows nothing whatever about fighting."[58]

In fact Ike intervened only once in the battle for Tunisia. He did so at the behest of Marshall, who protested about Alexander's plan to confine American forces to a subsidiary role in the final thrust. Even then Ike sought a compromise, but the chief of staff was adamant. Ike finally had to insist—Alexander had refused his request—that Second Corps be fully employed. Thanks partly to Patton's martinet methods and partly to the hardening process begun at Kasserine, the Americans acquitted themselves well. Ike was delighted. He wondered about designing a special uniform for himself with some "scrambled egg" on the cap and suggested that he and Butcher should get "good and drunk when 'Tunisia is in the bag.' "[59] Tunisia was duly bagged, and with it nearly a quarter of a million prisoners—an embarrassment to Ike, who told Marshall with uncharacteristic bloodthirstiness that it was "too bad we couldn't have killed more"[60]—on 13 May. This was just two days before the date Ike had set for the German collapse in a prophecy made four months earlier.

The German defeat in North Africa was greater even than that at Stalingrad. And the press, so long filled with news of Allied disaster, was wildly enthusiastic about this first triumph in the West. Butcher recorded that at the end of one interview the reporter practically nominated Ike for president—in private the general and his aide proceeded to pick a cabinet, selecting Bedell Smith to be "head of the Gestapo as he likes to cut throats."[61] Though outwardly modest, Ike was secretly proud of his achievement, which was marked by joyful celebrations. These he professed to hate, cursing the fact that he could not refuse a decoration from that "damned puppet" the bey of Tunis. He was indeed "noticeably uncomfortable" during the ceremony, a colorful affair complete with gold throne, turbaned eunuchs in white robes, and native troops in exotic uniforms, at which Ike was presented with a tinsel star on a pink and green sash.[62]

But Ike could not conceal his relish for the victory parade, a magnificent show in which thirty thousand Allied troops took part. They ranged from red-cloaked, sword-bearing Spahis on white horses, through kilted pipers of the Scots Guards, to beautifully equipped and newly confident American detachments. Ike repeated "ecstatically" to Harold Macmillan and others that "he had never believed it possible to dream of having such an honor as to command an army like this."[63] But he must have been uneasily aware that his own leadership had been irresolute. Had he made up for it by his unrivaled capacity for keeping the Allies working in concert? Omar Bradley's final verdict was just: Ike's African record "clearly demonstrates" that although he "did not know how to manage a battlefield," he was "a political

general of rare and valuable gifts."[64] Monty, who as a result of a
jocular bet with Bedell Smith demanded (and received) a Flying
Fortress for his personal use, demonstrated an uncanny knack of
offending his American partners at every opportunity. Eisenhower's
adroitness at coalition warfare was well illustrated in his reply to
Macmillan's congratulations on his victory in Tunisia. It was, Ike
insisted, a strictly Allied achievement—*our* victory.

7
★

The Navel
of the Underbelly

At the Casablanca Conference it had been agreed that once the enemy was defeated in North Africa the Allies would take Sicily, thus securing the sea route from Gibraltar to Suez. What strategy to adopt once Sicily had fallen was debated but not decided. Roosevelt, primed by Marshall, asserted that the quickest route to victory was across the English Channel. Churchill, who had at first been furious when Ike told him that the effort to light TORCH would extinguish any hope of invading France in 1943, now hankered to knock Italy out of the war. Ike himself was beset by characteristic hesitations. He assured Marshall that he had not lost faith in ROUNDUP, but at the same time he said that the coastal defenses of western Europe were now exceedingly formidable and thought it a waste not to employ the huge accumulation of Allied power (under his command) in the Mediterranean. Quite where it should be used he was not sure.

He explored Churchill's chimerical idea of moving eastward and bringing Turkey into the conflict. He nurtured irrelevant designs against Sardinia, until Churchill categorically refused to be "fobbed off with a sardine."[1] He even captured the island of Pantelleria, with its important airfield, treating the operation as a laboratory experiment in the use of heavy bombing. He lost not a single man in the process (though one Tommy was bitten by a mule) and gained a centime for every prisoner over three thousand, the number Churchill bet him would be captured—in fact eleven thousand were taken and at that rate Churchill offered to buy the whole Italian army. Ike was elated by this achievement, which was carried out (on 11 June) in the face of almost total opposition by his subordinates. But the decisiveness he here displayed (though he quaked internally, Butcher noted) was exceptional. Still, Ike cannot be judged too harshly for halting so long between various opinions, for he was only reflecting the strategic struggle that was being waged between his American and British masters.

Less defensible was Ike's vacillation over the Sicilian invasion itself, code-named HUSKY. At one point he said that it would be impracticable if there were more than two German divisions in Sicily. This "pusillanimous and defeatist" doctrine Churchill damned with much vituperation. He declared that it contrasted oddly with Ike's earlier endorsement of SLEDGEHAMMER, fulminated about the total absence of "directing mind and commanding will power" in Algiers, and asked what Stalin, facing 185 German divisions, would make of such a caveat.[2] Ike quickly reconsidered and was soon assuring the prime minister, "I always find my sentiments in full accord with any suggestion that seeks to avoid nibbling and jabbing in order to leap straight at the vitals of the enemy."[3] But Ike still could not make up his mind about which invasion plan of many to adopt, and Montgomery was not far wrong in likening Allied headquarters in Algiers to "an orchestra playing without a conductor."[4] It was not until the conference held on 2 May, when Monty cornered Bedell Smith in the lavatory and secured support for his invasion plan, that action was agreed.

Eisenhower told Marshall, somewhat disingenuously, that the plan conformed to the outline which he (Ike) had personally drawn up in the first place. The chief of staff, while warmly applauding incipient victory in Tunisia, responded coolly. He suggested that Ike was in the hands of the planners, who were notoriously conservative, orthodox, and lacking in boldness. The criticism perturbed Ike. He meekly agreed that commanders had sometimes to kick the planners out of the window and decide for themselves. He expressed gratitude to Marshall for loyally sustaining him through thick and thin. And he persuaded Patton to write to the chief of staff praising him (Ike) for working hard, taking risks, and handling the British so well. Patton did so, eulogizing Ike's "magnificent moral courage, self confidence and driving energy" and also licking Marshall's boots on his own account.[5] Privately Patton recorded that he had "largely overstated Ike's merits, but I felt that I owe him a lot and must stay in with him. I lied in a good cause." However, Patton added modestly, "I know of no one except myself who could do any better than Ike."[6] Ike was to repay Patton for his support with generous interest.

If anyone possessed the character of a trimmer that man was Ike. But his natural inclination to adjust his course to the prevailing wind and keep on an even keel was strengthened by the contrary pressures exerted on him by president, prime minister, and combined chiefs of staff, not to mention other political and military figures. Usually he had to justify his shifts in a series of wearisome long-distance essay contests, as he called them. But such was the strategic impasse reached by the Allies after the "Trident" Conference in Washington that Churchill and Marshall flew to Algiers at the end of May. With Ike's help they aimed to arrive at a decision about what to do after the conquest of Sicily. The prime minister was in an ebullient mood, exhausting the generals by his late hours and his insatiable appetite for food, drink, and talk. On one evening he got up steam after his third whiskey and, according to Butcher, gave Marshall "the razzberry for desiring to visit the south west Pacific. He said, in effect, Australia had no charm. He described it as 8,000 miles long, 4,000 miles wide and covered with brush. He said it was famous for a fur-bearing animal which laid eggs and made love to its mate only in the moonlight."[7] In fact Churchill had never been to the Antipodes but he was determined to prevent Marshall's going—or rather his dabbling seriously in any waters but those of the Atlantic and the Mediterranean. But although he lavished all his charm and "super-salesmanship"[8] on the chief of staff, Churchill did not manage to persuade him that the Allies should proceed to Italy if HUSKY proved successful. However, Marshall was by no means inflexible (as long as the invasion of France was not jeopardized) and Churchill achieved the next best thing. He induced Marshall to agree that Ike himself should decide what immediate strategy to pursue when the time came. And he had little trouble in convincing Ike that, as captain of the winning team, he should exploit the Allied victory by encompassing the fall of Mussolini's tawdry Roman Empire.

The prime minister also waxed eloquent about General de Gaulle, who had finally been allowed to come to Algiers in the hope that he would cooperate with Giraud in furthering the war effort. In fact de Gaulle, who bitterly resented the dominance of the Anglo-Saxons (as he, like Hitler, called the Americans and British), was much more concerned to destroy Vichy and establish his own power, which he regarded as synonymous with the revival of Gallic greatness. If de Gaulle felt any gratitude to the Atlantic Allies for liberating French North Africa it was surely gratitude as defined by Nietzsche—hatred wearing a mask. And the mask was sometimes allowed to slip, as Churchill noticed when damning the Frenchman's Anglophobia. The prime minister raged about de Gaulle to Ike, calling him an "egomaniac" and a "prime SOB," and threatening to break with him.[9] But at heart Churchill recognized that de Gaulle was the indomitable symbol of French resistance to Nazi Germany, and that Giraud was,

in comparison, a nonentity. Ike too came to realize this, though he
knew little and cared less about French politics, going so far as to
assure Marshall in June that de Gaulle was losing ground. This was
wishful thinking. It doubtless reflected Roosevelt's determination to
keep de Gaulle impotent. He told Ike, "I want you to remember that
you are in command in NORTH AFRICA and that means in effect that
while the BRITISH and ourselves would like to have the civilian functions of government run by the FRENCH the military objective is
absolutely paramount."[10] Ike was thus left in no doubt that he should
concede nothing to a man described by Harry Hopkins as "one of the
biggest sons-of-bitches who ever straddled a pot."[11]

However, civilian and military matters overlapped. Ike wanted a
secure base from which to launch HUSKY and as much help as the
re-armed French forces could give. Accordingly, when it became clear
that de Gaulle was ruthlessly outmaneuvering the antediluvian Giraud, Ike's inclination was to cooperate with this new power in the
land. This was difficult not only because of the presidential prohibition
but because de Gaulle made the other prima donnas with whom Ike
had to deal during the war—Roosevelt, Churchill, Montgomery, Patton—look like shrinking violets by comparison. In his early days, at
the École Supérieure, de Gaulle had been rebuked for behaving like
"a king in exile,"[12] a phrase that aptly sums up the fundamental
attitude of this awkward, brilliant, vindictive, intransigent, haughty,
and altogether extraordinary character.

De Gaulle, who could in private display great charm and even an
ironical brand of wit, gave Ike instead a taste of regal arrogance when
they met on 19 June. Two meters tall, dressed in full military uniform,
erect yet curiously ungainly—Churchill likened him to "a female
llama surprised in her bath"[13]—unsmiling and wreathed in his invariable halitosis, de Gaulle announced that he was there in his "capacity
as President of the French government."[14] This was not only untrue
—de Gaulle was only co-president, with Giraud, of the French Committee of National Liberation (FCNL)—but it was precisely what
Roosevelt intended at all costs to avoid. As usual Ike sought a compromise. He persuaded de Gaulle that Giraud (and thus, indirectly, Ike
himself) should maintain control of French forces in North Africa.
And, denying to Marshall that the thought of extending some form
of recognition to the FCNL had ever entered his head, he said that,
as a matter of fact, "some kind of limited recognition of the collective
body would be helpful here."[15]

This is exactly what he received in August and it opened the way
for future collaboration, if not concord, with de Gaulle. In this sort

The first known photo of Ike (bottom right), at age three, 1893, with his brothers. They slept four to a bedroom.

Huck Finns: the Eisenhower brothers in front of the first Abilene home, 1895. From left to right: Dwight, Edgar, Paul, Roy, Arthur.

Abilene, Kansas, c. 1900—traces of the frontier cow town remained.

The Belle Springs Creamery, Abilene, 1902. Ike became night foreman and purloined ice cream.

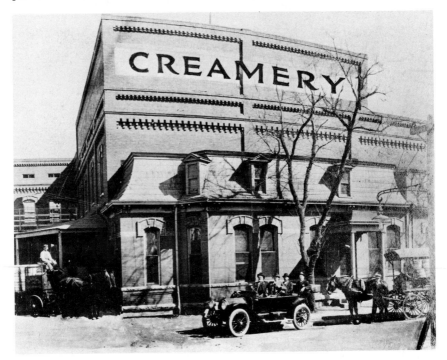

The Eisenhower family, 1902. Front row: David, Milton, Ida. Back row: Dwight, Edgar, Earl, Arthur, Roy.

"President of the roughnecks" on a camping trip, c. 1907.

The point of West Point
for Ike in 1912—football.

Ike at West Point, 1915—
the *Howitzer* portrait.

Ike and Mamie—the wedding portrait, 1 July 1916. Ike would not sit down for fear it would spoil the creases in his pants.

Major Eisenhower at the Tank Center, Camp Meade, Maryland, 1919, with a "coffin on wheels."

Mamie, Icky, and Ike, 1919.

Standardized citizens yet rugged individualists—the Eisenhower family, Abilene, 1925. From left to right: Roy, Arthur, Earl, Edgar, David, Dwight, Milton, Ida.

Major Eisenhower (partially obscured) and General MacArthur, intent on "breaking the back" of the Veterans' Bonus March, Washington, D.C., 1932.

Contrasting styles: Ike and MacArthur on display in the Philippines during the 1930s.

Ike during maneuvers amid "mud, malaria, mosquitoes and misery," Camp Polk, Louisiana, 1941.

General Ike looking after his aides, Harry Butcher and Tex Lee, October 1942.

Kay Summersby driving Ike's armor-plated gas guzzler, Algiers, 1942.

A smile "worth twenty divisions" and a chief of staff "as cold as a fish." Ike and General George C. Marshall, Algiers, May 1943.

President Roosevelt dines with his army commanders, Tunis, November 1943. He had not yet made up his mind about Ike's future.

Roosevelt with Ike, Sicily, 8 December 1943. "Well, Ike, you are going to command OVERLORD."

Wearing his famous multicolored dragon dressing gown, Churchill meets Ike in North Africa, 25 December 1943. Second from left: Tedder. Between Ike and Churchill: Alexander. Second from right: "Jumbo" Wilson. Far right: Bedell Smith.

Ike and Monty before D-Day, hoping to "crack the enemy a good one."

Churchill meets Ike in his trailer headquarters, Germany, 14 November 1944. The prime minister envied generals their "command of armies in the field."

Normandy, August 1944. Ike was "de Gaulle's best friend in the Allied camp."

The winning American team, 11 May 1945. From left to right (front row): Simpson, Patton, Spaatz, Ike, Bradley, Hodges, Gerow; (back row): center, Bedell Smith.

General de Gaulle presenting the Medal of Liberation, June 1945. Ike disliked being kissed on both cheeks.

"The valley of the Thames draws close to the farms of Kansas." Ike and Tedder parade victoriously in London, June 1945.

The conquering hero comes to New York, 19 June 1945.

Ike, Kay Summersby, and Mark Clark at Hitler's Berchtesgaden retreat, September 1945. Ike's chauffeur no longer sat in the driver's seat.

Ike and his son John at Culzean Castle, Scotland. Ike was given lifetime use of the castle.

Ike receiving the keys of Columbia University, 11 October 1948. Thinking of his academic brother Milton, Ike said that they'd asked the wrong Eisenhower to be president—some professors thought it no joke.

of negotiation, where poker-faced ambivalence was an immense asset, Ike was at his best and he received much praise for playing such a deft hand. Indeed, by the summer of 1943 various observers, including Secretary of War Henry L. Stimson, were commenting on Ike's growing maturity. Harold Macmillan was especially complimentary, saying that Ike "really has developed in an extraordinary way. He has a certain independence of thought which is very refreshing, and he is not afraid of taking responsibility for decisions—even when they do not exactly comply with his instructions from home!"[16]

Macmillan's opinion was doubtless colored by the fact that Ike had veered toward the Gaullism which he himself espoused, though he was also impressed by the general's manner with King George VI, who presented him with the Order of the Bath on 12 June. Ike was "interesting, amusing, not too shy or too much at ease—in fact, the real natural simple gentleman which he is."[17] (Macmillan might have been less effusive if he had heard Ike irreverently discussing with his staff how he should address the monarch in a cable—Dear Kingie, Dear Georgie, or Dear Rex). Whatever the motive behind Macmillan's praise it is clear that de Gaulle judged the worth of his contemporaries entirely by the criterion of whether they agreed with him. His tribute to Ike (in his memoirs) was correspondingly fulsome, though its inconsistencies are tinged with a certain irony. He found Ike prudent but audacious, adroit but generous-hearted, flexible but consistent, a great soldier who allowed de Gaulle to intervene in his strategy whenever France's interests led him to do so. To his face de Gaulle paid Ike a similarly ambiguous compliment, exclaiming that he was a man because he knew how to say "I was wrong."[18]

Ike was all too aware of the strategic errors which he had perpetrated in what was the largest amphibious assault ever launched—even larger, in terms of the number of men involved, than the D-Day landing—against the southern flank of Sicily on 10 July 1943. At the time he correctly forecast that the Germans would be delighted by this attack, which was merely (as Butcher said) "nibbling at the navel of the underbelly,"[19] and that history would condemn his "supercautious approach." He thought that the Allies should have either "island-hopped" straight to Italy or landed on both sides of the Messina Straits, thus cutting off the whole of Sicily and obtaining its surrender with minimal loss.[20]

In his war memoirs, however, Ike repudiated this argument and did not admit to any mistake, asserting that "we were wise . . . to proceed methodically to the conquest of an island in which the defending strength was approximately 350,000."[21] That figure was misleading, for there were only 60,000 Germans, the rest being more or less demoralized Italians, while the Allied force amounted to about half a million men. Moreover, thanks to Ike's courage in refusing to call off the armada when the weather turned unseasonably bad, the Axis forces were, to his joy, once again caught by surprise. Ike's stomach felt like a clenched fist before the assault. At his Malta headquarters he rubbed his lucky coins, chain-smoked, prayed for success, and waited. First news of the landings came in a BBC report from "General Eisenhower," to which Ike responded "Thank God—*he* ought to know!"[22]

Ike spent a further twenty-four hours agonizing about the fate of his men. He was so much at a loose end that he even went down to the seaside. Refusing to swim with his staff in "sand mixed with water," he lay down, stood up, had the fidgets, dug holes in the sand with a stick and then raced back to his communications center. The trouble was that, having done so much to prepare for HUSKY, Ike did not have direct control of operations as he had in TORCH. That responsibility rested with his scattered British deputies, Alexander for the army, Cunningham for the navy, and Tedder for the air force, while Ike himself attempted, not very successfully, to coordinate the services. In practice what happened was that when the troops landed, which they did with considerable ease on most of the hundred-mile shoreline, Alexander was effectively in command.

Ike admired and liked this charming, modest, and attractive figure. He regarded him as much abler than Montgomery and even said that he ought to be supreme commander, though he later changed his mind about that.[23] Ike was always most effective when working in tandem with a strong man like Bedell Smith. Ike and Alexander were too similar to make a good team, both being more inclined to win the cooperation of their subordinates by means of compromise than to compel obedience by a ruthless display of will. Patton correctly observed the "lack of force on the part of Alexander, who cut a sorry figure at all times." "He is a fence walker," Patton concluded, surmising, more problematically, that the cause of Alexander's shilly-shallying lay in his having an exceptionally small head.[24] Clark described Alexander, curiously but expressively, as acting like "a peanut and a feather duster."[25] As for Montgomery, he habitually deprecated Alexander behind his back and patronized him to his face. Neither man could forget that Alex had been a student at Staff College when Monty had been an instructor. Consequently Alexander always deferred to Montgomery in the field of tactics. He also failed to employ the immense driving force of Patton to best advantage.

The trouble was that Montgomery insisted on treating the Americans, who had so speedily assimilated the lessons of Tunisia and were from now on to be capable of more rapid maneuvers than the British, as auxiliaries. Monty's pretensions to infallibility matched his thirst for glory, and he consigned Patton's forces to a supportive and protective role during the landings. But after his initially quick advance up the coast toward Messina had stalled on the malaria-ridden Catanian plain in front of Mount Etna, Monty conducted the rest of the campaign, Ike complained, in slow motion. Finding a frontal assault too costly, Montgomery employed the "left-hook" which had served him well at Mareth. To achieve this he needed the road from Caltagirone to Enna, which had been designated as the route for Patton's advance. Alexander meekly re-allocated it to the British, causing confusion in the American ranks and provoking Patton to fury. Alexander then compounded his error by feebly allowing Patton to split his own forces. General Omar Bradley, who had succeeded to the command of Second Corps in Tunisia, was left to guard Montgomery's left flank, where he performed brilliantly, threatening to cut off the Germans and being (so the troops said) Patton's secret weapon.

Meanwhile Patton himself moved with astonishing speed . . . in the wrong direction. Entranced by the glamor of capturing a famous city, he made for Palermo, where he established himself in the Royal Palace (sleeping in the king's bed on three mattresses), ate K rations off china marked with the arms of Savoy, and hobnobbed with the cardinal. Unfortunately, Palermo was of historic but not strategic importance. Patton's westward drive permitted the Germans to retire eastward in good order and to disembark successfully. Much to Kesselring's surprise and satisfaction, Ike failed to concentrate the Allied naval and air forces, both vastly superior to those of the Axis, in order to prevent the evacuation or to destroy the enemy ferries, which completed their task in broad daylight. Ike had hoped that the conquest of Sicily would be accomplished in a fortnight: in fact, it took nearly six weeks. It was no wonder that he thought the team of Alexander and Montgomery "should be broken up as the two simply compound their individual conservatism." Bedell Smith was so disgusted by Alexander's vacillation that he told Butcher "confidentially that once the war is over he hoped he never again had to deal with the British. Yet," Butcher continued, "Beetle is Ike's most successful negotiator with them and is almost reverently respected by them."[26]

Nevertheless, despite the strategic blunders, Ike was not wholly wrong when he told Marshall that Patton's campaign would "be classed as a model of swift conquest by future classes in the War

College in Leavenworth. The prodigious marches, the incessant attacks, the refusal to be halted by appalling difficulties in communication and terrain, are really something to enthuse about."[27] In reaching Messina before the British and evicting the Germans from Sicily, Patton eradicated the stigma of inferiority which both Rommel and Montgomery had imprinted on the Americans in North Africa. He manifested not so much tactical flair as combat ferocity. War for Patton was a licensed orgy of the emotions in which he could indulge in violence, profanity, sentimentality, hatred, ambition, mysticism, and even lust—"I say fornication ain't fraternization! That is, if you keep your hat on and your weight on your elbows!"[28] Patton had fallen on his head too often while playing polo, but the Sicilian campaign, in which his men had sustained hideous casualties (the Germans going so far as to booby-trap their own dead), made him more unbalanced and uninhibited than ever. His lack of restraint was most memorably demonstrated when he abused and assaulted two shell-shocked American soldiers, whom he took to be cowardly malingerers, in a Sicilian field hospital. It was said that fifty thousand American troops in Sicily would cheerfully have murdered Patton, and their hostility was well expressed by their sardonic comment on his nickname—"Our Blood, his Guts."

Ike himself had no illusions about his most aggressive field commander, noting (as Butcher said) that "Patton personally pushed Bradley onward when he was ready to stop for rest and to obtain more supplies. Yet Ike feels that Patton is motivated by selfishness. He thinks Patton would prefer to have the war go on if it meant further aggrandizement for him. Neither does he mind sacrificing lives if by doing so he can gain greater fame."[29] But Ike recognized that Patton's vicious and manic qualities were better calculated to win victories than the sober virtues of less inspired generals. So he only hinted at the slapping episode when writing to Marshall and contented himself with giving Patton a stern rebuke and making him apologize (which he barely did, and that with the greatest ill-grace) to the soldiers concerned. Patton was only sorry about the effect which his outburst might have on his career, swearing that he would be careful as to the place he next had a tantrum and would certainly not choose a hospital. Ike himself vowed that he would never try to interfere with the freedom of the press—a plausible assertion in view of his having taken war correspondents into his confidence over HUSKY—but he managed to persuade them to suppress news of the slapping incident. This was unwise, for the story was bound to come out; though when it did, in November, Ike easily rode the storm.

Ike set great store by good public relations, so much so that Churchill complained that he gave too many press conferences and issued too
many official statements. But Ike recognized that this was a people's
war—or, as he put it, a GI and Tommy war—and that effective propaganda was essential for the achievement of high morale. Moreover,
journalists and others were already beginning to say that Ike was
presidential timber, and though he earnestly denied having political
ambitions he was as sensitive about his public image as any aspiring
candidate for office. Thus his first inspection trip to Sicily, on 13 July,
seems largely to have been conducted for the benefit of the press,
though he did take the opportunity to curse Patton for not keeping
him supplied with up-to-date information. When Ike's ship came
briefly under fire he rejected the small steel helmet which was offered
to him, declaring, "I'll need two men to hold it on," and murmuring
to the reporter, John Gunther, "They treat me like a bird in a gilded
cage." Apparently acting on Gunther's suggestion that it would make
a wonderful news item, Ike greeted the first soldier he met on shore
with the words, "My name is Eisenhower."[30]

This was certainly show business. But it was less autocratic and
egocentric than the manipulation of the media practiced by, say,
MacArthur or Mountbatten, both of whom carefully censored reports
about themselves and construed as criticism anything less than flattery
laid on with a trowel. It was also considerably less crude and raucous
than the cinematic means employed to advertise Montgomery, which,
as Butcher noted austerely, "are typical of Hollywood and to me stink.
To say the least, these methods would not work for an Allied Commander-in-Chief, whose greatest asset is naturalness and modesty."[31]
After the war Ismay confided to Ike his wish that someone would
"muzzle, or better still chloroform Monty. . . . I have come to the
conclusion that his love of publicity is a disease, like alcoholism or
taking drugs, and that it sends him equally mad."[32]

If Ike's military control of HUSKY was remote and ineffectual, his
exploitation of its political consequences was singularly adroit. Indeed, Ike was distracted from the business of war by the chance of
achieving a resounding victory by diplomatic means. The invasion of
Sicily helped to precipitate the downfall of Mussolini (on 25 July) and
Ike at once determined to induce the new government, appointed by
the king and headed by Field Marshal Pietro Badoglio, to make peace.
This, despite a statement by Badoglio professing loyalty to the Axis,
it obviously wished to do. But unfortunately the Allied governments,
committed to achieving the unconditional surrender of their enemies
since the Casablanca Conference and terrified that if anything could

be worse than a Darlan deal it would be a Badoglio imbroglio, imposed a series of crippling restraints on their senior man in the Mediterranean. Ike was harassed by a stream of "private," "personal," and "most immediate" telegrams, all contradicting one another, from the president, the prime minister, the chief of staff, the combined chiefs of staff, the U.S. secretary of state, and the British foreign secretary. As Macmillan wrote, Ike "was splendid about doing a good deal of Nelson blind-eye stuff,"[33] and he pressed forward with negotiations for an armistice on easy terms. But while the Allies debated and Badoglio dithered, Hitler acted, rushing reinforcements into Italy on the pretext of helping her to resist an invasion of the mainland.

Ike had, in fact, decided to proceed with this as soon as it became clear, by 15 July, that the Sicilian landings were a success. And he managed to convince Badoglio's secret envoys that the Allies would arrive in such overwhelming strength that Italy, or most of it, would have nothing to fear from Germany. Consequently, these emissaries accepted not only the initial, mild, "short" terms but a longer document containing much harsher stipulations. These, Bedell Smith promised vaguely, would not be implemented if Italy collaborated full-heartedly with the Allies. However, when it became plain, on 8 September, that the Allies were much weaker than he had thought, Badoglio threatened to back out of the agreement which they had signed. Ike was livid. But he decided, as he put it, to play a little poker. He sent a message to Badoglio saying that he would announce the armistice on the radio as planned and that unless the field marshal confirmed it Ike would "publish to the world the full record of this affair."[34] Caught between the German devil and the Allied deep blue sea, Badoglio capitulated. On the eve of General Mark Clark's landings at Salerno, he ordered his forces to change sides. A delighted Macmillan exclaimed that this extraordinary armistice had been brought about by "the biggest bluff in history."[35] Despite his triumph, Ike protested to everyone from Marshall to Mamie that he was a general, not a politician, and had been trained to wage war, not to engage in the diplomacy of peacemaking. He could not do both satisfactorily and he preferred bullet battles to the "straight and unadulterated venom" of politics.[36]

In practice, Ike found that the demands of coalition warfare were forcing him more and more to adopt political means to achieve military ends. In order to secure Allied cooperation he was constantly having to devise ambiguous formulas and compromise plans that would suit everyone. As he told Marshall, "In the various campaigns of this war I have occasionally had to modify slightly my own conceptions of campaign in order to achieve a unity of purpose and effort. I think this is inescapable in Allied operations but I assure you that I have never yet failed to give you my own clear personal convictions about every project."[37] However, Ike's convictions were seldom clear, let alone consistent, for he invariably adapted them to circumstances. His order, issued on 10 August, for the invasion of Italy was just such a compromise. It set out objectives and priorities which were barely compatible, if not downright contradictory—namely, the assaults on the toe of Italy (by Monty) and the shin (by Clark). Clark himself complained that Ike did not make a move without the "consent and approval" of Alex and Monty. "In fact, he is accepting their decisions instead of making them himself."[38]

This is too harsh. But there is no doubt that Montgomery obliged Ike to resort to equivocations. For, despite his poor showing in Sicily, Monty continued to behave as though he were Napoleon.[39] In August Ike assured Marshall that, although he preferred working with the "broad-gauged" Alexander, he felt that he had Monty's "personal equation, and have no lack of confidence in my ability to handle him."[40] And on 2 September Ike briefly and mistakenly expressed the view that Monty, to whom he had just given the Legion of Merit, had "decided to 'join the family.' He was seeking to become a member of the team and not simply the star player."[41]

In fact, Monty, who had real military talents and outstanding battlefield achievements to his credit, despised both Eisenhower and Alexander, who in his opinion had none. And such was his strange, sadistic, even megalomaniac personality that he could not resist boasting about his feats, rubbing the faces of his superiors in their inferior ability. His fanatical dedication to his profession could not be doubted, especially in an army that forbade discussion of military matters in the mess and assessed officers' ability on the basis of whether they knew (to give an example from Monty's *Memoirs*) how many times a day mules opened their bowels. But Monty had a compulsion to denigrate others and he constantly jeopardized the smooth working of the Alliance by a peacock display of self-esteem. Even when Monty wrote favorably about Ike there was a pronounced element of patronage in his compliments: "Eisenhower is a very 'big' man who takes the large view and keeps clear of all detail; BEDELL SMITH implements all the big decisions and keeps the whole show on the rails."[42]

The implication was plain: Ike did not, and should not, interfere; and left to himself Monty would continue to win battles. Ike's response to this attitude was equivocal. He was magnanimous enough to endure Monty's arrogance even at a cost of some personal humiliation—provided that the Alliance benefited. On the other hand, even when Monty failed to achieve results Ike did not give him firm orders. So it then became apparent that all Ike's talk about leadership by conciliation was irrelevant. Indeed, such talk seemed designed to conceal the fact that Ike was, like Alexander, intimidated by Montgomery's strong personality. Bedell Smith was not, and his celebrated remark to Monty was just: "You may be great to serve under, difficult to serve alongside, but you sure are hell to serve over."[43]

Montgomery's intransigence was well illustrated by the contribution he made to the invasion of Italy. Despite the reports of commandos, who had secretly crossed the Messina Straits, that he would meet no opposition, Monty was unconvinced. There followed what Ike later called a "long and unnecessary wait,"[44] while Monty arranged a creeping artillery barrage from six hundred guns. This achieved nothing except a waste of four hundred tons of shells, which blasted open the cages in the Reggio Zoo, with the result that a monkey and a puma escaped—the former attacked some men of the Third Canadian Brigade, who shot and wounded it. Monty, accompanied by his personal menagerie, which included birds, dogs, a peacock, and a young pig, landed in Italy on 3 September. He was under orders to advance up the leg and assist with Clark's landings at Salerno, scheduled for 9 September. But despite orders to hurry he moved, against very light resistance though over exceedingly difficult terrain, with ponderous slowness. On 10 September, when Clark was in danger of being pushed back into the sea, Monty allowed his men to rest for two days and wind up their logistical tails. A party of enterprising war correspondents actually preceded him into Salerno by some twenty-four hours. Monty himself arrived on 16 September, just in time to be too late to help Clark, who had helped himself and successfully repulsed the German onslaught. This did not prevent Montgomery from claiming that the Eighth Army had saved the Fifth. Ike had fumed at the unnecessary delay. Monty was unabashed and a few days later, on 20 September, he added insult to injury by sending Ike a pamphlet he had written entitled "Notes on High Command in War."

It was small consolation that the man who only two years before had been featured in the press as "Lt. Col. D. D. Ersenbeing" ("at least the initials were right," Ike remarked wryly)[45] now appeared on the front cover of *Time.* The magazine hailed him for the "tact and diplomacy," the "example, cajolery and compulsion" by which he achieved unity, and quoted a female admirer who said that he was "the handsomest bald man she had ever met."[46] But three days after Monty's slight, Ike received a much more direct slap in the face. General Marshall sent him a letter complaining that he was not showing "sufficient initiative" and criticizing his Italian strategy for want of boldness. Ike had canceled the planned airborne attack on Rome at the last minute, had dissipated his forces, and had been too cautious—climbing up the leg of Italy like a harvest bug (to employ Churchill's phrase) instead of striking at the knee.

Ike's reply cost him "a great deal of mental anguish."[47] Such was his concentration, as he paced the floor, that he walked right out of his office while still dictating. Ike had a reasonable case. He had been starved of bombers and of the landing craft that were being saved for the Normandy invasion, now code-named Operation OVERLORD. His experts there had advised that the drop on Rome was too hazardous. Despite fierce German resistance at Salerno and doubts about Clark, Ike supported him to the hilt and would not countenance any thought of withdrawal. Clark had consolidated the beachhead. Italy's fleet came over to the Allies after the armistice, but her land forces were effectively neutralized by the Germans. Indeed, Italy's *volte face* was in many ways less of a help than a hindrance to Ike. He might well have sympathized with Goering, who later remarked that if only the Italians "had been our enemies instead of our allies we might have won the war."[48]

However, Ike had not succeeded in properly coordinating the three services at Salerno. This caused major problems, not least of them the landing of Clark's reserve in the wrong place. Moreover, partly as a result of indecision by the Allied leaders, Ike had not worked out a coherent strategy to follow the capture of the Foggia airfields and the city of Naples, on 27 September and 1 October, respectively. Ike later claimed that these were "the first major objectives of the Italian Campaign. All later fighting in that area would have as its principal objective the pinning down of German forces far from" Normandy.[49] This was the standard American justification, as put forward constantly by Marshall, for remaining in the Mediterranean at all. At the time, however, Ike veered toward the British standpoint, summed up in Churchill's aim to slit open the soft underbelly of Europe. Ike wanted to assist OVERLORD by means of "a vigorous fall and winter campaign" that would attain for the Allies "a strong concentrated position in north Italy whence we can attack South France and threaten eastward as well."[50]

Of course, this turned out to be a vain hope because the Germans fought with such obstinacy in countryside ideally suited for defense, while the Allies, outnumbered by twenty-five divisions to eleven, concentrated their resources on the cross-channel invasion. It must also be said that neither Ike nor Alexander imposed a strategic plan on his subordinates, who largely arranged matters between themselves. Monty told Clark confidentially that if he received instructions from Alexander that he did not understand "just tell him to go to hell."[51] Yet, despite their show of friendliness, Monty and Clark were themselves bitter rivals. Thus Ike could not maintain the high degree of Allied unity by which he set such store, and which the Germans, with their obscene propaganda about Yanks lend-leasing British women, did everything they could to destroy. Monty systematically disparaged the American forces, while Clark developed paranoid suspicions that the British commanders in Italy were engaged in an anti-American conspiracy. It could have been said of Monty, as it was of Clark, that he believed war to be an extension of publicity by other means. In his eagerness to reach Rome first Clark not only refused to obey Alexander's orders but told him that he intended to shoot any British troops preceding him into the city.[52]

Ike's hopes of taking Rome by the end of October were dashed, and the autumn of 1943 became for him a time of frustration and demoralization. The war in Italy settled down into a bloody slogging-match, in weather so bad that Allied air superiority, which Ike reckoned to be worth ten divisions, was rendered useless. His frequent visits to the front line, where, as always, he inspired, and was inspired by, the troops, did little to galvanize the advance. Indeed, by November Butcher was hearing rumors to the effect that Ike would be dismissed because of the slow progress. Yet Ike refused to admit that a stalemate was developing, and he could not reconcile himself to the transfer of resources to OVERLORD. Ike never indulged in boasts—unlike Montgomery, who failed to breach the German line during his attack over the Sangro in November yet publicly announced that "the road to Rome is open"[53]—but Ike doggedly persisted with a strategy that made less sense every day.

He did, however, resist a further dispersal of effort to the eastern Mediterranean, thus embroiling himself in the sharpest dispute he ever had with Winston Churchill. The prime minister, who as a strategist combined volatility and tenacity to a bewildering degree, wanted to establish complete Allied control of the Aegean Sea. "All I am asking for," he told Ike plaintively, "is the capture of RHODES and the other islands of the DODECANESE."[54] His aim was to remind "Turkey that Christmas is coming" and to drag her into the war.[55] Eisenhower, supported by nearly all the political and military leaders on both sides of the Atlantic, refused to countenance this costly foray into a periph-

eral theater of operations. This did not, of course, stop Churchill's
pestering Ike with interminable arguments on the subject. In a letter
to Ismay, written after the war, Ike concluded sagely that Winston's
"uncanny judgements in the political-military field were of unques-
tionable value throughout the conflict." But, despite the "personal
affection" Ike felt for the prime minister, he could not agree with

many of his ideas about the tactical uses of troops and, sometimes, with his
calculations as to great results that would have resulted from minor adventures. Secondary and supporting attacks are one thing; but yielding to the
constant temptations that always present themselves so glitteringly in war for
dispersion and more dispersion has brought about more disappointment and
disaster than almost any other sin.[56]

While struggling against Churchill, Ike was also being harassed by
de Gaulle. The Free French leader was busy evicting Giraud from
power in North Africa and wreaking brutal revenge upon the supporters of Vichy. Roosevelt wanted to exert pressure on de Gaulle by
depriving him of military supplies. But Ike, less vain than the president and more concerned with measures than men, needed the French
divisions and prevented an open quarrel. Similarly, although Badoglio and King Victor Emmanuel were broken reeds tainted with
Fascism, Ike continued to sustain their authority, on the familiar
ground of military expediency. Harold Macmillan, by no means an
uncritical admirer of Ike—"he speaks a strange language of his own
which one has to learn"—was much impressed by his sure political
touch:

Although completely ignorant of Europe and wholly uneducated (in any
normal sense of the word), he has two great qualities which make him much
easier to deal with than many superficially better-endowed American or
British generals. First, he will always listen to and try to grasp the point of
an argument. Second, he is absolutely fair-minded and, if he has prejudices,
never allows them to sway his final judgement. Compared with the wooden
heads and desiccated hearts of many British soldiers I see here, he is a jewel
of broadmindedness and wisdom.[57]

Even so, Macmillan noticed that Ike was "going to seed" in the
Mediterranean.[58] And Ike himself told Mamie that the "eternal
pound, pound, pound seems a burden but when it once ceases it is
possible that many of us will be nigh onto [sic] nervous wrecks."[59] Ike
was worried about his personal prospects as well as the future of the
Italian campaign. Everything pointed to his being sent back to the
United States as chief of staff once OVERLORD became imminent and
Marshall, as everyone expected, took command of it. Ike felt himself

ill-suited for the post in Washington and he suggested several alternatives which would keep him fighting in Europe. But when, in mid-November, he met Roosevelt, who was on his way to the Tehran Conference, Ike received little hope of a reprieve. The president was at his most buoyant and fascinating as they inspected the Tunisian battlefields together and speculated about whether American tanks had been fighting on the site of Zama, where Hannibal (Ike's boyhood hero) had employed elephants against the Romans over two millennia before. Roosevelt remarked: "Ike, if one year ago you had offered to bet that on this day the President of the United States would be having his lunch on a Tunisian roadside, what odds could you have demanded?"[60]

But later Roosevelt told Ike that Marshall was entitled to command OVERLORD in order to establish his place in history as a great general. It was scant compensation for Ike to receive the Legion of Merit at the president's hands. And he was merely irritated to be told (in Cairo, on Thanksgiving Day—Ike had lost count of time and only learned the date during Marshall's turkey dinner) to take a brief holiday. He did so in Luxor, Jerusalem, and Bethlehem, before returning to grapple with the intractable problems of Italy.

Kay Summersby accompanied Ike on the trip to Egypt and the excursion to Palestine, during which their relationship apparently reached a new pitch of passion. The facts are impossible to ascertain because only Kay, now dead, left a record of the affair and this reads like cheap romantic fiction. Of course that by no means invalidates it, for life resembles pulp novelettes more faithfully than it imitates art. Moreover, where it can be corroborated Kay's story seems largely authentic. Omar Bradley found it quite accurate, for example, and even suggested that Kay's influence helped to make Ike "pro-British."[61] Her descriptions of Roosevelt's uncensorious affability, and the way in which Marshall (who had also had a close friendship with his English chauffeuse after the First World War) looked through her and seemed to wish that she did not exist, ring entirely true. And on the basis of internal evidence her account of her liaison with Ike is by no means implausible. According to Kay, then, Ike declared his love soon after her fiancé was killed, in the summer of 1943. At first he was hesitant, tender, tremulous, and apologetic. But soon he exclaimed, "Goddamnit, can't you tell I'm crazy about you?" She responded with coyness and "his kisses absolutely unravelled me."

Such was the goldfish-bowl existence he led that she quickly had to wipe the lipstick from his face and they conducted themselves with some discretion. But rumors that she was his mistress abounded, and

occasionally her behavior gave substance to them. Asked once if the
amour were not just a matter of gossip, John Thompson of the Chicago *Tribune* replied, "Well . . . I have never before seen a chauffeur
get out of a car and kiss the General good morning when he comes
from his office."[62] However, the raised eyebrows of officers and the
suggestive catcalls of soldiers who saw them out together left Ike
"rigid and red," and impotent. When traveling to the Cairo conference they availed themselves of the opportunity to embrace at length
in the darkened airplane, which Kay reckoned "as much an act of love
as a more physically intimate encounter." After their sightseeing trip
to Jerusalem, Ike sent her what seems to have been his solitary love
letter. It was a cryptic message, written, bizarrely enough, on a souve-
nir postcard from the Garden of Gethsemane: "Good night—there
are lots of things I could say—you know them. Good night."[63]

Meanwhile Ike's destiny was being decided at Tehran, where the
Big Three met in conclave, Roosevelt and Stalin enjoying on Churchill's birthday what one American newspaper called the "Most Important Meal since the Last Supper."[64] The Russian dictator, to the
Americans' delight, opposed Britain's continuing ambitions in the
eastern Mediterranean, favoring instead an attack on southern France
(Operation ANVIL). But he professed skepticism about the Western
Allies' commitment to open a Second Front in northern Europe when
a commander still had not been named. Roosevelt had perhaps by now
decided that Marshall, who took a prominent part in the Tehran
negotiations, was too valuable as a politician to be allowed to become
a general. As chief of staff he could continue to deal skillfully with
Congress and do much to prevent the British from going back on their
pledge to mount OVERLORD. The evidence is conflicting about
whether Churchill was inclined to renege over the cross-Channel
invasion: General Kennedy thought he was, while General Ismay
assured Ike that the prime minister had "definitely steeled himself to
take the plunge as far back as 1943, and that thereafter he never
wavered" though he did "continue to search for opportunities to
'nibble round the edges.' "[65] Roosevelt did not wholly trust the prime
minister and was determined to keep him up to the mark.

Marshall himself desired and expected to be Allied commander in
Europe—he had already sent some of his personal effects to England.[66] But he would not do the only thing needful to get the job
—ask for it. When given the chance to propose himself, Marshall
merely told the president that he must feel free to act in the best
interests of the country. Roosevelt took this proud act of self-abnegation as carte blanche not to appoint him, saying briskly: "Well I didn't

feel I could sleep at ease if you were out of Washington."[67] Eisenhower was the only alternative. Marshall sent him a cablegram which, though garbled in transmission, seemed to indicate that he had been chosen; and he followed it up by giving him Roosevelt's handwritten note informing Stalin of the decision, which Ike later had framed. The president, whom Ike met in Tunis on 7 December, confirmed the appointment: "Well, Ike, you are going to command OVERLORD."[68]

8

Overture to
OVERLORD

Having been entrusted with the most important assignment of the war, Ike had "ants in his pants," as he put it, to start the work of planning at once.[1] But he did not become officially operational until 1 January 1944 and he still nursed faint hopes of capturing Rome before he left Italy. In fact he had not yet properly arrived in Italy, though he had been planning to move his forward headquarters to Naples for a couple of months. Now he established it at the gigantic Bourbon Palace in Cazerta and briefly occupied Prince Umberto's hunting lodge in the hills, which had been requisitioned for his living accommodation—despite his dislike of pretentiousness and his habit of reprimanding senior officers who ensconced themselves in luxury while leaving their troops to their own devices. Butcher had advertised the hunting lodge as a "dream cottage," but it turned out to be notable mainly for having bugs in the beds and a rat in the general's bathroom. This was the kind of challenge Ike enjoyed and, putting on his glasses and taking careful aim at this creature, which was sitting on the lavatory seat, he fired his pistol at it. He missed. After three shots the rat, though wounded, was still alive and a sergeant had to polish it off with a stick. "Great marksmanship, Chief," said Butcher. "Just what we'd expect from the Supreme Commander."[2]

Ike was even less successful with the enemy than with the rodent. The front remained static despite all Ike's efforts, including the long and tiring final trip he made there in torrential rain. This expedition culminated in a fierce argument with Bedell Smith. But each recognized his need for the other and they apologized, rather sheepishly, after a decent interval. Smith, whom Ike insisted on taking to England, proved his worth in the new crisis with the French which blew up at the end of December. De Gaulle first infuriated Ike by suspending all departures of French troops to Italy until the Allies agreed that he should control them. He then enraged Roosevelt by purging Vichyite friends of America, like Peyrouton, in North Africa. The president told Ike to direct de Gaulle to desist from such action, a message which, had he delivered it, would probably have destroyed all hope of his receiving aid from Free French Forces and the Resistance. Ike took advice from Smith and Macmillan. He also consulted Churchill, who was recovering from pneumonia in Carthage, where he presented a remarkable spectacle in his padded silk Chinese dressing-gown covered with blue, red, and gold dragons. Then, at what Butcher called a "love fest," Ike worked out a compromise with de Gaulle.

French forces would place themselves at the disposal of Allied commanders in practice (though de Gaulle did not abandon the principle of control, a source of future trouble) and prominent Vichyites would not be tried until a constitutional government had been established in France. In return Ike promised arms and an important role for French contingents in the liberation of France. It is arguable that Ike became "de Gaulle's best friend in the Allied camp"[3] by consistently giving way to him. On the other hand, cooperation on de Gaulle's terms was more productive than confrontation on Roosevelt's. Ike was primarily interested in the military results of his political machinations. On the whole, during his time in the Mediterranean, his statesmanship had proved more adroit than his generalship. Now, as this exhausting tour of duty drew to a close, Marshall first urged, then ordered, him to return home. A rest was essential before he embarked on the enterprise which would, Ike told reporters optimistically, win the war in 1944. He departed on the last day of 1943, handing over his command to the aptly nicknamed British general, "Jumbo" Wilson. It was, said one officer, as though "Champagne and oysters had given way to beer and cheese,"[4] and very soon, Macmillan recorded, Anglo-American relations in the Mediterranean began to deteriorate.

Ike spent two weeks in the United States, most of the time engaged in frantic activity. He had secret conferences with the president (the last time they met), the secretary of war, the joint chiefs of staff, and others, during which he was told the frightening news about TUBE ALLOYS, the top secret Anglo-American atomic bomb program. He grappled with two major problems, the shortage of landing craft and the right of the supreme commander to control the Allied air forces during OVERLORD, but failed to solve either of them. He visited John at West Point and was so affable to his son's friends that before the evening was over they were giving him advice on how to defeat Hitler. He flew to Kansas for a reunion with his family, a not altogether happy one since his mother was now too feeble-minded to be able to understand what he had been doing across the Atlantic.

It is true that Ike did spend a few days relaxing alone with Mamie at White Sulphur Springs. But relations with her were uncomfortable. Ike sometimes called his wife Kay, which naturally infuriated her. She complained about his not having brought her presents from Naples and he was exasperated that she thought he had time to go shopping. The gift which he did bring home, one of Telek's offspring, was not a success since it left its mark on her oriental rugs at the Wardman Park. Her health was still poor. He was overweight and smoked incessantly, and his temper was not improved by a cold which lasted for most of the winter. Moreover, Ike had become surprisingly abrupt, almost brusque, in conversation, and he made it plain that he was eager to get to grips with his new responsibilities in Europe. When Mamie rebuked him for his sharp manner Ike replied crossly, "Hell, I'm going back to my theater where I can do what I want."[5] But despite these petty irritations Mamie depended on him and dreaded parting almost more than separation. Just before he left she said, "Don't come back, until it's over. I couldn't bear to lose you again."[6]

According to Kay, on the night Ike returned to England, after a seventeen-hour flight, a train journey from Prestwick, and a drive through one of London's pea-soup fogs, they came closest to consummating their affair. "Buttons were unbuttoned," she wrote. "It was as if we were frantic." But apparently Ike was unable to make love, either because he was too tired or, if Kay's hints are to be believed, because Mamie had somehow unmanned him, killed his capacity for passion. "Oh God, Kay," he allegedly exclaimed, "I'm sorry. I'm not going to be any good for you." So they dressed again. Kay was understanding, assured him that "It's all right," and "cuddled his head against my breast."[7] The obtrusive clichés do not necessarily convict her of falsehood or fantasy. Indeed, a deliberate liar would surely have claimed that they became lovers in the full sense. Kay's account, with its elements of guilt, anxiety, hesitation, preoccupation, and exhaustion, any or all of which could have led to the fumbling impotence she describes, is credible—if not verifiable.

What is certain is that Ike had practically no time to devote to his personal affairs during the hectic five months of preparation for OVERLORD. It is true that this operation, unlike TORCH and HUSKY, posed no fundamental problems in itself, as everyone accepted that the landings should take place during May in Normandy, away from the heavily defended Calais area but within range of air cover. Nor was there controversy about the size of the invasion. In October 1943 Ike had seen the preliminary plan, which was for a three-division assault, and had expressed reservations because it did not have "enough wallop in the initial attack."[8] But this was also the view of General Frederick Morgan, head of the original planning team, who had limited the size of the assault force only because of lack of resources, and it was echoed by Montgomery and others. So within ten days of his return to England Ike secured agreement to an initial attack of five divisions on a broad front (though not as broad as that from Dieppe to Brittany at first proposed by Montgomery).

Although the D-Day force would be smaller than the first wave to invade Sicily, the eventual buildup of troops and supplies was vastly greater, and it was a matter of the utmost complexity to organize such a massive transfer of military might to the Continent. Ike had to coordinate the work of various experts, American and British, in a host of different fields. By now he was the best qualified person in the world to do this: no one else could match his experience of mounting amphibious operations. He communicated to most, if not quite all, who encountered him a sense of boundless competence and self-confidence. One American officer, who met Ike as a result of his job in the Strategic Intelligence Branch, wrote on 21 January 1944, "Eisenhower impressed me as essentially a big man of great simplicity without the slightest affectation. He has a keen mind, great experience, and broad vision in his approach to all the problems we discussed. Like most great men, he drained me dry of every speck of information I had in a manner that seemed to show confidence in me."[9] The officer added that he was impressed by something else about the supreme commander—Ike always asked if he had consulted the British.

Even in uncontroversial matters cooperation between Allies was still the keystone of his policy. Indeed, the British leaders most inimical to Ike, men like Sir James Grigg, secretary of state for war, General Brooke (CIGS), and Montgomery, regarded Ike's commitment to coalition warfare as almost his sole raison d'être. Brooke, for example, harped constantly on Ike's lack of forcefulness and strategic understanding, but often concluded with some tribute to his skill at harnessing such heterogeneous forces. Even Monty, for all his vicious sniping about Ike's inadequacies, could acknowledge his intelligence, his "human qualities," and his "power of drawing the hearts of men towards him as a magnet attracts the bit of metal."[10] Monty did so, for instance, shortly before D-Day: "Eisenhower is just the man for the job: he is a really 'big' man and is in every way an Allied Commander." He led by personality, not authority. Monty concluded, "I like him immensely; he has a generous and lovable character and I would trust him to the last gasp."[11] Other prominent military figures in Britain scarcely tempered their praise with criticism at all. Tedder, Ike's deputy, paid unequivocal tribute to the supreme commander's "great inspiring leadership."[12] And in February, at a Claridge's dinner which Ike attended as guest of honor, Admiral Cunningham (ABC) presented him with an inscribed silver salver on behalf of senior British officers who had served with him in the Mediterranean and hailed him as a commander of outstanding integrity. Ike was too overwhelmed to formulate a suitable reply. But he enjoyed receiving lavish gifts as well as lavish testimonials, and the next morning Butcher found him in bed polishing a thumbprint off the salver with his sheet.

At the Supreme Headquarters of the Allied Expeditionary Force (SHAEF), which Ike soon moved from Grosvenor Square to Bushey Park, he managed again to build up a team spirit that transcended national and service rivalries. There was, indeed, as the journalist Harrison Salisbury noted, much personal and political intrigue at SHAEF. But this did not poison relations, for Ike's benign influence permeated the organization. As Air Marshal "Bomber" Harris (not one of Ike's most consistent supporters) told him after the war, "SHAEF, and all that it meant and always will mean, was yours. It was in fact you."[13] Such was the supreme commander's charisma—no doubt in part the product of his position, but in part stemming from his personality—that he became the focus of intense personal loyalty. Salisbury declared that he actually had a "court" of favorites and admirers,[14] though it can scarcely have been comparable to, say, MacArthur's, which was said to be so incense-laden that the atmosphere would have embarrassed Louis XIV.

But many Britons who came into close contact with Ike, such as General Morgan, displayed a devotion amounting to hero worship, thus contributing to international harmony. Morgan himself swapped a button from his tunic with his American deputy, General Ray Barker, as a symbol of unity. He also protected Barker's replacement, Bedell Smith, who was (said Barker) "a man given to Napoleonic decisions" and "a great chopper-off of heads," from the worst consequences of his own impulsiveness. However, as even Barker admitted, Smith was "a wonderful office manager."[15] He did much to make SHAEF, though top-heavy and overstaffed, the relatively efficient organization it became. Without Ike, though, the disparate elements could never have been welded into a successful joint command. Yet, paradoxically, as Bradley noted, Ike was always eager to escape from "that gaudy brass-bound prison known to the world as SHAEF," with its surfeit of "statisticians, logisticians and tacticians."[16]

The plans devised by the sixteen-thousand-strong bureaucracy at SHAEF, for whose soundness and implementation Ike bore ultimate responsibility, were so complicated that the supreme commander could only succeed by choosing able subordinates and delegating on a large scale. The best time to land in Normandy—at dawn, after a moonlit night, when a rising tide had not yet covered the beach obstacles—was calculated with minute precision. The troops and materiel were directed to the correct staging posts and southern ports, a feat that placed an almost intolerable strain on British ports and communications, not to mention the overloaded island as a whole. The standard joke was that Britain was only kept from sinking beneath the sea by the barrage balloons. The various deception schemes were worked out with such attention to detail that the most widely advertised invasion in history took the enemy by surprise. Two dummy armies, in Scotland and the southeast, helped to foster German suspicions that the landings would take place in the Calais region, where many Panzer divisions remained until long after D-Day. The ingenious technical devices were closely supervised. These included everything from the artificial harbors (MULBERRIES) and the underwater oil pipeline (PLUTO) to the tanks which swam or performed other specialized functions like destroying mines. Surprisingly, the British favored these "funnies," not all of which were practical, more than the Americans, though Ike himself was keen on them. Finally, of course, SHAEF had to coordinate the work of the three services in moving the armada of men and munitions safely across the Channel and in providing each division with the seven hundred tons of supplies it needed daily to keep fighting once a lodgment had been gained. Here Ike became involved in the main controversies, peripheral but still important, which were to plague him before D-Day.

There was, first of all, the tiresome question of landing craft, vessels about which Ike had for some time been obsessed. He once expressed the odd wish that when he died his body would be placed in a landing craft and started off "toward nowhere."[17] The shortage of landing craft was caused by Admiral King's refusal to divert them from the Pacific, and it was made acute by Marshall's insistence that an attack on the Mediterranean coast of France (ANVIL) should complement the Normandy invasion. In March Bedell Smith lamented that having to plan that invasion without knowing how many, and what kind of, landing craft he was to receive was "enough to drive a man insane." He was obliged to budget for the "very lowest, skimpiest, measliest figure" imaginable.[18] Delaying OVERLORD until the end of May or early June, and thus benefiting from an extra month's production of landing craft, eased but did not remove the difficulty. It was surely clear that the strategic coat would have to be cut to the logistical cloth.

Delay, at any rate, was the solution of the British chiefs of staff, spurred on by the pertinacious premier. He had various motives, among them a hankering to expand the Italian campaign (itself complicated by the relative failure of the landings at Anzio), and he was supported by Mediterranean commanders like Clark who reckoned that ANVIL might be "a fart in the dark."[19] The prime minister argued that the operation against southern France should be canceled in order to afford greater carrying capacity for the northern assault. Ike was caught, so to speak, between Churchill's hammer and Marshall's ANVIL. For all the impression which he conveyed in his memoirs of having been consistent, Ike squirmed dreadfully during the ordeal. First he seemed to recommend shelving ANVIL. Marshall's response was to suggest that he was suffering from "localitis," the disease afflicting American commanders who echoed the views of the local people, in this case the British. Ike then advocated the Mediterranean attack, only, in mid-February, to wobble again in the face of British pressure. However, Smith warned him against telling Marshall because "it would give the impression of changing our minds too quickly."[20] At various times Ike appeared to agree with Montgomery and Brooke but (the latter concluded) "he is too frightened of disagreeing with Marshall to be able to express his views freely."[21] Actually Marshall encouraged Ike to speak his mind and gave him a power of decision that astonished the British. In March Ike took full advantage of both, recommending the abandonment of ANVIL. But when it became clear that Admiral King would not release landing craft unless some sort of Mediterranean operation occurred, a compromise was finally evolved. ANVIL was to take place, but not until nearly six weeks after the D-Day landings in Normandy. Churchill opposed it to the last and the supreme commander, his resistance stiffened by Marshall, had to say no to him (as Ike put it) in every form of English at his command.

Ike's other main problem before D-Day was to gain control of the Allied air forces and ensure that their overwhelming superiority—the Luftwaffe had been reduced to a guerrilla air force by the spring of 1944—was employed where it would best assist OVERLORD. The

American and British "bomber barons," General Carl "Tooey" Spaatz and Air Marshal Arthur "Bomber" Harris, were reluctant to give up their independence. They mistrusted Air Marshal Trafford Leigh-Mallory, who was in command of the Allied Expeditionary Air Force though he only had fighter experience, and they both believed that it was possible to win the war by using the air arm alone. Spaatz thought that the "— — invasion can't succeed"[22] and wanted to smash the enemy by destroying crucial industries such as synthetic oil plants and ball-bearing factories. Harris hoped to make Germany surrender by blasting her cities and wrecking her morale—he liked big bangs and opposed the use not only of incendiaries but of paratroops because they did not explode on hitting the ground. After much expostulation and negotiation, during which Ike threatened to resign and almost let himself be persuaded to accept "supervision" of the air forces, he was finally given authority to "direct" their operations. This he virtually delegated to Tedder because, as Butcher wrote, "he knows Ike's desire to prevent the P.M. and the British Chiefs-of-Staff issuing orders direct to British units under his command and then short-cutting the formal organisation." Churchill had done this with Alexander, Butcher added, perhaps "from his love of showing his power."[23]

Ike's first priority was to engage the air weapon where it would have an immediate impact on the land battle, for SHAEF was fearful that the Allies would be driven back into the sea. He thus rejected Spaatz's "oil plan" in favor of Leigh-Mallory's "transportation plan," which aimed to wreck the enemy's communications and prevent his rushing reinforcements to the beachhead. Churchill had scruples about this strategy, fearing massive civilian casualties. But to this anxiety de Gaulle's lieutenants appeared airily indifferent, and with a well-calculated plea that only a successful OVERLORD could free the French people from slavery, Ike overcame the prime minister's opposition. So bridges, railroads, junctions, terminuses, and marshaling yards were systematically bombed—in such a way as to block routes to Calais as well as to Normandy, thus concealing the Allies' objective.

The debate about the two plans, oil and transportation, was highly technical and is still impossible to decide definitely. There is no doubt that the German lines of communication were severely disrupted by the interdiction campaign, particularly the bombing of bridges, and some of their military leaders thought this strategy "decisive."[24] On the other hand, it can be argued that there was so much excess capacity on the railroads that the traffic delayed was mainly civilian. Moreover, the oil plan might have achieved much better results had it been

implemented earlier. Actually, in May, Ike went into reverse and
plumped for a characteristic compromise when Spaatz himself threatened to resign over the issue. Ike then gave him verbal permission to
hit oil targets. The resulting raids quickly caused what Albert Speer
called "insupportable" shortages of aviation fuel,[25] which restricted
not only pilot training programs but operational flights. One German
general commented, however, that the attacks on "synthetic oil plants
came amazingly late. It was our Achilles heel."[26] Perhaps so, but Ike
at least insisted that the air forces should concentrate on "precision
bombing and not be deflected into morale bombing,"[27] which was
ineffective, if not counterproductive. And he induced the air arm to
cooperate with the other services, to their enormous mutual advantage. He was thus able to make much of contradicting, in his pep talks
to the troops, the GI who supposedly remarked while inflating his
Mae West, "This is the only bloody air support I'll get this day."[28]

Ike spent much of his time between January and June building up
the morale of those who would participate in OVERLORD. During that
time he visited twenty-six divisions, twenty-four airfields, five war-
ships, and many depots, hospitals, mock invasion beaches, and other
installations. (He even went to Bude.) Surprisingly, he evoked somewhat less enthusiasm than Montgomery. Monty's theatrical effects,
Blimpish manner, and schoolboy rhetoric today seem like master-
pieces of self-parody. But he was then, at a time that people were
unused to populism, hailed with such rapture that the British government feared he might become a military dictator. Nevertheless, Ike's
evident warmth, sincerity, and optimism (which he did not entirely
feel) were vividly projected, though some (including Patton) thought
his style was less that of an officer than an office-seeker. Certainly his
speeches made him well liked by the troops. He conveyed his concern
for their well-being. He joked with them like an indulgent first-class
man at West Point with a plebe, urging them to fight "so that we can
end this war and I can go home and go fishing."[29] He spoke to them
frankly, invariably asking them questions and inquiring especially
where each man came from—to his disappointment, he never found
anyone from Abilene. For their part they inspired Ike by clapping,
cheering, and openly showing "respect and admiration for him." As
many people observed, Ike loved being greeted by soldiers, by
crowds of any sort: "He waves back, yells back to them and gives a
broad grin. Whenever he sees troops coming he eagerly watches them
for signs of recognition."[30]

No doubt this sort of uncritical acclaim compensated Ike for what
he took to be willful lack of appreciation in other quarters. As he

completed his exhausting schedule in the months before the invasion he found time to resent, for example, the fact that British newspapers did not use words like "boldness" or "initiative" when describing him, commending instead his "friendliness in welding an allied team" together.[31] He now ceased to "chuckle"—if he had ever done so—about West Point's mistake in referring to him as a mere brigadier general. Other matters, great and small, harassed him. There was an impractical request from Marshall for a three-division air drop to secure airfields in the region of Evreux. Asserting that he too favored boldness rather than conservatism, Ike wisely rejected this plan (on grounds that he would have done well to ponder again before Arnhem). There was the problem of what to do about men who deliberately contracted venereal disease in order to escape combat. There was the difficulty of controlling the supply chief, General J. C. H. Lee, a religious martinet known as Jesus Christ Himself, who rode around Britain in his own special train and sometimes appeared booted and spurred and carrying a riding crop.

There was the question of whether to dismiss Patton for another indiscretion, a speech in which he had jovially remarked that the Americans and the British (he omitted other Allies) were destined to rule the world. Marshall passed the buck back to Ike, Patton got a sore lip from "boot-licking and ass-kissing," and the supreme commander finally heeded the advice of General Wedemeyer: "Get onto yourself, Ike. Georgie doesn't need you as much as you need him."[32] So Ike cleverly punished Patton and exploited his notoriety by giving him command of the dummy army in Kent. There was the absence of Telek: Ike and Kay sometimes visited him in quarantine but for the supreme commander the dog's incarceration was like "locking up a part of my heart."[33] All told, Ike lived during these spring months "on a network of high tension wires."[34] In his few moments of leisure at Telegraph Cottage he tried to relax. He read his Westerns, played games, tried to paint, enjoyed outdoor cooking—his black soldier-servants did the chores while Ike, like a culinary surgeon, demanded the implements—"measuring spoon," "chili powder," and so on.[35] He also delighted in listening to the cuckoos, which he had only heard before in clocks.

Nothing contributed more to the strain, as D-Day approached, than the continuing struggle with the French, compounded as it was by the prejudices of Roosevelt and the intractability of de Gaulle. Ike indignantly denied press suggestions that he was trying to achieve an accord with de Gaulle in defiance of the president's orders: "after working for two solid years as hard as I know how for the development of the spirit of unification and complete teamplay, it is disappointing to think that any single individual in the whole United States could be led to believe that I would myself be guilty of even a whisper of insubordination."[36] Actually Ike did want to conciliate de Gaulle because he was anxious to secure the full cooperation of the French Resistance both before and after D-Day. However, he was hamstrung by the president, who refused to allow the FCNL to administer liberated France on the grounds that the Allies must allow the French people the right to self-determination and not present the title deeds of the country to de Gaulle. Ike was similarly hampered by de Gaulle himself, whose London headquarters was "leaky" and liable to betray Frenchmen at odds with their self-appointed leader to the Gestapo. Consequently the Free French could not be trusted with advance information about Allied moves, which naturally annoyed them.

Matters were made worse in April when, at Ike's insistence, censorship was imposed on diplomatic communication from all foreign embassies in Britain (except those of America and Russia). This, together with the prohibition of unauthorized travel in southern England, was designed to ensure complete security about the invasion. But de Gaulle, in Algiers, bitterly resented being cut off from his headquarters in London and on 27 May the FCNL proclaimed itself the provisional government of France. This in turn offended the Allies, and when de Gaulle arrived in Britain on 4 June the scene was set for an acute crisis. Ike tried to mollify the French leader, but without success. Then, in the face of de Gaulle's denunciation of the Allied invasion currency as counterfeit money, his refusal to broadcast instructions to his compatriots to obey the supreme commander's orders, and his last-minute ban on the embarkation of 170 French liaison officers, Ike consigned him (in a private anathema) to hell. Churchill, even more furious, wanted to send "this obstructionist saboteur" back to Algiers in chains. Wiser counsels prevailed. The supreme commander and the prime minister, preoccupied with the most momentous event of their lives, permitted the door to be left open for future negotiations with de Gaulle. Thanks to their superhuman magnanimity his monstrous intransigence would prevail, for, as Roosevelt remarked, prima donnas do not change their spots.

Montgomery certainly did not changes his spots. After some hesitation Ike had confirmed that Monty would be in operational command of the invasion and its immediate aftermath. SHAEF was, Ike later wrote, responsible for the "broad strategy"[37] of OVERLORD, and although it seldom intervened over tactical details it did affect the course of battles. But the SHAEF planners were intensely preoccupied with securing a lodgment. They reckoned that the Allies stood a fifty-percent chance of being defeated on the coast, for they greatly overestimated the strength of Hitler's Atlantic Wall, which was afterward dismissed by Field Marshal von Rundstedt as "just a bit of cheap bluff . . . a few 'bunker' holes scratched in the sand."[38] Indeed, when Rommel first saw the Atlantic Wall he was appalled, describing it as a "figment of Hitler's cloud-cuckoo-land."[39] Consequently, Montgomery's plan for breaking out from the beachheads, containing as it did ambiguities that even now cannot be resolved, was never subjected to sufficiently close scrutiny.

At the famous meeting on 15 May, when the entire Allied high command in Britain gathered to sit on hard benches at St. Paul's School, Monty stole the show with a crisp display of optimism and self-confidence. He behaved, said Ismay, like King Henry V before the battle of Agincourt. Perhaps for this reason he was inclined to be unwontedly charitable to his impresario and supreme commander: "Throughout the day Eisenhower was quite excellent; he spoke very little, but what he said was on a high level and extremely good."[40] The American admiral Morton L. Deyo was even more struck by Ike's performance: "It had been said that his smile was worth twenty divisions. That day it was worth more. . . . Before the warmth of his quiet confidence the mists of doubt dissolved. When he had finished the tension was gone. Not often has one man been called upon to accept so great a burden of responsibility. But here was one at peace with his soul."[41]

Brooke disagreed, recording a hostile impression in his diary. Ike was no director of thought, plans, or energy, the CIGS wrote, "Just a co-ordinator, a good mixer, a champion of inter-Allied co-operation, and in those respects few can hold a candle to him." It was an opinion he never changed. Ike was "a past-master in the handling of allies" and "a charming personality." But he was "no real commander" and his deficiencies in leadership were mainly supplied by his subordinates, particularly by the abrasive Bedell Smith.[42] Brooke's allegation that "the staff 'ran' Ike" was dismissed by at least one of its British members as "ridiculous."[43] But the assertion that Ike was a passive figure, in thrall to his underlings, was to be repeated frequently, not least when he was president. There was undoubtedly something in it; throughout his life Ike was inclined to regard goodwill as a substitute for will. The fact was, however, that during the war at least Ike's weakness was also his strength. For only a "chairman of the board,"[44] prepared to delegate generously and to be accommodating to the point of self-effacement, could have done the job of Allied supreme commander at all, let alone have carried it to such a triumphant conclusion. Brooke never appreciated the supreme commander's concept of leadership, which Ike defined as "pulling a piece of spaghetti across a plate instead of trying to push it."[45] He did not understand that Ike measured his own skill as a captain by the strength of the team he built in the long term.

Ike often explained his views—being so sensitive to criticism he was a compulsive self-justifier—but never more persuasively than to his speech writer Emmet Hughes in 1953. Defending himself against the charge of inaction, which had been made against him in war as well as in peace, Ike wrote:

I learned that there is a priority of procedure in preparing for and carrying forward great tasks that the leader ignores at his peril. People close to a respected or liked commander fear he is losing his stature and urge the "squelching" of a Montgomery or a Bradley or a Patton; the seizing of the limelight in order to personalize the whole campaign for the troops and the public. But obviously in the hurly burly of a military campaign—or a political effort—loyal, effective subordinates are mandatory. To tie them to the leader with unbreakable bonds one rule must always be observed—Take full responsibility, promptly, for everything that remotely resembles failure—give extravagant public praise to all subordinates for every success. The method is slow—but its results endure!![46]

There was doubtless special pleading on the part of a general who did not display the necessary moral courage to lead from the front even when there was no decent alternative. It was also the testament of one whose high-mindedness and generosity of spirit have seldom if ever been equaled in a military commander. Years later Ike did not even blame Brooke, whom he regarded as "always honest, quick and generous,"[47] for the animadversions in his diaries, though he considered their publication a mistake. He left Ismay to comment that Brooke had been, in Churchill's opinion, not much better than a "bon generale ordinaire"[sic][48] and to conclude that the notion of a "partnership in genius" between the prime minister and the CIGS was nonsense. It was, Ismay said, ninety-five percent of Winston, five percent of Brooke.[49]

In setting out his plan on 15 May Montgomery emphasized that, once British and Canadian forces on the left had disembarked, they would quickly thrust south and east. Their vital aim was to capture airfields so that the Allies' chief asset, mastery of the skies, could be effectively maintained and to give themselves room to maneuver. "Once we can gain control of the main enemy lateral GRANDVILLE–

VIRE–ARGENTAN–FALAISE–CAEN, and the area enclosed in it, we shall have the lodgment area we want and can begin to expand."[50] Later, when this rapid penetration inland was forestalled, Montgomery stressed what may or may not have been its primary purpose. This was to draw the German forces onto the British front so that the Americans, having captured Cherbourg and the Brittany ports, could deliver a massive right hook. Whether this had always been Monty's intention is a vexed question. In his defense it can be said that months before D-Day he had put forward a plan always understood by Bradley "to maintain a very firm left wing" and to break out on the right.[51] At a general's briefing on 7 April he had spoken of occupying the high ground around Caen on D-Day itself, in order not only to assist further aggression against the enemy on his own front but to protect the Americans as they struck first north, then south and west, and finally east.[52]

On the other hand, despite his misleading phase lines on the map, which indicated where he would reach by certain dates, Monty was too cagey to commit himself to any detailed forecast of progress. His reputation for lucidity notwithstanding, many of his statements were conflicting or open to more than one interpretation, and he kept his options open in order to exploit any opportunities that might arise. It is at least arguable that he hoped the British would overcome German resistance in the good tank country to the east of Caen and that he expected the Americans would stall in the difficult "bocage" or hedge-row terrain of Normandy. They would thus be reduced to the supporting, flank-protecting role which he invariably advocated for them. The case can further be made that Monty, as guardian of his country's last reserves of manpower, altered his strategy when British losses became too heavy, giving himself what Bradley called a "decoy mission" while the Americans executed the coup de grace.[53]

The whole debate is bedeviled by national rivalry. And it is confused by the fact that Monty was often disingenuous and sometimes mendacious. His devotees claim that his shifts and evasions were calculated to obtain vital support from his superiors, from the air force, or from the press (in order to raise morale and dupe the enemy). His detractors assert that he lied in order to protect his reputation for success and that he changed his plan according to circumstances while pretending to a wholly spurious consistency and prophetic insight. Eisenhower's own reputation as a soldier is affected by the controversy about Montgomery's purposes because he is often accused of having culpably misunderstood them.[54] Freddie de Guignand, for example, Monty's chief of staff, said that Ike should not have misunderstood the intention to pivot on Caen, holding with the left and thrusting with the right, as he had personally explained it to the supreme commander.

But de Guignand also told Ike, after the war, that Monty erred in trying both to prove that he had always been right and to justify his "every action." For there was plenty of evidence which might remove Monty "from his present pedestal" and "some of us could tell a very damaging story."[55] Ike agreed, and in his private correspondence with Ismay he allowed his indignation about Monty's lack of consistency to boil over: "Do you remember the great promises that he made during the planning of OVERLORD about moving quickly to the southward beyond Caen and Bayeux to get ground fit for airfields, and his postwar assertions that such a movement was never included in the plan?"[56] So if Ike did fail to comprehend Montgomery's intentions he was given good cause to do so. Nor was he alone in his confusion. Churchill, Bedell Smith, and Patton were all led to believe that Monty meant what he said about the need to be offensive, to keep the initiative, to *"crack about* and force the battle to swing our way."[57]

A week before the St. Paul's conference of 15 May Churchill, with doubt in his mind and tears in his eyes, had told Ike "I am in this thing with you to the end and, if it fails, we will go down together." After that meeting the prime minister evidently felt more confident, for he assured the supreme commander, "I am hardening toward this enterprise."[58] It was the sort of remark that sharpened American suspicions about British commitment to OVERLORD, though Ike was wrong in concluding from it that Churchill had not until then really backed the operation.[59] In truth every preparation which Allied energy and ingenuity could contrive had gone into the making of the invasion. General Morgan, who had conducted the overture to OVERLORD and had dreamed of nothing else for years, was himself "astounded at the . . . vastness of the operation," the scope of which he only grasped when seeing an official film about it with Ike in Frankfurt in July 1945.[60]

Over 11,000 airplanes would be involved on D-Day, dropping three divisions of paratroopers, keeping the fleet safe from aerial attack, shooting the Luftwaffe out of the skies, softening the German defenses, smashing enemy communications. Nearly 7,000 ships would participate, including 7 battleships, 2 monitors, 23 cruisers, hundreds of destroyers, minesweepers, sloops, frigates, corvettes, patrol boats, launches, blockships, merchantmen, tugs, and specialized vessels of all sorts such as telephone cable ships. More than 4,000 landing craft of different types would convey 200,000 men (rising to about 600,000 in ten days) and 20,000 vehicles, which would disembark on fortified beaches over a fifty-mile front. It was the greatest armada and the mightiest amphibious operation the world had ever seen. But it had to perform a feat that had frustrated the power of Hitler, Napoleon, and King Philip of Spain and had last been accomplished by William the Conqueror.[61] And on its outcome the Allied victory depended. Hitler himself had said at the end of 1943, "If they attack in the west that attack will decide the war."[62]

Churchill was convinced that Ike's transports were filled not with bayonets but with dental chairs and YMCA institutions, a view shared by Patton, who protested that SHAEF put a lower priority on ammunition and gasoline than on pianos and Ping-Pong sets. There was a grain of truth in this complaint. German soldiers were allocated about half the rations and twice the ammunition of Allied troops and in every ground sphere except artillery and transport the enemy's equipment was superior. On the other hand, the sheer vastness of Allied resources was overwhelming. More ammunition was stored in dumps along English roadsides than had been used in all World War I.[63] Losses incurred as a result of Allied setbacks, such as the storm of 19 June or the failure of Monty's major attack in July (Operation GOOD-WOOD), were made up almost at once. The arsenal of democracy was seemingly inexhaustible. The Western Allies had other advantages. The Germans were already bleeding to death on the eastern front: they had lost two million men in that theater before D-Day; over two hundred of their best divisions still faced the Russians while only some sixty—most of them inferior formations, some of them consisting of foreign conscripts—remained in northern Europe.

The German units, to be sure, often gave a heroic account of themselves. But, unlike Allied troops, they did not enjoy the benefits of unified leadership. Indeed, Rommel requested that the German "Humpty-Dumpty" command in the west should be put together again under him.[64] Hitler's failure to do so—he kept von Rundstedt over Rommel—meant that the German strategy was never coherent. Rommel wanted to fight on the coast, from fixed defenses, because he believed that the counteroffensive favored by von Rundstedt could not succeed without air superiority. What emerged was a compromise in which the mobile reserve was effectively depleted without the Atlantic Wall being decisively strengthened. Finally, the Germans were fighting blind: the Allies had destroyed most of their radar installations, their aerial reconnaissance of southwest England was virtually nonexistent and, thanks to Allied action against their outlying meteorological stations, they had no reliable means of forecasting the weather.

The weather, that perennial subject of British conversation, dominated the minds of the Allied high command throughout the balmy days of May, which would have been ideal for a cross-Channel attack. The staff at SHAEF quipped that a meteorologist was "an expert who can look into a girl's eyes and tell whether."[65] But the weather was no joke. It was the one factor that could delay the invasion, now scheduled for 5 June, and on it depended the most historic decision of Ike's life. Actually another vital decision was demanded of him first. At the end of May Air Marshal Leigh-Mallory, oppressed by morbid fears, officially recommended the cancellation of the preliminary airdrops. A fresh German division had been transferred to the Cotentin Peninsula and he thought the paratroopers would be massacred. Ike himself was, as Butcher observed, the victim of "pre-D-Day jitters." He was afflicted by ringing in one ear, a sore eye, and a bad temper. But he responded calmly to Leigh-Mallory's panicky prognostications. Knowing that the airborne assault was vital if Bradley's forces were to make progress over the easily defended marshland behind UTAH beach, on the eastern neck of the Cotentin Peninsula, he insisted that the operation must proceed. It was a brave decision, taken in the face of expert advice, and it should have killed the canard that Ike invariably deferred to his British subordinates. Moreover, as Leigh-Mallory had the grace to admit afterward, he had been wrong and Ike right. Montgomery also acknowledged, less graciously, that if Ike had heeded his (Monty's) counsel to go ahead with the invasion on 5 June despite the deteriorating weather, the result might have been a catastrophe.

The circumstances leading to Ike's decision to launch OVERLORD itself—a decision as famous as Caesar's to cross the Rubicon or Napoleon's to invade Russia—are familiar to almost everyone. He arrived at Southwick House, the naval headquarters just outside Portsmouth, on Friday, 2 June. Then, although his chief meteorologist, Group Captain J. M. Stagg, was pessimistic about the weather prospects, Ike made the preliminary moves in the operation. He started the most distant flotillas and the midget submarines which were to guide landing craft to the correct beaches. A depression was coming in rapidly from the west and, it was said, there were six feet two of Stagg, and six feet one of gloom. Nevertheless, on 3 June Ike ordered more convoys to leave port. That evening, though skies were still clear, Stagg said that a storm was imminent. Ike was "very depressed"[66] by this news. But he took no action until, at four o'clock in the morning of Sunday, 4 June, it became evident that the cloud layer would be too low for airplanes to fly. The supreme commander canvassed the opinions of his subordinates and, supporting Tedder's negative vote against Montgomery's positive one (Admiral Ramsay and the navy were neutral), he postponed D-Day by twenty-four hours.

While the ships battled their way back to base in the gale, Ike spent Sunday in limbo. Having been harassed the night before by Churchill, who was disgruntled at the king's forbidding him to accompany the invasion fleet and punished Ike's stock of whiskey, the supreme commander stayed in bed late, surrounded by Westerns and newspapers, before getting up to engage in his dispute with de Gaulle at lunchtime. In the afternoon he walked up and down outside his trailer chain-smoking. For a few minutes he was accompanied by the journalist Red Mueller, but even then he was entirely immersed in his own problems and, one newsman was to say, each of the stars on his shoulders seemed to weigh a ton. In the evening Ike met his principal commanders in the library at Southwick House, which was used as a mess room. It was a large, comfortable sanctum, lined with dark oak bookcases, most of them now empty. Heavy double blackout curtains muffled the sound of gusting wind and rain outside. They sat together, not at the table with its green baize cloth, but informally on the sofas and easy chairs which were scattered about the other end of the room, Ike looking smart in his tailored battle jacket, Monty being more casual than the others in his outfit of corduroy slacks and sweater. At about 9:45 P.M. Stagg reported that a short break in the bad weather was approaching, enough to make the invasion a possibility. An extraordinary cheer went up from this company of middle-aged military men. Conditions would still be far from perfect (a moderate swell and a Force 5 wind) but again Montgomery wanted to go while Tedder reckoned that the operation remained "chancey."[67] What should be done?

Ike weighed all the considerations. If the sea was too rough or the sky too overcast the landings might become, as Brooke himself feared, "the most ghastly disaster of the whole war."[68] On the other hand, time and tide waited for no man and if he held back now conditions would not be right again for a fortnight; delay could harm the morale of seasick men and jeopardize the security of the entire enterprise; surprise would be an incalculable advantage. "The question is just how long can you hang this operation on the end of a limb," he said, "and let it hang there?"[69] The question was a rhetorical one, for, as Bedell Smith observed, at this moment Ike's "loneliness and isolation" were palpable.[70] The decision was his alone. This time he sided with Monty: "I'm quite positive we must give the order." Wires hummed, signals flashed, and the vast mechanism was set in motion again. But another meeting was arranged to confirm, or perhaps to cancel, the decision. On his way out for a few hours rest Ike implored Stagg, "For heaven's sake hold the weather to what you've forecast for us." When they foregathered once more, at 4:15 A.M. on Monday, 5 June, the rain was pelting down in horizontal streaks. However, Stagg stuck to his guns, though he would not commit himself to what the weather would be like over the French coast on D-Day, pausing for two dramatic minutes before declaring that an answer to that question would make him a guesser, not a meteorologist. Ike could not afford the luxury of pausing. But no one now, except Leigh-Mallory, had doubts about proceeding with the invasion. Ike announced unhesitatingly (and to further cheers), "O.K. We'll go."[71]

9

★

Military Statesman

The moment Ike had spoken the room emptied. As on previous occasions, he was left alone with his thoughts while his fate depended on the courage of others. Ike was not one to brood over his decision now that it had been taken, though he did apparently confide to Kay Summersby, "I hope I know what I'm doing. There are times when you have to put everything you are and everything you have ever learned on the line. This is one of them."[1] But Ike was prepared for the worst. Once on his own he drafted a press communiqué assuming full responsibility for the failure of the invasion and for the withdrawal of troops, while praising their bravery and devotion to duty. Then he put the note in his wallet and forgot about it, only discovering it later. Ike would have been blamed if the assault had been repulsed and he deserves the credit for its success. Success, indeed, is the ultimate criterion by which generalship can be judged, and it must always be remembered that, despite the frequent disputes and setbacks, Ike and his commanders did succeed. Perhaps they might have done better: they could certainly have done worse. So although it is understandable that attention should be focused on Ike's conflict with Monty, on "the war between the generals,"[2] on the rivalry between supposedly united nations, and on the debate over strategy, one must never lose sight of the fact that these were just unhappy accidents on the road to Allied victory. Nor must it be forgotten that, in the words of the distinguished historian K. R. Greenfield, "the Anglo-American Coalition in World War II was the closest and most effective partnership in war that two great powers had ever achieved."[3]

Eisenhower's achievement in preserving Allied harmony was comparable with that of the Duke of Marlborough over two centuries before. As Freddie de Guignand wrote, Ike's success was accomplished not by "a tremendous intellect" or "a ruthless disposition" but by his "human qualities: his sense of humor, his common-sense and his essential honesty and integrity. He inspired love and unfailing loyalty; and he knew how to find a solution along the lines of compromise, without surrendering a principle. He is, in fact, a great democrat. . . ." But such eulogies were sometimes used, not least by Montgomery, to denigrate Ike's qualities as a fighting soldier. In this sphere, of course, there can be no comparison with Marlborough, but it is worth quoting de Guignand again (who was, it will be recalled, Monty's chief of staff). He stoutly denied the suggestion that "Eisenhower functioned in Europe primarily as a politician commander, unfamiliar with the everyday problems of tactical war. This was grossly unfair, for Eisenhower showed himself to be a superb tactician with a sensitive and intimate feel of the front." De Guignand went on to say that he evolved many of their long-range plans in late-night discussions with Ike, who was Monty's superior as a field commander.[4]

De Guignand, a bon viveur who had received generous hospitality at Ike's hands in the White House before making this claim, surely protests too much. As the journalist-historian Chester Wilmot argued, Ike was first and foremost a military statesman rather than a generalissimo. The attributes, especially flexibility, which made him a successful supreme commander were liabilities in battle. Although Ike did have shrewd tactical insights, he was peculiarly hesitant about acting on them. But his own claim about overall strategy, which he made to de Guignand after Montgomery's television broadcast in 1959 ("a deliberate affront" in Ike's opinion), is difficult to challenge. "The fact remains," Ike wrote, "that the war in Western Europe was conducted under the program that I personally laid out in broad outline and victory was achieved much more rapidly than 'official' prophets [including Churchill] had foreseen."[5]

However, on the eve of D-Day Ike could do nothing but wait. It was a task that he found, as Kay Summersby said in a classic piece of understatement, "very trying."[6] He fretted, smoked, fingered his lucky coins, played "Hounds and Fox" and crackerbox checkers with Butcher, read Westerns, gossiped, talked to the press, and inspected departing troops. In the evening he visited the 101st Airborne Division, known as the "Screaming Eagles," at Newbury. "When he was recognized," Kay recorded, "the shouts that went up were tremendous."[7] He spent an hour talking to the men, their faces blackened, their mouths full of brave words, their eyes tense.

"What is your job, soldier?"
"Ammunition bearer, sir."
"Where is your home?"
"Pennsylvania, sir."
"Did you get those shoulders working in a coal mine?"
"Yes, sir."
"Good luck to you tonight, soldier."[8]

Ike had a final word with the Eagles' commanding officer, General Maxwell Taylor, who walked away from him stiffly in order to conceal the fact that he had torn a ligament in his right knee playing squash that morning. The 101st were to be harassed by clouds and anti-aircraft fire, and the paratroopers were scattered at the drop. But they did much to disrupt German defenses behind UTAH beach and they suffered nothing like the seventy-percent casualties that Leigh-Mallory had prophesied. Ike watched the huge C-47 airplanes lumbering off the ground, and Red Mueller noticed that the supreme commander's eyes were filled with tears.

After a fitful rest Ike learned, to his immense relief and delight, that the news from France was good. The Germans had been taken completely by surprise. There was virtually no opposition at sea or in the air. All the paratroopers, though widely dispersed, had landed much better than in Sicily and, like the French Resistance, they were creating chaos behind the German lines. The naval bombardment had been devastating and the engineers had cleared paths through the mines and beach obstacles, though these had done some damage. But the disembarkation had been successful everywhere, though not without hard fighting, except at OMAHA beach, on the American left. There the shore was overlooked by cliffs, the naval barrage was less prolonged than on other beaches because of tidal differences, and there were more German defenders, of better quality, than elsewhere. The Americans were pinned down by withering fire and suffered heavy casualties, only breaking out as a result of supreme heroism on the part of officers and men. Bradley was haunted for the rest of his life by OMAHA beach, which he called a "nightmare."[9] However, one figure from the grim statistics of war puts this in perspective and illustrates the relatively cheap cost of OVERLORD: the British lost more troops during the first two hours of the battle of Loos in 1915 than did the Allies and Germans combined during the whole of the D-Day landings.

Ike himself crossed the Channel on 7 June. His vessel, a fast minelayer called *Apollo*, mingled with the vast assemblage of craft, many of them towing barrage balloons, which jostled off the shore.

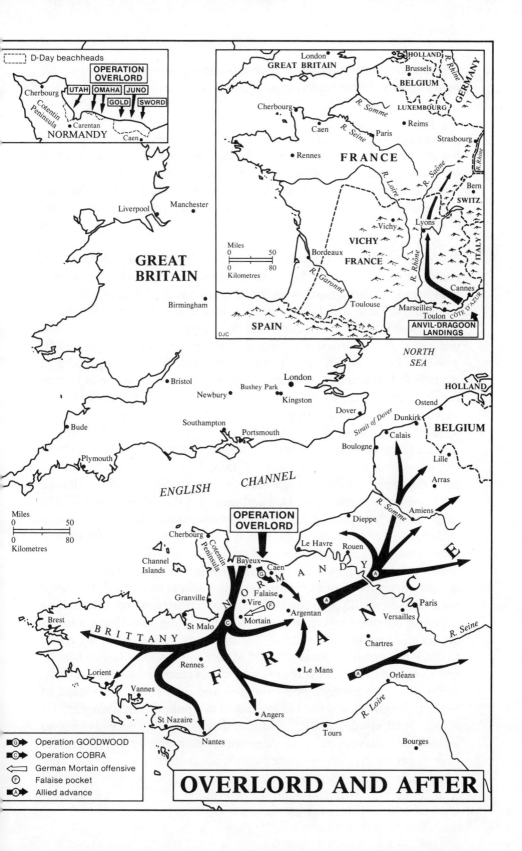

D-Day beachheads

OPERATION OVERLORD

Cherbourg

Cotentin Peninsula

UTAH OMAHA JUNO

GOLD SWORD

Carentan

NORMANDY

Caen

London
GREAT BRITAIN
HOLLAND
R. Rhine
Brussels
BELGIUM
GERMANY
LUXEMBOURG
R. Somme
Cherbourg
Reims
Caen
R. Seine
Paris
Strasbourg
R. Rhine
Rennes
FRANCE
R. Loire
R. Saône
Bern
SWITZ.
ITALY
Miles
0   50
0   80
Kilometres
Bordeaux
R. Garonne
Vichy
VICHY
FRANCE
Lyons
R. Rhône
Cannes
Toulouse
Marseilles
Toulon
CÔTE D'AZUR
DJC
SPAIN
ANVIL-DRAGOON LANDINGS

NORTH SEA

Liverpool
Manchester

GREAT BRITAIN

Birmingham

Bristol
London
Newbury
Bushey Park
Kingston
Dover
Strait of Dover
Dunkirk
Calais
Boulogne

HOLLAND
Ostend
BELGIUM
Lille
Arras
R. Somme
Amiens
Dieppe

Bude

Southampton
Portsmouth

Plymouth

ENGLISH   *CHANNEL*

OPERATION OVERLORD

Cherbourg
Channel Islands
Cotentin Peninsula
Bayeux
Caen
Le Havre
Rouen
N O R M A N D Y
F R A N C E
Granville
Falaise
Vire
Argentan
Paris
Versailles
St Malo
Mortain
R. Seine
Brest
B R I T T A N Y
Rennes
Le Mans
Chartres
Orléans
Lorient
Vannes
Angers
R. Loire
Tours
Bourges
St Nazaire
Nantes

Miles
0   50
0   80
Kilometres

Operation GOODWOOD
Operation COBRA
German Mortain offensive
Falaise pocket
Allied advance

OVERLORD AND AFTER

Ike could do little other than leave the initiative in the hands of his operational commanders. He supported their decision to devote the main immediate effort to linking the UTAH and OMAHA beachheads and promised them the aerial and logistical help they needed. All was not sweetness and light, however, as Ike made an angry fuss about not having been kept better informed (the messages had actually been held up by Monty's code clerks) and Bradley found his visit a "pointless interruption and annoyance."[10] Ike was so eager to see what was happening on the beaches that the *Apollo* ran aground and the supreme commander had to transfer to HMS *Dauntless* for his return journey. Perhaps it was an omen.

Montgomery had singularly failed to capture Caen, and enemy resistance was even stiffer than expected in the east, where the German armored formations were concentrating. And Bradley's forces were finding that the ditches, sunken roads, and thick hedgerows of the bocage made it "perfect natural defensive country." That was the verdict of Ike's hero-worshiping British aide, Colonel James Gault, who, like General "Lightning" Joe Collins and others, compared it to the jungle.[11] Ike said scarcely anything when he went ashore in France for the first time on 12 June, in company with the U.S. chiefs of staff, Marshall, King, and Arnold. But he was already beginning to worry about the lack of progress, especially on the British front. The matter was made more urgent by the arrival, that night, of the first V-1 (V for Vengeance) flying bombs in Britain. Telegraph Cottage was on their flight path to London and one near miss was enough to change Ike's mind about staying in bed and ignoring the "doodle-bugs." He spent his nights sensibly, safely but uncomfortably in a shelter along with the rest of his household, which for a fortnight included his son John, who had graduated from West Point on D-Day.

After the failure of his initial assault Monty tried to take Caen by envelopment. But Rommel, throwing in Panzers piecemeal, thwarted his every effort. Ike, though increasingly frustrated by the lack of progress, confined himself to exhortation, slipping into Monty's scoutmaster's jargon in the process: "I thoroughly believe you are going to crack the enemy a good one."[12] Monty himself now began for the first time to emphasize his role as a blocking force, which would resist Rommel's counteroffensive in the east and enable the Americans to break through in the west. He explained this policy to a military friend in his usual condescending fashion: Bradley was "very willing to learn" but "I have to take the Americans along quietly and give them time to get ready; once they are formed up, then they will go like hell. I have got to like them very much indeed, and once you get their confidence they will do anything for you."[13]

However, fearful that Ike might take over operational control, Monty insisted that his left wing would remain aggressive. When Ike, with growing impatience, urged that "we must blast the enemy with everything we have" and assured him that "Bradley understands the necessity of hitting hard and incessantly,"[14] Monty replied on 25 June that he would battle on "until one of us cracks, and it will not be us."[15] Actually his attack was delayed by the storm of 19 to 21 June, which caused havoc to shipping, destroyed one of the MULBERRIES and damaged the other, and severely disrupted the flow of supplies, already behind schedule as a result of congestion at the beach exits. Bradley nonetheless captured Cherbourg, despite the efforts of the Luftwaffe, which tried to lift the morale of its defenders by parachuting in a special consignment of Iron Crosses. Although this port (devastated by the enemy's demolition teams) was a vital acquisition, its fall scarcely raised Ike's spirits, for it now began to look as though a stalemate, like the one at Anzio or, even worse, that of the Great War, was beginning to develop.

Throughout this tense time Ike behaved, Bedell Smith said, like a football coach, running up and down the line encouraging everyone on his team to do their utmost. At the beginning of July he paid a four-day visit to France in order to examine the situation at first hand. As usual he was happiest when he could focus his beaming personality on those actually engaged in the conflict. Bradley recorded a scrap of conversation between the supreme commander and a soldier who came from the Kansas wheat belt.

"How many acres have you got?"
"Twelve thousand, Sir."
"Twelve thousand?" Ike said, "and how many do you have in wheat?"
"Nine thousand, Sir."
"What's the yield?"
"Forty-one bushels to the acre."
"Mister," Ike replied—and in telling the story he grinned at the recollection of it. "Just remember my name. When the war's over I'll be around for a job."
"When I was a kid," Ike concluded, "250 acres of Kansas wheatland would have represented an honest ambition for any Abilene boy. Yessir, it would have looked mighty good to me."[16]

Ike yearned to shed the cares of rank. He enjoyed sleeping in a tent on OMAHA beach (wearing only red pajama bottoms), shaving in cold water with a borrowed razor, and living off C rations, sometimes accompanied by a bottle of liberated champagne. Ike also longed to take a more active part in the fray. During his inspection trip he borrowed a jeep and, with only an aide and an orderly, he drove around the Norman countryside, once inadvertently wandering behind the German lines. He celebrated the Fourth of July, and the landing of the millionth Allied soldier in France, by flying over enemy-held territory squeezed into a Mustang. After the flight Ike grinned, "Marshall would raise hell if he knew about this."[17] Since Ike could not, and probably did not want to, avoid the attentions of the press, everyone soon knew about it and the chief of staff did send him a reprimand. But his rash exploits were symptomatic not so much of bravado as of frustration, the frustration of a man prone to furious impulses controlling himself in the face of mounting provocation.

On his return to England, 30 days after the first landings, a smoldering Ike complained to Churchill about the dilatoriness of Monty, who, worried about his heavy losses of infantry, was now suggesting that it was enough for him to maintain his position rather than to take Caen. Ike also wrote to Monty himself saying that he was "familiar with your plan for generally holding firmly with your left, attracting thereto all of the enemy armor, while your right pushes down the peninsula." This seems to indicate a pretty fair understanding of Monty's current intentions, though Ike was far from endorsing them. He said that Bradley was having difficulty penetrating the bocage country, added that he would back Monty in any measures to avoid a deadlock and tactfully suggested that "we have not yet attempted a major full-dress attack on the left flank supported by everything we could bring to bear."[18] In reply to Ike's cajolery (and perhaps in response to Churchill's threat that he should "get Caen or get out")[19] Monty vowed "to set my eastern flank alight and put the wind up the enemy by seizing Caen."[20] But once more his attack stalled before fully gaining its stated objective. Bradley too was making little progress. Patton blamed Ike for being a dupe of the British and for failing to assert himself, lamenting in his diary on 12 July, "we actually have no Supreme Commander—no one who can take hold and say this shall be done and that shall not be done."[21]

However, on the same day, as a result of further pressure from Ike, Monty again promised that "my whole eastern front will burst into flames."[22] He was preparing for Operation GOODWOOD, and Ike hoped for "a brilliant stroke that will knock loose our present shackles."[23] He assured Monty that he would support the new assault by getting the cooperation of the air force and by keeping Bradley "fighting like the very devil."[24] It is clear that Monty expected the attack, which commenced on 18 July, to blow an irreparable hole in the German line and that he hoped to advance southeast of Caen,

getting his armored cars as far as Falaise. But he also told Brooke that
"All the activities on the eastern flank are designed to help the [American]
forces in the west."[25] Thus Monty had it both ways and he was able to
claim success when his spearheads, assisted by such heavy bombing
that some German defenders went mad or committed suicide, were
halted after two days. Although he had lost four thousand men and
five hundred tanks (over a third of all British tanks in France) for a
gain of only six miles, Monty publicly expressed satisfaction at his
"break-through."[26]

In private he asserted that the enemy had been worn down and the
decks cleared for Bradley's drive, Operation COBRA. Ike was profoundly angry and disappointed about what he considered to be
Monty's dissimulation and "dilly-dallying." Butcher recorded that the
supreme commander was now showing signs of high blood pressure.
"The slowness of the battle, the desire to be more active in it himself,
his generally unspoken criticism of Monty for being so cautious: all
these pump up his system." Others at SHAEF were even more "disgusted" with Monty, whom they nicknamed "Chief Big Wind" because of his bombastic press pronouncements.[27] Ike was urged to
dismiss him. But that was politically out of the question—as Tedder
complained, the hero of El Alamein could be neither "removed nor
moved to action."[28] Denied "Monty's scalp,"[29] Tedder implored Ike
to give him firm instructions. But that seemed psychologically impossible, and the supreme commander continued to write letters containing vague exhortations which Monty could evade. On 21 July Everett
Hughes fulminated in his diary, "The man is crazy. He won't issue
orders that stick. He will pound the desk and shout."[30]

Actually Ike was sensitive to growing criticisms that he was being
too soft in his relations with the British. He was disturbed by the rising
volume of press complaint at home that the Americans were doing
more than their fair share of fighting and dying—U.S. casualties were
almost fifty percent higher than British. He was anxious about blunt
recommendations from Washington that "General Eisenhower be
told to get his advance headquarters into France at once and let the
American armies know that he is Commander-in-Chief."[31] And he
was "distraught" about Monty who, as Butcher wrote, "has issued
directives as lofty as the Ten Commandments but has so far not carried
through on them."[32] However, instead of assuming personal command in France, which would have been difficult but feasible, Ike
acted with his usual circumspection. Once again he discussed the
problems with the prime minister, who was sympathetic. Both Ike and
Churchill feared a deadlock. They also shared an instinctive penchant

for "attack all along the front."[33] In the prime minister's case this was an expression of his belligerent nature; the supreme commander seems to have borrowed Grant's strategy of employing superior resources to overwhelm the enemy on a broad front.

This was an unimaginative technique, quite the opposite to that of Monty, who preferred to unbalance the enemy and strike at a weak spot. It did correctly reflect the Allied preponderance of materiel, but it also encouraged Ike's critics to claim that he possessed a mass-production mind and had learned nothing about strategy since the Civil War. Certainly Ike's methods were not calculated to exploit the terrific American potential for maneuver and mobility—Sherman tanks, for example, were much faster but had much less firepower than Tigers. However, the fundamental raison d'être and the supreme merit of his strategy was that it kept the Allies fighting together. As he told Monty on 21 July, "We must go forward shoulder to shoulder, with honors and sacrifices equally shared."[34] The Germans were no match for such a combination.

Monty clearly sensed that his personal position would become precarious unless he obtained results quickly. In reply to further coaxing from Ike, he said that by "holding on the left" he had never meant to suggest that he would cease operations there. However, on 25 July, after an anxious wait for clear weather—Bradley spoke of court-martialing the chaplain if it did not improve—COBRA struck. Ike had encouraged Bradley to "Pursue every advantage with an ardor verging on recklessness."[35] Now his forces in the west, closely supported by aircraft and led by tanks with steel attachments (many made from German beach obstacles) for cutting through the hedgerows, burst through the enemy line. They swept southward, and by the beginning of August the entire Cotentin Peninsula was in Allied hands. At the local level, where Allied bombing had reduced areas held by the Germans to a lunar landscape, enemy resistance was disintegrating. As for the German high command, it was disorganized by the bomb plot against Hitler and by the fact that Rommel was seriously injured when his car was strafed by Spitfires. But the basic reason why the soft-spoken, hard-headed Bradley achieved his sudden victory was that on Montgomery's eastern front fourteen British divisions faced the same number of enemy ones (including six Panzer divisions and 645 tanks), while in the west fifteen American divisions confronted nine German (including two Panzer divisions and 190 tanks).

Did this mean that, despite tactical reverses, Monty's essential strategy had come to a triumphant conclusion? At the time Ike himself appeared to think so: "Am delighted that your basic plan has begun brilliantly to unfold."[36] And in his report to the combined chiefs of staff after the war Ike wrote of the operations preceding the Normandy breakout, "Field-Marshal Montgomery's tactical handling of this situation was masterly."[37] It is plain, however, that these were just anodyne platitudes, in the use of which Ike excelled, designed to cement personal relationships and political alliances. Not just in his private remarks then, but in those he made later, Ike was entirely skeptical about Monty's ex post facto justifications of his behavior in Normandy.

Thus, as Ike wrote to the historian Forrest Pogue in 1947, the Americans "had to make the eventual break-out."[38] According to Bedell Smith, as early as 24 June Ike himself had "already made up his mind that the full weight of U.S. strength should be used to break out into the open on our right."[39] As for the COBRA operation, it was essentially Bradley's both in conception and execution. Monty may have envisaged a breakthrough. Bradley achieved a breakout, brilliantly assisted by Patton, who on 1 August took operational command of the Third Army and proceeded to demonstrate his genius for mobile warfare. As late as 28 July Montgomery was still visualizing a full-scale American occupation of Brittany and on 2 August he talked of pushing the enemy back on the Seine. Ike, Bradley, and Patton all anticipated him in wanting to exploit the open flank and surround the German forces which Hitler so insanely ordered to counterattack toward Mortain.

So although in an important sense Montgomery did provide the conditions through which the Allied breakout in Normandy could occur, the extent to which he can be said to have planned it is much more doubtful. The issue, like others in the maze of ifs, buts, and might-have-beens which is military history, can never be finally resolved. Indeed, when one reads the conflicting accounts of soldiers— particularly the self-serving memoirs of generals—and the dogmatic antitheses of military historians, it is tempting to conclude that only novelists like Stendhal and Tolstoy can give a true picture of the ineffable muddle of war. A further temptation is to judge generalship on the basis of personality. Monty was insufferable: yet he understood his profession and his men better than any other British commander this century. Ike was likable: yet he failed to give decisive leadership in Normandy and to take a firm grip on the battle.

Monty's protestations, though the product of an ego that makes Nelson's seem stunted by comparison, cannot be altogether discounted. He wrote to Brooke on 14 August:

Ike is apt to get very excited and to talk wildly—at the top of his voice!!! He is now over here, which is a very great pity. His ignorance as to how to run a war is absolute and complete; he has all the popular cries, but nothing else. He is such a decent chap that it is difficult to be angry with him for long. One thing I am firm about; he is never allowed to attend a meeting between me and my Army commanders and Bradley.[40]

What Monty failed to grasp, of course, was the almost superhuman restraint Ike showed in *not* interfering overtly in operational matters or undermining Montgomery's authority over his American subordinates. Ike's task, to labor the point, was the infinitely delicate one of conducting the Allies to victory in tandem. For temperamental as well as political reasons, Ike held the reins too loosely and used the carrot more than the stick, but more coercive measures might have backfired, and Ike deserves full credit for his discreet, subtle, and effective contribution to the success in Normandy. A study of the campaign has actually led John Keegan, perhaps the best young military historian writing in Britain today, to conclude that "the greatness of Eisenhower as soldier has indeed yet to be portrayed fully."[41]

Meanwhile, on the home front, Ike was being harried by Churchill in the longest and most exhausting argument they had during the war. This was over ANVIL, the invasion of southern France, now renamed DRAGOON (see map on p. 149). The prime minister, of course, complained that he had been dragooned into it and asserted that, having opened the German front door, there was no need to break down the back door as well. Principally, it seems, because the British Empire's largest army was fighting in Italy under his favorite general, Alexander, Churchill wanted to employ it decisively. He advocated, instead of DRAGOON, plunging a dagger into the enemy's armpit, through the Ljubljana Gap. Ike protested that he could not even pronounce this gap and Marshall had to inquire of Harold Macmillan, "Say where is this Ljubljana?"[42] (But Marshall was in due course to amaze the British chiefs of staff by his knowledge of the Ljubljana area —all gleaned from an Italian barber.) Stiffened by the president and the chief of staff, Ike resisted all Churchill's blandishments, which ranged from pleas to threats of resignation and from suggesting ill-judged alternatives to misrepresenting the supreme commander's views to the president.

The ordeal left Ike limp, but on 15 August DRAGOON was set in motion. As the prime minister himself witnessed, the landings on the Côte d'Azur were virtually unopposed. Whether this fact, the swift occupation of the port of Marseilles (which kept half of Patton's army supplied), and the successful northward advance justified DRAGOON is still a matter of dispute. The British argued that it did not divert a single German division from the OVERLORD front and (in what seems to have been an afterthought) that it prevented the Western Allies from meeting the Russians further to the east in Europe. The Americans claimed that the southern ports played a vital role in Ike's victory, though this too was an afterthought, as they had originally championed the operation on strategic, not logistical, grounds. Still, it is extremely doubtful that Alexander, faced with mountainous terrain, could have made as spectacular progress as the DRAGOON divisions that sped up the Rhône Valley. On balance, Ike was probably right in sticking to his guns over this operation, simply because it concentrated the minds and the resources of the Allies on the crucial western route into Germany's industrial heartland.

As Patton continued to scythe around the German left flank (he took Rennes on 3 August and entered Le Mans five days later) Ike became, as Butcher said, "impatient, repeat impatient, and I mean impatient."[43] He was not so much interested in gaining territory as in achieving "the complete destruction of Hun forces."[44] Indeed, at this time Ike's detestation of the enemy seems to have been acute. He talked of exterminating the German general staff, all Nazi leaders from major up, and all members of the Gestapo. Despite later denials, he seems to have given Henry Morgenthau, Jr., the basic idea for "pastoralizing" Germany, reducing her to an agricultural nation, in what would have amounted to a peace of vengeance. Throughout the war, of course, he refused to accept the surrender of German generals personally and would never have entertained one to dinner, as Monty did—Churchill apparently commented that "no worse fate could befall an enemy officer."[45]

Ike must have felt that he was nearer coming to grips with the hated foe when, on 7 August, he transferred his forward headquarters to Granville, a town at the western base of the Cotentin Peninsula. SHAEF had found an agreeable location for his camp, in an apple orchard, and all domestic comforts were supplied, including Ike's black kitten, also named Shaef, to which Churchill delighted in giving milk from a saucer at the dinner table. (Ike could have obtained the milk himself, as he demonstrated to four GIs who had acquired a cow but could not "get it to work").[46] But from the point of view of communications Granville was disastrous, and the supreme commander's move there evidently owed less to military necessity than to prodding from Washington.

Still, Ike traveled energetically and, with the help of ULTRA, did manage to keep in touch with the rapidly changing military situation.

And on 8 August he enthusiastically endorsed Bradley's decision to trap the two German armies, which were suicidally attacking toward Mortain under Hitler's personal direction, in what became known as the Falaise Pocket. Ike supported Bradley again when he faltered, four days later. Bradley refused to let a rampaging Patton strike north from Argentan, where he had a "hard shoulder," for fear that in trying to close the pincers on the Germans at Falaise he would get a "broken neck."[47] Nor did Ike ensure that Monty reinforce the inexperienced Canadian troops over whose "slow going" he was only "a bit worried."[48] They had stalled outside Falaise in the face of fierce resistance and, if assisted, might have boxed the Germans in from the north. Finally, Ike failed to coordinate measures with American, British, and French forces to accomplish the wider envelopment which Monty then seemed to envisage. Consequently the Falaise gap was not closed until 19 August and over twenty thousand German troops escaped from the pocket, though they had had to "run a gauntlet of fire that stretched virtually from Mortain to the Seine."[49]

Ike's performance had been strong on general exhortation and weak on specific direction. Perhaps for once he had given way to euphoria. For although he told the press that Hitler would fight to the bitter end, as the German armies reeled backward he was tempted to believe that the end was nigh. Butcher recorded on 14 August that Ike's disposition was "sunny, if not almost jubilant."[50] Bradley's aide, Major Hansen, noted four days later that Ike was "feeling light-hearted and gay and he is taking an active part in determining the strategy—allocating missions to Bradley and Monty."[51] Despite shortcomings and disappointments, Ike had much to rejoice about, for, as he later wrote, the Falaise battlefield was "one of the greatest 'killing grounds' of any of the war areas." Ike went through it two days after the gap was closed and encountered "scenes that could be described only by Dante. It was literally possible to walk for hundreds of yards at a time stepping on nothing but dead and decaying flesh."[52] Over ten thousand Germans were killed, fifty thousand were captured, and nearly all the enemy tanks and guns were destroyed. Indeed, the catalog of destruction was never completed. For the stench of the putrefying corpses of men and animals prevented a thorough investigation—before the swift mass burials Allied pilots flying fifteen hundred feet above the carnage wrinkled their noses in disgust.

On 25 August Paris was liberated, de Gaulle having threatened that the Free French commander, General Leclerc, would take the city on his own if Ike did not issue the necessary orders. Two days later Ike, accompanied by Bradley (Monty refused to join them), paid the capital what (Kay Summersby said) was supposed to be a "secret" visit. But in his armored Cadillac, complete with escort and an entourage of war correspondents, Ike was inevitably "very quickly recognized by the people and given a tremendous welcome, especially at the tomb of the unknown soldier."[53] Recalling sardonically that Darlan had not needed American policemen, Ike got particular satisfaction from acceding to de Gaulle's request that some of his men should march through Paris in a demonstration of strength designed to show French factions, particularly the Communists, who was boss. By 1 September the Allied armies were streaming across the Great War battlefields, gaining miles for a fraction of the toll it had taken to gain yards a generation before. On that day Ike took operational command of the Allied armies (Monty's consolation prize being a field marshal's baton) and there were few who did not believe that he was about to preside over a German collapse similar to that of 1918—postal officials ordered that Christmas presents for the troops, already in the mail, should be returned to the United States. By 5 September Ike was convinced that "the defeat of the German armies is complete, and the only thing needed to realize the whole conception is speed."[54]

Speedy exploitation of the German retreat involved Ike in three associated problems, to do with command, strategy, and logistics, which were to plague him almost to the end of the war. It had now become Montgomery's thesis, first urged on the supreme commander on 13 August and repeated at a meeting on 23 August (from which Monty excluded Bedell Smith, Ike tamely acquiescing), that "the great mass of the Allied armies" should advance by a northerly route into the Ruhr. They should be under the "single control" of "one man"—and, though he made the impractical suggestion that he should serve under Bradley, there was no doubt who Monty thought that one man should be.[55] Without reducing himself to a complete cipher, incurring the wrath of Marshall, and losing the confidence of the government and people of the United States, Ike could not give way on the question of command, though he did waver from time to time on the amount of authority he was prepared to invest in his ambitious subordinate.

The supreme commander was more flexible over the strategic issue. In August he found Monty's arguments about the need to seize vital posts and V-weapon launching sites sufficiently convincing to justify a *temporary* (he stressed the word to Marshall) change of plan. But though he was willing, then and later, to accord priority to Montgomery's northern thrust, Ike always clung to the notion that the Allied

armies should advance on a broad front. It was the kind of contradiction in terms which Ike specialized in formulating. Certainly it satisfied
none of his principal subordinates, each of whom was convinced that
he could win the war alone if only he received more in the way of
resources. Monty, Bradley, and Patton all succeeded on occasions in
persuading the supreme commander to modify his directives, which
were invariably couched in the emollient language of compromise. In
late August, for example, swayed alternately by Monty and by Bradley
over the question of which of them was to control the left (First)
American army, Ike issued orders so ambiguous that he seemed to
give control to both.[56] Consequently, of course, his commanders,
American as well as British, damned Ike as an appeaser who agreed
with the last strong man who had spoken to him. But although his
emphases shifted and he often hedged his bets, Ike never capitulated
over the fundamental point: that the Allies must keep fighting shoulder to shoulder. Moreover he never ceased to condemn Monty's
"hair-brained"[57] conviction "that if he could merely get the entire
logistic support that we were capable of developing, he could thrust
a long, slender thrust-line to Berlin and as he said, 'end the war
instantly.' "[58]

Ike always accused Monty of proposing to make a slim, "pencil-
like" advance.[59] In fact the field marshal wanted a massive push, a
combination of new Blitzkrieg and old Schlieffen Plan (reversing the
vast wheeling movement through the Low Countries by which the
Germans had hoped to turn the entire French line in 1914). It is
possible that such a maneuver, which might have been employed, say
Ike's critics, if he had been a bold and decisive leader instead of
merely "a shrewd, intelligent, tactful, careful chairman," "could have
ended the war by Christmas."[60] But the proposition is doubtful for all
sorts of reasons, not least because it discounts the astonishing powers
of resistance which Germany displayed, notably when holding back
the Russian steamroller and when preventing the western retreat from
turning into a rout.[61] On the other hand, after the war many German
officers did say that their forces had been in such disarray by the end
of August that a single mass attack by the Allies would have succeeded. The case cannot be proved either way, though historians
continue to argue it with undiminished zest.

What can be said is that once again it was his concern for Allied
cohesion that led Ike to favor the advance on a broad front. And he
believed that no other mode of progression was either strategically
sound or "logistically feasible."[62] In a full and interesting letter written to Forrest Pogue after the war, Ike spelled out his position:

I did everything that was humanly possible to support Montgomery's attack in those days, but never for one instant at the cost of complete inaction throughout the remainder of the front, *which would have forced us to establish a defensive flank from St. Nazaire to the Rhine.* Such a move would have been sensible only in the event that the spearhead, fed at the cost of the rest of the Army, could have actually reached all the way into the center of Germany and ended the war. Such a conception was fantastic and consequently I favored my left by giving to Montgomery the vast bulk of all supplies and the entire Airborne Army, but I did insist upon a sufficient advance on the right to join up with [General Jacob L.] Devers' advancing [DRAGOON] forces and so establish the great logistic framework of ports, railroads, roads and forward depots that was absolutely essential to the knockout blow against Germany.[63]

The fact was that the Allies had advanced so much more swiftly than SHAEF had expected (Monty had moved even faster than Patton, who was himself so far ahead of the planners that he was relying on a Michelin road map) that by September the dearth of supplies, especially gasoline, was chronic. This was partly the fault of General J. C. H. Lee, whose bureaucracy seemed more concerned with supplying its own needs than those of the combat troops. Lee frequently sent an empty bomber from France to North Africa to bring back oranges for his breakfast. Ike was furious in September when Lee moved his whole organization to Paris, transporting typewriters at the expense of bullets, and tried to send him away from the fleshpots—without success. But he was characteristically unwilling to replace Lee, saying that the supply system "doesn't work very well but it works."[64]

Certainly heroic efforts were made to deliver the goods. Landing craft, beaching themselves as the tide ebbed and floating off at high water, deposited huge amounts of matériel in Normandy. Day and night from August to November, trucks of the famous Red Ball Express roared through France—British lorry drivers said that the way to avoid them was not just to get off the road but to climb a tree. The airlift made a small contribution. But Allied bombers had so wrecked French communications, the lack of a big port near the front was such a handicap, and the supply lines were so extended that it was becoming difficult to maintain fighting units at all—in early September three divisions were immobilized and their trucks used for haulage. As Ike said, Montgomery's airborne assault on Arnhem in late September "demonstrated again and very clearly, the limitations of supply lines where only a very narrow frontage is available. To have attempted to project similar methods all the way forward into Germany across the

Rhine would have been so stupid as to have warranted the relief of anyone who would have attempted it."[65]

However, Ike himself agreed to MARKET GARDEN, the code name for the assault on Arnhem, after ten bruising days of being in operational command of the Allied forces, during which time he had been pulled this way and that by his subordinates. He had irritated Bradley by giving him a pompous lecture on the subject of the future great battle for Germany. (Ike was increasingly inclined to deliver boring little homilies to captive audiences: his son John was the recipient of many such, on subjects ranging from the art of leadership, a favorite, to the importance of military hygiene.) The supreme commander had blasted Patton for stretching his line and creating logistical difficulties. But when Patton, who had urged his tank drivers to get out and push when their fuel was exhausted, promised to "go through the Siegfried Line like shit through a goose"[66] if only he received more gasoline —"My men can eat their belts, but my tanks have got to have gas"[67] —Ike went some way to meet him. If Patton, who thought Ike overcautious and lacking in any feel for the battle, was dissatisfied with his increased ration, Monty was furious about it. Montgomery insisted that he should be given all the resources, without compromise or qualification, for his single "full-blooded thrust towards Berlin."[68] Ike agreed with "your conception of a powerful and full-blooded thrust to Berlin" but immediately began to compromise and qualify. He said that without Antwerp "no allocation of our present resources would be adequate to sustain a thrust to Berlin" and that the Rhine must be crossed on a wide front in order to seize the Saar and the Ruhr.[69]

Monty interpreted Ike's reluctance to fall in completely with his clear-cut plans as the product of moral weakness and mental confusion. So, with his usual imperiousness, he summoned the supreme commander to his headquarters. A few days earlier Ike had suffered a nasty accident to his right knee, the "good" one, as the result of a forced landing made on the beach near Granville in his light plane. He had brooded in bed on Monty's rudeness and disloyalty but on 10 September, hardly able to walk, he made the journey to Brussels. The conference was held on the tarmac in Ike's B-25 and Monty at once showed himself to be in a manic mood. He excluded Ike's British chief administrative officer, Humfrey Gale, from the meeting and then proceeded to harangue the supreme commander. In insulting terms he stated that priority meant absolute priority and that he should have all the supplies even if this meant the immobilization of the southern armies. Ike demurred: "Steady, Monty! You can't speak to me like that. I'm your boss."[70]

Montgomery apologized. But he then persuaded Ike to agree to his plan for an airborne attack on Arnhem, a plan so daring and adventurous that Bradley said he would have as soon expected Monty to originate it as to see the teetotal field marshal wobble into SHAEF headquarters with a hangover. Its aim was to outflank the West Wall and, in effect, to continue Monty's full-blooded thrust by other means. The supreme commander had been under pressure from Marshall since before D-Day to employ his paratrooper divisions and he was now being urged by Churchill to eliminate the V-2 sites—the first rockets, against which there was no defense, had landed in Britain on 8 September. So Ike capitulated to Monty. It was probably the worst decision he made during the entire war. For the Arnhem assault, which was on too narrow a front to succeed, delayed the capture of Antwerp, or rather the approaches which would enable Allied ships to use the port. And so for three months Ike's endeavors to attack on a broad front were fatally hampered due to lack of supplies. Bradley concluded bitterly, and with some justice, "The force of Monty's personality seemed to mesmerize Ike and befuddle his thinking. I think in this instance Ike succumbed to Monty in part to stroke his ego and keep peace in the family."[71] It was the old story: Ike's attempt to maintain Allied cohesion led to strategic incoherence.

Ike still smelled victory. Having veered briefly back to favoring a "wide front" priority,[72] Ike tacked again when Montgomery threatened to delay the Arnhem operation unless he was given full logistical support. Ike obliged, at the expense of the American forces, in order to get MARKET GARDEN started as soon as possible. However, when he received intelligence of two Panzer divisions in the Arnhem area Ike was again afflicted by indecision. He said to Bedell Smith, "I cannot tell Monty how to deploy his troops. You must fly to 21 Army Group immediately and argue it out with Monty. I cannot order Monty to call MARKET GARDEN off when I have already given him the green light."[73] Smith did as he was told, Monty ridiculed his fears, and Ike did nothing to halt the operation, which began on 17 September (see map on pp. 166–67).

On that day Ike made the extraordinary statement to Marshall that his team of commanders was carrying out his plan of campaign in perfect harmony. In fact, as German defenses hardened and MARKET GARDEN resulted in little more than the creation of an awkward salient, the supreme commander's argument with Montgomery continued. Ike doggedly went on trying to distill concord out of contention, combination out of contradiction. He insisted that all Allied resources and energies should be concentrated on a rapid thrust to

Berlin and immediately asserted that strategic areas on the flanks should be occupied in a concerted operation. He assured Monty that he had never considered "an advance into Germany with all armies moving abreast" but he encouraged Bradley and Patton to keep on "acting offensively."[74] He said that it was vital to capture Antwerp but, by qualifying his statements confusingly, he allowed Monty to avoid making this his "unequivocal priority" until 16 October.[75] And when Hughes facetiously suggested that he might persuade the field marshal to cooperate by offering him a promotion, the supreme commander replied helplessly, "To what? When the King was in North Africa, he said he was delighted to discover that Monty wasn't after *his* job."[76]

Where Ike kept saying that they were in agreement Monty reiterated that they were not. He remorselessly exposed the inconsistencies in Ike's logic of compromise. He was also ungrateful for the real strategic opportunities Ike gave him, regarding concession as a sign of weakness. At the conference held in his luxurious new Versailles headquarters—from which Monty characteristically held aloof, sending instead his urbane chief of staff, Freddie de Guignand—Ike conceded almost everything except a complete ban on further advances by Bradley and Patton. They were so depressed by what they regarded as the supreme commander's capitulation to the British that, as Patton said, they wanted "to go to China and serve under Admiral Nimitz."[77]

Brooke, who was for once critical of Monty's strategy, recorded that "Ike nobly took all the blame on himself" for the Allied failure to reach the Arnhem objective.[78] But while Ike thought MARKET GARDEN had been a gamble worth taking, the result confirmed his gut feeling that it was fatal to attack—with vulnerable flanks and attenuated supply lines—on too narrow a front. Accordingly he was persuaded to give more scope to Bradley in the south. Ike's view that the Schelde estuary, the maritime approach to Antwerp, must be opened without delay, was also confirmed—though Monty refused to respond to his coaxing and only moved when he received an enraged telephone call from Bedell Smith threatening to cut off his supplies. However, by October it was clear that the Allies had lost the momentum which had carried them through France and that the Germans, fighting with renewed vigor to defend the frontiers of the Fatherland, had achieved "the miracle in the West."

The enemy actually mounted an autumn counterattack in the Peel Marshes and Monty persuaded Ike to give him two American divisions to clear them, which was not done until 3 December. The West

Wall, which Hitler had contemptuously said would not be able to stop a dog's fart, was effectively reinforced. And other formidable obstacles impeded Allied progress. Fighting from fixed defenses in the Huertgen Forest, the Germans took a terrible toll on Bradley's troops. Hemingway called it "Passchendaele with tree bursts,"[79] and another American observer said that battalion commanders emerging from this bloodbath "were as near gibbering idiots as men can get without being locked up for it."[80] The Germans had control of the Roer dams and could flood the river valley at will. Taking a calculated risk, Ike and Bradley held the Ardennes thinly, despite the former's fear that they might be exposing themselves to "a nasty little 'Kasserine.' "[81]

Patton did not clear defenders from the forts around Metz until 13 December. His most striking advances had been gained by the avoidance of fighting but here he showed his mettle, characteristically congratulating himself on being the first conqueror to take the city since Attila the Hun. In the far south Devers's forces made surprisingly good progress through the Vosges. But they had to contend with stiff pockets of resistance which Ike cautiously insisted on eradicating, thus perhaps missing the chance of turning the enemy's flank. Bad weather also slowed down the Allies and Ike "developed several new types of profanity" to characterize it.[82] But he did not restrict himself to swearing. He exhausted himself in trying to exhaust the enemy, traveling up and down the line incessantly and encouraging his commanders to engage in what amounted to a war of attrition. Like Grant before him, he was determined to wear down a weaker enemy by a sustained series of hammer blows.

The heavy cost of attrition, and the few obvious gains it brought, encouraged Montgomery in his autumn campaign against the supreme commander. On 10 October he renewed his attempt to be put in charge of the entire land battle. He suggested, in language that was barely diplomatic, that Ike was out of touch with the front and more inclined to formulate fuzzy political compromises than to take quick military actions. In a very plainspoken letter, drafted by his staff, Ike pointed out that Monty had failed to secure the approaches to Antwerp, which was "the real issue now at hand." He then contended that the front was too large for one man to exercise close "battle grip" on it, acknowledged that "it is quite often necessary to make concessions that recognize the existence of inescapable national differences," and said that if Monty was still unhappy he could refer the matter to higher authority.[83]

This was the last thing Monty wanted to do, for the American preponderance of troops was now so great that the combined chiefs

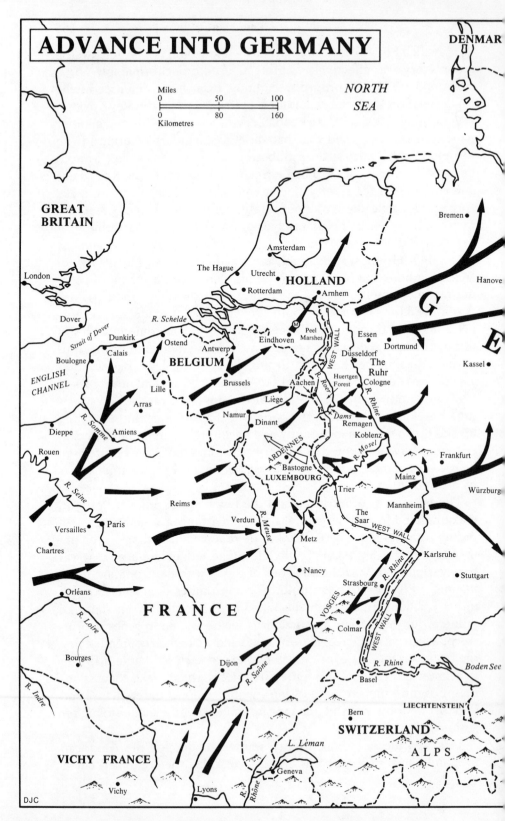

ADVANCE INTO GERMANY

Miles
0   50   100

0   80   160
Kilometres

NORTH SEA

DENMAR

GREAT BRITAIN

Bremen •

Hanove

London •

Amsterdam •

The Hague •

Utrecht •

Dover •

R. Schelde

HOLLAND

• Rotterdam

Arnhem •

Strait of Dover

Dunkirk •

Ostend •

Eindhoven •

Peel Marshes

Essen •

Dortmund •

Calais •

Antwerp •

Düsseldorf •

WEST WALL

The Ruhr

Kassel •

Boulogne •

BELGIUM

Brussels •

Huertgen Forest

Aachen •

Cologne •

ENGLISH CHANNEL

Lille •

Liège •

R. Roer

R. Rhine

G E

Arras •

R. Somme

Namur •

Dinant •

Dams

Remagen •

Dieppe •

Amiens •

Koblenz •

R. Mosel

Frankfurt •

Rouen •

R. Seine

ARDENNES

Bastogne •

LUXEMBOURG

Mainz •

Würzburg •

Reims •

Trier •

Versailles •

Paris •

Verdun •

R. Meuse

Metz •

Mannheim •

The Saar

WEST WALL

Chartres •

Nancy •

Karlsruhe •

R. Rhine

Orléans •

FRANCE

Strasbourg •

Stuttgart •

R. Loire

VOSGES

Bourges •

Dijon •

R. Saône

Colmar •

WEST WALL

R. Rhine

Basel •

Boden See

R. Indre

LIECHTENSTEIN

Bern •

SWITZERLAND

ALPS

VICHY FRANCE

L. Léman

Vichy •

Lyons •

Geneva •

R. Rhône

DJC

KIRKHAM STUDIOS — (TM/TB/TMI/AC-HM) — 18.12.85

BALTIC SEA

Gulf of
Danzig

• Danzig

GERMANY

• Lübeck

amburg

• Bromberg

üneburg R. Elbe

Stettin

POLAND

nswick

• Berlin

Magdeburg

• Poznan

HARZ MTS.

R. Neisse

Leipzig •

R Dresden •

Weimar

Gotha

M • Breslau

A

N

Y

• Cracow

Prague •

C

Z

E

Nuremberg • Pilsen

C

H

Regensburg

O

S

• Brno

L

O

V

A

K

BAVARIA R. Danube

I

A

Munich Linz • Vienna • Bratislava

Salzburg

• Berchtesgaden

HUNGARY • Budapest

Innsbruck A U S T R I A

• Graz

ITALY YUGOSLAVIA

	Operation MARKET GARDEN attack on Arnhem
	German Ardennes offensive
	Allied advances into Germany
	Russian advances into Germany

of staff were bound to support the supreme commander against his fractious subordinate. But although he promised that Ike would hear no more on the subject of command from him, Monty could not leave it alone. By now he was clearly being spurred on by personal ambition, for if a single-thrust strategy had been a doubtful prospect when the Germans were in disarray, it now stood virtually no chance of success. In any case Ike agreed that the main effort should take place on Monty's front, though this did not prevent him from giving Patton his head. But Monty was not simply eaten up by vanity and self-conceit. He was obsessed by the inadequacies of Eisenhower as a commander. In particular Ike's vice of military untidiness was an affront to his neat puritanical spirit. To his last gasp Monty maintained that "when it comes to war Ike doesn't know the difference between Christmas and Easter."[84]

Candid to the point of naïveté, Monty showed again and again that he was a babe in the woods when it came to politics. He never appreciated the political constraints under which Ike acted or the fact that they necessarily involved him in a degree of sophistry, even muddle. Nor would he heed Brooke's advice to drop the command issue. At the end of November he once again tackled Ike about it. He complained of past failure, the result of dissipating the Allied effort, and prophesied future failure unless he were given full operational control of a decisive thrust north of the Ardennes. Ike was more furious than Bradley had ever seen him. He replied firmly, deploring Monty's talk of failure and asserting that he would not stop Bradley and Devers. They were giving the Allies what he mysteriously called a *"capability of concentration"*[85] and would be a second string to their bow. For the first time, too, Ike stood up to Monty over the role of Bedell Smith at their conferences: his trusted chief of staff should not, as Monty had demanded, remain mute. However, as usual Ike's rage was short-lived and he quickly returned to a policy of conciliation. When Monty said that he had only been referring to their *recent* failure, Ike offered "prompt and abject apologies for misreading your letter."[86] And at their meeting on 7 December Ike again agreed to give priority to the northern attack, but without stopping the southern one. Then, in the face of all the evidence and despite a clear demur from Monty, he tried to say that there were no fundamental differences between them.

Montgomery, meanwhile, had appealed his case to Brooke, and thus to Churchill. At their invitation Ike met them in London on 12 December, when the CIGS at once launched into a condemnation of Ike's "double" invasion strategy. He accused the supreme commander of "violating principles of concentration of force" and deplored the fact that he apparently did not propose to cross the Rhine until May 1945.[87] In the event Brooke's position was undermined by Churchill, who also violated the principles of concentration, allowing himself to be distracted by an old fad—the possibility of floating "fluvial mines" down the Rhine. Brooke was in despair and considered resignation. But he cheered up the next day when the prime minister explained that he had only taken Ike's side because he was a guest, a foreigner, and in a minority of one. Churchill had already complained to Roosevelt that the Western Allies had lost the initiative and the British high command were now considering the best way to regain it.

These military arguments had taken their toll on Ike's psyche and he suffered further anguish that autumn on the domestic front. A fretful and jealous Mamie insisted that he ensure John's safety when he came to Europe and accused her husband of unspecified "dirty tricks." Ike wrote that he took a beating every day, that he could not interfere with John's career (though his son was found a place on Bradley's staff) and that he loved only her. He begged Mamie to "see me in something besides a despicable light—and please let me be *certain* of my welcome home when this mess is finished."[88] Even under stress or provocation Ike had an astonishing capacity for turning away wrath with soft answers. But it should never be forgotten that he could also be a formidable, even a terrifying figure. He was capable of being witheringly abrupt with his subordinates. In order to enforce discipline among his troops and to punish the crimes of rape and murder, he had staged what was virtually a public hanging in France —he later recalled its effectiveness as a deterrent in 1953 when refusing executive clemency to the convicted "atom spies" Julius and Ethel Rosenberg. Ike's occasional harshness, even brutality, provided a striking contrast to his usual sunny good humor. No one enjoyed having fun more than he did, which generally involved him in fantasies about his future leisure or in playing interminable games of bridge —if this was impossible he liked to replay, often with Bradley, old Army football games until everyone else was "bored blind."[89]

When Ike had reason to celebrate no one entered into the festive spirit more eagerly. Certainly it seemed that he had every reason to do so on 16 December when, indeed, the whole SHAEF headquarters was *en fête.* For the supreme commander had just been nominated for promotion to a newly created rank, General of the Army. That day, too, Mickey McKeogh got married to a WAC sergeant (in the beautiful but freezing chapel at Versailles) and Ike attended the wedding, drank champagne at the reception, and kissed the bride. Moreover, Kay Summersby, herself now a WAC lieutenant, was to be awarded the British Empire Medal—Churchill proving more amenable than Marshall when it came to handing out decorations. Finally, although Montgomery now demanded payment of a five-pound bet he had made with the supreme commander that the war would not be over by Christmas (Ike, who hated losing wagers, refused to pay for another nine days), he had firmly stated that the Germans "cannot stage major offensive operations"[90]—SHAEF's own view.

So confident was Monty that he requested permission to go on leave and spent 16 December playing golf. (This was an ironic circumstance in view of the comment in Brooke's published diary that Ike, himself so addicted to the game, was spending his time on the golf links at Reims; in 1959 Brooke apologized to Ike for the remark, acknowledging that this was merely where the supreme commander's forward headquarters had been situated.)[91] Anyway, all the auguries seemed good when Bradley arrived at Versailles on the evening of the 16th to discuss manpower shortages, to play bridge, and to take part in an orgy of oyster eating—Roosevelt's press secretary, Steve Early, had sent Ike a bushel and the supreme commander was proposing to eat a meal consisting of oysters on the half shell, followed by oyster stew, and concluding with fried oysters. But as Bradley arrived so did the first news of the German offensive in the Ardennes. Bradley was inclined to dismiss it as a little local difficulty. But Ike at once sensed the danger, saying firmly, "That's no spoiling attack."[92]

10

Crusade Accomplished

The Ardennes offensive caught Ike completely by surprise. Perhaps, as he later liked to suggest, he had taken into account the possibilities of such an attack. Certainly some of his intelligence officers claimed prescience after the event. The fact is, though, that Hitler had kept his secret well. The Allies received few positive indications of what the Führer had in mind—they were not even sure if he, rather than von Rundstedt, was still controlling operations in the West—and ULTRA, on which they relied too heavily, was of little help because most of the German signals went by land line. Ike was astonished by the enemy's power to push through such rugged terrain. Indeed, many Americans seem to have looked to the Ardennes chiefly as a source of pork for the barbecue—soldiers hunted wild boar with submachine guns from low-flying Piper Cubs.

At least Ike took the offensive seriously when he first heard about it. But he did not at once grasp the full scope of Hitler's plan, which was to send a force of twenty-eight German divisions through a sector defended by four American divisions and to drive all the way to Antwerp. Thus on 17 December Ike described the onslaught as "a rather ambitious counterattack," whereas the following day it became "a major thrust."[1] On the other hand Ike never wavered in his belief that the Allies could profit from the Germans' move out of their fixed defenses, even though he only had two airborne divisions in reserve. He did not go quite as far as Patton, who vociferated, "Hell, let's have the guts to let the —— go all the way to Paris. Then we'll really cut 'em off and chew 'em up." But Ike did see the Battle of the Bulge as a chance to destroy the enemy by means of vigorous flanking attacks. At a staff conference held at Verdun on 19 December and attended by Bradley, Patton, and Devers, the supreme commander announced,

"The present situation is to be regarded as one of opportunity for us and not of disaster. There will be only cheerful faces at this conference table."[2]

It was at this meeting that Ike asked Patton how soon he could disengage three divisions and strike northward, with the immediate aim of relieving the besieged garrison at Bastogne. Patton replied that he could do so in two days, causing the assembled company to gasp derisively and provoking the supreme commander to issue a sharp rebuke, "Don't be fatuous, George."[3] But although Patton was inclined to boast that the staff of his army consisted of himself and Sergeant Mims (his driver), he had learned much about detailed planning and organization since the slaphappy days in North Africa. He persuaded Ike that he really could wheel his divisions ninety degrees to the left in the specified time—one of the most remarkable maneuvers of the war. Yet in spite of the fame he deservedly gained by breaking the German ring round Bastogne (on 26 December), Patton himself later admitted that his main attack should have been directed at the base, not at the waist, of the bulge. Eager to cut off the enemy spearheads, Ike agreed in theory. But having radiated boldness at the Verdun Conference on 19 December he apparently succumbed, the following day, to the apprehensions of his staff at SHAEF.

The situation did seem alarming. Although small contingents of American troops were resisting fiercely and the Germans were hampered by a shortage of fuel, their advance was continuing apace. Allied aircraft were grounded by the weather—something Patton tried to correct with a specially printed prayer devised by his chaplain for the Saar offensive and now applied to the Ardennes: "Oh, the Lord won't mind. He knows we're too busy right now killing Germans to print another prayer."[4] (The weather cleared on 23 December.) Groups of English-speaking Nazis in American uniforms were causing disruption behind the Allied lines and rumors abounded that the supreme commander was one of their targets.

Ike responded with what seemed like panic measures. He allowed himself to be strictly confined by his own security guards. He imposed a news blackout. He issued orders that the Meuse bridges should be held at all costs. He tried to increase the supply of infantrymen by offering blacks the chance to fight in desegregated units—but quickly backed away from this explosive issue. It was easier to integrate long-term prisoners from military jails into frontline outfits—years later, when Bradley told him that he would enjoy a film called *The Dirty Dozen*, Ike recalled that he had anticipated the idea of the movie. Worst of all, Ike began to doubt the competence of General Courtney

H. Hodges, whose First Army was in the path of the Germans, and to fear that Bradley was losing touch with him and with General William H. Simpson's Ninth Army, on the British right. Accordingly the supreme commander fell in with the suggestion that he should temporarily place all American forces north of the bulge under the operational control of Field Marshal Montgomery.

This move, which even the loser Bradley admitted at the time to be logical from the military point of view, was fraught with dire political consequence. These the supreme commander should have foreseen, and Ike later said that if he had known what trouble the change would cause he would never have made it. Eisenhower himself was evidently impervious to the personal humiliation of seeming, at a time of crisis, finally to acknowledge the justice of Monty's arguments about command and, by implication, strategy. But, possessing not an iota of Ike's modesty and magnanimity, Monty regarded his new position as a personal triumph and a vindication of his case. As Brooke feared, he could not resist crowing about his victory. This further undermined British faith in the supreme commander, encouraging Brooke and Churchill in a prolonged but unsuccessful attempt to "kick him upstairs" and insert Alexander as his deputy with a central executive role. It also caused Marshall to worry that Ike was becoming "over-conciliatory in his dealings with the British."[5] Moreover, by rubbing the faces of the American generals in their supposed errors, Monty so damaged inter-Allied relations at the front that even Ike could barely mend them.

As an aide said, the field marshal arrived at the First Army's headquarters "like Christ come to cleanse the temple,"[6] and he was soon to propose the dismissal of its commander. But Hodges, admittedly exhausted and shaken by the German attack, was still thinking offensively, and Ike did not concur. Indeed, he reckoned that Hodges's only fault was that God had given him a face that always looked pessimistic.[7] Monty himself was intent on straightening and shortening his line on the principle that "you can't win the big victory without a tidy show."[8] This defensive approach infuriated Patton, who exclaimed, "To hell with Montgomery. We'll take the whole expurgated German Army and jam it up his expurgated."[9] In his diary Patton concluded that Ike, though not enough of a gambler, was a lion compared to Montgomery; and Bradley was better than both of them. Certainly Bradley favored aggression. In reply to Bedell Smith's prophecy that the Germans would shortly be over the Meuse, he plagiarized McAuliffe's celebrated reply to the German demand that Bastogne should surrender: "Nuts!"[10] All that Bradley received from

Montgomery was an infuriatingly condescending lecture, delivered on Christmas Day, about the folly of the "double thrust" strategy which was responsible for their present troubles. With superhuman self-control Bradley kept his temper.

The supreme commander himself was to become the next victim of Montgomery's vanity. At a characteristically confused meeting on 28 December Ike appeared to replay his role at Kasserine—urging, but not insisting on, a counter-strike now that the Germans were running out of steam—and Monty seemed about to repeat his performance at Falaise—squeezing the enemy out of the pocket instead of cutting them off. However, Ike came away convinced that Monty had agreed to attack on New Year's Day 1945. Instead, however, Monty sent him a message that the assault would not begin until 3 January, and he followed up this unwelcome news with what was perhaps the most arrogant letter a subordinate has ever sent to his commanding officer. In it he repeated that they had sustained "one very definite failure" and that in order to avoid another Ike should give him control of all the northern armies—"you cannot possibly do it yourself"—for a full-scale assault on the Ruhr. Monty then proceeded to dictate the style and content of the directive Ike should issue: "it will be necessary for you to be very firm on the subject, and any loosely worded statement will be quite useless . . . if you merely use the word 'co-ordination' it will not work."[11] Not only was the supreme commander enraged, but all the top American and British officers at SHAEF were "mad at Monty." And, as Kay Summersby wrote, it was Ike's "one aim to keep the staff together."[12] Ike resolved to have a showdown with Monty.

His determination was strengthened on 30 December by a cable from Marshall, who had been alerted by the British press which, in its enthusiasm for Montgomery, was scaling heights of chauvinism only reached in the United States by the McCormick-Patterson and Hearst newspapers. The chief of staff encouraged Eisenhower to make "no concessions of any kind" over the appointment of a single ground commander, on pain of causing "terrific resentment" in the United States.[13] (Public opinion at home could be gauged by the fact that *Time* magazine made Eisenhower its Man of the Year on 1 January 1945, but said that because of the Ardennes offensive he faced "the greatest setback of his career.")[14] So Ike prepared to refer the command dispute to the combined chiefs of staff, in the sure knowledge that they would support him against Montgomery.

But thanks to the astute and dramatic intercession of de Guignand, who flew to and from Versailles through fog in a frantic effort to prevent the crisis from coming to a head, Ike agreed to delay. Montgomery was completely unmanned by the prospect of dismissal and, at de Guignand's suggestion, drew back from the brink: "Very distressed that my letter may have upset you and I would ask that you tear it up."[15] Ike was quick to grasp this olive branch. But he made it plain that he would appeal to higher authority if their differences again became acute. He also assured Monty that in the matter of giving him command over Bradley he could go no further. But he did emphasize that Monty would direct the main assault, north of the Ruhr, after the reduction of the Ardennes salient.

Perhaps encouraged by this mark of confidence, Monty did not remain chastened for long. On 7 January he held a press conference, ostensibly to plead for Anglo-American unity and to compliment everyone from Ike to GI Joe for containing the German thrust, but actually to congratulate himself for having saved the Allies from disaster. Brigadier "Bill" Williams, Montgomery's intelligence officer, who had begged his chief not to talk to war correspondents, recalled that Monty "came in wearing a purple airborne beret and was like a cock on a dunghill."[16] The field marshal explained how he had thought ahead, had taken the necessary steps to avert danger, and had found the battle one of the most interesting he had handled. Monty later regretted using the word "interesting" to describe the occasion on which so many valiant lives had been lost.[17] At the time his vainglorious remarks were variously interpreted, but they were divisive enough to precipitate another crisis in Anglo-American relations.

German radio exploited them, issuing a distorted version purporting to emanate from the BBC. Bradley retaliated by stating publicly that the Ardennes offensive had been defeated in the south before Monty took temporary command in the north and by telling Ike privately that he would rather be sent home than serve under Montgomery. The supreme commander flushed and then protested at this unusual display of truculence on the part of his most trusted and balanced subordinate, but Bradley was adamant. Churchill finally had to damp down the hostility with a speech in Parliament that stressed that U.S. losses in the Ardennes almost matched those at Gettysburg on both sides, whereas the British had suffered relatively light casualties. The Bulge, he said, was an *American* battle. It was also a "famous American victory."[18]

This was perhaps claiming too much. Ike had allowed himself to be caught unawares, thus casting doubt on his personal competence. He had lost so much ground that his military strategy was also called into question, though if the Ardennes offensive proved to the British the danger of advancing on a broad front, it proved to the Americans that even an overwhelming assault on too narrow a front could be not only stemmed but repulsed. Ike had been forced to delay his own advance on the Rhine for two months. His leadership, admirable during the first stage of the attack, had later been marked by nervousness. He had even called for a Russian offensive to ease the pressure against the Americans. Finally, he did not impose his preferred strategy, which was to cut off the Bulge quickly at its base, and so the enemy was permitted to make a fighting retreat. On the other hand the Germans had suffered irreplaceable losses—100,000 men (compared to 75,000 Americans), 800 tanks, 1,000 planes. The final great effort of which the Third Reich was capable had been broken in the Ardennes. The long German front in the east had been so denuded of resources that it was actually weaker than the shorter western front, and the Russians were able to advance almost to Berlin following their attack on 12 January.

The Battle of the Bulge, in short, was a defeat for Hitler rather than a victory for Ike, a failure of the Führer's last desperate throw rather than a success for the supreme commander's calculating generalship. Of course, in public Ike preserved an unruffled facade: he told reporters that the Ardennes offensive had not frightened him at the time but had scared him stiff when he read accounts of it in the newspapers afterward. But in private Ike had every reason for feeling run-down, out-of-sorts and ill-tempered by mid-January. To a surprised GI who observed him giving blood in the SHAEF dispensary and expressed a desire to have some of it in order to make general, the supreme commander responded grimly, "If you do I hope you don't inherit my bad disposition."[19]

Montgomery was not the only person to have a deleterious effect on Ike's disposition during the Ardennes campaign. At the end of December the supreme commander instructed Devers to make a tactical withdrawal, in order both to defend himself better against the subsidiary German attack in the south and to provide a reserve for the northern conflict. This prompted de Gaulle to declare that it would be a national disaster for the enemy to reoccupy the city of Strasbourg, recently liberated by General Leclerc and now exposed to a hideous revenge. The supreme commander would not be moved by political arguments. But when de Gaulle, getting "quite heated to say the least," threatened to withdraw his forces from Ike's control, and Churchill, who was "magnificent,"[20] added a plea of his own, Ike found a good military reason to relent. He was obliged to relent again later in January when he tried to take several divisions away from

Bradley in order to help Devers. Ike was now chronically short of manpower, and the Colmar pocket of German resistance galled him as much as did the cyst on the back of his neck. But Bradley was "badly upset"[21] already over Ike's refusal to give him back the Ninth Army (the First had been returned when the Bulge was almost flattened, on 17 January). And with Patton egging him on he blasted one of Ike's senior staff at SHAEF: "I trust you do not think I am angry. But I want to impress upon you that I am *goddam well incensed.*"[22]

However, if Ike gave way to Bradley he continued to worry that pockets of German resistance like Colmar might yet be a source of further embarrassment to the Allies. For he believed that the Ardennes offensive was "only one episode and we must expect attempts in other areas."[23] So although he felt under a compulsion to stress his preference for boldness, Ike was now more determined than ever to defeat the enemy on a broad front, advancing his armies until they all reached the Rhine. There he planned to form "*a very firm* defensive line which can be held with the minimum of forces."[24] Thus he would minimize the danger of another surprise attack and Monty could cross the river in strength. Needless to say, Monty himself was dissatisfied with this plan, which contained the familiar provisos about maintaining flexibility and exploiting opportunities on secondary fronts, and he complained to Brooke that all the old snags of indecision and vacillation had once more appeared. However, Marshall supported Ike, and the two chiefs of staff had a blazing row on the subject when they met in Malta (before proceeding to Yalta with Roosevelt and Churchill) at the end of January. Brooke accused Marshall of conducting a personal vendetta against Montgomery and complained that Ike was not strong enough, to which Bedell Smith retorted that the supreme commander could only control his highly individualistic generals by a mixture of diplomacy and severity. Eventually Ike evolved a form of words which Brooke found confusing but, paradoxically, acceptable. The supreme commander promised to seize the Rhine crossings in the north as soon as possible and "without waiting to close the Rhine throughout its length."[25]

In practice Ike permitted Bradley to maintain an "aggressive defensive."[26] Patton took full advantage of this ambiguous directive to transform vigorous patrolling into reconnaissances in force, which in turn became full-scale attacks. He evidently thought that this transparent procedure fooled Ike and Bradley, an assumption which they agreed in conversation long after the war to be "ridiculous." As Bradley said, Patton's offensive "was not a major one until we turned him loose" and egged him on with the prospect of publicity—"we used to say, give him the headlines if he will go twenty miles."[27] Yet there is no denying that this was a strange mode of command. It was strategy by subterfuge, a generalship of nods and winks. Patton in particular raged about having "to wage war by inadvertence [and] to conquer by deceit."[28] Even when Ike was in a position to issue clear and direct orders he apparently preferred to work by more tortuous methods. He moved by stealth, directed through the allocation or retention of supplies, threatened to take Simpson's Ninth Army away from Montgomery if there was any recurrence of Fleet Street's campaign against Bradley. In fact, Ike did much to earn his cruel nickname, "General Eisenhowever."

At the beginning of 1945, Ike was perhaps especially inclined to exercise power in this elliptical fashion because he felt insecure about his position as supreme commander. Certainly he had cause to worry in view of Monty's intrigues, the Ardennes setback, and the scheme, not yet aborted, to appoint Alexander, an active ground commander, in Tedder's place, as his deputy. At any rate Ike arrived scowling at Monty's headquarters in Zondhoven on 14 February and banged the table during their interview. This was largely, the field marshal surmised, because Ike was anxious about being elevated into a figurehead. Actually Ike was also cross because he always had to call on Montgomery, who was seldom willing to return the compliment, and yet Churchill had said in Malta that he did not visit Monty enough and neglected the British. The supreme commander groused about "always being bullied by Marshall and the U.S. Chiefs of Staff for being too British, or by the P.M. and the British Chiefs of Staff for being too American." However, when Monty said that he was satisfied with the existing command situation Ike became "a different man" and drove away "beaming all over his face."[29] Ike's increased optimism and self-confidence were paraded at a press conference he held a few days afterward, which was attended by one of the best judges of such affairs in the world, Steve Early. He said, "It was the most magnificent performance of any man at a press conference that I have ever seen. He knows the facts, he speaks freely and frankly, and he has a sense of humor, he has poise and he has command."[30]

By the end of February it was becoming apparent that, whatever might be said about his means, Ike was achieving his ends. The Germans were not only fighting west of the Rhine, they were being defeated there. All along the line the Allies were making progress. The Colmar pocket was eliminated, the Roer dams were captured, and the West Wall was penetrated. The Rhineland and Saar battles were won at a terrible cost—96,000 Allied casualties—but the whole campaign was a decisive victory and 280,000 prisoners crowded into Ike's cages. As his forces reached or approached the Rhine all along its length from Switzerland to the sea, and Monty began preparing to cross the river in strength, one of Hodges's detachments seized the railway bridge at Remagen (on 7 March) before it could be demolished. Ike was thrilled. He encouraged Bradley to "get across with everything you've got" and "to hell with the planners."[31] However, the planners could not be dismissed that easily. They pointed out that the terrain east of Remagen was difficult to exploit and that the best route into Germany was the northern one. Bradley was furious with SHAEF for undervaluing his bridge—"what in hell do you want us to do, pull back and blow it up?"[32]

But when his initial enthusiasm for the coup had evaporated Ike himself took note of their objections. He would only let Bradley send five divisions across the river to defend the bridgehead. Yet Hitler's ferocious response to this breaching of the Reich's last great natural barrier, Germany's moat, showed how important it was—everything from bombers to frogmen was sent to destroy the bridge. Not until it became obvious, by 19 March, that Monty's preparations for crossing the Rhine just north of the Ruhr would be slow and cumbersome did Ike agree to reinforce Bradley and let him attack. By this time, anyway, German resistance was patently crumbling. Ike himself, exhausted, suffering from various minor aches and pains (his strained knee, for example) and, in the opinion of Bedell Smith, close to having a nervous breakdown, felt able to take some leave. Accompanied by Smith himself, Bradley, Kay Summersby, and a small entourage, he went off to Cannes on the French Riviera where he stayed in a sumptuous seaside villa lent by a rich American admirer. For much of the time Ike slept.

He also discussed strategy with Bradley, at the very time that Patton, who was determined to show himself more enterprising than Montgomery, beat him across the Rhine without any of the elaborate provisions—smoke, bombardment, airborne help—which the field marshal deemed necessary. Ike concluded that he could now take full advantage of the American successes and make a momentous change in his strategy—by transferring his main effort from Montgomery's northern to Bradley's central sector. Ike kept this change of plan to himself when he went off to watch Monty's crossing of the Rhine. He traveled by jeep, accompanied only by McKeogh, and watched excitedly from a church tower as the massive enterprise unfolded. It involved a quarter of a million British, Canadian, and American troops, the complex interaction of all three services and an artillery barrage from 1,250 guns. Ike was pleased when Churchill enthused, "My dear general, the German is whipped."[33] But he was delighted when Brooke "was gracious enough to say that I was right, and that my current plans and operations are well calculated to meet the current situation."[34] Brooke later denied having acknowledged this, though it is clear that he had said something of the sort. But the point is that he, Churchill, and Montgomery were all left in ignorance of the switch in emphasis that Ike was contemplating. Not until Monty wrote to him on 27 March, arrogantly assuming that he would keep control of Simpson's Ninth Army (which he had attempted to relegate to a minor job during the Rhine crossing) and laying down his line of advance toward Berlin, did Ike drop his bombshell.

On 28 March, Ike communicated with both Montgomery and Stalin. He told the former that the Ninth Army would revert to Bradley whose "main thrust," the "northern flank" of which Monty was ordered to protect, would be through the middle of Germany toward Dresden. There, in the area of the central Elbe, he would "join hands" with the Russians.[35] Ike informed Stalin of this proposed rendezvous, explaining that he first intended to destroy German forces in the Ruhr. And he asked for an agreed method of coordinating the Anglo-American and Russian armies so that they would not clash—the Soviets were so secretive that the western high command was almost always in the dark about their operations, which Bradley, for example, plotted on the basis of BBC news bulletins. Montgomery, whom Ike had assured as late as 15 September that Berlin was the "main prize," with the implication that he should carry it off, was naturally mortified when it was snatched from his grasp.[36] Stalin, on the other hand, rejoiced at Ike's decision. To his intimates he praised Ike's "decency, generosity and chivalry in his dealings with his allies."[37] He agreed to cooperate and told Ike that Berlin had lost its former strategic importance—which meant, as many surmised, that he attached supreme importance to capturing it himself. Ike himself said that he now regarded the city as a mere geographical expression. He proposed to aim for the economic heart rather than the political head of Germany, even though the Ruhr had been bombed into insignificance and the country was only being held together by the will of its Führer. But he intended to give Hitler no chance of making a bloody last stand in some Bavarian national redoubt, something which Bradley feared might extend the war for as much as two years.

Whatever Ike liked to claim, though, his reasons for abandoning Berlin to the Russians—perhaps the most controversial decision he made during the war—were not just military. It is true that he was unconcerned about the postwar political repercussions (which had begun to obsess Churchill) of shaking hands with the Bear so far to the west. But he did, rightly, reckon that it would be pointless to sacrifice Anglo-American lives (Bradley suggested that Berlin would cost the Allies 100,000 casualties, a much inflated figure) to gain a prestige objective that would immediately be handed back to the Russians. For he estimated, again correctly, that the Western Allies would not renege on their agreement with the U.S.S.R. to divide Germany into national zones. On the other hand, Ike's decision over Berlin was later a serious political embarrassment to him and, according to Robert Murphy, he once admitted that it had been a mistake.[38]

There was, though, a more personal consideration behind Ike's resolve to push Montgomery into the sidelines and to frustrate his ambition to enter Berlin (as a senior British officer at SHAEF put it) riding on a white charger and wearing two hats. His patience with the bumptious field marshal was finally exhausted. Ike went to enormous lengths to keep his friends, whom he divided, interestingly enough, into those he liked and those he did not. But it was not his practice to quarrel even with enemies, let alone with alienated colleagues. Instead he boycotted them, banished them from his mind, subjected them to a somewhat bizarre form of ostracism—writing their names on a piece of paper, putting it in the bottom drawer of his desk, and shutting the drawer. Monty was consigned to this oubliette. As Ike later told Cornelius Ryan, "Montgomery had become so personal in his efforts to make sure the Americans and me in particular got no credit, that in fact we hardly had anything to do with the war, that I finally stopped talking to him."[39] Bradley, for long Ike's most trusted and reliable subordinate, at last reaped the reward of loyal and skilled service. It remains an open question whether, if Bradley had commanded the northern armies, Ike would not have tried to race the Russians to Berlin.

The British protested strongly at Ike's communicating directly with Stalin and at his underestimating the political and psychological importance of Berlin. Churchill also complained that he was restricting the scope of Montgomery's advance and Brooke expostulated that it was unsatisfactory for Eisenhower to have to appeal to Stalin in order to control Monty. Ike defended himself with his usual skill. He said that he was instructed to deal with Stalin over military matters, that he aimed to destroy Germany's last military and industrial resources, and that the northern route was too cut up with waterways for rapid movement to be possible. Anyway, Ike argued, he was now doing what Brooke had always wanted—concentrating on a single major thrust. And he was acting in accordance with plans conceived before D-Day. This claim was specious. No doubt there was, among SHAEF's many contingency plans, one that proposed to cut Germany in half. But having for so long stressed that his main thrust was directed toward Berlin over the north German plain, Ike was disingenuous in declaring to Marshall, "I am still adhering to my old plan."[40] As usual, though, Marshall supported him. And as the enemy forces disintegrated, there was little Churchill could do but pay tribute to Ike's glorious victories. He expressed his "admiration of the great and shining qualities of character and personality which [Eisenhower] has proved himself to possess in all difficulties of handling an Allied command."[41] Sustained by his superiors at home, backed by a huge preponderance of American troops in Europe, with great triumphs to his credit and the prospect of greater to come, the supreme commander could no longer be patronized by the prime minister as "a good fellow who was amenable and whom he could influence."[42]

Still, Ike did assure Churchill that British and American soldiers would finish the war fighting side by side. Yet as German resistance in the west collapsed during the last few weeks of the war, he found it more difficult than ever to maintain Allied harmony and to impose an agreed strategy on his diverse forces. De Gaulle, for example, smarting at his exclusion from Yalta, proved even more recalcitrant than usual. In order to increase France's claim to receive a national zone of occupation in defeated Germany he instructed French troops to occupy Stuttgart in defiance of Devers's orders, which were confirmed by the supreme commander. To Ike's dismay, de Gaulle set national prestige above military exigency and by this démarche put the lives of American soldiers at risk. But whereas Ike delicately hinted that he might have to employ sanctions against the French, America's new president, Harry S. Truman, bluntly threatened to hold back supplies unless they withdrew. This was the sort of language which de Gaulle understood and it provides a vivid early example of the contrasting styles of Truman and Eisenhower.

Incidentally, the news of Roosevelt's death reached Ike at a time when he was already in a state of shock after having visited the German concentration camp of Ohrdruf Nord near Gotha on 12 April. Pale but resolute, the supreme commander toured every part of it. He, Bradley, and Patton witnessed terrible things, the gallows with its noose of piano wire, rooms piled high with lice-covered corpses, the marks left by starving prisoners who had torn at the entrails of the dead for food. They all felt nauseous and Patton vomited. Ike told Mamie that he had "never dreamed that such cruelty, bestiality and savagery could really exist."[43] He ensured that the evidence of these horrors was collected and made public so that there would be no room for doubt about the unmitigated evil against which the Allies had been fighting. Ike himself, however, wrote about the concentration camps in oddly inexplicit terms, as though he was reluctant to offend his own or his readers' susceptibilities by going into detail.

With the winning post in sight, Ike's own commanders became even more eager to gallop off on their own. Bradley was an exception, though it is arguable that he spent too much time clearing out the encircled Ruhr, instead of pressing eastward, perhaps because he feared that Simpson's army would be restored to Montgomery. No doubt remembering Falaise, Bradley declared, "I've got bags on my mind,"[44] and certainly his total bag of 317,000 prisoners was impressive. Monty made slow and sulky progress over difficult terrain. He was very angry, however, when Ike urged him on and (getting no results) persuaded Churchill to do the same. Without such goading, though, Monty probably would not have advanced his plans for crossing the Elbe to 29 April (from 1 May). This enabled him to reach Lübeck a few crucial hours before the Russians and, as Ike had intended, to seal off Denmark from Soviet penetration. Simpson, whose own vanguard crossed the Elbe at Magdeburg on 12 April, was appalled to be stopped from going on to Berlin. It was only sixty miles down the autobahn and, as one historian has written, "there was nothing between [Simpson] and Hitler except Eisenhower."[45] Perhaps he could have taken the city, for although Simpson was at the end of his logistical tether the Russians were still thirty miles away and the Germans, terrified of the murdering, raping, and looting inflicted on civilians by the victorious Red Army, were anxious to surrender to the Americans.[46]

Instead, Ike told the Russians (with British agreement) that he would halt at the Elbe. He was much less decisive about whether Patton, agog at the chance of taking Prague and fraternizing with friendly females (German women were "off-limits"), should be allowed to enter Czechoslovakia. Eventually, when Marshall expressed a wish not to sacrifice American lives for political ends and the Russians opposed such a move, Ike restrained Patton. That headstrong general had ideas of going on to the Urals and, as he put it, finishing the job. But Ike was clear that the Russians were Allies and made sure that no last-minute machinations by the Nazis, who tried to surrender to the Western partners alone, should disrupt the coalition. Ike later tried to suggest that he had seen the origins of the cold war in the embers of the hot one. In fact, he was willing to sacrifice Czechoslovakia to secure good relations with the Russians, who were pathologically suspicious about Western intentions. He labored to maintain mutual understanding until it became politically embarrassing to do so, and he was as slow to take offense at the brutalities of Stalin as at the incivilities of Montgomery.

It was enough, for the time being, that a coalition between East and West had defeated Germany, that Hitler was dead, and that his successors were suing for peace. It turned out, as Butcher observed ruefully, that war was easier to start than to stop. There were various hitches in the negotiations; Churchill bombarded Ike with telephone calls; there was a muddle about the surrender document; the publicity circus got out of hand; and the timing of the announcement was not properly coordinated with the Russians. Still, in the early hours of the morning of Monday, 7 May, General Jodl and Admiral von Friedeburg did sign the instrument of surrender at Reims in front of senior representatives of all the Allied forces.

The ceremony took place in the recreation hall of the school being used as SHAEF's headquarters and it was also witnessed by seventeen selected journalists, photographers, and film men. Butcher had decked the room, as Ike disgustedly remarked, "like a Hollywood setting." But Ike himself was determined to scotch any incipient myth, like that which had spread after the Great War, about the invincibility of German arms. After the signing the supreme commander met the Nazi plenipotentiaries for a few moments in a nearby office. He asked them sternly whether they understood the terms and would abide by them. Receiving an affirmative answer, he dismissed them curtly. Then he said a few words for the newsreel cameras, posed for pictures, and made a Victory sign with the gold fountain pens (provided by his friend Kenneth Parker, of the Parker Pen Company) with which the surrender had been signed. Afterward, rejecting various high-flown phrases suggested by his entourage, Ike dictated a stark communiqué to the combined chiefs of staff: "The mission of this Allied force was fulfilled at 0241 local time, May 7, 1945."[47] Ike decreed that the moment should be celebrated with a bottle of champagne. It was flat. And that seemed to sum up the mood of anticlimax now that the purpose which had informed all their lives for so long was achieved. Eisenhower went off to bed with his latest Western, which was entitled *Cartridge Carnival*.

The supreme commander was immediately deluged with congratulations, tributes, honors, decorations. In a matter of three years he had become one of the most famous, most trusted, and most beloved men on earth. He was hailed as a military genius who had commanded the most powerful army in the history of warfare and achieved the greatest victory over the forces of evil that the world had ever known. That he was no Caesar or Napoleon Ike himself would have been the first to admit, having decided before he came to Europe that such figures were an anachronism. What he had become instead was a supremely successful martial magnate, managing director of a vast conglomerate dealing in war. Ike himself once acknowledged that he was not really a general at all but more of a businessman. What he accomplished during the Second World War was a gigantic feat of military entrepreneurship. He acted as chairman of the board and retained the confidence of the stockholders' representatives, Roosevelt, Churchill, de Gaulle, and the combined chiefs of staff. He coordinated the work of his own team, arbitrating between rivals at the top and inspiring men at the bottom. He negotiated mergers or takeovers with more or less hostile competitors, the French and the Italians. He was senior executive of the firm which drove Adolf Hitler out of business for good. He ensured that America's huge military–industrial investment, her expenditure of blood and treasure, earned its just dividend—victory.

These were achievements enough. But Ike and his supporters had been brought up to admire the old-fashioned soldierly virtues. So frequent attempts have been made to represent him as a modern knight in shining armor, not least by Ike himself with his passion for "crusades." Randolph Churchill, for example, denied that Ike was a mere chairman of the board and hailed him as "a brilliant military figure."[48] However, when his record is scrutinized with care it becomes plain that, in the traditional sense of the term, Eisenhower was not a great military commander. Like Winston Churchill, Ike had good instincts, but he was too inconstant to be—as Marshall was—a master of grand strategy. Unduly influenced by strong personalities, by political expediency, and by a compelling desire for popularity, Ike was slow to make up his mind and quick to change it. He was not so much flexible as malleable.

He was cautious by nature yet was so anxious to seem daring that he sometimes endorsed plans that were rash, such as SLEDGEHAMMER and MARKET GARDEN. As everyone kept pointing out, Ike had always been a staff officer—a superlative one—and he was always hampered by his lack of fighting experience. It was no accident that his three ablest subordinates, Bradley, Patton, and Montgomery, agreed on one thing—that Ike, though an outstanding political general, was no battlefield commander. There is no disgrace in this; and as it happened, Ike did have a certain tactical flair. At least three times—during Kasserine, after the Ardennes, and at Remagen—his hunches were correct. But he lacked the will or the courage to play them to the full, opting instead for safety first. The strategy which Ike developed, often by fits and starts, was probably correct in essentials. His generalship was careful, orthodox, and uninspired. But it was sound. He never made a fundamental mistake and he was successful in the end.

The extreme difficulty of his task and the multitudinous pitfalls he avoided need no emphasis. What must be said is that Ike was able to bring his work as supreme commander to its triumphant conclusion because he embodied a unique combination of qualities. First there was his glowing personal charm and attractiveness, which when projected to a mass audience can only be called charisma. In private he could be, as one American officer noted, "gloriously cordial."[49] In public, as the New York *Herald Tribune* wrote in 1944, "he has the Lincoln touch."[50] To a considerable extent, then, despite his self-confessed ill temper and bad temperament, Ike could lead in accordance with his own ideal of leadership—because men wanted to follow him. Second, there was Ike's monumental discretion, that Washingtonian attribute which might be described as the beginning of political wisdom. No one possessed antennae so delicately attuned to the mood of the moment, and no one manifested such finesse in responding to it. Without his fusion of empathy and diplomacy Ike could never have achieved what he was to term (in a letter to Churchill written in 1948) "the miracle of Allied cooperation."[51]

Third, there was Ike's studious moderation, that instinctive cleaving to the golden mean which was to be the hallmark of his presidency. His frequent invocations to common sense and his denunciations of crazy extremes, though they accorded ill with his desire to be seen as a warrior both dashing and audacious, signified that he was a man who could be trusted. Finally, there were the simple virtues which made Ike appear to possess great moral stature. Everyone paid tribute to what Billy Graham later called Eisenhower's "honesty, integrity and spiritual power."[52] Ike displayed an engaging mixture of high-mindedness and fair-mindedness; he seemed a model of modesty, humanity, sincerity, and loyalty. In some ways this was, indeed, the true Ike. But in other respects the public image masked the private reality. Ike's closest associates knew that he was capable of duplicity and sophistry. But no one really plumbed the depths of his personality or came to an informed estimate of the calculating and self-regarding intelligence there enshrined. No one grasped the paradox that Ike combined common decency with uncommon deviousness, that he was not only a model of magnanimity but a dedicated opportunist. It was, in fact, Ike's guile, his ability to take the high moral line and lace it with low cunning, or even to ignore morality altogether in practice while paying elaborate lip service to it, which made him such a formidable military and political figure. As leader of the armed alliance which defeated Axis powers Ike was without equal. Field Marshal Montgomery himself concluded simply, "No one else could have done it."[53]

II

★

Backward into
the Limelight

Ike later asserted that he had reached his "historical peak" in May 1945,[1] and everything he said during the next seven years was designed to show that he had no political aims. Yet his every action indicates that he aspired to reach the topmost pinnacle, that scaled by Washington, Jackson, and Grant after their military triumphs. Better than anyone Ike understood that serving soldiers must not, even by implication, campaign for public office. It was worse than illegal, it was fatal—as MacArthur, and others who prematurely revealed that their eyes were set on the White House, discovered. So for seven long years Ike denied that his goal was the presidency. He denied it to his wife, to his relations, and to intimate friends like Harry Butcher: "Why, in the name of all that's holy, does everyone always have to think of the word politics in connection with the name Eisenhower?"[2] He denied it to public figures and to potential enemies like Harry Truman, who offered to campaign for him and was rebuffed with uneasy jocularity and odd grammatical pedantry: "Mr. President, I don't know who will be your opponent for the presidency, but it will not be I."[3] Most of all, Ike denied it to the press: "In the strongest language you can command you can state that I have no political ambitions at all."[4] Depending on how they are viewed, Ike's denials amounted to a brilliantly sustained feat of political legerdemain or to an epic of humbug.

Of course, he tried to preserve the fiction that he must do his patriotic duty and serve his country in any post to which he was drafted. So he refused to utter a categorical statement, as Sherman had done, that he would not accept if nominated and would not serve if elected. There may even have been a factual basis for the fiction, in that the West Point ideals were genuinely close to his heart and throughout the war he had conjured with notions of an idyllic retirement filled with golfing and fishing, together perhaps with a little writing and lecturing on the side. But his closest associates were quite certain that Ike was intent on seizing what Horace Greeley had called "the glittering bait of the Presidency."[5] In answer to the question of whether Ike wanted that office Bedell Smith replied, "Want it! He wants it so bad he can taste it!"[6] Butcher concurred, though he phrased it more delicately. So did another intimate who noted the general's postwar frustration and said that he "didn't regain his serenity" until he moved into the White House.[7] Patton noted that "Ike is bitten with the Presidential bug."[8]

On this subject Ike "never confided in journalists," as Harrison Salisbury said, not even in the aristocrats of their profession, men like Cyrus Sulzberger, with whom he played golf.[9] As late as December 1951 Ike assured Sulzberger, with every indication of veracity, that he "did *not*" want to run for the presidency—"It's a hell of a life." But Sulzberger and other reporters were convinced that Ike "definitely wants to be elected on a Republican ticket."[10] Newsmen agreed that Ike "itches to get into the political fight"[11] and "is 'running for the Presidency as fast as all get-out.' "[12] But while they did not believe his denials they did believe in his sincerity. Merriman Smith, for example, wrote, "I've never seen a man who gave more outward evidence of being sincere."[13] The paradox worried Ike, who was not prepared to admit that he subscribed to the code of cant which apparently governed the behavior of all professional politicians. He wrote to a friend, General Lucius Clay, after publicly declaring on 7 January 1952 that he would "under no circumstances" ask for relief from his military position to seek political office:

I do not see how people can state, on the one hand, that they believe implicitly in my integrity and honesty of intention and, in almost the same breath, imply that I did not mean at all what I said in that public statement. More than this, I fail to see why something of a virtue cannot be made of my refusal to have my attention diverted from my assigned duty. I have already admitted that if confronted with a greater duty, I shall strive to the best of my ability to perform it.[14]

Of course, it was not Ike's words, even ambivalent words like these, but his deeds which chiefly struck observers. He looked like a candidate for high office and he behaved like one. Even when confronting troops, as Patton noticed, his bearing was that of a man on the campaign trail. This impression hardened after the war. A U.S. Senator who witnessed Ike inspecting a camp full of released American prisoners of war on 21 May 1945 said to Butcher, "I hope that fellow never decides to run against me in my State. He's got what it takes. I can see now why the G.I.s worship him. He speaks their language, he isn't high hat like you expect from the brass, and he knows their problems and they know it." The soldiers themselves agreed. One was overheard to remark, "G.I. sure stands for General Ike."[15]

Ike's many public appearances, especially at the celebrations which marked the end of the war, all helped to build up his popular image. He was presented with a jeweled ceremonial sword by Marshal Zhukov in Frankfurt and a Napoleonic sword by General de Gaulle in Paris. He attended many dinners, receptions, and functions in other capitals, received the highest honors that nations could bestow, including the British Order of Merit—which means what it says and had never before been given to an American. And the only time he objected to publicity was when he was kissed on both cheeks by General de Gaulle.

Ike's most famous performance was his speech at London's Guildhall, when he was presented with yet another sword and (like General Pershing) with the freedom of the city. He wrote, rewrote, revised, and rehearsed this oration, and finally learned it off by heart. In the cold light of retrospect the Guildhall speech, as one literary critic has said, is chiefly distinguished by "a reliance on clichés, an uncertain diction and an effort to achieve grandiose effect by means of rhetorical devices that do not quite succeed."[16] However, in the mood of heightened emotion at the time they succeeded perfectly. Ike's praise for the courage of Londoners, who had been in the front line from the start, contrasted well with his own modesty—he claimed to be only a "symbol of great human forces that have labored arduously and successfully for a righteous cause." Ike's invocation to the victorious alliance, his assertion that he came from "the very heart of America," and his celebration of the values which the citizen of London shared with the citizen of Abilene, touched exactly the right note. He spoke earnestly about "those intangibles that are the real treasures free men possess. To preserve his freedom of worship, his equality before law, his liberty to speak and act as he sees fit, subject only to provisions that he trespass not upon similar rights of others—a Londoner will fight. So will a citizen of Abilene. When we consider these things, then the valley of the Thames draws closer to the farms of Kansas and the plains of Texas."[17] The newspapers compared his words to those of the Gettysburg Address and even Ike's sternest critic was moved to admiration. Field Marshal Brooke wrote in his diary, "Ike made a wonderful speech and impressed all hearers . . . I had never realized that Ike was as big a man until I heard this performance today."[18]

Obviously Ike was now so famous that publicity would surround his every act. When he went for a stroll in Hyde Park before delivering the Guildhall speech he was mobbed by autograph hunters and had to be rescued by two London bobbies—in the foyer of the Dorchester Hotel he was saluted by a British general who said, "Good morning, Sir. I see you are being brought home by the police." But Ike responded to the acclaim like a seasoned political trouper. He was seldom discomposed and he met almost every situation with marvelous tact and modesty. When he went with Kay and other members of the "gang" to see a musical, *Strike a New Note,* the theater audience shouted for a speech and he replied from his box: "It's nice to be back in a country where I can *almost* speak the language."[19]

Ike demonstrated a similarly sure touch during his rapid and jubilant return to the United States. In Washington he exclaimed, "Oh God, it's swell to be home." In Abilene he declared, "Oh boy, I'm glad to be back here."[20] His pronouncements were all recorded and many of them made headline news. His address to the two houses of Congress was particularly effective, even though Ike spoke off the cuff. He always preferred the extempore to the prepared speech, reckoning that he gained more in spontaneity than he lost in coherence. No doubt he was correct, since his talks usually impressed listeners by their warmth and sincerity—though when read they generally seem rambling and hackneyed. It is true that his brother Milton advised Ike against " 'ad lib' talking," on the grounds that it left a poor impression.[21] But journalists tended to think that Ike, like Truman, was better served by his own language "which can be graceful in spirit even when its cadences jar and its syntax is irregular." As Richard Rovere said, Ike would sometimes "put across, even to large audiences, a vivid sense of the blend of plasticity and firmness that has always been said to characterize his personality."[22] To some extent, though, Ike's responsiveness to his environment was a disadvantage, for his own behavior was liable to be determined by the prevailing mood. This partly accounts for his changeableness. Ike claimed that one of his horrors was a garrulous general, and he was given to a delphic reserve. But in the right company he could, as he acknowledged, become "very verbose," and John Gunther described him as "an extremely loquacious man."[23] Few politicians have been more sensitive to the susceptibilities of their audiences or have studied more carefully to please them.

Nothing would have offended the American people more than a public scandal over Kay Summersby. This in itself is enough to discredit the allegation made by President Truman in extreme old age, and published in Merle Miller's book *Plain Speaking* (1973) that Ike asked Marshall in June 1945 to be relieved of duty so that the could come home, divorce Mamie, and marry Kay. According to this story, the president and the chief of staff threatened to bust Ike "out of the Army" and make his life "a living hell" if he took any such action, and Truman eventually destroyed the letters.[24] Thus nothing exists to substantiate Truman's claim, which is thoroughly implausible in itself and is implicitly contradicted by circumstantial evidence that does survive. This shows that, far from contemplating a fatal *mésalliance,* Ike was determined to extricate himself from the dangerous liaison with Kay. Having apparently promised that she would continue as "a member of my personal official family,"[25] he used as an excuse for terminating their association the fact that she could not retain her commission as a WAC without becoming an American citizen, a process that would take five years. Ike confessed to Bedell Smith that Kay "feels very deserted and alone,"[26] and he tried rather half-heartedly to find her another job. He explained the situation to Kay herself and concluded dismissively, "I shall watch your future with the greatest interest. . . . Telek will, of course, go with you."[27]

Kay made periodic attempts to reestablish contact afterward. Once she bumped into him in the street (he backed away hastily) and on another occasion, in September 1946, she turned up at the War Department with a Scottie in tow whose collar bore the legend, "This dog belongs to Kay and Ike."[28] The general's aides kept her in a back room while Ike himself beat a retreat all the way to Kansas—sadly he had an impeccable reason for doing so, for he received news that his mother died. When Kay tried to arrange a meeting by letter he was stubbornly evasive: "I can scarcely estimate when there might arise an opportunity for you to come past the office. The days are an unending series of conferences and work. . . . My time is practically solidly booked."[29] Ike was similarly guarded when referring to Kay—"Irish and tragic"[30]—in his diary, always more of a public than a private document and now having the distinct air of being written for posterity. Kay was understandably hurt by Ike's treatment and, according to Butcher, she wrote her war memoir, *Eisenhower Was My Boss* (1948), partly "from pique."[31] That may be true, but she was as scrupulous as Ike himself not to damage his reputation by indiscreet revelations. Even so, Ike was embarrassed by this volume, a copy of which Kay sent him. When Montgomery, undoubtedly prompted by malice, asked about obtaining one, Ike professed not to have seen the book.

On 10 July 1945 Ike returned to his base in Frankfurt where he remained for four months to disband SHAEF, to command the shrinking number of American troops in Europe, and to act as military governor of the American military zone in Germany. These tasks were by no means to his taste. He missed the sense of unity and purpose which had informed the war years. He was bored by receiving honors and attending ceremonies. He complained to Mamie that, far from being able to relax now that the shooting had stopped, he was "busier than ever" trying to cope with the "destruction, disorder, and disease" which were "rampant in Germany."[32] His efforts were by no means altogether successful and he bitterly resented the severe criticisms to which he was subjected, especially for failing quickly to alleviate the living conditions of Jews and displaced persons. Nor was Ike entirely clear about the correct attitude to adopt toward the defeated foe. He began by sternly trying to enforce nonfraternization and de-Nazification orders, dismissing Patton from command of the Third Army after a blazing row in September for insubordination on these issues. But, peace general that Ike was, he soon took a more conciliatory line. He urged Truman to regenerate the Ruhr and to avoid the imposition of sanctions that would make it impossible for the Germans to develop their economy. He was also inclined to spare the Japanese from the horror of atomic bombing, though this humane and courageous plea was, of course, overruled.

Ike's attempts to preserve good relations with Russia were equally doomed. He had established a true rapport with Marshal Zhukov, "an affable and soldierly-appearing individual," despite being shocked by his manner of dealing with German minefields—he had simply marched his troops over them ahead of the tanks. (Zhukov was even more shocked by Ike's statement that he fed enemy prisoners of war U.S. army rations because he wanted American POWs treated decently: "But what did you care about men the Germans had captured? They had surrendered and could not fight any more.")[33] However, Ike did gain some understanding of the motives for Soviet ruthlessness when he visited Moscow in August and witnessed the appalling devastation wrought by the Nazis. From his airplane he did not see a single house standing between Russia's western border and her capital. In Moscow Ike was feted with a colorful display of folk dancing and mass gymnastics, accompanied by a thousand-piece band, which he watched for five hours with Stalin and other dignitaries from the top of Lenin's tomb.

Ike later claimed that he never had any illusions about the Soviet dictator. He portrayed Stalin in standard terms, as "a very cunning man who 'lived within himself.' . . . He mumbled when he talked, but one could tell he was thinking every minute." He was "strong and ruthless."[34] At the time, however, Ike described Stalin as "benign and fatherly."[35] For his part, Stalin seems to have been favorably impressed by Ike. He told the U.S. ambassador, Averell Harriman, that "General Eisenhower is a very great man, not only because of his military accomplishments but because of his human, friendly, kind and frank nature. He is *not* a 'grubyi' [coarse, brusque] man like most military."[36] It was a shrewd estimate and, until the cold war really set in, Ike doggedly strove to prolong the brief era of good feelings between West and East. He scorned the notion that the Soviet Union was bent on world domination and pleaded for a continuation of wartime cooperation. Ike only began to denounce the evils of Communism when they manifested themselves flagrantly abroad and when it became impolitic at home to do anything else.

To everyone from Mamie to Marshall Ike confided his wish to retire and "let someone else have the headaches and the headlines." So in November he was glad to leave Europe, with its "unholy mixture of irritations, frustrations and bewildering conflicts,"[37] and return to the United States. However, once there, though still toying with ideas of renunciation, he succumbed to the honorable ambition of reaching the top of his profession. Thus he willingly succeeded Marshall as chief of staff. The office proved a bed of nails, for Ike occupied it during a time that the largest military machine in history was being dismantled. Marshall himself admitted that he had bequeathed the most intractable set of problems: "I'm afraid I played an awful trick on Eisenhower, getting out so fast."[38]

Ike was harassed by the problem of how to retain an effective army when the pressure toward demobilization was becoming intense. By the beginning of 1946, for example, U.S. troops were close to mutiny, "Bring Back Daddy" clubs had sprung up all over the country, and Ike was deluged with appeals to release individuals from the service. He responded by passing the buck to subordinate commanders, whom he urged to let go of men for whom there was no further military need. But he was still the object of unwelcome criticism. Bernard Baruch said to him, "Remember in the circus and on Coney Island where they put a head in the circles and have people throw brickbats at them. Well, that's the way you are." Ike replied, "That's exactly where I am, Sir."[39] Ike was further vexed by the fact that neither of his pet military schemes, for universal military training and for unification of the three branches of the armed forces—war having now become "a triphibious affair"[40]—proved acceptable to the country. Nor would Truman take his advice about increasing military expenditure, though at this stage the president still admired Ike. He in turn lavished compliments on his commander in chief, who responded in the Midwestern idiom they shared, "That swells me up like a pizened pup."[41]

At the same time, immediately beneath him was Douglas MacArthur, who remained insubordinate to an embarrassing degree. Unable to control his former chief, Ike did his best to ignore him. They did meet once in the Far East, where each spent an evening denying his own presidential ambitions and trying to persuade the other to stand: afterward Ike privately warned Truman that he would have to face a MacArthur campaign, and MacArthur sent the president a personal message saying that Eisenhower intended to be a candidate. Ike suffered additionally from never being out of the public eye. The pace of work seemed to increase all the time. And he dubbed the Pentagon —vast, impersonal, labyrinthine, and noted for huge lavatory accommodation designed to segregate the races as well as the sexes—"a mad house."[42] Inevitably Ike got lost and had to be directed back to his office. He would have relished the standard joke about a woman found in labor in the Pentagon who protested that when she had entered the building she had not even been pregnant.

However, there were compensations for being incarcerated in the Pentagon "squirrel cage."[43] Ike and Mamie occupied the luxurious Quarters No. 1 at Fort Myer, where the chief of staff could drowse on the sun porch, or watch horse operas on his movie projector, or amuse himself with farming pursuits—he made sauerkraut from his own cabbages but, to his chagrin, all the chickens he inherited from Marshall died. Moreover, Ike managed to delegate the most onerous chores at work. As Bedell Smith explained to General Maxwell Taylor in January 1946, Ike "is an exponent of decentralization. He selects commanders and staff with care. He then accords them a full measure of confidence and a very large measure of independent authority. After this he backs them up completely; however, as a rule he allows only one serious mistake per officer."[44]

This technique enabled Ike to devote his time, much more than Marshall had done, to tours, public appearances, and speeches. He traveled widely, both at home and abroad, and was greeted everywhere with extraordinary manifestations of enthusiasm. In Brazil, for example, where he went in August 1946, the almost "hysterical" cordiality of the welcome actually made him ill.[45] As the U.S. ambassador, William D. Pawley, told Truman, "Even the late President Roosevelt's trip to Rio did not produce the magnificent gesture of spontaneous admiration that has been given to General Eisenhower." The banquet in his honor, set out in the Foreign Office dining room filled with "magnificent gold decorations, tremendous chandeliers, and elaborate furnishings," was reminiscent, said Pawley, "of the type of dinner that might have been given a hundred years ago by one of Brazil's Emperors."[46]

Having such an abundance to choose from, Ike was discriminating about the invitations he accepted. He set himself to attend and address important and well-reported gatherings all over the United States. And he began to acquire a circle of rich and influential friends among the leaders of the American commercial community. The chief members of this new "gang" (which was not complete until 1948) were Bill Robinson (vice-president of the New York *Herald Tribune*), Cliff Roberts (a banker), Ed Bermingham (a broker), Pete Jones (president of the Cities Service Company), Bob Woodruff (chairman of the board of Coca-Cola) and "Slats" Slater (president of Frankfort Distillers). The unspoken task of these Republican millionaires was to groom Ike for the White House. Of course, this was never articulated, for Ike's sensitivity on the subject was well appreciated. So the myth, in which he himself half believed, that Ike was not seeking the presidency—though he might succumb to the importunities of friends, to a draft, or to the call of duty—was sedulously maintained.

Politics thus seemed to be ignored as Ike became the beneficiary of lavish hospitality, was invited to shoot quail or duck on his friends' plantations, became through them a member of the best golf clubs, was entertained with bridge marathons lasting eight hours at a stretch. He also received, and was unembarrassed by, costly gifts (here a gold watch, there a "cottage" at Augusta National Golf Club) and fulsome adulation—Slater assured Ike, for example, that he was "the greatest living American and one of the great men of all times."[47] But in the haze of bonhomie and highballs no one forgot the primary purpose of their relationship, least of all Ike. He told Bedell Smith in September 1947 that it would be "an American miracle" for someone to be "named by common consent rather than by the voice and manipulations of politicians. So-called 'drafts,' since Washington's time, have been carefully nurtured, with the full, even though undercover, support of the 'victim.' "[48]

The "gang" became recipients of Ike's political lucubrations, studiously statesmanlike and direly platitudinous letters on current themes. They were written to be passed on to other friends and amounted to a sort of campaigning by proxy. The "gang" also ensured that Ike knew that if and when he did stand, his "personal expenses" would be "taken care of" and his candidacy would not be hampered for lack of funds.[49] And they saw to it that Ike was introduced to other top people in the nation's business hierarchy. These meetings were not always a success, as Ike's political ideas were painfully unsophisticated. He did not endear himself to a number of industrialists, for example, by suggesting that they would help cure inflation by holding down their companies' prices for a year. And when he did arouse the enthusiasm of the elite, as when he recommended that everyone in the United States should eat less and live more frugally, he was excoriated by the press—despite his assiduous attempts to cultivate it. However, Ike overcame all the political disadvantages imposed by his small-town Midwestern background and his long isolation in the artificial world of the army, by sheer force of personality.

Nothing illustrates this better than Bill Robinson's notes of a talk they had in 1947. Ike lit up when Robinson remarked that the only American to have had as much experience in dealing with Europeans as he had was Benjamin Franklin.

The General almost seemed to get on fire with his burning, patriotic feeling to be of helpfulness to the country he loves. He would, every few minutes, arise from the chair in which he was sitting and stride up and down the office, talking of his limitations at one moment, and in the next outlining the manner in which he would like to be of service. . . . [He was] completely free, unguarded to the point even of indiscretion. There was no pose, no pretence, no attempt to establish anything for the record, no attempt to build an impression of any kind. He was natural, alive, alert, spirited and gave the impression of having an intense amount of unloosened energy, both intellectual and physical. I came away with the conviction that no public man whom I have ever known or ever known about, had such intellectual honesty as Eisenhower. I also had the impression that here was a man who was realistic, practical and disciplined. His high spirit and his great emotional potentiality might conceivably develop a highly unbalanced entity in a person of lesser intellectual capacity.

Robinson did not discuss the "distasteful" subject of the presidency. But he received the clear impression that, although Ike would not "move a finger to promote himself for nomination," he would accept it if "one of the major political parties could demonstrate a preponderance of opinion in his favor."[50] As their friendship ripened Robinson concluded that it would be a tragedy if the nation "did not have the good fortune to benefit from the leadership of this great man."[51] He and his friends, as he told Ike years later, began "building up 'cells' of Eisenhower interest and enthusiasm among editors and publishers in every nook and corner of the country."[52]

Meanwhile it was plain that Ike had no solution to the intractable problems facing the United States after the war. It seemed impossible to accomplish the transition to a peacetime economy without reviving

unemployment, without stimulating inflation, and without causing
massive industrial disruption. Truman did his best with the Fair Deal.
But it failed to conciliate labor, which engaged in a large number of
damaging strikes. Consumers resented the black-marketeers who proliferated like bootleggers and grew rich on dearth; but they were hit
harder by soaring prices once controls were removed. The housing
shortage and power "dimouts" added further to public discontent and
seemingly confirmed the new adage that "To err is Truman."[53] As
conservative indignation over "the mess in Washington" grew, Ike
had to insist that, though in it, he was not of it. In public, of course,
he remained impeccably loyal to his commander in chief. But privately he assured friends that involvement with the government "carries no implication of my approval of governmental policies" or
philosophy.[54] Nor did he protest when Cliff Roberts sent him a
"worthwhile" newspaper cutting in which Westbrook Pegler viciously attacked the "little cigar-sport from Independence" as a "pathetic squirt" and a "tacky county commissioner."[55]

Ike relished the prospect of escaping from the confines of Washington, of detaching himself from an administration with which he was
out of sympathy, and of retiring from active military duty—though it
seems that Truman had also hinted that it was time for him to go. All
Ike's major initiatives at the Pentagon had failed and some high defense officials privately asserted that he was "the worst Chief of Staff
in Army history."[56] The "Eisenhower boom" for the presidency
might gather strength if he was seen to be independent. However, Ike
had no intention of being drafted by the Democrats—his new friends
would be shocked and chagrined by the idea—and he was convinced
that Thomas E. Dewey had both the Republican nomination and the
presidential election in his pocket. So he determinedly held aloof from
the political fray, waiting for a call so loud as to be irresistible. The
call did not come, and eventually Ike issued a categorical statement
removing himself from consideration as a candidate. James Forrestal
believed that his declaration "reflects the outcome of a genuine moral
struggle with himself" and was convinced of his "complete sincerity."[57] No doubt a part of Ike did truly want to repudiate the cares
and responsibilities of high office. He certainly talked of his desire to
settle down, after his "nomad's life," in a small town where he could
loaf and fish and "have fun" with children in the school playground.[58]
The fantasy was so real to him that he took months to make up his
mind, in 1947, to accept the offer (one of many he received) to
become president of Columbia University.

His famous predecessor, the aged Nicholas Murray Butler, had not been (it was cruelly said) fully in control of his faculties for some time, and Columbia needed a powerful figure to revive the university's waning fortunes. Ike laid down stiff conditions about what he would not do for his annual salary of $25,000: he refused to take part in academic affairs, do routine administration, raise funds, or entertain frequently. This left him little more than a figurehead, yet even before he went to Columbia, Ike was complaining about the "terrible de-mands" the post would make on his time. Robinson recorded that he had accepted it "without complete investigation of the functions and responsibilities. . . . This seems, in a way, to be a contradiction of Eisenhower's thoroughness and foresight—and it is!" But Robinson took comfort from the reflection that Ike's hasty acceptance of the Columbia position might have a "bearing on his susceptibility to the prospect of a Presidential nomination."[59] Ike himself gave some sub-stance to this inference by telling his friend Swede Hazlett that in going to Columbia he was simply changing "the location of my head-quarters."[60]

Before going to Columbia in June 1948, and after resigning as chief of staff in February, Ike did what he had sworn never to do: he wrote his war memoirs. Actually he had been making rough notes ever since 1945. But now he had the leisure and the incentive to complete the task. The incentive took the form of a deal, approved by the Treasury, whereby he would pay only light capital gains tax (instead of heavy income tax) if he sold the manuscript outright to his publisher, Dou-bleday, and thus net himself some half a million dollars. Ike acquired several assistants, ghost writers, and secretaries and, setting them-selves a crushing schedule of work, they completed the book in under three months.

When it appeared, in 1948, *Crusade in Europe* was greeted with immense enthusiasm. In many ways this was justified. Like its author, the book was unadorned by rhetorical flourishes or by pretensions to infallibility—in which respect it differed from, say, Churchill's massive tomes. Ike told his story plainly and lucidly, admitted to (some) mis-takes, exhibited a pawky sense of humor and portrayed himself in a characteristically self-deprecating manner. However, Ike was too prosaic and too bland to write anything really striking—despite his reported interest in forging a style that was both "epigrammatic" and "exquisite."[61] His pages lack astringency and incisiveness. He fudged awkward issues. He skated around personal and Allied disagreements. He never said a bad word about anyone. *Crusade in Europe* was not so much a work of history as an exercise in diplomacy. As such, of course, it was masterly. Ike made up for his lack of candor by being magnanimous to a fault. His book sold exceptionally well, it added further to Ike's popularity on both sides of the Atlantic, and it enhanced his stature as a global statesman.

No one could have been more modest than Ike about his qualifications to be president of Columbia, and many of those he met at the university agreed that he had a lot to be modest about. It was Ike himself who first suggested that the trustees had got the wrong Eisenhower, having mistaken him for his brother Milton, who was already president of Kansas State College. It was an amusing myth, but it gained wide currency. Ike disarmingly admitted that he knew nothing about running a university and that his own education had been radically defective. Far from reforming Columbia, Ike said, he would probably be reformed himself. The academics were somewhat mollified by his attitude, which did not stop them suggesting that he had never read a book and that he should not be sent long memoranda in case his lips got tired.

In some ways, of course, Ike invited sneers of this kind. He was apt to make naïve suggestions about adding the teaching of patriotism and citizenship to the curriculum. He was initially "so alert—and I might say, so allergic—. . . to the possibility of finding Columbia honeycombed with socialistic teachings that I made it my first business to acquaint myself with operations in Teacher's College, previously reported to me as practically a hotbed of this kind of indoctrination."[62] Such investigations did not endear him to most members of the university, particularly as he found little evidence to support the allegations. Nor was Columbia impressed by Ike's moral homilies, though one trustee enthused, apparently without irony, that "Emphasis on the obvious rather than elucidation of the obscure makes an Eisenhower talk something unique for a New York audience."[63] Ike was further criticized for his frequent absences on speaking tours or at golf links; for delegating most of his functions; for allowing his two military aides, Kevin McCann and Robert Schulz, to bar entry to all but the most favored members of the university to his office; and for valuing athletic above academic pursuits. For his part, Ike was irritated by excessive discussion and minimal action, maintaining that "Even in a University some things must stay decided." He resented undergraduate hostility to his views, and once threatened to boycott commencement ceremonies on account of their insubordination. He disliked raising funds, which he was expected to do. He found the work strange and bewildering. He complained of having an "appalling" schedule when he had hoped to "relax a bit," though Mamie was amazed by how much time he could spare for leisurely meals and games of bridge. It was generally agreed, in fact, that his appointment had been "a mistake" from all points of view.[64]

This was not entirely the case. Mamie had never seen her husband in better spirits. According to Kevin McCann, Ike had "a ball" at Columbia, making more friends in his two and a half years there than he had made in the whole of the rest of his life.[65] Most people at the university were, in turn, beguiled by Ike's charm. He had the ability to come into a crowded room, it was said, and give each person there a sense that he was smiling at him, or more especially, at her. When he was introduced to someone he seemed to radiate warmth and to study the face of that person with flattering intensity. At least one witness reckoned that there was nothing behind this mode of greeting except a natural flair for public relations and that new faces scarcely registered with Ike.[66] However, few could resist his animal magnetism. As for Ike himself, according to the secretary of the university, Frank D. Fackenthal, he "finally got over what I think was an inferiority complex about Professors. . . . By the time he left, he felt the University was home."[67]

Furthermore, Ike took initiatives which, although sometimes an embarrassment to those on the campus, augmented Columbia's wealth and prestige. Most notable among them was the American Assembly, a forum in which prominent citizens could discuss major issues of the day with the cloistered scholars of Columbia at a beautiful estate on the Hudson River, Arden House, donated by Averell Harriman. This was suspected of being a distinctly reactionary project, as was Ike's establishment of a "chair of Competetive [sic] Enterprise."[68] But the same could not be said of his program for the Conservation of Human Resources, his new Engineering Center, his Nutrition Center, or his Institute of War and Peace Studies. The last was the result of Ike's observation that, although millions of dollars were spent annually to cure cancer and tuberculosis, "no money had been provided for study or research of the greatest killer of them all—war."[69] Ike also raised large sums of money, increased endowments, and balanced Columbia's budget. By September 1949 he could report to a friend, "Compared to last year, it is my impression that there is a comforting hum of activity and forward-looking planning going on around this place."[70] In many respects the wholly unintellectual and partially absentee president had contributed to that hum.

It can scarcely be maintained, though, that Ike was cut out to be a university president. He was, paradoxically, too small and too big a man. His friends chaffed him for sounding like the secretary of a chamber of commerce in his new role. Yet he was also such a large fish in such a tiny pond at Columbia that he was bound to feel out of place. He chafed inwardly at his confinement and kept the eye of the public by accepting more invitations to address influential groups of people all around the country. Truman's surprise victory over Dewey —a soufflé that would not rise twice, as Eleanor Roosevelt remarked —meant that the Republicans were now desperate for a presidential candidate who could return them to power. Ike was obviously that man. As Walter H. Judd told Senator Taft, "You're the king, Bob, but Ike's the ace, as far as getting votes is concerned."[71]

Ike was the ace of trumps. It was not what he said that attracted people. He did little more than mouth safe, middle-of-the-road platitudes, always preferring to lapse into incoherence rather than to provoke controversy. He told the same joke so many times at the beginning of his speeches that he had to beg those in his audience who had heard it before to delay their yawns until he reached the punch line—it concerned a nervous paratrooper who was sitting next to him as they approached Washington airport and explained that he did not fear flying, having been in an airplane "seventeen times, but this is the first time I've landed."[72] Occasionally, too, Ike made gaffes, declaring that too many Americans aspired to live on caviar and champagne and should be content with hot dogs and beer; asserting that those who really wanted social security could find it in prison. No, Ike's orations would have been a frank disappointment, for all their sincerity, had it not been for the palpable aura of heroism which surrounded him. A *Saturday Review* poll in 1951 named General Eisenhower the greatest living American, and earlier polls, as Bill Robinson triumphantly announced, indicated that "no man since George Washington has ever had the degree of support and confidence from the American people."[73]

Ike had to work to maintain his preeminence, without at the same time losing his character as a modest, apolitical patriot. After Truman's victory—it was due, said Ike in his letter of congratulation, to the president's "stark courage and fighting heart"[74]—he stepped up his clandestine campaign. He increased his exposure by taking on various public duties. He served as informal chairman of the joint chiefs of staff (which did not diminish their quarrels). And he acted as consultant to Secretary of Defense James Forrestal, who once remarked to him, "Ike, with that puss you can't miss being President."[75] Ike also continued to educate himself politically, soliciting and taking advice from the experts. He once told Ed Murrow that when he heard of workmen contemplating strikes "I want to reach for my gun." Murrow replied, "General, you can't say that"—and Ike never did.[76]

While at Columbia Ike and Mamie lived in Morningside Heights. Both complained that their official, citified residence did not give them the privacy and repose which they wanted. They were reconciled to the fact that "a completely private life is denied us."[77] But Ike in particular had a passion to escape. He went for nighttime walks with his service revolver in his pocket. And he converted a structure that housed watertanks on the roof of his mansion into a den where he could paint and "be myself."[78] Ike described himself as a "deliberate dauber." Unlike Churchill he had no pretensions at all to being an artist, though he was vain enough, or anxious enough, to search the walls of friends' houses in order to see whether paintings he had given them were properly displayed. He frequently disparaged his paintings, though, as banal, stupid and "woefully bad," once going as far as to tell a journalist that they were "shit."[79] However, as he informed Swede Hazlett, painting "gives me an excuse to be completely alone and interferes not at all with what I am pleased to call my 'contemplative powers.' "[80] Yet there was a tension between Ike's yearning for solitude and his natural gregariousness, best summed up, perhaps, in his idea that it would be a "wonderful thing . . . to install a compact painting outfit on a golf cart."[81]

Similarly Ike bought a country retreat in 1950, the first house that he and Mamie had ever owned, and he was delighted when friends like George Allen protected him from having what he called "a bunch of hurdy-gurdy people" as neighbors by purchasing at high prices adjacent land as it came up for sale.[82] But to the amazement of some observers Ike chose to buy his farm at Gettysburg, a popular resort for tourists even before he moved there. Ike might rail about invasions of his privacy at Gettysburg—he was particularly indignant when reporters trespassed on the sacred turf of his putting green—but in a sense he had invited such irritations. His temper was not improved, incidentally, by the fact that (like General de Gaulle) he gave up a lifetime habit of smoking abruptly and completely—the result of medical advice after another (undiagnosed) ileitis attack in 1949. So despite his protestations, it is clear that Ike did not really enjoy isolation. He relaxed best in company. He needed the stimulus of his friends. He loved being surrounded by his growing family—John had married another "army brat," Barbara Thompson, in 1947, and Ike doted on his grandchildren, David Dwight II (born in 1948), Barbara Anne (1949), and Susan Elaine (1951).

In the autumn of 1950 Truman gave Ike a job that enhanced his stature as a statesman, while conveniently making it impossible for him to get his hands dirty as a politician by overtly campaigning for the presidency. The post, that of supreme commander of the armed forces of the North Atlantic Treaty Organization (NATO), which the United States had just entered in order to implement the policy of "containing" Communism, reminded voters of Ike's unique achievements in the field of coalition conflict. It restored him to a military position at a time that the country was once again at war, in Korea, while preserving his reputation from the vicissitudes which tarnished that of General MacArthur. It also enabled him to distance himself from the Democratic administration while presenting a sober alternative to the isolationist wing of the Republican party, led by the man who was obviously to be his chief rival for the nomination, Senator Taft.

Ike staged a little tableau at the Pentagon before he left for Europe, perhaps his first overt move toward the nomination. He ceremoniously tore up a Shermanesque communiqué renouncing the presidency, on the grounds that Taft supported Herbert Hoover's isolationist call for an "American Gibraltar." But Taft's act need not have been taken too seriously for, as a matter of fact, the senator was surprisingly flexible on the subject of isolationism. And Ike himself occupied a characteristically equivocal position, having at first firmly supported the senator's ratification of NATO but afterward qualifying his commitment:

although I recognize certain vital independencies between ourselves and foreign countries, I share most emphatically the average American's understanding that this country cannot carry the world on its shoulders. . . . This middle ground solution is, of course, unacceptable, both to the "do-gooders" and to the strict isolationsts. . . . For myself it is a solution that holds me to a job that is crowded with nothing but personal inconvenience and self-sacrifice.[83]

Despite such automatic grumbling it suited Ike perfectly to be away from home at this time. For in the United States the Korean conflict had thickened the atmosphere of bigotry and intolerance which had been forming during the early years of the cold war. Bitterness over the New Deal, the supposed betrayal at Yalta, postwar labor troubles and the Taft–Hartley ("Tuff-Heartless") Act, Soviet expansionism in Europe backed by a novel nuclear capacity (itself apparently the product of espionage), the "loss" of China, the case of Alger Hiss, the revival of the House Un-American Activities Committee, and the emergence of Senator Joseph McCarthy—these were the potent ingredients of a new Red scare. Despite his liberal protestations, President Truman himself had already succumbed to the national paranoia and imposed an inquisitorial "loyalty program" on the federal civil service. To his credit, Truman did try to resist the McCarran Act (1950) which imposed legal penalties on Communists, saying that in a free country men are punished for the crimes they commit, not the opinions they hold. But nothing could stop the new wave of heresy hunting which engulfed the United States. Investigations, FBI security checks, anonymous denunciations, quasi-judicial hearings, black lists, dismissals, loyalty oaths, book burning, and vigilantism darkened the domestic scene for a while.

American ideals were corroded by the thoroughly un-American concept of Un-Americanism, a term which implied that Americanism, like Communism, involved compulsory conformity. By 1950 to be controversial was tantamount to being subversive. Guilt by association was generally assumed, and a purge of the pink was proceeding apace. Constitutional safeguards crumbled before this onslaught, and the rule of law itself was threatened. Absurdities abounded. Atheism, homosexuality, and the fluoridation of water were all seen as part of a fiendish Kremlin plot. Loyalty oaths were imposed on professional wrestlers in Indiana and on amateur fishermen in New York. Protesting about Communists in Hollywood, the American Legion urged the banning of *Abbott and Costello Meet the Invisible Man.* Many states made it a felony to display the red flag. The Harvard Russian Club changed its name to the Slavic Society and the Cincinnati Reds changed theirs to the Redlegs.

To liberal friends Ike privately deplored the "current lynch-law atmosphere"[84] and the "hysterical folly" of the anti-Communist witch-hunt. He asserted that it was ridiculous that a Columbia professor should be harassed now for the radical convictions he had held two decades before.[85] However, there is no doubt that Ike himself was affected by the scare. After all, if Marshall could be attacked as a traitor by McCarthy, so could the man who allowed the Russians to take Berlin and went on professing friendship with them for several years afterward. Accordingly, Ike was anxious to establish his bona fides with conservative supporters as a staunch anti-Communist. He told Ed Bermingham, for example, that he had come out of World War II with a profound conviction that the United States was in danger from "the Communist threat from *without*" and by 1951 he was no less convinced that the Communist menace within "has now reached a peak where definite, prompt, and comprehensive measures are necessary if we are to survive."[86] Luckily, in his new post Ike could avoid making public pronouncements on partisan matters and there was no need for him to try to reconcile his conflicting private views. He was above the

grubby political fray at home but in the front line of the cold war
against Communism abroad.

On indefinite leave of absence from Columbia, Ike set off for
Europe at the beginning of January 1951, and quickly discovered that
NATO's front line was in a parlous state. It was said that the only thing
the Russians needed in order to reach the English Channel was shoes.
In a little over three weeks Ike visited the eleven NATO countries of
Europe, and everywhere he urged the need for unity and strength.
Only if individual states were prepared to forgo narrow nationalistic
advantage and invest seriously in an international force could they
hope to create an effective system of defense. Ike had less success in
obtaining support for NATO from the Europeans, who were intent
on their economic recovery, than he did from the United States, which
was obsessed by the bugbear of Communism. In a cunningly wrought
speech to Congress, delivered on 1 February, Ike argued that the
United States could sustain Europe by sending a large amount of
military aid and a small number of troops. Walking a tightrope between isolationism and internationalism, between expenditure and
security, Ike tried to suggest that the American involvement would be
both limited and temporary, that the cost would be low but the effect
in deterring the Russians would be substantial. However disingenuous, it was one of Ike's cleverest dialectical balancing acts. And it
earned him the approval of that distinguished former isolationist Senator Vandenberg, who exclaimed, in the last letter he ever wrote:
"what a mess our beloved nation is in. (Thank God for Eisenhower!)"[87]

Ike returned to take up his military duties in April 1951, sailing
with Mamie on the *Queen Elizabeth*. On their arrival in France, during
the small hours, they were greeted with grandiose toasts. Ike replied
in French so halting that it sounded, he later wrote, like "a Kansas
threshing machine with gear trouble."[88] Despite such linguistic problems Ike's popularity in Europe had, if anything, grown with the years.
In Britain, for example, the Labour prime minister hailed him as "the
man who had won the war," the foreign secretary called him "the first
citizen of the Atlantic," and the leader of the opposition, Winston
Churchill, described him as "a great statesman."[89] Privately, of
course, some Europeans had reservations. Frenchmen who came into
contact with Ike were always inclined to think him rather naïve and
dull. As the politician Jules Moch recorded, they "described him as
a small man, dispassionate, cold, occasionally sardonic, never in a
hurry to take a decision, reconciling a life which the most slanderous

tongues sometimes judged to be very profane with a very American form of religiosity."[90]

Ike's title was Supreme Allied Commander in Europe (SACEUR), about which he commented deprecatingly to Marshall, "I think we are hurling the adjective 'Supreme' around rather carelessly these days. . . . Soon we'll have to use 'Colossal Supreme.' "[91] He was housed in a beautiful château outside Paris once occupied by Napoleon III, where Mamie soon organized the plumbing to her satisfaction and established such a select Club Eisenhower that she found staying at home more fun than visiting the capital. Ike was guarded from Russian assassins by secret service men; he was looked after by a new "official family" of aides and soldier-servants; he could play golf on his personal course, and he could fish for trout in his private lake. However, he was still somewhat embarrassed to be living in such elaborate style, and he assured Averell Harriman that he was setting up his headquarters on an "austerity basis."[92]

Actually, as Ike soon discovered, the plaudits and the perquisites were not an indication of, but a substitute for, full-hearted European cooperation with SACEUR. The Europeans had not learned, Ike complained, the lessons about unified command which World War II had taught. Montgomery, Ike's deputy, was indeed somewhat subdued, and Ike now found him "a fine team-mate."[93] But all the old national jealousies and divisions remained. And they were compounded by atavistic French fears about German rearmament and pathological British suspicions of continentals in general and Ike's notions of a United States of Europe in particular. As he told Harriman in an expressive jeremiad,

The confusion and the irritations are multiplied by the hazy, almost chimerical character of the organization to which I am officially responsible. For example, the job of obtaining a site for headquarters, of constructing the necessary buildings and temporary barracks, of obtaining quarters in which officers can live together and in harmony (particularly when the scale of pay of these officers varies from that of the American down to that of the Norwegian), of devising an organization that satisfies the nationalist aspirations of twelve different countries or the personal ambitions of affected individuals, is a very laborious and irksome business but one that must be done before we can get very far along the road to real progress. Yet there is no budget, not even for housekeeping, and there is no clear line to follow in getting these things accomplished, because each government is 1/12 responsible and to refer them to committees will condemn us to inaction. When we get into the more difficult chores of producing troops and training them, of bringing over munitions and new American units, we begin to realize just how necessary it is that a few key figures in the whole development have commonly understood purposes.[94]

In his frustration, Ike soon claimed that he had come to Europe "laboring under a misunderstanding," having assumed that all the details had been settled. This was not the case. But the lack of preparation did give Ike the opportunity to play his part in mounting "a dynamic and forceful campaign of enlightenment of all N.A.T.O. populations."[95] Ike was always a passionate believer in the worth of propaganda, covert as well as overt, and his main achievement during the fourteen months he spent as supreme allied commander was to establish NATO as the notional basis of the European defense system. The muddy reality fell far short of the pristine purity of the idea, something Ike did not acknowledge in his unduly optimistic final report. But the idea itself could scarcely have developed in such potent form without Ike as its advocate.

Ike had initially feared that, because of being detached from the soldier's "traditional chain of responsibility" to one government as SACEUR, he would "become a modern Ishmael."[96] The opposite occurred. His absence from the United States at a time of vicious controversy was sheer gain, and his contribution to the fight against Communism in Europe confirmed his position as America's favorite son.

12

★

Forward into the
White House

In September 1951 a Talbart cartoon was published featuring a big
bass drum resounding to the "Eisenhower boom" while two drum-
sticks, one labeled "Ike's intentions" and the other "Ike's politics,"
lie unused on the ground. Viewing the spectacle a mystified man
remarks, "It must be done with mirrors." To the uninitiated the
Eisenhower boom did seem inexplicable. But it was being deliberately
orchestrated and conducted by Ike's backers, with the tacit connivance
of the general himself. The gang, led by Cliff Roberts and sustained
by other wealthy Republicans, had formed a "non-partisan" Citizens
for Eisenhower organization and fertilized the grass roots, where
support was already flourishing, with generous applications of cash. In
the summer of 1951 Ike Clubs had sprung up throughout the country
like mushrooms, and the professional politicians began to cabal with
Ike's friends. Governor Thomas E. Dewey and his former campaign
manager, the lawyer Herbert Brownell, Senator James Duff of Pennsylvania, and Senator Henry Cabot Lodge, Jr., were the most important. They met General Lucius Clay, one of Ike's most trusted
intermediaries, and a campaign team was formed led by Lodge. It was
their hope that, thanks to the Eisenhower magic, the Grand Old Party
would "become the Grand New Party."[1]

Ike himself cooperated to the extent of meeting as many of the
politicians and journalists who made the pilgrimage to Paris as he
could, talking inspiringly about his ideals and aims, and exposing them
to a charm that Drew Pearson found more "contagious" even than
Franklin Roosevelt's.[2] Ike also embarked on a course of self-education
in the mysteries of economics. He quizzed experts like Dulles on their
specialisms, and before returning home he had studied several thorny
current issues and read a simple book on the history of the United

States. He also gave his blessing to Kevin McCann, who was writing what amounted to a campaign biography. And he ensured that his friend Sid Richardson, the oil billionaire, did not make a killing on his behalf with money which Ike had given him to invest. He evidently recognized even then the need to be "as clean as a hound's tooth." What Ike would not do, however, was to "make a positive announcement of political intent," or even of party affiliation—he refused forty thousand dollars from *McCall's* magazine to say whether he was a Republican. For, as he told Cliff Roberts and reiterated interminably to others, "To my mind it would be a dereliction of duty —almost a violation of my oath of office. . . . It has always worried me to realize that too many people did not believe me when I told them I do *not want* a political career, and, moreover, that I would do nothing of any kind to get a nomination. I have promised only that I would not repudiate their efforts."[3]

Like many conservatives, Ike preferred the passive to the active mood and he was frequently impressed by the advantages of doing nothing. Faced with the problem of whether to remove a troublesome Italian general from his command, for example, Ike said that "no decision is better than any decision I could make."[4] Happily for Ike, apparent self-abnegation was the best form of self-promotion throughout 1951. No doubt it always is in the United States, where there has been (at least until the 1980s) a perennial ambivalence toward power, a feeling that although necessary it is somehow illicit, a weary acknowledgment that someone must exercise it but a healthy suspicion of anyone who shows himself eager to do so. As Ike shrewdly observed to Bill Robinson, "the seeker is never so popular as the sought. People want what they think they can't get."[5]

However, playing hard to get is a tricky game. Ike risked both discouraging his followers and losing the larger contest for the Republican nomination if he did not make some positive move early in 1952. Backers like Herbert Brownell, Ed Bermingham, and Cliff Roberts insisted that "The public are beginning to doubt that Ike can be nominated. Many warm admirers are losing hope." Absentee leadership and masterly inactivity were no longer enough. Even a victory in New Hampshire "would not assure you enough steam to carry you through unless you breathe some life into the effort."[6] In order to prepare himself for the fray Taft had had his tonsils out—which somehow strengthened his knees[7]—and he was accumulating an impressive number of pledged delegates. In short, Ike's hope of being "honestly drafted" by a unanimous party was doomed.[8]

Accordingly, acting on a hint from Eisenhower or perhaps determined to precipitate matters on his own account, Henry Cabot Lodge entered Ike's name as a Republican in the New Hampshire primary and declared that, if offered it, the general would accept the GOP's nomination. Ike responded by issuing a statement on 7 January 1952 in which he went some way to confirm what Lodge had said. He declared that future political duty might transcend present military responsibility and swore that "under no circumstances will I ask for relief from this assignment in order to seek nomination . . . and I shall not participate in pre-convention activities."[9] Privately Ike professed to feel "a bit of bitter resentment" toward Lodge for having exceeded his brief, and he told Cliff Roberts, "Already I have gone much further in making myself 'available' than I ever thought I would."[10]

To all and sundry—and, indeed, to himself, in his diary—Ike vowed he would go no further. His statement of 7 January had been firm and genuine, he assured Bill Robinson, and not based on "transitory expediency." But, he continued, "At the risk of appearing pontifical, I can only abide by my hope of doing my *duty*—as quickly as my political future is removed from the category of duty and placed in the realm of personal ambition or desire, its automatic destruction is assured."[11] Ike never came close to admitting that the path of duty and the course of expediency lay in the same direction and that his chief hope of winning was to display, for as long as possible, a personal reluctance to compete. Well into February he went on insisting, even to Lucius Clay, that his statement of 7 January "meant exactly what it said" and that "I do not intend to do anything that would, to my mind, be clearly 'participation' in a pre-convention campaign."[12] However, Ike had always encouraged his backers by acknowledging that "eventualities could create a personal duty taking precedence over the one I am now performing,"[13] and soon these eventualities began to materialize.

Ike discovered that he was "a sort of prisoner to some of my friends' enthusiasm and exuberance" and he "had a natural horror of allowing them to feel let down."[14] He was much moved by the film of an Eisenhower rally held at Madison Square Garden. He wrote, "I've not been so upset in years. Clearly to be seen is the mass longing of America for some kind of reasonable solution for her nagging, persistent and almost terrifying problems. It's a real experience to realize that one could become a symbol for many thousands for the hope they have."[15] Finally, when Ike met Clay at King George VI's funeral in London on 17 February he was persuaded that, with 450 delegates, Taft would win by default unless he entered the contest. But not until after Ike had scored a convincing victory in New Hampshire and received an impressive number of write-in votes in Minnesota did he let his intentions be known. "Harassed and baggy-eyed,"[16] Ike announced that he would return to the United States at the end of May and seek the Republican nomination. Even then Ike pretended that he would not become involved in a political campaign and ever afterward he tried to maintain the fiction that he had engaged in "no 'electioneering' as such."[17]

At a touching ceremony a tired and pale supreme commander, still suffering from an attack of conjunctivitis, handed over the reins to his successor—about whom, to Eisenhower's amusement, French Communists proclaimed on posters stuck up around his headquarters, "We don't like Ike but we hate Ridgway."[18] For the first time in his life, Ike told Cliff Roberts, he really dreaded the prospect of coming back to his own country. He was right to be apprehensive. His farewell address at SHAPE (Supreme Headquarters of the Allied Powers in Europe) scarcely suggested that he was an effective orator. Ike forgot to stop for the interpreter, who eventually summed up his rambling discourse in a few crisp sentences, thus earning the supreme commander, to his amazement, an unprecedented round of applause from French officers.[19] Moreover, seething beneath the glossy surface of American life, its nascent consumerism symbolized by icons like the man with the eye patch wearing the Hathaway shirt, was a political snake pit.

The Democrats had been in power too long, and they seemed to be doing their best to justify Senator Richard Nixon's charge that the president headed a "scandal-a-day administration."[20] The splenetic Truman himself hardly contributed to domestic calm: for example, when in May Ike supported state ownership of tidelands oil, the president expostulated, "That would be robbery in broad daylight on a colossal scale. It would make Teapot Dome look like small change."[21] The Republicans had been out of office for too long. They were bitterly divided between the liberal Eastern establishment, which was intent on returning to power, and the conservative old guard, who wanted to preserve the party's ideological purity at all costs. The most vociferous exponent of the latter cause was Colonel McCormick's Chicago *Tribune,* which declared that "The Eisenhower organization ought to be called Republicans for Truman" and denounced Ike as the "candidate of effeminates."[22]

The cold war, itself intensified by Korea and by American testing of the hydrogen bomb, raised the political temperature at home still further. So did McCarthyism, now well into its Red-baiting, scare-mongering, character-assassinating stride. All the front-rank politicians—Truman, Adlai Stevenson, Taft, and Ike himself—were influenced by the power McCarthy supposedly wielded over the voters, and all made more or less shameful efforts to appease him. Aspirant leaders were no less craven: at a Harvard dinner in February 1952 John F. Kennedy went out of his way to defend McCarthy as "a great American patriot."[23] Finally, television had become a potent factor in the political equation for the first time. The first coast-to-coast TV linkup had occurred in September 1951, and the following year's election focused with unprecedented immediacy on the personalities of the candidates, magnifying the issues and heightening the tensions all around.

Ike's initial performance, televised nationally from Abilene on 4 June, was a hopeless flop. In the pouring rain, to a half-empty stadium, a weary, mufti-clad Ike mumbled through a prepared text so full of clichés that one congressman remarked, "It looks like he's pretty much for home, mother and heaven."[24] Despite this fiasco journalists at once agreed that Ike was an "amazingly good campaigner." At a parade in his home town Ike had nudged Mamie when the first float, a replica of his parents' house, went by; he did a little caper when the high-school musicians played "Alexander's Ragtime Band"; and he hugged his wife as a marriage float passed—it consisted of two youngsters on pink clouds in front of a heart-shaped lattice. "Ike's natural warmth," reporters concluded, "could not be caught by headlines."[25] And when he ad-libbed his way easily through a press conference at Abilene, no less a person than James Reston expressed the general view that Ike was in some ways a greater master of that art than Franklin Roosevelt. The "paradox of the General's Abilene adventure," said Reston, was that when Ike calculated his effects in advance he got into trouble, but when "doin' what comes naturally" he was "a political manager's dream."[26] Opinions changed. Where journalists now admired Ike's lucidity they would later mock his obscurity. Many reporters would consider that Ike wore his five stars when he met them and treated them like GIs. As for Ike, he was to say within a year, at the opening of a press conference, that he would now mount the usual weekly cross and let reporters drive in the nails.

Perhaps the most effective part of Ike's technique was to pose as a political innocent, a novice. It was a role that he tried to sustain even to his closest friends, referring to "my vast ignorance of things political."[27] On 19 June, for instance, he wrote to his former chief of staff and bridge partner, Al Gruenther:

The life I lead now is made more difficult because of my complete strangeness in politics. Everything is calculated; the natural and the spontaneous are frowned upon severely. All of this would be easier if I had any real personal

ambition to be a political leader. The nearest I come to this is a burning desire
to do my duty and be of service. This carries me through and keeps me
plugging away and, I think, with some enthusiasm.[28]

The truth was, of course, as Ike himself acknowledged after his first
day in the White House, being president seemed like "a continuation
of all I've been doing since July 1941."[29] Elsewhere he admitted,
correctly enough, that his political training had begun as early as
1929. If Ike had more experience of managing coalitions than anyone
since Metternich, he had more experience of politics at the highest
level than any president since Washington.

For the rest of June Ike engaged in the increasingly bitter struggle
to capture delegates, and by the end of the month he was catching up
with Taft. His advantages were that most of the press supported him,
as did many Democrats and independents. In domestic policy he was
actually more right-wing than Taft, and there was more confidence in
his ability to handle foreign affairs, particularly in the Far East. Furthermore, it was widely trumpeted and believed that only Ike could
win in November. Taft was dour, unbending, and singularly devoid
of charm, at least in public. Ike seemed to live up to his claim that he
was the most optimistic man in the world. He was, said an aide,
"totally at ease at all times."[30] He even kept calm when an anxious
delegate from Nebraska questioned him about the persistent rumors
of Mamie's alcoholism. Ike's measured reply, the most authentic information available amidst the welter of gossip and innuendo, suggests
that she had pretty well renounced hard liquor—on which she had
clearly been dependent to ease the tedium of being an army wife—
in the interests of her husband's political career: "I don't think
Mamie's had a drink for something like eighteen months."[31]

Ike might shock delegations by asking what parity payments were,
or surprise journalists by coining words like "skyhootin'" to describe
prices that were rising. But he could also convince them that he was
a man of destiny. He possessed an animal magnetism that Taft singularly lacked. Ike could reduce groups of Republican ladies to tears by
explaining how it was that women had more developed spiritual values than men. As one of his staff, Bernard Shanley, noted: the "look
of almost adoration in the eyes of the women just waiting to touch Ike
was startling."[32] However, the Grand Old Party's deep-seated loyalty
to "Mr. Republican," as Taft was called, could not be overcome that
easily. The Minneapolis *Star* summed it up well in a cartoon by Justus
which portrayed the Republican elephant being crushed by a huge
basketful of Taftites, who sported a placard saying: "We'd rather lose
with Taft than win with Ike."

Like his father in 1912, Taft was additionally strengthened by support from the Southern states. There tiny Republican organizations—all rank and no file—survived largely on party patronage. They elected Taftite delegates despite the opposition (which became violent at some local caucuses) of pro-Eisenhower factions, most of whom were thought to be Democrats. A great cry of corruption went up from Ike's followers, who brandished signs saying "Graft with Taft" and "Rob with Bob." It was estimated that the Eisenhower camp spent $3 million publicizing the Texas theft, and wherever Taft went loudspeakers could be heard blaring "Thou shalt not steal." Taft, who was loudly denouncing the mess in Washington, was sensitive about the mess in Texas and offered a compromise. Characteristically, Ike accepted it with enthusiasm, only to be told by Lodge that splitting the Texas delegation would be fatal to his campaign. So the Eisenhower camp insisted that there could be no compromise with wrongdoing. Meanwhile, thanks to some crafty politicking by the rude but shrewd Governor Sherman Adams of New Hampshire, who became Ike's chief of staff, a national governors' conference at Houston had unanimously urged the Republican National Committee not to permit the contested delegates to vote until they had been officially seated.

This view was formulated as the "Fair Play Amendment" when the Convention assembled, at Chicago's air-conditioned International Amphitheater, on 7 July. After much acrimonious debate and complex procedural maneuvers in which Taft's managers displayed notable ineptitude, the amendment was carried. Eisenhower's agents, by contrast, had been extremely skillful. They had dropped hints to Senator Richard Nixon that he might be selected as Ike's running mate, thus gaining his powerful intercession with the eighty-strong California delegation which was nominally pledged to Earl Warren. Warren himself was given some kind of commitment about being promoted to the Supreme Court. Arthur Summerfield, who held the balance on the Michigan delegation, and Governor John S. Fine, who brought with him most of the Pennsylvania delegates, had been seduced away from Taft.

Add to this the immense ballyhoo on the general's behalf: the "I like Ike" buttons; the carefully organized impromptu demonstrations; the illuminated barrage balloons (the one hoisted near Colonel McCormick's gothic Tribune Tower was brought down by rifle fire); the uniformed "Eisenhowerettes" (the "Belles for Bob" were generally reckoned prettier, but Ike's forces alleged that Taftites had cleaned out the model agencies to make up for their candidate's lack of sex appeal); the campaign song, "The Sunshine of Your Smile"; and it was plain that the Eisenhower bandwagon was rolling. It was helped by the complete breakdown of the MacArthur bandwagon. MacArthur was ushered in to the strains of a Swiss choir playing angelic music and hailed as the greatest general since Washington. But, almost visibly fading away, as he had promised after Truman dismissed him, MacArthur delivered a dull, wordy speech which was "a dead pigeon as far as starting any boom" was concerned.[33] Nor did anti-Communist cant from Senator Joseph McCarthy, or rant against Dewey and the Eastern establishment from Senator Everett Dirksen, assist Taft.

Ike was strangely detached from the proceedings. He stayed in the Blackstone Hotel reminiscing about Abilene with his brothers, worrying about Mamie who had a painfully infected tooth, and watching the convention on television—it was the first one to be covered live. On the first ballot he gained 595 votes to Taft's 500. At once Minnesota switched its nineteen votes to Ike. (The favorite son, Harold Stassen, vainly protested, though he was always afterward to assure Eisenhower that, in line with his earlier pledge, it had been his initiative which had pushed the general over the magic figure of 604.) Anyway, thus it was that Eisenhower won the nomination. In "a curious mood of dazed elation,"[34] Ike made one of those spontaneous gestures of reconciliation which gained him such immense popularity. He struggled through the crowds to the Hilton Hotel in order to shake hands with Taft. Alarmed by the emotional scenes and moved himself, Ike confided to his rival, "I was telling my wife that when I really have a nightmare it's when I imagine I have been nominated—and elected." A cool Taft replied, "You'll win the election all right."[35] Back at the Blackstone Ike sat alone on a sofa for a few minutes, amid his champagne-drinking friends, "as if he were an invisible man." As Cyrus Sulzberger observed, he looked pale and stunned and his thoughts were "obviously far, far away."[36]

Of course no one was more adept at the art of harmonizing conflicting interests than Ike, and he at once set about the task of unifying the Republican party. His first move was to agree with "the collective judgement" of its leaders that his vice-presidential running mate should be Richard Nixon.[37] The ill-starred senator was ideal from the viewpoint of balancing the ticket. He was young where Ike was, at nearly sixty-two, the oldest man then to have stood for the presidency. He was invulnerable on the Communist issue where Ike had actually been made by MacArthur, in his convention speech, the subject of veiled criticism for losing Berlin. He represented the West Coast where Ike was associated with the liberal Eastern establishment. And, as Nixon wrote, "to maintain his above the battle position" Ike "needed a running mate who was willing to engage in all-out combat."[38] Partly for that reason Nixon was not to everyone's taste. Taft, for example, thought he possessed "a mean and vindictive streak" and described him as "a little man in a big hurry."[39]

Ike's own relationship with his running mate was characteristically ambiguous. He never really warmed to Nixon, toyed with the idea of dropping him during the slush-fund scandal, connived at the scheme to remove him from the ticket in 1956, and casually damaged his chances of succeeding to the presidency in 1960. On the other hand, Ike declared that he chose Nixon because "his political philosophy generally coincided with my own,"[40] even though the Californian's views were widely regarded as being McCarthyism in a collar and tie. And although Ike maintained his distance from Nixon, he would not break with him. Indeed, according to Milton's somewhat implausible story, Ike secretly "began grooming Nixon for the Presidency" before 1956.[41] However, the prominent position given to the vice-president in Ike's administration was misleading, for he never exercised any real power, though he did prove more useful than a fifth teat on a cow (to employ Truman's colorful characterization of the office). As the journalist Robert J. Donovan said, Nixon was "a political Mr. Fixit, and Eisenhower gave him chores . . . he was a kind of Throttlebottom."[42]

Ike made other moves to bind the GOP together. He took his stand firmly on the party platform despite the vicious Republican attack on the Democrats, traitors who not only coddled Communists but aimed at "national socialism." Even more difficult for Ike to swallow was the condemnation of Truman's containment policy because, as Truman himself pointed out in a reproachful letter to the general, "You had a part in outlining it."[43] But Ike evidently reckoned that some concessions must be made to the old guard, even though it was (to paraphrase Stevenson) still fighting valiantly to keep the United States out of World War II in Western Europe, while threatening to unleash World War III in Eastern Europe and Asia. Actually the foreign policy plank, carved by Dulles to make himself acceptable as secretary of state to both wings of the party, did seem to reject the "Fortress America" concept of the extreme isolationists. But it also eagerly favored the idea of rolling back Communism and was a considerable embarrassment to the candidate.

Ike was on firmer ground at home. In his acceptance speech he promised to work with his defeated rivals and to crusade for progressive Republican policies. What these were he was not anxious to say. At a press conference that he gave before leaving Chicago Ike declared, after superfluously disclaiming any pretensions to eloquence, "I hope to bring a message of militant faith and hope to the American people in what they have got the capacity to do, gol darn it, rather than go into details of a specific program." Ike then urged his supporters to work "endless hours,"[44] while he himself went off to the Colorado ranch of his old friend Aksel Nielsen for a ten-day holiday of painting, fishing, and cooking outdoor meals. He also tried to teach Nixon the art of fly-fishing. Casting from twenty feet Ike could often hit a cigarette stub, but his running mate, looking distinctly uneasy in country clothes and rubber boots, showed a disappointing lack of aptitude for the sport.

Actually Ike was preparing to embark on a campaign that would be much more strenuous than Stevenson's. But it was one carefully calculated to steer a middle course between the gentle "me-tooism" of Dewey's 1948 effort and the strident "Give 'em hell, Harry" tactics of Truman. The famous criticism from the Scripps–Howard press that he was "running like a dry creek" was made in August when he was standing still. During that month Ike patiently laid his plans, raised money, consulted his advisers, gathered his strength, and held his fire. He calculated that both he and the electorate would be exhausted by much more than eight weeks of barnstorming. Ike had little respect for his oversophisticated Democratic opponent, reckoning him too clever by half. Probably he shared the view of two other presidents, though he might not have expressed it in such robust terms: Truman said that Stevenson was "a man who could never make up his mind whether he had to go to the bathroom or not,"[45] while Lyndon Johnson thought "he's the kind of man who squats when he pees."[46] Ike switched off the television in disgust after hearing Stevenson begin his acceptance speech, "So, 'If this cup may not pass from me, except I drink it, Thy will be done.' " Ike commented that Stevenson was "a bigger fake than the rest of them," though he himself was capable of referring publicly to his "Gethsemane."[47] And this was actually a rare lapse of taste on the part of the Democratic candidate, who went on to "talk sense to the American people."[48] Despite Stevenson's *faux pas* Ike had no illusions that the majority party would be easy to beat.

However, he thought the South vulnerable to his conservative appeal and proposed to campaign there in spite of an aide's forecast, which proved quite wrong, that he would not draw a crowd larger than a "corporal's guard."[49] Otherwise Ike took the advice of his staff. He even changed from steel-rimmed to horn-rimmed glasses in response to a plea from his advertising men—whereas the only time Stevenson consulted his television expert was when the set in his hotel went wrong. The truth was that Ike's campaign was conducted more professionally as well as more energetically than Stevenson's. Ike spent more money. He made more use of advertising and public relations than any previous candidate. His press arrangements, managed by James C. Hagerty (formerly Dewey's press secretary), were highly efficient, right down to the scrupulous care taken to ensure that black reporters did not have to face discrimination in Southern hotels—the schedule was so organized that they could always sleep aboard the campaign train, the "Look Ahead Neighbor Special."

Ike seldom kept people waiting, whereas Stevenson was often late for appointments. It amused Ike to be given a thirty-five-page document full of details about his itinerary to Philadelphia when, he said, the plan for the invasion of Normandy had been compressed into five pages. Certainly Ike's entrances were elaborately contrived. Indeed, one journalist, Cabell Phillips, thought Ike's homespun appeal might be impaired by the contrast it afforded to the slick techniques being used to sell him. But then Phillips reflected that the public was largely unaware of these gimmicks. All they saw was a man of "rugged, incorruptible honesty."[50] And for all Ike's shifts and evasions this was not entirely an illusion. Ike did manage, for example, to create a remarkably high-minded team, and he won the allegiance of both his token Jew and token black. As Bernard Shanley wrote, there was "no knifing which was something almost unheard of in the political game."[51] Another member of the team, the economist Gabriel Hauge, remarked that Ike was "very fair," "very decent, wholesome in his instincts, terribly free of the little meannesses that often plague great men's lives."[52]

Ike needed all the help he could muster because he was an erratic performer, who was sometimes puzzled and confused by the campaign. He lit up in response to the enthusiasm of crowds, and he found the thousand miles he covered in motorcades particularly wearisome because he could not keep himself from shouting and waving in acknowledgment to the applause. But he was bored and irritated by small, quiet gatherings and he often reacted to them in a halting, wooden manner. Still, he was better as a campaigner, projecting his ebullient personality and smiling his radiant smile, than he was as an orator. He seemed so much more at ease amid "the raucous intimacy of a friendly mob" than in trying to communicate his ideas. These were "delivered like unfamiliar quotations from a textbook" or came out as "banal platitudes."[53]

Inevitably, during his fifty-thousand-mile odyssey, particularly at the seven-minute whistle stops, Ike repeated himself over and over again. His most notorious speech, about the hundred or so concealed taxes on eggs, was ridiculed as "The Egg and Ike."[54] Yet the name that his opponent gained for being an egghead was much more damaging—"Eggheads of the world arise," Stevenson quipped. "You have nothing to lose but your yolks."[55] Stevenson's polished periods earned him the suspicion that always attaches to intellectuals in politics (though he was actually more of a journalist than a scholar), whereas the very artlessness of Ike's orations helped to make him the more popular candidate. Stevenson's studied elegance was less attractive than Ike's almost equally studied folksiness—the farmer's boy from Abilene was after all the cosmopolite who had been on easy terms with Churchill, Stalin, and de Gaulle.

The difference was manifest in everything from their manner— Ike's modestly self-confident, Stevenson's skeptically self-deprecating —to their clothes—Ike's acquired for little or nothing from a friend in New York and designed to look smart, Stevenson's expensively tailored to look casual. Even Stevenson's wit rebounded against him in the end. He derided Ike's "pompous phrases," "marching across the landscape in search of an idea."[56] Yet Ike's suggestion that his opponent was not taking the issues seriously, and should not therefore be taken seriously himself, hit home. By defying "the Republican law of gravity,"[57] Stevenson fell flat on his face. Anyway, it profited Stevenson nothing to win the voters' minds because Ike won their hearts. To quote Robert J. Donovan again, "Adlai was a warm man, and yet his effect on audiences was often quite cool, despite his eloquence. Eisenhower, on the contrary, is quite a cold man, and yet that smile of his, that expression, throws a whole light over a hall. It's a genius, I guess."[58]

If Ike possessed a genius, which is doubtful, it was for commanding a coalition. Moreover, it was for doing so without (on the whole) losing the respect of the coalition's disparate elements, in spite of the inevitable compromises involved. Early in September he displayed in the field of party politics precisely the qualities which had made him so successful as supreme commander of the Allied armies during the war. He sacrificed clarity of principle for unity of purpose. Stevenson's view of Ike, expressed shortly after his defeat, is difficult to refute: "I can not put much stock in the belief of the Alsops, Reston, etc., that the 'real' Eisenhower will now emerge. . . . I think this last campaign amply disclosed the real Eisenhower—a man with little content of his own, infatuated with the idea of compromise as a solution to everything."[59] Of course this was partly sour grapes, and the charge did not come particularly well from a civil rights liberal who had run with a Southern Democrat, Senator John Sparkman of Alabama. Nevertheless, in his attempts to bind the Republicans together Ike underwent some humiliating experiences.

In Indianapolis, for example, on 9 September he shared a platform with Senator William Jenner, a Neanderthal member of the old guard, who had denounced General Marshall as "a living lie" and habitually supported the Red baiting of McCarthy. Ike made no direct reference to Jenner, implying, however, that he was "part of our team." But Ike delivered what he acknowledged to be "a very partisan speech"[60] on the celebrated K_1C_2 formula—blaming the Democrats for Korea, Communism, and corruption. Throughout the address Jenner, whom Ike professed to loathe, kept grabbing his arm and raising it into the air. And during the terrific ovation at the end Ike allowed himself to be photographed, smiling, in Jenner's embrace—though afterward one witness described him as being "almost purple with rage,"[61] and he himself expressed his disgust for the man, "You know, he is just slimy."[62]

Three days later came the famous "Surrender of Morningside Heights." (Ike retained his Columbia headquarters, much to the annoyance of many on the campus who were "madly for Adlai"; they flew a flag at half-mast when he lost). Taft called on Ike for a breakfast of honeydew melon, scrambled eggs, toast, and coffee, and together they arrived at a settlement. Stevenson might memorably jibe that "Taft lost the nomination and won the nominee," but there was actually an element of surrender on both sides. Ike endorsed Taft's domestic program (restrictions on executive power and labor, freedom from federal controls and "creeping socialization"). He also accepted that their disagreement over foreign policy, which he had once given as his main reason for running, amounted to no more than "differences of degree."[63] At this stage Ike and Taft regarded each other as abysmally stupid. In particular Taft considered that Ike did not read enough to understand the issues. Certainly Ike's method of reaching his agreement with Taft seemed to confirm the common view that he was allergic to the printed word. For it emerged that Ike had done no more than glance at Taft's draft statement and offer a few minor suggestions before accepting it.

However, as always, Ike was interested in the final result, not the concession he had made to achieve it. He had won Taft's unqualified support and thus that of the Republican party as a whole. Stevenson could no longer talk about "two Republican Parties," though he did say that he suspected he was now running against Taft, not Ike.[64] But it was Ike who had brought harmony to the GOP (though his truckling to the right did provoke a few liberal defections), which may well have clinched victory for him in November. As one of Stevenson's supporters remarked, "the lower Eisenhower sinks, the harder he gets to beat."[65] Actually it had merely been a tactical descent, for there was ever a great gulf fixed, where Ike was concerned, between emollient words and executive action. During the campaign Ike called for the liberation of Eastern Europe and condemned Truman's Asian policy. But once elected he conducted foreign policy wearing, with only slight signs of discomfort, the clothes he had stolen from the Democrats, not those he had borrowed from the old guard.

Ike's campaign now seemed to be set fair, but it was driven off course by a totally unexpected squall. This was caused by Richard Nixon, who was stumping the country urging that "the experts in shady and shoddy government operations" should be driven "back to the shadowy haunts in the subcellars of American politics from which they came."[66] As if in revenge the New York *Post* appeared on 18 September with a headline that blared, "Secret Rich Man's Trust Fund Keeps Nixon in Style Far Beyond His Salary." Nixon at once denounced this "smear" as the malevolent product of "Communists and crooks."[67] But the accusation undermined the entire Republican crusade. Two newspapers in three opposed Nixon; the New York *Herald Tribune* and the Washington *Post* called for his resignation; and Ike was deluged with telegrams hostile to his running mate. He was shocked by the charge and his campaign team was demoralized. But the candidate resisted their almost unanimous plea that he should at once remove Nixon from the ticket.

Ike ignored this advice and acted with his usual caution, publicly expressing confidence in Nixon and saying that a "complete accounting" should be made. At the same time, Ike began to distance himself from his running mate. He let it be known that "even a great man could make a mistake" and that he was "disturbed" that Nixon had not conferred with him before issuing a statement about the charges. But to Nixon's dismay Ike made no attempt to communicate with him directly. Instead the candidate said that his running mate must be as "clean as a hound's tooth—or else."[68] What this meant nobody knew, though Nixon received clear indications from Ike's headquarters that the general wanted him to resign. Not being a quitter, as he tautologically remarked on television, Nixon would not quit. But he was now being harassed at meetings by demonstrators waving placards bearing messages such as: "Sh-h-h, anyone who mentions $16,000 is a Communist." When Ike did finally telephone him, on 21 September,

Nixon's resentment at the general's failure to give him unequivocal support, or to decide on his fate immediately after he had made a clean breast of his financial affairs on television, boiled over. "There comes a time in matters like this," he told Eisenhower, "when you've either got to shit or get off the pot."[69] Controlling his temper with difficulty, Ike refused to be stampeded by such rudeness into such incontinence.

Instead he waited for his running mate's telecast, which has gone down in history and in legend as "the Checkers speech" because of Nixon's tremulous invocation to the dog which an admirer had given to his family and which he would not give back. Nixon claimed that the fund was neither illegal nor immoral. He solemnly denied having "feathered his nest" and bared his financial soul to the viewers, listing his assets and debts. Then he declared memorably, "Pat and I have the satisfaction that every dime we've got is honestly ours. I should say this, that Pat doesn't have a mink coat. But she does have a respectable Republican cloth coat, and I always tell her that she would look good in anything."[70] A Hollywood gossip columnist named Adela Rogers St. Johns, mindful of Roosevelt's successful conjuring with his dog Falla, had suggested that Nixon should mention Checkers, and the whole speech provoked an emotional landslide in the candidate's favor. It was easy for cynical journalists or hard-boiled operators from the GOP's machine to laugh at such schmalz. Tom Stephens, for example, joked that the best part of Nixon's speech had been omitted—when Checkers crawled up on Dick's lap and licked the tears off his face. One of Nixon's professors, incidentally, remembered teaching him how to cry in a Whittier College play, and the candidate needed so much time to rehearse his cocker-spaniel act that his aides were unable to buy the half-hour slot they had wanted, immediately after the *I Love Lucy* show. But the fact was that Nixon had correctly gauged the naïveté of a nation for whom televised senatorial soap opera was a novelty. (His presidential forays into that art after Watergate, however, revealed his failure to grasp the increasing sophistication of the public and proved that it *was* possible to become a political bankrupt by underestimating the intelligence of the American people.)

According to Sherman Adams, Ike himself was visibly moved by Nixon's performance and, turning to Mamie, who was wiping her eyes, he said that in his opinion Nixon was a completely honest man. This conclusion is difficult to reconcile with another story about Ike's reaction when Nixon called for full financial disclosures by the two opposing candidates. Ike apparently recognized that this gambit was really a way of putting him on the spot and furiously broke the point of a pencil on his yellow pad. Certainly Ike raged and swore that he would never reveal his personal accounts, though he did eventually declare his income (but not the gifts in kind which he had received). However, he quickly mastered his wrath where Nixon was concerned and praised his running mate warmly in the speech he now made in Cleveland. Ike then instructed Nixon to meet him at Wheeling, West Virginia, his next port of call. But only after Nixon was assured that he could come as vice-presidential candidate would he comply. Ike weakly allowed his legitimate doubts about his running mate's honesty to be overborne by the weight of favorable telegrams.* When Nixon arrived at the airport Ike bounded aboard his plane, smothered him in a bear hug, and blurted out, "You're my boy."[71] It was not an auspicious opening to Ike's Great Crusade.

The rapprochement which Eisenhower achieved with Joseph McCarthy was less satisfactory still, from every point of view. The candidate was constantly being implored to disavow the senator. For example, Arthur Hays Sulzberger, publisher of the *New York Times,* wrote, "if you would cut yourself loose affirmatively from McCarthy, I think the heart of the world would rise up to you." And as early as August Sulzberger rebuked Ike for watering down the text of a speech which, in its original form, had condemned "the assassins of character and the promoters of witch hunts."[72] Ike rejected such private pleas. In public he invariably refused to discuss personalities and used every trick he knew to avoid facing the issue of McCarthy, even pretending not to hear when reporters questioned him on the subject. Ike was unusual in not considering McCarthy to be a great vote winner, even among Roman Catholics, but he did realize that the senator could became a major liability if not handled with kid gloves. So Ike's failure to break with him was obviously motivated by a desire to preserve the fragile Republican unity and to limit the damage the senator could do if he went on the rampage.

Ike was also hampered by the fact that he shared some of McCarthy's feelings on the bugbear of Communism. It is difficult now to recall, or even to imagine, the depth of the fears on which McCarthy played: no demagogue, before or since, has been able so to dominate the political life of the United States. Like everyone in the public arena, Ike was apprehensive of being contaminated by the slightest taint of Communism. The finger of suspicion could point at anyone. Ike apparently stood up to McCarthy when they met in Peoria

*Later Ike would question Nixon personally about rumors of other financial scandals.

on 2 October and on the following day during his whistle-stop tour through Wisconsin. According to Sherman Adams, who recorded their somewhat less than Homeric dialogue, Ike told McCarthy: "I'm going to say that I disagree with you." "If you say that, you'll be booed." "I've been booed before and being booed doesn't bother me."[73] Actually nothing bothered him more. And when it came to the point, Ike only said that he differed from McCarthy over methods, not aims.

Worse still, in response to pressure from McCarthy, Governor Kohler of Wisconsin, and some members of his staff, Ike gloweringly agreed to delete from his speech in Milwaukee a paragraph defending General Marshall from the senator's wild abuse. There Ike gave full expression to the rhetoric of the Red scare, claiming that Communism had poisoned two decades of American life and had infiltrated schools, unions, news media, and government. He was cheered to an echo and, in the opinion of Gabriel Hauge, he "could have called for the impeachment of McCarthy and they would [still] have cheered."[74] Few journalists cheered, and some people, most notably President Truman, never forgave Ike for apparently betraying the man who had backed him throughout the war. Truman said it was "one of the most shocking things in the history of this country. The trouble with Eisenhower . . . he's just a coward . . . and he ought to be ashamed for what he did."[75] The curious thing is that Ike seemed almost to concur with this harsh verdict. He told Bernard Shanley that he disliked the Milwaukee speech because it sounded like an endorsement of McCarthy, that he deplored a "wishy-washy" approach to the senator, and that those who recommended the changes lacked "basic character."[76] What is more, in a long reply to Harold Stassen, Ike wrote, "In principle I agree with the criticism you make on revisions made in the Milwaukee talk."[77]

Ike then went on to explain why he had accepted them, blaming the insistence of his staff and Governor Kohler, claiming that he had tried to achieve a balance between approving the purpose of hunting Communists but insisting on ethical means, and suggesting that McCarthy had not specifically alleged that Marshall was "traitorous in design." Ike promised to emphasize "the liberal side of our program" in future and said that he had already stressed the need for "real Americanism in method" when it came to uprooting "subversion and disloyalty in government."[78] What is so striking about this apologia is its lameness. It revealed, once again, that Ike's instincts were sound but that he somehow lacked the will to act on them. He evidently recognized that what most commentators took to be his capitulation to McCarthyism was one of the least glorious moments in his life. And he might have reflected that he had achieved the integrity of his party by sacrificing to some degree his personal integrity. Yet he was not alone. For all his moral indignation about Ike's lack of backbone, Stevenson agreed not to criticize McCarthy in Massachusetts in case he damaged the senatorial campaign of John F. Kennedy. Moreover, after Wisconsin Ike did denounce witch-hunts and character assassination, though never in the virulent manner of a Truman. And he declared that "We cannot pretend to defend freedom with weapons suited only to the arsenal of tyrants."[79]

However, it was not in the field of home affairs that Ike made certain of the election. His policies, in any case, were largely negative. They consisted mainly of attacks on the Fair Deal and on government expenditure, and he was vague about his positive goals. Even on foreign policy Ike avoided specifics and was quite reticent about the need for collective security. But he did appreciate the central position which the Korean conflict occupied in the mind of the American people. Thus in Detroit on 24 October he took up the proposal of his ablest speech writer, Emmet Hughes, and promised that if he were elected he would go to Korea. It was a marvelously ambiguous pledge, and it conformed to Ike's general stance on the conflict, which was to support a limited war while seeking an honorable peace. On the other hand it suggested a reversal of Ike's earlier position, which was that he had no easy answer to the Korean conflict. The pledge smacked of action but committed Ike to nothing more than making the journey. It implied to hawks that he would win the war and to doves that he would end it. It reminded voters of Ike's paradoxical military record, the soldier of democracy, the crusader for peace. It also took the sting out of Truman's increasingly bitter attacks—his assertion, for example, that GOP stood for "General's Own Party" and that General Motors, General Foods, and General Electric were endangering the country by trying to foist on it yet another general.[80] In the face of such an inspiring initiative it was impossible to believe the president's charge that Ike was conducting "one of the lowest gutter campaigns I have ever seen."[81] Nor did Stevenson's accusation that Ike was planning a Far Eastern Munich carry much weight. And Stevenson's flippant counter-pledge—he promised that if elected he would go to the White House—merely seemed to underline his lack of gravitas.

The Korean promise is often said to have put Ike's election win beyond doubt. But, merely on the principle that the political pendulum was swinging his way, it seems probable that a Republican victory was inevitable. After twenty years of Democratic rule there was a widespread wish for change. And while the unsophisticated were primarily concerned about the involvement of the party in power with Communism and corruption, opinion makers like Walter Lippmann and the Alsops worried about the dangerous effects on the Republicans of prolonged opposition. Lippmann thought the nation needed someone to bind up its wounds, a symbol to rally to, just as it had needed George Washington in 1789. Joseph Alsop expressed his disgust for the "really horrible" campaign of 1952—"like a trip through the Paris sewers"—and concluded from it that whereas Stevenson was "admirably qualified" to be president, Ike was not. But, he continued (in an interesting letter to Isaiah Berlin), "I find myself constantly black-mailed by the virtual certainty that we shall have a first class fascist party in the United States if the Republicans don't win. The real need for a change in this country arises, not from the decay of the Democrats, but from the need to give the Republicans the sobering experience of responsibility."[82] Only a victorious leader of the GOP, many liberal and intelligent people thought, could lance the boil of McCarthyism, which was threatening to poison the entire body politic. So whether it was a case of throwing the Democratic rascals out or of preventing the Republicans from becoming worse rascals by putting them in, Ike's triumph at the polls was assured. That he did even better than his party was a personal tribute to him as an authentic American hero. As Emmet Hughes reminded Ike, the seal of victory bore "the initials D.D.E. not G.O.P."[83]

At the stroke of midnight on the last day of campaigning Ike had his picture taken under a large wall clock which promptly fell on top of his bald head, drawing blood. He was unperturbed, celebrated with his campaign workers to the strains of Fred Waring and his orchestra, and, on arriving in New York, cast what he was confident would be one of a large majority of votes. He spent most of polling day, 4 November 1952, in bed. That evening, surrounded by members of the gang, Ike watched the results coming in on television at the Commodore Hotel. At the final count Ike got 33.9 million votes to Stevenson's 27.3 million, winning 442 electoral votes to his opponent's 89 and all but nine states. As the scale of this victory became apparent Ike's grin grew wider, while Mamie was overcome. She had stood up surprisingly well to the campaign and, with her quiet, demure, smiling manner, she had been a considerable asset to Ike—Pat Nixon admired her more than any other woman. But now, doubtless hit by the realization that she would soon change from "homebody"[84] into First Lady, Mamie wept. Ike himself succumbed to irritation as the minutes ticked by and Stevenson failed to concede. "What in God's name is the matter with that monkey?" he kept asking.[85] Finally, at 1:30 in the morning, the desired announcement came over the air. After making a short speech, Ike returned in triumph and exhaustion to Morningside Heights. He and Mamie were accompanied by two Secret Service guards whom they had never seen before. These were shades of what Truman had called "the Great White Jail" on Pennsylvania Avenue,[86] in which they were to be incarcerated for eight years, and shadows that would follow them for the rest of their lives.

The president-elect and his wife quickly went off to Augusta National Golf Club to recover from the rigors of the campaign. There Ike was able to enjoy "privacy without seclusion" to revel in sport, to whistle interminably the theme song of High Noon, which he could not get off his mind, and to bask in the discreet hero-worship of his affluent fellow members in their green-blazered, gray-trousered uniforms. Bill Robinson wrote that Ike was "the greatest American I have ever known." He thought that he could detect the future president's "latent and unused powers" emerging despite his tiredness.

These seemed to have come to the surface in full flower for the complete rounded-out development of an amazing human being. [After his return to New York] the clarity, the restraint, the decisiveness with which he discussed Britain's foreign affairs with [Foreign Secretary Anthony] Eden was a remarkable thing to see. His stature and his character seemed to transcend everything and everybody around him. . . . Here is a bigger man than we thought.[87]

Ike's early holiday, however, set a pattern for the presidency, one that was to be much criticized.

Ike was similarly relaxed over making the senior appointments in his administration. For although he often asserted that his method of governing was to choose the best subordinates and then delegate to them as much power as possible, Ike actually delegated the selection procedure as well. That he was so casual about such a crucial matter is not to say that Ike was idle or incompetent, as was so frequently suggested at the time. In fact he worked hard—though he also played hard—and his capacity for intense concentration, whether at work or play, amazed everyone who observed it at close quarters. But sometimes Ike simply failed to focus his attention, which perhaps helps to explain the conflict between the many witnesses who reported that he was grossly ignorant about the business of government and the many others who said that he was astonishingly well informed. At any rate, when the spirit moved him Ike seemed to disengage himself from affairs of state and slip into a condition of intellectual indifference and moral neutrality. Thus he gave Lucius Clay, now president of the Continental Can Company, and Herbert Brownell, who was to be his attorney general, the main responsibility for picking his Cabinet. And when he himself took a hand in making the most vital appointment, the result was an unfortunate muddle.

Ike seemed to want John J. McCloy as his secretary of state, a man described by Richard Rovere as chairman of the board of the American Establishment—that "legitimate Mafia."[88] Though he later denied it, Ike was initially bored by the droning moralistic monologues of John Foster Dulles, whom he likened to an "Old Testament Prophet."[89] Moreover, he had several times been obliged to insist that when Dulles, in discussing the party platform, spoke publicly about liberating enslaved nations from Communist dictatorship he should add the rider, by "all peaceful means." Ike was quite prepared to be flexible in small matters, he told Dulles, but there would be global chaos if Western "collective security" were abandoned: "Exclusive reliance upon a mere power of retaliation is not a complete answer to the broad Soviet threat."[90] As it turned out, Ike had to be flexible in large matters during the election. In the field of foreign policy, particularly, he made major concessions to the old guard. One of them was evidently to prefer Dulles to McCloy as secretary of state. According to one authority, however, Ike told Dulles that he wanted him in the post for only a year, after which he would come to the White House as special adviser on foreign policy and McCloy would take over. Dulles was apparently deputed to put this proposition to McCloy and did so in such a way as to make it seem that he, Dulles, would retain the substance of power over foreign affairs while McCloy merely became administrative head of the State Department. McCloy refused.[91]

So for most of Ike's time in the White House his secretary of state was a "card-carrying Christian"[92] who saw the world in starkly Manichean terms—as a battleground between the powers of righteousness and godless Communism. But Dulles was a Christian *lawyer,* if that is not a contradiction in terms. Certainly contradiction had been the stuff of his life as an exponent of American foreign policy over the years. He had favored appeasement before the war and the dismemberment of Germany after it. He had been so widely rumored to be Dewey's choice for the State Department that on the morning after the Republicans' shock defeat in 1948 Dulles had told a CBS interviewer, "You could introduce me as the former future Secretary of State."[93] He had held ambassadorial rank under Truman (when he negotiated an excellent treaty of reconciliation with Japan), whose foreign policy he was denouncing by 1952 in language that won Taft's support. Aided by Eisenhower such an accomplished advocate was always able to find some casuistical reason why the hostile forces in the cold war should not, in the last resort, destroy one another.

Nevertheless, Dulles's rhetoric, with its incantatory references to "rolling back" Communism, "massive retaliation," "agonizing reappraisal," and going to the "brink," seemed stridently bellicose. Ike was understandably worried about what he said were Dulles's two main weaknesses—his tendencies to oversimplify and to overdramatize. Yet these were acceptable faults because they helped to disguise the essential ambiguity of Ike's foreign policy. For while Dulles was mouthing the fierce slogans of old-guard isolationism he was actually implementing, under Ike's rather loose direction, the Democratic program of internationalism. Whether this strategy was a Machiavellian attempt to achieve a measure of détente in a hostile world, whether it was designed to be a middle way between the opposites of liberation and containment, or whether it was just confusion worse confounded is not, even now, clear. But its effect was to achieve peace in Ike's time.

After he became president Ike always professed a profound affection and admiration for Dulles, saying that he was the most distinguished secretary of state of his time (previous incumbents included Dulles's grandfather and his uncle). Ike could evidently ignore the unattractive features of Dulles's person and personality which alienated almost everyone else—his pervasive aura of bad breath, his eccentric habits (he liked chewing candle grease), and his rumpled appearance. Dulles's manners were crude—he would twirl his pencil in his hair, nose, and ears—when they were not rude. He would stir his whiskey with a thick finger and then suck it, and (like Henry Luce) he would absentmindedly eat everything in sight, emptying bowls of peanuts, for example, when he was hungry. He was gauche enough in mixed company to remind one journalist of something "out of Kansas."[94]

So perhaps Ike felt an affinity for him. Certainly the secretary was as compulsive a doodler as the president, who decorated the margins of many of his papers with weird heads, most of them sporting long straight noses. Maybe, too, Ike was intrigued by Dulles, who was a curious mixture of Spartan—hiking, sailing, bathing in freezing water—and sybarite—drinking fine wines, smoking large cigars, visiting six cabarets in an evening. Undoubtedly Ike admired the smashing force

of Dulles's intellect, his technical mastery of the detail of foreign
affairs, and his marvelously lucid formulation of a case. Dulles spoke
in a strange, strangled fashion. Harold Macmillan said that "his speech
was slow but it easily kept pace with his thought."[95] But when the
words did emerge they were, said Ike, "just like a printed page."[96]
Moreover, while Dulles was liable to be cold, abrupt, and arrogant
with inferiors, he could display a nimble wit as well as an elephantine
charm among people he wanted to impress. Nor was Ike put off by
Dulles's self-righteous sermonizing, being rather inclined to mount
the pulpit himself. He certainly would not have agreed with William
Clark, who had known Dulles for most of his life and expressed what
was, both at home and abroad, the standard conclusion about the
secretary of state—that he was "a pious and hypocritical ass."[97]

Among the major figures in Ike's Cabinet was George Humphrey,
president of a huge conglomerate, the Mark A. Hanna Corporation
of Cleveland, who became secretary of the Treasury. From Ike's point
of view this amiable Midwesterner was an ideal choice. Humphrey
thought and talked and even, as the equally bald president-elect remarked when they were introduced, parted his hair like Ike. Humphrey was generally reckoned to be a typical captain of industry, safe,
conservative, given to uttering portentous platitudes: "In business,
it is results that count."[98] But Ike found him very intelligent, he
liked the "imaginative orthodoxy" which was said to characterize
Humphrey's approach to everything,[99] and they became close
personal friends. Ike was particularly struck by the fact that their
gut reactions to financial and other matters were almost invariably
identical. He once wrote that Humphrey had come into office, his
face aglow with the humanitarian possibilities of improved housing and expanded unemployment insurance, when all his instincts,
like Ike's, told him to *"save money* and *balance the budget* and *cut
taxes."*[100]

If Humphrey was the most congenial member of the Cabinet as far
as Ike was concerned, Charles E. Wilson, president of General Motors
(known as "Engine" Charlie to distinguish him from his namesake,
"Electric" Charlie at General Electric) was probably the least congenial. Clay and Brownell successfully recommended Wilson to be secretary of defense and before long he was reducing Ike to paroxysms of
rage by his rambling discourses in the White House and his appalling
gaffes outside it. The joke was that Engine Charlie had invented the
automatic transmission in order to have one foot to put in his mouth
—but that the real disasters occurred when he took it out again.
Actually the most flagrant indiscretion was to appoint Wilson in the

first place. Ike was wedded to the idea that Big Dealers were the best men to govern the country, partly because they had proved their worth in business and partly because they would not be serving the public in order to feather their own nests. Wilson, for example, was the highest paid executive in the world, and he said that no one but Ike could have persuaded him to accept a government salary of $22,-500 a year. But Wilson also owned $2.5 million dollars worth of stock in General Motors, which was the country's largest defense contractor. To put him in charge of the Pentagon produced a stark conflict of interest, as well as tightening the bonds of the military–industrial complex.

Stevenson's jibe that the car dealers had taken over from the New Dealers gained added point from the fact that Clay and Brownell selected as secretary of the interior Douglas McKay, who before becoming governor of Oregon had been a successful automobile salesman. Other tycoons also received prominent positions in the administration: the industrialist Sinclair Weeks became secretary of commerce: the banker Joseph M. Dodge went to the Bureau of the Budget. Senior Republicans who had worked in the campaign were rewarded: Henry Cabot Lodge was to serve as ambassador (with cabinet rank) at the United Nations; Arthur Summerfield became postmaster general; and Harold Stassen was put in charge of mutual security.

There were also three rather anomalous appointments. Mrs. Oveta Culp Hobby, who had been director of the Women's Army Corps during the war and who published the Houston *Post,* was Ike's token woman in the Cabinet. He tended to patronize her—in the nicest possible way—and he could never remember the name of the department which he created for her, calling it "Health, Welfare and Whatnot."[101]

On Milton's advice Ike made Ezra Taft Benson, one of the Twelve Apostles of the Mormon Church (and later a pillar of the John Birch Society), his secretary of agriculture. Ike soon surmised that "Ezra is less concerned with his Department than with making sure I open every [cabinet] session with a prayer."[102] This was, indeed, occasionally omitted and Ike was liable to exclaim, "Jesus Christ, we forgot the prayer."[103] More seriously, however, during the campaign Ike had given a pledge to farmers, "without any 'ifs' or 'buts,' " that he and the Republican party stood behind "the price support laws now on the books." But Benson, who was said to have a talent for making enemies and a genius for keeping them, did not agree. Only a few days after taking office he delivered a statement of faith: "A completely planned and subsidized economy weakens initiative, discourages industry, destroys character, and demoralizes the people." "The epistle from the apostle," as this was dubbed, roused much opposition and it required all Ike's ingenuity to reconcile his stated position with Benson's (from which, in truth, he did not radically dissent).[104] It was no wonder that Ike advised Benson to do "a lot of zigging and zagging": "that's the way you run a military campaign . . . that's also the way you run a political enterprise."[105]

Ike's final appointment outraged Benson's cousin, Robert A. Taft, and astonished the nation. He made Martin Durkin, president of the Plumbers' Union and a Democrat, secretary of labor. Ike's aim was to conciliate organized labor, for Durkin was an opponent of the Taft–Hartley Act. But all he did was to provoke a public expostulation about this "incredible" appointment from Mr. Republican, whom he then had to appease.[106] Moreover, Durkin resigned within a year, never having "taken off his AF of L hat" and always having remained, according to Bernard Shanley, under the control of George Meany.[107] Ike was convinced that "the right kind of team is evolving"[108] and that Durkin had just been unable to fit into it. Democrats were more cynical about Durkin's departure, having long derided the incongruousness of a Cabinet consisting of eight millionaires and a plumber.

In the first cabinet meeting he held as president Ike announced: "I believe in decentralization—that's why I took as much care in picking this gang."[109] Actually the selection of his principal aides was more significant as far as the business of conducting the administration was concerned. Of these the most important was Sherman Adams, Ike's chief of staff, whom he did not actually appoint to the post at all in so many words—"What I'd like to have you do is to stay around where I am."[110] Adams was said to boss "the Cabinet members with all the finesse he learned as a lumber camp foreman."[111] Ed Bermingham had told Ike, "You need Sherman Adams. He's an Al Gruenther."[112] Really he was more of a Bedell Smith, brusque, sarcastic, impatient, and ungracious. He took over the functions which had formerly been performed by Smith, who, in a fit of unwonted emotion, once confessed to Richard Nixon:

I was just Ike's prat boy. Ike always had to have a prat boy, someone who'd do the dirty work for him. He always had to have someone else who could do the firing, or the reprimanding, or give any orders which he knew people would find unpleasant to carry out. Ike always has to be the nice guy. That's the way it is in the White House and the way it will always be in any kind of an organization that Ike runs.[113]

Adams worked so hard that he apparently had no time for the normal courtesies of "please" and "thank you," "hello" and "goodbye." When he had finished talking on the telephone he simply hung up—doing so once on Ike himself. Similarly he would go to bed when he was tired even when he had guests. He expected complete dedication from his staff, reducing secretaries to tears and assistants to fury. When one of them sighed, "I feel like I've done three weeks' work this morning," Adams retorted: "Well take three weeks' vacation tonight."[114] Some thought Adams "insane." Others considered him merely inhuman, an impression he sometimes tried to dispel, as when he told the mother of one staff member, "You know *I* had a mother!"[115] Actually Adams exerted a liberal influence on the administration as well as making it run with considerable efficiency. He did what Ike did not, or would not, do. He acted as a Cerberus at the president's door. And he exercised an enormous amount of power. Bernard Shanley called Adams "the Rock," a tribute to his rugged New Hampshire strength as well as to his features, which seemed to be chiseled out of granite.[116] Echoing Bedell Smith, James Hagerty described Adams as "the official son-of-a-bitch," "the 'no' man," who said no "a thousand times a day."[117] Some called him "the Abominable No-Man."[118] Others joked that it would be a tragedy if Adams died and Ike became president.

This sort of remark was often made, too, about Jim Hagerty, perhaps the best presidential press secretary in history. Hostile newspapers ran stories comparing Adams, "a harsh little buzz-saw from the woodlands of New England," to Hagerty, "an effusive gayblade from the sidewalks of New York," and claiming that together they ran the government while Ike was "working himself to a frazzle on the 19th hole."[119] In general, however, Hagerty kept Ike's press coverage so favorable that critics accused journalists of indulging in fawning sycophancy toward the president and suggested that the fourth estate was falling down on its job. The tough, "stocky, chain-smoking, hard-drinking Hagerty," it has been said, "looked and talked like a character out of *The Front Page,* but his instincts towards news manipulation and techniques of mass psychology were as smooth and sophisticated as [those of] any Madison Avenue executive."[120]

Hagerty managed to retain the confidence of the press by showing that he was in the president's confidence while simultaneously giving the impression of being completely frank and fair. But he was an expert at focusing attention on (or manufacturing) silver linings rather than clouds. He exploited the new medium of television, which marvelously conveyed the warmth of Ike's personality. And he invariably presented the chief executive and his colleagues in the most flattering light, though even Hagerty could be flummoxed. After trying to persuade a busload of reporters that Ike was going to stay at George Humphrey's Georgia *farm*—actually a breathtakingly luxurious establishment, filled with antiques and swarming with servants, set in thirteen thousand acres—he was silenced by a sign proclaiming "Milestone Plantation." Hagerty had what Ike called a "healthy Irish temper"[121] and every evening he would amuse the president by proclaiming, "This has been the worst day of my life."[122] But in his cool, astute, balanced handling of Ike's public relations Hagerty made an inestimable contribution to Eisenhower's administration and to his reputation.

Gone were the days when presidents had personally replied to their own mail, as Lincoln had done, or picked up the White House telephone when it rang, like Grover Cleveland, or stood ready, like Warren Harding, to shake hands with any citizen who cared to call. Since Roosevelt's inauguration the business of government had grown apace and the number of federal employees had risen from 600,000 to 2.5 million. Yet when Ike prepared to take office he found that one man, Bill Hopkins, had been permanent executive clerk since Hoover's day and observed that he was the only form of continuity between presidents. Improving on procedures that he had learned from the British, Ike created a White House secretariat, headed first by General Paul Carroll and after 1954 by General Andrew Goodpaster. Other administrative changes were also made. The most important was to promote the National Security Council (NSC) to be the central forum for making cold war policy, though in practice the president and the secretary determined significant matters. Ike also appointed Foster Dulles's brother Allen to direct a growing and, as it turned out, increasingly ungovernable CIA.

Other committees proliferated. Arguably Ike merely expanded a governing bureaucracy that was already too cumbersome. Critics of his regime said that the official world he created was stuffy, self-satisfied, and "intensely hierarchical, in the manner of the staff of a large industrial company."[123] However, Ike felt at home in such an organization, though he complained in moments of irritation that if his White House staff had been with him at SHAEF, the Allies would have lost the war. What is more, Ike employed able men from outside the military–industrial complex, speech writers like C. D. Jackson and Emmet Hughes of Time–Life, to prevent any ossification of ideas or initiative. In any case, as another assistant, Bryce Harlow, remarked: "the only thing you can do in the White House is to arrange your crises in some form of priority."[124] This Ike's staff could accomplish easily and, as a matter of fact, his record of crisis management compares well with that of John F. Kennedy, who despised his organizational methods.

Apart from picking his team and preparing to take office, Ike had one other major task to perform before his inauguration. This was to fulfill his pledge to go to Korea. He left in a fog of secrecy, at the end of November, accompanied by several of his senior appointees. The trip was a hard one, reminiscent of the tours that Ike had made during the Second World War. It was made in bitingly cold weather, often by puddle-jumper airplane and four-wheel-drive vehicle—everyone but Charlie Wilson was amused when a sergeant unwittingly told him that Ike's party must transfer from sedan to jeep because "this God-damned Chevrolet he can't go up a hill like this."[125] Ike inspected troops, watched an artillery duel from a distance, and flew over the front line. He would refuse to allow Mark Clark, who commanded the American forces, to mount the full-scale offensive by which he hoped to gain victory. But he would agree to let Clark bomb certain civilian targets hitherto prohibited, the North Korean capital Pyongyang, the Yalu River hydroelectric plants, and irrigation dams protecting the rice fields. This last was a vicious measure, one branded by the Nuremberg Tribunal as a war crime. But Ike was determined to find some way to resolve what looked to him like a bloody stalemate. He also toyed with the idea of using the atomic bomb.

This solution of last resort was advocated by some, including General MacArthur, who confided his plan to Ike when he returned to the United States and afterward damned his former aide for lacking the courage to implement it. But Ike's policy was a characteristically subtle and ambiguous variation on the crass nuclear blackmail recommended by MacArthur. He employed hints rather than threats, and always succeeded in keeping his options open. Ike revealed his capacity for ruthlessness by bombing the irrigation dikes but concealed his ultimate intentions behind a smoke screen of verbiage. Ike was more attracted to the cheap nuclear alternative to conventional warfare after a return voyage from Guam to Pearl Harbor on board the cruiser *Helena,* where he was joined by the cold warrior Dulles and the fiscal conservative Humphrey as well as other colleagues. From Hawaii, he issued a statement saying that his Korean visit had convinced him that "we face an enemy whom we cannot hope to impress by words, however eloquent, but only by deeds—executed under circumstances of our own choosing."[126] What Ike meant, of course, was that he hoped his words, rather than the deeds which he darkly adumbrated, might impress the North Koreans enough to make them agree to an armistice.

In denouncing Ike's excursion to Korea as a piece of demagoguery Truman further embittered relations between them, making the transfer of government much more fraught than usual. When the two men had met in November to discuss the handover of power Ike's expression, Truman said, was one of "frozen grimness." Dean Acheson wrote that Ike's loquacious good nature had deserted him, and as he sat embarrassedly chewing the earpiece of his spectacles the president-elect seemed "wary, withdrawn and taciturn to the point of surliness."[127] The final meeting between Truman and Eisenhower (until they shook hands at Marshall's funeral in October 1959) occurred on Inauguration Day itself. Prior to it Ike had given vent to uncharacteristic little outbursts of antipathy toward Truman, wondering aloud, for example, "if I can *stand* sitting next to that guy."[128] Ike remained firmly seated on 20 January itself, refusing to get out of the car to greet Truman at the White House. This was his second breach of protocol on that day, for Ike had earlier announced that *he* would be wearing a homburg hat (along with his black jacket, striped gray trousers, dark blue double-breasted overcoat, and white silk scarf), thus dictating Truman's headgear. So their journey to the Capitol was a chilly one. And when Ike moved into the White House he eradicated all traces of his predecessor, even hanging a picture over the marble plaque, in the ground floor corridor alcove, which commemorated the reconstruction of the building during Truman's term of office.

All inaugurations are a mixture of solemnity and festivity, and Ike's was no exception. The largest crowd Washington had yet seen for such an occasion, some three-quarters of a million people, had gathered to witness what would be half somber ceremony and half political circus. Ike particularly wanted to emphasize the former aspect, ritual as opposed to spectacle. As he phrased it, "Religion was one of the thoughts I had been mulling over for several weeks."[129] And on the morning of the inauguration he composed a special prayer to read before his address. Ike was visibly moved as he took the oath, administered by Chief Justice Fred Vinson on two Bibles, to "execute the Office of President of the United States," and "to preserve, protect and defend the Constitution." At this "high moment of his life," wrote one observer, he "looked lonely and a little sad."[130] But as he spoke a ray of sunshine forced its way through the thin mist and illuminated him like some celestial spotlight.

Ike turned, grinned, and raised both hands in his familiar victory salute. Then, when the cheering had died down, he gravely intoned his prayer: "Almighty God, as we stand here at this moment my future associates in the Executive branch of Government join me in beseeching that Thou will make full and complete our dedication to the service of the people in this throng, and their fellow citizens everywhere. . . ."[131] As Ike read on he stumbled briefly over the stilted, bureaucratic prose. But the very awkwardness of his style and delivery convinced almost everyone of the president's passionate sincerity. Much was made of this prayer subsequently: it was printed, set to music, carved in stone at the Eisenhower Memorial Chapel. Cynics, however, believed that the deity was invoked simply to suggest that Ike and the GOP had obtained endorsement from the cosmic Chief Executive. The radical journalist I. F. Stone became especially critical of presidential pronouncements "nauseatingly larded with the wholly artificial religious sentiments now considered de rigueur in all American state papers and designed firmly to anchor God on our side in the Cold War."[132]

How artificial Ike's sentiments were, if at all, it is impossible to say. But his Inaugural Address was, despite his stated reluctance to preach, essentially a lay sermon based on the text "God Bless America." Its tone of political moderation satisfied Democrats like Lyndon B. Johnson and Republicans like Robert R. McCormick that the speech "might have been written at Mr. Truman's order."[133] But most people found it an inspiring statement, a clarion call, at a time of fear and danger, to faith in "the abiding creed of our fathers."[134] It was immediately followed by what Arthur Krock called "the mightiest pageant ever to pass before a President,"[135] at the head of which was "God's float"—an icon somewhat tarnished by the fact that it had been included in the parade as an afterthought.

Following it was a fantastic ten-mile-long procession containing everything from eighty-five-ton atomic cannons to a California sheriff's posse riding palomino horses, from the Governor's Foot Guards of Connecticut and the Georgia Hussars of Savannah in their Revolutionary uniforms to ten floats depicting scenes from Ike's life and a live turtle waving the American flag with its front leg, all accompanied by competing bands and whirling drum majorettes, while above circled two navy blimps. With special permission from the Secret Service a television cowboy was even allowed to lasso the president—the cowboy was so nervous that on his first try he missed. Bringing up the rear, at almost seven o'clock, were two Republican elephants. Ike and Mamie then had to attend two inaugural balls—one was too small to hold the Grand Old Party's party. They were engulfed by "a mob scene" that would have staggered Cecil B. de Mille, according to *Time* magazine,[136] and they submitted to more raucous razzmatazz. Not until two in the morning could Ike settle down for his first night in the White House, as thirty-fourth president of the United States.

13

★

The Shadow of
McCarthyism

Despite the late night, Ike began his first day in the White House early. As a countryman he preferred to be at work by 7:30 and he would mock the likes of Herbert Brownell, who was sleepy in the mornings, for their decadent, citified habits. Ike's first major task was to inspire his team with a spirit of unity and selfless service, and he gave them a pep talk when they gathered to take the oath: "I want the White House to be an example to the nation."[1] Dulles, meanwhile, insisted that his officials at the State Department should display "positive loyalty."[2] And Adams tried to ensure that the new dispensation at the White House would have a tone of impeccable puritanism. Despite his curious expressions—"Joyful Appomatox Jesus"—and his unusual behavior—he sometimes brought his lunch to work in a cardboard box—Adams was by nature conventional and conservative. He cautioned the assembled staff against "eccentric habits" in "deportment" such as smoking in the corridors, gossiping with the secretaries, and putting their feet on the desks.[3] So anxious was Adams to ensure that staff members should be clear, even at mealtimes, about the difference between the present reign of morality and the past mess in Washington that he had a gold sticker placed over the legend on matchbooks that read "The White House Mess."[4] It was ironic that this stern guardian of righteousness should himself be forced to resign over an issue of what Democrats considered corruption and Republicans considered imprudence.

That lay in the future. Ike's immediate problem was that the Senate would not confirm the appointment of "Engine" Charlie Wilson as secretary of defense until he had sold the stock he held in General Motors. Wilson, who faced heavy capital gains tax, was reluctant to oblige, professing to see no conflict of interest. He resented being singled out for the senatorial inquisition (George Humphrey, who would have made just as good a target, was ignored) and allowed his resentment to show. Wilson was a combative character who once said that "A little bit of aggression is like a little bit of pregnancy," and he in turn annoyed senators by addressing them as "you men." Finally he blurted out, "I thought that what was good for our country was good for General Motors and vice versa."[5] This indiscretion was much cited and much inverted. The "vice versa" seemingly entitled everyone to quote Wilson as having said that "what was good for General Motors was good for the country." And though the secretary's defenders piously denounced this as a wicked distortion at the time, he himself later acknowledged, "I have never been too embarrassed by the thing, stated either way."[6] Stated any way, it appeared to confirm a general suspicion that Ike's government was on the side of the big-business battalions. However, Ike persuaded Engine Charlie to sell his stock, though he came to the sad conclusion that Wilson, "able as he is, is just a bungler when it comes to handling any delicate situation."[7]

But the president himself revealed an odd flexibility of conscience over such matters of financial propriety. He implied that Wilson would not have been open to criticism if he had kept his stake in General Motors. Yet Ike had put his own shareholdings in a trust, about which he was to know nothing for eight years, so that his decisions could not be affected by concern for his own interests. Moreover, as president he sternly refused gifts of money and of deep freezers. But he accepted almost everything else he was offered, an astonishing assortment of presents ranging from prize cattle to half a ton of coffee from the emperor of Ethiopia.[8] The president even persuaded Dulles to smuggle cases of wine home for him from France so that he could avoid paying the duty. And before he had properly settled into the White House, Ike laid himself open to criticism from none other than Alf Landon by expressing "satisfaction with the ridiculous explanation of National Republican Committee Chairman C. Wesley Roberts for his prostituting of his political influence in a raid on the public treasury of Kansas, which stinks to high heaven."[9] When he passed on Landon's indictment to Adams with the comment, "This looks more and more serious to me all the time,"[10] Ike was clearly remarking on the political rather than the moral implications of the scandal, which advisers feared was hurting him.

These were strange lapses in a man whose watchword was discretion, who waxed pontifical on the subject of ethics at every opportunity, and whose first aim was to root out the corruption and disloyalty which had supposedly permeated Washington under his predecessor. At his first cabinet meeting Ike urged "positive action" against security risks.[11] At his second he recommended that a "sympathetic attitude" should be taken toward Congressional inquiries into government departments,[12] though in his State of the Union message Ike asserted that the removal of the nation's "false servants" was essentially the responsibility of the executive branch.[13] However, it is impossible to view Ike's commitment to clean out subversives simply as part of his great crusade. He did want to purify public life and to rid the federal government of Communists and "perverts" of every kind. He even went as far as to agree with Senator Jenner, in a private letter, that "the work of the Soviet Communist Fifth Column does indeed constitute an international conspiracy" and added that the government was "determined to use every appropriate means to counteract it."[14] But he also felt bound to satisfy the Republicans' craving for the spoils of office after twenty years in the wilderness. As Ike astutely wrote to Emmet Hughes at the end of the year, "Old-time leaders of the winning party heaved such a great sigh of relief, when they imagined themselves again free to dip their arms to the elbows in the patronage trough. . . . They did not look upon the results of the election as the threshold of opportunity: rather it was the end of a long and searing drought."[15]

Yet, despite his elaborate pretense of being disgusted by, or at least indifferent to, all considerations of patronage, Ike was realistic enough to know that it was, as Bryce Harlow put it, "the mortar between the political bricks."[16] The president professed to make all appointments strictly on merit and to disqualify those who solicited positions. "I just can't begin to connive the way you have to," he said, "[to] get the best out of a congressman."[17] But in secret he connived like a seasoned ward boss, even for Republicans whom he detested on both political and personal grounds. In August 1954, for example, Ike reluctantly approved the appointment of a certain Cale J. Holder as a judge in the Federal District Court of Indiana when he was told that Senator Jenner's future depended on it.[18] Similarly, Ike was determined to make changes in the foreign service. He proposed to point out "the facts of life . . . about patronage" to Bedell Smith, Dulles's deputy, when a congressman told him, in January 1954, that half the American embassies still displayed Truman's picture where his own should be.[19] Ike agreed with Len Hall, new chairman of the GOP's National Committee, who at an early cabinet meeting stressed the importance of putting "sympathetic" Republicans in official positions now occupied by "leaky" Democrats. Hall quoted Jim Farley to the effect that "a party exists when it handles patronage right."[20]

However, there was an even more powerful motive behind the purge of officials over which Ike presided. This was his desire to appease the right wing of the Republican party. Such a policy was not altogether reprehensible. For, as Emmet Hughes wrote to Ike in December 1953, the president had inherited "a divided, clannish and often confused Party." The process of welding it into "a responsible instrument of government" not only required a "titanic effort," it also imposed "thousands of obvious restraints" upon the leadership.[21] In order to make the party work as a unit Ike had to make concessions to its more extreme members. Thus in his State of the Union message, for example, although he did not repudiate Yalta, Ike rejected "secret understandings of the past with foreign governments" which permitted the "enslavement of any people."[22] He also proclaimed his order to stop the Seventh Fleet's patrols of the waters between Formosa and Nationalist China, something which had originally been instituted, it was said, to keep the two sides apart. Ike's famous "unleashing" of Chiang Kai-Shek was rather like unleashing a mouse against a cat. But it was intensely gratifying to the old guard. However, these sops were designed to conceal the fact that Ike was not going to provide the full meal advertised in the more expansive Republican menu—the rolling back of Communism in Europe, the dismantling of the New Deal, victory in Asia. Ike was a born pragmatist. No one better understood that if the GOP continued to eschew moderation in favor of such impossible dreams it could not, as he wished, transform itself into the natural party of government. The trouble was, as Richard Nixon was quick to observe, it would take time to get the Republicans in Congress to adopt a " 'majority' attitude."[23]

Chiefly responsible for this doctrinaire reluctance was the new chairman of the Senate Committee on Government Operations, Joseph McCarthy. What made Joe run is a puzzling question but not beyond all conjecture. The junior senator from Wisconsin had sprung to prominence early in 1950, when he began to make specific (though never consistent) allegations about Communists in the State Department. The fact that McCarthy was totally ignorant about Communism —like Ike he read only pulp Westerns—and had never even heard of Earl Browder, supported the view held by many commentators that he was simply an unscrupulous politician recklessly exploiting an inflammatory issue. The scruffy, boozy senator, with his dark jowls and his shifty eyes, with his penchant for gambling and womanizing, with his public speeches full of bluff and bombast and his private conversation replete with scurrilous obscenities, seemed typecast as a crook. The impression was apparently confirmed by the contrast between the vicious brutality of McCarthy's political tactics and his back-slapping, hail-fellow-well-met manner on social occasions. But if McCarthy was amoral he was not necessarily cynical. Had he been driven merely by ambition he would not have persisted with his campaign until it ruined him. The evidence suggests that McCarthy came to believe his own propaganda about Communism. Indeed, his terrific effectiveness as a demagogue stemmed largely from his fanaticism on the subject. Probably Emmet Hughes was right when he told Ike that McCarthy was "not simply an unusually recalcitrant, hot-headed legislator with violent and slightly eccentric ways. He is a psychopathic case, and whether the ultimate sickness be mind or vanity, the result is the same —to presume to set his purposes above those of all others, including the government of the United States."[24]

McCarthy did just that. Using his official position as a base he went on the rampage. He investigated civil servants, concentrating first on the Voice of America and then on the State Department, both organizations allegedly riddled with Communists and homosexuals. He forced the dismissal of hundreds of federal employees, caused libraries to be closed and books to be burned, challenged government appointments, and in certain instances, actually seemed to usurp the power of the executive itself. The marble caucus room in the Senate office building, where McCarthy's Investigations subcommittee often met, was said to stink "with the odor of fear."[25] But fear of the witch-hunt permeated American society as a whole. It spread from the civil service into industry, from the teaching profession to Hollywood. Perhaps fewer than twenty thousand people were dismissed altogether. But many more resigned and, it has been estimated, some twenty million Americans were affected by the loyalty-security program—intimidated, screened, forced to take oaths, and so on. Not a single Soviet agent was discovered as a result.

For this state of affairs Ike was ultimately to blame. He often pretended ignorance of current affairs during his presidency; but this was largely a charade, enabling him to slough off inconvenient responsibilities and to adopt a pose of monumental detachment when presented with awkward issues. He knew precisely the poisonous effect that McCarthy was having on the American body politic. As early as 27 March 1953 Ike read out to the cabinet a letter that he thought was indicative of public opinion. It complained of the "pall of fear spread by McCarthy," said that "his growing power" and "unscrupulous" "demagoguery" were actually intimidating his fellow senators, and urged the president to restore confidence: "You have allowed other men to usurp the leadership." To the Cabinet Ike explained his respect for persuasion. He argued that it was the job of Congress to tackle McCarthy and "it would be completely wrong [for me] to challenge a single man." Patience was necessary: in only two months they had already come "a long ways" and seen an "almost revolutionary change."[26]

This early discussion of McCarthy foreshadowed countless others, held over the next two years, in which the president was urged to declare his opposition to the senator and consistently refused to do so. Some of the most eloquent voices speaking up for intervention against McCarthy came from within Ike's own administration. C. D. Jackson, for example, was worried about Ike's propensity to "twist and turn" on the issue or to brush it off entirely. "The President's instinct is, as Southerners put it, 'not to get into a fuss.' " But, said Jackson, he "cannot keep up the three little monkeys act" forever. It was all very well to refuse to "indulge in name calling or talking about any individual," but "Olympian dialectics" were irrelevant "when your house is on fire." Jackson pleaded for an end to presidential "pussyfooting" and told Ike that "there is a vacuum that can't be filled by his associates, he has got to say it himself."[27] Similarly, Jackson's Time–Life colleague, Emmet Hughes, insisted to Ike that McCarthy "can *not* be 'handled' as if he were a kind of cussed but essentially affectionate house-dog who needs only to have his ego massaged occasionally . . . he will *have* to be confronted sooner or later." And "ways—and words—can be found" to do this. Hughes wanted clear, unambiguous, unfuzzy government, and he begged Ike to "trust *your own* judgement above all the professional politicos." The president was too modest: "Your own wisdom and instinct are the greatest resources at your command."[28]

These were persuasive arguments, but again and again Ike rejected them. To Hughes he retorted that (as he had proved where Montgomery and Patton were concerned) criticizing subordinates in public, though it might magnify the stature of the leader, was no way to build a strong team. To Jackson he replied, "I will not get in the gutter with that guy."[29] To his brother Milton Ike asserted that he refused to "get into a pissing contest with that skunk" (a phrase he had earlier used about Truman).[30] To Aaron Berg Ike affirmed, "I personally deal in principles, ideas and national purposes—I shall not demean this office by indulging in personal Donnybrooks."[31] To his diary Ike confided that, because McCarthy was so avid for headlines, the best tactic was to ignore him. To his secretary, Ann Whitman, Ike "said that he had heard a new one: 'A man is just as big as the people and things that annoy him.' "[32] Writing to Swede Hazlett, Ike compared McCarthy to Huey Long and claimed that "every attack" on such demagogues merely "increased their idolators."[33] To another correspondent Ike wrote, "When any individual or any idea goes completely outside the realm of logic and of reason, I doubt that elimination can be achieved through argument."[34] To Bill Robinson Ike declared that "the President can properly attack un-American practices and condemn unfair procedures, but that he cannot be one of the parties in a gutter brawl. . . . We have sideshows and freaks where we ought to be in the main tent with our attention on the chariot race."[35] To reporters at innumerable press conferences Ike refused to comment adversely on McCarthy.

Ike's defenders have always claimed that his strategy—to ignore McCarthy publicly while trying to undermine him in private—was right in that it was the only effective one open to him. Milton Eisenhower, for example, who at the time tried to persuade Ike to come into the open and cut McCarthy down to size, subsequently concluded that his own policy had been "100% wrong" while his brother's had been "completely correct."[36] Truman, it is pointed out, who had early denounced McCarthy, calling him among other things a pathological character assassin and "the Kremlin's best asset,"[37] afterward became reluctant to give the senator more notoriety or to get his hands dirty in the process. Ike's advocates further say that, like most senior members of the GOP, such as Hoover, Taft, and Nixon, plus nearly all Republicans in Congress, the president was committed to the McCarthyite purpose of rooting out Communism in government. Thus he supposedly had little option but to employ what a recent academic analysis has called "hidden-hand" techniques for "defusing McCarthy,"[38] techniques which proved successful. At any rate, the argument goes, within two years of Ike's taking office McCarthy had been censured by the Senate and the president could crow that McCarthyism had become McCarthywasm.

There is undoubtedly something in this defense. Yet in the last resort it is unconvincing. It ignores the fact that "the Presidency is pre-eminently a place of *moral* leadership,"[39] something about which Eisenhower agreed with Roosevelt. Moral leadership precludes the adoption of clandestine strategies to deal with manifest evils. It requires the open diagnosis of social ills and the clear prescription of remedies, not woolly platitudes about the desirability of health. After the inauguration Ike could have used his enormous prestige and popularity to convince Americans that there was nothing to fear about McCarthyism but fear itself. He might, like Major——de Coverley in Joseph Heller's *Catch-22* (as much a satire on the 1950s as on the war), have demolished the fatuities of the great loyalty oath crusade at a stroke. An inspirational statement condemning in specific terms, as it might have done, the perversion of American values, could in no sense have reduced the dignity of the presidency. It could not have been mistaken for Trumanesque mudslinging. It would not have inflated McCarthy—quite the reverse. Moreover, it would have reflected Ike's personal dislike of Red scaremongering and his private skepticism about his own security program. "If [there are] 2,500 security risks in one office," he once exclaimed to the Cabinet, "I'm going to quit."[40]

Of course Ike was right in his guess that Communism was virtually moribund in the United States—the *Daily Worker* was only kept alive in 1956 because the CIA, anxious to preserve that sorry emblem of Red menace, took out thousands of annual subscriptions. But insofar as the security program was at all desirable—and in bullish moods Ike claimed that it had "an imposing and terrific record"—McCarthy was actually hampering it. As Ike said, the "worst thing about McCarthy [is that] he's impeding all this work. [The] Kremlin ought to pay him."[41] If so, the White House ought to have put paid to him. And according to an internal government report based on surveys taken around the country, the president could have acted without political risk. The report concluded that "McCarthyism [was] disapproved of, and should be curbed."[42] Why then did Ike remain, vis-à-vis McCarthy, such a mute, inglorious president? Why did Emmet Hughes find himself quoting Edmund Burke: "The only thing necessary for the triumph of evil is for good men to do nothing"? Why did Eisenhower, despite his public pieties, abdicate the moral leadership conferred on him by his high office?

It is clear that Ike's own explanations—anyway mutually inconsistent—were primarily efforts at self-justification. The truth was at once more simple and more complicated. At its most complex, there is once again evidence of the familiar dichotomy between Ike's sound instincts and his infirmity of purpose. As Senator Jacob Javits said, Ike's "heart was in the right place" but "he could never bring himself to do what needed to be done." If his "follow-through" had been as good as his original instincts, "the President could have ended the McCarthy operation very decisively."[43] At its simplest, the president merely succumbed to the prevailing climate of fear. Ike once acknowledged to Dulles, when faced with some diplomatic embarrassment,

"that his only defense would be to go fishing"[44]—the invariable recourse of yellow sheriffs in his Westerns when the bad men rode into
town.

This, morally speaking, was Ike's frequent response to circumstances in which he might get hurt. His sometime assistant, William
B. Ewald, went so far as to write that "sensitivity to personal attack"
was Ike's "tragic flaw."[45] Or, as Marquis Childs put it, Ike's chalice
of fame had been filled to the brim in 1945 and he was reluctant to
spill a drop. So he seldom committed himself to any course of action
that would provoke hostility.[46] The hostility of McCarthy at this time,
when his capacity for besmirching reputations had been enhanced by
his new position, was to be avoided at all costs. As Richard Rovere
recorded, "In 1953, the very thought of Joe McCarthy could shiver
the White House timbers and send panic through the whole executive
branch." Rovere cited a revealing instance of what he meant. When
he mentioned McCarthy's name to one of Ike's more courageous and
responsible aides, the man adopted a supplicating mien, begged not
to be asked to talk about the senator, and seemed ready, in return for
silence on the subject, "to get me an ambassadorship or even to
declassify the recipe for the hydrogen bomb."[47]

The revised history of Eisenhower's presidency is now driving out
the received wisdom about it, perhaps through the operation of some
Cliometric Gresham's Law. So much has been written recently about
the concealed methods by which Ike helped to destroy McCarthy that
the terror which the senator inspired is in danger of being forgotten.
What struck most contemporaries as obvious, almost as soon as Ike
took office, was the fact that his administration was engaged in a fairly
consistent "retreat," sometimes amounting to a "cowardly flight,"
from the specter of McCarthyism.[48] The evidence that this was so is
actually much more full and unambiguous than the testimony which
supports the view of Ike as a secret activist. Thus, for example, his
government was at once thrown into acute disarray over McCarthy's
opposition to some of its appointments.

The most notorious case was that of Charles E. Bohlen, who was
nominated for the post of ambassador to the Soviet Union. Bohlen
was a career diplomat who had served in Russia and acted as translator
at Yalta. He also had the misfortune to be extremely handsome and
to play the balalaika. Naturally, McCarthy's worst suspicions were
aroused. He opposed Bohlen's confirmation. He also demanded that
the FBI files on him, which contained rumors of homosexuality,
should be shown to the Senate. This was refused. But eventually a
compromise was reached, Taft and Nixon working as intermediaries,

whereby two senior senators read the reports. They turned out to be the usual mishmash of suspicion and speculation. Ike endorsed his own candidate at a press conference, saying that he knew Bohlen well and had played golf with him. Bohlen's appointment was confirmed by a large majority and the administration chalked up a victory for itself, which historians have ratified.[49]

If so, it was a Pyrrhic victory. Taft instructed the White House that there must be "No more Bohlens."[50] Ike had hoped that Bohlen might resign on grounds of ill health, while admitting that "it would look bad" if he did. He now told Dulles, "Let's never mention another name until we have all these [security] clearances before us and know that we aren't going to get into this again." Dulles was reduced to a jelly by the whole episode. He assured various Republican senators that Bohlen was not really being promoted at all but being taken "out of a policy-making role" and reduced to the status of a mere reporter.[51] He expressed his confidence to Ike that "Bohlen has a normal family life" but he would not accompany him to the Hill in case they were photographed together.[52] Having supported Alger Hiss for a time, Dulles was terrified that he would be attacked on the security issue in Congress. He prepared an elaborate statement demonstrating his hostility to Hiss and exclaimed to Bohlen, "I couldn't stand another Alger Hiss."[53]

In his panic Dulles even allowed his McCarthyite security officer, an ex-FBI agent named Scott McLeod, to defy him in the State Department. Dulles was content that McLeod should investigate and dismiss hundreds of civilian employees on more or less unsubstantiated charges. The secretary was already, at Ike's behest, conducting a purge of his own among senior officials—George Kennan and John Carter Vincent were two innocent victims. But when McLeod leaked departmental secrets to McCarthy, Dulles talked of demanding his resignation. He told Ike that "the characters are minor but the issue is great: it will decide whether McCarthy, Bridges and Jenner are dominating the Executive Branch of this government." Hagerty was convinced that either Dulles or McLeod would have to go. But Ike remained passive, and in the end Dulles accepted his subordinate's apology and a promise of good behavior—only to fume impotently when the leaks continued.[54]

Morale at the State Department plummeted and, as Bohlen later wrote, "the miasma of fear and suspicion infected American life."[55] American diplomacy was pushed off its correct course abroad. Bohlen himself was virtually incapacitated by the State Department's mistrust. Dulles was so terrified about "adverse political possibilities on the

Hill" that he consulted Nixon about the advisability of bringing Bohlen to Washington for foreign ministers' meetings; the vice-president advised the planting of stories illustrating the new ambassador's sound judgment "to build Bohlen up and prove that it was a good appointment."[56] But Bohlen was prevented from playing any part in scaling down the cold war or even from keeping his government informed of the Sino–Soviet split and thus dispelling their illusions about the monolithic character of Communism.

Other ambassadors were similarly affected. Chester Bowles in India, for example, privately complained that "no one in the State Department dares show initiative any more. They are scared of having something unorthodox in their record for McCarthy to pounce on. With Dulles under fire himself, many don't believe the department will protect them if they stick their necks out."[57] The president knew all about the virtual paralysis afflicting the State Department though he variously denied it and said that it must not get any worse. But it did get worse: for Ike issued his Executive Order 10450, which enabled the government to fire anyone considered a security risk (for any reason—drinking, loose living, talkativeness), thus extending Truman's order, which had merely specified disloyalty as the ground for dismissal. The president made this order after consultation with right-wing senators, including McCarthy, whose approval he obtained. It was widely interpreted as proof that Joe had Ike firmly in his pocket.

This was not the case. But since many influential people thought of McCarthy as what Joseph Alsop called "an American Hitler-figure,"[58] it was a deplorable impression to convey. The impression was strengthened by other events during Ike's presidency, most notably the book-burning episode. In April 1953 two of McCarthy's young acolytes, Roy M. Cohn and G. David Schine, went off on an inquisitorial trip to Europe. It was an extraordinary jaunt, replete with farcical details (such as Schine's chasing Cohn around a hotel lobby bashing him on the head with a rolled-up magazine, and a gaggle of diplomats in pursuit of a lost pair of trousers) gleefully reported by the press. Its purpose, at first scarcely clear even to the principals, turned out to be an investigation of subversion among Americans abroad, particularly as manifested in the libraries of the International Information Administration (of which the Voice of America was a part). McCarthy's wild charge that thirty thousand books in U.S. embassies were written by Communists completely unmanned the administration, which issued a series of contradictory instructions to deal with the problem. Some books were banned, some screened, some burned. But most badly burned were the government's fingers.

For once again censorship proved to be the father of absurdity as well as the child of prejudice. As one cabinet memorandum rightly concluded, "We cannot screen without looking like a fool or Nazi."[59] Nevertheless, much time was spent in a vain effort to find a criterion which the censors could apply. Nixon, for instance, wanted any author who took the Fifth Amendment to be banned, while Ike objected to the disqualification of Dashiell Hammett, whose work he admired.

However, Ike's overall response was typically equivocal. In a speech made at Dartmouth College on 14 June he extolled courage: "I forget the author, but one many years ago, you know, uttered that famous saying, 'The coward dies a thousand deaths, but the brave man dies but once.'" He went on to exhort his audience, "Don't join the book burners. Don't be afraid to go into your library and read every book, as long as that document does not offend your own ideas of decency. That should be the only censorship." But at a press conference three days later, the president performed a characteristic maneuver and, to the dismay of many Republicans and all liberals, he backed away from the bold stand. Ike qualified his original appeal so heavily as to make it virtually meaningless, saying that he would not tolerate "any document or any other kind of thing that attempts to persuade or propagandize America into communism."[60] McCarthy praised the president for this "commendable clarification."[61] But the government itself could not disagree with a grass-roots opinion poll taken in California which concluded alliteratively that the "Book burning [business] was badly bungled."[62]

The same poll stated that Senator McCarthy's "publicity far overshadows the President's in quantity," though the "President's golf game is on the front page of every paper daily."[63] Certainly Ike seemed about the only person in the United States who was able to ignore McCarthy. He appalled Dulles by being unwilling even to read one of the senator's speeches: when the secretary said that he thought the president "should know what he said," Ike replied, "McCarthy was never interested in facts, just something to shoot at."[64] The press was, of course, McCarthy's involuntary instrument. Newsmen well knew that (as one said), "Joe couldn't find a communist in Red Square —he didn't know Karl Marx from Groucho."[65] However, convention bound them to report the sensational statements of a U.S. senator but, in general, not to make the sort of comment which would expose their absurdity. As president, Ike could easily have beaten McCarthy in any contest for publicity, but he chose not to compete. Thus the senator got away with his brazen manipulation of the press, which recorded his every charge and the administration's every retreat.

Occasionally McCarthy himself suffered a reverse. In July, for example, a member of his staff made an intemperate attack on Communism in the churches and, thanks largely to frantic efforts by Emmet Hughes, Ike was persuaded to condemn such generalized assaults (in general terms) before McCarthy had time to repudiate his own man. The president also refused to let the senator investigate the CIA and certain aspects of the executive. But McCarthy managed to throw the Government Printing Office into such disarray that it went onto a wartime security footing. He caused other departments to make ignominious shifts in policy and personnel. And he provoked the administration as a whole to take a stronger line against "Communists in government." Bernard Shanley was one who urged even tougher action, on the grounds that "we had fully abdicated to McCarthy [over] this vital issue."[66] Sinclair Weeks wanted better press coverage for their efforts, complaining that when McCarthy exposed one Communist he got publicity whereas "we fire many and get none." The fact that Nixon could sound like a moderate demonstrated how far McCarthy had moved the axis of American politics to the right. "We don't want to give [a] 'witch hunt' impression. But there is a middle ground," said the vice-president. "Government is [the] first object of infiltration. We've got to get them out. We promised Executive Action."[67]

Thus in November Herbert Brownell, with Ike's approval (later denied), attempted to convict a dead Treasury official, Harry Dexter White, of spying, and a live ex-president, Harry Truman, of complicity in his treason. This was a futile exercise. Moreover, it led to awkward questions being asked about what one journalist called this "pretty squalid" investigation, at the next presidential press conference.[68] It was also a transparent attempt to steal some of McCarthy's thunder, an attempt that failed because the senator (in a performance Jim Hagerty described as "sheer Fascism"[69]) managed to grab the headlines with subsidiary charges directed against both Truman and Eisenhower.

Yet Ike continued to reject the counsel of C. D. Jackson and "advocates of the beat-McCarthy-over-the-head" policy[70] and to seek ways of mollifying the senator. At a cabinet meeting on 15 December he canvassed various ways of crushing Communism in America—outlawing the party, the deportation of its members, a British-style Official Secrets Act, even (he joked) doubling their taxes. But Ike was not convinced that these measures, however desirable, were practical, and he doubted if the law could be changed "without arousing [the] suspicion [that] we are beating [the] bushes for subversives where none exist."[71] Nevertheless, four days later he had a conference with McCarthy and other members of the old guard at which further sanctions against subversives were discussed. They included proposals to make wiretap evidence legal and to compel witnesses to testify despite the Fifth Amendment. McCarthy, whose private nickname for Ike was "Stupe,"[72] praised the president for affording him "cooperation of the highest type."[73] It was praise which many regarded as a disgrace.

Ike himself later claimed to regard McCarthy's criticisms as an honor, but he never admitted to trying to propitiate the senator. However, after reading an article by Larry Martin in the Denver *Post* that catalogued instances of appeasement, he did concede, "I sometimes feel that I have been let down by my staff officers who do appease; but the orders I have given are all to the contrary."[74] There were occasions, it is true, when Ike's writ did not run throughout the administration, and sometimes two contradictory policies were pursued at the same time. But where McCarthy was concerned the government undoubtedly reflected the irresolution of its leader. And the best that can be said about such indirect efforts as Ike made to undermine the senator—mainly via feeble general appeals for American standards of fair play—is that by the end of 1953 they had proved singularly ineffective. The disillusionment felt by many of Ike's erstwhile supporters was summed up in a letter written by Nicholas Roosevelt. He assumed that the president's "failure to stand up to [the neo-Fascist] McCarthy, and his apparent approval of Dulles's truckling to him," were due to Ike's having become an unwitting tool of the old guard. "The picture of President Eisenhower washing his hands of McCarthy like Pontius Pilate," Roosevelt concluded, "serve[s] to shake the confidence of many persons who voted for him."[75]

The thin-skinned president was stung by this criticism and with the help of his aide, Bryce Harlow, drafted a long reply. Ike made his standard assertion that indulgence in "bitter personal indictment . . . smacks more of the coward and the fool than of the leader." He declared that the forces of reaction "have not only *not* been allowed to gain control over policy or to exert undue influence over leaders in the Administration, but they have been defeated, soundly defeated, in some of their most determined efforts." To prove his point, Ike cited the extension of the Reciprocal Trade Act, the maintaining of the Excess Profits Tax, the emergency Immigration Bill, and the continuance of foreign aid. The president increasingly resorted to listing his government's positive accomplishments in order to demonstrate the irrelevance of McCarthy. This was a sound tactic. For the senator's ballyhoo obscured the fact that Ike's first year in the White House was distinguished by some solid successes. Yet, as Nixon complained to the Cabinet, people failed to recognize the administration's achievements: "They see only McCarthy."[76] Still, in a way they were right. For even Ike's most signal achievements cannot be viewed outside the grim context of McCarthyism.

Thus his foreign policy was vitiated by fears of a right-wing backlash at home. The president's greatest feat, the armistice in Korea, was achieved in the teeth of the Republican old guard, who believed that there was no substitute for victory in the only place the United States was actually fighting the forces of Communism. Ike therefore had to balance his pacific overtures with a bellicose rhetoric that was liable to frustrate them. In this endeavor he was both hampered and helped by his secretary of state: hampered in that Dulles was opposed to making any concessions to Communism; helped in that he could be used to deliver the hawkish utterances which were alien to Ike. It was once generally assumed that Dulles determined American foreign policy, "thwarting Eisenhower's benign impulses" in the interest of "rigid moralism."[77] This is "simply incorrect,"[78] according to the new orthodoxy, which states that Dulles took no important initiatives without Ike's approval and often concluded their discussions by saying, "Mr. President, you've got to tell me what to do."[79]

The truth surely lies somewhere between these categorical extremes. Dulles consulted Ike very thoroughly and the president often modified his drafts and policies. On the other hand, as C. D. Jackson observed, it was not Ike's habit to initiate strategy: he preferred his staff to present him with a brief plan of action which he could then approve, disapprove, or alter. Dulles had a lawyer's knack of putting forward a convincing case, and he treated the president like a respected client who would probably accept his expert advice. Such was the secretary's moral force, intellectual cogency, and diplomatic acumen that the president generally did defer to him. There were, of course, times that Ike contradicted him sharply or ticked him off bluntly. But, as the president told Gruenther, "I cannot tell you how definitely I lean upon [Dulles's] wisdom, judgment and integrity."[80]

Nevertheless, as Sherman Adams noted, Ike's approach to foreign problems was more conciliatory than that of Dulles. Thus, during their association the United States was inclined to adopt two different diplomatic postures. The very confusion this engendered produced enormous political dividends. At home Ike could conceal his crucial purpose of implementing a policy of containment rather than rollback. Abroad he was able so to baffle the Communists about his true intentions that they were willing to make and preserve the peace. In short,

Ike spoke softly while Dulles carried a big stick. Whether the ambiguity of this foreign policy occurred by accident or by design remains obscure. The president himself asserted forcefully that peace did not just happen by itself. So perhaps most of the credit should go to Ike, whose unrivaled power of equivocation never operated to better effect.

A striking example of this equivocation was to be heard on 16 April 1953, when the new president delivered his first major speech, entitled "The Chance for Peace," on the cold war. The U.S. government had been thrown into something of a turmoil by Stalin's death a few weeks earlier and by the friendly overtures made shortly afterward by Malenkov. No preparation had been made to deal with either eventuality. Dulles was darkly suspicious of every Russian move, even perhaps inclined to wonder why Stalin had chosen that particular moment to die. Ike saw the chance of a thaw in the cold war and wanted to make a serious peace proposal. It is impossible to doubt the sincerity with which he discussed the proposition. His eyes gleaming, his jaw set, his head martially erect, Ike spoke eloquently to Emmet Hughes about the costly armaments which were robbing people everywhere of the fruits of their labor. He wanted to make a real bid for peace. "Let's talk straight: *no* double talk, *no* sophisticated political formulas, *no* slick propaganda."[81]

Yet the address Ike finally gave (while in agony from an ileitis attack) was everything he had said it should not be. It conveyed in vividly idealistic terms the tragic waste caused by the arms race and the fell plight of "humanity hanging from a cross of iron."[82] But although Ike hoped that the tide of history might turn toward peace, he ensured that it did not. For, at Dulles's behest, he reiterated all the traditional denunciations of Soviet aggression and all the familiar demands for Communist withdrawal from Eastern Europe and elsewhere. Ike was a man divided against himself. His genuine bid for peace was an equally genuine maneuver in the cold war. It was designed to trump Malenkov's initiative, perhaps to "pry one or two [Russian] satellites loose,"[83] and to satisfy right-wing and McCarthyite opinion at home that he was not making any concessions to Communism. The propagandist nature of the speech became more apparent when, despite the immense enthusiasm it generated, the magnanimous impulse behind it petered out. It became increasingly obvious that the chance for peace, or at any rate for détente, had been lost.

Ike continued to keep everyone guessing. Dulles's private fulminations were even more aggressive than his public ones. To colleagues he expressed his wish to "bury the containment policy,"[84] for example, or to postpone a settlement in Korea "until we have shown— before all Asia—our clear superiority by giving the Chinese one hell of a licking."[85] But, unlike Chiang, Dulles was kept on a leash. When disturbances occurred in East Germany in June he was only allowed to protest verbally, which suggested that "liberation" was more pontification than policy. In Korea, on the other hand, Ike pushed ahead with stern measures, dispatching more air power, bombing the irrigation dikes, revealing plans to expand the South Korean army, and placing nuclear missiles in Okinawa. In a coded statement whose meaning was all too clear, Dulles was even permitted to threaten an atomic attack. But when Syngman Rhee, the South Korean president, attempted to sabotage the peace negotiations by freeing enemy prisoners of war due for repatriation, Ike threatened to withdraw U.S. support. Rhee was eventually induced to cooperate, in return for promises of generous U.S. aid, and the truce was agreed in July.

Ike did not greet it with "wild rejoicing" but claimed that "we have shown, in the winning of this truce, that the collective resolve of the free world can and will meet aggression in Asia—or anywhere in the world."[86] This belligerent announcement was designed to pacify the old guard at home, who were muttering about Munichs and complaining that this was the first time in history that the United States had agreed to an armistice without honor or victory. However, Ike had every reason for congratulating himself. He had extricated his country from a bloody, expensive, and dangerous war without compromising his anti-Communist position. This was something that could perhaps only have been accomplished by a general who was not a militarist and a Republican who was not a reactionary. Radicals now reckoned that the Democrats were the party of the cold war, and I. F. Stone coined the slogan "Back Ike for Peace."[87]

Ike often stressed that there would be no victors in a nuclear war —Russia exploded her first hydrogen bomb in August 1953—and that peace was therefore essential. He could, it is true, mention with terrifying casualness the prospect of using atomic weapons, seeming to regard them as a mere extension of conventional arms. In general, though, this was a propaganda tactic, a warning that he too could envisage more or less massive retaliation. But while the Soviet Union might be intimidated enough to refrain from large-scale aggression, Ike was convinced that their policy of fomenting world-wide revolution would continue. He was sufficiently a victim of cold-war terrors to be obsessed by the danger of "losing" more countries to Communism, especially those achieving independence from the declining

European empires. In 1951 Ike had shrewdly written to Averell Harriman,

The Moslem world grows restive—I firmly believe that, in this case, the Russians are getting far closer to the masses than we are; I sometimes have the uneasy feeling that in those countries our side deals primarily with the classes that have been exploiting their own people since time immemorial. The Soviet method is, through bribery, the use of agents, and the skillful use of propaganda, to appeal *directly to the masses.* [88]

Yet in the same breath Ike remarked that it was vital for the French to gain a quick victory in Indochina. Moreover, despite an antipathy to imperialism, he was always inclined to view popular anti-colonial leaders as puppets controlled, so to speak, by a hidden hand in the Kremlin.

As president, Ike was determined to resist the advance of Communism in the guise of nationalism. But so as not to risk a general war he preferred to avoid open confrontation and instead pursued a variety of clandestine methods—mutual security, propaganda, psychological warfare, counterinsurgency, and "dirty tricks" of all sorts,[89] including, perhaps, political assassination.[90] Ike may not have been personally responsible for the worst excesses of his main instrument in this work—the CIA, which expanded greatly during the 1950s— though in view of his penchant for distancing himself from unpleasant decisions it is impossible to be certain. But if not, he was at least guilty of losing control of a powerful and potentially lawless undercover force. Ike claimed that covert operations were "just about the only way to win World War III without having to fight it."[91] But this argument, still heard today, both denies and impedes the possibility of peaceful coexistence. It also suggests that the United States, whose greatest glory is a system of open government, should ape the Soviet Union by taking its foreign affairs out of the realm of diplomacy and into that of conspiracy. Ike did his country no honor by turning it into a global secret policeman.

One of the first fruits of his policy was the coup which the CIA staged in Iran. That country's prime minister, Mohammed Mossadegh, had nationalized Iran's oil resources, thus offending the British who had formerly profited from them and now organized a boycott. The United States, whose oil companies had a vast stake in Saudi Arabia, reaped enormous benefits from the boycott. But by 1953 Iran, cut off from her markets, faced bankruptcy. Mossadegh wrote to Ike in May pleading for financial help and suggesting that if it were not forthcoming he would have to appeal to Russia. The

American ambassador in Iran, Loy Henderson, passed on this letter, emphasizing its confidential nature. He was appalled when Ike made it public—an action Henderson thought "not worthy of the U.S. government"[92]—brusquely rebuffing Mossadegh in the process. Mossadegh was, in fact, an amiable and civilized Iranian nationalist. He was ridiculed in the West as a clown because he appeared in public in his pajamas and held conferences in bed—he did so because of his tendency to faint (he even fainted when horizontal). Somewhat inconsistently, Mossadegh was also reviled as a Communist. In the words of one CIA agent, "the British understood the extent of paranoia" about Communism in McCarthy's America and "consciously played on that fear" in order to persuade Ike and Dulles that he must be overthrown.[93] In this atmosphere any evidence was good enough to convict the Iranian premier.

With inimitable logic the president remarked of the August plebiscite which gave Mossadegh 99.4 percent of the votes, "Iran's downhill course toward Communist-supported dictatorship was picking up momentum."[94] Mossadegh, it is true, was now being supported by the Communists, and Ike promptly authorized the coup. With some difficulty and delay, the expenditure of much money and the limited use of force, the shah was placed firmly on the peacock throne. Iranian oil was then vested in a new international consortium, with American companies (exempted from antitrust legislation at home) holding a 40 percent share. The president and some of his friends in the oil business were delighted by the settlement. However, it was not so good from the point of view of Iran, where the oil consortium secretly held back production for their own benefit. Ike was as much thrilled by the dime-novel aspects of the coup as by the black eye it gave to Communism. When its CIA instigator, Kermit Roosevelt, told his story Dulles's eyes gleamed and "he seemed to be purring like a giant cat."[95] In fact, according to the British Secret Intelligence Service, "Roosevelt really did little more than show up in Iran with C.I.A. funds to encourage agents the British had organized and then released to American control."[96] But Ike later decorated Roosevelt at a private ceremony in the White House. However, the coup was more of a tragedy than a triumph. Contrary to all his protestations about nations' inalienable rights to self-determination, Ike had uprooted a legitimate government and planted a royal despotism in Iran. He had simultaneously sown dragon's teeth which would spring up as armed men, imbued with a fanatical hatred of the United States.

In December 1953 Ike made a second major peace initiative. This one, like its April predecessor, was replete with enough dialectical contradiction to baffle the most ardent Marxist. Responding to the new threat of the hydrogen bomb, Ike proposed that the United States, the Soviet Union, and Britain should give some of their uranium to a United Nations agency, which would employ it to serve "the peaceful pursuits of mankind,"[97] such as the generation of energy. Ike's aim was at once to slow down the nuclear arms race and to leap ahead in it. As he later wrote, the United States "could afford to reduce its atomic stockpile by two or three times the amount the Russians might contribute, and still improve our relative position."[98] He was intent both on scoring a spectacular propaganda victory and on promoting genuine mutual trust. He wanted to offer the world new hope, to replace terror by joint humanitarian endeavor. But he ensured that McCarthyite charges of appeasement could not be made to stick by blowing the atomic trumpet and stating that American nuclear weapons had virtually acquired conventional status. Ike's speech was the product of several hands and innumerable drafts. Its original candor and idealism were diluted in the interests of cold-war strategy, and it became exactly what its antithetical name suggested—a peace offensive.

Even Winston Churchill played a small part in revising the speech. Ike met him and the French premier, Joseph Laniel, for a three-power conference in Bermuda just before going on to address the United Nations. The president disliked such summit meetings. He deprecated Churchill's "old-fashioned, paternalistic approach" toward colonial peoples and thought that his idea of resuscitating the wartime "British–American partnership" in order to direct world affairs was "fatuous."[99] Ike was also apprehensive about being charmed or cajoled into some wayward course by Churchill, whom he described as "a man of improvisation and expediency."[100] Moreover, Ike yearned for the chance to take some recreation. But he was fussed about whether it would be seemly to bring his golf clubs to Bermuda —and anyway he had cut his hand when showing Mamie how cowboys "fanned" their six-shooters.

However, the occasion was agreeable if not very profitable. Ike was amused by Churchill's devotion to a goat, the mascot of his guard of honor. And he reported to Hazlett that "At times Winston seemed to be his old and hearty self, full of vim and determination. At others he seemed almost to wander in his mind," though this may have been "a deliberately adopted mannerism" to keep boredom at bay. The French, by contrast, were futile, always saying " 'Yes, but' or 'No, unless.' "[101] But Ike not only hid his contempt for Laniel, he tried to make Churchill treat him with ordinary politeness. Ike was glad to depart for New York. During the flight he urged on his staff, who were duplicating, collating, and stapling the pages of his final draft as though their lives depended on it. Even the ponderous Dulles helped and Ike amused him by saying, "Hurry up, Foster. Pick up some more copies."[102]

The thunderous ovation which greeted Ike's "Atoms for Peace" proposals—even the normally dour Russians applauded—suggested that the United Nations believed their lives might depend on it. But, on second thoughts, the Soviet Union restrained its enthusiasm, and the implacable men of the Kremlin refused to make any reciprocal gesture. Unfortunately, the president had given them cause to doubt his good faith because, as an American historian has phrased it, Ike's "dual goals of military invulnerability and reduction of international tension were in conflict."[103] What is more, as C. D. Jackson complained to Ike some six months later, "there was *no* follow-through," and "Foreign policy by Presidential speeches, without follow-through, just doesn't work." Jackson continued forthrightly (and Ike hinted to Adams that he was a little too forthright) that this failure, in such an important and urgent situation, suggested to some observers that "You don't like your job." In psychological warfare "the action comes first and the propaganda second," and, Jackson argued, the president's reversal of this process was "utterly incomprehensible to really serious people abroad." Jackson came close to blaming Ike directly for lack of leadership in this matter: "people have got to feel that you want [a scheme] to come off, otherwise it gets frittered away."

Naturally Ike disagreed with these criticisms, saying that it had taken months to obtain a negative answer from Russia and that subsidiary initiatives were proceeding. But he did acknowledge, somewhat lamely, that the country "has always been lacking in an organism here in Washington to pull together, except only in the person of the President or someone very close to him." And he concluded that the United States should not talk about world leadership: "We ought first of all to be content with little steps, even if you use the occasional dramatic appeal."[104] It was a fair, if dispiriting, summary of Ike's method of waging peace during the cold war.

On the domestic front Ike was also inclined toward wary pragmatism as he tried to find a safe course between extremes. He was convinced that unless the Republicans made themselves "the militant champions of the Middle Way, they are sunk."[105] The president was thus neither a reactionary nor a liberal. He was a moderate conservative, so much so that Joseph Alsop likened him to Britain's Tory Prime

Minister Stanley Baldwin, and others thought, since he also talked
"Gamalielese," that he resembled Warren Harding. Ike deplored the
advance of "creeping Socialism," all the more sinister because, he
said, it was "striking in the United States."[106] But he made no attempt
to dismantle the New Deal—the number of people covered by old-
age benefits rose during his two terms from about two million to ten
million. Ike privately longed to sell the Tennessee Valley Authority,
but in public he defended it, making only tentative efforts to stop its
expansion. Ike was widely viewed as the president of big business, and
his ceding of the tidelands oil rights to coastal states was seen as a
massive subvention to the oil tycoons who had supported him. But
when Southerners complained that "Truman offered us more than
that," Ike retorted, "Brother, I'm not competing in giving away
money . . . we're not going to be bludgeoned."[107] While he was
sensitive to the interests of industry, Ike often reminded the Cabinet,
"We've got to show and prove to him that we're going after the little
man's interest directly."[108] Yet when Durkin went ahead in the summer with plans to reform the Taft–Hartley law Ike backed down in
the face of business pressure, and his secretary of labor resigned.

However, Ike did preside over the birth of the affluent society: in
one of the greatest booms in history, the gross national product rose
by almost fifty percent, to over $500 billion. Naturally progress was
not uniform, and there were peaks and troughs. Yet Ike was willing
to regulate the economy in the manner of the New Deal, especially
by his highway building program, despite his general opposition to
interventionism. There was a minor recession after the end of the
Korean War, for example, and George Humphrey produced the familiar Republican bromides about building up the confidence of 160
million Americans: "Government can't make or break prosperity.
. . . What government can do is remove restrictions on enterprise,
stimulate initiative," and so on. Ike, who was determined that the
GOP should not once more become the party of depression, responded firmly: "Now look. Let's not begin to quote too much Mr.
Hoover. I remember 1929 and prosperity around [the] corner, and
[the] basically sound economy. [We] can't put government in [the]
position of [being] unable to act positively."[109]

Nevertheless, like Humphrey, Ike stressed the vital importance of
fiscal responsibility. He was particularly anxious to economize on
defense spending and often asserted that there was no point in being
both armed to the teeth and bankrupt. However, in his first budget
Ike was only able to cut the deficit down to $2.5 billion. This pro-
voked a table-pounding tirade from Taft: "With a program like this,

we'll never elect a Republican Congress in 1954. You're taking us down the same road Truman travelled. It's a repudiation of everything we promised in the campaign."[110] Ike flushed angrily and might have retorted in kind had the talk not been diverted along harmless channels by the quick intervention of colleagues. Taft soon recovered his good temper, and by the time he died from cancer in the summer of 1953, Ike had (somewhat to his surprise) no better friend on the Hill.

Taft's death was a serious blow to Ike because his successor as Republican leader in the Senate, William Knowland of California, was an old-guard diehard. He was nicknamed "the Senator for Formosa" because of his intense hostility to Red China, and he condemned the Korean settlement as a "Munich in the Far East."[111] Ike always reckoned himself a constitutional president in that he believed in the separation of powers and scrupulously respected the prerogatives of the other branches of government. "We can't risk cutting across the customs of Capitol Hill," he said.[112] Accordingly he needed able ambassadors in Congress willing to argue his case, as Taft had been (up to a point) prepared to do. This was particularly so because the Republicans, anyway barely a majority, were so reluctant to abandon the delights of opposition and face the responsibilities of power. As Ike put it, "we're getting exceedingly tired of having people in Congress who are supposed to be supporting us engage in kicking our shins and bickering."[113] Unfortunately, Knowland was the voice of the old guard in the White House rather than the voice of the president in the Senate. His stupidity and obscurantism drove Ike almost frantic with rage. Nor could the president exert much influence on Knowland's followers. "I made as much of an impression [on Pat] McCarran," Ike exclaimed bitterly, "as a sponge would on a steel lid."[114]

Nothing, in Ike's view, indicated "the complete readiness of the Republican party to tear us apart"[115] more than the Bricker Amendment. This was Senator John Bricker's proposal, put forward on January 1953, to curtail the president's treaty-making powers. It was the GOP's revenge for Yalta and Ike had opposed it from the start, though the long and frustrating process made him "so sick . . . I could scream."[116]

Ike never screamed but he did grouse continually about his lot. He complained to Field Marshal Montgomery, "No man on earth knows what this job is all about; it's pound, pound, pound. . . . Not only is your intellectual capacity taxed to the utmost, but your physical stamina. This week every morning my first meeting is at breakfast, business breakfasts."[117] Ike's schedule was indeed so packed that he blamed his staff for filling it "right up to the brim with appointments in order to show how busy I am."[118] But actually it was impossible for him to fulfill his functions at all without being busy. There were the incessant meetings—with officials who briefed the president every day (especially on intelligence and foreign affairs), with members of the Cabinet, with the Security Council and other government committees, with senators and congressmen, with military chiefs and church leaders, with ambassadors and foreign dignitaries, with important groups and individuals, with speech writers and journalists. Ike had to sign his name hundreds of times a day, and he was bombarded with print.

Of course, he saw only a tiny fraction of the six million letters and telegrams delivered during his eight years at the White House, many of his formal replies being drafted by an official, Dr. Fred Fox, known as the "Holy Ghost writer"—who himself lamented, "It has got so that a bridge foursome cannot meet in Des Moines without Presidential wishes of best luck."[119] But Ike liked to sample his mail; he had to read interminable reports and memoranda; and he scanned the newspapers attentively, despite an elaborate pretense to the contrary —he even told Emmet Hughes, "Anyone who has time to . . . read columnists obviously doesn't have enough work to do."[120] In addition there were endless ceremonial functions about which Ike grumbled vociferously, saying that he never had any time to think.

Thus the sunny good nature for which Ike was renowned was by no means invariably present during his working life in the White House. But his infectious charm was on display frequently enough. He could and did face appalling pressure with remarkable equanimity, something he attributed to his mother's happy temperament. He was capable of bearing bad days with "wonderful grace," and his secretary once wrote that he appeared after a long stormy period "in an angelic frame of mind."[121] But the storms, when they did rage, were frightening. Bernard Shanley remembered a time when "The President blew up every fifteen or twenty minutes," and so fierce were these explosions that, Ike later thought, they probably helped to bring about his heart attack. It was on one such occasion that Ike, who seldom directly rebuked his senior staff, castigated Adams so violently that he emerged from the Oval Office "like a man hit over the head with a hammer."[122] Ike was most frequently bad-tempered not, as rumor had it, when he was wearing a brown suit (though this, as he remarked, might have reflected the disposition of his valet, who put out his clothes), but when he was shackled to his work with no remission in sight. Even so, it did not take much to cheer him up. At one Cabinet meeting, for example, Jim Hagerty managed to get the hook on an elaborate fishing trophy, which had been presented to Ike, attached to the seat of his pants, and the embarrassed press secretary had to be cut free with a penknife by Ezra Benson. Ike's "foul mood" at once evaporated, and he laughed until he cried.[123] Still, Ike usually gave the impression that his job was a chore and a bore. Close friends had reason to believe that he hated his office. After a hard day the president was liable to announce that he was going to look for "a good tall building."[124]

However, it was not Ike's seeming aversion to his office, but his passion for recreation that gained him the reputation of being the most work-shy president since Calvin Coolidge. His yearning to escape from the White House, at once a prison, a treadmill, and a goldfish bowl, and to seek refuge in the surrogate world of sport, was palpable. Golf, in particular, had become almost an alternative form of existence for him. He had a putting green constructed outside the Oval Office and ordered Sergeant Moaney to shoot the squirrels (which had been fed scraps by Truman) for burying nuts in it—at the insistence of the Secret Service most of these creatures were trapped and transferred to Rock Creek Park, a laborious process since an indignant conservationist kept releasing more squirrels through the White House railings, but he too was eventually caught. The president installed a driving range in the grounds, and there was a "hysterical" scene when workmen nearly dug a hole in it to plant a tree.[125] He practiced chip shots at all possible and some impossible moments. He issued invitations that could not be refused for friends to fly halfway round the world to make up a foursome and interrupted his work to plan his leisure. On 7 February 1953, for example, the new president kept peering gloomily into the rain-filled sky and, finally deciding that he would have to play bridge rather than golf that afternoon, he exclaimed (to Ann Whitman's amusement), "Sometimes I feel so sorry for myself I could cry."[126] And when, several times a week, the president did get onto the exclusive golf courses (such as Burning Tree) which he loved, he invested all his manic concentration in the game. When winning he treated partners and opponents to sustained bouts of raillery. He swore profusely and furiously banged his clubs into the ground when his play was not up to scratch.

Hostile reporters computed the impressive amount of time, about 150 days out of 365, which Ike spent on the golf links. His addiction to fishing, shooting, cooking, and playing bridge also drew adverse comment. From some accounts it seemed that he was always on holiday—actually it was for about ten weeks a year. Mamie involuntarily contributed to the impression of presidential idleness. She seldom woke before ten in the morning and solemnly announced that "every woman over fifty should stay in bed until noon."[127] Sometimes she did not get up at all, and her afternoons were usually spent watching soap operas on television, playing bolivia (a form of canasta) with her friends, or fussing about domestic trivia. Even the stag dinners which Ike regularly gave for influential people, mainly those engaged in business and politics, were seen by critics as another means by which he neglected the affairs of state, a gastronomic equivalent to golf. By the end of his second term influential journalists like the Alsops, whom the president himself reckoned to be the "cleverest of G-2 people there are" and "not . . . vicious,"[128] could remark dismissively that "Eisenhower remains the same, like a dead whale on a beach, or rather, like a nice old gentleman in a golf cart."[129] Yet someone like Bernard Shanley, who observed Ike hard at work by 7:15 A.M.—the president having already digested the contents of four or more newspapers—found the reports about his being "ineffective" or "not doing his job" to be "startlingly incorrect."[130]

It was equally incorrect to say that Ike disliked being president. His inclination to mask his real feelings apart, Ike was by nature too modest to revel in his new role. Indeed, he pretended to be shocked and hurt and to realize all of a sudden the loneliness of his position, when Omar Bradley addressed him for the first time as "Mr. President." Yet other old friends, who continued to call him Ike, received the distinct impression that he was uncomfortable about such familiarity and would be happier if accorded the title. Furthermore, as he wrote in his diary after a year in the White House, ever since 1942 he had been accustomed to the isolation at the top, to being unable to visit restaurants, theaters, and other public places freely, to being hemmed in by security and protocol, so he was "psychologically prepared" for the presidency.[131] Anyway, to his associates in government Ike admitted that he enjoyed the interest and stimulus of occupying the most testing post on earth. He told Gabriel Hauge:

It isn't that I don't like the job; the very challenge of working with people —great minds around to help you. In many ways I think I am pretty well qualified for this thing, even if in the political angles of it the reason I am not qualified is that I don't understand what these fellows are getting at, but I so despise their methods that there is just a resentment in me that finally renders me relatively ineffective.[132]

In the last part of this statement, however, Ike was surely once again being disingenuous. It was not the devious shifts as much as the bruising hostilities of politics that so upset him. This emerged clearly

in his letter to Sid Richardson in August 1953. The president wrote
that he was looking forward to forgetting "all this political yammer-
ing" during a vacation devoted to fishing, frying pancakes, and playing golf, and he continued: "I am going to declare my independence
of partisan quarrels and let others fight such things out to the bitter
death."[133]

Ike was obviously referring here to his troubles with McCarthy.
Without doubt the senator had become the central issue in America's
domestic life during the first year of Ike's presidency. As *Time* wrote,
no one who read the newspapers, attended to the broadcasting media,
or discussed politics "needs to be told how all-pervasive the McCarthy
topic has become." On the other hand, it continued, 'The specter of
the U.S. in the grip of a hysterical witch hunt, of the President cower-
ing before McCarthy's power, bears only a specter's relation to reality." There was something in this, as in the magazine's contention that
much of the fuss abroad was aggravated by anti-Americanism. The
senator, whose political techniques were those of improvisation, mendacity, smear, and self-advertisement, had no constructive program to
put in the place of the president's, which remained largely inviolate.
And Ike himself put the matter in perspective by pointing out how
absurd it was to pretend that McCarthy could seriously imperil the
Constitution of the United States. Nevertheless, insofar as the Constitution is an instrument to protect the rights of citizens, it often failed
—thanks in part to the connivance of the chief executive. Even *Time*,
which warmly supported Ike, could not but acknowledge that
McCarthy had imposed a "paralyzing fear" on the administration,
which it was the president's duty to dispel, and that there had been
a number of "disgraceful episodes" of appeasement.[134]

Many considered that the most shameful of these was the execution
of Julius and Ethel Rosenberg, who had been convicted of betraying
atomic secrets to Russia. Much to Ike's amazement the case aroused
international concern, about which he was kept well informed by
ambassadors such as Clare Boothe Luce in Italy and C. Douglas Dillon
in France. The latter wrote that Roy Cohn, on his recent trip to
Europe, had tried to convince critics of his maturity (he was twenty-
six) by claiming to have prosecuted the so-called "atom spies."
"Nothing could be better calculated than this claim to convince wav-
erers that the Rosenbergs, if executed, will be victims of what the
European press freely terms 'McCarthyism.'"[135] The European press
was substantially correct. Ike himself was a victim of the McCarthyite
climate of fear in which Charlie Chaplin could not be tolerated, let
alone the Rosenbergs. The president could find no reasons of state,

which would be the only ground, he considered, for exercising executive clemency. He admitted to John that it went against the grain to execute a woman. But Ike was, as usual, more alive to practical than to moral considerations and he appears not to have agonized over the decision. He reasoned that Ethel Rosenberg was a recalcitrant character and that to commute her sentence would simply encourage the Russians to recruit their agents from among women. So Ike ignored pleas made by almost everyone, from the pope downward, on behalf of the Rosenbergs, telling Dulles that "it would be better to go ahead, and not let the Commies brag that they had influenced our justice."[136] The Rosenbergs died in the electric chair on 19 June 1953. They were a pathetic sacrifice to the spirit of an age which in some respects deserved the outrageous lampooning it received, a generation later, in Robert Coover's novel *The Public Burning.*

Needless to say Ike took a positive view of his administration's record in its first twelve months. He reflected on peace with honor, on moderate policies, on keeping NATO solid, on having become president not of a faction but of all the people, most of whom admired his integrity. Ike was even prepared to boast about the government's anti-Communist crusade, saying that fifteen hundred "security risks" had been rooted out of the civil service.[137] Privately, however, he was inclined to agree with Dulles, who thought the whole security program "a mess" because no one had "a clear idea of what security risk means." The secretary told the Cabinet that the screening process cost between six hundred and seven hundred dollars per case and had turned up a number of officials who were drunks, who consorted with "immoral women," or who had pacifists in their families. "Should we fire them?" he asked rhetorically. Ike merely observed that it was "terrible how few reports are entirely clear" and how many relied on gossip. He was "anxious to have Foster say 'we're finished' so as to end [the] cloudy situation [and restore] employee morale." He was also willing to get more money from the Appropriations Committee "to speed things up."[138] It was obvious from this exchange and others like it that the security program was primarily a lightning conductor to divert the wrath of McCarthy.

Thus for all Ike's positive achievements he had not only failed to discredit the senator, he had implicitly encouraged him by weakly following a similar path. By the end of 1953 many people, even in his own government, were calling on the president for "more 'ruling'" and "less 'reigning.'"[139] One memorandum concluded with a flourish, "Mr. President, your play is still on in the most important theater in the world. Your audience—most of it—is seated. Some are patient, many are impatient, some have already left. You are on the stage but the lights are out. Please go on with the play—talk to your audience —be the *leader* of the United States and the world!"[140] Henry Cabot Lodge echoed this advice, asserting that Ike must become the first television president, as Roosevelt had been the first radio president, and must thus "seek to dominate public opinion." At present he was regarded as a fine, good man, "sitting in the background modestly allowing others to do the work. This may be sound administration but it is not good politics. The people voted for Eisenhower."[141] Here he was obviously right. However, Lodge had surely hit on the opposite of the truth in the rest of his argument. Ike's refusal to lead from the front, particularly in the matter of McCarthy, was good politics, in that the president never risked wrecking his popularity on the sharp reef of the Communist issue. But as administration it was unsound. For Ike permitted the junior senator from Wisconsin to intimidate his government on important matters and to become what Walter Lippmann called "a national obsession."[142] All this damaged the prestige of the United States in the eyes of the world, and it was a sadly inauspicious opening to Eisenhower's presidency.

14

★

The Dawn of Tranquillity

In 1954 the McCarthyite abscess burst and the American body politic began to return to its fundamental state of health. In one sense the senator's decline and fall vindicated Ike's policy of refusing to dignify him with a mention, of prohibiting his investigation of the executive branch, of upholding decent values, and of allowing demagoguery to reap its just reward. But this view ignores the fact that during the months of McCarthy's apocalypse Ike's administration presented a picture of panic. Far from coolly masterminding the senator's downfall, it appeared to have lost the initiative and, in the face of McCarthy's onslaughts, to quake from one expedient to the next. For all Ike's determination to focus on high policy and stern principle, he continued to be distracted by the obnoxious behavior of his political Old Man of the Sea.

The government's fearful disarray was particularly apparent in the way it handled the case of J. Robert Oppenheimer, the father of the atomic bomb. At the end of 1953 Ike was told that hoary charges of Communism were being revived against Oppenheimer and that McCarthy had got wind of them. There was no new evidence against the scientist and anyway, as Ike remarked, "If this man is really a disloyal citizen, then the damage he can do now as compared to what he has done in the past is like comparing a grain of sand to an ocean beach."[1] Actually it seems that Ike did not take the accusations against Oppenheimer very seriously. It is true that he was ready to impute guilt by association: he told Churchill, "It isn't that anyone believes that Oppenheimer is really disloyal—but when you have a Communist brother and a Communist wife. . . ."[2] The president also took circumstantial evidence into account: when the scientist made public details of the security panel's adverse decision in June 1954, Ike exclaimed,

"This fellow Oppenheimer is sure acting like a Communist. He is using all the rules that they use to try to get public sentiment in their corner on some case where they want to make an individual a martyr."[3] Essentially Eisenhower was claiming that Oppenheimer was a dangerous animal because, when attacked, he defended himself. But perhaps this line of reasoning was the product of temporary presidential annoyance: in the end Ike agreed that since the investigating committee had found Oppenheimer to be both loyal and discreet, its decision against him "did not make a great deal of sense."[4]

It made sense only in the sinister context of McCarthyism. Rather than face further scares, Ike tried to anticipate the senator in his hunt for Communists. "We've got to handle this so that all our scientists are not made out to be Reds," declared the president. "That goddam McCarthy is just likely to try such a thing."[5] So first Ike ordered a "blank wall" to be placed between Oppenheimer and all secret information,[6] and after the official investigation the scientist's security clearance was revoked altogether. The investigation itself was a sordid affair. The committee chairman, Gordon Gray, not only impugned the integrity of Oppenheimer's supporters but told an audience that the scientist's "private morals would 'horrify the mothers of America.' " It is difficult to disagree with Joseph Alsop, who told Gray that his committee's decision was "base and ignoble." Alsop was particularly "outraged by our existing apparatus of security, with its gaggles of hired perjurers, files full of poison pen letters, smug flatfeet, shocking secret revenges and flagrant trampling on all that America stands for."[7] Ike himself, though having successfully preempted McCarthy, had provoked a storm in the scientific community, and he clearly felt disquieted by the case. When questioned about it by the press, he exploited his talent for obfuscation to its utmost and lapsed into almost total incoherence: "this is something that is the kind of thing that must be gone through with what I believe is best not talked about too much until we know whatever answers there will be."[8]

Alsop—he and his brother were nicknamed the Allslops by McCarthy—was similarly eloquent in pleading with Dulles against the dismissal of John Paton Davies from the State Department. Davies was supposed to have had some responsibility for the "loss" of China and McCarthy demanded his head on a charger. Alsop made a case not only for justice but for expediency:

I am certain you and the President will be the next victims if the administration continues to build up McCarthy by surrenders and seeming surrenders to him. . . . It does not matter what you say or do; if Davies is now dropped

from the Department, you and the administration will be universally regarded as bowing down in Moloch's temple in the most public and decisive
manner.[9]

Dulles rejected this admirable advice, vainly trying to release the news
of Davies's dismissal in such a way as not to make it seem a capitulation
to McCarthy.[10] In fact, as the cabinet discussion revealed, Ike's government had neither the courage of McCarthy's convictions nor the
courage of its own skepticism.

Dulles began by saying that Davies's case had inspired a great
defense by those opposed to McCarthy, when Ike chimed in, "A
feeling I can share." The secretary continued that Davies was "unreliable" because his "record [was] spotted with irregularities—undisci-
plined actions and conduct, talk, unauthorized diaries showing great
flippancy." Under Executive Order 10450 the doubt about him must
be resolved in favor of the government, though, Dulles admitted,
"standards are so high almost anyone could be tossed out." Realizing
that the admission invalidated Dulles's verdict, Ike replied, "This
does suggest questions on [the] Order—as to the possible injustness
of putting [the] burden of proof on [the] individual. At the same time
[we] cannot go all the way to the opposite. What about some intermediate procedure—[such as his] transfer to [a] non-sensitive position."
This was thought possible but nothing was done about it. Davies, with
a wife and three children to support, was dismissed, even though the
president explicitly recognized the "trouble a man has in getting a job
after [being] relieved [as a] security risk." Once again Ike's instincts
seemed sound—as might be expected in one who gloried in having
been raised on Wild Bill Hickok's code, which forbade shooting in
the back and secret character assassination. The president sympathized
with the anti-McCarthyites, appreciated that an injustice was being
done, and worried that "we are building up in public opinion an
image of a Star Chamber approach."[11] But he would not endanger his
prestige or his popularity by putting matters right. Nor, shockingly,
would President Kennedy, who admitted that Davies had suffered a
terrible injustice but said that it would have to wait for correction until
his second term.[12]

Ike also kept his head down as McCarthy engaged in his final, fatal
campaign, which was directed against the U.S. army, or at any rate
against the supposed Communists within its ranks. Thanks to the
"official" policy of "appeasement"[13] followed by Robert T. Stevens,
the amiable textile executive who was secretary of the army, McCarthy
had already been permitted to cause chaos at Fort Monmouth. At the

beginning of 1954 he unearthed the famous "Red Dentist," Dr. Irving Peress, who had been promoted to major despite having refused to answer questions about his membership in subversive organizations, and obviously posed a serious threat to the security of the Army's teeth. McCarthy went on the rampage. He interrogated Peress, who took the Fifth Amendment and was honorably discharged. He subpoenaed and insulted Peress's commanding officer, General Ralph Zwicker, telling him that he had "the brains of a five year old child," was "not fit to wear the uniform," and "should be removed from command." He threatened to kick Stevens's brains out for trying to protect Zwicker. And at a chicken lunch in the Senate building he maneuvered the hapless secretary into a humiliating form of cooperation, which included rescinding his order that the general should not testify again. The administration was apparently astonished by the response of the press, which almost universally condemned the surrender. James Reston called it "the worst deal since Yalta" and Stevens, who had been known as "Fighting Bob," was now nicknamed "Retreating Robert."[14]

In "a state of shock and near hysteria," Stevens came to Ike and offered to resign. The president refused to let him go, commenting mildly to General Lucius Clay that Stevens had "made an error in agreeing too quickly."[15] Ike said that he was not going to take the senator's onslaught lying down because "My friends tell me that it won't be long before McCarthy starts using my name instead of Stevens's." Lodge was one of these friends. He had informed Ike that the army investigation was "actually a part of an attempt to destroy you politically." Each cabinet member, he insisted, "should be urged once again to give top priority to getting his own department in shape so as to meet a McCarthy type investigation." Meanwhile the government should counterattack, using as a weapon the senator's attempts to press the army into giving favorable treatment to the newly drafted G. David Schine, the only private, it was said, whose morale was not in his boots. Despite all this, Hagerty did not have much confidence in Ike's willingness to stand up to McCarthy. He noted in his diary that "everyone" was "jittery" about the row and that the president "must take a stronger lead."[16]

Hagerty was right in the sense that Ike mounted only a temperate defense of Stevens and Zwicker, without condemning their assailant. At a press conference he asserted that nobody should be diverted from the nation's "grave problems—of which one is vigilance against any kind of internal subversion—through disregard of the standards of fair play recognized by the American people."[17] Journalists were astounded by Ike's weasel words and Joseph Alsop expostulated to a colleague under his breath, "Why, the yellow son of a bitch."[18] Indeed, Ike's coded rebuke and the outspoken riposte with which McCarthy at once greeted it received about the same amount of newspaper coverage, much of it unfavorable to the administration. It became a commonplace to say that the president and the senator were sharing command of the army and leadership of the GOP. Ike rightly scoffed at such nonsense, but he failed to scoff, except to his aides, at "what a silly business this screaming of the Armed Forces being full of Communists was."[19] Three days after the presidential press conference, on 6 March 1954, Lodge told Ike that he seemed to have "delegated political strategy to everyone in general and no one in particular," and he recommended the appointment of a special adviser who would deal with all "actions and decisions which involve your popularity, prestige and influence . . . to avoid repetitions of the Stevens incident." For, Lodge concluded in matter-of-fact tones, McCarthy had managed to engineer a confrontation not with Stevens but with Eisenhower himself, and had won a "major victory."[20]

That victory marked the high point of McCarthy's career. Within a few months the senator had accomplished his own ruin. He was destroyed by the very force which had made him—publicity. For his brutal tactics were exposed to the popular gaze on television during the "Army–McCarthy hearings," which took place in front of his own subcommittee. The subcommittee had now to investigate itself, specifically to consider the army's charge that McCarthy had tried to obtain preferential treatment for Schine by improper means. Thus the senator himself was virtually in the dock. Even so he tried to remain a judge in his own case, a move that was stopped when Ike publicly disapproved of it. But, though McCarthy was deprived of his vote, he dominated the subcommittee. The rotund Senator Mundt was nominally chairman but, torn between his McCarthyite sympathies and his need to appear impartial, he was said to resemble a "tormented mushroom."[21] McCarthy himself retained the right to subpoena and to cross-examine witnesses. It was this which really worried the president. For he was determined not to have himself or members of his official family dragged into the Roman circus which McCarthy was staging.

The first performance took place on 22 April. McCarthy began a systematic process of bullying, hectoring, and smearing—the obsequious Stevens being his prime target. Ike followed the hearings with the same fascination as did millions of other Americans—it was reported that the nation's housewives were neglecting their work because they were glued to their television sets. Like decent people everywhere, Ike, who had the advantage of regular inside briefings from Hagerty and Senator Charles Potter (who sat on the subcommittee), was revolted by the proceedings. He told Hazlett on 27 April, "The McCarthy–Army argument, and its reporting, are close to disgusting. It saddens me that I must feel ashamed of the United States Senate."[22] However, Ike had a compulsive need to detach himself from this gutter brawl and even attempted to persuade posterity that he knew nothing about it. In his private diary he wrote, "I have not followed the hearings either in the press or by television or radio."[23] When asked at a press conference on 29 April whether he had known that McCarthy had exerted pressure on the army over Schine, Ike responded, "I never heard of him. I never heard of him."[24] Amid incredulous laughter from the reporters, the president refused to answer further questions on the subject. In an atmosphere described as electric, he strode from the room, his face flushed, his eyes moist, and his jaw set.

Yet, paradoxically, Ike's very anxiety to remain uninvolved in the hearings helped to finish off McCarthy. The president was not at first averse to assisting the subcommittee. He even overruled a furious General Ridgway, the army's chief of staff, on 11 May, saying that the names of all involved in the Peress case should be released to avoid the appearance of a cover-up. Almost immediately, however, the army's counsel, John Adams, revealed to the subcommittee, and to an excited press, that the White House had played a part in the January decision to use Schine as a stick with which to beat McCarthy. Ike felt himself in danger of being sucked into the maelstrom.[25] At once Adams was ordered to say no more about the matter and, on 17 May, Ike invoked what later came to be called "executive privilege," the right to withhold information from the legislature on the ground that this was "essential to efficient and effective administration." The president stated that government employees must be able to give candid advice on official matters and that all details of their communications with the executive branch should therefore be kept confidential.

Political leaders advocating official secrecy in "the public interest" almost invariably do so to suit their private convenience. Ike was no exception. But he was able to disguise the fact convincingly, asserting that the suppression of information was designed "to preclude the exercise of arbitrary power by any branch of the Government," an obvious reference to the perils of a McCarthyite Senate.[26] Not until President Nixon attempted to use the same argument, during the Watergate scandal, was it widely appreciated that an imperial presidency might pose more serious dangers, and that the great American traditions of open government and freedom of information were in jeopardy. As Arthur Schlesinger, Jr., wrote in 1973, the extension of presidential privilege "represented a claim of boundless and unreviewable executive control of information in which the Whig Eisenhower outdid all his activist predecessors, including such renowned exponents of presidential power as Jackson, Lincoln and the two Roosevelts."[27] Ironically, however, Ike received nothing but praise from liberals at the time for denying McCarthy access to the raw facts which he devoured and distorted. By a further irony, Ike to some extent merited the praise, for what he wanted was not more power but less responsibility. With his street-fighter's eye for weakness, McCarthy sensed this, accusing the executive of having taken the Fifth Amendment. As it happened, the Fifth Amendment was the best form of defense. McCarthy's rant revealed his impotence in the face of it, and did Ike nothing but credit with the increasing number of Americans who were growing disillusioned with the senator.

These provocations caused Ike to fulminate in private. He compared McCarthy to Hitler, threatened "a finish fight"[28] with him, railed against Republican senators who lacked the guts to defend his administration, and complained to Engine Charlie Wilson that "McCarthy daily calls Stevens a perjurer and that Stevens just sits and takes it."[29] But the president still would not denounce the senator in public, and at a press conference on 19 May he categorically, and mendaciously, denied having approved the army's assault on McCarthy over the Schine affair. Furthermore, when, on 29 May, a demoralized Stevens asked if he could call the FBI's chief, J. Edgar Hoover, to the witness stand in his support, Ike replied that

he knew so little of [the] actual hearings, tried to keep the poison out of his system. He could not make a decision but . . . the Secretary of [the] Army should try to get in touch with Herb Brownell, failing him [his deputy] Bill Rogers, to see what their opinion might be. . . . [The] President suggested that Stevens take his family and go away for a vacation after this thing is over.[30]

This was a classic abdication of responsibility. There were even more astonishing instances of equivocation. For example, as late as August Ike actually defended McCarthy to a journalist. He acknowledged that the senator "is in many ways objectionable. But take a look at his voting record and he has got probably about as high a political record as anyone in the country."[31]

Yet if Ike's personal position was humiliatingly amorphous he did

manage to preserve a facade of dignity, and his aloofness paid handsome political dividends. For McCarthy, like Montgomery a decade
before, had been given enough rope to hang himself. There was a
national mood of revulsion against the senator. The mood was
strengthened in June, when McCarthy gratuitously blackened the
character of a lawyer in the firm of the opposing counsel. The counsel
was John Welch, who memorably condemned McCarthy for "cruelty
and recklessness," asking, "Have you no sense of decency, Sir, at long
last?"[32] Ike's Communist Control Act, a primitive measure passed in
August, which came so close to outlawing the Communist Party that
some believed it violated the constitution, at least had the merit of
making nonsense of McCarthy's accusations of "twenty-one years of
treason"—the final year indicating that under Ike's presidency the
Republicans were simply aping the Democrats. It also helped to restore confidence shattered by the Red scare, a boon to the many
purchased at the cost of injustice to a few. McCarthy was then ar-
raigned before a select committee of the Senate. This forbade him to
use his famous tactic of disruption—"A point of order, Mr. Chairman"—a prohibition that he described as "the most unheard-of thing
I ever heard of." The Senate concluded, in December, by censuring
him. To Ike's dismay only half the Republican senators voted for the
censure motion. Still, it killed McCarthy politically, it destroyed a
major source of domestic friction, and it ushered in a new era of
tranquillity. Soon Ike was being blamed for lacking charisma, excitement, inspiration, and for presiding complacently over a torpid America.

Such criticism was doubtless to be expected from the sort of "smart-
aleck columnist" whom Ike defined as "one who doesn't agree with
us."[33] But after the heady adventurism of Roosevelt and Truman most
Americans were content to have a dependable grandfather figure as
president. They wanted a respite after the strains of the Great Depression, the Second World War, and the Red scare period of the cold
war. As Samuel Lubell wrote, "Rarely in American history has the
craving for tranquility and moderation commanded more general
public support."[34] The 1950s, admittedly, has sometimes been called
an age of anxiety. But if so, it was an anxiety from which most men
and women seemed bent on escaping, whether in the church pew, or
on the psychiatrist's couch, or even slumped in front of the hypnotic
new medium of television clutching a bottle of tranquilizers (sales of
which boomed). People tried to forget worries about politics or nuclear war, and they focused instead on more manageable concerns
such as mortgage repayments and pension plans. The era was one of

crew-cut conformity, a period in which the suburbs expanded, the consumer revolution was the dominant feature of life, and fantasy was safely confined to unidentified flying objects and Disneyland, opened in 1955. It was a time of "togetherness," a term coined by *McCall's* magazine in 1954. Many more women were going out to work, it is true. But women's liberation from the old-fashioned stereotypes about their role had yet to occur. Indeed, Mamie Eisenhower, "feminine to the point of frivolity," was in many ways Mrs. Average America.[35]

Even the youth seemed reluctant to flout convention. As Lubell noted, "No collegians are swallowing goldfish, or eating phonograph records."[36] Sexual intercourse, as the British poet Philip Larkin poignantly observed, was not invented until 1963. In the fifties students went on panty raids or got married instead, and those who did violate sexual taboos suffered for it. Drug experiments and the chanting of mantras also lay in the future. Admittedly adolescence had come into its own and *Catcher in the Rye* was a campus cult. But the nearest teenagers came to revolt in 1954 was to listen to Bill Haley singing "Shake, Rattle and Roll." In the same year, too, the Beat Generation was born, but the measure of its iconoclasm can perhaps be found in the fact that Jack Kerouac liked Ike. Almost everyone liked Ike, who was a comforting symbol of the age and summed up its orthodox spirit by adding to banknotes the motto "In God We Trust."

The quiescence of the country was vividly exemplified in its attitude toward civil rights. Few exerted themselves to remove the injustices that disfigured American society. Instead the fuel for a future racial conflagration was simply allowed to accumulate. The kind of prejudice that existed in both government and nation was epitomized in the career of E. Fred Morrow. As the first black man to hold an executive position in the White House, Morrow was subjected to an appalling series of humiliations. His appointment was delayed. At the pre-inaugural religious service members of the National Presbyterian Church's congregation audibly complained of his presence, and Morrow was ignored by his colleagues who apparently did not want to have to introduce him to their wives. The secretaries and clerks at the White House threatened to walk out when he arrived. At official functions guests sometimes treated him like a servant. He could find nowhere suitable to live in Washington and the only place downtown where he could eat or get a drink of water was Union Station. He was exposed to crude racist jokes at work. He was "anathema" to Ike's Southern cronies and his presence in the White House, he remarked, almost gave George Allen "a nervous breakdown."

Ike responded to pressure from these Southern friends. He contravened his own custom by failing to attend Morrow's swearing-in, which did not occur until 1959. Morrow himself thought that the president, born in Texas and raised in Kansas, had a "little Southern touch himself." On the campaign train in 1952 Morrow asked Ike why he had vetoed racial integration in the army. The general reddened and inquired if Morrow's father, a minister, had taught him anything about forgiveness. "Yes, he did." "Well, that's where I am now." Ike explained that he had unwittingly taken the advice of staff officers with a "Southern exposure." But he would never forget the heroic self-sacrifice of black troops, despite their lack of training—some had not even held a rifle before—during the Battle of the Bulge. "They fought nobly for their country and I will never forget," Ike repeated. Morrow was inspired by this reply. "I had a relationship with this man that was, it was just a beautiful thing," he said, and it gave him the "inner strength" to work for Ike through all adversities.[37]

Nevertheless, the president's ambivalent attitude toward the race issue was profoundly troubling. Undoubtedly Ike saw himself as a liberal—which in the Southern context, of course, he was. In 1953 he moved to end the practice of racial segregation in the District of Columbia. And after Representative Adam Clayton Powell had publicly urged him to "assert your integrity" and cease "standing between two moral poles," the process was extended to the armed forces.[38] Behind the scenes Ike called on Southern politicians to follow his example, vainly pleading with men like Governor James Byrnes of South Carolina for "constructive advances."[39] The president even enlisted the evangelist Billy Graham, urging him to preach for "moderation and decency" in the field of race relations.[40] There is no doubt that these impulses were benevolent. Morrow went as far as to say that his reaction to the school integration crisis in Little Rock was "wonderful . . . fair, decent and honest."[41] The Washington *Post* praised Ike for "curbing racial discrimination" in public places, saying that this was "one of the strongest features" of his administration.[42] Nothing could have been finer than Ike's statement to Nixon on the race issue: "No man is discharging his duty if he does nothing in the presence of injustice . . ."—or at least nothing would have been finer than this if Ike had not added a characteristic rider: ". . . even though these matters might not be ones for punitive legislation."[43] There was the rub. At a deeper level in his complex psyche Ike shared many of the atavistic biases of his Southern friends. The president laughed at, and repeated, their jejune witticisms about "darkies." He hesitated to ask Dr. Ralph Bunche to dinner.[44] He thought it wrong that "a Negro should court my daughter."[45] And he told Earl Warren that the Southern segregationists "are not bad people. All they are concerned about is to see that their sweet little girls are not required to sit in school alongside some big overgrown Negroes."[46]

Warren was by this time chief justice of the Supreme Court. Ike had appointed him after Fred Vinson's death, in September 1953, as payment for his political support at the convention. Of course, the president denied this. When criticized for the appointment he defended Warren on the grounds that he was a reliable, moderate liberal-conservative and "we need statesmanship on the Supreme Court."[47] Actually Warren had demonstrated his capacity for immoderation during the war, when he had taken a leading part in hounding Japanese Americans out of California. But he proved to be an outstanding chief justice, something which Ike occasionally recognized, though he was more apt to lament that Warren's appointment was "the biggest damn fool thing I ever did."[48] This was after the Supreme Court had made its famous ruling, in May 1954, on the case of *Brown v. Topeka,* that racial segregation in education violated the Fourteenth Amendment. Ike had earlier told Brownell, half in jest, that he hoped the Supreme Court could defer its decision until it became the next administration's problem. He added seriously, "I don't know where I stand, but I think I stand that the best interests of the U.S. demand an answer in keep[ing] with past decisions."[49]

In other words Ike clung to the discredited doctrine, established by the *Plessy v. Ferguson* case in 1896, of "separate but equal" education. Nevertheless, Ike's ambivalence remained. He was privately shocked by the Supreme Court's decision, even though it was unanimous and supported by his own attorney general. But though he considered it wrong at the time, he wrote in his memoirs that he thought it was right. And though he firmly refused to endorse (or condemn) the decision, he announced that he would uphold the constitution. He also told his right-wing brother tartly, "I should like to point out that the meaning of the Constitution is what the Supreme Court says it is."[50] Fundamentally, however, Ike held to the passive view that only persuasion would win the hearts and change the minds of white Southerners. Legislation might achieve school integration, he said, at the cost of social disintegration. Federal compulsion would set back the course of progress, Ike told Byrnes. So although the president urged Billy Graham to preach favorably about the desegregation of certain schools, he cautioned, "Such approval on your part would not necessarily imply that the same thing could be done in all schools and without delay."[51] Ike exploited fully the Supreme Court's ambiguous guideline that desegregation should occur "with all deliberate speed." And he wished that the court had demanded integration even more gradually—first in graduate schools, later in colleges, and finally in public schools—"as a means of overcoming the passionate and inbred attitudes that [Southerners had] developed over generations."[52]

But if Ike showed himself delicately sensitive to white susceptibilities he was much less well attuned to those of blacks. In 1956, for example, the president said that he was "all for" a Negro getting a federal judgeship "but felt that St. Louis was a little too far 'South' to accept such an appointment at this time."[53] He manifested extreme reluctance to meet or address representatives of the black community. And when he did so, in June 1958, the president appalled them by abandoning Morrow's set speech and mouthing the most exhausted cliché he could find: "Now you people have to be patient."[54] But if blacks thought his words pharisaical, they considered his deeds pusillanimous. The president refused to interfere in a number of cases in which the Supreme Court's decision was blatantly flouted, as it was, for example, in 1955 when the University of Georgia would not enroll a black student named Autherine Lucy. Not until he was faced with a violent challenge to his authority, at Little Rock, did he intervene, and then only with the utmost reluctance. Morrow himself felt ridiculous trying to defend such a record, and some regarded the token black man in the White House as Ike's very own Uncle Tom.

It may be said in the president's defense that, in his attitude toward the thorny subject of civil rights, he was typical of his age and background; that he did as much as was politically advisable to improve matters; and that Adlai Stevenson, for example, was even more guilty than he was of what Adam Clayton Powell called "middle-of-the-road shilly-shalling, pussy-footing, double-talking"[55] on the question of desegregation. All this is true. As Fred Morrow said, although Ike was a "decent" man he was not "tough-minded" over the race issue and he could not "bring himself to come to grips" with it.[56] There was thus "no strong clarion, commanding voice from the White House, righteously indignant over the plight of the 18,000,000 Negroes in the United States."[57] So, to quote the verdict of a recent student of the subject, Eisenhower's civil rights policy was "paralyzed by over-caution, ineptitude and indecision."[58] Earl Warren, who could not forgive Ike's "wishy-washy" conduct,[59] believed that if such a popular president had condemned the discrimination which continued after the Supreme Court's decision "we would have been relieved . . . of many of the racial problems which have continued to plague us."[60] If the president is judged, as is proper, by the highest standards, there can be no doubt that he failed even to make a serious attempt to implement the noble words of the pledge: "One nation indivisible, with liberty and justice for all." The fact that the words "under God" were added to the pledge by his authority in 1954 made Ike's failure, if anything, more palpable and more culpable.

The president was more successful in dealing with the other major issue which tormented him during the early part of his administration —the Bricker Amendment. Ike was convinced that Senator Bricker was moved by a "psychopathic"[61] desire to write his name in the statute book. He thought it so dangerous to unbalance the Constitution by limiting the chief executive's treaty-making powers that everyone in favor of the amendment must have "lost all their brains."[62] He pronounced himself "unalterably opposed" to Bricker, for any compromise "would be notice to our friends as well as our enemies abroad that our country intends to withdraw from its leadership in world affairs."[63] In the event Ike did manage, by the narrowest possible margin, to prevent the adoption of Bricker's amendment, early in 1954. Assiduous lobbying played an important part in this. So did the astute manipulation of argument.

It was all too easy for those whose measure of brain power was articulacy of speech to conclude that Ike was stupid. Richard Rovere, for example, thought him "a fuzzy-minded man . . . [who] didn't have much grasp of ideas."[64] And after the censure, McCarthy went as far as to begin one speech, "If Eisenhower were alive. . . ."[65] Those who witnessed Ike's surprising preoccupation with accuracy over the written word were impressed, like Emmet Hughes, by his "penetrating sense of the structure of an argument and precise concern for the balance of a sentence, the tense of a verb, or the force of an adjective."[66] Hughes, who was prone to overwrite, doubtless protests too much. Yet there was an astonishing discrepancy between the military-bureaucratic gibberish Ike so often talked and the relatively clear, concise prose he could write. His clever and lucid memorandum demolishing Dulles's draft on the Bricker Amendment provides a good illustration of an intellectual capacity which Ike was so strangely loath to display.

At another place in your paper (page 17), there is the plain implication that, with a different kind of administration, it might be a good thing to adopt such a Resolution. If this is true, *then I am for the Resolution.* If we must have some amendment to protect our government and our people from what might happen to them under the treaty-making powers of a stupid President and a partisan Senate, then the mere fact that we believe there is no danger during the next four years is not a *good* argument. All through your paper, you make the point that there exist many kinds of influences in and out of government to maintain necessary balances and protect our people. You show that this has been our history through good administrations and bad administrations for one hundred and sixty years. Then suddenly your paper says, ". . . what might, under other circumstances, be a desirable Constitutional Amendment."

As a consequence of the point just made, there should not be too much emphasis on the contention that the current one is a *good* administration. Of course, we pray and believe that we are seeking what is good for all the people, that we are not merely working for personal aggrandizement, and that this administration is one of good will and intent. But the whole argument of your paper *should* be based on principle and on Constitutional wisdom, rather than on personal ability and wisdom of individuals.[67]

Dulles was sufficiently impressed by the president's dialectical skill to say that he could write his own briefs and needed no lawyer. Yet although Ike won his case he had been less stanch in his opposition than his rhetoric suggested. Bricker left one interview at the White House walking on air because he thought that the president had capitulated. In January 1954 Ike told Brownell, "I come closer and closer to believing in giving up trying to beat the Bricker Amendment."[68] And Dulles himself complained to Sherman Adams that if Ike did not "take the lead" more firmly against Bricker his views might be "ineffectual" and his administration suffer "a serious defeat." Adams apparently agreed, saying that Ike "was in an embarrassing position to be in possession of two letters—one from the Attorney General and one from me, both advising that this Amendment would throw serious doubt on the traditional treaty-making power and negotiating power of the President—and then do nothing about it. If this should ever come out, it would certainly be awkward."[69] However, although he continued to be harassed by the issue, not least because it demonstrated Republican lack of teamwork, Ike's opposition was enough to prevent the Constitution from being demolished (to quote a joke he liked to repeat) "brick by brick by Bricker."

For most of 1954 domestic matters, notably the Army–McCarthy struggle, monopolized the attention of America. But Ike himself was also concerned about what he took to be the advance of Communism on a global scale. The president was already being criticized in some quarters for the "loss" of North Korea. He well knew that if other countries succumbed to the Red embrace there would be a fierce

reaction at home, which would strengthen McCarthy's hand. But if the
United States conducted a successful crusade against Communism on
an international scale, the witch-hunt in the United States would probably die down. In short, Ike's purpose was to export McCarthyism.
However, having escaped from one bloody foreign entanglement he
was anxious to avoid another. What is more, the "New Look" defense
policy, which increased America's nuclear arsenal at the expense of
conventional arms in order to give "a bigger bang for the buck,"[70]
was ill-adapted for limited conflict. So if Ike were to fight Communism, but to avoid the ultimate catastrophe of a nuclear world war, he
had to rely on propaganda, diplomacy, saber rattling, and covert
action.

The last he applied with particular effectiveness in Guatemala,
where the CIA mounted a coup on the Iranian pattern to overthrow
Jacobo Arbenz's supposedly Communist government. In Ike's terms
the operation was a signal success. In the light of hindsight it is
possible to discern "a pattern of U.S. deceit and corruption toward
Guatemala that establishes the affair as one of the most sordid and
inane foreign 'security' operations in American history."[71]

Actually Arbenz was a Social Democrat, his government was
elected by a popular vote, and it operated under a liberal, Jeffersonian
constitution. Moreover, it was concerned with the well-being of its
people, which unfortunately brought it into conflict with the American United Fruit Company (UFCO). Wanting to improve the economy and feed an industrial workforce by growing staple foods instead
of export crops, Arbenz nationalized vast tracts of UFCO's uncul-
tivated land, paying compensation. He aimed, it has been said, at a
"green revolution," not a Red one.[72] UFCO, a rapacious, racist giant
of the robber-baron era, and almost a state within the state of
Guatemala, was determined that the country should remain, quite
literally, a banana republic. The company was known in Guatemala as
"El Pulpo," "the Octopus that strangled all it touched,"[73] and its
tentacles extended into the highest echelons of Ike's administration.
Both the Dulles brothers, Bedell Smith, Robert Cutler, Lodge, and
several others had such "close relations" with the company that Foster
Dulles evidently found it embarrassing.[74] Ed Whitman, husband of
Ike's devoted secretary Ann, was actually head of UFCO's public
relations department, and he asserted (in a distant echo of Charlie
Wilson's remark about General Motors), "Whenever you read
'United Fruit' in Communist propaganda, you may readily substitute
United States."[75] UFCO spent millions of dollars employing
McCarthyite lobbyists to persuade the American government to inter-

vene in Guatemala. As the historian Richard Immerman has noted,
Ike's administration relied on "McCarthy-like techniques" to impute
Communism to the Guatemalan government, and "the most widely
cited indications of Communist penetration were the hardships encountered by the United Fruit Company." Ambassador John E. Peuri-
foy might have taken lessons in assessing evidence from McCarthy.
He testified to the House of Representatives that Arbenz "talked like
a Communist, and if he is not one, Mr. Chairman, he will do until one
comes along."[76]

Ike needed no convincing and he was directly responsible for the
operation which toppled Arbenz's regime. It was given special top-
secret classification, but by January 1954 Guatemala broadcast evidence of the plot and the State Department was obliged to issue an
official denial. "The charge is ridiculous and untrue. It is the policy
of the United States not to intervene in the internal affairs of other
nations."[77] Actually, the CIA was employing a remarkable range of
"dirty tricks" against Guatemala. It placed anonymous articles in Chilean newspapers naming Guatemalan officials as Communists and then
reprinted them elsewhere with a Chilean attribution. It blackened
Arbenz's character, taking full advantage of its connections with the
American press, which failed to subject the Guatemalan episode to
thorough investigation. It parachuted Russian-made arms into
Guatemala in order to be able to claim that the Soviet Union was
supplying Arbenz. It tried to undermine the loyalty of the Church, the
army, and, by means of virulent propaganda, the people of
Guatemala. It decided against assassinating Arbenz but did attempt to
bribe him, without success. It also organized a tiny "army" of
Guatemalan mercenaries, led by a puppet called Castillo Armas and
supported by the neighboring dictators in Nicaragua and Honduras.
When Arbenz tried to arm a peasant militia with a shipload of Czech
weapons, Ike isolated Guatemala diplomatically and ordered that the
coup should proceed.

He also imposed a unilateral naval blockade on Guatemala, an
action that contravened the American tradition of freedom of the seas
and outraged international opinion. Britain and France, who had not
been consulted, were particularly upset. To Ike's horror and rage,
they proposed to support Guatemala's appeal to the United Nations.
This would have meant one of two things: either the United States
would be forced to take the damaging and unprecedented step of
using its veto; or U.N. peace-keeping units might be appointed, which
would reveal the fact that American aircraft were being used to ensure

Arbenz's downfall. Luckily for Ike he was able to prevail on his colonialist allies to abstain, threatening that "if they take [an] independent line backing the Guatemalan move . . . we would feel entirely free" to oppose them in Egypt, Cyprus, Algeria, and so on.[78] Arbenz was so demoralized by further CIA subversion and by the obvious American determination to oust him that at the end of June he resigned. Armas was installed at the head of a brutal dictatorship which took away the rights, and in some cases the lives and property, of the people, and gave back the land to United Fruit. Within a year Vice-President Nixon was telling the Cabinet that Armas was a "good middle-roader" with "overwhelming popular support." That this was an idiosyncratic view may best be indicated from Nixon's further observation that Somoza's repressive rule in Nicaragua was "encouraging" and that although families lived in caves only a hundred yards from his palace, which was more luxurious than the White House, the president of Mexico had "a real feeling for his people."[79]

Ike's fear was that precisely because of the gross disparity between rich and poor, Latin America was ripe for Communist infiltration. He also took seriously the warnings of his brother Milton, who (to Dulles's annoyance) became chief presidential adviser on South America and asserted that "What is now [the] back door may become [the] front door."[80] It is true that Ike himself knew little about Guatemala: its ambassador was struck by his "frightening ingenuousness" and his refusal to believe in the "exaggerated privileges" which UFCO enjoyed.[81] But abroad, as at home, Ike was so haunted by the specter of Communism that he felt bound to exorcise it wherever it was said to appear and by whatever means were most convenient. He appreciated that "intervention in Central America and Caribbean affairs earlier in the century had greatly injured our standing in all Latin America."[82] He also recognized that if the United States pursued policies inimical to nationalist aspirations "we will almost certainly arouse more antagonism" and the "possibility of these countries turning Communist would mount rapidly."[83] But he did not conclude from this that a generous, open, sustained "Good Neighbor Policy" would encourage the countries of the southern hemisphere to accept the Monroe Doctrine and shun Communism. Instead he determined on a policy of clandestine coercion, with the CIA as his chosen instrument.

Nor had he any doubt that he was on the side of the angels. He could, and frequently did, congratulate himself on the immediate outcome of his Guatemalan operation. Indeed, he was so pleased with

it that soon afterward he held a White House briefing attended not
only by cabinet members and staff but also, to Allen Dulles's dismay,
by Mamie.

His intervention had disastrous long-term effects. It inspired future
American presidents to pursue hidden and sometimes iniquitous policies abroad, from which Congress was excluded and press and people
were kept in ignorance or deceived. It frustrated moderate improve-
ments in Guatemala, condemning that country to the rule of a succession of military juntas who wrecked its economy and violated human
rights on a scale seldom rivaled elsewhere. It did not quell, as much
as foster, Communism elsewhere in Latin America, for, as President
Kennedy said, "Those who make peaceful change impossible make
violent change inevitable."[84] Indeed, it fueled the fires of mistrust and
resentment toward "Yankee imperialism" which burn brightly in
Nicaragua today. It also encouraged the use of an absurdly overconfi-
dent CIA while, as Richard Immerman has shown, warning prospective victims what to expect—hence the Bay of Pigs fiasco. Worst of
all, Ike's Guatemalan coup d'état strengthened the basic premise of
the cold war, namely that the world was divided into two hostile
political camps and that there was no prospect of compromise, neutrality, or peaceful coexistence.

This view seemed to be confirmed in the Far East, where, by the
spring of 1954, French colonial forces were facing defeat at the hands
of Vietnamese guerrillas led by Ho Chi Minh. This was a war of
national independence and Ho's Vietminh army took supplies—
though not orders, as even the State Department had to admit—from
Moscow and Peking.[85] However, like most Americans, Ike was convinced that "the struggle against Communistic dictatorship is a global
one" and that the conflict in Indochina was merely "a phase and part
of the whole."[86] It was a very important part, for his administration
regarded Vietnam as "the keystone of the arch of South East Asia,"[87]
the removal of which, to mix contemporary metaphors, would topple
its neighbors like a row of dominoes. If "we should lose South East
Asia," Ike exclaimed, it would be "a calamity of the most terrible
immediate and eventual consequences."[88] Accordingly, the United
States was giving France almost every assistance short of formal participation.

It was financing some three-quarters of the French war effort and
supplying huge amounts of equipment. The government in Paris "acknowledged that U.S. aid in many areas exceeded French capacity to
absorb it,"[89] and in February 1954 Ike was persuaded to send in not
only more bombers but two hundred American technicians, the first

American servicemen to go to Vietnam. Even so the French continued to lose the war. The best evidence for this was that by March their garrison in the jungle fortress of Dien Bien Phu was cut off and threatened with annihilation. The French high command had neglected the fiendish military potential of the bicycle, by which the besieging Vietminh forces kept themselves supplied against all the odds. Throughout the whole thirty-year war the Western powers consistently underestimated their Vietnamese opponents, no doubt partly as a result of the racial arrogance which Ike himself shared— he thought them a "backward people."[90]

When the French appealed for more assistance toward the end of March, Ike was caught on the horns of several dilemmas. He wanted to help decisively, both to prevent Indochina from going Communist and to convince France that Communism was the enemy not only in the East but in the West—where Gallic fears of a rearmed Germany wrecked Ike's cherished plan for a European Defense Community in August 1954. However, he was anxious not to be tarred with the imperialist brush, telling Al Gruenther that for three years he had been "trying to convince the French that they could *not* win the Indo-China war and particularly could not get real American support in that region unless they would unequivocally pledge independence to the Associated States [Vietnam, Cambodia, and Laos] upon the achievement of military victory."[91] In making such a plea Ike was the victim of two fallacies: first, that the French were fighting not for colonial spoils but to keep Southeast Asia safe for democracy; and second, that it was possible to give the Indochinese the right of self-determination while somehow depriving them of the freedom to embrace Communism. Anyway, the French were uncooperative, Ike found, to the point of decadence. Sometimes he wished for the recall of General de Gaulle[92] (who did have the courage to pull out of Algeria). However, Ike informed Gruenther that the "inspirational leader" he had in mind for France was not one "6 feet 5 . . . who considers himself to be, by some miraculous biological and transmigrative process, the offspring of Clemenceau and Jeanne d'Arc"[93]— a crack which he plagiarized from Roosevelt. To confuse matters still further: when Vietnamese nationalists pressed too hard for immediate French withdrawal early in 1954, it turned out that Ike did not want this after all, fearing that it would lead to a Vietminh victory. One American diplomat in Saigon commented wryly, "We are the last French colonists in Indochina."[94]

Finally, Ike could not decide how to help the French. The army chief of staff, General Ridgway, confirmed his own view that sending

American troops after guerrillas in the tropical jungle would be, to quote Churchill's analogy, like going into the water to fight a shark.[95] Nor was there any possibility of partial intervention in Vietnam, of using, say, air or naval units only. As Admiral A. C. Davis pointed out: "One cannot go over Niagara Falls in a barrel only slightly."[96] So Ike rejected the course proposed by the chairman of the joint chiefs of staff, Admiral Radford, who favored a tactical nuclear strike against the forces surrounding Dien Bien Phu; but the main reason for Ike's refusal to mount a massive air attack was apparently not military but political. He could get no support from Congress or from his closest allies. United action was essential because, as Ike liked to say, "without allies or associates the leader is just an adventurer like Genghis Khan."[97]

The president was particularly cross with the intractable British, telling Dulles that they "must not be able merely to shut their eyes and later plead blindness as an alibi for failing to propose a program."[98] But the program of allied intervention, eloquently proposed by Ike, appalled Churchill. The British foreign secretary, Sir Anthony Eden, informed Dulles he had "grave doubts" that "Britain would cooperate in any active fighting to save Indo-China." He also "expressed fear that United States intervention might initiate World War III."[99] And, as Churchill told Ike when they met in June and the prime minister vainly tried to commit the president to holding a summit conference with the Russians, "I am sure you will not overlook the fact that by the Anglo-American [air] base in East Anglia we have made ourselves for the next year or two the nearest and perhaps the only bull's eye of the target."[100] Dulles found the British attitude "most disheartening." Yet, paradoxically, he was by no means clear about his own attitude. He concluded that armed intervention was not warranted because "it would seem to involve us very deeply on an unsound basis."[101] But he denuded the Dulles household of pencils because he chewed up so many in the agonizing process of veering from hawk to dove.

Ike's own attitude was, if possible, even more vacillating, so much so that it confused friends and foes at the time and historians subsequently. A recent study maintains that the maneuvering of his administration on the Indochinese issue between March and July 1954 "can be characterized either as egregious bumbling saved only by the unwillingness of allies to participate and the restraint of enemies or as a dazzling display of neutralizing potential domestic opposition and of deterring hostile states bent on total victory."[102] Ike's defenders interpret his various shifts and inconsistencies as part of a deliberate plan to keep the Communists guessing, to stop the French from capitulating at the five-power conference convened at Geneva (April–July 1954), to resolve Far Eastern problems, and to protect himself from attack by the old guard, while at the same time preventing the United States from being drawn into the Vietnamese quicksand. There is something in this, no doubt.

However, Ike frequently contradicted himself in private, when there was no need for duplicity—quite the reverse. He seemed at once to be furious with the British for preventing armed intervention and pleased that they gave him an excuse to keep American forces out of Vietnam. It has been claimed recently that Ike deliberately placed impossible conditions on American involvement in Vietnam with the aim of blocking it.[103] But if, say, his oft-repeated plea for united action really had been a disingenuous maneuver, designed perhaps to exonerate him at home from the charge of appeasement, it seems incredible that Ike should have persisted with it to the point of seriously damaging relations with his closest ally.[104] On the other hand, if he genuinely wanted to forge a coalition to defeat Communism in Vietnam he was evidently willing to risk a world war. Ike's policy bore every sign of being extemporized from day to day, sometimes from hour to hour. It is arguable that in their eagerness to make sense of his changes tidy-minded scholars impose an entirely artificial coherence on a policy that was at best inconsistent and at worst a muddle.

Take the question of employing nuclear weapons, for example. Ike could quite casually mention that they might have to drop tactical atomic bombs around Dien Bien Phu, adding, "of course, if we did, we'd have to deny it forever."[105] He approved a recommendation by the joint chiefs of staff which called for "employing atomic weapons wherever advantageous . . . against . . . military targets in China."[106] The president was even capable of raising the possibility, during a National Security Council meeting on 29 April, of whether, instead of intervening unilaterally in Indochina,

the right decision was not rather to launch a world war. If our allies were going to fall away in any case it might be better for the United States to leap over the smaller obstacles and hit the biggest one with all the power we had. Otherwise we seemed merely to be playing the enemy's game—getting ourselves involved in brushfire wars in Burma, Afghanistan, and God knows where.[107]

Yet it was Ike's most cherished axiom that there would be no victors in a nuclear war and there was thus "no longer any alternative to peace."[108] What is more, the day after the NSC meeting, when Robert Cutler brought Ike a paper exploring the possibilities of using atomic weapons in Vietnam, the president declared (so he later claimed): "You boys must be crazy. We can't use those awful things against Asians for the second time in less than ten years. My God."[109]

Still, the result was more important than the method. Perhaps more by improvisation than by sound judgment, Ike did manage to keep the United States out of the Vietnam War—no small achievement. The president's perennial optimism was not even dashed when Dien Bien Phu surrendered on 8 May. As late as 26 April he had told Gruenther that the fortress "*can* hold out" if adequately supplied,[110] though on the same day, in a characteristic counterpoint, he assured Hagerty and others that it would probably fall within a week. However, as the French foreign minister, Georges Bidault, told Dulles, his country regarded the event as one of "tremendous symbolic importance."[111] Accordingly, France reached a settlement with the Vietminh at Geneva. This provided for a cease-fire, a temporary partition along the 17th parallel, and the holding of elections, scheduled for 1956, in which North and South Vietnam would be reunited. It was at this point that Ike and Dulles missed a momentous opportunity—to disengage the United States from Vietnam for good. Unfortunately, they were stultified by fears that the Republican old guard and McCarthy would accuse them of having perpetrated another Yalta. So they rejected a diplomatic solution and refused to allow the Geneva accords to become a full-scale treaty with multilateral guarantees. Dulles, in particular, was nervous about even seeming to appease the Communists. Before the first session at Geneva he announced that the only way he could possibly meet Chou En-lai was if their cars collided, and when an attempt was made to introduce them Dulles turned his back.

Ike turned his back on the Geneva settlement, which he regarded as a disastrous concession to Communism. He would not be bound by it, though the United States did agree not to upset the accords by force and to support the 1956 elections, to be supervised by the United Nations, which would unify Vietnam. Ike broke both promises. Even before agreement had been reached at Geneva, CIA teams were doing their best to sabotage North Vietnam by methods which ranged from pouring destructive contaminant into the engines of Hanoi buses to printing astrological almanacs full of dire predictions for Ho Chi Minh's regime and good omens for the new government in the south led by Ngo Dinh Diem. Ike was soon elbowing aside France (which had granted Vietnam full independence in the summer of 1954 but still hoped to retain influence in Indochina) in order to prop up Diem, not only with massive financial help but with military aid, in violation of the Geneva accords.

Meanwhile, Dulles organized a new defensive pact against Communism, the South East Asia Treaty Organization (SEATO). This was a factitious association which only included one member state from Southeast Asia—Thailand—the others being Pakistan, the Philippines, Australia, New Zealand, Britain, and the United States. Moreover, while it was supposed to deter aggression, SEATO increased the chances of creating the kind of war coalition which might involve the United States. Finally, Ike's support enabled Diem to refuse even to discuss the elections in 1956. The stated reason was that they could not be held freely; but, with candor amounting to naïveté, Ike admitted in his memoirs that if they had taken place in 1954 "possibly 80 per cent of the population would have voted for the Communist Ho Chi Minh as their leader."[112] There was an embarrassing similarity between Ike's rejection of democratic procedures when they threatened to get Communists elected and the Kremlin leaders' acceptance of democratic procedures as long as only Communist candidates were allowed to stand.

Still, Ike's luck held. Almost until he left the presidency Ho Chi Minh was preoccupied with assimilating North Vietnam and it took some time for Diem's corrupt and oppressive government to provoke violent opposition in the south. But as the historian George Herring has written, only "the quirks of the electoral calendar spared Eisenhower from facing the ultimate failure of his policies in Vietnam."[113] The neocolonial state of South Vietnam was virtually Ike's creation, and the attempt to sustain it, in the absence of solid indigenous support, was soon to draw the United States into a tragic morass—the longest war in America's history. Whether the cautious Ike would have allowed this to happen remains an open question. But it is interesting to note that the sort of domestic calculations which had helped to make Ike such a stanch cold warrior were still being heard in the White House as late as 1963. In that year President Kennedy said, "If I tried to pull out [of Vietnam] completely now, we could have another Joe McCarthy scare on our hands."[114] So Ike must be given full credit for keeping the peace in the 1950s. He must also bear some responsibility for sowing the seeds of the war in the 1960s.

Americans were naturally concerned with the present. Although by the autumn of 1954 Ike had suffered a couple of setbacks abroad, over the failure of the European Defense Community and the "loss" of North Vietnam, his stock at home was high. Germany and Italy were soon brought into NATO, thus nullifying the EDC disappointment—

in any case few had set such store by it as Ike, who thought a completed EDC would be "the greatest thing since Charlemagne."[115]
And most people were so pleased that the United States had not
become embroiled in another Korea that the defection of a far country, of which they knew little, scarcely mattered. Admittedly members
of the old guard were indignant. The president was harried by his
right-wing brother, Edgar, though, as Ike chided, he had no reason
"to make the bland assumption that I am surrounded by a group of
Machiavellian characters who are seeking the downfall of the United
States and the ascendancy of socialism and communism in the
world."[116] The president was also worried about Senator Knowland,
whose idea of foreign policy, said Ike, was to develop high blood
pressure at the mention of China. Ike feared that Knowland might
advocate a preventive war after the Red Chinese started bombarding
the offshore islands (occupied by Chiang's forces) of Quemoy and
Matsu in September. The president spent a great deal of time trying
to persuade the senator that the Republicans must "make bipartisan-
ship work" in foreign affairs.[117]

In domestic matters Ike could point to quite a satisfactory record.
The economy was recovering. Unemployment fell as productivity
rose. The St. Lawrence Seaway was approved, a project about which
he had initially been dubious but which he later hailed as "a historic
victory."[118] The budget was reduced, and there had been tax reforms
and tax cuts. Two billion dollars was voted for the highway program.
Modest advances in housing and social security had occurred. And
where there had been defeats—over health care, farm prices, and
attempts to improve the Taft–Hartley Act—people blamed diehard
Republicans, not the Republican president. All told, Ike had a wonderful knack of associating himself with the administration's successes
and detaching himself from its failures. The columnist Fletcher Kne-
bel astutely quipped: "Half the people think this is a good Administration. The other half think it is terrible and are proud of Ike for not
being mixed up in it."[119]

Needless to say, as the midterm Congressional elections approached the Republicans were eager that the president should impart
some of his popularity to them. Senior members of the GOP, such as
Dewey, put pressure on him to "campaign on an intensive basis." At
first Ike refused, having long contended that he must be seen as
president of all the people. In any case a president could not get a
party elected, he argued. And he was sixty-four. A few television
appearances, during which he would discuss major issues in a nonpar-
tisan fashion, would be more effective and more dignified. "Nothing

that Mr. Truman did," he concluded piously, "so shocked my sense of the fitting and the appropriate as did his barnstorming activities while he was actually President of the United States."[120] True to form, however, Ike changed his mind. He might pretend to be above party politics but he was completely committed to a Republican victory in what looked to be a close contest. So he did his best to stimulate the economy in time for the elections and he "conducted a coast-to-coast off-year campaign unprecedented in the Presidency," traveling ten thousand miles and delivering nearly forty speeches.[121] He also urged members of his team to play their part, telling them that somebody had to do the hard-hitting in-fighting and he did not object to this as long as no one expected him to do it.[122]

The president might have done better to restrain his colleagues. Nixon actually felt it unnatural to conduct a decorous political campaign, and some of his speeches were distinctly McCarthyite in character. Ike was quite aware of this, having in June chided Nixon for his "castigation of Democrats" when the government was trying to get support for its foreign policy "on a bi-partisan basis."[123] But the president complimented Nixon publicly for his energetic campaigning while privately saying that the vice-president occasionally interpreted him in "colorful language."[124] Similarly, Charles Wilson felt free to make one of his notorious gaffes during the election. He compared unemployed automobile workers to "kennel-fed dogs," as opposed to "bird dogs," and said that he preferred the latter: "You know, one who'll get out and hunt for food rather than sit on his fanny and yell."[125] Given all these conflicting opinions, Adlai Stevenson found it a simple matter to accuse the GOP, "caught between contradiction, apathy and McCarthy," of "having as many wings as a boarding-house chicken."[126] And the more Ike tried to present Republicanism as "dynamic conservatism," or "progressive moderation," or "positive progressivism"[127] (to cite a few of the phrases be favored), the more he drew attention to the extremist elements in the GOP, led by his own vice-president, who conformed to no such formulas. In protecting himself Ike exposed his party. The Republicans lost control of Congress by two seats in the Senate and twenty-nine in the House. The Democrats won by attacking the Republicans but not the president, just as the English opposition had once attacked the monarch's "evil counsellors" but never the sacred person of the sovereign. Speaker Sam Rayburn had pioneered the process in 1952. When he was lambasting the GOP in Texas a heckler asked if Ike had not been born in the Lone Star State. "Yes," replied Rayburn generously, "and he was a wonderful baby."[128]

Actually, Ike found it easier to work with Southern Democrats like Rayburn and the new Senate majority leader, Lyndon B. Johnson (despite mutual feelings of contempt and distrust, well camouflaged by an effusive show of cordiality), than with the old guard. This circumstance aggravated the recriminations which followed the Republican defeat. The GOP's right wing blamed it on Ike, saying that he had abandoned the party's principles. He claimed that the defeats would have been worse if he had not campaigned and in turn accused the old guard of blighting his hope of creating a modern Republican party. Not for the first time, or the last, he toyed with the idea of founding a new party of the center, one which would appeal to the majority of people in America who were middle-class and believed in common sense. He even tried to find a name for it, without success. Later, of course, he denied all this. But, nettled by the criticism, he railed against the obscurantists on his own side: "far from appeasing and reasoning with the dyed-in-the-wool reactionary fringe, we should completely ignore it and when necessary repudiate it."[129] He threatened, "If the right wing wants a fight they're going to get it."[130]

In practice, of course, Ike tried to avoid anything of the kind. He even seemed put out when Hagerty released the news that he had congratulated Arthur Watkins, chairman of the Senate committee which recommended McCarthy's censure, on having done a superb job—though he was apparently "not at all displeased" by the resulting publicity.[131] Moreover, just after the Senate did censure McCarthy, as Ike was completing his second year in the White House, the president revealed that he was as keen as ever to dissociate himself from controversy that was likely to anger the old guard.

At the end of 1954 Ezra Benson summarily dismissed Wolf Ladejinsky from his post in the Department of Agriculture, on the grounds that he was a security risk. This provoked an outcry because the distinguished land-reform expert was firmly anti-Communist and had already been cleared by the most obsessive Red hunter in America, none other than Scott McLeod of the State Department. The flagrant injustice done to Ladejinsky was pointed up by the fact that within a couple of weeks he was cleared again, this time by Harold Stassen, who gave him a job in the Foreign Operations Administration. Ike had originally heard what he admitted to be a brief and partial statement of the case from Benson. The president then promised to "back" the secretary "all the way" and assured him that there would be "no backing down." But Ike quickly backed away from the whole issue when the uproar occurred and it became clear that Ladejinsky was only a security risk in the fevered imagination of Benson.

Hagerty declared that the president had "no involvement" in the case.[132] At a press conference Ike confirmed that he condemned no one and supported both Benson and Stassen "in their right to make different judgements."[133] Even in private Ike refused to exert his authority, remarking plaintively to Hagerty, "Benson could end this once and for all by saying he was mistaken, but he is a stubborn man and I don't suppose we can get him to do that."[134] A recent study of the Ladejinsky affair contends that it showed Ike to be a "shrewd political leader."[135] Almost all the evidence cited by its author militates against her interpretation, which reveals more about historiography than history, more about the revisionist fashion in Eisenhower scholarship than the truth of a fiasco so blatant that even newspapers which normally endorsed Ike's government were moved to condemn it. Indeed, a two-party Senate investigation into the matter concluded that the security program was not doing enough to safeguard the rights of individuals. As usual, Ike, with his infallible instinct for self-preservation, had pursued what seemed (amid much fudging of the issue) to be a moderate course. He had bent over backward to defend Benson in order not to antagonize the old guard. But he had conceded just enough to mollify the liberal opinion which was becoming more vocal as the Red scare receded.

A president who could retain considerable dignity and immense popularity, while his administration floundered in a quagmire partly of his own making, was no mean politician. A president who could conjure peace, prosperity, and tranquillity out of brinkmanship abroad and detachment at home attracted not just admiration but adoration. Ike's popularity was, indeed, as James Reston wrote soon after, "a national phenomenon, like baseball." The president was the focus of "a national love affair, which cannot be analyzed satisfactorily by the political scientists and will probably have to be turned over to the head-shrinkers."[136] Naturally the Republicans hoped that this fine political romance would be consummated at the polls in 1956. But they were now less inclined than they had been in 1952 to infuriate Ike by talking about exploiting his name and fame while implying that he hadn't a brain in his head.

By the time he was halfway through his first term, plans were well in hand to ensure that he would serve a second term. Ike was adamant that nothing would induce him to be a candidate. He suggested that his brother Milton should call in a psychiatrist if he even considered it. To Swede Hazlett Ike stated flatly, "I shall never again be a candidate for anything. This determination is a fixed decision."[137] But to Jim Hagerty Ike had confessed in July 1954, "I kind of think that the answer will be that I will run for another term."[138] And when, at the end of 1954, Lucius Clay proposed to work for his reelection, the president, after rehearsing all the reasons against running again, permitted him to do so.

15

★

Much Better, Thanks

On Ike's huge uncluttered desk in the Oval Office stood a small, black piece of wood bearing the Latin inscription, "Suaviter in modo fortiter in re." It meant, "Gently in manner, firmly in deed," and it proved, as the president jestingly informed an inquirer, that he was after all an egghead. With his tigerish rages and his chameleon changeability, Ike did not live up to either part of this motto, certainly not in the way of Truman, who had proved that "The buck stops here." Nevertheless, Ike managed to convey the spirit of his Latin tag. He exuded confidence and optimism. His serene bearing contributed signally to easing the atmosphere of tension generated by the Red scare. Having been coached by the actor-producer Robert Montgomery, Ike was supremely relaxed as a television performer, so much so that he was quite willing to go on the air without rehearsal, though he once remarked blithely that he would probably die of fright. Usually, though, his public appearances were carefully stage-managed, and he resented it when the press revealed details of the elaborate behind-the-scenes machinery which sustained them. Still, the combination of his naturalness and the professionalism of his advisers was highly effective. The president projected an image of benign self-assurance which was all the more convincing because it pretty well reflected the truth.

The White House staff who knew him best were unanimous in admiring his composure under stress. Arthur Larson was particularly impressed by the deliberate way in which the president took the only time he could find in his crowded day, their speech-writing conferences, to manicure his fingernails—his hands were so large that he employed a paper knife and a foot-long pair of desk shears. Ike was not even flustered by the importunate behavior of some of his guests.

When the British ambassador specially requested that Churchill should be provided with his usual midday feast one Sunday during his visit in June 1954, Ike responded to Dulles, "I suppose we have enough food in the White House to give Churchill his huge luncheon, but I'll be damned if I'm going to change my habits for the Prime Minister—I'll have a light luncheon."[1]

It has been said, of course, that Ike assuaged the febrile temper of the time not just by being unruffled but by being positively torpid. He certainly gave the impression, because of his unabashed need for recreation and vacations, of taking life easy. In some respects he did. Ike was waited on hand and foot and received the best service in the world. His valet even helped him to step into his undershorts. He only had to pick up the telephone to get instant attention—after he left the presidency, like some latter-day Rip van Winkle, he did not know how to dial a number. He was surrounded by every convenience and many luxuries. Anthony Eden was amazed, for example, by the "remarkable comfort" and silence of the presidential airplane, the Columbine, which made it possible for him and his staff to make long journeys and to arrive "fresher than when they left."[2] Ike's friends entertained him with a lavishness that was all the more marked for being inconspicuous —Sid Richardson was an exception to the rule of inconspicuousness, and Ike thought it "not smart" of him to complain, "It's getting to be terrible when a man can't lose ten million dollars without causing a lot of fuss and talk."[3]

Ike himself, though he warned his colleagues never to speak disrespectfully of a billion dollars, was the reverse of ostentatious about his comforts. He put the presidential yacht into mothballs as an economy measure and rechristened Shangri-la (Roosevelt's mountain hideaway) Camp David, a less pretentious name and that of his father and grandson. Ike did, to be sure, "let Mamie go hog-wild" over the rebuilding of their Gettysburg farm, a costly and somewhat inefficient undertaking. But he thought she "probably would have a nervous breakdown" without the opportunity to make them a permanent home.[4] Actually, of course, it was impossible not to work hard at Ike's job, and he needed all the help he could get not to exhaust himself. But the fact that he seemed able to relax and enjoy himself as president helped to assuage anxieties about McCarthyism and the cold war. Others followed his example: the sale of playing cards increased apace and golf boomed as a sport. People swapped unworried jokes about the president's addiction to the game. A favorite quip concerned his request to drive through the four ahead: he was in a hurry because New York had just been bombed.

It is possible to reject the argument that Ike deliberately employed Fabian tactics in order to defeat McCarthy without fighting him, while accepting the view that the president did contribute to the senator's downfall by establishing a reign of decency in Washington. Ike certainly paid elaborate homage to the proprieties. In private, or in a fury, he might occasionally curse like a trooper. But all expletives were deleted in anything approaching a formal situation, and Ike never went in for the crude conversational gambits of, say, his three immediate successors in the presidency. He never told obscene stories, preferring instead the crackerbarrel maxims which he repeated endlessly: "Take your job seriously but not yourself," "Never miss too many opportunities to keep your mouth shut," "Don't make any mistakes in a hurry."[5] And if anyone else overstepped Ike's puritanical mark he could be withering. Early in 1955 at a meeting of senior political figures in the White House, Senator Alexander Wiley made a flippant remark: "the public be damned." Ike was livid. The skin on the back of his neck reddened and, as Bernard Shanley recorded, "the President, with a look in his eye that I would hate to have him ever look at me with, said, 'Senator, don't you ever use that language in this office.' Everybody just kind of froze—even way off in the back of the room, I almost fell off my chair. I think Senator Wiley will next time be a little more circumspect."[6]

There was doubtless an element of stuffy sanctimoniousness in Ike's White House, though this was sometimes leavened with a refreshing dash of humor, often provided by the president's first appointment secretary, Tom Stephens. He was irreverent enough to guy even the current obsession with security, once typing on the top of an interoffice memorandum, "Please destroy before reading."[7] Ike himself was a victim of the obsession and went as far as to protect himself by secretly recording the conversations that took place in the Oval Office. He was not the first or, of course, the last president to do so; nor was he, like Nixon, a systematic self-bugger. Still, bugging and wiretapping were unsavory practices, and Ike's justification for them was unsatisfactory. He told one of his staff that he had no objection to monitoring telephone calls when the person at the other end of the line knew it, adding inconsistently, "I did it for years with people I didn't trust."[8] However, Ike's capacity for unscrupulous action was carefully concealed and no one beat the big bass drum of morality in political life with more vigor. Sophisticated commentators like Joseph Alsop might complain that the president "uttered every noble cliché in the modern statesman's yearbook."[9] Those who knew Ike better were convinced of his "transcendent integrity."[10] The man in the street—or as Ike liked to put it, the man digging a ditch in Kansas—warmed to, and put his trust in, a president who seemed to desire and pursue the wholesome. Ike was thus able to restore a measure of calm to a nation that had been suffering from an acute attack of nerves.

Paradoxically, however, in the first few months of 1955 the United States probably came closer to nuclear war than at any other time during Ike's presidency, and it was over an issue that even he regarded as fundamentally trivial. Ever since the previous September a crisis had been blowing up over the islands off the coast of Communist China, which had been occupied by the forces of General Chiang Kai-Shek after his defeat in the civil war. As Ike acknowledged to Gruenther, some of these islands were almost within "wading distance" of the continent. Quemoy, the Matsus, and the Tachens, he said, "have always been a part of the Chinese mainland both politically and, in effect, geographically."[11] Others, notably the Pescadores, were closer to the Nationalist stronghold of Formosa (Taiwan), about a hundred miles from the mainland. Chiang had reinforced the nearby groups, using them as a base from which to attack shipping and to mount raids on the coast. For the Communists it was, as Robert Divine has observed, rather "like having a foreign power on Staten Island."[12] But the offshore islands were important chiefly because they were stepping stones for the much-trumpeted Nationalist return to China or, conversely, for the equally heralded Communist conquest of Formosa. So, when the Red Chinese started to bombard Quemoy in September 1954, it seemed like a prelude to the larger invasion.

Having warned laconically that this "would have to run over the Seventh Fleet," Ike restrained his more excitable advisers, such as Admiral Radford, who were advocating a nuclear assault on China. Ike sensibly observed that this would take them to the "threshold of World War III," for "if we get into a general war, the logical enemy will be Russia, not China, and we'll have to strike there."[13] Evidently he shared General Ridgway's view that a preventive war over this issue would "tragically demonstrate our complete and utter moral bankruptcy,"[14] and, as an observer recorded, Ike personally saved the situation. A contemporary reporter paid the president this just compliment:

Considering the hysteria over Communism of the past two years, it is a tribute to Mr. Eisenhower that he has somehow thrown off those who would drive him into a dead end from which war would be the only escape. This is also a reflection of his innate caution, of his feeling against extremes, of his ability to gauge the temper of the mass of Americans and the masses elsewhere in the world on both sides of the Iron Curtain.[15]

Ike could not escape from contemporary pressures that easily. McCarthyism had virtually suppressed objective discussion of China in America's academic, journalistic, and diplomatic spheres. For example, Dulles's assistant secretary of state for Far Eastern affairs, Walter S. Robertson, was so rabidly anti-Communist that his speeches were "an unceasing diatribe against the puppets of Peking" and he was, as Anthony Eden noted, "impervious to arguments or indeed to facts."[16] Ike thus came under terrific pressure, especially from Senator Knowland and the China lobby, who regarded anything less than a blockade of the yellow Reds as tantamount to appeasement. Furthermore, though he was furious when Ridgway revealed this, the president was trapped by the New Look defense policy, which inhibited him from retaliating against the Chinese threat other than massively. As he told Churchill, the "principal weakness" of the nuclear deterrent policy "is that it offers, of itself, no defense against the losses that we incur through the enemy's political nibbling." The enemy knew that "there is a great area of fruitful opportunity open to him lying between the excitation of a global war on the one hand and passive acceptance of the status quo on the other." However, Ike reckoned, "there can be local deterrents as well as global deterrents."[17] Among the former, presumably, was the mutual defense pact which the United States concluded with Formosa in December 1954. It was Ike's attempt to put Chiang back on a leash, to intimidate potential warmongers among the Chinese Communists, and to placate bellicose members of the old guard.

Unfortunately the treaty failed on all three counts. First, Chiang continued to make aggressive noises and proved to be as intransigent an ally as Syngman Rhee. Indeed, there was a danger that the American dog might be wagged into war by the Formosan tail. Anthony Eden employed a similar but stronger metaphor, saying that the United States "had a bear by the tail."[18] But none of Ike's Western allies could sympathize with his plight, for, as Gruenther told him, "most Europeans think that Chiang Kai-Shek is a palooka."[19] Second, the Communist Chinese took full advantage of the pact's ambiguity— it had specified that Formosa and the Pescadores would be defended, while leaving American intentions toward the other offshore islands vague. In January 1955 they attacked the Tachen group and captured a small outpost to the north of it. Thus, third, Ike came under renewed

pressure to take hostile action. With typical circumspection he moved
in two directions at once. He insisted on the evacuation, with American
help, of the peripheral Tachens. And he sent a special message to
Congress asking for authority to use American forces to defend Formosa,
the Pescadores, and "other territories"—a deliberately cryptic
allusion to Quemoy and the Matsus. Just before Ike broadcast this
portentous message Dulles told Hagerty, "I'm as nervous as a kitten.
I feel just the same way I did waiting for my son to be born. It's a
ticklish and very delicate question, and of course, none of us knows
how the Chinese Communists are going to react."[20]

Dulles's apprehensions were well founded, for Ike himself, who
was wont to pontificate on the unpredictability of the "Oriental
mind," had no idea whether the Chinese Communists would call his
bluff—if it was bluff—over the offshore islands. But whether the carte
blanche he received from Congress frightened his enemies, it certainly
frightened his friends. Ike had to reassure the public that U.S.
forces would only be used defensively. He also tried to convince
America's Western allies that his policy was reasonable and right,
telling Churchill,

God knows I have been working hard in the exploration of every avenue that
seems to lead toward the preservation and strengthening of the Peace. But
I am positive that the free world is surely building trouble for itself unless
it is united in its declared determination to resist all forceful Communist
advance, and keeps itself ready to act at a moment's notice, if necessary.[21]

Ike had certainly served due warning on the Communists; though
being already authorized by the Constitution to do what he had asked
Congress for the authority to do, the president had also, as his critics
alleged, to some extent passed the buck at home.

But the old master of coalition warfare was unable to share the
burden of his responsibilities with traditional allies abroad. As Eden
said, "No great power could seriously want to fight" about Quemoy
and the Matsus. And since the Chinese Communists lacked the military
capacity to "run over" a strengthened U.S. fleet, the British
foreign secretary continued, "Formosa would be stronger without the
commitment of the offshore islands."[22] Curiously enough, Ike did not
altogether disagree. He told Gruenther that the offshore islands
should be defended because their loss would damage Nationalist
morale, but "militarily it makes sense to abandon them."[23] However,
Ike could not risk being accused of appeasement. He assured Knowland
that "we can't just try to fight another war with handcuffs on as
we did in Korea"; that if any Chinese threat to Formosa built up "we

are going to have to go in and break it up"; and that Quemoy was "only important because it . . . can be used to break up any offensive."[24]

Ike's policy was to deter the Communists by not revealing what lengths he would go to if they attacked the offshore islands, though, as he remarked, "the problem now is how to make it work."[25] If he actually had any definite intentions, they seem to have been to retaliate massively only when he judged that the Chinese Communists were attacking the offshore islands as a preliminary to invading Formosa. How Ike was to distinguish this from a mere assault on Quemoy and the Matsus themselves was a difficult question. It was posed in an acute form at the end of February, when Dulles sent a message home from Bangkok saying that from their preparations he was convinced that the Chinese Communists soon intended to take Formosa by force. He concluded with all sorts of dire prognostications: "we are in a battle for Taiwan . . . further retreat could swing Asia . . . loss of Formosa would convince Japan [that] Communism [is the] wave of the future."[26]

Ike responded in March by permitting Dulles to make explicit the fact that American support for the offshore islands would "require the use of atomic missiles."[27] The secretary said that these would be "clean" and aimed only at military targets—something contradicted by a CIA report he subsequently received, to the effect that an atomic strike on the coastline opposite Quemoy and the Matsus would kill between 12 and 14 million Chinese. The president was apparently unmoved by this estimate. On 16 March he informed journalists that tactical nuclear weapons could be employed on "strictly military targets" and "I see no reason why they shouldn't be used just exactly as you would use a bullet or anything else." Ike added that he was intent on giving the facts about nuclear war "without terrifying people."[28] In this case he failed, and there was a fearful outcry which echoed around the world. The Formosan situation was so fraught and so delicate, Hagerty told Ike just before his next press conference, that he should avoid saying anything about it whatever question he was asked. "Don't worry, Jim," the president replied, with a confidence that proved amply justified, "if that question comes up, I'll just confuse them."[29]

This remark has been subjected to the sort of exegesis traditionally reserved for Holy Writ. It has become a key text—illustrating Ike's Machiavellian capacity for obfuscation—for those bent on revising the old, hostile interpretation of his presidency.[30] Indeed, Ike's entire handling of the problem of the offshore islands has recently earned fulsome praise from historians. For apart from a few more anxious moments, the Formosan crisis had passed. By April the Chinese foreign minister, Chou En-lai, was making conciliatory overtures. By August, thanks to diplomatic discussions, the shelling of Quemoy had ceased. Although the issue was not resolved—it was to recur in 1958, when Ike employed the same tactics with the same results—the tension had eased and the antagonists had found a modus vivendi. Thus Ike's "strategy of deliberate deception"[31] has been hailed as a "tour de force."[32] There can be no doubt that it worked: Chiang kept the offshore islands; Ike made no gestures of appeasement; there was no nuclear war. This was a triumph.

But it was a triumph purchased, surely, at an unacceptably high price. It aroused such apprehensions in the American people that Ike kept having to issue calming statements. Above all it took the greatest possible risks for manifestly insignificant objectives. As late as April one worried State Department memorandum recommended that the United States should accept a Communist buildup opposite Formosa rather than "now be responsible for initiating active hostilities which could readily spread into a major war."[33] Ike himself was generally confident that the worst would not happen. But as he admitted in his diary, he could never be sure that the Chinese Communists, indifferent to human life, might not assume that he was crying wolf. They might have been particularly inclined to take the gamble if they had heeded Engine Charlie Wilson. To Ike's fury,[34] the secretary of defense announced that the loss of Quemoy and Matsu would make little difference in the long run. He further revealed his estimate of the islands' importance by getting them in the wrong place—"One thing about him," said Ike bitterly, "he certainly does his homework."[35] The president himself was of course the soul of discretion, and he consistently maintained his public position that the loss of the offshore islands would do "serious damage to our security position in the Western Pacific."[36] But he was at the same time secretly trying to persuade Chiang that Quemoy and the Matsus were "outposts, not citadels," and that the Nationalists should withdraw from them voluntarily.[37]

Chiang refused, and Ike did not insist for fear of impairing Formosan morale. It was that nebulous factor, therefore, for which Ike risked a third world war. Alternatively, since he was at once willing to give up the islands and prepared to utter terrifying threats in order to keep them, Ike himself had become a victim of the confusion which he was so adept at disseminating. No doubt his ambivalent position had as much to do with placating the China lobby as with refusing to appease

Senator McCarthy greeting Ike during his campaign visit to Wisconsin, October 1952. The president refused to "get into a pissing contest with that skunk."

Adlai Stevenson, a political egghead twice thwarted by Ike.

Ike whistle-stopping in Washington state, October 1952, aboard the "Look Ahead Neighbor Special."

Ike and "Mr. Republican," November 1952. Taft "lost the nomination but won the nominee."

Truman and Ike discussing the handover, 19 November 1952. Ike wondered if he could *"stand* sitting next to that guy."

"I will go to Korea." Ike fulfills his election pledge, December 1952.

Ike's victory sign, Columbia, 1953.

Ike's first inaugural, 20 January 1953. A ray of sunshine broke through the clouds just as he took the oath.

Ike's first Cabinet, May 1953—rather more than "eight millionaires and a plumber."

Playing games with the president—more of a duty than a pleasure for the vice president.

Herblock's famous cartoon of McCarthy and Ike.

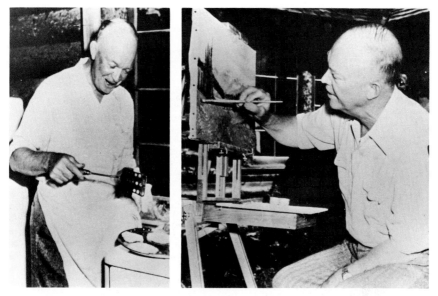

Ike was proud of his cooking but called his painting "shit."

Churchill and Eden try to maintain the "special relationship" with Ike and Dulles, White House, 25 June 1954.

Geniality hid antipathy. Ike thought Nixon was perpetually maturing, perpetually immature.

MUCH BETTER, THANKS—Ike after his heart attack, Denver, 25 October 1955.

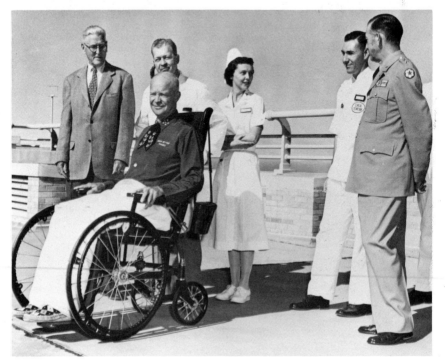

Ike and Mamie at their first permanent home, the Gettysburg farm, September 1956.

Inaugural, 21 January 1957. Ike's grandchildren, David and Barbara Ann; Nixon's daughters, Julie and Tricia. The dynasties were to merge.

Ike and the British Prime Minister Harold Macmillan, Bermuda, 10 March 1957—trying to patch up their friendship after the British invasion of Suez.

Two star players on the President's "team," Sherman Adams and John Foster Dulles, Washington, April 1957.

Ike was enraged by the "stupidity and duplicity" of Orval Faubus, governor of Arkansas, during the Little Rock crisis, September 1957.

Grandfather Ike. Christmas at the White House with son John and family, 1957.

When he could not play golf, Ike lamented, "I feel so sorry for myself I could cry."

Gone fishing—West Greenwich, Rhode Island, August 1958.

Ike and Khrushchev, Camp David, 25 September 1959. The Communist hoped to "bury" capitalism; the president sought to put the Russian argumentatively "in a box."

Ike in India, December 1959. Nehru talked nonviolence and cleared their path through the crowds with a big stick.

Ike and John F. Kennedy, 6 December 1960. Ike repeated, "You can always tell a Harvard man, but you can't tell him much."

Ike and Barry Goldwater, September 1961. The president thought the senator "nuts" but supported him just the same.

Ike and Lyndon B. Johnson, Palm Springs, 1968. LBJ sought help from his fellow Texan when he got his "tail in a crack."

Taps. Ike's funeral in Washington, D.C., March 1969.

Red China. An American olive branch might actually have led Mao Tse-tung to renounce the use of force in seeking to liberate Formosa. This was a naïve hope, perhaps, but it was shared by both Eden and Stevenson. The latter was shocked by Dulles's willingness "to play Russian roulette with the life of the nation" and he described the missed opportunity of establishing détente in the Far East as "the greatest political crime of our times."[38] However, Stevenson was speculating and exaggerating. When all is said and done, the fog of equivocation Ike generated gave him the supreme diplomatic advantage of flexibility.

This was something which the doctrinaire Dulles lacked. Thus when, in April, Chou made his offer to talk, the State Department automatically rejected it. At his next press conference Ike claimed that this was "an error of terminology" and, while denying any "reversal of attitude," he indicated that the offer had been accepted.[39] No doubt the president and the secretary collaborated closely, but there were persistent reports of splits between them over Far Eastern policy, which perturbed Dulles at the time.[40] Later he was eager to take full credit for the successful outcome, telling Emmet Hughes that "of all the things I have done, *I* think *the most brilliant* of all has been to save Quemoy and Matsu."[41] In fact such credit as is due for that obscure, devious, dangerous, but ultimately effective maneuver, belongs almost exclusively to Ike.

He also deserved much credit for fostering the "spirit of Geneva," the first sign of a relaxation in the cold war, which occurred as a result of the four-power summit meeting in July 1955. Actually Ike was hostile to the idea of such a top-level encounter, asserting that every time a president had gone abroad in person to treat with foreign leaders "he's lost his shirt."[42] Ike leaned heavily on Dulles for advice about venturing into the international arena, acknowledging that "this was one field where he was completely inexperienced in the kind of negotiations, and he was therefore unsure as to exactly what was the right thing to do." He added, "I am not afraid to meet anybody face to face, but the world gets in the habit of expecting a lot."[43] Unhappily Dulles was so haunted by the ghost of Yalta that he was opposed to conjuring up a spirit of Geneva. He easily succeeded in confirming the president's opinion that "summit meetings were not only futile but had many dangers."[44] However, in the spring of 1954 Ike found it impossible to resist any longer the pressure, from allies as well as antagonists, to attend a Big Four Conference.

Ever since Stalin's death the Soviet Union had been taking modest initiatives in an effort to achieve some sort of rapprochement. At the

Geneva Conference in 1954, for example, Bedell Smith reported that
Molotov was a changed man: "He went further, was much more
frank, made no charges, by implication or otherwise, [and indulged
in] no recriminations."[45] Dulles had always insisted that Russia should
prove its good intentions by deeds, not words. In April and May the
new Soviet leaders, Nikolai Bulganin and Nikita Khrushchev, did just
that. They signed a treaty giving Austria her independence, something Russia had been withholding ever since the war. Furthermore,
they suddenly accepted Western proposals on disarmament and suggested the establishment of an international agency to inspect the
manufacture of nuclear and conventional weapons. Having for years
condemned the Soviet Union for being a closed society, Ike and
Dulles were severely embarrassed by this démarche. For all their
rhetoric about ending the arms race, neither was prepared to sacrifice
the nuclear advantage which the United States possessed. But whereas
the secretary feared some sort of diplomatic trick, the president was
more concerned that the Russians had scored a propaganda coup. He
was reduced to doing an about-face and adopting what had been the
Soviet position. "Are we ready to open up every one of our factories,
every place where something might be going on that could be inimical
to the interests of somebody else?" he asked plaintively.[46]

While not acceding to the Soviet proposal, then, Ike felt bound to
respond to the Soviet gesture. Overcoming his own reluctance and
Dulles's resistance, he decided to go to Geneva. Their differing attitudes were graphically summed up in Herblock's famous cartoon
showing Dulles muffled up to his ears in overcoats while Ike, dressed
in summer clothes, says into a telephone, "Yes, We'll Be There, Rain
and Shine." Robert Divine further observed that American foreign
policy bore "a schizophrenic appearance"[47] as the secretary dourly
pursued the cold war and the president optimistically sought peaceful
coexistence. Yet this appearance surely owed less to a split between
the two men than to a split in Ike's personality, or at any rate to a
disjunction between the elements of extrovert cheerfulness and self-
protective caution.

In a sense Ike comprehended Dulles, who embodied a single aspect
of his antithetical character. The president was just as vigorous a cold
warrior as the secretary, just as fearful of making concessions to the
Communists, and just as darkly suspicious of Russian good faith. Ike
told Herbert Hoover, for example: "You can't trust them, the Soviets,
when they are talking nice and you can't trust them when they are
talking tough."[48] And he informed Eden that the Russians were either
Communist zealots or power-mad dictators, and that it was difficult to

deal with either. At the same time Ike was genuinely anxious about
the nuclear arms race, he was eager to reduce global tensions, and he
longed to satisfy the "common desire for peace . . . that is a terrific
force in the world."[49] What is more, Ike felt sure that by exposing the
Russian leaders to a forceful display of charm, openness, and sincerity,
he could achieve some measure of concord. He ignored Dulles's
advice to maintain an unsmiling and "austere countenance" while
publicly in their company and to avoid meeting them in private.[50]

Thus Ike attended the July summit in Geneva with characteristically
ambivalent intentions. He was determined, at the very least, to win
a propaganda victory. He had told Dulles that in his parting broadcast
to the nation he wanted to counter "hostile propaganda" which portrayed Americans as "worshipers of might, people with no culture and
no real longing for peace." "The thought I have is a peculiar one,"
he said—with some justice, for it was to stress that the United States
believed in "Divine Power" and, avoiding the pitfall of seeming
"helpless or mawkishly sentimental," to urge them to go to church
and pray for peace.[51] This he did, in a sermonlike address that had the
advantage of implicating the national congregation in his pacific endeavors and providing a celestial guarantee that Geneva (as Ike had
promised senior members of Congress) would be no Yalta. The response to this homily, according to Ike's new special assistant for
psychological warfare, Nelson Rockefeller, was "tremendous," and
the USIA gave it massive publicity.[52] Meanwhile, Rockefeller had
been working, with Harold Stassen and others, on another presidential project, which was designed to trump the Russian proposal for the
supervision of arms control—namely a system of unfettered aerial
reconnaissance.

The first few days of the summit were devoted to sparring, mutual
appraisal, and the fruitless recapitulation of familiar positions. The
conference was held in the hall at the Palais des Nations, a great
amphitheater decorated with blue, gray, and gold frescoes, depicting
humanity's struggle against the scourges of famine, slavery, and "sub-
human beasts drop[ping] babies down the muzzles of monstrous cannons, tilted at crazy angles."[53] To Harold Macmillan these murals
seemed to portray "the End of the World, or the Battle of the Titans,
or the Rape of the Sabines, or a mixture of all three," and he could
"conceive of no arrangement less likely to lead to intimate or useful
negotiations."[54] Outside this apocalyptic forum Ike, surrounded by
Secret Service men, exuded goodwill. By contrast the Russian leaders,
though free of bodyguards, "seemed to exercise surveillance" over
each other. Ike reestablished friendly relations with General Zhukov,

who was evidently a mere shell of his former self. And he found Khrushchev and Bulganin, who like the others "drank little and smiled much," wary and amicable but ultimately implacable.[55] For his part, Khrushchev considered Ike "a good man but he wasn't very tough." He observed Dulles slipping Ike scribbled notes under the table, which the president read "like a dutiful schoolboy taking his lead from his teacher," and he concluded that the secretary "determined the foreign policy of the United States."[56]

But it was the president who, on 21 July, put forward what came to be known as his "open skies" plan. He had, in fact, discussed it with his advisers but, according to his later account, he "extemporized some of the proposal" and "just threw it right in [the Russians'] faces."[57] Declaring that he had been "searching my heart and mind for something that I could say here that could convince everyone of the great sincerity of the United States in approaching the problem of disarmament," he looked the Russian leaders straight in the eyes. He proposed that they should "give each other a complete blueprint of our military establishments" and provide "facilities for aerial photography to the other country." As Ike finished his earnest and impressive peroration, in which he pleaded for peace with security, there was a great clap of thunder like some cosmic round of applause, and all the lights went out.

Metaphorically speaking, the Russians were also thunderstruck. Bulganin was at a loss for words, but, having stated that he believed Ike's earnest pledge never to take part in an aggressive war, he said that the proposal would receive sympathetic study. After the meeting, however, Khrushchev (incidentally revealing who was boss) told Ike that the "open skies" plan was a "transparent espionage device" and quite unacceptable.[58] Whether Ike actually intended it to be accepted remains a matter of debate. He himself later admitted, "We knew the Soviets wouldn't accept it—we were sure of that." Nevertheless, it was "a good move."[59] The initiative, which would have been almost impossible to implement, bore all the hallmarks of a propaganda ploy, and the U.S. Cabinet talked of it in those terms.[60] As Ike recorded in his memoirs, the American "plan was to keep the Soviets on the defensive" by proposing measures of general appeal.[61] This was certainly true of the "open skies" plan, which had the additional advantage that the open United States would gain by it more new information about the closed Soviet Union than vice versa. On the other hand, one of Ike's closest confidants, his staff secretary Colonel (later General) Andrew J. Goodpaster, asserted that the proposal was not disingenuous or made for propaganda purposes.[62] Ike talked and wrote to his own friends and advisers as if the offer were a genuine attempt to ease tensions and augment trust. And his sincere and candid manner spoke for itself. Or did it? Was the whole performance an elaborate charade?

On balance, it seems, Ike was hoping to have it both ways. He wanted a propaganda advantage that would also reduce the risk of nuclear war and might just lead to some form of agreement that would clearly benefit the United States. Such objectives were mutually exclusive: Ike could not achieve peace by means of psychological warfare. So nothing emerged from the conference except a nebulous "atmosphere of friendliness," a diluted "spirit of Geneva."[63] Actually, in the strained conditions of the cold war this was no mean achievement. It was due largely to the fact that Ike's open personality was more in evidence than Dulles's closed mind. Eden could say that Geneva had quite simply "reduced the dangers of war."[64] The French Foreign Office waxed "lyrical" over the conference.[65] In the United States Ike's prestige and popularity rose to unprecedented heights.

Yet the fact that Geneva produced no more substantial results was surely attributable to Ike's timid velleities. Wanting to improve international relations but "letting 'I dare not' wait upon 'I would,' " he had not been able to make an unequivocal gesture. He had looked on the summit as a hazard to be circumvented rather than an opportunity to be grasped. The administration's terror at being accused of capitulating to the Communists was well illustrated when the *Columbine* flew back into Washington airport on 24 July. Although it was raining, Nixon had ordered that officials there to greet the president should not carry umbrellas—people might be reminded of the famous return of Prime Minister Neville Chamberlain after his trip to Munich. Ike at once announced that "no secret agreements had been made" at Geneva.[66] He talked to Dulles, with obvious relief, about having "come through unscarred" from meeting the "top Communists."[67] President and secretary were so anxious to keep their political skins whole that they seriously debated whether to use the words "friendly intent" in a personal letter to Bulganin which was to be published.[68]

Of course, it may have been impossible, in view of internal and external hostility, to reach an agreement on arms control with Communist Russia. Dulles expressed the difficulties with his usual cogency when Ike tried to revive and combine his "atoms for peace" and "open skies" proposals early in 1956. In a long memorandum to the president, the secretary said that the Soviets were untrustworthy, that there were no effective international controls for eliminating nuclear arms, and that no international organization would be effective either.

Moreover, he stressed, *"Only atomic weapons provide the United States with the needed worldwide power at bearable cost."* At the same time, Dulles acknowledged, there was a "growing, and not unreasonable, fear that nuclear weapons are expanding at such a pace as to endanger human life on this planet." But while recognizing that this terrifying state of affairs imposed a duty on the United States to take a lead "in the struggle for a durable peace," Dulles treated the question of disarmament primarily as a question of propaganda. The "atoms for peace" and "open skies" proposals had won worldwide support, he argued, because they "seemed to prepare the way for disarmament." Both schemes had "now largely lost their popular influence," leaving a "vacuum" which the Soviet "ban the bomb" campaign had filled. Because of it the "masses feel that at least the Russians *want* to end the thermonuclear danger while we are represented as stalling and trying to think up good reasons for perpetuating the danger and making it even greater. Thus, ironically, our moral leadership in the world could be stolen from us by those whose creed denies moral principles."

Dulles's solution was to take a "major and sustained initiative" with the idea of "vesting nuclear weapons in a vetoless Security Council." The USSR would probably oppose this, but it would put them, instead of the United States, in a "negative position."[69] Ike, too, while appalled by Defense Department reports of what nuclear bombs could do to the country, was intent on denying the Soviets "propaganda ammunition."[70] And when revised proposals were put to the Russians in March 1956, he did not expect them to be accepted; though, if they were, he considered that the United States would suffer no disadvantage. The fact was that Ike could create little international harmony because he persistently added propaganda overtones to his pacific overtures. He was unable to reduce the balance of terror significantly or to slow down the arms race because he was always looking over his shoulder at the old guard. As Professor John Kenneth Galbraith suggested, Ike's administration "perhaps rightly, has deeply mistrusted its intellectual ability and, in particular, its ability to bargain." It had lacked the moral certainty to try making a deal with the Communists, and as a result, Galbraith said, "we present a kind of tortoise-like appearance to the outside world and sometimes to ourselves."[71]

Ike had no need to be defensive, as he went off on holiday in the summer of 1955. For an astonishing 84 percent of Americans approved of his conduct as president, and he was in the process of becoming, as Murray Kempton wrote, the great tortoise on which everything rested (people never recognizing, Kempton added, the cunning beneath the shell). As such, Ike was well armored against the various domestic reverses suffered by his administration in that year.

There was, for example, the Dixon–Yates affair. A private firm of that name was shown to have employed a government consultant, Adolphe H. Wenzell, to arrange its contract to build a plant for supplying Tennessee Valley Authority electricity to the city of Memphis. Ike had taken an all too "perfunctory"[72] part in the decision thus to restrict the growth of the "socialistic" T.V.A.,[73] and he tried to deny the obvious conflict of interest. Invoking executive privilege, he also held back relevant government files from a congressional investigating committee on the grounds that they were "honey-combed" with "personal notes from my own staff."[74] Here were all the ingredients for a classic scandal and cover-up, made more piquant by the revelation that the president's golfing friend, Bobby Jones, was a director of the Yates part of Dixon–Yates. Ike became extremely sensitive about the issue, complaining about the implication that his administration was guilty of "chicanery and dishonesty, and that only demagogues are honest."[75] Luckily for the president, Memphis announced that it would build its own power plant, the Dixon–Yates contract was canceled, and the issue died a natural death.

Ike also emerged unscathed from Oveta Hobby's failure to organize the speedy distribution of the new Salk vaccine against polio. The delay was caused in part by her conservative reluctance to draw on federal funds, as well as by her admitted mistake in not foreseeing public demand. There was an understandable outcry, and Senator Wayne Morse, accusing her of administration so bad that it "borders on immorality," read into the record a pre-feminist newspaper editorial entitled "Send Hobby to Hubby."[76] Mrs. Hobby did resign, thus freeing Ike from a serious embarrassment, and he scored points for remaining publicly loyal to her.

Harold E. Talbott also had to resign, because he had used his position as secretary of the air force to advance his business affairs. But Ike incurred little or no guilt through their bridge-playing association. This was largely because the mass media, mostly owned by rich Republicans, thoroughly absolved the president. In April 1955, the attorney general exposed, during the H. W. Grunewald case, what he called the biggest bribery scandal in American history, even bigger than the Teapot Dome scandal, proving "in court that the Internal Revenue Service was utterly corrupt" and tracing kickbacks of a quarter of a million dollars. But the president still remained immune from criticism, and there was no loose talk about the mess in Washington.

"Funny it makes so few headlines," Ike remarked, and it was impossible to tell whether he was being artless or artful.[77]

However, Ike's popularity did not stem just from the appealing image he projected. Its foundation was the combination of peace and prosperity which the United States enjoyed during his presidency. People could ignore the inevitable scandals. They were unperturbed by Ike's failure to get various modest reforming measures, in such fields as health and education, through a Democratic Congress—for all the president's talk of the efficacy of leading by persuasion even Sherman Adams was "never too much impressed by the results."[78] No, what mattered was the fact that American soldiers were not being sent to die abroad, and that at home inflation stood at one percent and unemployment at four percent, the budget was almost balanced and the economy was buoyant. Real family incomes were rising steadily, the evidence of which was everywhere to be seen or heard—hi-fi sets blasting out "Rock around the Clock," women having their hair tinted all colors of the rainbow, the proliferation of credit cards, the spread of chrome-plated suburbia, the sale of mink-handled can openers.

By 1955 just about half the population wore white collars to work and went on summer vacations. Big commercial organizations were growing richer, and so were the organization men who ran them. The industries of consumerism—advertising, public relations, packaging—flourished. The American Federation of Labor and the Congress of Industrial Organization finally merged in 1955, and their new head, George Meany, rightly proclaimed that labor had "never had it so good."[79] It is true that deep pockets of poverty remained, startling inequalities of wealth persisted, and public amenities did not keep pace with private affluence. But the nearest Ike came to dismantling the New Deal was to rename the Boulder Dam the Hoover Dam. He was determined that the Republicans should lose the stigma of being the party of depression. He cautiously expanded social welfare programs. He spent significantly more (though not enough) on education ($14 billion in 1960, or 3 percent of the gross national product, as compared to $2.34 billion in 1940, or 2 percent) and massively more on highways. Nothing testified better to the national mood of optimism than the continuing baby boom—America's birth rate was actually higher than India's, and during the 1950s the U.S. population increased by almost 30 million.

Although Ike heard with delight at the end of July that he was set to become a grandfather for the fourth time, his own prevalent mood, by contrast, was gloomy. At Geneva he had occupied the center of the world's stage. His return to prosaic and intractable affairs at home was a dismal anticlimax. He came back, as Bernard Shanley said, like "a lead balloon" and gave his immediate staff "a pretty rough time."[80] Nervous before his departure, he had frequently reduced Ann Whitman to tears. His bouts of ill-temper intensified afterward, rising and subsiding with the sudden ferocity of a Kansas tornado. He cheered up momentarily when going off for his long summer vacation in Colorado. Here he took his usual energetic delight in fishing, cooking, and golfing. But he could not slough off the pressures of the presidency. According to Richard Rovere he spent only an average of forty-five minutes a day at his desk. But there were other demands on his time, not least the mounting Republican effort to ensure that he ran for a second term. When Richard Nixon paid him a visit to urge this course, Ike displayed more than usual testiness and refused to discuss politics while on holiday.

Early in the morning of 23 September, having fried and eaten breakfast, Ike left Aksel Nielsen's ranch and drove the eighty miles to Denver at high speed, descending over five thousand feet in the process. He quickly completed some outstanding office work and went off, at mid-morning, to play twenty-seven holes of golf at his favorite club, Cherry Hills. He was in poor form and, to turn his irritation into rage, the game was twice interrupted by abortive telephone calls from Dulles. For lunch Ike had a double hamburger garnished with slices of raw onion dipped in vinegar, which (not surprisingly) gave him heartburn during the afternoon. But that evening he ate dinner at his mother-in-law's house and, after playing billiards with George Allen, went to bed. At about 1:30 A.M. he awoke with agonizing chest pains. He had suffered a heart attack.

It was a moderate one, to be sure, but still a grave matter for a man of sixty-four. Worried about the effects on the morale of both Ike and America, his personal physician, Dr. Howard Snyder—whom Mamie had summoned at once—next morning issued a statement saying that the president had "suffered a digestive upset."[81] To support the deceit he had Ike walk to a car, instead of being carried by stretcher to an ambulance. The president was then driven to Fitzsimons Army Hospital, where he was placed in an oxygen tent. That afternoon reporters were told that Ike had had "a mild coronary thrombosis."[82] On the following Monday, 26 September, the Dow Jones share index fell by over thirty points, wiping twelve billion dollars off the value of stocks —its worst day since the Crash of 1929.

The United States became obsessed by the question of heart disease, and Hagerty, with Ike's approval, provided what must have been the most comprehensive medical bulletins ever issued. American jour-

nalists were sour about Snyder's initial announcement. They might
have reflected that when Prime Minister Winston Churchill had suffered his stroke, two years before, the press barons—Beaverbrook,
Camrose, and Bracken—successfully concealed it from the British
public. By contrast they themselves were now being encouraged to
print every conceivable detail about President Eisenhower's state,
down to and including the nature of his bowel movements.[83] This
news, incidentally, caused a crisis in some newspapers, which were not
used to dealing with such indelicate information and indulged in an
orgy of euphemism.

As the American press charted the president's gradual progress
toward recovery over the next few weeks, Hagerty was able to suggest
adroitly that Ike was taking the important decisions while doing nothing to strain himself. The president was keeping his finger on the pulse
of events while not being allowed to see the newspapers or listen to
the radio. Sometimes the implausibility of these claims became apparent, for example when Dulles let slip the fact that Ike knew nothing
of the Franco-Algerian crisis. But public attention was so fixed on the
popular president's state of health that few concerned themselves
about his capacity to do the job. In any case, as Dulles said, "we were
able to carry on the business of government effectively without serious
interruption" because the harmonious Cabinet "had so good a back-
log of forward thinking."[84] Such paradoxical special pleading
abounded, and it was particularly difficult to reconcile the argument
that Ike's team functioned superbly in his absence with the view that
his leadership was indispensable.

Nevertheless, it must be said that the administration did continue
to run quite smoothly. This was partly because Adams, Dulles, and
Hagerty continued to play their dominant roles, partly because Nixon
evinced calculating statesmanship (presiding over cabinet meetings,
for instance, but not from the president's chair), partly because no
controversial issues presented themselves, and partly because it was
clear that the president was on the mend. On 7 October Ike told
Snyder, "Howard, if I didn't know this heart attack belonged to me
I'd say it belonged to the other guy."[85] The doctors told Ike that he
had a small heart and it could stand some enlargement. The president
was photographed on 14 October, his sixty-fifth birthday, wearing a
gift from the press—bright red pajamas with five stars on the collar
and this legend embroidered over the breast pocket: MUCH BETTER,
THANKS.

On 11 November Ike left the hospital and began a period of convalescence, spent mainly on his Gettysburg farm, which lasted for about

two months. For most of that time he was in such low spirits that his mood amounted to a depression—of a kind that often afflicts heart-attack patients. Ike mooched about the house using a golf club for a stick. He referred to himself as an old dodo. He chafed because the weather was too cold for him to use the putting green. He became a prey to boredom and lassitude. He sat "immobile for long periods of time, brooding silently about the future."[86] Actually he did attend to some official business, though his chief preoccupation was whether he would be fit to run for a second term, and if so whether Nixon should be on the ticket. Ike broached the latter subject with his vice-president when he returned briefly to Washington over the Christmas period.

He suggested that Nixon could best prepare himself to occupy the highest office by getting some executive experience, and offered him a cabinet post. It was better to be a "half-back in his own right," Ike argued, than "the understudy to the star of the team."[87] Nixon knew full well that it was better to be a heartbeat away from the presidency, particularly when the president had a weak heart and a penchant for fried mush. Nixon resented what he rightly took to be Ike's attempt to maneuver him out of his position. The vice-presidency may not in itself have been worth, in John Nance Garner's phrase, "a pitcher of warm piss,"[88] but remaining in that office provided Nixon with the best chance of one day moving into the White House. So although he was himself tormented by "agonizing indecision,"[89] the vice-president resisted Ike's characteristically oblique campaign. While telling the press that he had never talked to Nixon about his future, and otherwise negatively endorsing him, the president weighed the qualifications of other candidates. He continued privately to let it be known that Nixon "is making a mistake by wanting the job." He explored all the angles: "I'm not going to say that he is the only individual I would have for Vice President. There is nothing to be gained politically by ditching him."[90] Doubtless Ike reckoned that what he might have gained in popular votes he could have lost in support from the old guard. Anyway Nixon, correctly gauging that the president would not take the decision himself, clung to his post like the tightest of barnacles. After four awkward months, Ike told Hagerty to announce that he was delighted by the vice-president's decision to run with him.

Meanwhile Ike had arrived at his own much more important decision. He did so after much earnest cogitation and a good deal of superfluous consultation with colleagues who had a vested interest in advising that it was his duty to complete the business he had begun. Shortly before his heart attack Ike had evidently decided on a long campaign of prevarication and misinformation. When asked about running again he replied, "I'll jump off that bridge when I come to it."[91] Ike told his brother Milton that he wanted to "retain as long as possible a position of flexibility—that is, to wait until the last possible moment before announcing any positive decision."[92] In other words Ike was intent on staging a repeat of his performance in the contest of 1952. Milton suggested that the best method was to spread the rumor that Ike would not be a candidate.

The heart attack itself had certainly seemed to rule out a second term. But in fact the heart attack, or more precisely the subsequent depression, convinced both Ike and Mamie that the fuller his life was the longer it would last. Furthermore, the doctors said that it was not the big problems that upset Ike but the "little petty annoyances." They prescribed a regimen that seemed to enable him to carry out his duties. He must control his temper, take frequent rests, attend no difficult meetings that went on for longer than an hour, compensate for evening engagements by cutting his daytime program, and so on. On 9 February 1956 Ike declared that such changes of method made it hard for him to work and provided an additional reason for quitting.[93] Four days later he told Len Hall, chairman of the Republican National Committee, that he would run again. Ike gave a number of inconsistent accounts about what had made him change his mind. He told Swede Hazlett, for example, that one vital consideration had been "a guilty feeling on my own part that I had failed to bring forward and establish a logical successor for myself,"[94] whereas the previous August he had assured his friend that "the absence of an obvious successor provides no valid reason for my considering a second term."[95]

The truth was that Ike wanted to go on being president, reckoned that he could do a better job than anyone else, and was confident of victory. Although his pulse remained jumpy, his temper erratic, and his indigestion troublesome, Ike had generally cheered up with the New Year as his resolution hardened. In February Ann Whitman described him as being in "radiant spirits," and by the end of the month his frame of mind was more serene than in any of the previous weeks. Having spent an enjoyable vacation shooting quail and golfing on George Humphrey's plantation, Ike coyly made known his decision on 29 February. It was swathed in language of such bureaucratic opacity that for a moment even reporters used to interpreting Ike did not catch his meaning. His answer could not be expressed just in the simple terms of yes or no. . . . I would not allow my name to go before the Republican Convention unless they, all the Republicans, understood, so that they would not be nominating some individual other than they thought they were nominating. . . . I don't know, certainly for certain, that the Republican convention after hearing the entire story, want me . . . my answer will be positive; that is, affirmative.[96]

16

★

Three Spectaculars

In the eight months leading up to the 1956 election Ike was constantly harassed as the two parties fought for political advantage. For example, the president tried to solve the continuing problem of agricultural surpluses by means of a Soil Bank, a system of paying farmers to conserve their land. But when, in the spring, the Democratic Congress insisted on tacking price supports to the measure, he vetoed it. This was a courageous act under the circumstances, but Ike knew that Ezra Benson, cold, tactless, and self-righteous, would serve "quite effectively as a lightning-rod on agricultural policy."[1] Charles Wilson was Ike's lightning-rod on defense policy, though he angered the president by failing to stop the quarrels, and hence the adverse publicity, between the three services. In fact, Ike himself had initially encouraged their rivalry, hoping that it would speed up the development of nuclear missiles. But he had qualms about doing so and before long was saying "we must eliminate competition among ourselves."[2] It had, indeed, become so ferocious that Wilson could explain it only on the assumption that the services "plan on fighting each other."[3] It also led to a diffusion of effort and a duplication of resources, already scarce because Ike insisted that Wilson should run the Defense Department on a "Spartan basis," asserting that "the patriot of today is the fellow who can do the job with less money."[4] Nevertheless in attacking the nation's most famous soldier over the issue of military preparedness, the Democrats were on shaky ground—though after the Russian Sputnik had bleeped its way into the American psyche they were able to exploit a chimerical "missile gap."

In 1956 it was much easier to stultify Ike's school construction program. Congressman Adam Clayton Powell did so by moving an amendment to deny federal funds to any state that refused to implement the Supreme Court's verdict on racial segregation. When cautioned about being controversial the president liked to tell his advisers, "You don't make hay by always being afraid of things because they are hot."[5] This was bravado. Ike instinctively steered clear of issues which might burn his fingers, especially cases of political and racial bigotry. In 1955, for example, over the contentious matter of whether to give a passport to McCarthy's whipping-boy, the China expert Owen Lattimore, Dulles warned Ike, "I have a feeling that it is better if you are not consulted about it as it is hot." Nothing loath, the president at once "agreed with the Secretary's view that it is better he doesn't know."[6] Now Ike did his best to distance himself from the Powell amendment. He made vague appeals for moderation and progress, a contradiction in terms as far as the blacks were concerned. He maximized the part that lower courts and states should play while minimizing his own role. He said, in effect, that he wanted schools at once and was content to have integration gradually.

The lines were hardening on the racial issue by 1956. The black attempt to end segregated seating on buses in Montgomery, Alabama, by means of a boycott, had begun the previous year under the leadership of the Rev. Martin Luther King, Jr., a charismatic figure who inspired his followers to meet physical force with moral force. Since the Supreme Court's decision white Southerners had been organizing both legal and illegal resistance. In March 1956, J. Edgar Hoover delivered a long report to Ike's cabinet on the growing racial tension. Particularly sinister was the revival of the Ku Klux Klan, a 400 percent increase in the sale of pistols in Alabama, and the employment of violence and sanctions of other kinds against blacks who supported integration. The FBI could elicit few details because of the "iron curtain of silence" drawn by "negroes afraid to talk." There were a few hopeful signs, Hoover said. Lynchings were less common, and some schools and colleges had begun to admit black students. On the other hand, Governor White of Mississippi had referred to the Department of Justice as a "bunch of meddlesome jackasses," and there was a concerted effort both inside and outside Congress to overturn the Supreme Court's ruling.

At a cabinet meeting Ike supported Brownell's proposals for civil rights legislation, a move that would in turn gain Ike additional support in the Northern cities. Ike declared, "In [the] long run [the] Constitution is going to be enforced. That's my duty. But [the] Supreme Court gave some time. Our complaint is that [the] time is not being used. Instead states have merely sat down to say 'We Defy.'" Ike thought the South had made two mistakes: it should have started integration from the top and worked down, and it should not have opposed the moderate demands of blacks on the Birmingham buses.[7] This was a sound response, as far as it went, to the institutionalized violation of black people's rights in the South.

Unfortunately, however, Ike was only prepared to talk morality in terms so general that they never seemed to have a specific application. His aim, he told his colleagues, was "to interpret [the] conscience of the entire nation and try to get [the] Southern conscience closer to it."[8] But when he was asked to condemn the horrible murder of a black boy named Emmett Till at the end of 1955 he remained silent, heeding the cautious advice of his staff that he could not afford to alienate the white South. When a journalist asked Ike how he felt about "Negroes being brought to trial for refusing to ride the Montgomery buses," he replied: "You are asking me, I think, to be more of a lawyer than I certainly am." It was a matter for local courts. "We should not stagnate," he believed, "but again I plead for understanding, for really sympathetic consideration of a problem that is far larger both in its emotional and even in its physical aspects than most of us realize."[9] When the president was asked to force the University of Georgia to accept Autherine Lucy he remained passive. "I'm all at sea on this," he told the Cabinet. If he acted "they could just stop education. Could be chaos." He was on the horns of a dilemma: "[I] must enforce the law—or would you ignore it?"[10]

This was an extraordinary question for one who set such store by his oath of office. But Ike was no less indefinite over his own government's proposed legislation. When pressure was put on him by Knowland and others to water down Brownell's civil rights measures he duly obliged. The attorney general was only allowed to send two bills to Congress which, Ike said, were "the most moderate thing we could have asked for . . . the real criticism was going to come because of [their] lack of vigor."[11] They were, indeed, designed to investigate the racial problem rather than to solve it. Even so there was widespread doubt about whether the president supported the proposals and general certainty that they were in any case disingenuous, calculated simply, as the *New York Times* put it, "to cause maximum embarrassment to the Democratic Party."[12] Without much evident embarrassment the Democractic party duly strangled Brownell's bills in a Senate committee, and although Ike did pay lip service to civil rights during the 1956 election campaign he did so in a decidedly lukewarm fashion.

The president explained his equivocal stance to Brownell: "he was between the compulsion of duty on one side, and his firm conviction, on the other, that because of the Supreme's Court's ruling, the whole issue had been set back badly."[13] When violence broke out in Texas over school desegregation orders in September, Ike condemned extremists on both sides. He treated civil rights workers and lynch mobs with monumental even-handedness, and, as I. F. Stone said, he adopted "at home the moral neutralism he deplores abroad."[14] His lamentable failure to make a serious start in the process of eradicating racial injustice was pregnant with consequences for the 1960s. Indeed, the only merit in Ike's civil rights policy was that it was marginally more inspiring in rhetoric and marginally less feeble in intent than Adlai Stevenson's. The moral bankruptcy of Ike's leadership over this issue emerges plainly, but so does the immense political capital he accumulated as a reward for his skillfully sustained balancing act.

The smooth progress to Ike's nomination by the Republican convention, in August, was interrupted by the second major crisis in his health while he was president. On 7 June he suffered a severe attack of stomach pains which were, for the first time, correctly diagnosed as ileitis. At Walter Reed Hospital, Dr. Snyder told him that he required immediate surgery. Echoing the words he had used before D-Day Ike replied simply, "Well, let's go." The major but straightforward operation, in which a diseased section of the small intestine was bypassed, was a complete success. As Ike said, it also provided "the sternest test that my heart could have."[15] During his six weeks of convalescence the depression which Ike had suffered after his heart attack returned. But, although it was to recur at intervals, Ike had shaken it off by 21 July. On that date he proved to himself and to the nation that he had made a full recovery. He went off on a strenuous trip to Panama for a meeting of leaders from all the Americas.

Ike reckoned that he would have to campaign less energetically during the 1956 election. By this time, anyway, he had become so enamored of television that he actually questioned whether it would not be "unseemly" for a president to conduct a noisy whistle-stop tour. The fact was that the Republicans had refined the techniques of promoting their candidate along commercial lines. In 1952 C. D. Jackson had excitedly proclaimed, "We will merchandise the hell out of the Eisenhower Program."[16] Now Len Hall was more matter-of-fact about the process. "Politics these days is like a business," he said. "You sell your candidate and your programs the way a business sells its products."[17] Once again Ike's image was burnished by the advertising agency, Batton, Barton, Durstine and Osborn—whose initials, according to Harry Truman, stood for "bunko, bull, deceit and obfuscation."[18] Under the careful tutelage of Robert Montgomery, Ike actually looked younger and fitter (and, as even the Washington *Post* admitted, altogether more impressive)[19] on television than his Democratic rival, once again Adlai Stevenson. Ike was quite confident of being able to beat him. As the current jest went, Stevenson could not be a virgin twice—though Doris Day seemed to manage it. The president undoubtedly shared the shrewd view of the Augusta *Chronicle*'s cartoonist who pictured the two candidates on the golf links, Ike striding out with the Republican elephant in his bag, while the Democratic donkey struggles along with Stevenson in his.[20] The president had even less respect for Stevenson's running mate, Senator Estes Kefauver. Ike enjoyed repeating the story, no doubt apocryphal, about a voter who told Kefauver that he was his second choice. To the senator's enquiry about who his first choice was, the man replied, "Almost anyone else."[21]

A number of people in the liberal wing of the Republican party might have echoed this response if asked the same question about Richard Nixon. Ike himself was perhaps among them, for in July he once more seemed to revive the possibility of running with another mate. He did so in a characteristically elliptical fashion—refusing either to stop Harold Stassen from backing Governor Christian Herter of Massachusetts for the vice-presidential post or to express a positive preference for Nixon. Ike's motives are more obscure, and probably more confused, than usual. Maybe he was worried about the six percent of the vote which, it was estimated, Nixon's presence on the ticket would cost him. Maybe Ike wanted to gauge the strength of Nixon's following in the GOP. Maybe he was persuaded, in view of his age and state of health, to make better provision for the possible future of his country. Ike thought Stassen "so honest that he is naive."[22] However, he recognized too that Stassen was so eager for office that "he would take dog-catcher—just anything."[23] Ike may have exploited this naked ambition, perhaps hinting that Stassen himself might be chosen at an open convention to replace Nixon on the ticket. At any rate, it was clear that Herter, an aging Easterner who was himself in poor health, could contribute little to Ike's campaign. Bernard Shanley, for one, was convinced that Stassen had planned all along "to substitute himself" and that Sherman Adams "knew all about the operation."

Ike was cross when the chairman of the Republican National Committee attacked Stassen and supported Nixon. "I told Leonard Hall," he said, "to stay neutral."[24] But when it became obvious that Hall spoke for the bulk of the party, Ike got Herter to state that he (Herter) would not be a candidate. So, ironically, at the convention Herter successfully proposed Nixon's nomination and Stassen found himself in the humiliating position of having to second it. Altogether it was a curious, though not atypical, episode in Ike's career. The president appeared to be willing to wound Nixon but afraid to strike. Ike had threatened to cause "a commotion" in his office if anyone proposed a "dump-Nixon movement" but, when asked about it, he denied that this was what Stassen had done.[25] Ike declared that if he had decided on a change of running mate he would have said plainly, " 'Dick, I just don't want you this time.' You see that would be the soldier's way."[26] What makes this claim so absurd, of course, is that the president could just as easily have told Nixon that he did want him. Ike seldom went far along the soldier's way without deviating into the politician's maze. It was not for nothing that during Eisenhower's administration, John Kenneth Galbraith coined the tart axiom that "men of high position are allowed, by a special act of grace, to accommodate their reasoning to the answer they need. Logic is only required in those of lesser rank."[27]

Logic had certainly been lacking in Ike's policy toward the Middle East, which helped to precipitate the Suez crisis during the 1956 election campaign. However, the situation there was so complicated and America's various interests were so incompatible that this was not difficult to understand. Broadly speaking, there were four major considerations, each at odds with the others, which Ike had to take into account. These were, first, to preserve friendship with the Arabs, chiefly in order to protect American oil interests; second, to maintain the state of Israel, which could exert considerable pressure inside the United States; third, to prevent the Soviet Union from extending its sphere of influence to the southwest; and finally, to fill the power vacuum left as the British and French empires reluctantly receded, supporting efforts to close the anti-Communist ring around Russia while avoiding any taint of colonialism. In view of these conflicting aims it was perhaps inevitable that Ike's approach to Middle Eastern problems was characterized, in the words of a recent authority, by "half-measures . . . indecisiveness, and the lack of any well-defined policy." The ambiguity of Ike's policy, indeed, was epitomized in the notorious gift he sent to Egypt's ruler in 1953—a golden pistol. As the Suez crisis erupted, Gamal Abdul Nasser, the new charismatic leader who had effectively freed Egypt from the British, remained bewildered by Ike. He remarked to his advisers, "That man puzzles me; which side is he on?"[28]

The American government's first mistake was to support the Baghdad Pact in February 1955. This was Britain's attempt to salvage its position in the Middle East by signing what purported to be an anti-Soviet treaty with Turkey, Iran, Iraq, and Pakistan. Nasser condemned it as a form of diplomatic imperialism and responded by conducting a drive for the leadership of the nonaligned Arab nations. Dulles and, to a lesser extent, Ike regarded such neutrality as political immorality. In September 1955, therefore, they denied Egypt the arms she needed to combat Israel, thus opening the door for the Communists, who at once supplied them on easy terms. Having thrust Nasser into the enemy's camp, Ike then tried to wean him back with offers of aid for what Dulles called the "largest single project yet undertaken anywhere in the world." This was the construction of the Aswan High Dam, which would revolutionize the economy of the Nile Valley. By November 1955 Dulles told Ike, "we were fairly well agreed to proceed" with this enterprise, though the secretary wondered darkly whether "Nasser is playing an honest game or is in the Communist pocket."[29]

During the spring and summer of 1956 Dulles's suspicions hardened as Nasser continued to forge links with the Soviet Union. Worse still, in May, he recognized Red China, a move that seemed definitely to brand him as a Communist, though it was really an assertion of independence from big-power tutelage—essentially an expression of Arab nationalism. Meanwhile, Ike was being influenced to withhold the Aswan loan by powerful lobbies at home—cotton growers, supporters of Israel, and "trade-not-aid" fundamentalists in the GOP. Though himself trying to remain neutral between the Israelis—whom he thought boastful and intransigent—and the Egyptians—whom he considered prickly and "arrogant"[30]—Ike gradually veered toward the former. Thus, at the end of April, he refused to give weapons to Israel because he wanted "to be able to exert an influence throughout the area for peace," and he professed not to care about the political repercussions at home. But at the beginning of May he did send a small consignment of arms to Israel.[31] And in July, using as his excuse Egypt's objections to conditions that the United States placed on the Aswan loan (though, despite his later denials, Ike knew that Nasser was now prepared to accept them), the president reneged on the offer. Dulles announced the withdrawal in such an offensive manner that Ike queried it at the time and later admitted that the secretary might have been undiplomatic. Dulles said in his defense that by now the Egyptians "knew they would get an adverse decision."[32] He was probably right, but this did not take the sting out of his rebuff. Nasser was particularly outraged by Dulles's disparaging remarks about the Egyptian economy. They were an attack on his regime, he said, and a deliberate "slap in the face."[33]

Military dictators are not in the habit of turning the other cheek, and Nasser at once retaliated by nationalizing the Suez Canal Company. It was owned largely by the French and the British, who paid Egypt only three percent of its annual revenue of more than $30 million. Now all the money could be devoted to modernizing Egypt, for, as Ike said, crossly and unfairly, "Nasser had started the whole business by wanting to build the Aswan Dam."[34] However, Ike at once appreciated the seriousness of the Suez situation and remarked that they were "sitting on a keg of dynamite."[35] Nasser's action gave the two European powers the opportunity they had long been seeking to attempt to overthrow him.

Anthony Eden, who had succeeded Churchill as prime minister in April 1955, had developed a paranoid hatred of the Egyptian leader, seeing him as a Fascist who had his hands on Britain's imperial lifeline and must under no circumstances be appeased. Eden now told Ike that he was prepared to "use force to bring Nasser to his senses."[36] Ike, who had sharply observed that "the British have never had any sense in the Middle East,"[37] thought Eden's proposal to "break Nasser" "unwise," "out of date," and calculated to rouse the whole Muslim world. For the United States to support it might well be to array everyone "from Dakar to the Philippine Islands against us." Dulles, by contrast, feared the loss of Middle East oil, believed that the canal should be internationalized, and maintained that Nasser could be, and "must be," made to "disgorge his theft."[38] This was precisely the expression Dulles used on 1 August when speaking to Eden,[39] and it was indicative of America's equivocal attitude toward the employment of force.

From the first Dulles seemed to hint to the Europeans that military intervention might have its place (though not until after the American election, in which Ike was standing as a peacemaker) and could at any rate be used as a threat in negotiations with Egypt. Thus, on 2 August, Dulles cabled Ike from London to the effect that the British and French probably would "move into the Canal area with force." "I am not (repeat not) sure from their standpoint they can be blamed," he said, because if Nasser got away with his expropriation it would end European power in the Middle East. But, Dulles added, with minimal regard for consistency, "I believe I have persuaded them that it would be reckless to take this step."[40] Over the next couple of months the U.S. embassy in London went "white with rage and red with embarrassment" at what one of its inmates called the "zigging and zagging, today-we'll-say-we-will-and-tomorrow-we'll-say-we-won't tactics that Dulles adopted."[41] But if the secretary of state was torn between his own pugnacious instincts and the president's pacific caution, Ike himself, with his allergy to categorical statements, did not absolutely rule out the use of force.

He certainly informed Eden that the American public "flatly rejects the thought" that an invasion would not achieve a "successful result," and that it would "vastly increase the area of jeopardy."[42] But at the same time he said that the situation might eventually "deteriorate to the point where such action would seem the only recourse,"[43] though there should be no resort to arms until after Dulles's attempts to negotiate a settlement were exhausted and an appeal to the United Nations had failed. He told Eden that Anglo–American solidarity would increase "the chance that Nasser will give way without the need for any resort to force," and implied that force was indeed a justifiable last resort.[44] Furthermore, although Ike described Hugh Gaitskell, leader of the opposition Labor Party, as a "sound fellow" because he favored the use of "peaceful means" over Suez,[45] the president seemed to share something of the prime minister's attitude toward Nasser. Eden told one of his junior ministers that he "wanted Nasser murdered."[46] Eisenhower remarked to Bernard Shanley, "I just can't understand why the British did not bump off Nasser. They have been doing it for years and then when faced with it they fumble [sic]."[47]

As Dulles engaged in tortuous maneuvers to gain time and find a compromise, and Ike assured the press that no one thought "we had been vacillating,"[48] Britain and France acted to topple Nasser. Encouraged by the ambiguities of American policy, they were able to believe what they wanted to believe. This was that if Ike (who would anyway be hamstrung by the election) were presented with a fait accompli, he was bound to side with his traditional allies. Searching for a casus belli, the Europeans withdrew their pilots from Suez in September, but the Egyptians proved quite capable of operating the canal themselves, something about which Ike had at first been confident, though later he had doubts.[49] However, the Europeans were able to manufacture a pretext for aggression in mid-October, when they secretly hatched a plot with the Israelis. Israel agreed to attack Egypt, whereupon the European powers (whose forces were massing in Cyprus) would be able to intervene, ostensibly to separate the combatants but actually to occupy the canal areas and get rid of Nasser.

For the next fortnight an eerie silence settled over Anglo-American relations. Ike became involved in the election campaign and the concurrent crisis caused by the Hungarian uprising. He received a number of indications that war was imminent, and on 24 October he agreed with Dulles, who was frankly bemused by Eden's policy, that the British and the French might "commit suicide by getting deeply involved in colonial controversies in an attempt to impose their rule by force in the Middle East."[50] But as late as 28 October the president could not "believe the British would let themselves be dragged into" an invasion.[51]

The following day he learned that, despite his stern warnings to Prime Minister David Ben-Gurion, the Israelis had attacked Egypt and were rapidly pushing their way through Sinai. Ike was outraged and, according to James Reston, "the White House rang with barracks-room language that had not been heard at 1600 Pennsylvania Avenue since the days of General Grant." Dulles, too, was "personally affronted," and their initial impulse was to give vent to their feelings by adopting extreme and punitive measures.[52] However, Ike responded with a statesmanlike blend of firmness and moderation. He let Eden know that the American government would "redeem our word about supporting any victim of aggression," not least because failure to do so was likely to cause Russia "to enter the situation in the Middle East." It was "important" that the United States and Britain should "stick together," but "perhaps we cannot be bound by our traditional alliances." There was much to be said on the British side of the dispute, he concluded, but "nothing justifies double-crossing us."[53]

Eden ignored all this, being determined to embark on what Lord Tedder, in a letter to his wartime chief, called the "mad action" of making Nasser "the victim of aggression."[54] On 30 October the British and French issued an ultimatum demanding that both Egypt and Israel should withdraw from the Suez Canal area. This was not just "pretty rough," as Ike said,[55] it was obviously ridiculous. For, in the words of the Israeli ambassador, Abba Eban, "Since we were nowhere near the Canal, we would have to 'remove ourselves' forward in order to obey."[56] The ultimatum therefore confirmed American suspicions that the British and French were acting in collusion with the Israelis.

When Dulles asked Ike how they should handle the prospective Anglo-French invasion, the president replied in his inimitable manner that his "off-hand judgement is hands off." He did "not think we should help them," and he wanted to "let them stew in their own juice for a while." He particularly resented Eden's attempt to give the impression that the United States had been kept informed, and he wished "to get over to him that we are a government of honor and stick by what we say."[57] Accordingly Ike called for a cease-fire in the United Nations, only to hear, on 31 October, that the British were bombing Egyptian targets—something that scarcely accorded with the fine impartiality which they professed. Ike was appalled. Though hurt and angry at having been duped by his allies, he preserved throughout the crisis a remarkable degree of calm. On 4 November he even took part in a bridge game with members of the gang, in which they jovially gave each other insulting nicknames, like Nasser and Ben-Gurion. But now he was incensed. "Bombs, by God," Ike expostulated. "What does Anthony think he's doing? Why is he doing this to me?"[58] Ike then telephoned Eden and delivered a military "tongue-lashing" which, according to one account, reduced the ailing premier to tears, and according to another account, astounded an aide whom the president mistook for the prime minister.[59]

Whatever the truth of that, Eden resisted Ike's pressure, both personal and diplomatic. The invasion proceeded, though it was hampered by inept planning and a capacity for amphibious lift which one American admiral found "nothing short of pitiful"—some landing craft of World War II vintage which had been pensioned off as pleasure boats had to be brought back into service. However, the British were responsive to economic sanctions. As Ike remarked on 5 November, with ironic understatement, "the purposes of peace and stability would be served by not being too quick in attempting to render extraordinary assistance" to the Europeans in the matter of oil supplies.[60] But although he was willing to use America's economic might to stop Britain's final, doomed attempt at gunboat diplomacy, Ike rejected as "unthinkable" Bulganin's proposal that the United States and the Soviet Union should combine forces to end the conflict.[61] On 3 November Dulles had gone into the hospital for surgery on the stomach cancer that would eventually kill him, and Ike, who found that the State Department could not make up its mind without the secretary, was now directing his own foreign policy. He had always been "very clear that the Soviet Union was not going to get into a major war" over Suez.[62] But for a few hours, just before election day, he began to have doubts. The president told Emmet Hughes that "we may be dealing here with the opening gambit of an ultimatum. . . . And if those fellows start something, we may have to hit 'em—and, if necessary, with *everything* in the bucket."[63] Just in case, he put U.S. forces on alert all over the world.

The following day, however, 6 November, Ike received two welcome prizes. The first was an overwhelming victory in the election, though, as Ann Whitman recorded, "there was no anxiety or even doubt about the outcome."[64] The second was a statement from Eden that Britain, whose currency was on the verge of collapse, would accept a cease-fire. Ike was almost incoherent with delight:

Anthony, this is the way I feel about it. I have not ruminated over this particular situation at length. I am talking off the top of my head. You have got what you said you were going to get in that you have landed. . . . I would go ahead with the cease-fire, not putting any conditions into the acceptance . . . and after the cease-fire talking about cleaning up the Canal [which Nasser had blocked] and so on.[65]

The President agreed to meet Eden and the French premier, Guy Mollet, in Washington. But when his staff opposed the meeting on the sensible ground that it would antagonize the Arabs, Ike withdrew the offer, telling Eden that the "timing is very, very bad."[66]

He was more decisive about ensuring that the Anglo-French forces actually did leave Suez. Ike refused to provide oil or financial support until the deed was done. He was prepared to supply an economic "fig leaf"[67] to cover the Europeans' nakedness. He also provided a political ploy to save their faces, the creation of a United Nations force to occupy the canal zone—the Tory claim for credit on this score was neatly punctured by the Labor politician Denis Healey, who said it was "like Al Capone taking credit for improving the efficiency of the Chicago police."[68] In the end the cease-fire held and the first British troop withdrawals actually took place while later units were still landing. General Stockwell, the British commanding officer, informed the War Office sarcastically, "We've now achieved the impossible. We're going both ways at once."[69] Obviously he did not know General Eisenhower.

Despite Ike's professed opposition to the Suez invasion he afterward said that if Britain and France had "done it quickly, we would have accepted it."[70] As late as Saturday, 3 November, the deputy director of the CIA telephoned his man in London with instructions to tell the British "to comply with the goddam cease-fire or go ahead with the goddam invasion. Either way, we'll back 'em up if they do it fast. What we can't stand is their goddam hesitation waltz while Hungary is burning!"[71] After the event Dulles reproachfully asked the British foreign secretary, Selwyn Lloyd (whom he despised as a "civil servant"),[72] "Well, once you started, why didn't you go through with it and get Nasser down?"[73] Yet despite American vacillation before the invasion, despite Ike's failure to stop Dulles using diplomatic double-talk, despite his own wobbles during the crisis, the fact remained that Suez was in many ways the president's finest hour.

Quite simply, Ike stood up to be counted on the side of international peace and righteousness. He publicly supported a weak and underdeveloped country against two great colonial powers who were also old allies. He scarcely flinched over agreeing with Socialists opposed to Eden's Tory government, though Nixon thought it "too bad that [Aneurin] Bevan is allowed to make political capital" out of the coincidence, "since any swing to that school of thought would be tragic for us."[74] Ike ignored the Jewish vote in the United States (which he variously regarded as insignificant and capable of causing his defeat) and opposed Israel, America's cherished Middle Eastern protégé. He sustained the cause of decency when the supposedly civilized states of Britain and France had become international bandits. He stopped the war. Moreover, he did so with such tact that the NATO alliance was unscathed and no aid or comfort was given to the Russians.

Ike was furious with the Europeans for having made "such a complete *mess* and *botch* of things."[75] He was particularly offended by the British, who had compounded the immorality, illegality, and stupidity of their action against Egypt by duplicity toward America and its president. His well-developed amour propre had been wounded by this betrayal. His self-esteem—described by a historian who met him as "simple, naive, and charming, but enormous, a tacit sense of total faultlessness"[76]—had been hurt. Yet, once again, Ike displayed that astonishing capacity for magnanimity which was his most transcendent virtue. In a letter to Gruenther on 2 November he remarked sympathetically that "Eden and his associates" must have become "convinced that this is the last straw and Britain simply *had* to react in the manner of the Victorian period."[77] Perhaps he was right, though there are less charitable explanations for Eden's conduct. For if Suez was the epilogue of empire it was also Britain's Watergate, a sordid conspiracy by the rulers to deceive the ruled. The difference was that the British press was too impotent to reveal the truth—the London *Times* actually knew all about the plot and elected to keep it a secret.[78] Still, one British politician did learn a trick from Ike. When Harold Macmillan, who soon succeeded Eden, was asked in a television interview whether there had been collusion with Israel, his answer was couched in such gobbledygook that no one was any the wiser.

The United States, or rather the old guard of the Republican party, also bore some responsibility for the other international crisis which occurred in the fraught autumn of 1956. All the loose talk about freeing the captive peoples behind the Iron Curtain encouraged resistance movements in Eastern Europe to hope that the Americans would give them practical assistance. The reaction against Stalinism inside the Soviet Union, expressed most vigorously by Khrushchev, who enumerated the dictator's crimes at the twentieth Communist Party Congress in February 1956, prompted the satellites to break out of the Russian orbit. Disturbances in Poland induced the Soviet Union to accept a more liberal government, though it still professed Communism and adhered to the Warsaw Pact. The Hungarian uprising, which began on 22 October, might have produced a similar result; for, despite the violent anti-Russian demonstrations, Khrushchev was prepared to tolerate the moderate regime which emerged under Imre Nagy, a Communist who had opposed Stalin.

However, Dulles, apparently inspired by an apocalyptic vision of the decline and fall of the Russian empire, egged on militant nationalist forces in their attempts to eradicate Communist rule in Hungary altogether. He told Ike on 27 October that "the Nagy government in Hungary included a number of 'bad' people, associated with the Molotov school."[79] If the United States had supported Nagy, instead of permitting Radio Free Europe, the CIA's propaganda station, to urge on the rebels with promises of American aid, he might have achieved a considerable degree of independence for Hungary, because Khrushchev was uneasy about the traditional policy of repression. On 30 October he expressed a willingness to negotiate a complete withdrawal of Soviet troops and to establish a new relationship with Russia's Eastern European satellites based on "non-interference in each other's internal affairs."[80] Ike saw this as "the dawning of a new day."[81]

Dulles was struck by "What a tragedy it is just when the whole Soviet policy is collapsing the British and French are doing the same thing in the Arab world."[82] The tragedy grew more bloody when the Hungarian nationalists, by calling for a repudiation of the Warsaw Pact, provoked the Russians to reassert their brutal despotism. On 4 November, the day before the Anglo-French landings at Suez and two days before the American election, the Red Army moved in to crush the revolt, at a cost of some thirty thousand Hungarian lives. Khrushchev acted not only under cover of the Suez invasion but partly in response to it, for Russia could not take a defeat in Eastern Europe as well as a defeat in the Middle East. Ike prepared to meet any further "Russian threat"[83] and made humanitarian gestures in the direction of Hungary. Otherwise he did nothing, because there was nothing he could do without precipitating a third world war. Although he had said, "We cannot . . . subscribe to one law for the weak and another law for the strong,"[84] the truth was that he could coerce his feeble friends over Suez but not his powerful enemies over Hungary.

Ike hinted in his memoirs that he might have responded differently if Hungary had not been "as inaccessible to us as Tibet."[85] But this was surely just a futile attempt to endow the spurious threat to liberate Eastern Europe with some retrospective substance. At the time Ike was obviously perturbed not only by his powerlessness but also by having been implicated in the rhetoric of rollback. He telephoned Dulles anxiously to pass on Henry Cabot Lodge's "feeling that we have excited the Hungarians for all these years, and [are] now turning our backs on them when they are in a jam." Dulles replied comfortingly that "we had always been against violent rebellion." Ike agreed, saying that he "had told Lodge so, but was amazed that he was in ignorance of this fact."[86] The president, who had always insisted that the conquered nations should be liberated by all peaceful means, was on firmer ground than the secretary in this disingenuous conversation. But Ike himself had never boldly repudiated the inflammatory language of GOP fundamentalists, and he must bear some of the blame for encouraging a hopeless rebellion in Eastern Europe. He must also receive much of the credit for resisting the siren calls of those dogmatists and opportunists who favored intervention there. Once again he had preserved the peace.

A cartoon in the *Christian Science Monitor* picturing a man with his head in a whirl as he tried to watch "Three Spectaculars at once" on separate television sets, summed up the mood of American voters, now over 100 million of them, as the election approached. That domestic event was certainly overshadowed by the two international crises. But it would probably have excited relatively minimal interest even if the invasions of Suez and Hungary had not taken place. For once it became clear that Ike was a candidate—and even after his ileitis operation most people assumed, as Stevenson did, that "if he can walk he can run"[87]—the result was a foregone conclusion. The patrician Stevenson and his folksy running mate, Estes Kefauver (whose symbol, the coonskin hat, testified both to his Tennessee background and to the Davy Crockett craze), never stood a chance. It must be said, however, that Stevenson's electioneering efforts were singularly inept. Robert Kennedy accompanied him for a while to learn how to run a presidential campaign and later said that he had learned how not to run one. (And after campaigning for Stevenson, Robert Kennedy quietly voted for Ike.) It has been argued in Stevenson's defense that he was ahead of his time, that with his concern about such matters as

Medicare and nuclear disarmament he laid the groundwork for John Kennedy's New Frontier and Lyndon Johnson's Great Society. But to be successful a politician must ride the wave of the present. This was exactly what Ike did—despite quoting Ibsen at the celebratory Republican convention to the effect that the "man is right who is most clearly in league with the future."[88]

In his efforts to prove that the Democrats were not the party of war, Stevenson attacked Ike where he was strongest, on matters of defense and foreign policy. Actually Stevenson did manage to exploit real fears that atomic tests were poisoning the atmosphere. But Ike was able to make enormous capital out of the fact that Bulganin, who called for a test ban in October, endorsed his opponent's views. Moreover, in advocating the abolition of the military draft and an increase in U.S. missile strength, Stevenson was perceived to be inconsistent. Ike was also invulnerable to his personal assaults. Stevenson portrayed Ike as the "part-time President" of "fusion and confusion."[89] He produced a catalogue of crises which had occurred when Ike was on vacation or playing golf. He concluded in a final desperate allusion to the president's health that Ike "lacks the energy" for the job.[90] Thus a vote for him would be a vote for President Nixon, who had "put away his switchblade and now assumes the aspect of an Eagle Scout."[91]

Ike was stung by such personal attacks, as his letter to Gruenther in September, which clearly said the opposite of what it meant, indicates: "When I begin to question the right of anyone to make some of the extraordinary statements that are made, involving distortions and even disregard of fact, I am apt to get very heated. It never occurred to me, though, that anyone thought that I was personally hurt or irritated by those things."[92] However, Ike was so revered that any criticism of him seemed close to blasphemy, and Stevenson's attacks did little more than redound to his own discredit. Suez and Hungary seemed to make nonsense of the charge that Ike was incapable of fulfilling his functions. Anyway, his supporters said, they would rather have a half-time Ike than a full-time Adlai. The president himself made much of the fact that he was interrupting what had turned out to be quite an energetic campaign (designed to prove his fitness) in order to act as national leader, while his opponent continued his partisan sniping from the sidelines.

As the votes were counted Ike abandoned his pose of indifference. He told Emmet Hughes (who had made what Ike gratefully called a "tremendous and unique contribution" to the campaign)[93] that he would be content with nothing less than a landslide. "I just want to win the whole thing." He succeeded, to the delight of 2,300 Republicans who celebrated victory with Ike and Mamie at the Sheraton Park hotel. Ike carried all but seven states and received nearly 58 percent of the total votes cast, some 35.5 million, compared to Stevenson's 26 million. For the first time since 1876 the Republicans even took Louisiana. "Louisiana?" said Ike. "That's as probable as leading in Ethiopia."[94] Ike also attracted an impressive amount of support from the cities and from blacks—even Adam Clayton Powell, despite having earlier likened Ike to Pontius Pilate washing his hands of the race issue, backed him.

However, Ike's coattails proved surprisingly short. The Republicans failed to carry either the Senate or the House, the first time this indignity had been visited on a president-elect since 1848. Thus Ike's claim that his was a triumph of modern Republicanism rang particularly hollow. It was a personal victory. During Ike's first term peace, prosperity, and serenity had descended on America. So, too, had a degree of complacency. But the nation surely had a good deal to be complacent about. Ike got a lot of mileage out of the joke about a man who said he was going to vote for Stevenson—on the grounds that he had voted for him in 1952 and everything had been just fine ever since. But the American people had not voted for measures so much as for a man, not for policies so much as for personality. Quite simply, they liked Ike.

17

★

Winds of Change

On 8 November 1956, Ann Whitman noted that the "President was in a wonderful frame of mind, with the lifting, if only temporarily, of the tensions."[1] The lift was very temporary. Ike was bitterly disappointed to be deprived by the crises of the golfing holiday he had promised himself immediately after the election. He remained so cross with Eden and Selwyn Lloyd that most of his relations with Britain were channeled through the aged Churchill, who, while eating a gargantuan breakfast in bed, would discuss matters with the American ambassador Winthrop Aldrich.[2] Ike had to deal not only with routine business but with bizarre suggestions like Stassen's plan (which intrigued the president) that the United States should buy the Sinai peninsula and the Gaza Strip and internationalize them. Ike was plagued by visits from two types of people, he complained: one lot who thought him "awfully ignorant and tried to tell him all they knew," and the other lot who "thought only he could do anything about any problem that came up."[3]

Dulles's recovery was a relief to Ike in many ways. But the secretary apparently came out of the hospital even more of a prosecuting archangel than he had been on entry. In December he sent the president an earnest memorandum asking whether they should not "shape our policies towards a 'showdown' with Russia . . . having in mind that the persistent injustices and threats perpetrated by the Soviet and Chinese Communists become increasingly intolerable?" Dulles acknowledged that this "showdown" "would not have more than a one chance in three of working, and two chances out of three in making global war inevitable." He therefore actually recommended the continuation of present policies, a course with which Ike, who preferred showdowns of the OK Corral variety, found himself in "complete agreement." As the president mildly observed, he was "very doubtful that a showdown with Russia would work."[4] This was a sound and comforting conclusion. But Ike surely wondered whether anyone willing to present the chief executive and commander in chief with such a reckless exercise in intellectual brinkmanship was fit to conduct the foreign policy of the most powerful nation on earth. It was scarcely surprising that by Inauguration Day, 21 January 1957, Ike was fussing about the many pleasurable things he and Mamie might have been able to do as private citizens. During the ceremony Ike's fingers grew numb with cold and he was so keyed up that he could not sleep before the inaugural balls. But he did finally concede that he had enjoyed himself, or at any rate that he would have been more unhappy to be handing over the presidency to Adlai Stevenson.[5]

Amid the misty, high-sounding platitudes of Ike's Inaugural Address one idea did emerge with reasonable clarity. This was that isolationism was dead, that Fortress America was not a stronghold but a prison. "We are called to act a responsible role in the world's great concerns or conflicts," Ike proclaimed. It was obvious from Suez and Hungary that great powers risked moral censure and political damage if they attempted to impose their will on small countries by force. Ike sensed that these "new nations" were beginning to stir and strive as the "winds of change blew harshly" across the globe.[6] Accordingly he put greater emphasis on the policy of winning the struggle for the hearts and minds of the Third World. Ike had previously maintained that waging the cold war involved "trying to arouse disaffection among our enemies."[7] Now he began to concentrate more on making friends among the emerging countries, through the medium of American aid. He argued persuasively that this was an "investment for peace." The vast military budget only brought "the policeman on the corner to see that the burglar doesn't get into our house," said Ike. The mutual security program was calculated to neutralize the threat altogether. Aid was required to assist the developing countries for whom, Ike rightly observed, nationalism was even stronger than Communism. It was impossible to wage peace "from the pulpit," he urged. It must be paid for in hard cash and then "if we make mistakes, [it] is in terms of dollars not lives."[8]

As the president enunciated it, this was an attractive and intelligent policy. But it was frustrated by a number of factors. First, Ike could not persuade members of his own government to support generous "expenditure on aid"—most parsimonious of all was that dyed-in-the-wool fiscal conservative George Humphrey (whose mother had always spelled the New Dealer Roosevelt with a small *r*). Second, to

Ike's dismay, Senator Styles Bridges spoke for most of the Republican party when he described the scheme as nothing but "a do-gooder act."[9] Third, Congress cut the funds which the president had requested by a third, to $2.7 billion, only about two and a half times more than was spent on the CIA. Finally, despite all his professed hostility to colonialism, Ike felt an atavistic sense of superiority toward lesser breeds without the law, which tended to nullify even his best efforts to appeal to the Third World.

It emerged in his instinctive feeling that Algeria was not yet fit for self-government. It was evident, too, in the cultural and personal antipathy he felt for leaders of underdeveloped nations whom he tried to cultivate. He did, it is true, find some common ground with King Ibn Saud of Arabia (who did not, as Ike had feared, bring his harem to Washington): they discussed hunting. But Ike felt stifled by the musky smell of the monarch's robes and embarrassed by his constant references to Allah. The president also found it difficult to get on with Pandit Nehru. His talk, uttered in such low tones that Ike's primitive listening devices could not pick it up, was a disconcerting series of harangues punctuated by long silences. Ike reckoned that the Indian prime minister was eaten up by "terrible resentment . . . to the domination of the white." "The fellow is a strange mixture, intellectually arrogant, and of course at the same time suffering from an inferiority complex . . . schizophrenia."[10] Actually Ike was not alone in this view. The Progressive Henry Wallace told him that Nehru was "a very intelligent, self-contained person who, in spite of his western education, is sufficiently oriental to go in two directions at the same time very politely." Or perhaps Wallace was just being ironic at Ike's expense.[11]

If Ike's enlightened impulses to aid the Third World were hampered by his neocolonial mentality, they were quite stultified by his (and even more, by Dulles's) compulsion to treat the developing countries as pawns in the cold war. Now that Anglo-French power in the Middle East was dissolving, Ike did not, despite his protestations, visualize the evolution of Arab states with "full sovereignty and independence." Instead he feared the intervention of a Soviet Union bent on controlling two-thirds of the earth's known oil deposits and the "crossroads of the continents of the Eastern Hemisphere."[12] "The existing vacuum in the Middle East must be filled by the United States," he declared, "before it is filled by Russia."[13] Thus he formulated what became known as the Eisenhower Doctrine, his demand for congressional authorization to give economic aid and, if requested, military assistance to Middle Eastern countries. His motive here was probably much as it had been when he had applied for the authority he already possessed during the Formosan crisis: he wanted to share responsibility with Congress and to warn the Communists to keep their distance. What he achieved was unsatisfactory on all counts. The congressional debate revealed a marked American reluctance to become involved in the Middle East. But the Arabs naturally suspected that the president intended Uncle Sam to take over the roles vacated by John Bull and Marianne.

In order to keep the Arab states out of the Russian camp, Ike thought it essential to allay this suspicion. He also considered it vital to start oil flowing through the Suez Canal again, for the European economies were in danger of drying up. But Nasser refused to clear the canal until Israel had withdrawn from strategic outposts in the Gaza Strip and Sinai. So, during February, Ike put pressure on Ben-Gurion, though he tried to conceal the resultant hostility by issuing news bulletins so fuzzy that they left matters "in a state of confusion." Ike found it "funny" that "the whole world is balked by two little countries worrying about local prestige etc., and other countries torn by troubles have to take this and make it their major business and get nothing else done." Eventually Ben-Gurion succumbed to a mixture of financial threats and blandishments—which Ike called, to Dulles's amusement, "not really bribery."[14] By March 1957, therefore, the president had successfully restored the status quo in the Middle East and had shown himself to be an honest broker. In the Arab world (and in the Third World generally) American prestige had never stood so high. Even Egypt, which disliked the Eisenhower Doctrine, could scarcely protest about it.

However, Ike could not leave well alone, and his Doctrine was applied, particularly by the doctrinaire Dulles, with increasingly muddled results. These were, first, that American aid and interference, far from stabilizing the region, created further rifts between rival countries and blocs. Second, an American success with one state—for example, King Hussein of Jordan's suppression of nationalist opposition with American assistance in the spring—provoked its neighbors to look toward the Soviet Union as a countervailing force. Third, any serious threat to intervene directly or by proxy—for instance, in strife-torn Syria during the autumn of 1957—crystallized Arab opposition to the United States. Thus, in a paradoxical way, the implementation of the Eisenhower Doctrine actually did help to neutralize any Communist threat to the Middle East. But it did so only by stirring up a virulent Arab nationalism that was more hostile to the United States than to the Soviet Union.

Arab countries were as much inclined to view the West as a mono-lith as America was to view the East in that light, and the impression hardened when Ike sought a rapprochement with Harold Macmillan, who had now become prime minister of Britain. Of course, their friendship went back to North Africa and, when Eden proved that he was not "a good first man,"[15] Ike had hoped that Macmillan, rather than his rival R. A. Butler, would succeed him. Macmillan was "a straight, fine man," Ike said, "the outstanding one of the British he served with during the war."[16] However, Macmillan had been a hawk over Suez, vowing that he would rather pawn the National Gallery than be humiliated by Nasser—though as chancellor of an Exchequer facing bankruptcy he had felt bound to recommend an early with-drawal, and Harold Wilson sneered that he was first in and first out. Still Macmillan had evidently made it clear that Britain felt "let down, if not betrayed, by the vacillating and delaying tactics" of the Ameri-cans.[17] Before long, therefore, Ike was saying that "Butler would have been easier to work with—that Macmillan and Eden were somewhat alike in the fact that both could not bear to see the dying of Britain as a colonial power." Ike himself was convinced that, having lost an empire, Britain must find a new role in the European Common Market and become "leader of a Western European coalition."[18]

Anxious to press this point and to patch up the Atlantic Alliance, Ike tactfully proposed a meeting, in March, on the British island of Bermuda. Realizing that Bermuda would not be Canossa, that he would not have to appear as a suppliant in a white sheet, and that there would be no recriminations, Macmillan accepted with alacrity. Nor-mally astringent, the British premier etched an unusually malicious caricature of the American president at the conference. Macmillan depicted Ike as a lonely, garrulous figure, "half king, half Prime Minister," as a bumbler who relied on Dulles for his foreign policy and on Hagerty for his attitude to home affairs, as a part-timer who spent 150 days of the year on the golf course, had only come because he liked the Mid-Ocean Club in Bermuda, and was disappointed when the weather prevented him from playing more than a few holes. No doubt much of this was the product of badly bruised pride. Yet it is clear that Ike handled Macmillan with consummate delicacy. There were, to be sure, some plain words spoken on both sides. Macmillan supported the Eisenhower Doctrine though he felt it was nothing more than "a gallant effort to shut the door after the horse had bolted."[19] Ike urged Macmillan to use his influence to tone down anti-American excesses in the more chauvinistic British newspapers. But in general the president effaced, even diminished, himself. He subtly and successfully insinuated his own ideas. He restored confidence by means of beaming cordiality and transcendent charm. He bound up the wounds as only a master of coalition diplomacy could.

Ike found the Bermuda Conference "most profitable"[20] and a bright moment in a time of growing gloom. For as he embarked on his second term everything began to go wrong, so much so that soon even Republican newspapers were wondering if the president, who was anyway a lame duck thanks to the Twenty-second Amendment, was too old and infirm to carry out his duties. Before long Ike's friends were worried that he did not seem to be a dominant leader,[21] and his enemies were pronouncing him to be "nine-tenths figurehead."[22] A mood of disillusionment with the administration began to pervade the country. Taking a morning walk past the White House, Harry Truman wondered "who lives there now."[23] Inside the White House, according to Arthur Larson, "negativism" was triumphant. The government's policy appeared to be "postpone, delay, or better still don't do anything."[24] Ike himself seemed more than ever to be affected by that kind of broad-mindedness that is almost indistinguishable from intellectual paralysis. He actually found it in him to endorse Barry Goldwater's view of himself as "a true liberal" because the senator opposed compulsory unionization. "The liberal of today," Ike declared, "says that everyone should agree with him, or else he is NOT a liberal, which is against the basic meaning of liberalism."[25] Later, of course, Ike changed his mind (though he retained a crippling degree of ambivalence), asserting that Goldwater was "nuts," that he was "a nice guy" who had "got everything but brains."[26]

Emmet Hughes, who came to regard Ike as a man fatally divided against himself, attributed the president's loss of initiative in 1957 to the fact that the frugal Kansan was at odds with the earnest New Republican.[27] It was, indeed, the prolonged debate over the budget which most seriously damaged Ike's prestige during the first nine months of 1957, when this financial measure was struggling to be born. The president baffled everyone by appearing to argue on both sides, putting forward his generous fiscal plan and then supporting its parsimonious critics inside as well as outside the administration. He submitted his 1958 budget, which envisaged expenditure of just over $70 billion, to Congress on 16 January 1957. The same day George Humphrey deplored "this terrific amount" of spending and the consequent heavy taxation, and predicted that if cuts were not imposed "you will have a depression that will curl your hair."[28] This remark evidently indicated a major rift between the president and his secretary of the Treasury. But when questioned about it, Ike astonished his fellow Americans by saying that he had helped to draft Humphrey's statement, which "expresses my convictions very thoroughly." If Congress could find ways of trimming the budget, he added, "it is their duty to do so."[29]

The truth was that Ike wanted to oblige both the big spenders and the big savers. He was anxious to promote a progressive Republicanism, investing in areas like social security, public housing, schools, and highways, and to "do for the people" (as Larson had said that Lincoln had said) "what they cannot do for themselves."[30] He was also under tremendous pressure from the Pentagon to provide their increasingly expensive hardware—Charles Wilson noted that the B-47 airplane had cost its weight in silver, whereas the new B-52 cost its weight in gold.[31] And behind the military lay the even more potent industrial complex—as Barry Goldwater said, "The aircraft industry has probably done more to promote the Air Force than the Air Force has done itself."[32] To Ike's annoyance Wilson was more inclined to support the joint chiefs of staff than the commander in chief, who complained that the Defense Department "blows with the wind."[33] But it was the president who blew with the wind, for he was also trying to appease the advocates of sound money and fiscal integrity. Or rather, having encouraged Congress to cut the budget—encouragement which the Democrats gleefully heeded, incongruously joining the conservatives in a blatant attempt to embarrass the government—he now swung uneasily between spenders and savers. He supported both, but qualified his support in such a way as to satisfy neither. To bewildered journalists he maintained at once the need to "reduce our spending" and the need to retain every project "that was provided for in the budget."[34] He refused to recognize that these objectives were mutually exclusive.

As Congress hacked away at the budget, the GOP became anxious about what seemed an unprecedented abdication of authority on the part of the executive. The press grew so restive that one reporter was bold enough to ask whether Ike would economize to the extent of doing "without that pair of helicopters that have been proposed for getting you out to the golf course a little faster than you can make it in a car?"[35] Ike angrily denied that any had been procured for that purpose. But the story rumbled on and Hagerty had to explain that the helicopters could be used to evacuate the president in an emergency.[36] The president tried to defend his anomalous budget procedure by going over the heads of Congress and speaking directly to the American people on television. In his first broadcast, on 14 May, he argued that, provided it satisfied the national interest, there was no right size for a budget. The discussion reminded him of the question put to Lincoln about how long a man's legs should be, to which the spindle-shanked president had sagely replied, "long enough to reach the ground."[37] Such unhelpful pieces of vernacular wisdom did not satisfy Ike's audience, and Emmet Hughes was called in to devise a more convincing fireside chat. But in spite of it Congress finally slashed four billion dollars from the budget. The whole episode was a notable defeat for Ike, exposing as it did his penchant for chronic vacillation. When he was asked in August if he had any comment on the accomplishments of the Eighty-fifth Congress, Ike replied sourly, "Nothing printable."[38]

However, Congress, and in particular the "ruthlessly ambitious" Senate majority leader Lyndon Johnson,[39] received more credit than Ike for the first civil rights bill in over eighty-two years, which became law in September 1957. For although the president supported the bill he did so in such a half-hearted fashion as to suggest that it was fundamentally distasteful to him. This is not to say that Johnson himself liked what he privately dubbed "the nigger bill."[40] Indeed, he was responsible for emasculating it. But he was also responsible for passing it. For in his perpetual campaign for the presidency—he even campaigned abroad where, it was said, he once shook hands with a leper—Johnson reckoned to gain more in national popularity than he would lose in Southern hostility. Ike himself shied away from offending any powerful constituency. Throughout the year, as racist violence mounted in the South over the integration issue, he had adopted a distant manner toward its victims. Invited by Martin Luther King to tour the troubled region and speak out on the moral aspects of the desegregation conflict, Ike had been characteristically evasive. He said: "I have just got as much as I can do for the moment" and "as you know, I insist on going for a bit of recreation every once in a while."[41] In short, he was prepared to visit the South to shoot quail but not to meet Jim Crow.

As the civil rights bill was attacked on the Hill, Ike proved notably inept at defending it in the White House. James Reston asked him, for example, whether he would be willing to answer Senator Richard Russell's charge that the bill was a cunning attempt to enforce integration in schools, by rewriting it in such a way that it only guaranteed the right to vote. As a matter of fact, suffrage was its main purpose in Ike's view. And he had suggested that it might be thus restricted during a sympathetic private talk with Russell,[42] a talk that he had misleadingly represented to Swede Hazlett as a complete dialectical triumph for himself.[43] So the president responded to Reston in his best know-nothing manner: "Well, I would not want to answer this in detail, because I was reading part of that bill this morning, and there were certain phrases I didn't completely understand."[44] But this reply, whether true or false, was ill-calculated to get him out of trouble. His admission of ignorance about his own legislation was, in the opinion of Fred Morrow and others, a "shocking" one.[45] Not only did it testify to his lack of interest in civil rights, it encouraged opponents of the bill to draw such teeth as it had. This they proceeded to do, and a number of compromises were proposed which Ike accepted. Finally, however, an amendment was passed whereby anyone refusing to obey the orders of a federal judge in a civil rights case, and being cited for contempt of court, could opt for trial by a jury. This, being composed of registered voters, would be all (or mostly) white, and would automatically deny convictions to federal prosecutors and justice to black plaintiffs.

Ike said that the "country took an awful beating"[46] as a result of this clause, which obviously made a mockery of the whole bill. It was, he declared, the most serious political defeat he had suffered in four years. But though he expressed his bitter disappointment Ike did not veto the bill, as many (including Fred Morrow) urged him to do. The deputy attorney general, William Rogers, exclaimed indignantly that "the law is like handing a policeman a gun without bullets."[47] However, the nearest Ike came to condemning those who had disemboweled the bill was to question mildly "whether it would be out of character for him to say [in a press conference, that] a "lot of people seem to be working to protect the right of a man who might interfere with another's voting rights, rather than protecting the right of a citizen to vote.' "[48] Eventually the president acceded to a further compromise whereby federal judges could forbid jury trials but could impose only minimal penalties. In his memoirs Ike congratulated himself on having deliberately steered "a difficult course between extremist firebrands and extremist diehards."[49]

But while this claim acknowledged his role as captain it ignored Lyndon Johnson's as helmsman, and it provided an unfortunate reminder of the president's habit of equating civil rights activists and members of the Ku Klux Klan. Still, the civil rights bill was hailed by the New York Times as "incomparably the most significant domestic action of any Congress in this century."[50] And it was certainly a token acknowledgment that black people were full citizens of the United States. In practice, though, it did little to improve their lot. Between 1957 and 1960 the Department of Justice brought only ten suits to secure electoral rights for blacks. Moreover, only about a quarter of blacks eligible to vote had been registered by the time Ike left office —hardly surprising since so few of them were able to qualify by answering questions like, "How many bubbles are there in a bar of soap?" The bill's feebleness was a reflection of the racial attitudes of a president who was committed to benign, if hesitant, moralizing in public and who privately shared many of the prejudices of his Southern friends.

However, thanks to the Supreme Court's ruling on integration, a major domestic crisis was brewing which forced Ike to take a clear stand on the school issue; it proved to be one of the most painful decisions of his career. On 2 September Governor Orval Faubus of Arkansas defied a federal court order to admit nine black students to Central High School in Little Rock, calling out the state's National Guard to prevent their entry. The previous July Ike had declared that he could not "imagine any set of circumstances that would ever induce me to send Federal troops . . . into any area to enforce the orders of a Federal Court, because I believe that common sense in America will never require it."[51] Such optimistic sentiments, themselves almost an invitation to Faubus, now looked fatuous, and Ike was faced with having to uphold the law. The president received a report on the adverse publicity which events in Little Rock had generated around the world, particularly in the United Nations where (to the dismay of America's allies) the Russians were afforded a marvelous opportunity to turn the tables on Lodge, who was complaining about their violation of human rights in Hungary. But he remained reluctant to intervene. He fell back on the conservative cliché that it was impossible to change the human heart by laws, which anyway ought to be "executed gradually." And he conjured with the segregationist cliché that the South saw "a picture of a mongrelization of the race, they call it."[52] Then he went off on a golfing vacation to Newport, Rhode Island. As he departed with Mamie, who was convalescing after a recent hysterectomy, photographers asked her for a big smile, which she bestowed on them saying, "I still have that."[53]

The situation in Little Rock grew uglier, and on 9 September a new school in Nashville, Tennessee, was dynamited to prevent the entry of one black child. As Cabell Phillips wrote, the segregationists "invested their cause with searing emotional impact."[54] Ike recognized this and did everything to avoid getting burned. As the legal proceedings dragged on, he arranged for Faubus to ask to come to Newport, though he would not see black leaders like Adam Clayton Powell and Martin Luther King, who were clamoring for a meeting. Brownell and Adams both advised Ike against trying to work out a compromise with

Faubus. The governor was described as "a slightly sophisticated hillbilly" who hailed from Greasy Creek and was looking for the redneck votes which would give him a third term in office.[55] He could not afford to back down on this domestic issue, and an interview with the president would just give him more publicity.

Nevertheless, on 14 September, at Ike's insistence Faubus flew to Newport for a talk with the president. Like so many of his wartime conferences with Monty, this one ended in amiable concord and did nothing to remove the fundamental discord. Ike "got definitely the understanding"[56] that Faubus had agreed to keep the National Guard at the school but to admit the black pupils, in which case the legal proceedings would be dropped. According to Faubus, Ike promised not to use force. Whatever the truth of this, Ike, having praised Faubus's "constructive and cooperative attitude,"[57] felt that he had been betrayed; for the governor continued to exclude the black children. And when the court once more insisted that he proceed with integration Faubus withdrew the National Guardsmen and turned over the streets to a howling white mob, which abused, beat, and spat at the black pupils.

Ike issued a strong statement condemning these "disgraceful occurrences." He threatened to use "the full power of the United States" to prevent "violations of law and order by extremists" and hoped that "the American sense of justice and fair play will prevail."[58] It did not. The next day, 24 September, the disturbances grew worse. Ike had told a colleague that if he did make a move over Little Rock it would be "quick, hard and decisive."[59] But he spent several hours vainly and agonizingly trying to find some moderate solution. He did not act until the mayor of Little Rock sent him a telegram reporting that the police could no longer control the mob and appealing urgently for federal troops. Ike then put the National Guard under federal control and dispatched one thousand paratroopers to Little Rock.

As the violence had mounted the president was increasingly criticized for remaining on holiday in Newport. Ike argued that he did not want to invest Little Rock with unnecessary significance by rushing back to the capital. He also claimed that his headquarters were wherever he happened to be. But when the crisis broke he changed his mind. He observed that communications were too difficult from Rhode Island. He also heeded advice that "it did not sound well to have it said that his speech to the nation came from the vacation White House" and that he required "the dignity of the White House" proper behind him.[60] So it was from the "house of Lincoln, of Jackson and of Wilson" that Ike made his broadcast. He justified the use of force, which was necessary not to compel integration but to uphold the rule of law against mob rule.[61] Nevertheless, Ike was furious about having to return to Washington and he was soon complaining to Nixon that he did not know whether he could play golf "because of the stupidity and duplicity of one called Faubus."[62]

For the first time since Reconstruction federal troops had been sent to the South to protect the rights of blacks. Ike was thus subjected to the kind of vilification which he detested. Senator Russell, for example, compared the president's soldiers to "Hitler's storm troopers."[63] Others lambasted him as a destroyer of states' rights. Ike himself said that now his "main effort would be to play down the Little Rock situation."[64] He did so by expressing his understanding of the white South, his faith in patience, moderation, gradualism, and his insistence that coercion had been the last resort of a government concerned with maintaining order rather than with desegregating schools. According to a Gallup poll, nearly two-thirds of all Americans and more than one-third of Southerners thought that Ike had been right to send in troops. The result certainly vindicated his action. The protests gradually died down, and although Faubus (who was duly reelected) fought a lengthy rearguard action in and out of the courts, Little Rock's Central High School was operating satisfactorily on an integrated basis within two years. The same could not be said of other schools in the South, where segregation was the rule. Indeed it remained so in every sphere of Southern life during Ike's presidency, despite a growing volume of protest—which was met with increasingly violent resistance.

Ironically the president had shown during his admirably firm action at Little Rock that the law could, by affecting behavior, change minds if not actually win hearts. But for all his addiction to crusades Ike was disinclined to try to repeat the process elsewhere. Nor was his timid rhetoric calculated to alter the outlook of his countrymen. As Martin Luther King, who praised Ike's conduct over Little Rock, said after their long-deferred meeting the following year:

His personal sincerity on the issue was pronounced, and he had a magnificent capacity to communicate it to individuals. However, he had no ability to translate it to the public, or to define the problem as a supreme domestic issue. . . . His conservatism was fixed and rigid, and any evil defacing the nation had to be extracted bit by bit with a tweezer because the surgeon's knife was an instrument too radical to touch this best of all possible societies.[65]

In his high-minded, pharisaical, lazy, and sheepish attitude toward civil rights Ike was typical of his time. To the casual listener he

sounded like a mere echo of orthodoxy. Yet he was able to convey
a deep understanding of, and a passionate sympathy for, the black
human condition to men as intelligent as Morrow and King. Once
more, Ike's instincts were sound but his purpose was infirm. It would
be easier to pardon him if his speech and writing had not been so
thickly larded with unctuous remarks about his personal "regard," in
the sleazy world of politics, "for moral and ethical standards."[66] It
would be easier to condemn him if he had not given so much evidence
of being a president of rare decency and integrity. Yet again Ike
emerges as that paradoxical hybrid, the sincere hypocrite, the honest
Tartuffe.

Little Rock seriously harmed America's moral prestige throughout
the world, but on 4 October the country's military prestige suffered
an equally damaging blow. That day the Soviet Union challenged the
technological supremacy of the United States by firing the Sputnik
into space. The literal meaning of *sputnik,* ironically enough, was
"fellow traveler," and it was the first artificial earth satellite—the only
satellite, humorists quipped, with which the Russians had no trouble.
The "red moon" was the size of a beachball, it weighed just over 184
pounds, and it circled the globe in about 96 minutes at a speed of
18,000 miles an hour. The Sputnik was only just visible to the naked
eye, but its sinister radio signals were all too audible. Those "chilling
beeps" not only announced the dawn of a new era, they proclaimed
that Soviet scientists had taken the lead in the space race.[67] In the
words of Clare Boothe Luce (whom Ike had denied the cabinet post
she wanted after her unsatisfactory term as ambassador to Italy), the
beeps were "an intercontinental outer-space raspberry to a decade of
American pretensions that the American way of life was a gilt-edged
guarantee of our material superiority."[68] The shock to American
morale, it was frequently stated, compared to that administered by the
Japanese at Pearl Harbor. The physicist Edward Teller said so, and
when asked what American space travelers would find if they ever
reached the moon he replied: "Russians."[69]

Yet it seemed inconceivable that a state like the Soviet Union,
economically backward, devastated by the war, and hampered by the
Communist system, could have overtaken the richest, strongest, and
freest country on earth. Visceral doubts began to be felt in the United
States about flaws in the capitalist way of life, in the consumer society,
in public education, and in the government. Ike's friend Bill Robinson
waxed indignant, complaining that the American press was doing the
Daily Worker's job and asking the president, "is there any justification
for a Sputnik to create a cacophony of petulant and frantic voices
which are intent on substituting fear, terror and dissension for the

nation's natural virtues?"[70] But it was clear to most people that democracy was "on the defensive" and that Uncle Sam had been in a snug, smug doze until roused by that insistent bleep. The *New York Times* reprinted a telling cartoon that simply showed a Sputnik whirling past a golf ball.[71]

Although Ike's administration announced that the Sputnik "did not come as any surprise" it was evidently "highly surprised."[72] It should not have been. Only a few days before the launch the Russians, who had successfully tested their intercontinental ballistic missiles in the summer, virtually announced their intentions, though the American press reported the story like a piece of science fiction.[73] But the government certainly did not expect the domestic crisis of confidence which the Sputnik brought in its train. As a result it miscalculated badly, trying to disparage the Russian achievement or to treat it simply as a propaganda coup. The retiring Charles Wilson, for example, described it as "a nice technical trick."[74] Clarence Randall, a White House economics adviser, called it "a silly bauble."[75] Sherman Adams thought the Russians had just scored a point in "an outer-space basketball game."[76] Ike himself pooh-poohed its importance from the security point of view, said that he "didn't know what we could have done better," and declared that there could be no more money for missiles.[77] But far from calming public fears, this sort of response seemed to reveal an invincible complacency. The Democrats, seizing a priceless opportunity, denounced what Hubert Humphrey called this "pseudo-optimism." Senator Stuart Symington declared that the president was "paternalistically vague." At a time that the Ford Edsel was in the process of becoming the greatest automobile fiasco of all time, Lyndon Johnson ridiculed promises that the United States would build a better satellite: "Perhaps it will have chrome trim and automatic windshield wipers."[78]

Ike was thus faced with what he later called a "wave of near-hysteria"[79] and what was at the time a "demand for more dynamic leadership."[80] His response was twofold, to win the propaganda battle and to accelerate the missile program. Ike told the Cabinet that they had all become "so convinced of the rectitude of our position, we have often forgotten some of the techniques of presentation." He urged that the Soviet achievement should not be belittled. But, he said, "we can still destroy Russia. We know it. We've got to convince the world we're doing well. We just have to do a little less buttering and more gunning."[81] Rather than substitute guns for butter, the government abruptly changed its strategy in the war of words. Nixon now acknowledged that the Sputnik could not be brushed off as a "scientific stunt of more significance to the man in the moon than to men on earth."[82] Soon Ike himself admitted that the satellite had "real military significance."[83]

As October passed the president's luck seemed to hold. The visit of Queen Elizabeth II pushed the red moon off the front pages— according to Ike she "expressed shock at how much hysteria there was here over Sputnik. It had died down almost at once in Britain."[84] But on 3 November Russia launched Sputnik II, a 1,120-pound space capsule—or rather space kennel, for it contained a canine astronaut of the Laika breed whose plight, rather than flight, really did upset the British. The Americans too were upset, seeming to believe, as Ike sardonically phrased it, that the "exile of one Russian dog to outer space means the end of the world."[85] Actually Senator Knowland expressed the general anxiety about the Sputniks, telling Ike that they "seemed to negate the impact of our large mutual security program." Because of the "psychological factor" he wanted a speedy "lunar probe." Ike was not interested in "glamor" projects regardless of cost,[86] nor in rockets that could hit the moon. As he remarked sagely, "We have no enemies on the moon."[87]

James R. Killian, whom Ike now appointed as his special assistant for science and technology—popularly known as his "missile czar"— noted that the president had a correct grasp of the military strength of his enemies on earth.[88] The flight of the Sputnik revealed to Ike that the Russians had developed huge rockets because they were incapable of miniaturizing their technology. And the spying flights of high-altitude U-2 aircraft revealed to him that the Soviet Union could not match the United States in the sphere of aviation. Thus when, three days after the launch of Sputnik II, H. Rowan Gaither, Jr., of the Ford Foundation presented his independent report on national security in a nuclear age, the president remained unimpressed. According to Gaither the United States would be "critically vulnerable" to missile attack by 1959, casualties of up to fifty percent could then be expected, and "today our deterrent force is inadequate." Ike replied that the United States was stronger than Gaither recognized. He said that "the free world holds the periphery and can pose a threat from a multitude of points" and that "maximum massive retaliation remains the crux of our defense." Indeed, "there is in reality no defense except to retaliate."

Accordingly Ike insisted that the country's main efforts should go into securing the safety of its strike force. He also rejected the costly option of building fallout shelters on a huge scale.[89] Still, all too aware of burgeoning national anxieties, he favored publication of only "a sanitized version" of the Gaither Report.[90] Ike remained reluctant to pour more cash into defense, especially in view of the first signs of another recession and an inflation rate edging above four percent, not to mention the long struggle to cut the budget. But although he resisted the worst of the panic, he bowed to the inevitable. Ironically his next budget—the product of his much-admired protégé Robert B. Anderson, who had succeeded George Humphrey at the Treasury— was criticized by the Democrats for being too penny-pinching. It made modest increases in military expenditure and compensated for them by restricting federal funds for urban development, hospitals, farms, welfare, and so on. More guns, Ike repeated, had to be provided by "at least a token reduction in the 'butter' side of government."[91]

Ike's initial efforts to speed up missile development were disappointing. On 6 December the Navy's much-heralded "Vanguard" rocket exploded on its launching pad in front of the television cameras. This provoked further disquiet and gave punsters a field day— they coined endless sputnicknames for the U.S. Kaputnik. An American satellite was not put into orbit until the end of January 1958, this time fired by the Army's "Redstone" rocket. Popular anxiety was to some extent allayed. But the continuing competition between the services while the Soviet Union, by concentrating its resources, was still winning what everyone except Ike called the space race, caused further worries. Lyndon Johnson skillfully exploited them during a Senate investigation. The fact was that no fewer than "eleven major organizational changes pertaining directly to the missile programs" had taken place since Ike had entered the White House. According to one missile manufacturer, obtaining a contract from the Department of Defense for your product was just like playing a slot machine: it took "a lot of nickels and a lot of time" but eventually you hit the jackpot.[92]

It was perhaps understandable that the president should have allowed himself to be unduly swayed by that powerful new hieratic caste, scientists. They were, of course, gratified to discover that he was "exceptionally responsive to innovative ideas" in the field of military technology.[93] Ike had, for example, throughout the year overcome his own hankering to reach some sort of accord with the Soviet Union over banning nuclear tests in the face of the scientists' opposition. Actually they disagreed amongst themselves, but the president tended to accept the advice of the hawkish Strauss. As a professional military man, however, Ike might have been expected to quell the damaging squabbles not only between the services but within them. For all three were riven by internal disputes: the Navy over submarines versus big aircraft carriers, the Army over tactical nuclear weapons versus conventional forces, the Air Force over bombers versus missiles. Ike neither gave a decisive lead nor imposed an effective discipline—quite the reverse.

He continued, for example, to support in public the provision of aircraft carriers while expressing his private belief that "the flattop is becoming obsolete."[94] He claimed in his memoirs that as early as February 1947 he had urged the chiefs of staff to get on with building rockets and missiles, the neglect of which "could bring our country to ruin and defeat in an appallingly short time."[95] But as late as December 1956 he told the Defense Department that he "did not think too much of" ballistic missiles "as military weapons." They were too expensive and possessed only "psychological importance." He tried to cut back production.[96] After the Sputniks, though, Ike changed his tune again: "we were talking about bows and arrows at the time of gunpowder when we spoke of bombers in the missile age."[97]

When the commander in chief's trumpet gave such an uncertain sound each service head naturally prepared for battle in his own way —hence the duplication, waste, and delay. In 1958 Ike tried to impose a radical reorganization whereby Charles Wilson's successor, Neil McElroy (formerly head of Procter and Gamble), should be given a stronger hold over the joint chiefs of staff. Ike said that if the Pentagon did not "develop an effective plan" he himself "would have to take the bull by the horns, otherwise he would lose his own self-respect after having been into this business for eleven years."[98] But once again Ike was thwarted, partly by Congress, partly by McElroy's feebleness, partly by the military bureaucracy, and partly by his own laissez-faire approach. This last was epitomized by the president's extraordinary response to the Pentagon's intransigence at the beginning of 1958. Ike said that he believed in the right of people to express themselves—even, apparently, military subordinates who were resisting the controls, financial and otherwise, which their commander in chief was trying to impose. But he felt worried and frustrated by the "revolt of the generals" because no one knew how to stop it.[99] If such a remark proves that Ike was not the stuff of which tyrants are made, it might also suggest that he was not entirely solid presidential timber.

By November 1957 an increasing number of Americans were beginning to fear the worst. Few went as far as the beatnik Lawrence Ferlinghetti who entitled one of his poems "Tentative Description of a Dinner to Promote the Impeachment of President Eisenhower." But Ike's popularity rating dropped to only 57 percent. Despite two

television addresses on defense, critics were now questioning his judgment over what ought to have been his strongest suit. Harold Macmillan noted that Ike's "policies are said to have failed everywhere." The
president complained to the prime minister "a good deal about 'politicians' and the attacks upon himself. This is a new experience for him.
Up to now he has been immune."[100] All this took its toll on the
president, so on 16 November he went off to Augusta for a week's
golfing. When he returned the cares seemed to have fallen from his
shoulders. He was cheerful and well. Then on 25 November he got
cold waiting to greet the king of Morocco. That afternoon in the Oval
Office he was suddenly overcome by dizziness and found that he could
talk "nothing but gibberish."[101] He had had a stroke. Technically, it
was a mild cerebral occlusion and resulted in a form of aphasia.

The statements about his illness given to the press were so confused
that they might have been uttered by the president himself. But it was
clear enough to the American people that their aged chief executive
had been afflicted by his third major illness in two years. There
seemed every reason to expect his resignation on health grounds, and
many newspapers called for it. Such was his initial frustration at not
being able to attend to his duties that Ike himself threatened to give
up his job. But his usual determination quickly reasserted itself. An
anxious Dulles told Nixon that the president's refusal to realize that
he needed to rest indicated poor judgment. He wondered whether
Ike's new sensitivity about the vice-president was "a reproduction of
the [Woodrow] Wilson problem, jealousy and the usurpation of
power."[102] Perhaps so, but within a couple of months Ike had made
an unprecedented arrangement whereby Nixon would take over if the
president became incapacitated. Luckily it was never needed. Within
a few days Ike had returned to light duties and in mid-December he
flew to Paris to attend a NATO meeting. He still had occasional
difficulties with words. But otherwise he had made a remarkable
recovery from what the United Press, bemused by the White House's
garbled account of his illness, had at first called "a heart attack of the
brain."[103]

18

★

Worst Year

As the United States twirled to the hula hoop and twisted to the sound
of Elvis Presley, Ike struggled, during the first few months of 1958,
to make up the ground he had lost the previous year. Thanks to the
therapeutic effects of bridge, golf, and Wyatt Earp on television, not
to mention a strong constitution and a stronger will, he seemed little
the worse for his stroke. He lacked stamina, it is true, and "at the end
of a day his performance is admittedly below par."[1] As Sherman
Adams told the White House staff, "This man is not what he was."[2]
But Ike had cut his work load by some twenty-five percent and was
still able to take the big decisions. However, he found it more difficult
to recover politically and the "Ike-can-do-no-right cries were louder
than ever before."[3] The nation was still reeling from the Sputnik
shock and from the leaked revelations of American vulnerability contained in the Gaither Report. The president himself seemed to be
suffering from an uncharacteristic loss of confidence. He began his
first cabinet meeting of the year by saying, "One nice thing about the
silent prayer—for at least a minute I can't make any mistake."
  Ike was certainly torn between his familiar contradictory impera-
tives as the New Year dawned. He could not make up his mind
whether to save in order to protect the economy or to spend in order
to strengthen defense. He instinctively plumped for fiscal conservatism, though he worried about the effect on the country's morale. "In
some ways we've got to put on [a] hairshirt and sackcloth," he said.
"At [the] same time, not to scare people [we] have to talk about [the]
sturdiness of the American character."[4] In the end Ike decided on a
predictable compromise. He invested more in missile building, in
aircraft construction, and in scientific education. Very reluctantly, too,
he overcame his aversion to "glamor" projects. He initiated the space

program to be run by the newly created National Aeronautics and
Space Administration (NASA).

These concessions were moderate and sensible, but they did not
assuage national anxiety. The president was criticized in the press and
in Congress for doing too little too late. He was simultaneously as-
sailed by organized labor for not dealing more decisively with the
growing recession. Actually it did not concern him too much, though
by the spring unemployment had risen to over five million, the highest
figure since 1941. Ike did some modest pump-priming, but he was
determined to avoid "wild-eyed schemes," even at the risk of being
called "a reactionary old fossil."⁵ On 13 March the president held
what he reckoned was a "friendly," and what Gabriel Hauge thought
a "tough," meeting with the executive committee of the AFL–CIO.
The union leaders went over gloomy statistic after gloomy statistic and
they kept asking, "And *why* don't you act now?" Eventually Ike told
them a story that amused them and broke the ice—without satisfying
their demands. He had been faced with similar questions during the
war, he said, and had finally replied that "he guessed he was too dumb
to act precipitately."⁶

Ike's dilemma in the field of foreign policy was even more acute.
He could not decide whether to negotiate seriously with the Soviet
Union over the question of a test-ban treaty. To do so might gain him
a valuable propaganda coup and freeze American nuclear technology
in a position of advantage. On the other hand he might be represented
as appeasing the Russians, who were not to be trusted and could steal
a march on the United States during any moratorium. Ike frankly
dithered over this issue. He opposed an agreement in February, favored it in March, and then quickly changed his mind again. Meanwhile the exchanges with the Russian leaders became more sterile and
repetitive. Ike protested to Dulles, "If we are to continue this Bulganin–Eisenhower squirrel cage exercise, it seems to me that we should
attempt, at the very least, such divergencies in pace and running style
as may partially prevent the whole thing from becoming completely
monotonous." But the president confessed that he had no "completely new ideas."⁷ The trouble was that the secretary had none
either. And when Ike suggested an imaginative scheme for exchange
visits with ten thousand students from the Soviet Union, Dulles's
disapproval killed it. Ike, it was said, "believed devotedly, even mysti-
cally, in the value of people-to-people contacts" in order to break
down "barriers of misunderstanding between nations."⁸ Dulles was
horrified by the prospect of all those young Communists running
loose in the United States.

Ike was actually beginning to recognize that Dulles was something of a handicap to the government, even though he drew hostile fire away from the president himself. A "surge of anti-Dulles feeling" was going around the globe,[9] and Ike was influenced by it. He was anyway dismayed by the secretary's rigidity and aridity, by his sanctimonious international prosecuting attorney's style and his small-minded "sensitivity" about encroachments into his sphere by men like Nelson Rockefeller and Harold Stassen, whom he regarded as potential rivals.[10] But although Ike evidently hankered to replace him with C. D. Jackson, he would not let Dulles resign. Indeed, the president went to great lengths to defend Dulles. Early in 1958 Cyrus Sulzberger wrote a scathing indictment of the secretary in the *New York Times*. He asserted that the "free world has lost the initiative in its propaganda contest with the Soviet bloc." Moscow had been allowed to take the lead in the quest for peace, and to make it appear as though "we are being forced into talks against our desire." This was all the fault of the secretary of state. "Dulles has emerged as a kind of tragic–comic figure, the greatest no-man since Molotov was in his prime. He lets himself seem to accept diplomatic paralysis as an act of faith."[11] Ike tried to refute Sulzberger's arguments and asked their mutual friend Al Gruenther to rebuke him for voicing them.

As it happens Sulzberger was largely correct. Toward the end of March Ike himself stressed to Dulles the "desirability of our seizing the initiative."[12] But before they could decide to act against the cautious advice of the military, Khrushchev had seized it instead. He announced a unilateral halt to nuclear testing. Ike came close to admitting that he had been completely out-maneuvered. His first response was to say that the Soviet move was not "to be taken seriously," that it was a "gimmick"—a fair criticism since the Russians had just finished a series of tests, while the Americans were about to start one.[13] But after a global outcry over the radioactive fallout caused by the American explosions, Ike had to go into reverse once again. At the end of April the president agreed to begin technical talks on evolving an inspection system, with a view to negotiating a full test-ban treaty.

Despite Khrushchev's démarche, Dulles "had a feeling that the Communist bloc might now be pushing all round the perimeter to see whether our resolution was weakened by the Soviet possession of nuclear missiles." But, he told Ike, "I felt confident that if it appeared that we were standing firm, then they would not take action that would risk precipitating a large-scale war."[14] There were snippets of evidence to support Dulles's first hypothesis, with which Ike apparently agreed. In Venezuela an allegedly Communist mob attacked Nixon's motorcade. Communists were stirring up trouble in Burma. In Indonesia Communists were playing a part in Sukarno's "guided democracy"[15] (this had provoked a military revolt: Ike professed "careful neutrality,"[16] but the United States both covertly assisted the rebels and overtly sustained the government, a policy that so confused the American president that he asked plaintively, "which side are we on?").[17] Anyway, the Communists were the obvious scapegoats when a new crisis blew up in the Middle East during the spring and summer of 1958.

Actually the unrest in Lebanon resulted from the deep divisions which have afflicted that country ever since it gained independence from the French after World War II. To simplify a complex situation: the Muslim section of the population, inflamed by pan-Arab propaganda, began a series of violent protests in May. They were directed against the Maronite Christian president, Camille Chamoun, who had (alone of Middle Eastern leaders) accepted the Eisenhower Doctrine and was trying to alter the constitution in order to stay in power for another term. Chamoun had been elected in the first place with CIA help and he now called on the United States for military assistance. However, Ike and his advisers agreed that the Eisenhower Doctrine could not be invoked because there had been no external Communist aggression against Lebanon. On what authority, Ike asked, had "our former so-called 'gun-boat diplomacy' " rested? Dulles answered that this was no longer "an acceptable practice," though it was agreed that the president could argue that U.S. forces were going in at the request of the Lebanese government in order to protect American lives and property. Dulles warned, however, that "the move might create a wave of anti-Western feeling in the Arab world comparable to that associated with the British and French military operation against Egypt."[18] As it happened, the Lebanese army gained a degree of control over the disturbances and the tension eased. But Ike would have done well to have heeded Dulles's admonition a couple of months later when, for the only time during his presidency, he formally initiated a military action.

On 13 July 1958 a "carefully prepared" coup occurred in Iraq, a stanch member of the Baghdad Pact. The king, his prime minister, and many leading supporters were killed, and a new nationalist government, which looked toward Cairo rather than London, took power. The other pro-Western states, Saudi Arabia, Jordan, and most of all Lebanon, felt threatened. Chamoun once again appealed to the United States for help, and King Saud sent word to Ike that "if [the

Americans did] not come in [they were] finished in the Middle East."[19] The president at once consulted his senior advisers, who were struck by his calm, confident, and relaxed air. He seemed to have already made up his mind to intervene. Cutting short the discussion, Ike asked General Nathan Twining, "How soon can you start, Nate?" Twining replied, "Fifteen minutes after I get back to the Pentagon." Ike said, "Well, what are we waiting for?"[20] The president then explained his plans to congressional leaders, who expressed grave reservations about participating in what looked like a civil war with no Communist involvement. Ike's determination was not shaken. Nor was he put out by Harold Macmillan's response to his telephoned explanation that, although sticking by Chamoun might open a Pandora's Box, the alternatives were disastrous.[21] The prime minister, who regarded Ike's new Middle Eastern policy as "a recantation . . . unparalleled in history,"[22] retorted: "You're doing a Suez on me." They both laughed.[23] The following day the U.S. Sixth Fleet arrived off Beirut. Five thousand Marines, supported by atomic cannons, splashed ashore—to the astonished dismay of bikini-clad bathers and ice-cream vendors on the beach.

Why did the president act with such unaccustomed speed, belligerence, and resolution? The superficial answer is that he believed an independent Lebanon could only be preserved from Communism by force. He told his colleagues, "if we move quickly and decisively the Soviet Union—which is undoubtedly behind the whole operation—may feel that Nasser has gone too far too fast and may call on him to pull back." Ike was not sure whether Nasser was playing his own game, but clearly "the Soviets have a tremendous interest in this."[24] On a more fundamental level Ike was concerned about the threat posed to the West by the possible interruption of Middle Eastern oil supplies. He told Nixon that they had reached a crossroads. "Since 1945 we have been trying to maintain the opportunity to reach vitally needed petroleum supplies peacably." Now Nasser was trying to get hold of them. With his shrewd eye for public opinion, Nixon replied that "you cannot allow it to appear that the Mid East countries are simply a pawn in the big power contest for their resources." What was required, Nixon suggested, was an argument to the effect that "the Communists have developed the device of foreign-inspired revolution to create a civil war."[25] This was precisely the case Ike put forward in his television address justifying the "stationing" of U.S. troops in Lebanon. Of course, he referred to the need to protect American lives. But his central contention was that the civil strife in "tiny Lebanon" had been fomented by Communists. It was a form of "indirect aggression" and part of their familiar "pattern of conquest."[26] Ike stuck to that story in his memoirs, recording his "deep-seated conviction that the Communists were responsible for the trouble."[27]

However, it is clear that the president did not really believe his own account. There was little or no evidence of Communist subversion in Lebanon. Certainly Ike cited none, though the CIA did report on the "wide scope of Nasser's clandestine activities" in Lebanon.[28] As Ike's talk with Nixon reveals, he was exploiting the fears, and employing the rhetoric, of the cold war. On the day of the invasion itself the president gave "deep thought to finding a moral ground on which to stand if we have to go further." He tried to convince himself that Nasser was a Soviet "puppet, even though he probably doesn't think so." But as Ike well knew, the Communist party was banned in Egypt, and as he told Nixon, the trouble was that "the people are on Nasser's side."[29] In other words, Ike recognized at heart that Nasser was an Arab nationalist. He also admitted that the Arab masses would object to the arrival of American troops in Lebanon.[30] From the first Ike was aware that he might be opening a Pandora's Box. He must have been told that the American embassy in Lebanon was "severely critical" of his policy.[31] On 18 July he even confessed to the Cabinet that he was "not under any illusion it would solve the situation—might even make it worse. Using outside forces to stem [the] tide of nationalism is not good." Nevertheless, he added, "failure to act would have shaken the foundations of the free world from Morocco to China." Thus Lebanon was a crucial "test case" for his government.[32]

As he explained it to his colleagues, this was the fundamental reason for American intervention. Lebanon was a test of American political will, even of American political virility. It was proof that the Eisenhower Doctrine was not just an empty formula. Ike told Robert Murphy, whom he sent to pick up the diplomatic pieces after the military operation, that "sentiment had developed, especially in Egypt, that Americans were capable only of words, that we were afraid of Soviet reaction if we attempted military action."[33] To his senior advisers Ike said that it was better to take "a strong position rather than a Munich-type position. . . . Our action would be a symbol of American fortitude and readiness to take risks to defend the values of the free world." This is plausible as far as it goes. But it does not explain why Ike should now suddenly be echoing Dulles, who had always "felt that if the world comes to believe that we will not take risks we are heading for a series of disasters."[34] In previous foreign policy crises just as acute as this Middle Eastern one, the cautious Ike had always kept the impetuous Dulles on a tight rein. The president had employed his matchless talent for prevarication and procrastination to fudge issues and blunt hostilities. He had invariably guided the United States away from the brink. Now, for the only time during his eight years in the White House, he was unequivocally taking an aggressive lead. Why?

The answer must surely be that Ike saw Lebanon not as a test of America's virility but as a test of his own. For if his political motives were unsatisfactory where they were not self-contradictory, his personal motives were compelling and coherent. Since his reelection almost everything seemed to have gone wrong for Ike. Actually, this was an illusion. His second term had not been without its bright aspects. He had restored the status quo in the Middle East after the Suez war. Although he had bent somewhat on defense spending after the Sputnik, he had not given way to panic. He had refused to take alarmist measures during the third recession of his presidency, and recovery was now imminent. But even Ike's successes, which were usually of a passive rather than an active kind, could easily be represented as failures. By the spring of 1958 only 49 percent of the population approved of his conduct and he was being subjected to unprecedented personal attack. It tended to focus on his feebleness, physical, moral, and mental.

Ike was increasingly depicted as an amiable, bumbling grandfather. His failure to reorganize the military establishment, despite his obvious qualifications to do so, had counted particularly heavily against him. Indeed, Ike's backing away from controversy of any sort had provoked his warmest admirers to complain that he should "carry a big stick while he talks softly."[35] Ike so smarted under this sort of criticism that he once ordered his secretary to assemble all the tributes he had been paid by world leaders. As Emmet Hughes recalled, the president's serene surface of humility suddenly foamed with "little bursting bubbles of hidden vanity."[36] The last straw was the outcry which greeted Ike's admission, when Sherman Adams was facing investigation for unethical conduct in June 1958, that "I need him."[37] Ike meant thus to acknowledge the vital role Adams played in the administration. But the remark was taken as a desperate *cri de coeur* from an ailing and incompetent president.

The further eruption of the Lebanese crisis gave Ike the perfect opportunity to correct this impression of weakness at a time that, as Arthur Krock said, the president was "more heavily on the defensive than at any time" since he had taken office in 1953.[38] Ike was determined to invest the doctrine which bore his name with substance. He would prove that American forces were capable of a flexible response and would remind his countrymen of his achievements in the field of amphibious warfare. He would impress Nasser. He would make his mark on the Middle East in the confident assumption that the Russians did not want to risk a "general war" over a country as insignificant as Lebanon.[39] He would rebuild his reputation at home and abroad. If this hypothesis is correct, these were the worst possible motives for a clumsy intrusion into the fractured world of Lebanese politics.

The operation was mismanaged from the start. When the U.S. Marines arrived in July only the last-minute mediation of the American ambassador averted a clash with the Lebanese army, which they were supposed to be helping—still, bloodshed *was* avoided, the best that can be said of the enterprise. The occupying force achieved nothing positive except to replace Camille Chamoun, who, as Admiral Holloway remarked with amazed disgust, had "had the impertinence to call in American armed forces to protect his own personal interests."[40] On the negative side, the United States, by seeming to support Christians against Muslims, exacerbated the process by which Lebanon was to tear itself apart. The intervention of fourteen thousand troops (a larger force than the Lebanese army) who remained for just over a hundred days, did irretrievable damage to American prestige in the Middle East. It wiped out the good effects of Ike's behavior during the Suez war and sowed seeds of Arab hatred for the United States, the bitter harvest of which is still being reaped. It is difficult to disagree with Professor D. C. Watt's harsh verdict: Ike's "incursion into the Middle East with the Eisenhower Doctrine was an unmitigated disaster."[41]

For Ike the case of Sherman Adams was also a disaster, though on a much smaller scale. In June 1958 a Congressional committee discovered that the White House chief of staff had accepted gifts from a textile manufacturer named Bernard Goldfine, whose business he had helped by interceding with federal agencies. These presents—notably free hotel accommodation, a rug, and a vicuña coat—were not bribes, Adams maintained, but tokens of affection from an old friend. He therefore pleaded guilty only to "imprudence." Ike agreed and paid a thumping tribute to Adams: "I admire his abilities. I respect him because of his personal and official integrity. I need him."[42] But if Ike needed Adams, the Democrats needed him too. He provided them with a marvelous issue in the forthcoming midterm elections. They remembered all too well Adams's indictment of Truman's "Augean Stables."[43] They joyfully exploited the similarity between freezers and vicuña coats. And the cartoonists pulled the rug from underneath Adams, attached hotel bills to the Republican elephant's tail and depicted the Democrats laughing like jackasses.

Ike claimed that there was no parallel between his own and the previous administration. Adams, he said, "is all business and all work."[44] But Ike was "forced into an unhappy and vulnerable position."[45] Worse still, the president himself had accepted some vicuña material from Goldfine, though, according to Hagerty, he had given it to a friend whose name he could not recall. This mysterious circumstance drew attention to the hundreds of thousands of dollars worth of gifts which Ike had received. Ike was embarrassed, though his moral stature was so overwhelming that he was not really harmed by innuendos of corruption. As one newspaper wrote, "the river of gifts flowing over the Eisenhowers has not become a political issue."[46]

The impression of weakness which Ike gave as a result of the Adams episode was much more damaging. It was summed up in a cartoon reprinted in the *New York Times* which showed the president stumbling along with a broken crutch marked Adams. The caption read, "I need. . . ."[47] Unfortunately for Ike he was trapped between his stated need and his oft-repeated pronouncements about ethical practices in government. He privately asserted that he "could not be a party to crucifying the Governor for political reasons."[48] But he was widely criticized for not being prepared to sacrifice the man for the principle. Even the Republicans refused to stand by Adams. Many of them remembered how he had flayed Taft in 1952, when he had gone around proclaiming "Thou Shalt Not Steal." Others had been victims of his brutal and laconic style of doing business—Adams's rudeness even extended to his wife, though she was said to have retaliated by filling his lunchtime sandwiches with soap. Only Richard Nixon rallied, at least in public, to Adams's defense. He stated, "The trouble with Republicans is that when they get into trouble they start acting like a bunch of cannibals."[49]

Nixon was born to trouble and he knew whereof he spoke. For although Ike needed Adams, he needed his resignation more. As the elections drew nearer the president was perturbed by news of party morale being badly hit and campaign contributions drying up. He was also disturbed by messages from supporters like Winthrop Aldrich, who said that "this man has got to go or we are done." Ike was upset and resentful, but he felt bound to agree. However, he himself would take no direct action.[50] He had first commissioned Nixon to talk Adams into resignation, to no avail. So in September Ike called in Meade Alcorn, who had succeeded Len Hall as chairman of the Republican National Committee. "You've got to handle it," the president said; "It's your job, the dirtiest job I could give you."[51] Alcorn did handle it. Perhaps on the principle of murdering the messenger,

Adams never forgave him. But he continued to respect Ike, despite having ascertained that Alcorn was acting on the president's instructions. Even more curiously, when Adams told Ike that he would resign, on 17 September, the president tried to maintain the fiction that he was not involved. He told Adams, "If anything is done and we make any critical decision, as I have always said, you will have to take the initiative yourself." Ike stressed that he was "very anxious that we do not do anything that can be interpreted as pressure from [me]."[52] Nixon obviously despised Ike for, as it were, deserting Adams by proxy. During the Watergate scandal he bitterly recalled Ike's determination to "be sure he was clean" at all costs, and, Nixon declared, "we're going to protect our people if we can."[53] It is a nice question as to which was the more reprehensible, Eisenhower's moral cowardice or Nixon's immoral courage.

There is no question, however, that the efficiency of Ike's administration suffered as a result of Adams's departure. His replacement, General Wilton B. ("Jerry") Persons, was less liberal-minded than Adams and also much less ruthless. His career had been mainly spent in lobbying Congress on behalf of the army, and except on the civil rights issue—he came from Alabama—Persons was one of nature's appeasers. Fred Morrow was not alone in finding that "the White House machine has stalled almost completely. . . . There is vacillation, indecision and lack of leadership."[54] Soon Ike himself was complaining that "the staff seemed to descend upon him in droves and dump everything in his lap—much more than when Adams was here." Ann Whitman commented, "It is perfectly true. Even worse, which I do not think he realizes, is the tendency of the staff to have staff conferences, endless I am told, at which nothing but nothing, is accomplished."[55] The president talked to his new chief of staff, but the problem was never solved. His decision to appoint Persons in the first place is difficult to explain, for Ike always needed to work in association with a strong man, either as his boss or as his deputy, someone prepared to shoulder responsibility and to take hard decisions. As James Reston had observed soon after the Adams scandal broke, "when the President said this week, 'I need him,' he spoke the plain truth. The whole White House Staff is built around Adams. It is a weak staff."[56]

It was further weakened by Persons's promiscuous tendency to interfere in matters that did not concern him. Before long Ike was having to restrain him, saying, "there comes a time when you have to make a declaration of independence from your staff."[57] Part of the trouble was that Ike's staff so loved and revered him that they tried to shield him from worrying issues and disagreeable information. According to Joseph Alsop, Bobby Cutler's hero worship of Ike was such that he not only assumed "the President's instincts are more relevant to our problems than the hard facts of our national situation," but went "to great and dangerous lengths to shield the President from anything that might make him unhappy."[58] Ike complained furiously that his staff treated him "like a baby."[59] Paradoxically, however, the resignation of Adams and the death of Dulles in 1959 prompted the emergence of a "new Eisenhower."[60] No doubt this was largely a journalistic myth. But in the last two years of his presidency Ike actually did make a sterling effort to meet the challenge of being thrown onto his own resources.

Meanwhile, the dormant issue of the Chinese offshore islands had flared up once again. In August 1958 the Communists began to shell Quemoy and Matsu, which had been heavily reinforced by Chiang Kai-Shek. Before the bombardment started Dulles had warned Ike that the "amputation" of the offshore islands could not occur "without fatal consequences to Formosa itself." Ike denied that this was true from a military point of view. Dulles agreed, but he said that "the connection from a political and psychological standpoint had become such that I thought now it would be quite dangerous to sit by while the Chicoms took Quemoy and Matsu."[61] So it was that history virtually repeated itself. The offshore islands were to be defended to preserve Nationalist morale.[62] Chiang was straining at the leash. Dulles and the joint chiefs of staff urged aggression. The secretary of state alarmed America's allies by saying that small tactical nuclear weapons might be used to defend the offshore islands—"our entire military establishment assumes more or less that the use of nuclear weapons will become normal in the event of hostilities."[63] As before, Ike forbade the use of nuclear weapons while seeming to dice with megadeath. He staggered reporters by not even knowing, apparently, all the circumstances under which local commanders were empowered to use atomic weapons: "I would have to make certain. My memory is not quite that good this morning."[64]

Once again, too, Ike's purpose was clouded in ambiguity. He insisted on the need to maintain a "firm demeanor, but [to] avoid making statements from which we might later back off."[65] But he did precisely that. In a television address to the nation, broadcast on 11 September, he hoped for a negotiated peace but, employing the language of the China lobby, he rejected any idea of a "Western Pacific Munich."[66] His statement met with an almost universally hostile reception. Ike himself expressed concern that two-thirds of the world and half the United States population opposed his policy. Actually the proportions were probably higher. Some eighty percent of letters on the issue sent to the State Department were critical. So, yet again, in what Harold Macmillan called this dangerous "game of threats and bluffs," Ike seemed to be approaching "the brink of World War Three."[67]

Most people agreed with Dean Acheson that the offshore islands were not worth a single American life, and Ike himself had recently declared that modern warfare was "preposterously and mutually annihilative."[68] However, Ike was confident that the worst could be avoided, a view supported by reports from U-2 spy planes that the Chinese Communists were not preparing to invade the offshore islands. The president said at the time, "I felt that if we stand firm against the Communists, the outcome will be in our favor."[69] As usual, Ike's firmness was tempered with flexibility. Faced with global trepidation, he and Dulles—and Chou En-lai—began to drop conciliatory hints about negotiating what the *Rocky Mountain News* called "a reciprocal loss of face."[70] By the end of September the crisis was evaporating. In October the Communist Chinese restricted their artillery to firing on alternate days and Ike wondered whether he was engaged in "a Gilbert and Sullivan war."[71] Yet again Ike had taken massive risks for insignificant ends. And yet again he had won.

As the United States floated "pleasantly out of recession and into the football season,"[72] Ike himself seemed to be blown to and fro by shifting winds of opinion. The president's greatest achievement during the autumn of 1958 was to assert himself in the matter of a nuclear test-ban agreement. The rash of tests, which occurred on both sides before the autumn conference at Geneva, had alarmed a world increasingly aware of the dangers of radioactive fallout. Ever sensitive to popular opinion, Ike overcame the opposition of his technical and military advisers. He volunteered to stop exploding nuclear devices above ground if the Russians would follow suit, which, after a couple of thermonuclear hiccups, they did. This was a complete reversal of the president's former insistence that such a moratorium was impossible without a satisfactory system of inspection. The nuclear powers continued to wrangle about that in what one scientist called an "Alice in Wonderland" fashion—"The same words used by the two sides had opposite meanings and neither side was willing to state its clear intentions."[73] But Ike gained a major political and propaganda advantage, which he sensibly reckoned would outweigh any technical disadvantage, by halting the apparently inexorable process of poisoning the earth's atmosphere. Most Americans applauded his determination to walk the "extra mile" for peace, though some believed that he had "walked too far for security's sake."[74] They would not have thought so if they had known that Ike had capitulated to the military–industrial–scientific complex over continuing to build up America's nuclear arsenal.

Once again the president's instincts in the matter seemed entirely sound. Again and again he decried the "incredible," "fantastic," and "ridiculous" capacity for "overkill" which the United States was acquiring. America would soon have enough bombs "to destroy every conceivable target all over the world," he exclaimed, "plus a threefold reserve."[75] The radiation from so many nuclear blasts in the Soviet Union would, he asserted, destroy the United States as well. However, Ike did nothing to correct this Strangelove logic. Preoccupied as he was by the "fiscal dangers ahead" and the "rapidly and immensely increasing cost of the military establishment,"[76] Ike did manage to hold down defense spending. But, according to Stephen Ambrose, nuclear weapons continued to be manufactured at a rate of more than two per day. Presumably Ike allowed cold-war fears to overwhelm his natural common sense. His failure to insist that his instinctive judgment should prevail, in an area where he was professionally equipped to lay down the law, permitted the arms race to continue on its course.

Ike also vacillated in his approach to the midterm elections. In August he appeared determined to fight "liberal and leftish" tendencies even if this meant giving vociferous support to his most reactionary allies. He asserted, for example, that Bill Knowland, who was standing for the governorship of California, "*must* win," despite his being, as the president thought, "somewhat dense."[77] By October, though, Ike had decided to keep his own appearances "nonpolitical," leaving the aggressive speechifying to Nixon. One reporter described the president's own electioneering as a "Give 'em Hello Campaign."[78] But in November, Ike changed tack again and made a rousing partisan defense of his record. He accused the Democrats of being "hopelessly split" between Northern radicals and Southern conservatives, saying that they, and not the Republicans, suffered from "political schizophrenia."[79] But Ike could not hold back the landslide. The Democrats increased their majority from 2 to 28 in the Senate and from 235 to 281 in the House. No president in the twentieth century had faced a heavier opposition on the Hill, and no president had ever faced three hostile Congresses in succession.

After the defeat Ike remarked to Hagerty that "it looks as though what the United States wants is to go directly to the left."[80] It was true that the old guard, Knowland included, had been almost annihilated, whereas liberal Republicans, such as Nelson Rockefeller in New York, had made a better showing. But there was no escaping the fact that the result also reflected disenchantment with Ike's second-term performance. The Denver *Post* expressed the widespread view that millions of people had been "shaken by Republican doubletalk over the budget two years ago, the U.S. lag in missiles and the race for outer space, the incredible confusion over civil defense, the Sherman Adams case, Little Rock, and the antics of John Foster Dulles. It all adds up to a weak, distracted and irrationalized leadership."[81] Ike seemed to have lost his way. He was accused of having presided over "the great postponement" in a land where the loudest sound was "the oink-and-grunt of private hoggishness."[82] The nation seemed to have given him an overwhelming vote of no confidence. And he was visibly shaken by it. The president spent most of the rest of the year out of the public eye, much of it on holiday in Georgia. He told members of the gang that 1958 had been the worst year of his life.

19

★

The "New Eisenhower"

The first few months of 1959 were dominated by a looming crisis over Berlin, which seemed to frighten everyone except Khrushchev, who had provoked it, and Ike, who had to resolve it. Actually the fundamental cause of the crisis was the American rejection of various plans, the most imaginative being that put forward by the Polish foreign minister Adam Rapacki in 1957, for creating a nuclear-free zone in central Europe. Having seen the devastation caused by the Nazis in Russia, Ike must have appreciated Soviet motives for wanting to incorporate Germany into such a demilitarized bloc. Knowing, too, the extent to which West Berlin was used as a center for Western propaganda and espionage (the CIA had achieved a notable coup by burrowing its way into the telephone system of East Berlin), the president probably understood why the city was a bone in Khrushchev's throat. But, like Dulles and the ancient, stubborn chancellor of West Germany, Konrad Adenauer, Ike was immured in the attitudes of the cold war. The United States was gradually equipping West Germany with nuclear weapons, and it was American policy that the country should be reunified on the basis of free elections. This meant that a united, rearmed Germany might add its formidable strength to NATO, in a nightmare for the Russians.

So in November 1958 the Kremlin had announced that it was signing a peace treaty with East Germany. According to the Soviet Union, this would mean that the United States, Britain, and France would have to quit the zones they had occupied in West Berlin since the war. Khrushchev then issued an ultimatum. Unless negotiations were begun to make West Berlin a free city within six months, by 27 May 1959, the Soviet Union would hand over to East Germany control of all its access routes. This would either cut the NATO allies off from West Berlin or force them to deal with the East German regime, whose legitimacy they did not recognize. That, in turn, might perpetuate a divided Germany. Khrushchev's hostile move alarmed the Europeans, and Ike's own advisers reacted in a predictably hawkish manner. As the tension mounted so did the pressure on Ike to respond aggressively and to increase the defense estimates. He resisted, declaring that "the Communist objective is to make us spend ourselves into bankruptcy."[1] But he was increasingly impressed by the power and art of the military–industrial complex, observing sourly that in 1935 the army's entire public relations staff had consisted of "Dave Surles and two stenographers."[2]

In the strategy of the cold war Ike may have been dourly and conventionally intransigent, but his Fabian tactics were well adapted to prevent skirmishes from becoming battles. He was seldom seen to better advantage than during the Berlin crisis, when he defused Khrushchev's time bomb by the simple expedient of treating it as a dud. He did "not believe that the Soviets want war, but pointed out that Khrushchev is quite ready to engage in military bluffs to advance Soviet foreign policy."[3] He insisted to his colleagues that the United States should not go "frantic" each time Khrushchev behaved provocatively somewhere in the world. If America did not act calmly, he said, "we may miscalculate and become involved in a general war." The only sensible course was to stand by the established program, "based primarily on deterrence, our air power, our missiles, and our allies."[4] Ike saw the current scare in perspective, as a little local difficulty in a long cold war. "We do not want to, and should not, look upon this situation as a 'Berlin crisis'; instead . . . we can anticipate two or three decades of tension."[5] It is true that he did toy with the futile idea of breaking off diplomatic relations with the Soviet Union. But in the main he was firm, cautious, conciliatory, and confident. Ike rejected the Russian ultimatum and declared that the United States would fulfill its responsibilities over Berlin. But he remained studiously vague about how this would be done, havering between his ultimate reliance on massive retaliation and his immediate acknowledgment that "Destruction is not a good policeman."[6] Naturally he did his best to exploit this ambiguity, though it was not easy to intimidate the Russians while simultaneously reassuring the Americans.

Nor was it easy to keep the NATO allies in line. The French were particularly recalcitrant now that the formidable figure of General de Gaulle had returned to power. Ironically Ike, who was keen that France should cease to be such a weak link in NATO, had (through the CIA) secretly subsidized the Gaullist party, which was to take the country out of the alliance. (Even more ironically—a paradigm of presidential ambivalence—the United States supported both France and the rebels against French colonial rule in Algeria.) Of course, Ike had few illusions about de Gaulle, whom he knew to be obsessed "with the honor, strength and glory of France." Ike said that "de Gaulle merely wants to make France the first nation in the world with himself the first Frenchman."[7] But even Ike miscalculated the degree to which de Gaulle's chauvinism, his suspicion of the Anglo-Saxons, and his belief that cooperation eroded French independence would hamper the Western alliance. As it was, de Gaulle deliberately tried to discredit Ike's flexible approach toward the Russians by adopting a hard line and encouraging Adenauer (who actually needed no encouragement) to do likewise.

The British, by contrast, were in Ike's view much too anxious to be conciliatory. Most of all Macmillan wanted a summit meeting, and in March 1959 he flew to America to press for it. Ike stuck to the traditional view that America had never lost a war or won a conference. But he wanted to help the Conservative prime minister, who was preparing for a general election later in the year. Ike therefore devised what Macmillan called a "somewhat ambivalent formula" to the effect that he would participate if "developments" in a preliminary foreign ministers' meeting "warrant holding a Summit conference."[8] As usual Macmillan was bewildered by Ike. Like many others—not least Ike's son John, who admitted that "the folks' tastes are strictly cornball"[9]—the prime minister was pained by the president's philistinism. He was obliged to sit through a Western called *The Big Country* which lasted for three hours and which he found "inconceivably banal." (He may not have known that Ike was seeing it for the fourth time at least.) But Macmillan could not help being impressed by Ike even while he was patronizing him. He was especially struck by the president's notion of trying to "institutionalize" cooperation between the countries of the free world, instead of relying on personal factors like their own friendship. (Macmillan may also not have known that, in the wake of giving statehood to Alaska and Hawaii, Ike was contemplating some sort of United States of the English-speaking peoples.) "He is certainly a strange mixture," Macmillan concluded. "With all his crudity and lack of elegance of expression, he has some very remarkable ideas."[10]

As the Berlin crisis approached its climax, three of Ike's oldest colleagues were fading away. Early in May Churchill paid his final visit to the United States. Ike treated him, Ann Whitman observed, as a son would treat an aging father. Churchill was, indeed, tragically old.

For years he had been slipping in and out of senility—as long ago as 1954 Bedell Smith, meeting him at Geneva, had pronounced him "completely finished."[11] But flickers of animation remained, usually when Churchill's pugnacious instincts were engaged. At Gettysburg, for example, he was interested not in the cattle but in the battle—Ike took him on a tour of the battlefield by helicopter. Churchill also noticed with pleasure that the picture of Montgomery was hanging in its accustomed place in the White House, an indication that Ike felt "disappointment not rancor" toward the field marshal, despite his disagreeable writings. Still, as Ann Whitman noted, Churchill was very "feeble and has difficulty in talking, so much so that communication is at times practically impossible." This was certainly what journalists found. As Churchill was boarding the *Columbine* to leave Washington, Bernard Baruch urged him, "For God's sake, Winston, say something, anything, in front of the cameras." Churchill obliged: "Bow wow, bow wow, bow wow!"[12]

One of Ike's guests at the White House remarked of Churchill that it was possible to live too long, and the president may well have agreed. But he seldom dwelled on the subject of mortality and was rarely shaken by the death of friends, even close ones. For a time, though, he was "hard hit" by the news that Dulles's cancer was incurable. He was even inclined to "mope."[13] But he soon recovered his sang-froid. He coolly discussed with Dulles the matter of his successor and they agreed on his deputy, Christian Herter. He became secretary of state on Dulles's resignation in April. Herter was six feet four and a half inches tall but, bowed by arthritis, he joked that he was "shrinking all the time."[14] Certainly he lacked the international stature of Dulles, whom Ike continued to consult to the end. On 19 May the president found it "ironic" that two of the men he considered great, Dulles and Marshall, were in Walter Reed Hospital so ill that they could hardly recognize him.[15] Dulles died on 24 May. A couple of days later, according to Ann Whitman, Ike was "in fine fettle despite the death of Mr. Dulles."[16] The president's good spirits may have stemmed from the fact that it was now clear that Khrushchev had been bluffing. On 27 May, a stifling day, Dulles's funeral took place, and the Soviet ultimatum on Berlin expired without evil consequences to the world.

However, the Soviet threat had not been withdrawn, merely postponed. Both the foreign ministers' meeting and the test-ban talks had reached deadlock, and Khrushchev continued to fulminate ominously from Moscow. In June, for example, he met Averell Harriman, who described his attitude over Berlin as "more intransigent and threatening" than before. Khrushchev exuded confident amiability while simultaneously making "terrifying" remarks about the Soviet capacity to destroy every industrial center in the West. Harriman "considered him a more dangerous man than Stalin."[17] He also recommended that Khrushchev should be invited to see the strength of America in person. This idea had been in the air for some time, though Ike had rejected it on the familiar ground that such a visit "would lead both the American and the Russian people to expect unattainable results." But he did consider that an invitation was "a possible 'ace in the hole' in dealing with the Berlin crisis."[18]

In July, urged on by Herter, Ike decided to play that ace. He instructed Robert Murphy to invite Khrushchev on condition that there was progress at the stalled foreign ministers' meeting in Geneva. But, as he admitted, Ike failed "to make myself unmistakably clear"[19] about the proviso, and Murphy misunderstood him. He issued an unqualified invitation, which the surprised Khrushchev promptly accepted. Ike was "staggered" and "extremely disturbed" by this faux pas.[20] He had been saying for months that there had been no "detectable progress that to my mind would justify the holding of a summit meeting."[21] Now he would have to go into reverse once again, apparently confirming the criticism increasingly voiced that "Eisenhower just doesn't know his own mind—which maybe is just as well."[22] He proposed to cover his confusion by claiming that "if the Geneva negotiations show some progress" this would be "fruitful in promoting . . . mutual understanding" during Khrushchev's visit.[23] Dulles had been accused of adding the planned mistake to the art of diplomatic blundering, but here was an accidental error that, as Ike wryly remarked, could not have occurred under his auspices.

It was a matter of supreme irony that an administrative muddle should have initiated a thaw in the cold war and that the man chiefly responsible for it should be hailed as the "new Eisenhower," not a lame duck but a dove of peace. As a matter of fact, sharp-eyed journalists had detected a change in Ike well before the invitation to Khrushchev was sent. In May, for example, *Time* magazine commented that in recent months the president "has been looking better, working harder and more effectively than at any time since his heart attack."[24] In June one of the news agencies noted the transformation which seemed to have occurred in Ike at press conferences. "None of his sentences lost their predicates and swam away, as often used to happen. He did not duck any questions, and did not take off into a haze of moralizations." Admittedly, when faced with certain queries Ike was "too courteous and, in truth, not quick-witted enough to turn a thrust to his own advantage, as Mr. Truman sometimes did." But "Mr. Eisenhower, toward the end of his tenure in office, is reaching a high and unexpected plateau of performance" and moving "more like a stake horse than . . . a lame duck."[25]

In July there was an extraordinary break with tradition which concerned reporters themselves. Encouraged by Hagerty, whose influence was now enhanced and who believed in building bridges, Ike initiated a series of stag dinners for regular White House correspondents. They were not, to be sure, altogether successful. At the first one the journalists complained that they did not "know" Ike, comparing "his formality unfavorably with that of Mr. Truman, who used to 'drop in' at the Press Room and ask for peanuts or join in a poker game."[26] There was also a misunderstanding about the rules governing the reporting of the dinner. Ike wanted newsmen to use the material they gathered as background for future articles, but they wrote direct stories. Nevertheless, until now Ike had held more aloof from the press than any president since Calvin Coolidge. The "new Eisenhower" at least seemed to be trying to make himself more accessible.

Still, the media did not give the "new Eisenhower" massive coverage until Khrushchev's visit was announced in early August. Then Ike's "bold effort to sweep aside the Cold War's barriers" was widely acclaimed, though conservatives harped on the fact that the Soviet Union had made no concessions, the Berlin crisis having been postponed, not resolved.[27] There was fevered speculation about what had prompted the presidential change of front and why Ike now evidenced a determination to rule as well as reign. The metamorphosis did, indeed, seem a dramatic one. It was as if an extinct volcano had suddenly erupted. At home and abroad people wondered at Ike's restored confidence and vitality. They also wondered whether he really had been a "captive President" (as Marquis Childs's recent book argued) who was at last free of his steely mentors, Sherman Adams and John Foster Dulles. Only a few of the more discerning commentators expressed doubts. In a particularly thoughtful article, for example, Cabell Phillips wrote, "Mr. Eisenhower has exhibited spurts of determination and jut-jawed stubbornness before, only to lapse again into ambiguity and indecisiveness." Phillips suspected that nothing fundamental had changed. He noted that Ike was the same genial, superficial man dealing with issues at arm's length like a staff officer. He opined that the president remained unconcerned by, and incurious about, other people, whose worth he measured by the size of their fortunes. Phillips concluded, "They still clear the corridors of the White House when he walks through."[28]

Needless to say, the "new Eisenhower" was largely a myth fostered by the media. The concept was as spurious as the diplomatic initiative which chiefly provoked speculation about it. What had really changed was not Ike but his circumstances: he had regained his health; Adams and Dulles were gone; the end of his presidency was nigh. This was the perceptive view of James Reston and it was endorsed by Ann Whitman. In her diary she suggested that the newspapers had now discovered that Ike was not "old and sick and feeble" but a man who could be reelected save for the Twenty-second Amendment—by mid-August Gallup put his popularity rating back to 62 percent. The papers were now trying to correct their mistake by creating "the 'new' Eisenhower." Reston was right to deride this notion and to assert that because the political situation had altered "the President was acting freer, more sure of himself, than at any time since war days." Ann Whitman did admit, however, that Ike had recovered from his early fear of the legislature,

a carry-over from the days when he appeared before committees . . . kowtowing to Congress. And I think that in these last six years he has learned how to handle Congress, that you must fight them to win their respect. To that extent I believe there has been a change. And, while decisions were always the President's, I think also that Herter and Persons are more inclined to remain in the background than were Adams and certainly Dulles.[29]

This was a shrewd summary but it did not tell the whole story. With nothing more to lose since the Republican defeat in the midterm elections, Ike had certainly taken a tougher line with Congress. For he also had nothing more to gain, electorally speaking, and he discovered that being a lame-duck president increased his moral authority more than it decreased his political power. The president was also assisted by the GOP's new minority leaders, Everett Dirksen, who succeeded the obscurantist Knowland in the Senate, and Charles Halleck, who took over (in January 1959) from the bumbling Joseph Martin in the House. "The Ev. and Charlie show," as the hard-nosed Halleck termed it, was a highly professional operation.[30] It helped Ike to prevent Democratic expenditure—government by veto, they called it—and to balance his budget. He was also able to resist Congressional encroachments into his sphere and even to intervene, for the first time, in fights on the Hill. In the summer of 1959, for example, Ike managed to secure legislation against racketeering in the labor unions.

A cartoon depicted Johnson and Rayburn, with Ike's bootmarks on the seats of their pants, saying to each other, "I can't get over it—and he's a fellow Texan, too."[31]

However, there were distinct limits to what Ike could achieve in Congress, and he was enraged and mortified in June 1959 when the Senate refused to confirm Lewis Strauss as his new secretary of commerce. Furthermore, the president's increased impact on the Hill was probably due less to Ike than to inflation. For all their rhetoric about investing in social welfare, Johnson and Rayburn were not anxious to take the blame for preventing the economic recovery from turning into a boom. Finally, it must be said that Ike obtained support from the Southern Democrats by a thoroughly old-fashioned, unspoken accord over civil rights.

Since 1956 a wave of violence had been sweeping the South as the civil rights movement began to gather momentum. Churches and synagogues were bombed. Activists were attacked and murdered. In a vile parody of the Communist treatment of dissidents, a black college professor attempting to enroll for a doctoral course in Mississippi was taken to a psychiatric hospital by the state police. The police chief of Dawson, a town in Terrell County, Georgia, declared that "terror was necessary in order to keep Negroes in their place, and that killing a few of them once in a while was always good medicine for the rest of them." When an outraged Fred Morrow raised this issue with the assistant attorney general "his coolness and nonchalance about the whole matter disturbed me no end."[32] He should not, however, have been surprised. Ike made "essentially moderate"—in other words, ineffectual, equivocal, and uncomprehending—efforts to stop the worst abuses. But, the president told a Legislative meeting, he "did not wish to make any proposal that gave rise to arguments and dissension."[33] On the issue of civil rights, the old Eisenhower remained firmly in the ascendant.

The old Eisenhower's open, amiable, and peace-loving instincts could return to the ascendant now that Dulles was no longer around to bring out the dour, suspicious, and belligerent side of his character. Dulles had discouraged Ike from traveling, from meeting foreign (especially Communist) statesmen, and from taking diplomatic initiatives. Ann Whitman went as far as to say that Dulles's State Department regarded the president as its "chattel."[34] Ike had endured all that because he half agreed with the secretary's method of waging the cold war. Even now he considered using wrangles with the Russians over procedure and protocol as an excuse for canceling Khrushchev's visit. He also decided not to confer special distinction on the Russian leader by inviting him to Camp David, though the under-secretary of state Douglas Dillon persuaded him to change his mind. (That invitation caused consternation in the Kremlin because no one knew where Camp David was, and the Russians feared an American plot to humiliate Khrushchev by taking him to a leper colony or a place where stray dogs were sent to die.) Finally, Ike had no new policy to advance. He assured everyone, from Cardinal Spellman downward, that "the exchange of visits implied no hint of surrender."[35]

On the other hand, as James Reston noted, "Eisenhower's personal inclination has always been to try to talk and to conciliate."[36] Even before the invitation to Khrushchev was sent, Ike had been privately saying that "what we have to do is to 'thaw out' the Russian defenses" by means of personal discussions.[37] After the meeting was agreed upon the president "expressed dissatisfaction with being cornered in the diplomatic stalemate of the last two years, and he showed his pleasure at the thought of breaking free into a wider field of maneuver."[38] There must be "no gun unfired and no individual effort spared" to end the cold war.[39] The United States must try to find "some little break, some little avenue yet unexplored through which we can possibly move to a better situation."[40] Of course, Ike went to great lengths to demonstrate that his new approach was consistent with Dulles's old one. But he was, in fact, busily standing Dulles's former arguments (and his own) on their heads. Before long, for example, he had reversed their earlier view that "preliminary low-level talks must precede a summit meeting" on the grounds that "where you do have a dictatorship there is only one man who can make the decisions."[41] No president in history was more adept at making "About face!" sound like "Forward march!"

Like many chief executives nearing the ends of their terms of office, Ike was beginning to think about his place in history and was seeking some sort of monument to mark it. One small monument which he did inaugurate in 1959 was the Eisenhower Library near his boyhood home in Abilene. He insisted, too, that the road-building program should proceed apace. But Congress limited his opportunities to establish a great political memorial in the United States. Moreover in some respects he felt increasingly out of tune with life in America. He was disturbed by the fact that many people dressed badly and so few kept their shoulders back. He was "bewildered" by the fact that Charles Van Doren was found guilty, in a celebrated case, of cheating in televised quiz games.[42] He disapproved of contemporary styles of dancing and thought moral standards were slipping. The postmaster-general convinced him that *Lady Chatterley's Lover* was "a 'filthy' book,"[43] but when the government tried to have it banned it went straight to the top of the best-seller list. Inevitably, then, as Ike contemplated his position he looked abroad. Foreigners revered him as a war hero and subjected him to none of the partisan darts he had to endure from domestic critics. Could not the president of the United States establish himself as an inspiring global statesman? Could he not perform a memorable final act on the international scene? At all events (to quote from James Reston's verdict on the "new Eisenhower" once again) "the mood and setting have changed once more, and he has moved out of the shadows into the center of the stage."[44]

Ike's first foray, made to Europe in the new, luxurious presidential jet *Air Force One* on 26 August, was designed to reassure his chief allies and to concert NATO policy toward the Soviet Union. Ike found a large measure of agreement in Bonn and London, though Adenauer was worried that he would make concessions and Macmillan was worried that he would not. But in Paris, where de Gaulle was intent on disengaging France from NATO, Ike made no progress at all. By contrast, the public everywhere greeted the president with spontaneous and heart-warming enthusiasm. The crowds were enormous and hailed Ike not only as the savior of Europe from the Nazis but as the messiah of world peace. The feeling of hope was palpable, and Ike responded to it in his staged television conversation with Macmillan: "I think that people want peace so much that one of these days governments had better get out of the way and let them have it."[45] Unfortunately the exchange between president and prime minister creaked in every joint, as did the second floor of No. 10 Downing Street under the weight of people and television equipment. As Ike remarked, the cameras might have recorded the curious spectacle of "both principals falling out of sight of the viewing public while expressing confidence in the future."[46] Macmillan noticed that during their official talks, held in good golfing weather, Ike was "pretty restless."[47] But he was able to play a bit. He also had a few days off in Scotland, staying first with the royal family in Balmoral, and then at the residence he had been given for his lifetime, Culzean Castle. Here he was joined by members of the gang, who had flown halfway around the world to play bridge with the president.

After his return home on 7 September, Ike only had a week to prepare for the arrival of Khrushchev. This was a momentous event, the first time a head of the Soviet government had set foot in the United States. In the confrontation both sides were proud, prickly, sensitive, and suspicious. Both wanted to gain some political or propaganda advantage. Yet there was also a degree of goodwill on both sides, a tentative hope that some measure of détente, or at any rate of mutual understanding, might emerge from the visit. Actually it was dogged by mutual incomprehension. This stemmed largely from the enormous differences between the two countries, their systems, their culture, their society. Khrushchev, for example, accused Ike of being able by a "wink" to determine the kind of reception he would get, and he seemed unconvinced by the president's assurance that this was utterly impossible in a free society.[48] Ike was unable to convey the mysteries and delights of golf to Khrushchev. Nor would the Russian admire American highways and automobiles, which Ike showed him from a helicopter. (But he liked the helicopter itself so much that he asked to be given a couple, and when this request was refused he purchased three.) Even when the two leaders did discover a common bond, their weakness for Westerns, Khrushchev told Ike that Stalin had always denounced such films, after watching them with great enjoyment, for their "ideological content."[49]

Language, too, was a barrier. When Nixon had become embroiled in his celebrated debate with Khrushchev in the kitchen of the American Exhibition which had been sent to Moscow, the Russian had baffled him by threatening, "We'll show you Kuzma's mother."[50] This expression simply meant, "We'll teach you a lesson," but it illustrated the difficulty of grasping the thought of such an earthy and ebullient figure. Ike took advice from his vice-president, who explained Khrushchev's "penchant for light-hearted needling." Nixon also warned that the Russians tried to wear out the opposition and that, although Khrushchev saw "everything through Communist glasses" and had a "closed mind," the trip would "give him a subtle feeling of the power and will of America."[51] This assessment was not far wrong.

When his giant TU-114 landed at Andrews Air Force Base on 15 September, Khrushchev was "terribly impressed" by the reception. Everything was "shining and glittering," a contrast to the "proletarian" way of conducting such affairs in the Soviet Union.[52] However, fears engendered by the cold war ensured that Khrushchev received a guarded welcome from the American people. The crowds were reserved, and few Russian flags flew in Pennsylvania Avenue. The most eccentric manifestation of antipathy, William Buckley's plan to fill the Hudson with red dye so that it would resemble a river of blood, did not take place. But as Khrushchev and Ike drove to the White House a sky-writing plane traced a large white cross overhead, and church bells pealed "Nearer My God to Thee." Cardinal Spellman had decreed that parochial school children should say three extra

"Hail Marys" to ward off the evil effects of Khrushchev's presence, and in the White House itself such a gesture seemed anything but preposterous. Bubbles of suspicion and hostility kept coming to the surface. Ike was "privately annoyed"[53] by Khrushchev's gift of a model of Lunik II, a projectile which the Russians had just landed on the moon. The president could not make up his mind whether the gift was a blatant piece of propaganda or a simple token of sincerity.

Other circumstances also irritated him. A grim-faced Ike was not amused by Khrushchev's suggestion that the KGB share sources with the CIA—the Russian told Allen Dulles, "We should buy our intelligence data together and save money. We'd have to pay the people only once."[54] The president was fussed by the Soviet men's refusal to wear bourgeois dress suits at the state dinner and he remarked, somewhat oddly, that their womenfolk, "being feminine even though Communist," were made equally uncomfortable by their husbands' sartorial sloppiness.[55] For his part Khrushchev resented the barely concealed antagonism of some members of Ike's government. Douglas Dillon, for example, fumed and sputtered at the proximity of the Russians so much that, Khrushchev later wrote, it seemed "as though he were about to explode, as though something inside him had short-circuited."[56] In this atmosphere it was not surprising that the initial discussion, anyway intended to be general, was unproductive—though everyone agreed that no one wanted war. Khrushchev found that the president did not contribute much. Ike found that his effort "to soften up the Soviet leader even a little bit" met with no success. When they were alone the president pointed out Khrushchev's "opportunity to go down in history as a towering statesman if he would use his power constructively."[57] As Ike well knew, they both had this opportunity. Neither embraced it. Neither could escape from domestic constraints or cold-war inhibitions. The prospect of peaceful coexistence was a tantalizing one but neither statesman had the political will, the courage, imagination, or intelligence to grasp it. Each blamed the other. "Those sweet words," Ike said of Khrushchev, "but he won't change his mind about anything."[58]

So, with the promise of more discussions to come at Camp David, Khrushchev set off on his whirlwind tour of the United States. The media dogged his footsteps, recording his every movement and mood. The nation became hypnotized by his responses, his unpremeditated fury at being insulted by Los Angeles's boorish Republican mayor, his vociferous disgust at the Hollywood film Can-Can, his petulant frustration at being denied a sight of Disneyland, his flamboyant geniality among San Francisco longshoremen, his folksy charm

with Midwestern farmers, and his brutal joviality toward hecklers—
to those who urged the virtues of capitalism he replied, "Only the
grave can correct a hunchback."[59] All told it was a bravura performance, and the president was soon having to allay anxieties that the
human face of Communism was attractive enough to undermine the
American way of life.

Ike not only read the newspapers, he received private reports from
Khrushchev's American guide and mentor, Henry Cabot Lodge. He
told the president that after "hitting bottom" (the pun was presumably unintentional) with the "vulgar, even obscene show on the set in
Hollywood," the tour had gone well. Khrushchev was "a remarkable,
although very difficult man" who had been impressed by what he saw
and wanted peace and cooperation.[60] Ike was left in no doubt that he
faced a dynamic and capable opponent. The president echoed his
brother Milton's verdict that Khrushchev had "a quick mind, and is
good at polemics. He has a primitive approach."[61] However, what
chiefly concerned Ike was the speech Khrushchev had made at the
United Nations on 18 September advocating complete disarmament.
As Khrushchev later admitted, such proposals were disingenuous,
being "intended to serve a propagandistic, rather than a realistic,
purpose."[62] Nevertheless, Ike was troubled. He mused that "if we
could now really eliminate all atomic weapons we would not be badly
off." However, verification was still the problem. As the Camp David
conference approached he looked for a way to put Khrushchev argumentatively "in a box."[63]

Ike was no more able to accomplish this, during the long weekend
they spent in the Catoctin Mountains, than Khrushchev was able to
carry out his oft-quoted threat to bury America. In fact it was Khrushchev who initially took the dialectical offensive. Whether he was
driven by the fitful impulses of a capricious personality, or was simply
employing the familiar Russian technique of alternately blowing cold
and hot, it is impossible to say. But he first talked at length about his
war experiences, as if to outflank Ike on the military front. He then
waxed eloquent about the strength of Russian defenses. Finally, at
lunch on 26 September, he tried to renew the "kitchen debate" with
Nixon. According to George Kistiakowsky (Ike's new scientific adviser, who understood Russian) Khrushchev was so "personally insulting," that Ike remained "completely silent." The vice-president
"behaved as if he didn't notice the offensiveness." Nixon and Kistiakowsky interpreted Khrushchev's "almost violent" outburst as the
product of "an extreme inferiority complex exhibiting itself as arrogance."[64]

That afternoon, whether by accident or design, the atmosphere improved. Ike went off by helicopter alone with Khrushchev (and an interpreter) to inspect his farm at Gettysburg. The Russian leader was impressed by his Black Angus herd and Ike offered him a heifer. Khrushchev accepted and in return arranged to send Ike a planeload of birch trees (something Ike did not record in his memoirs, though he mentioned his own gift). Khrushchev met and "mesmerized" Ike's grandchildren, telling them the Russian versions of their names and inviting them to accompany the president on his trip to the Soviet Union, now arranged for the following spring.[65] Ike called this a "heartwarming family scene,"[66] and it helped to break the ice. The two men discovered that they were each forced to capitulate to the extravagant demands of their respective military establishments, which were determined not to fall behind in the arms race. Ike remarked, "You know, we really should come to some sort of agreement in order to stop this fruitless, really wasteful rivalry." Khrushchev endorsed the end but they could not find the means: "We couldn't agree then and we can't agree now."[67]

However, they did manage to agree that the deadline, and thus the element of duress, should be removed from the negotiations over Berlin in return for Ike's participation at a summit meeting. Actually both commitments were hedged about with ambiguous qualifications. Ike told journalists that the Berlin "negotiations should not be prolonged indefinitely but there could be no fixed time limit on them,"[68] which was only a whisker away from being a contradiction in terms. He was also less than categorical about the summit: most of his objections to it had been removed, he said, but the agreement of America's allies was essential. Ike was not happy about this rather vague outcome, especially as the last part of the conference was spent in wrangling over the joint communiqué. It emerged as a singularly amorphous document because Khrushchev would permit no mention to be made of his lifting the ultimatum over Berlin. This could only be announced, he finally insisted, after his return to Russia. Consequently the leaders' car journey to Washington was a dismal affair. According to Khrushchev, Ike resembled "a man who had fallen through a hole in the ice and been dragged from the river with freezing water still dripping off him."[69]

When Khrushchev had taken off for home Ike would not even admit to a press conference that his visit had begun a thaw in East–West relations. Soon afterward he told the Cabinet that, despite Soviet suave talk, "there is *no question* about the efforts they are making in this field of world domination." However, he was now less concerned about their political intentions than about "the growing threat posed by a singly controlled, hostile, atheistic, growing economy."[70] Accordingly Ike spent much of the fall endeavoring to win the fight against "that demagogue" Khrushchev by balancing the budget.[71] He complained that the Sputnik had given "a surge to defense spending from which we have not recovered" and said that "if he was to approve another unbalanced budget he would regard his Administration as discredited."[72] He urged that "our real effort should go into making some meaningful move toward disarmament."[73] He did not see why the United States should bear such a heavy burden in NATO and wanted a reduction of American forces in Europe, even though John Foster Dulles "used to grow violent when the suggestion was made."[74] He protested about the cost of bringing freeways into cities, which was not what he had visualized. He resisted an inflationary settlement in the long steel strike and argued for tougher laws because "we were practically being blackmailed by the Unions."[75] He insisted, "We must get the Federal Government out of every unnecessary activity,"[76] but he admitted that matters like cutting farm subsidies, though economically simple, were "baffling" politically.[77]

Ike could only concentrate on the economic struggle with the Soviet Union because he believed the political threat was receding. So, although the meeting with Khrushchev had produced few concrete results, it did give a hope of détente that was not completely chimerical. As I. F. Stone wrote, "Quite suddenly," thanks to Ike, "peace has become a respectable word again." He continued, "with Mr. Eisenhower at our head we had been proceeding on the assumption that the world was menaced by a diabolic conspiracy run from Moscow, and that our own safety lay in piling up an ever larger supply of ever more destructive arms. With Mr. Eisenhower at our head we have now executed an about face and are proceeding on the assumption that the Russians want peace as much as we do, and that we must slowly by patient negotiation disentangle the issues which hinder peaceful coexistence."[78] Everyone talked optimistically about the "Spirit of Camp David."[79]

The mere fact that Ike was widely praised for having conjured up this new spirit encouraged him to try to invest it with substance. Paradoxically, though, his final effort in 1959, after an extended November rest at Augusta, was not a diplomatic mission but a goodwill trip to the Third World. As he told Congressional leaders at a breakfast on 5 December, "I am going abroad, therefore, in an effort to pay them the personal compliment of visiting them in person and to tell them in person what our true beliefs are rather than seeking anything else.''[80] But although Ike insisted that his tour was not tourism and that he was going to improve the morale of underdeveloped nations, it is clear that he was also intent on improving his own morale and seeing famous sights in style.

The Taj Mahal, which he had admired since boyhood, was a prime attraction, and Ike spent five days in India, his longest stay anywhere. He was quite overwhelmed by his reception, which "has been cordial beyond words."[81] He was also amused that the nonviolent Nehru could wield such a big stick to clear a path through the enormous crowds. The almost hysterical fervor of their greeting doubtless owed something to India's need for American support against China. Indeed, the prospect of American aid may have added warmth to his welcome everywhere. But Ike's magnetic charm, his personal standing, and his pacific aspirations were chiefly responsible for the acclamation. For he was doing what he did best—communicating human warmth and sympathy.

Accompanied by John and Barbara Eisenhower, the president covered 22,370 miles in nineteen days. Even in the five-star luxury of *Air Force One*, with everything scrupulously arranged for his convenience—right down to the twelve cases of Mountain Valley drinking water which accompanied him—it was an exhausting jaunt for a man of nearly seventy. Ike stood up to it well, and one Pakistani commented that he had "the stamina of a Karachi camel." All told he visited eleven countries—Italy, Turkey, Pakistan, Afghanistan, India, Iran, Greece, Tunisia, France, Spain, and Morocco. As *Time* magazine said, without hyperbole, "the world's best-known, most respected statesman lifted personal prestige and national influence to new highs from Rome to New Delhi to Paris."[82] It was a triumphant journey that achieved virtually nothing more concrete than this. But it was a suitable conclusion to, and perhaps a fair reward for, an encouraging year. And it showed that there was life in the old Eisenhower yet.

20

⭐

Down from the Summit

Not the least wearisome part of the president's overseas trip had been his meeting in Paris with leaders of the chief NATO powers. Ike was furious with de Gaulle who, because of his "great preoccupation" with "the honor and prestige of France,"[1] had been dragging his feet over the summit. But now that Khrushchev had agreed to visit France, which was shortly to become a member of the nuclear club, the "Big Four" conference could proceed. It was arranged for May 1960. Ike was still showing signs of strain and exhaustion after Christmas, when he had been home for nearly a week. At a conference held in Augusta, George Kistiakowsky noted that the president's "difficulty in express-ing his thoughts was far greater than I have ever encountered before, and the result was that it was almost impossible to conclude what he wished done." By the New Year, however, Ike was restored to "rare good form, laughing, kidding various people present" at a National Security Council meeting.[2] No doubt his mood reflected the confi-dence he felt in the simple, positive program he had in mind. Ike wanted to use his last year in office to secure his place in history as a crusader for peace. It was an understandable and laudable ambition for one who had earned his fame in war. Winston Churchill had also nursed such aspirations, only to be frustrated by force of external circumstances. Ike was to be thwarted by his own internal contradic-tions.

These were manifested with peculiar clarity in Ike's attitude toward his Latin American neighbors, which was a mixture of benevolence and coerciveness. His benign intentions were demonstrated in an-other goodwill tour, which he made in February, visiting Puerto Rico, Brazil, Argentina, Chile, and Uruguay. "With its combination of dust, crowded days and summer heat," he said, this fifteen-thousand-mile trip was even more exhausting than his previous one.[3] However, except in the Argentine, where his routes had to be carefully arranged to avoid demonstrators chanting *"Viva* Castro!" and "Death to Ike," he was greeted with scarcely less rapture. Ike's message, constantly reiterated, was that in its own hemisphere the United States wanted to encourage progress with freedom but that it adhered "strictly to a policy of non-intervention and mutual respect."[4] He told the Brazilian Congress that if any nation chose to adopt an "unenlightened system of tyranny," the United States would pity them but would "respect their right to choose such a system. Here is the key to our policy—the right to choose." However, he at once denied this fine sentiment by warning that the United States "would consider it intervention in the internal affairs of an American State if any power, whether by invasion, coercion or subversion, succeeded in denying freedom of choice to the people of any of our sister Republics."[5]

In other words, as he had demonstrated in Guatemala, Latin Americans were at liberty to choose anything as long as it was not Communism, or could not be mistaken for Communism. Thus Rafael Trujillo, vicious right-wing dictator of Dominica, was an embarrassment to the United States. But Fidel Castro, vicious left-wing dictator of Cuba, was anathema. It was as clear to Ike as it had been to Rousseau that some people must be forced to be free—whether through invasion, coercion, subversion, or even assassination. Shortly after the president's return from South America his policy toward Cuba moved from open hostility to secret aggression. Before long the CIA was engaged in a series of plots so bizarre that any writer of spy thrillers would have rejected them on grounds of total implausibility. They ranged from employing the Mafia to shoot Castro to booby-trapping a seashell in the area where he went skin-diving, from poisoning his coffee and cigars to spraying his shoes with a depilatory powder which would cause his hair and beard to fall out. Thus, like some modern Samson, he would be deprived of his virile appearance and the source of his strength.

Relations with Castro, who had seized power from the corrupt and brutal Batista regime at the beginning of 1959, had deteriorated for much the same reason that they had with Jacobo Arbenz of Guatemala five years previously. Though a less legitimate and more repressive ruler than Arbenz, Castro had it as his main aim to make Cuban independence a reality. Since 1898, when the United States had fought for that independence, it had been a myth. Cuba had become a neocolonial state, its freedom constrained in every sphere of life, political, social, economic, and cultural—according to the film star

Down from the Summit 385

Errol Flynn, Havana was simply the "best place to get drunk." In an effort to break the American stranglehold, Castro confiscated the huge sugar plantations and cattle ranches (paying compensation, as Arbenz had done, on the value their owners had declared for tax purposes) and redistributed them to the peasants. Such actions, in Ike's view, stamped Castro as a Communist. But although he was moving in that direction, the best estimates of the CIA at the time concluded that Castro was actually an "anti-Communist."[6] Nevertheless, like so many of his fellow Americans, the president was sensitive almost to the point of paranoia about anything resembling a Communist presence in the "back yard." Having toyed with a scheme to blockade Cuba, the president resorted once more to the CIA. But he was dissatisfied with Allen Dulles's early proposal to sabotage a sugar refinery. "Allen, this is fine, but if you're going to make any move against Castro, don't just fool around with sugar refineries. Let's get a program that will really do something about Castro."[7]

There is no evidence that Ike specifically authorized assassination attempts on Castro, or, in August 1960, of the Congolese leader Patrice Lumumba. It would, indeed, have been quite out of character for a man who instinctively employed the language of euphemism, ambiguity, and morality, to issue such direct and ruthless orders. According to Andrew Goodpaster a red-faced Ike replied angrily to an aide's jocular remark about "bumping off Lumumba": "That is beyond the pale. We will not discuss such things. Once you start that kind of business there is no telling where it will end."[8] Actually Ike was quite capable of using the prohibited term himself—he had been unable to "understand why the British did not bump off Nasser."[9] Still, with his preference for operating by indirection and delegating his authority, Ike was unlikely to have used such words to give instructions about Castro or Lumumba. The fact is, however, that Allen Dulles did order their assassination and that serious—or rather, farcical—attempts were made to carry out his orders.

It is just possible that Dulles was acting on his own. By 1960, as George Kistiakowsky observed, "the whole intelligence business is in chaos."[10] The CIA was "virtually unbridled."[11] Having encouraged the growth of a Frankenstein's monster, Ike had made sporadic efforts to restrain it, and especially to restrict its activities to intelligence gathering as opposed to covert operations. He had failed. The American intelligence community was increasingly a law unto itself. For example, Ike had several times forbidden the floating of camera-carrying balloons over the Soviet Union. They aroused hostility in Russia and caused embarrassment to America, particularly when they came down behind the Iron Curtain. On one such occasion Ike had summoned John Foster Dulles, who exclaimed, "Oh my God, the Boss is going to give me absolute hell."[12] He did, but he did not manage to control the balloon project. So there was something in the criticism, loudly repeated and angrily rejected after the U-2 incident, that Ike was not fully in command of his own (vast) administration.

Historians now attempting to rehabilitate Ike are loath to admit this. To do so, indeed, would be inconsistent with their opinion of him as "an active and politically skillful President, a strong leader and policy maker who ran his own administration—though often circumspectly."[13] However, proponents of this view are caught in a cleft stick when they come to consider the crimes and follies perpetrated by the CIA, especially in 1960: for Ike must bear the blame for them if he was fully in control, whereas to exonerate him is to admit his ineffectiveness. Thus, for example, W. B. Ewald, the scholar who helped Ike to write his memoirs, tries to deny both propositions. He says that Ike did not trust Allen Dulles and that, to control the CIA, he set up an elaborate apparatus, which did not work.[14] But it was Ike's job to make it work. The truth is, surely, that he veered between strength and weakness, guilt and innocence. As befitted a soldier who owed so much to secret intelligence Ike was, in the words of his special assistant Gordon Gray, "as security conscious as any President we've had."[15] He never hesitated to pull his commander-in-chief's rank on Allen Dulles. To quote Goodpaster, who was a great admirer of Ike's strength in the intelligence field, the president "insisted that he have access to everything." Goodpaster immediately qualified this, however, by adding that "there were things that he deliberately did not inform himself about."[16]

By the same token Ike would not have explicitly instructed Dulles to kill foreign leaders. Both the president and the director of the CIA accepted the convention of "plausible deniability." A ruler should be able to claim clean hands, just as King Henry II of England did after his rhetorical question—"Who will rid me of this turbulent priest?" —had provoked the murder of Thomas Becket. According to one cabinet member, Allen Dulles "felt very strongly that we should not involve the President directly in things like this." But Ike must surely have been involved indirectly. It is almost inconceivable that Dulles would have taken such a drastic step as ordering homicide without a nod or a wink, or some form of "implicit authorization" from above. That this was given, Richard Bissell, deputy director of the CIA, had no doubt: "When you use language that no particular means are ruled out, that is obviously what it meant, and it meant that to everybody in the room. . . . You don't use language of that kind except to mean, in effect, the Director is being told, get rid of the guy, and if you have to use extreme means up to and including assassination, go ahead."[17] It was therefore reasonable to infer Ike's involvement, as Senator Church's investigating committee did in 1975. Although the evidence submitted to that committee, and the conclusions it reached, have been challenged, the inference remains a reasonable one. Only proof is lacking.

There is no doubt, however, that Ike did order a comprehensive attempt to destroy Castro's government. This involved economic sanctions, infiltration, guerrilla operations, the recruitment and training of Cuban exiles, and a search for someone to lead them. In fact preparations were made to repeat the Guatemalan coup, and a momentum was being built up which culminated in the disastrous Bay of Pigs invasion. Central to this endeavor was the need to prove or, failing that, to assert, that Castro was a Communist. In March 1960 Herter had to tell Ike that the "latest National Intelligence Estimate does not find Cuba to be under Communist control."[18] But by April the secretary of state was working to "impress upon Latin Americans the nature and seriousness of Communist penetration of Cuba."[19] Despite his conviction that Communism was a monolith, Ike had no difficulty in reconciling his decision to attack the Communists in Cuba with his intention to conciliate the Communists in Russia.

More contradictory still was his attitude toward the Soviet Union itself, as the summit approached. On the one hand he was keen to wage peace successfully, to achieve a test-ban treaty and an agreement over disarmament, to set the seal on his presidency by ending the cold war. Thus he continued to resist calls for more defense spending, calls amplified by the presidential election campaign from which Ike was trying to hold aloof. He spoke with the voice of sanity as he argued against the insensate race for weapons and the mad capacity for overkill. On April Fool's Day 1960 he sarcastically interrupted a discussion in the National Security Council about building more missiles, "Why don't we go completely crazy and plan on a force of 10,000?"[20] (By 1983 the United States had built those 10,000 strategic missiles, not to mention 1,300 intermediate range missiles and 17,700 tactical nuclear weapons.)[21]

On the other hand, Ike behaved like someone quite conditioned by cold-war fears. Despite the proximity of the summit he subjected Khrushchev to a number of pinpricks. He permitted the Voice of America to make provocative broadcasts. This was particularly unfortunate because at Camp David Khrushchev had promised to stop

jamming this "legitimate" radio station in return for Ike's agreement
to shut down "clandestine" stations, ones pretending to be run by
dissidents and issuing "black" propaganda.[22] Similarly Ike allowed
both Herter and Dillon to make speeches so hostile to the Soviet
Union that Khrushchev thought he had taken a calculated decision to
"revive the Cold War."[23] Most chilling of all, Ike demonstrated his
continuing mistrust of, and antagonism toward, the U.S.S.R. by au-
thorizing flights of the high-altitude U-2 reconnaissance aircraft over
its territory. However anxious Communist leaders were to believe in
American good faith, it was difficult to do so under the sinister gaze
of what *Soviet Aviation* called "the black lady of espionage."[24]

The U-2 had been flying over Russia since 1956. It had brought
back photographic information which enabled Ike to gauge Soviet
defense achievements and intentions with great accuracy. He knew,
for example, that the "missile gap," about which politicians like John
F. Kennedy and columnists like Joseph Alsop fulminated, was nonsense. But he also knew that the Russians passionately resented the
violation of their air space, and he even admitted that in their position
he would have felt this was a legitimate cause of war. Soviet radar,
which was more advanced than American, could trace the U-2s'
flights, and the Soviet government protested about them through
diplomatic channels. This was all the Russians could do, since they had
no airplane or missile capable of shooting down a U-2, which flew at
a height of about fifteen miles. Against his better judgment, Ike allowed his national security advisers to persuade him that he gained
more in intelligence than he lost in goodwill. So the president paid
scant attention to the protests, though he did try, not altogether successfully, to keep a tight hold on the U-2 program.

Even so, he was uneasily aware that it was jeopardizing the chance
of improving relations with the Soviet Union. He also appreciated the
fact that Russian technology was improving and that the days of his
spy in the sky were numbered. Several times he warned that eventually "one of these machines is going to be caught and then we're going
to have a storm."[25] According to Goodpaster, Ike had, of all his
colleagues, "the greatest sense of what the turmoil and turbulence was
likely to be if we lost one."[26] As the summit drew nearer Ike became
even more nervous that his one "tremendous asset," namely his "reputation for honesty," might be impaired. "If one of these aircraft were
lost when we are engaged in apparently sincere deliberations, it could
be put on display in Moscow and ruin the President's effectiveness."[27]

Never had Ike's ambivalence over his own "honesty" and "sincerity" been more clearly expressed. Never had his instinctive judgment

been more uncannily and tragically accurate. This was the sort of cleverness to which George Kennan referred in his incisive and illuminating assessment of Ike as "a man of keen political intelligence and penetration, particularly when it came to foreign affairs." Kennan considered Ike to be "one of the most enigmatic figures of American life." He noted that in casual company Ike repulsed, "with charming, baffling evasiveness," any political discussion. But "when he spoke of such matters seriously and in a protected official circle, insights of a high order flashed out time after time through the curious military gobbledygook in which he was accustomed both to expressing and concealing his thought." However, Kennan added, "whether Ike used this understanding effectively is another question."[28] It is obviously a question begging the answer no. Certainly over the U-2 incident his first intuitions had been almost miraculously prescient. It was his tragedy that he allowed them to be negated by obscure second thoughts. Once again Ike's pronounced duality of mind had asserted itself. He saw the right course but he took the wrong one. In the midst of a genuine campaign to achieve peaceful coexistence, Ike acted in a way calculated to perpetuate the cold war.

Admittedly the president had been assured by the CIA that even if a U-2 aircraft were shot down, it would disintegrate and its pilot would be killed. But just to authorize a flight within sixteen days of the summit was incredibly provocative and, as de Gaulle said, "absurdly ill-timed."[29] Indeed, it was the timing which attracted the most outspoken condemnation. Arthur Krock, for one, stated flatly that it "implies incompetence and/or irresponsibility."[30] But as the whole world knows, Ike did permit the flight of Francis Gary Powers, whose plane was brought down near Sverdlovsk, probably by a surface-to-air missile, on 1 May. The president took no action until, on 5 May, Khrushchev announced that the Russians had shot down the spy plane. To Hagerty's fury Goodpaster delayed telling him the news for an hour. Even then, despite the abuse heaped on the American militarists, Ike was not anxious to elaborate on the story, already given out by NASA, that one of their meteorological aircraft had crashed. But he abandoned this policy of cautious reticence when all his staff opposed it.

Assuming that the pilot was dead and the U-2 destroyed, they thought it would be safe and sound to confirm the cover story that a weather plane had strayed off course. So the first strand was woven in the web of deceit which was to enmesh Ike and his administration. For it was the mendacity, not the espionage, which did most to discredit Ike. The spying could be defended because it was directed against the Russians. But since the Soviet Union knew the truth about the U-2, official lies about it from Washington were not defensible on the usual grounds of security. Ike's government was obviously intent on deceiving the American people, in whose name it was supposedly acting, in order to protect itself. It was also seeking to mislead the world. But its various shifts—from pleading innocence to admitting guilt, from claiming that the U-2 was vital to America's security to halting its operations—were worse than lies: as Adlai Stevenson was quick to point out, they were blunders. The London *Times* was right in saying that the United States had "handed Mr. Khrushchev his propaganda triumph on a plate."[31] In view of his own cover-up, Ike's assertion that the U-2 flights were necessary because of the Soviet "fetish of secrecy"[32] rang particularly hollow. Khrushchev's reply was telling. He said that the Americans were asserting "it is not the burglar who is guilty, but the owner of the house he broke into, because he locked it, thereby compelling the burglar to break in. But this is the philosophy of thieves and bandits."[33] Ironically, at what might have been the culminating moment of his political career, the president who so valued his own reputation for honesty had to play the starring role in a hypocritical charade—and on the international stage.

On 7 May Khrushchev sprang his trap. At a crowded, jubilant, and vituperative session of the Supreme Soviet, he announced that Gary Powers was alive and gave full details of his spy mission. Khrushchev did not, however, accuse Ike personally of responsibility for the flight, being content to vent his spleen on the "bandits" and "aggressors" in the Pentagon.[34] Ike's own impulse was to distance himself from the whole unsavory affair, partly, no doubt, in the hope of saving the summit. So he agreed that the State Department should issue a statement saying that the U-2 flight had "probably" taken place, though without "authorization" from the "authorities in Washington," and that such surveillance was essential in view of the danger of a surprise attack. Naturally the Russians pounced on the inconsistency. They replied that since the United States justified espionage its claim that the flight was unauthorized "does not correspond to reality."[35] And by trying to pass the buck Ike was just confirming opposition charges of his ineffectiveness. John F. Kennedy concluded, for example, that Ike's leadership was "palsied" and that the whole U-2 episode had been characterized by a "shocking lack of presidential directive."[36] So on 9 May Herter issued another statement, which Ike himself helped to draft and later claimed to be "utterly and meticulously accurate."[37] Actually it told half the truth, admitting that Ike had authorized espionage in general but denying that he had ordered Powers's flight.

Furthermore it gave the impression that such flights would continue.

Needless to say, this was an unsatisfactory compromise. First of all it put Khrushchev in an impossible position. He was already bitter about America's "two-faced policy . . . approaching us with open arms . . . and stabbing us in the back."[38] Now he was supposed to establish détente with, and later act as host to, someone who apparently avowed his intention of sending over more spy planes. Khrushchev understandably expostulated, "The people of Russia would say I was mad."[39] Second, by admitting only indirect responsibility for Powers's U-2 flight, Ike was presenting his critics with their usual target once again. James Reston took a thoughtful shot at it, attacking Ike for having created an "institutionalized Presidency." "The Presidency has been parceled out, first to Sherman Adams, then to John Foster Dulles, and in this case to somebody else—presumably to Allen Dulles." The criticism, through no fault of Reston's, was wide of the mark. But his summary of the lamentable consequences of the U-2 affair for the president hit the bull's eye:

He wanted to reduce international tension and he has increased it. He wanted to strengthen the alliance and he has weakened it. He has glorified teamwork and morality, and got lies and chaos. Everything he was noted for —caution, patience, leadership, military skill, even good luck—suddenly eluded him at precisely the time when he needed them most.[40]

Ike was momentarily cast down by the U-2 affair. He remarked sadly: "That it had to be such a boo-boo and that we would be caught with our pants down was rather painful."[41] He even told Ann Whitman that he "would like to resign."[42] But his natural resilience and ebullience quickly triumphed. He took a philosophical attitude to what was admittedly a bad experience, saying that there was no point in breaking one's neck worrying about it.[43] As for the newspaper darts, he appeared to be far angrier about reports that he had caught more than his statutory allowance of trout in Colorado than about journalistic disparagements of his handling of the U-2 crisis.[44] This may have been because he always refused to admit that it was responsible for the failure of the summit. Before he set off for Paris Ike assured a meeting of Senators that "the United States would not be encumbered by the U-2 incident." Khrushchev, he said, was a "strong man," much "too smart" to be deflected from his political goals by what he knew to be just a routine case of espionage. Afterward Ike explained that the Russian premier had wrecked the conference in response to hard-line pressure from the Kremlin.

There may have been some truth in this opinion, for certainly at the summit Khrushchev was always flanked by the grim figure of Marshal Malinovsky. But until the U-2 incident Khrushchev had successfully resisted the Moscow (and Peking) hawks. He was definitely looking forward to entertaining Ike in Russia, had built a bijou palace for him overlooking Lake Baikal, had learned golf so that he could play the president, had even planned to construct his own version of Disneyland outside Moscow.[45] Khrushchev had been assisted in his pacific endeavors by the fact that his admiration for Ike was shared by many among the Soviet military. As Harold Macmillan surmised, the "inept American handling" of the U-2 affair was a "blow to the image" of Eisenhower which had been built up in Russia. Khrushchev complained to Macmillan that "his *friend* (bitterly repeated again and again) his friend Eisenhower had betrayed him." And the British prime minister reckoned that the Communist leader, a creature of impulse and emotion, had acted not only under pressure but also "under a real sense of indignation."[46] It is difficult to dissent from Adlai Stevenson's view that "we handed Khrushchev the sledge hammer and the crow bar to wreck this meeting."[47]

The story of the summit that never was is soon told. Ike flew to Paris on 14 May, two days before it was due to begin. He conferred with de Gaulle, who warned him that Khrushchev was threatening to end the conference unless the United States repudiated U-2 flights, apologized, and punished those responsible. "Depressed and uncertain," Ike discussed tactics with Macmillian at the American embassy over breakfast—the prime minister was appalled by the president's meal, which consisted of cereal, figs, steak, and jelly.[48] Ike also held a series of consultations with his advisers. Bohlen reckoned that the Russians intended to break off the conference and that they would try to make Ike "grovel." The president had no intention of doing that. But he did wonder if the United States should not terminate the conference first, only to be told by Bohlen's successor in Moscow, Ambassador Llewellyn Thompson, that "we needed a better posture on which to break it off than the matter of spy flights." Instead Ike simultaneously made aggressive and conciliatory moves. He placed U.S. forces on alert. And he decided to restrict "all intelligence operations of a "provocative" nature and "to renounce the use of the U-2."[49] This renunciation he planned to affirm at the conference.

Before he could do so Khrushchev, his face red, his hands shaking, rose to his feet. "With a gesture reminiscent of Mr. Micawber," he pulled a large wad of typed papers out of his pocket and launched into a long and offensive polemic against the president and the United States.[50] His speech, which accused Ike of lies and hypocrisy, was punctuated, according to de Gaulle, by Marshal Malinovsky's "peremptory gestures and warlike grimaces."[51] As the labored abuse and humiliating requirements were translated, paragraph by paragraph, Ike's own responses apparently varied. He had difficulty in controlling himself and, for the first time in years, he longed to light a cigarette. But at one point he caught Khrushchev's eye and could not refrain from flashing a broad grin, which so disconcerted the Russian that he afterward kept his head firmly buried in his papers. Khrushchev finished by saying that the summit should be postponed for six to eight months, by which time Ike would not be a lame duck but a political dead duck, and that he was no longer welcome in the Soviet Union.

The president replied with dignity that U-2 flights were suspended and that he wanted the summit to continue for the sake of world peace. But though Macmillan and de Gaulle were of the same mind, it was hopeless. As Ike said immediately after the first session, Khrushchev had been "completely intransigent and insulting to the United States and had presented impossible demands."[52] The president devoted some strong language to the Russian leader and it was clear that Macmillan's desperate attempts to rescue something from the wreck were doomed. Bitterly disappointed, Ike flew home. He stopped in Lisbon, evidently unperturbed to be honoring Salazar's dictatorship at such a time. In the gardens of the Queloz Palace Ike encountered a reporter throwing coins into a fountain. He was doing it for luck. The president said, "Then you'd better throw some in for all of us."[53]

Ike's luck had run out. But the clouds did have a little silver lining. The European allies had responded to America's predicament with admirable loyalty, and Macmillan and de Gaulle had done their best to support the distressed president. So did the people of the United States, who welcomed him home as though he had achieved a triumph and inundated him with "letters of praise."[54] As Ike remarked, they had been "infuriated" by Khrushchev's boorish behavior and stood "stanchly behind" their own man.[55] So did many of the more popular newspapers. Ike was moved to write to William Randolph Hearst, Jr., expressing satisfaction over "the balanced and reasonable way the Hearst papers handled the recent U-2 incident and the 'summit' meeting. . . . I never forget the old saw—'He is a great man; he agrees with me.' "[56]

Despite the debacle Ike's popularity remained a phenomenon to arouse the awe of journalists. One wrote a long article about it in July quoting, without irony, Ike's own solemn explanation of why he stood so high in public esteem. It was "because the people think I am honest and sincere, as I hope I am." Evidently the bungled U-2 cover-up did

little to change the general opinion that Ike had a "superior character," an opinion that cast "a golden glow over his Presidential presence."[57] The politicians themselves were transfigured in that glow. At
a breakfast of congressional leaders late in May Ike admitted that,
although the weather-plane story should have worked, "on reflection
it would have been a good idea to count ten." The legislative leaders
were sympathetic, and Senator Fulbright suggested that the president
should not have taken full responsibility. Ike said that "if he didn't
take responsibility someone else would have to." Then he added with
a smile, "if anyone were punished they should punish me first,"
though the only way to do so would be by impeachment. In a jocular
vein Sam Rayburn replied, "You haven't got long enough to go for
that." But he continued seriously: "We are all in this together."[58]

Still, amid all this more-or-less false bonhomie, stern and sensible
voices could be heard calling for a more realistic assessment of the
situation. Walter Lippmann, for example, pronounced that "The damage to our prestige would be irreparable if we all rallied round the
President and pretended to think that there was nothing seriously
wrong. . . . It is the dissenters and the critics and the opposition who
can restore the world's respect for American competence."[59] Even
inside the administration there was whispered censure. Gordon Gray,
for instance (who later lauded Ike as a dedicated activist), told George
Kistiakowsky that he "felt that actually Truman did a better job of the
presidency because he really applied himself." Gray said that Ike's
frequent holidays and games of golf were causing "paralysis of government."[60] One or two staff members injudicious enough to mention
the seriousness of the U-2 setback in Ike's presence received withering
rebukes. But the president's irritation points to his uneasy awareness
that he had just suffered one of the most damaging reverses in his
career.

When George Kistiakowsky seemed to blame him for the fiasco, the
president flared up angrily and was mollified only by the assurance
that those really culpable were the bureaucrats. The president, who
was consistently in a "bad humor,"[61] kept looking for scapegoats. He
said that the scientists had failed him. "The intelligence people," he
asserted, "had failed to recognize the emotional, even pathological,
reaction of the Russians regarding their frontiers."[62] No one in America, of course, appreciated that Soviet sensitivity better than the president. Thus somewhere in the complex recesses of his heart Ike could
hardly avoid the conclusion that the fault was his, and he told Kistiakowsky "very sadly that he saw nothing worthwhile left for him to
do until the end of his presidency."[63] The summit conference was

destroyed. The test-ban treaty was doomed. Ike's chance to end the cold war, and to achieve a just and lasting peace between East and West, had vanished. He too would shortly disappear from the center of the world's stage. The president had denied himself the chance he craved to make a "splendid exit."[64]

As it was, Ike's presidency ended in miserable anticlimax, and the months leading up to his departure saw the administration running down like an ancient clock. Ike tried to compensate for the cancellation of his Russian odyssey by going on another goodwill trip, this time to the Far East. He left in June to visit the Philippines, Korea, Formosa, and Japan. But this time his tour was greeted with some cynicism at home and was marred by opposition abroad. One newsman remarked sardonically, as the president sailed through the Formosa Strait (escorted by the Seventh Fleet) while the Chinese Communists bombarded Quemoy, "Ike's the only Chief of State who ever got an eighty-thousand-gun salute."[65] The journalist Harrison Salisbury went as far as to call this "the most macabre Presidential trip that ever could be imagined"[66] because its crowning glory—the Japanese element—also had to be canceled. In Tokyo anti-American crowds, displaying placards which proclaimed "I Dislike Ike," demonstrated violently, and it was thought the president might become the victim of "a Kamikaze-type operation."[67] Not wishing to make an exit quite that dramatic, Ike settled instead for a delightful holiday in Hawaii. But many Americans were less than delighted. They wanted more domestic bread and fewer foreign circuses.

Back in the United States, Ike was anxious not to initiate any major new undertakings. So he kept his temper in the face of Khrushchev's provocative words and actions. He could not quite match the suave hauteur of Harold Macmillan who, when the Russian leader hammered on the table with his shoe at the United Nations, asked for a translation. But he did resist a fleeting temptation to launch an attack on Russia while Khrushchev was in New York. Ike also resisted exhortations to go openly on the offensive against Cuba, contenting himself with stepping up economic sanctions and pushing forward covert measures. Employing the CIA and the United Nations peacekeeping force as proxies, he also tried not to become directly involved in the chaotic situation which the Belgians had created in the Congo. If Ike's responsibility for the assassination plot against the nationalist leader Patrice Lumumba cannot be proved, the direction of the president's policy toward the Congo itself is hard to mistake. Ike first rebuffed Lumumba, then complained that he had become a Soviet stooge, and finally supported neocolonialist forces ranged against him.

The CIA did not murder Lumumba, but it assisted in his capture by the new military ruler, General Joseph Mobutu, who did execute him.

On the home front Ike was even less active than he had been in preceding years. His main effort was devoted to securing a balanced budget, the campaign for fiscal responsibility now having become his primary crusade. Admittedly, he did give way a little further over defense expenditure, simply because the pressures were so great. But throughout 1960 his social legislation was penny-pinching and tepid. A new civil rights bill, for example, was scarcely an improvement on its predecessor, and it did little or nothing to prevent the continuing deterioration of race relations in the South. Modest progress was made over fair labor standards, minimum wages, assistance to needy areas, and old-age medical insurance. But Ike dithered on the last item, for which he was cruelly lampooned in the press. One cartoon represented him as saying, "If all the aged want is security they should've joined the government as I did."[68]

Of course, throughout the summer and autumn of 1960 all eyes were focused on the electoral struggle between Richard Nixon and the glamorous young Democratic contender, John F. Kennedy. Ike was about to become a has-been. His chief interest to press and public now revolved around the question of whether he could pass on his mantle to the vice-president. Naturally Ike said that he was looking forward more than ever to retirement and told everyone that, even had it been possible, nothing could induce him to run again. In fact, he had dropped hints to Republican leaders in Congress that he would not be averse to the repeal of the Twenty-second Amendment. Had this happened Ike would surely have found persuasive reasons for deciding that, after all, he was not too old to embark on a third term. He would almost certainly have been elected, as Kennedy admitted. But whether Ike could, or would, transfer his popularity to Richard Nixon remained open to the gravest doubt. He had, it is true, preferred Nixon to his Republican rival, Nelson Rockefeller. Ike disliked Rockefeller's high spending plans, especially on arms, and thought he was "being too much influenced by a man who has no capacity for giving sensible advice."[69] This was Emmet Hughes, whom Ike had once considered brilliant but now could not forgive for having expressed cogent reservations about his government.

But although Nixon was his political heir, Ike remained ambivalent toward the vice-president. He avowedly supported Nixon, but seemed incapable of giving him an unqualified endorsement. In his speech at the Republican Convention in July, which was a paean of praise for the achievements of his own administration, Ike did not once mention Nixon's name. When pressed by journalists about the vice-president's personal achievements, Ike insisted that only the president had taken decisions. "Now if just when you talk about other people sharing a decision, how can they?" he luminously inquired.[70] It was as if Ike were chiding Nixon retrospectively for not having accepted his offer to take an executive post in the Cabinet. Finally, when asked to name a major idea which Nixon had contributed to the government's program, Ike snapped, "If you give me a week, I might think of one. I don't remember."[71] Ike at once appreciated that this was a gaffe, but the subsequent "clarification" was so threadbare that it could only augment Nixon's discomfort. Even when talking to Nixon, Ike was painfully two-edged in his remarks. At the beginning of the campaign, he advised the vice-president not to be too glib and to think before he spoke. Toward the end of it, when visiting Nixon who was in the hospital with a badly bruised knee, Ike remarked of his loud pajamas that "this was a side of your personality the voters had not seen."[72]

However, although Ike apparently made it harder for Nixon to do so, he did want the vice-president to win in November. He described Kennedy as a "young whippersnapper"[73] who was far more incompetent than Nixon. As for his Democratic running mate, Lyndon Johnson, he was "the most tricky and unreliable politician in Congress."[74] It is true that neither Kennedy nor Johnson attacked Ike personally, as Truman had done, being all too aware of his popularity. But it was clear that Kennedy's calls for a renewal of national purpose and a recovery of national prestige, his appeals for a more vigorous and intelligent leadership in order to get the country moving again, were barely veiled criticisms of Ike's stewardship. Nixon, too, subtly tried to distance himself from the personal and political weakness of the Eisenhower administration, while simultaneously basking in the president's reflected glory. He cynically gave way, for example, to the mounting national hysteria about inadequate defense spending, knowing full well that the missile gap was a myth. Ike considered that this was "little short of outright repudiation of his competence as Commander-in-Chief,"[75] and he angrily whipped Nixon back into some semblance of conformity.

In general, of course, the vice-president was bound to support the policies he had been espousing for eight years. Accordingly Ike did some campaigning on his behalf. But he invariably concentrated on the Republican successes of the past two terms rather than the future benefits which would be conferred on the nation by Nixon and his running mate, Henry Cabot Lodge. Ike was privately concerned that

Lodge, "a blue blood from Boston," was a dubious electoral asset,[76] though he balanced Nixon well. Ike's lack of enthusiasm for his chosen successor may well now be considered evidence of a rare political clairvoyance struggling to find expression. But it naturally embarrassed the vice-president and may help to explain why he requested Ike to limit his efforts, though according to Nixon's own account he was motivated by a concern for the president's health. However, Nixon was not above trying to enlist Ike's help in casting doubt on Kennedy's health. Jim Hagerty called this a "cheap, lousy, stinking political trick," and the president would have nothing to do with it. He also forbade Nixon to say that, if elected, he would use Ike to visit Communist countries in return for their leaders coming to the United States. When Nixon ignored the prohibition Ike was "so mad" that he wanted to make him retract—only to let Hagerty persuade him to send the vice-president a congratulatory telegram about his speech.[77]

The result of the election was so close that almost any adverse factor can be blamed for Nixon's defeat. Many observers attributed the late surge in his favor to Ike's more energetic campaigning in the last week. As Theodore H. White wrote, "No cavalcade I have followed in the entourage of any other political figure in this country has ever left so many smiling, glowing people behind as the Eisenhower tour."[78] On the other hand, there were many placards saying, "We Like Ike but We Back Jack." And the vice-president himself could hardly have been unaware that Ike's earlier behavior might have cost him the few thousand votes he needed to win. Nevertheless, after conceding he telephoned Ike from California and dutifully intoned, "You were magnificent as far as I am concerned."

Nixon also said that he was "not downcast particularly."[79] Ike himself was deeply disappointed and said that he felt as if he had been hit in the solar plexus with a baseball bat. Going off to Augusta for a holiday of golf and quail shooting, he remarked to Slats Slater, "Well, this is the biggest defeat of my life."[80] Soon, though, in a more relaxed vein, he reckoned that the defeat was not a repudiation of his brand of Republicanism. Having at first felt that "the work of eight years was down the drain," he now considered that Kennedy was talking more responsibly.[81] Certainly the president-elect paid flatteringly close attention when Ike "hit the high spots in the problem of transferring federal control from one administration to another."[82] He also took a respectful and intelligent interest in other presidential mysteries as expounded by Ike. And he appeared duly impressed when Ike told him, "There are no easy matters that will come to you as President. If they are easy, they will be settled at a lower level."[83]

Afterward Kennedy commented enigmatically that Eisenhower was "better than I had thought."[84]

Ike's approval of Kennedy, such as it was, soon soured. He resented the growing assumption that the Democratic hero had arrived in the nick of time to save the country from helpless stagnation. If Ike's popularity remained intact, his prestige during the last weeks of his administration began to fall toward the nadir of benign contempt which it reached during the 1960s. Jokesters now called Ike's White House "the Tomb of the Well-Known Soldier." A sensational NBC television documentary on the U-2 affair concluded that (as one critic wrote) it had been "one of the worst snafus in the history of statesmanship" and that the president's handling of it had been "totally and limply incompetent."[85] It seemed ironically apt that the Commission on National Goals, which the president had established after the demoralized drift of 1958, should report right at the end of Ike's second term. Yet the president could not believe that a meretricious regime like Kennedy's would be an improvement on his own moral administration. He did not understand how a future incumbent of the White House could allow entertainers such as Frank Sinatra and Sammy Davis, Jr., to become so prominent in his retinue. He deplored some of the new appointments, especially "a menagerie in the State Department comprising one individual who is no less than a crackpot, another noted for his indecisiveness, and still another of demonstrated stupidity, and, finally, one[86] famous only for his ability to break the treasury of a great State."[87] Ike's contempt for Kennedy grew with the years. As an elder statesman he was fond of repeating the old saw, "You can always tell a Harvard man, but you can't tell him much."[88]

Ike did his best to tell Kennedy about the outstanding political problems he was going to face. A Communist Cuba remained a serious threat, and Ike explained the covert operation being planned to oust Castro. Later, of course, Ike was "terribly distressed" over the "fiasco" of the abortive invasion of Cuba at the Bay of Pigs and knew "it could not have happened in his administration."[89] He afterward claimed to have told Kennedy that he could disband the force of Cuban exiles being trained in Guatemala "in ten minutes."[90] But as Kennedy himself ruefully observed after the Bay of Pigs disaster, "victory has a hundred fathers and defeat is an orphan."[91]

According to a memorandum of their meeting in the White House on 19 January 1961, Kennedy asked Ike if he favored "guerrilla operations in Cuba" even if the United States government was publicly involved. Ike replied, "Yes, as we cannot let the present government there go on." Robert Anderson supported him with the argument that "large amounts of United States capital now planned for investment in Latin America" were "waiting to see whether or not the United States can cope with the Cuban situation." Ike did caution that the United States could handle a " 'one-Korea type' situation" but not more. He added that it was difficult to distinguish between a limited and a major war—"in other words when do you go after the head 'of the snake' instead of the tail."[92] But this was the only note of warning he struck. He showed no "reluctance or hesitation" about the policy of helping Cuban exiles "to the utmost," stating that the effort should be "continued and accelerated."[93] Thus Kennedy was left under the firm impression that the Cuban operation, which had built up a big head of steam, had the unequivocal blessing of America's most distinguished soldier. Of course, whether Ike would have proceeded with the invasion in the manner of Kennedy, or at all, remains a matter of speculation. Maybe his natural caution would have prevailed, especially in the absence of a convincing alternative to Castro's government—something Ike had urged the CIA to provide. Or perhaps he would have tried to achieve a trio of triumphs, adding Castro's scalp to those of Mossadegh and Arbenz.

Actually Cuba was not the most acute foreign problem which Ike bequeathed to Kennedy. For some time Vietnam's small jungle neighbor, Laos, had been riven by fierce internal strife, and it was only exacerbated by American aid and intervention. Not for the first time, the Eisenhower administration had conducted two contradictory foreign policies, with the State Department supporting one Laotian faction and the CIA another. As a bewildered Lao leader remarked, "Since so many voices are heard it is impossible to tell which has the authoritative ring."[94] In December 1960 an alliance of left-wing forces took advantage of the chaos to stage a coup, and the government appealed for help. Ike thought "we should act vigorously now that we have the cover of legality."[95] However, he could get no support from his European allies. De Gaulle was particularly arrogant, and Ike described him as "a curious combination of the medieval and modern, whose mental picture of the conduct of world affairs is the meeting of Napoleon and Alexander on a raft in the Dnieper [actually Nieman] River settling the affairs of the world."[96] Ike talked of sending in "the Seventh Fleet, with its force of marines" to keep Laos out of Communist hands.[97] But he took fright at the prospect of becoming engaged in another Korea. Anyway, time was running out for him, and in the end he did little but huff and puff and pass on his alarm to Kennedy.

Ike was still more alarmed by the likelihood that Kennedy would dissipate Ike's own hard-won credit balance in an orgy of fiscal irresponsibility. What troubled him most "in the whole security picture," Ike said, "was the danger of excessive, unnecessary spending."[98] It was with this in mind that he made the most famous and oft-quoted remarks of his presidency. In his televised farewell address to the nation he spoke of the novel "conjunction of an immense military establishment and a large arms industry." He then issued his classic warning: "we must guard against the acquisition of unwarranted influence, whether sought or unsought, by the military–industrial complex."[99] The ungainly phrase sounded as if it might have been coined by Ike, but apparently his speech writer Malcolm Moos was responsible for it. How far Ike is entitled to credit for the thought behind the expression is more difficult to gauge.

Ike had fought long and hard on several fronts to end the arms race. He had become almost obsessed by the political power and financial voracity of the defense lobby. He had spoken urgently about the social price which had to be paid as a result of high military expenditure. Many expert witnesses, among them scientists like Killian and Kistiakowsky, have testified that Ike's concern was no final flash in the pan but the culmination of a deeply felt and continuing, albeit unsuccessful, campaign.

But by a supreme irony Ike himself had done much to foster a powerful defense establishment and to advocate its integration with industry. As chief of staff he had declared, "The future security of the nation demands that all those civilian resources which by conversion or redirection constitute the main support in times of emergency be associated closely with the activities of the Army in time of peace." As a soldier-president with a Cabinet full of business tycoons, Ike had asserted that the United States must maintain a "permanent armaments industry of vast proportions."[100] He had quadrupled defense spending during his two terms, partly as a result of cutting back the government's own research and manufacturing capability, which was cheap to run, while encouraging the profiteering private sector. In the farewell speech itself, he uttered other admonitions with equal solemnity—about the "hostile ideology" of Communism, about the perils of "a scientific technological elite"[101]—but they did not strike a chord. In retirement, far from speaking out clearly against the military–industrial complex, Ike obscurely qualified his opposition to it.

Today it is little more than a commonplace to denounce the enormous vested interest embodied in the military–industrial complex; to dwell on the sinister symbiotic relationship between producers and consumers of weapons; to point to the ramifications of their influence and to their acolytes in academe, in public relations, and in politics; to lament the cost and the waste of it all. In his farewell address, rightly said to be the most memorable since that of George Washington, Ike anticipated all this. Unfortunately no one can be sure how much he meant it.

Hearing the sound of workmen erecting a reviewing stand across Pennsylvania Avenue for Kennedy's inaugural, Ike observed to a friend: "it's like being in the death cell and watching them put up the scaffold."[102] Few presidents can have expressed their reluctance to quit their office in such graphic terms. The White House servants were also sad about his departure. On the cold, snowy morning of 20 January, some of them wept as Ike and Mamie shook hands with them and said goodbye. Ike had dressed up in a morning suit as his successor, turning the clock back, had requested. Mamie amused Kennedy by remarking about Ike's top hat: "Till seeing you in *that,* I never noticed how much an Irishman *you* look."[103] During their car journey to the Capitol, Kennedy asked Ike what he thought of Cornelius Ryan's vivid account of D-Day. According to his brother Robert, the president-elect was intrigued to discover that Ike had not read the book and, in fact, did not seem to have read anything. Even so, John Kennedy thought that Ike had "a rather fascinating personality, could understand talking to him why he was President of the United States . . . [but] just felt that he hadn't done any homework, didn't know a great deal about areas that he should know."[104] Robert Kennedy added that his brother always felt Eisenhower to be unhappy with him, particularly because he was so young. There was no denying this. Whereas Ike, aged seventy, had just overtaken Andrew Jackson's record as the oldest man to occupy the White House, Kennedy now became the youngest. The new president made a guarded allusion to this change in his Inaugural Address, saying that the torch had now been passed to a new generation. Shortly afterward, the Eisenhowers inconspicuously left the proceedings. They had lunch with friends and former cabinet members and then drove home—to what the newspapers insisted on calling Eisenhower's Gettysburg address. As Ike later wrote, apparently with enthusiasm, he and Mamie made "a fantastic discovery. We were free."[105]

★

Death of a Statesman

Unlike Rip van Winkle, after nearly two decades at the summit of affairs Ike had plenty of help in easing his return to everyday life. Thanks to a special act of Congress, his five-star rank was restored and with it his right to a servant, driver, and aide, to free transport and medical care. Ike also retained his annual pension of twenty-five thousand dollars, plus a large office allowance. The latter was very necessary as he continued to receive nearly two thousand letters a week. Ann Whitman agreed to continue as his secretary. She had found herself rather pushed into the background after Persons had succeeded Adams—at times the president had looked through her rather than at her—and she had contemplated resignation. Nevertheless, when the president asked her to set up an office for him at Gettysburg she said that "my dedication to him was ten times my dedication to my country."[1] This sort of dedication, in the more intimate surroundings of Ike's new headquarters, caused problems with Mamie, and before long Ann Whitman did leave. Still, until then she conducted Ike's business with her usual efficiency. And his rich friends rallied around to help with other mundane matters, such as providing him with private airplanes and luxurious accommodation on his trips around the country. However, none of this prevented Ike from grumbling about his new and unfamiliar lot. In July 1961, for example, he informed Bill Robinson that he was "harassed by tourists, inefficient staff work, lack of protection when I venture out of doors, endless requests for appearances (of course I realize I would feel just as irritable if I weren't asked to do such things), pressures from the Republican National Committee—and with it all, my unrelieved concern about the state of the world and my inability to do anything about it."[2]

For all his fantasies about loafing away the evening of his days, Ike simply could not retire and vegetate. He did, it is true, take life more gently than before. He enjoyed mooching around the farm. He engaged in his usual outdoor recreations with his usual concentration. He made several trips abroad and reveled in his winter stays in California. He spent as much time as possible with his son's family, who lived in a house on the farm. He got pleasure from merely lounging in his large glass sun parlor with Mamie. This was their favorite retreat, for the living room, with its elaborate marble mantelpiece, candelabbra, and glass cabinet full of gifts, was more of a showplace. So, amid the cozy clutter on the porch, Ike would paint or enjoy the funny papers while Mamie watched television or searched for mail-order bargains—something she had surprised staff by doing from her bedroom-cum-office at the White House. The Eisenhowers even liked to entertain and take their meals in the sun parlor, preferring it to the more formal dining room, with its plush red chairs, polished silver, and huge chandelier. The last Club Eisenhower was, of course, very select indeed. But it continued to flourish, with small parties and familiar games, in their retirement home. As always, to quote one of their friends, "Mamie wants her soldier boy around, and Ike likes to be around her."[3]

But Ike could not escape the fact that he was a great national figure, almost the state's most senior senior citizen. He was deluged with requests to talk, to raise funds, to attend functions, to lend his name and presence to every conceivable cause. As he wrote to Winston Churchill, "there seems to be little cessation from the constant stream of demands on my time and energy. I do know that I am not as resilient as I once was and I approach a speaking engagement now with no sense of zest. The hard part is constantly to say 'No' to the various requests that come my way; but discourage them I must if I am to accomplish the writing chores I have undertaken."[4] In fact, Ike seemed to have the energy and the inclination to say "Yes" surprisingly often. When questioned about his retirement, he replied that Mamie "thinks it's nothing but a word in the dictionary."[5] Ike was particularly helpful to educational endeavors, notably to Eisenhower College, a liberal-arts institute at Seneca Falls, New York, on which he was glad to bestow his name and patronage. He also did some well-paid magazine writing and television work, his most memorable program being a poignant documentary entitled *D-Day Plus 20,* which he made with Walter Cronkite. But, as Ike had suggested to Churchill, his main effort was devoted to writing his presidential memoirs, *The White House Years.*

These two large volumes were Ike's least successful literary work. They read as though they had been compiled by committee and intended as apologia—which was indeed the case. They are bland, dull, complacent, and self-righteous. They lack intellectual insight and historical perspective. At times they reveal an awesome failure on Ike's part to understand the problems with which he was engaged or to treat them as anything more than a succession of disparate events. Although full (but not comprehensive) and factually accurate, these volumes resemble Coolidge's rather than Grant's *Memoirs*. They do not compare, save in respect of special pleading on their subject's behalf, with Churchill's grand autobiographical exercises or with the mordantly intelligent *oeuvre* of de Gaulle. Thus Ike was savaged by the critics. Of course, they were writing at the height of the reaction against the Eisenhower age, "that historical intermission when America stopped to snooze while the world churned inconsiderately on . . . [that] era of insufferable moral posturing abroad and irresponsible political abdication at home." Undoubtedly this sharpened the tone of their notices. In what was perhaps the most devastating review, Ronald Steel denounced Ike for his assumption of infallibility.

In page after page we are treated to the exhilarating spectacle of Ike immediately grasping the essentials of every situation, weighing an infinity of possibilities against the yardstick of morality and national interest (usually interchangeable), suffering his critics with a Christ-like patience, and invariably doing exactly the right thing. No wonder everybody loved him. No wonder he remains a semi-sacrosanct figure, the nearest thing to a Big Daddy this nation has known since George Washington.

Among the pieces of evidence Steel cited was Ike's suggestion that the U-2 incident had not been important because it was inevitable that the 1960 summit would fail, which would have caused disillusionment in the West. "Thus did Ike, by *seeming* to commit a blunder, cleverly save the Free World from the hands of an unscrupulous Khrushchev." Steel concluded that Ike's memoirs revealed the mind of a great staff officer rather than a great president, "a mind which sought consensus at the expense of conviction."[6]

Much of this is fair comment. Yet, paradoxically enough, Ike's one-dimensional book does have a three-dimensional hero. The personality of the president does emerge, almost by default, from these strangely impersonal pages. Tom Wicker suggested this in his review, detecting beneath the calm, unruffled surface of Ike's account, as of his leadership, "familiar hints of things not fully seen—of a determined composure laid at all costs over turbulent events." He concluded that Ike "succeeds better than he perhaps knew or intended in conveying the essential mood, the central character of his Administration."[7] Similarly, Ike managed to epitomize in these tomes the paradoxical nature of his presidency. James Reston, who found the memoirs "so like the Eisenhower administration in spirit," noted that "By his own testimony in this book, General Eisenhower constantly seems to be doing precisely what he insisted he would not or should not do."[8] Willy-nilly Ike appears in *The White House Years* as a bundle of contradictions. He is devious yet simple, evasive yet sincere, equivocal yet without guile. He is open, straightforward, even shallow. Yet he is also an opaque figure who exhibits almost nothing of his interior life or the process by which he made decisions. He is universally benevolent, yet he imputes base motives to everyone who opposes him, and his charitableness is selective even toward his supporters. He demonstrates modesty, even humility, but he never admits errors or suggests that his judgment was open to doubt. Ike's volume of informal reminiscences, *At Ease: Stories I Tell to Friends* (1967), was much better received. It is, indeed, far more readable. Yet precisely because of its relaxed charm, that book does not so well convey the sphinxlike quality of Ike's personality. As different reviewers wrote, from the pages of *The White House Years* "a peculiar fuzzy nimbus seems to arise";[9] "A gray fog of dignified reticence . . . enshrouds the book."[10] Ike himself is swathed in it, a man of mist and mystery to the last.

By a strange twist, the first volume of *The White House Years* was overshadowed by the assassination of John F. Kennedy, and the second one was eclipsed by the appearance of two distinguished memorials to the dead president, written by Theodore Sorensen and Arthur Schlesinger, Jr. What emerges clearly from their books is that much of Kennedy's conduct as chief executive was a deliberate attempt to escape from the cautious methods of Eisenhower, to fling off the bureaucratic shackles and break the chains of command. For, like Winston Churchill, Kennedy believed that organization was the enemy of initiative. The new president also aimed to transform the White House from a dreary, philistine officer's club into a vital focus of all that was brightest and best in America. This meant, for example, that Pablo Casals superseded Fred Waring and that French cuisine was preferred to home cooking—though in truth Kennedy did not much like either improvement and sometimes made late-night trips to the kitchen for a corned-beef sandwich and a beer.

Be this as it may, Ike naturally resented the much-trumpeted contrast between the two regimes. Although he maintained cordial relations with Kennedy, Ike thought his manner flashily vulgar and his policies dangerously irresponsible. No doubt Ike's carping was partly inspired by jealousy, for at a time when his own reputation was in decline Kennedy's brio dazzled the world. His tragic death enshrined him for years as a mythopoeic hero. But now the legend has been shattered, the tawdriness of Camelot has been exposed, and Kennedy's presidency has been dismissed as a triumph of style over substance. The pendulum has surely swung too far, for there is much to admire in his achievement. Yet if the president who enjoyed Westerns was a less inspiring, he was also a more wholesome, figure than the president who enjoyed James Bond. Ike had some reason, apart from personal pique, to chortle delightedly over a bumper sticker that appeared within a year of his leaving the White House: "I Miss Ike. Hell, I Even Miss Truman."[11]

Ike's substantive criticisms of Kennedy's conduct were pertinent but not entirely consistent. He denounced the president's deficit spending, especially that devoted to closing the nonexistent missile gap. But having at first deplored the extravagant moonshot project, in 1964 he opposed its abandonment on the ground that too much money had already been invested in it.[12] Ike regarded the Bay of Pigs debacle not as a failure of the policy of intervention but as a failure on Kennedy's part to implement correct staffing and consultation procedures. Kennedy had indeed taken decisions haphazardly, mocking those of his advisers opposed to the operation for "grabbing their nuts" in fear. Thus he was chastened by the disaster while Ike was not. Partly out of deference, but chiefly out of caution, the president invited his predecessor to Camp David for consultation.

According to his brother Robert, Kennedy "went out of his way to make sure that Eisenhower wouldn't hurt the Administration by going off at a tangent, and that's why he made such an effort over Eisenhower, not that Eisenhower ever gave him any advice that was very helpful."[13] According to Ike's account of their meeting, he gave the president very firm and forthright counsel. Ike encouraged him to "solidify the O.A.S. against Communism" and promised to support any future notion "that had as its objective the prevention of Communist entry and solidification of bases in the Western hemisphere." However, he qualified this sharply by warning Kennedy that "the American people would never approve direct military intervention, by their own forces, except under provocations against us so clear and so serious that everybody would understand the need for the move."[14] No ex-president has offered his successor a wiser caveat.

Unfortunately Ike paid no heed to it himself. He became increasingly bellicose in the advice he gave to the White House. Of course, he would not accept any blame for the Bay of Pigs failure and furiously denounced the "falsity of Schlesinger and Sorensen," who had suggested that a "plan for [the] invasion of Cuba was . . . discussed during [the] Eisenhower Administration." For the only time in his career, he even went as far as to alter the printed record, which stated that there had been planning. Yet he himself referred to "the plan" which Kennedy had "agree[d] to" and had subsequently changed.[15] And in an interview with Malcolm Moos, in 1966, Ike said that his administration had been thinking of invading Cuba "further to the east in the Oriente Province, so that first we would get into the very mountains where Castro first started to organize the revolution."[16] But if Ike dodged responsibility for past intervention he was willing to back Kennedy's tough line during the Cuban missile crisis in 1962. He declared that a blockade, with the aim of getting the Soviet long-range missiles removed, was the best plan. He later claimed that he tried, though without success, to make Kennedy insist that inspection teams be allowed in to ensure that all the missiles were gone. Ike also wanted the United States to take some kind of retaliatory action over the building of the Berlin Wall.

On the home front Ike was equally pugnacious. He did, it is true, create a moderate organization of Republican Citizens (which proved quite ephemeral) to counter extremist tendencies within the GOP. But his purpose was to smash the Democrats in the midterm elections. Faithful to his pledge "to keep on slugging [for the Republicans] in a different capacity,"[17] Ike campaigned with much energy, though little success. Kennedy whimsically blamed Ike's activities on Arthur Schlesinger, Sr. His poll of seventy-five historians had put Eisenhower so far down the list, way below Truman, in terms of presidential greatness that, Kennedy asserted, "Now he's out to save his reputation."[18]

Actually, in the months after Kennedy's assassination, Ike lost such reputation as he possessed for consistency and decisiveness. The crusader for peace allowed himself to be seduced into supporting a land war in Asia, the very disaster from which he had rescued the United States during his own presidency. The flail of nepotism now had no hesitation in recommending his brother Milton as the GOP's presidential choice, though when Robert Kennedy started to campaign for the Democratic candidacy Ike remarked, "The Kennedy family evidently is trying to control the United States."[19] Worst of all, the proponent of moderate Republicanism first dithered over opposing, and then brought himself to support as the GOP's candidate, a political primitive.

"In your heart you know he's right" was Barry Goldwater's slogan, to which opponents answered brusquely, "In your guts, you know he's nuts." Ike agreed with the latter formulation. He had even used the term "nuts" to describe Goldwater, who had never apologized for calling the Eisenhower administration "a dime-store New Deal."[20] Yet Ike refused to sustain liberal Republicans in their efforts to stop Goldwater's getting the nomination. To be sure, he ignored the wild suggestion that he should run as Goldwater's vice-presidential candidate, the only way in which the Arizona senator might have stood a chance. But Ike did throw his cloak of respectability over Goldwater during the campaign itself. No wonder, as an anxious Ike told Governor William Scranton of Pennsylvania, "my mail is amazing. So many are saying that I have split the party."[21] Small wonder that Richard Nixon, temporarily in political limbo and permanently embittered by the humiliations he had suffered as vice-president, was prompted to describe Ike as "that senile old bastard."[22]

In 1963 Ike had encouraged both Henry Cabot Lodge and William Scranton to enter the Republican race. But they held back, and Ike would not say of either one "here is my man."[23] Nor would he come out explicitly for Goldwater's main rival, Nelson Rockefeller, for whom he privately nursed an even stronger antipathy. He did issue a guarded account of the ideal Republican candidate, "responsible," "positive," and "forward looking," which seemed to fit the New York governor.[24] But he quickly redefined his statement and denied that it had any specific intent. Anyway, Goldwater won in the primaries and Ike became the focus of desperate appeals to save the GOP from a new old guard. In June, therefore, Ike met Scranton—who looked to optimists like a Republican Kennedy—and seemed to give him his blessing. The newspapers reported that Ike would endorse Scranton when he declared his candidacy. At this point George Humphrey intervened. He favored Goldwater, and on the telephone he strongly advised Ike not to take sides. Ike himself then called Scranton and said that, in order to clear up any misunderstanding, he would not be part of a "cabal" to halt Goldwater.[25]

Scranton thus stumbled hopelessly into the fight while Ike remained uncommitted, though he kept having to deny that he would nominate the Pennsylvania governor at the Republican National Convention. Ike used a military metaphor to cover his embarrassment and to describe his neutrality. He told Len Hall that "perhaps he was wrong in the beginning (in not picking a candidate) but he thinks it best he stick to his guns."[26] A more apt representation of his state was given in a brutal cartoon which depicted Ike as an ancient baby crying because he could not make up his mind. Ike admitted the criticism, but refuted its force, when he quoted to a reporter, at length and with enormous vehemence, the lines which Stephen Vincent Benét put into Lincoln's mouth in *John Brown's Body:*

> They come to me and talk about God's will
> In righteous deputations and platoons . . .
> But all of them are sure they know God's will
> I am the only man that does not know it.[27]

At the convention in mid-July Ike also tried to remain above the battle. He spent much of his time commenting on the proceedings for ABC television, a role which, in the opinion of the gang, did not comport with his dignity. He almost agreed to condemn Goldwater's alarming views on vesting the control of nuclear weapons in military hands, but at the last moment he repudiated the statement to which he had apparently committed himself. Nor could he quite bring himself to endorse Scranton's declarations against the John Birch Society or for the constitutionality of the civil rights bill. However, he did manage to provoke an extraordinary outburst of aggression among the GOP fundamentalists who had gathered at San Francisco's Cow Palace. In the course of a speech riddled with illiberal comments, which Ike, perhaps sensing the mood of the delegates, had added at the last moment, he told them to pay no attention to "sensation-seeking" journalists, who "couldn't care less about the good of our party." As an observer recalled, "the convention exploded into a pandemonium of rage against the news media. The delegates stood on their chairs, shouting, raving, shaking their fists and cursing the reporters in the press section."[28] One delegate was even heard to scream, "Down with Walter Lippmann!"[29]

Ike professed to be astonished by all this. But, having contributed nothing to the liberal resistance and something to the revivalist atmosphere, he should not have been surprised when Goldwater was nominated. The candidate at once declared that *"Extremism in the defense of liberty is no vice . . . moderation in the pursuit of justice is no virtue."* ("My God," exclaimed one reporter, "he's going to run as Barry Goldwater.")[30] Needless to say, Goldwater's uncompromising philosophy contradicted everything Ike stood for—yet the apostle of the middle way made no protest. Norman Mailer, who viewed the GOP's assembly as "a convention of hangmen who subscribe to the principle that the executioner has his rights too,"[31] remarked that Ike "obviously had a deep fear of the forces which were for Goldwater." The novelist attributed Ike's failure to stand up and be counted to an old man's willingness to be despised as long as he was not detested. "He was hooked on love like an addict, not large love, but the kind of mild tolerant love that shields an old man from hatred."[32] This was a shrewd assessment, though Mailer's suggestion that Ike's longing for love was some kind of senescent aberration is surely wrong. It was, despite Ike's expressed contempt for Hubert Humphrey as "the type of politician that went along with what was popular,"[33] a perennial characteristic. Just as Ike had gone out of his way to avoid bruising confrontations with MacArthur in the 1930s, Montgomery in the 1940s, and McCarthy in the 1950s, so he did with Goldwater in the 1960s.

Ike's detachment was less than serene, however, especially as he was lambasted by the press for having missed "one of the great opportunities of his political career in his failure to take a clear and unmistakable stand against" a man who was "totally unfit" to be president.[34] Soon after the convention Ike admitted to Lewis Strauss, "I am mentally tired, I am so pressured by friends. . . ."[35] He resented these pressures and occasionally succumbed to self-pity: "I don't see why they are always dragging out an old retired man."[36] Ike was further perturbed by the barely hidden racism in Goldwater's opposition to Johnson's civil rights bill. He told Bill Paley, boss of CBS, "I have no sympathy with a 'white back lash.' I will not encourage it and if it is encouraged I will vote for the other side." But characteristically he refused Paley's offer to "go on the air about your stand on these issues." Ike revealed that he had no stand—rather a wobble—in a letter to Milton. He wondered "why some responsible persons don't call [the] leaders of [the] Civil Rights movement and tell them they are playing into Goldwater's hands."[37] Ike was always inclined to preserve his own influence by not exercising it, but this was like telling the victim of an assault that any form of self-defense would shift public sympathy to his attacker.

Ike's personal capitulation to Goldwater was not quite total: he suggested mildly that the end did not justify the means, and he refused to sign a statement in support of the candidate unless forty or fifty prominent Republicans did so first. But in private as well as in public he rooted for this revolutionary of the right. He informed Jim Hagerty that Goldwater's public image was much worse than the man himself. He assured Nelson Rockefeller that Goldwater was "sincere and honest and dedicated to his country."[38] Ike told Goldwater himself that "he was baffled by businessmen going to Johnson," who "is so avid for popularity." Ike said he could not "do barnstorming" for Goldwater but that he would endorse him on television.[39] They duly appeared together on the screen, an incongruous pair, the peace crusader and the champion of total victory over Communism. Ike assured an audience consisting largely of the converted that it was "silly" to regard Goldwater as a right-wing extremist and "tommyrot" to talk of his wish to use nuclear weapons.[40] Richard Rovere remarked that "one hesitates to attribute political adroitness to a man who has revealed as much political ineptitude as Eisenhower."[41] Ike's current defenders claim that the converse is true, but there is no denying that the Goldwater episode affords a spectacular instance of Ike's political *mal*adroitness.

Ike's innate conservatism was becoming ever more pronounced. Perhaps as chief executive he had at times suppressed his natural bias in order to achieve national consensus. But shortly before the 1964 election he told George Humphrey that the records of his presidency showed that "domestically, except for one or two things, he was always to the right of Senator Taft."[42] After Lyndon Johnson won his landslide victory over Goldwater, Ike showed that his right-wing views did not stop at the water's edge and that his cold warrior's ardor had, if anything, increased with age. And as Johnson stepped up the conflict in Vietnam he was naturally anxious to benefit from the general's counsel and support.

Few presidents have been more adept at the art of personal and political manipulation than Johnson. He was a master of lapel holding and arm grabbing, of pulling strings and granting favors, of ward-boss wheeler-dealing and men's-room horse trading. His unabashed hucksterism had earned Johnson the juvenile nickname of "Bull" (for Bullshit). In Washington his febrile energy provoked the comment, "The guy's just got extra glands."[43] Jim Hagerty thought Johnson had "a 'Messiah' complex."[44] Certainly he did his utmost to convert Ike, charming, flattering, caressing, and cajoling like a born-again talkshow host. Ike and Mamie were paid every kind of small courtesy and minute attention that Johnson's fecund ingenuity could devise. The president wanted, in return, permission to come running to Ike on the subject of foreign affairs if he got his "tail in a crack."[45] Most of all Johnson was eager to invest his baneful Southeast Asian policy with Ike's unique moral authority and military prestige. No one could help him to bridge the yawning "credibility gap" better than Eisenhower. Soon the president was telling Ike that he was a "tower of strength" over Vietnam.[46]

It is true that Ike did endorse Johnson's war and did give him hawkish advice on how to fight it. On 17 February 1965, for example, Ike held what amounted to a seminar on the conduct of the war for

the president and his senior advisers. He lectured them on the purpose of the conflict, "that of denying Southeast Asia to the Communists." He quoted Napoleon to the effect that "in war morale is to the
material element as three is to one," adding that he himself rated it
higher than this in a guerrilla war. He stressed the importance of
improving morale by obtaining allied support, disseminating propaganda, and conducting air strikes—though bombing would not stop
infiltration. To do that it was vital to win the support of the South
Vietnamese people. He cited as an example the operations of Colonel
John S. Mosby, who had retained the affection of the inhabitants of
northern Virginia where he fought as an irregular during the Civil
War. Ike also quoted the old adage that "centralization is the refuge
of fear."[47]

Over the next two years Ike urged Johnson to give General Westmoreland the tools and let him alone to finish the job. He condemned
defensive strategies, "acting by 'driblets'" and taking "piddling"
steps. Rather, he recommended, the United States should swamp the
enemy with overwhelming force.[48] In public he supported the bombing which, despite the civilian casualities, he knew to be directed at
military targets. In July 1967, fed up with what he considered to be
a policy of gradualism, Ike declared that the United States should
"take any action to win" the war. He "would not automatically preclude" the use of nuclear weapons.

Within a couple of weeks, however, Ike said that this was a "silly"
idea.[49] The characteristic about-face points to the fact that Ike's attitude toward the whole Vietnam conflict was riddled with anomalies.
First of all, the advice which he proffered about the need to give
Westmoreland his head was difficult to reconcile with his insistence on
winning the hearts and minds of the Vietnamese people. At one
moment, Ike seemed almost to agree with General Curtis Le May that
North Vietnam should be "bombed back to the Stone Age."[50] The
next, Ike told Johnson that he wanted a greater understanding between Americans and Communists in Vietnam. He favored stern
measures; but he warned Johnson that "No country can be saved
unless the people's hearts are in the right place." It was necessary
therefore to "talk morals and spiritual facts" to the Vietnamese. Their
government could not be kept in place "with bayonets"; the "consent
of the people" was crucial.[51]

Second, Ike had private reservations about the Vietnam War which
were not entirely consistent with his pugnacious public utterances.
The master of coalition warfare was naturally troubled by the fact that
the conflict had produced a "loss of friendship and mutual confi-

dence" between the United States and its European allies.[52] By 1966 he was worried about fears that the war was "dragging on inconclusively."[53] He told Goodpaster that "open conflict . . . is something that should . . . be brought to an end as soon as possible. . . . Our people inevitably get tired of supporting involvements of this kind which go on and on for a long time with no end in sight."[54] Perhaps after all, Ike was hankering for a nuclear final solution to the Vietnamese problem. Or perhaps, despite his strictures against those who whined and whimpered about the war, he was toying with the notion that peace in Vietnam in 1966 might be just as desirable as peace in Korea had been in 1953. Certainly Ike was sensitive about Democratic efforts to "tie our commitments [in Vietnam] back to Eisenhower."[55] He went out of his way to tell Johnson that the situation had been quite different during his administration. "There was no military problem," and he had not "started military plans."[56]

This deplorable lapse was doubtless one factor among many which prompted the John Birch Society to denounce Ike as a "dedicated conscious agent of the Communist conspiracy."[57] The irony was that he shared the revulsion which conservatives of all sorts felt for the iconoclastic trends of the 1960s. Ike's had been a decade of Dial-a-Prayer, and he was shocked by topless dancers. In the 1950s the most unconventional hair cut had been the DA: now men cultivated long, androgynous tresses and later sometimes decorated them with flowers. When Ike was president males had worn charcoal-gray suits and females mid-calf-length dresses; now caftans and miniskirts were in fashion. Elvis Presley had attained a degree of respectability by joining the army: the Beatles lauded the culture of drugs—"Lucy in the Sky, with Diamonds." Wherever Ike looked he was appalled by new manifestations of decadence, by hippies and Hell's Angels, by pop art and nude theater, by Women's Lib and black power, by pornography and violence.

He was understandably most upset by the Watts riots in 1965. Ike acknowledged that they had not taken place in a "vacuum." But it did not occur to him that his own chickens might be coming home to roost, that his failure to tackle the problem of racial discrimination might have helped to cause the mayhem. Instead Ike explained it as part of a growing, nationwide "disregard for law and order, and weakening of morals." The state of affairs was epitomized by the "dancing you see teenagers doing on television, [which] was not allowed in vaudeville in [the] old days."[58]

In Ike's view the extreme phenomena which he now condemned were, like the Vietnam War, purely products of the 1960s. But such hoary social panaceas as he proposed were increasingly those of a much earlier age. In the 1950s, for example, Ike had been firm in his resolve to keep the government out of the messy business of birth control. Now, harking back to a noxious fad that had been popular with eugenicists and others in his youth, Ike favored the compulsory sterilization of unmarried mothers. Otherwise he reiterated the familiar lessons and the crusty prejudices he had learned at West Point—about respect for elders and betters, tidiness in thought and appearance, the practice of old-fashioned virtue and patriotism. He manifested his own patriotism by going on television with Omar Bradley and demanding victory in Vietnam, which might involve hot pursuit of the Vietcong over international frontiers. He condemned the anti-war movement as a quasi-treasonable conspiracy of "kooks" and "hippies."[59] Actually Senator Fulbright's hearings on Vietnam, not to mention other things, had demonstrated that responsible and respectable citizens also opposed the war. Many of them made representations to Ike, and his private doubts about "whether it would be better to get out of it than to continue" apparently increased.[60]

Nevertheless he persevered on the rightward path. He deplored the fact that Ronald Reagan, having made some "splendid appointments" as governor of California, had "all the intelligensia [sic] against him."[61] And he supported Richard Nixon's reviving efforts to obtain the Republican presidential nomination. As always, there was a degree of hesitation and ambiguity in Ike's attitude toward Nixon, whom he considered perpetually maturing, perpetually immature. It was somehow appropriate that the final entry in Ike's diary concerned a misunderstanding about the former vice-president. His name, along with Reagan's, came up at a noisy press conference in March 1967. Ike said that he was "one of the ablest men I knew and a man that I admired deeply and for whom I had a great affection."[62] Journalists thought Ike was referring to Reagan, and it was thus that his statement was reported. This was an embarrassment, since any correction would seem like a slight on the governor of California, whom Ike did admire, no doubt as much for his cinematic as for his political performances. Anyway Ike compensated for this gaffe by his unqualified endorsement of Nixon in 1968. He must have found this easier to give as Nixon was shortly to become a member of the family, when his daughter Julie married Ike's grandson David. But Ike surely went above and beyond the call of loyalty when he described Spiro Agnew as a man well qualified to be Nixon's vice-president because he was "intelligent, honest and straightforward."[63]

It might be thought that by this time Ike's judgment had been

impaired by illness and old age. Throughout the early 1960s he had
been in and out of the hospital with a variety of more or less serious
ailments. But in November 1965, just over ten years after his first
health crisis as president, he suffered a second heart attack. Again he
recovered, this time more slowly, and despite worsening arthritis, he
was able to play golf once more. Indeed in 1967, to his immense
delight, he scored his first hole in one. He even felt well enough to
consider visiting South Africa as a guest of the government—he was
assured that there were be "no problem at all" about his black servants, the Moaneys.[64] But in April 1968 Ike had a third heart attack.
In Walter Reed Hospital he rallied again briefly before complications
set in. It became clear that his heart was failing.

In spite of all this Ike retained a clear grasp of affairs and an astonishing capacity to impress even the most sharply skeptical. Henry Kissinger, who had "held about him the conventional academic opinion
that he was a genial but inarticulate war hero who had been a rather
ineffective President," called on the invalid twice and entirely
changed his mind. Ike was terribly emaciated and largely immobilized, but his "forcefulness was surprising. His syntax, which seemed
so awkward in print, became much more graphic when enlivened by
his cold, deep blue, extraordinarily penetrating eyes and when given
emphasis by his still commanding voice." Ike even managed to display
a flash of his celebrated temper when he thought Nixon's foreign
policy was insufficiently bellicose, and Kissinger was struck by "a
graphic vocabulary at variance with his sunny smile."[65]

Ike struggled manfully against the inevitable. Life still had its compensations—the Army–Navy game, the poignant manifestations of
public sympathy and affection, the visits he continued to receive from
the wise and the great, and above all his family. Like the methodical
old soldier he was, Ike had made his dispositions in readiness for the
end. He had settled his affairs. He had provided for Mamie, who was
living in a small suite next to his in the hospital. He had arranged to
be buried in the Eisenhower Memorial Chapel at Abilene next to Icky,
whose tiny remains had been moved from Denver. It was as well, for
Ike's cardiac condition deteriorated. It became plain that both heart
and body were giving up. Almost to the last he was hoping to put on
a little weight, to gain a brief respite. But on 28 March 1969 he died.
His last words, uttered in the presence of Mamie, John, and David,
were, "I want to go; God take me."[66]

So, amid a sincere but dignified display of national mourning,
passed the supreme commander of the victorious Allied armies in
Europe and the thirty-fourth president of the United States. Ike was

a richly kaleidoscopic figure. Of course, in democracies all major politicians tend to be or to become protean personalities, in order to embody the widest possible range of opinion. One American president, Martin van Buren, even gave his name to describe an evasive straddling of the issues. But no president, not even van Buren—who refused to commit himself to the proposition that it was a fine day— was more vanburenish than Dwight D. Eisenhower. As his son John acknowledged, Ike was "very, very changeable in a way."[67] He was, in Dryden's words,

> A man so various that he seem'd to be
> Not one, but all mankind's epitome.

Manuscript Sources
and Abbreviations

The following original sources were consulted and the abbreviations for them used in the notes are here given in bold type.

A. Eisenhower Library, Abilene, Kansas

1. Pre-Presidential Papers   **Pre PP**
2. Papers as President of the United States, 1953–61:
   Ann Whitman File
   - Name Series   **AWF NS**
   - Ann Whitman Diary Series   **AWF DS**
   - Eisenhower Diary Series   **AWF DDE DS**
   - Administration Series   **AWF AS**
   - Dulles–Herter Series   **AWF DHS**
   - Legislative Meeting Series   **AWF LMS**
3. White House Office
   - Office of Staff Secretary (Cabinet Series)   **WHO OSS**
   - Legislative Meeting Series   **WHO LMS**
4. Post-Presidential Papers
   - Principal Files   **Post PP PF**
   - Augusta–Gettysburg Series   **Post PP AGS**
   - Special Name File   **Post PP SNF**
   - Appointment Books   **Post PP AB**
5. Ruby Norman Lucier Papers   **RNLP**
6. Kevin McCann Papers   **KMP**
7. Harry Butcher Diary   **HBD**
8. Walter Bedell Smith Papers   **WBSP**
9. William E. Robinson Papers   **WERP**
10. John Foster Dulles Papers
    - White House Memoranda Series   **DP WHMS**
    - Telephone Call Series   **DP TCS**
    - Subject Series   **DP SS**
11. Bernard Shanley Diaries   **BSD**
12. Oral History Transcripts   **OH**

420 IKE

B. Library of Congress

1. Patton Diaries — LCPD
2. Spaatz Papers — LCSP
3. Alsops' Papers — LCAP

C. Columbia University Library

1. Bermingham Papers — CUL
2. Columbia Oral History Transcripts — COH

Abbreviations have also been used for the following published sources:

The Papers of Dwight D. Eisenhower, vols. 1–5, ed. A. D. Chandler, Jr., et al., vols. 6–11, ed. L. Galambos et al. (Baltimore, 1970–). — EP

Public Papers of the Presidents of the United States: Dwight D. Eisenhower (Washington, D.C., 1954–62) — PPP

New York Times — NYT

Notes

All the books mentioned below are published in New York unless otherwise indicated. Books listed in the Bibliography are referred to by short title in the Notes.

Introduction

1. A. Bryant, *Triumph in the West* (London, 1959), p. 339.
2. See R. L. Lane, *Ruddle's Rangers* (Manasses, Va., 1979), pp. 36, 44, passim.
3. D. D. Eisenhower, *At Ease,* p. 388.
4. Pre PP, C. Roberts, 1951.
5. Perrett, *Dream of Greatness,* p. 554.
6. *Chicago Tribune,* 1952.
7. Goldman, *Crucial Decade,* p. 221.
8. OH, R. J. Donovan, p. 39.
9. D. MacDonald, ed., *Parodies* (London, 1960), pp. 447, 449.
10. L. Morrow, "Dreaming of the Eisenhower Years," *Time,* 28 July 1980, p. 33.
11. T. A. Bailey, *Presidential Greatness: The Image and the Man from George Washington to the Present* (1966), p. 328.
12. Post PP AGS, 19 Sept. 1966.
13. Ewald, *Eisenhower the President,* p. 52.
14. G. H. Quester, "Was Eisenhower a Genius?," *International Security,* February 1979, p. 160.
15. LCAP, Box 17, David D. Barrett to J. Alsop.
16. S. Lubell, *The Revolt of the Moderates* (1956), p. 25.
17. See A. Krock, "Impressions of the President—and the Man," *New York Times Magazine,* 23 June 1957, pp. 34–39; and R. Rovere, "Eisenhower and the New President," *Harper's Magazine,* May 1960, pp. 31–35.
18. M. Kempton, "The Underestimation of Dwight D. Eisenhower," *Esquire,* September 1967, p. 109.
19. See especially R. Rhodes, "Ike: An Artist in Iron," *Harper's Magazine,* July 1970, and Lyon, *Eisenhower.*
20. E.g., Ambrose, *Eisenhower.*
21. A. M. Schlesinger, Jr., "The Eisenhower Presidency: A Reassessment," *Look,* 14 May 1979, p. 42.

22. BSD, 3. Two good accounts of the recent "Eisenhower Revisionism" are by V. P. de Santis in *Review of Politics* 38 (April 1976); and M. S. McAuliffe in *Journal of American History* 68, no. 3 (December 1981).
23. See especially Cook, *The Declassified Eisenhower,* and Greenstein, *The Hidden-Hand Presidency.*
24. LCAP, Box 10, William Clark to Stewart Alsop, 3 Mar. 1954.
25. Parmet, *Eisenhower,* p. 176.
26. Wilmot, *The Struggle for Europe* (London, 1965 ed.), p. 336.
27. Hamilton, *Monty,* p. 791.
28. COH, Barry Bingham, p. 105.
29. Hughes, *Ordeal,* p. 148.
30. AWF NS, Box 18, Eisenhower to Hazlett, 5 Apr. 1957.
31. WHO OSS, Box 3, 3 Jan. 1958. Since I completed this book Eisenhower's letters to Hazlett have been published by R. Griffith, ed., *Ike's Letters to a Friend.*
32. BSD, p. 567.
33. D. E. Lilienthal, *The Journals of David E. Lilienthal,* vol. II, *The Atomic Energy Years, 1945–1950* (1964), p. 375.
34. OH, Andrew Goodpaster, 26 June 1975, p. 118.
35. COH, Barry Bingham, p. 28.
36. BSD, p. 2283.
37. Hughes, *Ordeal,* p. 149.
38. *Time,* 11 June 1952.
39. Kempton in *Esquire,* p. 108.
40. Hughes, *Ordeal,* p. 149.
41. H. C. Lodge, *As It Was* (1976), p. 12.
42. Pre PP, Eisenhower to Butcher, 12 Oct. 1945.
43. OH, Robert D. Murphy, p. 26.
44. R. M. Nixon, *Six Crises* (London, 1962), p. 161.
45. OH, Gabriel Hauge, p. 120.
46. Kempton in *Esquire,* p. 108.
47. DP WHMS, Box 5, 8 Aug. 1956.
48. BSD, p. 2266.
49. S. Ambrose, "The Ike Age," *New Republic,* 9 May 1981, p. 30.
50. AWF NS, Box 20, Eisenhower to H. Luce, 8 Aug. 1960.

Chapter 1: President of the Roughnecks

1. B. Kornitzer, *Great American Heritage,* p. 49.
2. P. Brock, *Pacifism in the United States* (Princeton, N.J., 1968), p. 796.
3. OH, Rev. Roy I. Witter, p. 7.
4. OH, Rev. Roy I. Witter, p. 9.
5. See J. R. Hertzler, "The 1879 Brethren in Christ Migration from Southeastern Pennsylvania to Dickinson County, Kansas," *Pennsylvania Mennonite Journal,* January 1980, pp. 13ff.
6. J. A. Hawgood, *The American West* (London, 1967), p. 289.
7. Eisenhower, *At Ease,* p. 65.
8. H. B. Jameson, *Heroes by the Dozen* (Topeka, Ks., 1961), pp. 36, 27.
9. K. S. Davis, *Kansas* (1976), p. 112.
10. Kornitzer, *Great American Heritage,* p. 278.
11. AWF DS, Box 5, 1 May 1955.

12. H. C. Allen, *The United States of America* (London, 1964), p. 166.
13. AWF NS, Box 11, Eisenhower to Edgar Eisenhower, 30 June 1953.
14. Butcher, *My Three Years*, p. 521.
15. OH, Nettie Stover Jackson, p. 2.
16. EP, I, p. 431.
17. EP, III, p. 1882.
18. EP, III, p. 1815.
19. Eisenhower, *At Ease*, p. 33.
20. Ibid., p. 31.
21. Ambrose, *Eisenhower*, I, p. 21.
22. AWF NS, Box 11, Eisenhower to Edgar Eisenhower, 30 June 1953.
23. Kornitzer, *Great American Heritage*, p. 25.
24. Eisenhower, *At Ease*, p. 31.
25. Davis, *Soldier of Democracy*, p. 73.
26. Gunther, *Eisenhower*, p. 56.
27. BSD, 27 Apr. 1955, p. 1907.
28. AWF DS, Box 9, 30 Dec. 1957.
29. Kornitzer, *Great American Heritage*, p. 254.
30. AWF NS, Box 16, Eisenhower to James Hagerty, Sr., 30 June 1954.
31. RNLP, Eisenhower to Ruby Norman, 24 Nov. 1913.
32. Davis, *Soldier of Democracy*, p. 102.
33. RNLP, Eisenhower to Ruby Norman, 24 Nov. 1913.
34. AWF NS, Box 27, Eisenhower to Cliff Roberts, 29 July 1952.
35. EP, I, p. 398.
36. HBD, A207.
37. Becker, *Everyman His Own Historian* (1935), p. 9.

Chapter 2: Duty, Honor, Country

1. M. Sullivan, *Our Times*, vol. 5 (1933), p. 222.
2. RNLP, Eisenhower to Ruby Norman, 20 Nov. 1913.
3. Eisenhower, *At Ease*, p. 4.
4. Ibid.
5. EP III, p. 1198.
6. T. J. Fleming, *West Point* (1969), p. 270.
7. S. E. Ambrose, *Duty, Honor, Country* (Baltimore, 1966), p. vii.
8. OH, J. W. Leonard, pp. 3, 9.
9. RNLP, Eisenhower to Ruby Norman, 20 Nov. 1913.
10. Eisenhower, *At Ease*, p. 14.
11. RNLP, Eisenhower to Ruby Norman, November 1913.
12. Fleming, *West Point*, p. 290.
13. RNLP, Eisenhower to Ruby Norman, 24 Nov. 1913.
14. AWF NS, Box 9, Eisenhower to Natalie Brush, 1 Dec. 1914.
15. Fleming, *West Point*, p. 291.
16. RNLP, Eisenhower to Ruby Norman, November 1913.
17. W. Manchester, *American Caesar* (London, 1979), p. 121.
18. L. Farago, *Patton, Ordeal and Triumph* (1966), p. 37.
19. S. Forman, *West Point* (1950), p. 155.
20. A. Hatch, *General Eisenhower* (London, 1946), p. 33.
21. J. Elki and R. Moore, *School for Soldiers* (1974), p. 12.

22. OH, J. W. Leonard, p. 4.
23. Eisenhower, *At Ease,* p. 24.
24. RNLP, Eisenhower to Ruby Norman, 17 Jan. 1916.
25. KMP, n.d.
26. RNLP, Eisenhower to Ruby Norman, 17 Jan. 1916.
27. Hatch, *Red Carpet,* p. 81.
28. Ambrose, *Eisenhower,* I, p. 58.
29. RNLP, Eisenhower to Ruby Norman, 17 Jan. 1916.
30. Brandon, *Mamie Doud Eisenhower,* pp. 75, 94, 48.
31. Eisenhower, *At Ease,* p. 127.
32. Blumenson, *The Patton Papers,* I, p. 171.
33. AWF DDE DS, Box 7, Eisenhower to P. A. Hodgson, 19 July 1954.
34. R. Weigley, *History of the United States Army* (1968), p. 392.
35. AWF DS, Letter from Lieutenant Edward C. Thayer to his mother, January 1918.
36. H. Hagerdom, *Leonard Wood,* vol. II (1931), p. 237.
37. L. Mosley, *Marshall: Organizer of Victory* (London, 1982), p. 29.
38. OH, James Hagerty, p. 435.
39. Ambrose, *Eisenhower,* I, p. 65.

Chapter 3: Bald-headed Major

1. L. Farago, *Patton, Ordeal and Triumph* (1966), pp. 40, 44.
2. D. D. Eisenhower, "A Tank Discussion," *Infantry Journal* 17 (November 1920): 457.
3. Ibid.
4. Eisenhower, *At Ease,* p. 173.
5. Blumenson, *Patton Papers,* I, p. 94.
6. Farago, *Patton,* p. 35.
7. Pre PP, Patton to Eisenhower, 4 Feb. 1943.
8. J. S. D. Eisenhower, *The Bitter Woods* (London, 1969), p. 332.
9. LCPD, Box 1.
10. Pre PP, Patton to Eisenhower, 15 Nov. 1942.
11. EP, II, p. 939.
12. Blumenson, *Patton Papers,* II, p. 637.
13. Blumenson, *Patton Papers,* I, p. 96.
14. Eisenhower, *At Ease,* p. 167.
15. KMP.
16. Neal, *Eisenhowers,* pp. 64–65.
17. Eisenhower, *At Ease,* p. 183.
18. Davis, *Soldier of Democracy,* p. 200.
19. J. S. D. Eisenhower, *Strictly Personal,* pp. 1, 9.
20. KMP.
21. Eisenhower, *At Ease,* p. 196.
22. Ambrose, *Eisenhower,* I, p. 79.
23. B. H. Liddell Hart, *Foch: Man of Orleans,* vol. 1 (London, 1937), p. 119.
24. KMP.
25. Kornitzer, *Great American Heritage,* p. 248.
26. EP, IV, p. 2140.
27. Davis, *Soldier of Democracy,* p. 214.

28. Lyon, *Eisenhower*, p. 62.
29. B. F. Cooling, "Dwight D. Eisenhower at the Army War College, 1927–1928," *Parameters* 5, no. 1 (1975), p. 34.
30. Hatch, *Red Carpet*, pp. 146, 151.
31. New York *Herald Tribune*, 27 Sept. 1943.
32. KMP, 24 Sept. 1929.
33. J. K. Galbraith, *The Great Crash 1929* (Harmondsworth, 1961 ed.), p. 93.
34. F. Freidel, *America in the Twentieth Century* (1966 ed.), p. 48.
35. F. D. Mitchell and R. O. Davies, eds., *America's Recent Past* (1969), p. 201.
36. KMP, 9 Nov. 1929.
37. McCann, *America's Man of Destiny*, p. 65.
38. Hoover Oral History Program, D. D. Eisenhower, 13 July 1967.
39. Pre PP, Moseley to Eisenhower, 18 Feb. 1933.
40. J. F. Vivian and J. H. Vivian, "The Bonus March of 1932: The Role of General George Van Horn Moseley," *Wisconsin Magazine of History*, Autumn 1967, p. 30.
41. KMP.
42. Neal, *Eisenhowers*, p. 84.
43. Pre PP, Moseley to Eisenhower, 11 May 1943.
44. Pre PP, Moseley to Eisenhower, 29 Sept. 1943.

Chapter 4: Best Officer in the Army

1. KMP, 30 Dec. 1931.
2. KMP, 15 Feb. 1932.
3. KMP, 2 June 1933.
4. KMP, June 1932.
5. Pre PP, MacArthur to Eisenhower, 30 Sept. 1935.
6. KMP, 1 Dec. 1931.
7. Ambrose, *Eisenhower*, I, p. 93.
8. KMP, June 1932.
9. C. M. Green, *Washington* (Princeton, N.J., 1963), p. 371.
10. F. Daniels, *The Bonus March* (Westport, Conn., 1971), p. 167.
11. J. F. Vivian and J. H. Vivian, "The Bonus March of 1932: The Role of General George Van Horn Moseley," *Wisconsin Magazine of History*, Autumn 1967, p. 34.
12. *Baltimore Sun*, 31 July 1932.
13. OH, L. D. Clay, p. 160.
14. KMP, 28 Feb. 1932.
15. Eisenhower, *At Ease*, p. 21.
16. KMP, 15 Mar. 1933.
17. W. E. Leuchtenberg, "The Roosevelt Reconstruction: Retrospect," in F. D. Mitchell and R. O. Davies, eds., *America's Recent Past* (1969), p. 234.
18. E. Wilson, *The Thirties* (London, 1980), p. xvi.
19. KMP, 28 Feb. 1933.
20. KMP, 15 Mar. 1933.
21. Report of the Chief of Staff U.S. Army, 1935 (drafted by Ike), p. 3.
22. KMP, 18 June 1933.
23. Pre PP, Eisenhower to Hughes, 9 Sept. 1934.
24. KMP, 26 Apr. 1934.

25. Pre PP, Eisenhower to Hughes, 9 Sept. 1934.
26. Davis, *Soldier of Democracy,* p. 243.
27. Hatch, *Red Carpet,* p. 158.
28. KMP, 30 Jan. 1932.
29. Pre PP, Eisenhower to Moseley, 26 April 1937.
30. Eisenhower, *At Ease,* p. 223.
31. Ferrell, ed., *Eisenhower Diaries,* p. 20.
32. Ibid., p. 21.
33. Lyon, *Eisenhower,* p. 78.
34. Ferrell, *Eisenhower Diaries,* p. 22.
35. J. S. D. Eisenhower, *Strictly Personal,* p. 23.
36. Davis, *Soldier of Democracy,* p. 455.
37. Pre PP, A. Gruenther to Mamie, 24 Feb. 1942.
38. A. M. Schlesinger, Jr., and R. Rovere, *The General and the President* (London, 1952), p. 63.
39. OH, L. D. Clay, p. 201.
40. W. Manchester, *American Caesar* (London, 1979), p. 173.
41. Lyon, *Eisenhower,* p. 79.
42. Ferrell, *Eisenhower Diaries,* pp. 44, 49.
43. BSD, 1956, p. 2130.
44. Pre PP, Eisenhower to MacArthur, 7 Dec. 1948 and 15 May 1951.
45. Pre PP, MacArthur to Eisenhower, 18 May 1951.
46. Pre PP, Eisenhower to Gerow, 25 Nov. 1940.
47. Pre PP, Eisenhower to Gruenther, 24 Feb. 1942.
48. Lyon, *Eisenhower,* p. 79.
49. A. Hatch, *General Eisenhower* (London, 1946), p. 65.
50. Pre PP, Eisenhower to Gerow, 11 Oct. 1939.
51. Pre PP, Eisenhower to Hughes, 26 Nov. 1940.
52. Ibid.
53. McCann, *America's Man of Destiny,* pp. 2, 7.
54. Pre PP, Eisenhower to Hughes, 26 Nov. 1940.
55. D. D. Eisenhower, *Crusade in Europe,* p. 9.
56. KMP, "Fort Lewis Diary," 26 Sept. 1940.
57. Pogue, *George C. Marshall,* II, p. 22.
58. R. Weigley, *History of the United States Army* (1968), p. 434.
59. Pre PP, Patton to Eisenhower, 1 Oct. 1940.
60. Pre PP, Eisenhower to Hughes, 26 Nov. 1940.
61. Pre PP, Eisenhower to Moseley, 28 Aug. 1941.
62. McCann, *America's Man of Destiny,* p. 17.
63. J. M. Brown, *Through These Men* (1956), p. 146.
64. Manchester, *Glory and Dream,* p. 233.
65. Blumenson, *Mark Clark,* p. 54.
66. Ambrose, *Supreme Commander,* p. 3.

Chapter 5: Commanding the Whole Shebang

1. C. E. Bohlen, *Witness to History 1929–1969* (1973), p. 269.
2. L. Mosley, *Marshall: Organizer of Victory* (London, 1982), p. 15.
3. Ferrell, *Eisenhower Diaries,* p. 52.
4. D. Lohbeck, *Patrick J. Hurley* (Chicago, 1956), p. 164.

5. EP, I, p. 13.
6. Ferrell, *Eisenhower Diaries,* p. 46.
7. KMP.
8. EP, I, p. 109.
9. EP, I, p. 142.
10. Lyon, *Eisenhower,* p. 113.
11. EP, I, p. 227.
12. Lyon, *Eisenhower,* pp. 119, 112.
13. A. Bryant, *The Turn of the Tide* (London, 1957), p. 344.
14. Eisenhower, *Crusade in Europe,* p. 185.
15. Ibid., p. 75.
16. P. Ziegler, *Mountbatten* (London, 1985), p. 528.
17. Summersby [Morgan], *Past Forgetting,* p. 25.
18. Lyon, *Eisenhower,* p. 122.
19. Ambrose, *Supreme Commander,* pp. 29–30.
20. Hatch, *Red Carpet,* p. 181.
21. OH, Arthur Nevins (15 Aug. 1972), p. 23.
22. Pre PP, Butcher to Eisenhower, 26 July 1945.
23. Summersby [Morgan], *Past Forgetting,* p. 43.
24. Ibid., p. 27.
25. D. D. Eisenhower, *Letters to Mamie,* pp. 32, 24.
26. Butcher, *My Three Years,* p. 5.
27. L. Farago, *Patton, Ordeal and Triumph* (1966), p. 84.
28. Butcher, *My Three Years,* p. 4.
29. Davis, *Soldier of Democracy,* p. 316.
30. O. Bradley, *A Soldier's Story* (1951), p. 207.
31. HBD, p. 251.
32. Davis, *Soldier of Democracy,* p. 317.
33. OH, H. Salisbury (6 Oct. 1972), p. 2.
34. M. J. McKeogh and R. Lockridge, *Sgt. Mickey and General Ike* (1946), p. 31.
35. Pre PP, Eisenhower to Ismay, 13 July 1946.
36. EP, I, p. 628.
37. Butcher, *My Three Years,* p. 55.
38. Lord Ismay, *The Memoirs of Lord Ismay* (London, 1960), p. 263.
39. Blumenson, *Patton Papers,* II, pp. 123, 181, 284.
40. N. Longmate, *The G.I.'s* (London, 1975), p. 116.
41. Eisenhower, *Crusade in Europe,* p. 99.
42. WBSP, Box 7, Smith to Marshall, 22 Oct. 1942.
43. HBD, 20 Dec. 1942, A103a.
44. HBD, 26 Aug. 1942, p. 161.
45. Summersby [Morgan], *Past Forgetting,* p. 44.
46. P. Brendon, *Winston Churchill* (1984), p. 137.
47. Pre PP, Eisenhower to Conner, 20 July 1942.
48. Pogue, *George C. Marshall,* II, p. 346.
49. EP, I, p. 389.
50. K. R. Greenfield, *American Strategy in World War II: A Reconsideration* (Baltimore, 1967), p. 43.
51. M. Howard, *The Mediterranean Strategy in the Second World War* (London, 1968), pp. 23, 36.
52. EP, I, p. 464.

53. HBD, 26 Sept. 1942.
54. EP, I, p. 471.
55. Eisenhower, *Letters to Mamie,* p. 48.
56. Macmillan, *War Diaries,* p. 122.
57. HBD, 20 Oct. 1942, p. 332.
58. EP, I, p. 628.
59. Summersby, *Eisenhower,* p. 32.
60. Blumenson, *Patton Papers,* I, p. 407.
61. Summersby [Morgan], *Past Forgetting,* p. 62.
62. Ibid., p. 124.
63. Ferrell, *Eisenhower Diaries,* p. 81.

Chapter 6: From TORCH to Tunis

1. Butcher, *My Three Years,* p. 136.
2. EP, I, p. 658.
3. Eisenhower, *Crusade in Europe,* p. 112.
4. Pre PP, Eisenhower to Smith, 9 Nov. 1942.
5. Pre PP, Patton to Eisenhower, 15 Nov. 1942.
6. Lyon, *Eisenhower,* p. 171.
7. HBD, 9 Nov. 1941.
8. Murphy, *Diplomat Among Warriors,* p. 176.
9. A. L. Funk, *The Politics of Torch* (Lawrence, Ks., 1974), pp. 243, 245.
10. *Time,* 29 March 1943.
11. A. Viorst, *Hostile Allies* (1965), p. 124.
12. A. Eden, *The Reckoning* (London, 1965), p. 406.
13. Gunther, *Eisenhower,* p. 84.
14. Pre PP, McCloy to Eisenhower, 1 Mar. 1943.
15. HBD, G–84, 15 Nov. 1942.
16. R. E. Sherwood, *The White House Papers of Harry L. Hopkins,* vol. II (London, 1949), p. 648.
17. Pre PP, Smuts to Churchill, 20 Nov. 1943.
18. H. Macmillan, *The Blast of War* (London, 1967), p. 221.
19. HBD, A46 and A68A, 5 and 12 Dec. 1942.
20. HBD, A-92.
21. HBD, A176, 20 Jan. 1943.
22. Pre PP, Eisenhower to Tex Lee, 30 Nov. 1942.
23. Ibid.
24. Eisenhower, *Letters to Mamie,* pp. 68, 69.
25. Butcher, *My Three Years,* p. 188.
26. Pre PP, Churchill to Eisenhower, 7 Dec. 1943.
27. L. Farago, *Patton, Ordeal and Triumph* (1966), p. 107.
28. Pre PP, Patton to Eisenhower, 15 and 19 Nov. 1942.
29. Pre PP, Churchill to Eisenhower, 16 Dec. 1942.
30. M. Blumenson, *Rommel's Last Victory* (London, 1968), p. 91.
31. EP, II, p. 846.
32. Murphy, *Diplomat Among Warriors,* p. 209.
33. EP, II, p. 690.
34. EP, II, p. 945.

Notes 429

35. G. F. Howe, *North West Africa: Seizing the Initiative in the West* (Washington, D.C., 1957), p. 405.
36. Blumenson, *Rommel's Last Victory,* p. 177.
37. Butcher, *My Three Years,* p. 231.
38. Eisenhower, *Crusade in Europe,* p. 161.
39. Pre PP, Eisenhower to Bradley, 16 Apr. 1943.
40. Hamilton, *Monty,* p. 166.
41. HBD, 4 Mar. 1942, A265.
42. HBD, 7 Mar. 1943, A265.
43. HBD, 7 Mar. 1943, A250.
44. Pre PP, McCloy to Eisenhower, 8 Mar. 1943.
45. EP, II, p. 997.
46. Davis, *Soldier of Democracy,* p. 399.
47. Eisenhower, *Letters to Mamie,* p. 127.
48. HBD, A315.
49. D. Irving, *The War Between the Generals* (London, 1981), p. 47.
50. Eisenhower, *Letters to Mamie,* pp. 76, 105.
51. EP, II, p. 997.
52. Eisenhower, *Letters to Mamie,* p. 137.
53. Ferrell, *Eisenhower Diaries,* p. 86.
54. HBD, 8 Apr. 1943, A306.
55. HBD, 17 Apr. 1943, A298.
56. Macmillan, *Blast of War,* p. 261.
57. AWF DS, Box 10, 21 Nov. 1958.
58. Hamilton, *Monty,* p. 213.
59. HBD, 1 and 5 May 1943.
60. Irving, *War Between Generals,* p. 96.
61. Butcher, *My Three Years,* p. 287.
62. HBD, A417.
63. Macmillan, *War Diaries,* p. 91.
64. Bradley and Blair, *General's Life,* p. 130.

Chapter 7: The Navel of the Underbelly

1. P. Brendon, *Winston Churchill* (1984), p. 180.
2. Lyon, *Eisenhower,* p. 208.
3. EP, II, p. 1262.
4. Hamilton, *Monty,* p. 271.
5. Pogue, *George C. Marshall,* III, p. 191.
6. Blumenson, *Patton Papers,* I, p. 245.
7. HBD, 31 May 1943.
8. HBD, 30 May 1943.
9. Ibid.
10. Pre PP, Roosevelt to Eisenhower, 11 June 1943.
11. D. Cook, *Charles de Gaulle* (1984), p. 277.
12. Ibid., p. 36.
13. Lord Moran, *Winston Churchill: The Struggle for Survival, 1940–1965* (London, 1966), p. 763.
14. Pogue, *George C. Marshall,* III, p. 238.

15. EP, III, p. 1273.
16. Macmillan, *War Diaries*, p. 119.
17. Ibid., p. 121.
18. C. de Gaulle, *The War Memoirs of Charles de Gaulle*, vol. II, *Unity* (1959), pp. 216–17.
19. Butcher, *My Three Years*, p. 302.
20. Ibid., p. 329.
21. Eisenhower, *Crusade in Europe*, p. 181.
22. Ambrose, *Supreme Commander*, p. 217.
23. D'Este, *Decision in Normandy*, p. 49.
24. Hamilton, *Monty*, p. 268.
25. Blumenson, *Mark Clark*, p. 163.
26. HBD, 18 and 23 Sept. 1943, A789 and A810.
27. EP, III, p. 1353.
28. Hamilton, *Monty*, p. 391.
29. HBD, 21 Aug. 1943, A682.
30. Lyon, *Eisenhower*, p. 230.
31. HBD, 4 June 1943, A455.
32. AWF NS, Box 19, Ismay to Eisenhower, 8 June 1959.
33. Macmillan, *War Diaries*, p. 171.
34. A. N. Garland and H. M. Smyth, *Sicily and the Surrender of Italy* (Washington, D.C., 1965), p. 507.
35. Macmillan, *War Diaries*, p. 211.
36. Eisenhower, *Letters to Mamie*, p. 149.
37. EP, III, p. 1714.
38. Blumenson, *Mark Clark*, p. 123.
39. Sometimes Monty compared himself to Napoleon, to the latter's detriment: see, e.g., A. Brett-James, *Conversations with Montgomery* (London, 1984), p. 93.
40. EP, II, p. 1354.
41. HBD, A711.
42. Hamilton, *Monty*, p. 380.
43. Ibid., p. xxv.
44. AWF NS, Box 19, Eisenhower to Ismay, 14 Jan. 1959.
45. Eisenhower, *Crusade in Europe*, p. 15.
46. *Time*, 13 Sept. 1943.
47. HBD, A814.
48. LCSP, Box 134.
49. Eisenhower, *Crusade in Europe*, p. 209.
50. EP, III, p. 1492.
51. M. W. Clark, *Calculated Risk* (1950), p. 186.
52. R. Trevelyan, *Rome '44* (London, 1981), p. 303.
53. R. Lamb, *Montgomery in Europe* (London, 1983), p. 56.
54. Pre PP, Churchill to Eisenhower, 7 Oct. 1943.
55. Brendon, *Winston Churchill*, p. 181.
56. Pre PP, Eisenhower to Ismay, 2 Oct. 1951.
57. Macmillan, *War Diaries*, pp. 259–60, 285.
58. Ibid., p. 321.
59. Eisenhower, *Letters to Mamie*, p. 15.
60. Eisenhower, *Crusade in Europe*, p. 214.

61. Bradley and Blair, *General's Life,* p. 133.
62. J. M. Gavin, *On to Berlin* (1978), p. 142.
63. Summersby [Morgan], *Past Forgetting,* pp. 119, 100, 178, 144.
64. Brendon, *Winston Churchill,* p. 182.
65. AWF DDE DS, Box 54, Eisenhower to Ismay, 3 Dec. 1960.
66. OH, General Ray Barker, p. 93.
67. Pogue, *George C. Marshall,* III, p. 321.
68. Eisenhower, *Crusade in Europe,* p. 227.

Chapter 8: Overture to OVERLORD

1. Butcher, *My Three Years,* p. 456.
2. Summersby [Morgan], *Past Forgetting,* p. 146.
3. A. Viorst, *Hostile Allies* (1965), p. 189.
4. K. Strong, *Intelligence at the Top* (London, 1966), p. 126.
5. J. S. D. Eisenhower, *Strictly Personal,* p. 23.
6. Davis, *Soldier of Democracy,* p. 457.
7. Summersby [Morgan], *Past Forgetting,* pp. 152, 156.
8. Butcher, *My Three Years* (U.S. ed.), p. 434.
9. AWF DDE DS, Box 8, W. J. Jackson to his mother, 21 Jan. 1944.
10. B. Montgomery, *Memoirs* (London, 1958), p. 484.
11. Hamilton, *Monty,* p. 608.
12. Pre PP, Tedder to Eisenhower, 28 July 1945.
13. Pre PP, Harris to Eisenhower, 17 July 1945.
14. OH, H. Salisbury (6 Oct. 1972), pp. 2–3.
15. OH, Ray Barker, pp. 18–19.
16. O. Bradley, *A Soldier's Story* (1951), p. 310.
17. M. J. McKeogh and R. Lockridge, *Sgt. Mickey and General Ike* (1946), p. 127.
18. EP, III, p. 1773.
19. Blumenson, *Mark Clark,* p. 174.
20. Pogue, *George C. Marshall,* II, pp. 335, 338.
21. A. Bryant, *Triumph in the West* (London, 1959), p. 108.
22. W. W. Rostow, *Pre-Invasion Bombing Strategy* (Aldershot, 1981), p. 45.
23. HBD, 3 Mar. 1944, A1122.
24. LCSP, Box 134. See also R. Overy, *The Air War, 1939–1945* (1980), p. 76.
25. LCSP, Box 135.
26. LCSP, Box 134.
27. LCSP, Box 15, note by Spaatz of conversation with Eisenhower on 15 July 1944.
28. Davis, *Soldier of Democracy,* p. 470.
29. Blumenson, *Patton Papers,* I, p. 468.
30. HBD, 7 Feb. 1944, A1065 and 1384.
31. Ferrell, *Eisenhower Diaries,* p. 111.
32. L. Farago, *Patton, Ordeal and Triumph* (1966), pp. 221, 205.
33. Butcher, *My Three Years,* p. 411.
34. Eisenhower, *Letters to Mamie,* p. 183.
35. Summersby [Morgan], *Past Forgetting,* p. 662.
36. EP, III, p. 1794.
37. Pre PP, Eisenhower to F. Pogue, 10 Mar. 1947.

38. LCSP, Box 134.
39. C. Ryan, *The Longest Day* (1959), p. 25.
40. Montgomery, *Memoirs,* p. 236.
41. Bradley and Blair, *General's Life,* p. 241.
42. Bryant, *Triumph in the West,* pp. 189–190.
43. AWF AS, Box 17, Whiteley to Gruenther, 8 Nov. 1959.
44. Lyon, *Eisenhower,* p. 267.
45. AWF DDE DS, Box 3, Eisenhower to Eden, 16 Mar. 1953.
46. AWF AS, Box 20, Eisenhower to Hughes, 10 Dec. 1953.
47. AWF NS, Box 19, Eisenhower to Ismay, 14 Jan. 1959.
48. AWF AS, Box 17, Ismay to Gruenther, 9 Nov. 1959.
49. AWF DDE DS, Box 54, Ismay to Eisenhower, 30 Dec. 1960.
50. Pre PP, Box 5, quoted by F. Pogue to Eisenhower, 15 May 1947.
51. L. F. Ellis, *Victory in the West,* I (London, 1962), p. 81.
52. M. Blumenson, "Some Reflections on Immediate Post-Assault Strategy," *D-Day* (Kansas, 1971), p. 207.
53. Hamilton, *Monty,* p. 588.
54. For a recent apologia by a participant see D. Belchem, *Victory in Normandy* (London, 1981), pp. 49–55. For criticisms of it see D'Este, *Decision in Normandy,* pp. 92–98.
55. Pre PP, de Guignand to Eisenhower, 13 Jan. 1948.
56. AWF NS, Box 19, Eisenhower to Ismay, 14 Jan. 1959.
57. Wilmot, *Struggle for Europe,* p. 216.
58. Butcher, *My Three Years,* p. 458.
59. D'Este, *Decision in Normandy,* p. 87.
60. F. Morgan, *Overture to Overlord* (1950), p. 142.
61. Of course these invaders had been attempting the operation in reverse, and I discount William of Orange's effort of 1688 because most of England rallied to his standard.
62. W. Warlimont, *Inside Hitler's Headquarters* (London, 1962), p. 403.
63. A. A. Michie, "The Great Decision," *Reader's Digest,* August 1944, p. 83.
64. G. Harrison, *Cross-Channel Attack* (Washington, D.C., 1951), p. 247.
65. Butcher, *My Three Years,* p. 481.
66. Pre PP, Box 40, Summersby Diary, 3 June 1944.
67. Lord Tedder, *With Prejudice* (London, 1966), p. 545.
68. Bryant, *Triumph in the West,* p. 206.
69. Ambrose, *Eisenhower,* I, p. 307.
70. Smith, *Eisenhower's Six Great Decisions,* p. 55.
71. Wilmot, *Struggle for Europe,* p. 226.

Chapter 9: Military Statesman

1. Summersby [Morgan], *Past Forgetting,* p. 166.
2. To quote the title of David Irving's distasteful but informative book (London, 1981).
3. K. R. Greenfield, *American Strategy in World War II* (Baltimore, 1963), p. 47.
4. F. de Guignand, *Generals at War* (London, 1964), pp. 192–93, 103. De Guignand was evidently endorsing—indeed, plagiarizing—Bradley's verdict. Cf. O. Bradley, *A Soldier's Story* (1951), p. 354.
5. AWF NS, Box 7, Eisenhower to de Guignand, 29 June 1959.

6. Pre PP, Box 40, Summersby Diary, 6 June 1944.
7. Pre PP, Box 40, Summersby Diary, 5 June 1944.
8. G. E. Koskimaki, *D-Day with the Screaming Eagles* (1970), p. 34.
9. Bradley and Blair, *General's Life,* p. 251.
10. Ibid., p. 257.
11. HBD, 1433C.
12. Lord Tedder, *With Prejudice* (London, 1966), p. 553.
13. Hamilton, *Monty,* p. 689.
14. Tedder, *With Prejudice,* p. 555.
15. Hamilton, *Monty,* p. 691.
16. Bradley, *Soldier's Story,* pp. 323–24.
17. Davis, *Soldier of Democracy,* p. 501.
18. Weigley, *Eisenhower's Lieutenants,* p. 135.
19. D'Este, *Decision in Normandy,* p. 311.
20. Lyon, *Eisenhower,* p. 294.
21. Blumenson, *Patton Papers,* I, p. 480.
22. Lyon, *Eisenhower,* p. 294.
23. Tedder, *With Prejudice,* p. 561.
24. Pogue, *Supreme Command,* p. 188.
25. L. F. Ellis, *Victory in the West,* I (London, 1962), p. 330.
26. London *Times,* 19 July 1944.
27. HBD, 2 Aug., 19 and 20 July 1944.
28. Tedder, *With Prejudice,* p. 559.
29. HBD, 25 July 1944.
30. Irving, *War Between Generals,* p. 217.
31. LCSP, Box 15, Robert A. Lovett to Spaatz, 25 July 1944.
32. HBD, 2 Aug. 1944, 1561.
33. Pre PP, Box 40, Summersby Diary, 26 July 1944.
34. Pogue, *Supreme Command,* p. 190.
35. EP, III, p. 2028.
36. EP, IV, p. 2041.
37. Report by the supreme commander to the combined chiefs of staff (London, 1946), p. 41.
38. Pre PP, Eisenhower to Pogue, 10 Mar. 1947.
39. EP, III, p. 1969. Ike himself claimed that he and Bradley had begun an intensive study of the breakthrough possibilities in the American sector on 20 June.
40. Hamilton, *Monty,* p. 791.
41. Keegan, *Six Armies in Normandy* (1982), p. 66.
42. H. Macmillan, *The Blast of War* (London, 1967), p. 416.
43. Butcher, *My Three Years,* p. 543.
44. Eisenhower, *Letters to Mamie,* p. 204.
45. AWF NS, Box 32, Bill Attwood's diary.
46. D. Greene, "The Human Side," *The American Legion,* May 1983, p. 22.
47. Bradley and Blair, *General's Life,* pp. 298–99.
48. Pre PP, Box 40, Summersby Diary, 12 Aug. 1944.
49. M. Blumenson, "General Bradley's Decision at Argentan," in K. R. Greenfield, ed., *Command Decisions* (Washington, D.C., 1960), p. 416.
50. Butcher, *My Three Years,* p. 551.
51. Hamilton, *Monty,* p. 798.

52. Eisenhower, *Crusade in Europe,* p. 306.
53. Pre PP, Box 40, Summersby Diary, 27 Aug. 1944.
54. EP, IV, p. 2121.
55. B. Montgomery, *Memoirs* (London, 1958), p. 240.
56. Ellis, *Victory in the West,* I, pp. 462–63, 475.
57. AWF DDE DS, Box 54, Eisenhower to Ismay, 3 Dec. 1960.
58. Pre PP, Eisenhower to Pogue, 10 Mar. 1947.
59. Pogue, *Supreme Command,* p. 255.
60. R. Ingersoll, *Top Secret* (1946), p. 219.
61. Cf. Pogue, *Supreme Command,* pp. 245, 259, and B. H. Liddell Hart, *History of the Second World War* (London, 1970), p. 558.
62. R. G. Ruppenthal, "Logistics and the Broad-Front Strategy," in Greenfield, *Command Decisions,* p. 427. But see also J. A. Huston, *The Sinews of War* (Washington, D.C., 1966), pp. 675–77.
63. Pre PP, Eisenhower to Pogue, 10 Mar. 1947.
64. OH, L. D. Clay, p. 351.
65. Pre PP, Eisenhower to Pogue, 10 Mar. 1947.
66. Blumenson, *Patton Papers,* II, p. 539.
67. Liddell Hart, *Second World War,* p. 562.
68. Tedder, *With Prejudice,* p. 587.
69. EP, III, p. 1935.
70. Ambrose, *Eisenhower,* I, p. 346.
71. Bradley and Blair, *General's Life,* p. 328.
72. Butcher, *My Three Years* (U.S. ed.), p. 661.
73. R. Lamb, *Montgomery in Europe* (London, 1983), p. 226.
74. EP, IV, pp. 2164, 2147.
75. C. B. MacDonald, *Siegfried Line Campaign* (Washington, D.C., 1963), p. 220.
76. Irving, *War Between Generals,* p. 286.
77. Blumenson, *Patton Papers,* II, p. 553.
78. Bryant, *Triumph in the West* (London, 1959), pp. 291–92.
79. C. B. MacDonald, *The Mighty Endeavor* (1969), p. 355.
80. Ingersoll, *Top Secret,* p. 240.
81. EP, IV, p. 2186.
82. Ibid., IV, p. 2243.
83. Ellis, *Victory in the West,* II, pp. 85–91.
84. D'Este, *Decision in Normandy,* p. 50.
85. EP, IV, p. 2324.
86. Ambrose, *Supreme Commander,* p. 548.
87. Bryant, *Triumph in the West,* pp. 351–52.
88. Eisenhower, *Letters to Mamie,* p. 220.
89. Summersby [Morgan], *Past Forgetting,* p. 203.
90. Liddell Hart, *Second World War,* p. 639.
91. AWF NS, Box 1, Alanbrooke to Eisenhower, 9 Nov. 1959.
92. J. S. D. Eisenhower, *The Bitter Woods* (London, 1969), pp. 214–15.

Chapter 10: Crusade Accomplished

1. EP, IV, pp. 2355–56.
2. Eisenhower, *Crusade in Europe,* p. 382.
3. J. S. D. Eisenhower, *The Bitter Woods* (London, 1969), p. 257.

4. Ibid., p. 337.
5. D. Irving, *The War Between the Generals* (London, 1981), pp. 383.
6. Lyon, *Eisenhower*, p. 322.
7. C. B. MacDonald, *The Mighty Endeavor* (1969), pp. 406–7.
8. J. Toland, *Battle* (1959), p. 162.
9. R. Ingersoll, *Top Secret* (1946), p. 272.
10. O. Bradley, *A Soldier's Story* (1951), p. 482.
11. L. F. Ellis, *Victory in the West*, II (London, 1968), pp. 199–200.
12. Pre PP, Box 40, Summersby Diary, 29 Dec. 1944.
13. Pogue, *George C. Marshall*, III, p. 487.
14. *Time*, 1 Jan. 1945.
15. B. Montgomery, *Memoirs* (London, 1958), p. 319.
16. R. Lamb, *Montgomery in Europe* (London, 1983), p. 330.
17. Montgomery, *Memoirs*, pp. 311ff.
18. Ellis, *Victory in the West*, II, p. 207.
19. Butcher, *My Three Years*, p. 631.
20. Pre PP, Box 40, Summersby Diary, 3 Jan. 1945.
21. Ibid., 1 Feb. 1945.
22. Weigley, *Eisenhower's Lieutenants*, p. 581.
23. EP, IV, p. 2407.
24. EP, IV, p. 2416.
25. Ibid.
26. EP, IV, p. 2489.
27. Post PP, Box 3, 16 June 1967.
28. Blumenson, *Patton Papers*, I, p. 538.
29. Montgomery, *Memoirs*, pp. 324–25.
30. Butcher, *My Three Years*, p. 648.
31. Ibid. (U.S. ed.), p. 768.
32. Weigley, *Eisenhower's Lieutenants*, p. 628.
33. Eisenhower, *Crusade in Europe*, p. 426.
34. EP, IV, 2543.
35. Ellis, *Victory in the West*, II, p. 297.
36. Montgomery, *Memoirs*, p. 331.
37. S. Talbott, ed., *Khrushchev Remembers*, I (London, 1971), pp. 220–21.
38. OH, R. D. Murphy, 12 Oct. 1972, p. 41.
39. Lamb, *Montgomery*, p. 376.
40. EP, IV, p. 2559.
41. W. S. Churchill, *History of the Second World War*, vol. VI (1954), pp. 406–7.
42. Bradley and Blair, *General's Life*, p. 345.
43. Eisenhower, *Letters to Mamie*, p. 248.
44. Weigley, *Eisenhower's Lieutenants*, p. 673.
45. J. Toland, *The Last 100 Days* (1966), p. 386.
46. But see S. Ambrose, *Eisenhower and Berlin, 1945* (1967), pp. 93–96.
47. Butcher, *My Three Years* (U.S. ed.), p. 834.
48. Pre PP, Bedell Smith, Box 4.
49. Bradley and Blair, *General's Life*, p. 371.
50. New York *Herald Tribune*, 3 Feb. 1944.
51. Pre PP, Eisenhower to Churchill, 12 July 1948.
52. Pre PP, Graham to S. Richardson, 20 Oct. 1951.
53. E. K. G. Sixsmith, *Eisenhower as Military Commander* (London, 1973), p. 219.

Chapter 11: Backward into the Limelight

1. M. Smith, *Meet Mister Eisenhower* (1954), p. ix.
2. Pre PP, Eisenhower to Butcher, 15 Feb. 1950.
3. Eisenhower, *Crusade in Europe*, p. 485.
4. Lyon, *Eisenhower*, p. 27.
5. W. H. Hale, *Horace Greeley* (1950), p. 351.
6. Lyon, *Eisenhower*, p. 348.
7. S. Lubell, *The Revolt of the Moderates* (1956), p. 237.
8. Blumenson, *Patton Papers*, II, p. 798. Patton added that Ike was "also yellow," by which he may have meant that he was too cowardly to acknowledge his ambitions.
9. OH, H. Salisbury, 6 Oct. 1972, p. 23.
10. Sulzberger, *Long Row of Candles*, pp. 606, 586.
11. Rovere, *Eisenhower Years*, p. 6, quoting *Look* magazine.
12. D. E. Lilienthal, *The Journals of David E. Lilienthal*, vol. II (1964), p. 283.
13. Smith, *Meet Mister Eisenhower*, pp. 13–14.
14. Pre PP, Eisenhower to Clay, 28 Jan. 1952.
15. Butcher, *My Three Years* (U.S. ed.), p. 854.
16. L. T. Milic, "Eisenhower's First Inaugural Address: Composition and Style," *Style* 16, no. 1 (Winter 1982): 1, 35.
17. Eisenhower, *At Ease*, pp. 388–89.
18. D. Fraser, *Alanbrooke* (London, 1982), p. 468.
19. Summersby [Morgan], *Past Forgetting*, p. 197.
20. Lyon, *Eisenhower*, p. 27.
21. AWF NS, Box 12, Milton to Eisenhower, December 1952.
22. Rovere, *Eisenhower Years*, p. 39.
23. Gunther, *Eisenhower*, p. 8.
24. M. Miller, *Plain Speaking* (London, 1974), p. 340.
25. Pre PP, Eisenhower to Summersby, 22 Nov. 1945.
26. Pre PP, Eisenhower to Smith, 4 Dec. 1945.
27. Pre PP, Eisenhower to Summersby, 22 Nov. 1945.
28. L. Mosley, *Marshall: Organizer of Victory* (London, 1982), p. 351.
29. Pre PP, Eisenhower to Summersby, 1 June 1948.
30. Ferrell, *Eisenhower Diaries*, p. 145.
31. Pre PP, Butcher to Eisenhower, 13 Dec. 1948.
32. Eisenhower, *Letters to Mamie*, p. 255.
33. Eisenhower, *Crusade in Europe*, pp. 475, 510, 512.
34. AWF DS, Box 49, Eisenhower in an interview with H. Feis, 6 Apr. 1960.
35. Lyon, *Eisenhower*, p. 356.
36. EP, VI, p. 320.
37. EP, VI, pp. 310, 406.
38. Mosley, *Marshall*, p. 353.
39. Pre PP, Baruch to Ike on telephone, 8 Apr. 1946.
40. Pre PP, Eisenhower to Hazlett, 27 Nov. 1945.
41. Pre PP, telephone call, 4 June 1946.
42. EP, VII, p. 581.
43. EP, VII, p. 618.
44. WBSP, 25 Jan. 1946.

45. EP, VIII, p. 1267.
46. Pre PP, Truman, Box 3.
47. Slater, *The Ike I Knew,* p. 22.
48. Cook, *Declassified Eisenhower,* p. 75.
49. Pre PP, Eisenhower to C. Roberts, 4 Apr. 1952.
50. WERP, 17 Oct. 1947.
51. WERP, Robinson to Mrs. Helen Reid, 24 Mar. 1948.
52. AWF NS, Box 29, Robinson to Eisenhower, 25 Nov. 1959.
53. C. Phillips, *The Truman Presidency* (1966), p. 144.
54. CUL, Eisenhower to E. J. Bermingham, 8 Feb. 1951.
55. Pre PP, C. Roberts.
56. *American Mercury* (1948) quoted by Childs, *Eisenhower: Captive Hero* (London, 1959), p. 99.
57. W. Millis, *The Forrestal Diaries* (1952), p. 349.
58. WERP, Box 1.
59. WERP, 17 Oct. 1947.
60. Pre PP, Eisenhower to Hazlett, 19 July 1947. Ike grew rather fond of this phrase and later used it to explain that his frequent absences from the White House were not really holidays at all.
61. Gunther, *Eisenhower,* p. 29.
62. CUL, Eisenhower to Bermingham, 12 May 1951.
63. McCann, *America's Man of Destiny,* p. 137.
64. COH, James Gutman, pp. 46, 47.
65. OH, K. McCann, 21 Dec. 1966, p. 16.
66. COH, James Gutman, pp. 43–44.
67. COH, F. D. Fackenthal, p. 54.
68. CUL, Eisenhower to Bermingham, 15 May 1951.
69. Ibid., 9 Mar. 1950.
70. Ibid., 24 Sept. 1949.
71. COH, W. H. Judd, p. 4.
72. McCann, *Man of Destiny,* p. 137.
73. WERP, Robinson to Mrs. H. Reid, 24 Mar. 1948.
74. Pre PP, Eisenhower to Truman, 18 Nov. 1948.
75. A. Krock, *Memoirs* (1968), p. 280.
76. Lilienthal, *Journals,* II, p. 283.
77. Pre PP, Eisenhower to Hazlett, 25 Aug. 1947.
78. Eisenhower, *At Ease,* p. 310.
79. Richard Cohen to the author, 25 June 1984.
80. Pre PP, Eisenhower to Hazlett, 12 Aug. 1948 and 4 Sept. 1951.
81. Eisenhower, *At Ease,* p. 341.
82. AWF DDE DS, Box 9, Eisenhower to Allen, 8 Feb. 1955.
83. CUL, Eisenhower to Bermingham, 8 Feb. 1951.
84. Lilienthal, *Journals,* II, p. 378.
85. Sulzberger, *Long Row of Candles,* p. 597.
86. CUL, Eisenhower to Bermingham, 29 Sept. 1950 and 28 Feb. 1951.
87. A. R. Vandenberg, ed., *The Private Papers of Senator Vandenberg* (London, 1953), p. 576.
88. Eisenhower, *At Ease,* p. 362.
89. WERP, Box 8.

90. Moch, *Rencontres*, p. 213. (My translation.)
91. Pre PP, Eisenhower to Marshall, 12 Mar. 1951.
92. Pre PP, Eisenhower to Harriman, 2 Apr. 1951.
93. Ibid., 20 Apr. 1951.
94. Ibid., 24 Feb. 1951.
95. Ibid., 2 Apr. 1951.
96. Ibid., 14 Mar. 1951.

Chapter 12: Forward into the White House

1. J. M. Brown, *Through These Men* (1956), p. 9.
2. T. Abell, *Drew Pearson Diaries* (London, 1974), p. 154.
3. Pre PP, Eisenhower to Roberts, 8 Dec. 1951.
4. OH, R. Thayer, June 1972, p. 3.
5. Ambrose, *Eisenhower*, I, p. 521.
6. Pre PP, Roberts to Eisenhower, 3–6 Mar. 1952.
7. J. T. Patterson, *Mr. Republican* (Boston, 1975), p. 520.
8. WERP, Robinson memorandum, 1 Apr. 1948.
9. NYT, 8 Jan. 1952.
10. Pre PP, Eisenhower to Roberts, 11 Jan. 1952.
11. Pre PP, Eisenhower to Robinson, 19 Jan. 1952.
12. Pre PP, Eisenhower to Clay, 28 Jan. and 9 Feb. 1952.
13. CUL, Eisenhower to Bermingham, 18 Dec. 1951.
14. Pre PP, Eisenhower to Roberts, 28 Jan. 1952.
15. Ferrell, *Eisenhower Diaries*, p. 214.
16. *Time*, 21 Apr. 1952.
17. Ferrell, *Eisenhower Diaries*, p. 376.
18. Sulzberger, *Long Row of Candles*, p. 650.
19. I am grateful to Field Marshal Lord Carver for telling me of this incident.
20. E. Mazo and S. Hess, *President Nixon* (London, 1969), p. 101.
21. *Time*, 26 May 1952.
22. *Chicago Tribune*, 6 July and 25 Aug. 1952.
23. H. S. Parmet, *Jack: The Struggles of John F. Kennedy* (1980), p. 245.
24. Eisenhower, *Mandate*, p. 32.
25. *Time*, 16 June 1952.
26. NYT, 6 June 1952.
27. AWF AS, Box 27, Eisenhower to Roberts, 19 June 1952.
28. AWF NS, Box 16, Eisenhower to Gruenther, 19 June 1952.
29. Ferrell, *Eisenhower Diaries*, p. 225.
30. BSD, p. 493.
31. Ambrose, *Eisenhower*, I, p. 532. I am grateful to Sally Quinn for the information about Mamie's earlier dependence on alcohol.
32. BSD, pp. 555, 513.
33. BSD, p. 439.
34. Sulzberger, *Long Row of Candles*, p. 664.
35. Patterson, *Mr. Republican*, p. 563.
36. Sulzberger, *Long Row of Candles*, p. 664.
37. Mazo and Hess, *President Nixon*, p. 86.
38. Nixon, *Memoirs*, p. 88.

39. Neal, *Eisenhowers,* p. 288.
40. Eisenhower, *Mandate,* p. 46.
41. M. Eisenhower, *President Is Calling,* p. 325.
42. OH, Robert J. Donovan, p. 20.
43. AWF NS, Box 33, Truman to Eisenhower, 16 Aug. 1952.
44. Parmet, *Eisenhower,* pp. 106–7.
45. M. Miller, *Plain Speaking* (London, 1974), p. 28.
46. J. B. Martin, *Adlai Stevenson and the World* (1977), p. 101.
47. BSD, 16 Oct. 1952, p. 548.
48. Manchester, *Glory and Dream,* p. 623.
49. Eisenhower, *Mandate,* p. 56.
50. NYT, 19 Oct. 1952.
51. BSD, p. 498.
52. OH, Gabriel Hauge, p. 13.
53. NYT, 19 Oct. 1952.
54. Brown, *Through These Men,* p. 33.
55. Martin, *Adlai Stevenson,* p. 254.
56. Parmet, *Eisenhower,* p. 118.
57. NYT, 3 July 1960.
58. OH, Robert J. Donovan, p. 26.
59. Martin, *Adlai Stevenson,* p. 5.
60. NYT, 10 Sept. 1952.
61. OH, G. Hauge, p. 15.
62. BSD, p. 502.
63. NYT, 13 Sept. 1952.
64. NYT, 13 and 21 Sept. 1952.
65. J. B. Martin, *Adlai Stevenson of Illinois* (1976), p. 683.
66. Mazo and Hess, *President Nixon,* p. 91.
67. NYT, 20 Sept. 1952.
68. NYT, 20 and 21 Sept. 1952.
69. Nixon, *Memoirs,* p. 98.
70. F. M. Brodie, *Richard Nixon* (Cambridge, Mass., 1983), p. 283.
71. Nixon, *Memoirs,* p. 96.
72. AWF NS, Box 32, A. H. Sulzberger to Eisenhower, 18 and 28 Aug. 1952.
73. S. Adams, *Firsthand Report,* p. 40.
74. OH, G. Hauge, p. 17.
75. Miller, *Plain Speaking,* p. 130.
76. BSD, pp. 524–25.
77. AWF AS, Box 34, Eisenhower to Stassen, 5 Oct. 1952.
78. Ibid.
79. Reeves, *Life and Times,* pp. 443, 452.
80. NYT, 3 Oct. 1952.
81. NYT, 19 Oct. 1952.
82. LCAP, Box 8, J. Alsop to I. Berlin, 20 Oct. 1952.
83. AWF AS, Box 20, Hughes to Eisenhower, 1 Dec. 1953.
84. Brandon, *Mamie Doud Eisenhower,* p. 274.
85. Hughes, *Ordeal,* p. 46.
86. R. H. Ferrell, ed., *Off the Record: The Private Papers of Harry S. Truman* (1980), p. 368.

87. WERP, Robinson to Robert T. Jones, 21 Nov. 1952.
88. R. Rovere, *The American Establishment* (London, 1963), pp. 240, 234.
89. R. D. Challoner and J. M. Fenton, "The Past Comes Alive in Dulles 'Oral History,'" *University*, Spring 1967, p. 5.
90. AWF DHS, Box 1, Eisenhower to Dulles, 20 June 1952.
91. Hoopes, *Devil and Dulles* (London, 1974), p. 136.
92. Challoner and Fenton, "The Past Comes Alive," p. 5.
93. Hoopes, *Devil and Dulles*, p. 74.
94. Ibid., p. 40.
95. Ibid., p. 426.
96. OH, Eisenhower on Dulles.
97. LCAP, W. Clark to S. Alsop, 9 June 1953.
98. Hughes, *Ordeal*, p. 71.
99. *Time*, 26 Jan. 1953.
100. AWF AS, Box 20, Eisenhower to Hughes, 10 Dec. 1953.
101. BSD, p. 1004.
102. Hughes, *Ordeal*, p. 54.
103. Ewald, *Eisenhower*, p. 13.
104. E. L. and F. H. Schapsmeier, "Eisenhower and Ezra Taft Benson: Farm Policy in the 1950s," *Agricultural History* 44 (October 1970): 369–70.
105. Richardson, *Presidency*, p. 32.
106. Patterson, *Mr. Republican*, p. 584.
107. BSD, p. 1188a.
108. AWF AS, Box 20, Eisenhower to Hughes, 10 Dec. 1953.
109. WHO OSS, Box 1, 23 Jan. 1953.
110. OH, S. Adams, p. 127.
111. New York *Post*, 31 March 1958.
112. CUL, Bermingham to Eisenhower, 19 July 1952.
113. Nixon, *Memoirs*, p. 198.
114. New York *Post*, 1 Apr. 1958.
115. Gray, *Eighteen Acres*, pp. 52, 34.
116. BSD, p. 555.
117. OH, J. C. Hagerty, p. 272.
118. Perrett, *Dream of Greatness*, p. 555.
119. New York *Post*, 31 Mar. 1958.
120. Quoted by J. Tebbel and S. M. Watts, *The Press and the Presidency: From George Washington to Ronald Reagan* (1985), p. 466.
121. Eisenhower, *Mandate*, p. 117.
122. AWF AS, Box 33, Eisenhower to Bedell Smith, 4 June 1957.
123. LCAP, Box 13, J. Alsop, 17 Oct. 1956.
124. OH, B. Harlow, February–May 1967, p. 23.
125. OH, J. Hagerty, p. 64.
126. NYT, 15 Dec. 1952.
127. Acheson, *Present*, p. 706.
128. Hughes, *Ordeal*, p. 54.
129. Eisenhower, *Mandate*, p. 100.
130. NYT, 21 Jan. 1953.
131. PPP, 1953, p. 1.
132. I. F. Stone, *The Haunted Fifties* (London, 1963), p. 10.

133. Chicago *Tribune,* 21 Jan. 1953.
134. PPP, 1953, p. 3.
135. NYT, 21 Jan. 1953.
136. *Time,* 2 Feb. 1953.

Chapter 13: The Shadow of McCarthyism

1. Eisenhower, *Mandate,* p. 108.
2. Lyon, *Eisenhower,* p. 505.
3. Hughes, *Ordeal,* p. 61.
4. Gray, *Eighteen Acres,* p. 34.
5. E. B. Geelhoed, *Charles E. Wilson and Controversy at the Pentagon 1953–1957* (Detroit, 1979), pp. 182, 48, 46.
6. *Time,* 14 Oct. 1957.
7. AWF DS, Box 3, Eisenhower to Brownell, 2 Dec. 1954.
8. D. A. Frier, *Conflict of Interest in the Eisenhower Administration* (Ames, Ia., 1969), p. 208.
9. *New Republic,* 23 Mar. 1953, p. 11.
10. AWF NS, Box 12, Eisenhower to Adams, 16 Mar. 1953.
11. WHO OSS, Box 1, 23 Jan. 1953.
12. WHO OSS, Box 1, 30 Jan. 1953.
13. PPP, 1953, pp. 24–25.
14. AWF DS, Box 1, Eisenhower to W. Jenner, 30 Nov. 1953.
15. AWF AS, Box 20, Eisenhower to Hughes, 10 Dec. 1953.
16. OH, B. Harlow, p. 125.
17. AWF DS, Box 5, 25 May 1955.
18. AWF DS, Box 3, 2 Aug. 1954.
19. DP TCS, 11 Jan. 1954.
20. WHO OSS, Box 1, 8 May 1953.
21. AWF AS, Box 20, Hughes to Eisenhower, 1 Dec. 1953.
22. PPP, 1953, pp. 13–14.
23. WHO OSS, Box 1, 30 Jan. 1953.
24. AWF AS, Box 20, Hughes to Eisenhower, 1 Dec. 1953.
25. Reeves, *Life and Times,* p. 476.
26. WHO OSS, Box 1, 27 Mar. 1953.
27. DP TCS, Box 1, 1 and 2 Dec. 1953.
28. AWF AS, Box 20, Hughes to Eisenhower, 1 Dec. 1953.
29. Lyon, *Eisenhower,* p. 521.
30. Ambrose, in *New Republic,* 9 May 1981, p. 30.
31. AWF NS, Box 2, Eisenhower to Berg, 7 Apr. 1954.
32. AWF DS, Box 5, 17 May 1955.
33. AWF DS, Box 3, Eisenhower to Hazlett, 21 July 1953.
34. AWF DS, Box 8, Eisenhower to J. McCrary, 4 Dec. 1954.
35. AWF DS, Box 6, Eisenhower to Robinson, 12 Mar. 1954.
36. OH, Milton Eisenhower, p. 64.
37. NYT, 31 Mar. 1950.
38. Greenstein, *Hidden-Hand Presidency,* p. 227.
39. O. Burnham, "Eisenhower the Man, Eisenhower the Mystique," *Commonweal,* 27 Dec. 1963, p. 408.

40. WHO OSS, Box 1, 20 Oct. 1953.
41. WHO OSS, Box 1, 2 Apr. 1954.
42. AWF DDE DS, Box 3, October 1953.
43. OH, J. Javits, 20 Jan. 1968, pp. 4, 14, 8.
44. AWF DDE DS, Box 7, 1954.
45. Ewald, *Eisenhower,* p. 240.
46. Childs, *Eisenhower: Captive Hero* (London, 1959), p. 85.
47. R. Rovere, *Senator Joe McCarthy* (London, 1960), pp. 19–20.
48. *Time,* 9 Mar. 1953.
49. Greenstein, *Hidden-Hand Presidency,* p. 167.
50. J. T. Patterson, *Mr. Republican* (Boston, 1975), p. 596.
51. DP WHMS, Box 8, 17 and 6 Mar. 1953.
52. DP WHMS, Box 8, 17 Mar. 1953.
53. Parmet, *Eisenhower,* p. 241.
54. DP WHMS, Box 8, 20 Mar. and 3 Apr. 1953.
55. C. E. Bohlen, *Witness to History, 1929–1969* (1973), p. 311.
56. DP SS, Box 6, 10 July 1953.
57. AWF NS, Box 32, Bill Attwood's Diary, p. 4.
58. LCAP, Box 8, J. Alsop to P. Viereck, 26 Feb. 1953.
59. WHO OSS, Box 1, 17 July 1953.
60. PPP, 1953, pp. 413, 415, 427.
61. Reeves, *Life and Times,* p. 495.
62. AWF DDE DS, Box 3, 9 Sept. 1953.
63. Ibid.
64. DP TCS, Box 10, 27 Nov. 1953.
65. A. Marro, "When the Government Tells Lies," *Columbia Journalism Review,* March–April 1985, p. 36.
66. BSD, 14 July 1953, p. 1037.
67. WHO OSS, Box 1, 2 Oct. 1953.
68. PPP, 1953, p. 763.
69. AWF DS, Box 1, 27 Nov. 1953.
70. BSD, 30 Nov. 1953, p. 1312.
71. WHO OSS, Box 1, 15 Dec. 1953.
72. OH, J. L. Bell, p. 26.
73. Reeves, *Life and Times,* p. 532.
74. AWF DS, Box 2, 28 May 1954.
75. AWF NS, Box 12, N. Roosevelt to Milton Eisenhower, October 1953.
76. WHO OSS, Box 1, 25 Sept. 1953.
77. B. J. Bernstein, "Foreign Policy in the Eisenhower Administration," *Foreign Service Journal,* May 1973, p. 17.
78. Cook, *Declassified Eisenhower,* p. 150.
79. R. D. Challoner and J. M. Fenton, "The Past Comes Alive in Dulles 'Oral History,'" *University,* Spring 1967, p. 32.
80. AWF AS, Box 16, Eisenhower to Gruenther, 22 Dec. 1954.
81. Hughes, *Ordeal,* p. 104.
82. PPP, 1953, p. 182.
83. The phrase was that of C. D. Jackson, a seasoned psychological warrior: WH OSS, Box 1, 10 July 1953.
84. WHO LMS, 2 Mar. 1953.

85. Hughes, *Ordeal,* p. 105.
86. PPP, 1953, p. 549.
87. I. F. Stone, *The Haunted Fifties* (London, 1963), p. 8.
88. Pre PP, Eisenhower to Harriman, 20 Apr. 1951.
89. W. Colby and P. Forbath, *Honorable Men: My Life in the C.I.A.* (London, 1978), p. 115.
90. M. G. Kalb, "The C.I.A. and Lumumba," *New York Times Magazine,* 2 Aug. 1981, pp. 44–46.
91. Cook, *Declassified Eisenhower,* p. 177.
92. OH, L. Henderson, 14 Dec. 1970, p. 14.
93. London *Times,* 27 May 1985.
94. Eisenhower, *Mandate,* p. 163.
95. K. Roosevelt, *Countercoup: The Struggle for the Control of Iran* (1979), p. 210.
96. C. Andrew, *Secret Service* (London, 1985), p. 494.
97. PPP, 1953, p. 821.
98. Lyon, *Eisenhower,* p. 584.
99. Ferrell, *Eisenhower Diaries,* pp. 223–24.
100. Larson, *Eisenhower,* p. 16.
101. AWF DDE DS, Box 4, Eisenhower to Hazlett, 24 Dec. 1953.
102. OH, J. C. Hagerty, p. 207.
103. T. F. Soapes, "A Cold Warrior Seeks Peace: Eisenhower's Strategy for Nuclear Disarmament," *Diplomatic History* 4 (Winter 1980): 70.
104. AWF DS, Box 3, 11 Aug. 1954.
105. AWF DS, Box 6, 1 June 1955.
106. Goldman, *Crucial Decade,* p. 243.
107. WHO LMS, 23 Mar. 1953.
108. WHO OSS, Box 1, 30 Oct. 1953.
109. WHO OSS, Box 1, 15 Jan. 1954.
110. Adams, *Firsthand Report,* p. 32.
111. Neal, *Eisenhowers,* p. 324.
112. WHO LMS, 16 Mar. 1953.
113. WHO OSS, Box 1, 8 May 1953.
114. BSD, 20 July 1953, p. 1063.
115. AWF DDE DS, Box 4, Eisenhower to Brownell (telephone call), 23 June 1953.
116. Manchester, *Glory and Dream,* p. 674.
117. AWF DS, Box 3, Eisenhower to Montgomery, 24 Nov. 1954.
118. BSD, Diary, p. 1904.
119. Gray, *Eighteen Acres,* p. 112.
120. Hughes, *Ordeal,* p. 150.
121. AWF DS, Box 7, 11 Nov. 1956 and 2 Nov. 1959.
122. BSD, 11 Nov. 1955, p. 2088.
123. BSD, 10 July 1953, p. 1015.
124. AWF DS, Box 10, 25 June 1958.
125. AWF DS, Box 10, 8 May 1956.
126. Lyon, *Eisenhower,* p. 511.
127. J. B. West, *Upstairs at the White House: My Life with the First Ladies* (1973), p. 178.
128. WHO OSS, Box 1, 6 Feb. 1953.

129. LCAP, Box 16, J. Alsop, 20 July 1960.
130. BSD, p. 617.
131. Ferrell, *Eisenhower Diaries*, p. 267.
132. AWF DS, Box 4, 25 May 1955.
133. AWF NS, Box 27, Eisenhower to Richardson, 8 Aug. 1953.
134. *Time*, 29 June 1953.
135. AWF AS, Box 34, Dillon to Dulles, 15 May 1953.
136. DP TCS, Box 10, Eisenhower to Dulles, 23 June 1953.
137. PPP, 1953, p. 802.
138. WHO OSS, Box 1, 15 Jan. 1954.
139. Branyan and Larsen, *Eisenhower Administration*, I, p. 207.
140. AWF DDE DS, Box 3, 9 Sept. 1953.
141. AWF DDE DS, Lodge to Eisenhower, 15 Oct. 1953.
142. Reeves, *Life and Times*, p. 587.

Chapter 14: The Dawn of Tranquillity

1. AWF DDE DS, Box 4, 3 Dec. 1953.
2. AWF DS, Box 2, Eisenhower to Churchill, 25 June 1954.
3. Ferrell, *Diary of Hagerty*, p. 61.
4. BSD, 11 June 1953, p. 1586.
5. Ferrell, *Diary of Hagerty*, p. 43.
6. L. L. Strauss, *Men and Decisions* (London, 1963), p. 268.
7. LCAP, Box 11, J. Alsop to F. Wisner, 2 Sept. 1954; and Box 10, J. Alsop to G. Gray, 10 June 1954.
8. PPP, 1954, p. 435.
9. LCAP, Box 10, J. Alsop to J. F. Dulles, 27 Feb. 1954.
10. DP TCS, Box 10, Dulles to Hagerty, 4 Nov. 1954.
11. WHO OSS, Box 2, 19 Nov. 1954.
12. D. Halberstam, *The Best and the Brightest* (London, 1972), p. 103.
13. J. G. Adams, *Without Precedent: The Story of the Death of McCarthyism* (1983), p. 109.
14. Ibid., pp. 127, 138–39.
15. AWF DDE DS, Box 5, 25 Feb. 1954.
16. Ferrell, *Diary of Hagerty*, pp. 20–21.
17. PPP, 1954, p. 291.
18. Reeves, *Life and Times*, p. 558.
19. BSD, 5 Apr. 1954, p. 1500.
20. AWF AS, Box 24, Lodge to Eisenhower, 6 Mar. 1954.
21. Goldman, *Crucial Decade*, p. 272.
22. AWF DDE DS, Box 6, Eisenhower to Hazlett, 27 Apr. 1954.
23. Ferrell, *Eisenhower Diaries*, p. 281.
24. PPP, 1954, p. 438.
25. PPP, p. 490.
26. PPP, pp. 483–84.
27. A. M. Schlesinger, Jr., *The Imperial Presidency* (London, 1954), p. 157.
28. Ferrell, *Diary of Hagerty*, p. 59.
29. AWF DS, Box 2, 10 May 1954.
30. AWF DS, Box 2, 29 May 1954.

31. AWF DS, Box 2, Eisenhower to Joe Morris, 11 Aug. 1954.
32. NYT, 10 June 1954.
33. WHO OSS, Box 2, 20 Jan. 1954.
34. S. Lubell, *The Revolt of the Moderates* (1956), p. 4.
35. J. B. West, *Upstairs at the White House: My Life with the First Ladies* (1973), p. 130.
36. Lubell, *Revolt of Moderates,* pp. 4–5.
37. OH, E. F. Morrow, 23 Feb. 1977, pp. 19, 22, 17.
38. Donovan, *Eisenhower,* 156.
39. AWF NS, Box 3, Eisenhower to Byrnes, 3 Aug. 1953.
40. AWF DS, Box 8, Eisenhower to W. Graham, 21 Mar. 1956.
41. OH, E. F. Morrow, p. 18.
42. Washington *Post,* 22 Apr. 1955.
43. Lyon, *Eisenhower,* p. 560.
44. Sulzberger, *Long Row of Candles,* p. 566.
45. Larson, *Eisenhower,* p. 138.
46. E. Warren, *The Memoirs of Earl Warren* (1977), p. 291.
47. AWF NS, Box 2, Eisenhower to Milton Eisenhower, 9 Oct. 1953.
48. Warren, *Memoirs,* p. 5.
49. AWF DDE DS, Box 5, Eisenhower to Brownell, 25 June 1954.
50. AWF DDE DS, Box 8, Eisenhower to Edgar Eisenhower, 8 Nov. 1954.
51. AWF NS, Box 16, Eisenhower to Graham, 22 Mar. 1956.
52. AWF DS, Box 8, 14 Aug. 1956.
53. AWF DDE DS, Box 18, 5 Oct. 1956.
54. OH, Morrow, p. 12.
55. J. W. Anderson, *Eisenhower, Brownell, and the Congress* (Montgomery, Ala., 1964). p. 22.
56. Ibid., pp. 22–23.
57. Morrow, *Black Man,* p. 130.
58. M. S. Katz, "E. Frederick Morrow and Civil Rights in the Eisenhower Administration," *Phylon,* June 1981, p. 134.
59. J. D. Weaver, *Warren: The Man, The Court, The Era* (London, 1968), p. 342.
60. Warren, *Memoirs,* p. 291.
61. Ferrell, *Eisenhower Diaries,* p. 233.
62. AWF DDE DS, Box 4, 11 Jan. 1954.
63. Branyan and Larsen, *Eisenhower Administration,* I, p. 308.
64. OH, R. Rovere, 22 Feb. 1968, pp. 28, 38.
65. Reeves, *Life and Times,* p. 665.
66. Hughes, *Ordeal,* p. 150.
67. AWF DHS, Box 1, 1 Apr. 1953.
68. AWF DDE DS, Box 5, Eisenhower to Brownell, 29 Jan. 1954.
69. DP WHMS, Box 4, 9 May 1956.
70. Parmet, *Eisenhower,* p. 363.
71. S. Schlesinger, "How Dulles Worked the Coup d'Etat," *Nation,* 28 Oct. 1978, p. 439.
72. R. H. Immerman, *The CIA in Guatemala* (Austin, Tex., 1982), p. 183.
73. Cook, *Declassified Eisenhower,* p. 221.
74. DP TCS, Box 10, J. F. Dulles to R. Cutler, 26 May 1954.
75. Cook, *Declassified Eisenhower,* p. 228.

76. R. H. Immerman, "Guatemala as Cold War History," *Political Science Quarterly* 95 (Winter 1980–81): 636–37.
77. Branyan and Larsen, *Eisenhower Administration,* I, p. 309.
78. AWF DDE DS, Box 7, 24 June 1954.
79. WHO OSS, Box 3, 11 Mar. 1955.
80. WHO OSS, Box 2, 5 Mar. 1954.
81. S. Schlesinger and S. Kinzer, *Bitter Fruit* (London, 1982), p. 141.
82. Eisenhower, *Mandate,* p. 426.
83. Immerman, *CIA in Guatemala,* p. 16.
84. Schlesinger and Kinzer, *Bitter Fruit,* p. 255.
85. *The Pentagon Papers as Published by the New York Times* (London, 1971), p. 9.
86. Pre PP, Eisenhower to Harriman, 6 Sept. 1951.
87. AWF DHS, Box 2, Operations Coordinating Board Memorandum.
88. AWF DDE DS, Box 7, Eisenhower to Gruenther, 8 June 1954.
89. AWF DHS, Box 2, Operations Coordinating Board Memorandum.
90. Ferrell, *Diary of Hagerty,* p. 35.
91. AWF DDE DS, Eisenhower to Gruenther, 26 Apr. 1954.
92. Eisenhower, *Mandate,* p. 364.
93. AWF DDE DS, Eisenhower to Gruenther, 26 Apr. 1954.
94. E. Hammer, *The Struggle for Indochina, 1940–55* (Stanford, 1966), p. 319.
95. M. B. Ridgway, *Soldier: The Memoirs of Matthew B. Ridgway* (1956), p. 277.
96. A. L. A. Patti, *Why Viet Nam?* (Berkeley, Calif., 1980), p. 428.
97. Washington *Post,* 22 Aug. 1982.
98. AWF DDE DS, Box 6, Eisenhower to Dulles, 23 Apr. 1954.
99. AWF DDE DS, Box 6, Dulles memorandum, 23 Apr. 1954.
100. AWF DDE DS, Box 7, 21 June 1954.
101. AWF DHS, Box 2, 25 Apr. 1954.
102. L. H. Gelb and R. K. Betts, *The Irony of Vietnam: The System Worked* (Brookings Institute, Washington, D.C., 1979), p. 56.
103. Ambrose, *Eisenhower,* II, p. 177.
104. M. Gravel, ed., *The Pentagon Papers,* I (Boston, 1971), p. 103.
105. Ferrell, *Diary of Hagerty,* p. 39.
106. Divine, *Eisenhower and Cold War,* p. 51.
107. Washington *Post,* 22 Aug. 1984.
108. PPP, 1954, pp. 915, 917.
109. Ambrose, *Eisenhower,* II, p. 184.
110. AWF DDE DS, Box 4, Eisenhower to Gruenther, 26 Apr. 1954.
111. AWF DHS, Box 2, 25 Apr. 1954.
112. Eisenhower, *Mandate,* p. 372.
113. G. C. Herring, *America's Longest War: The United States and Vietnam, 1950–1975* (1979), p. 72.
114. B. W. Tuchman, *The March of Folly* (London, 1984), p. 303.
115. BSD, July 1953, p. 1004.
116. AWF DS, Box 8, Eisenhower to Edgar Eisenhower, 8 Nov. 1954.
117. AWF DS, Box 3, 15 and 24 Nov. 1954.
118. Eisenhower, *Mandate,* p. 301.
119. Gray, *Eighteen Acres,* p. 147.
120. AWF DDE DS, Box 9, Eisenhower to Dewey, 8 Oct. 1954.
121. Eisenhower, *Mandate,* p. 432.

122. Adams, *First-Hand Report,* p. 140.
123. AWF DS, Box 2, 29 June 1954.
124. AWF DDE DS, Box 8, Eisenhower to Hazlett, 23 Oct. 1954.
125. Ambrose, *Eisenhower,* II, p. 223.
126. Nixon, *Memoirs,* p. 159.
127. Manchester, *Glory and Dream,* p. 693.
128. Donovan, *Eisenhower,* p. 312.
129. Ferrell, *Eisenhower Diaries,* p. 288.
130. Ferrell, *Diary of Hagerty,* p. 129.
131. AWF DS, Box 3.
132. M. S. McAuliffe, "Dwight D. Eisenhower and Wolf Ladejinsky: The Politics of the Declining Red Scare, 1954–1955," *Prologue,* Autumn 1982, p. 124.
133. PPP, 1955, p. 194.
134. Ferrell, *Diary of Hagerty,* p. 156.
135. McAuliffe in *Prologue,* p. 125.
136. Parmet, *Eisenhower,* p. 407.
137. AWF DDE DS, Box 4, Eisenhower to Hazlett, 24 Dec. 1954.
138. Ferrell, *Diary of Hagerty,* p. 100.

Chapter 15: Much Better, Thanks

1. Ewald, *Eisenhower,* p. 96.
2. A. Eden, *Full Circle* (1959), p. 332.
3. AWF DDE DS, Box 5, Eisenhower to G. Allen, 1954.
4. BSD, 9 July 1954, p. 1597; 29 July 1955, p. 2012.
5. WHO OSS, passim.
6. BSD, March 1955, p. 1830.
7. Gray, *Eighteen Acres,* p. 130.
8. BSD, 16 July 1954, p. 1610.
9. LCAP, Box 13, J. Alsop, 29 Nov. 1956.
10. Killian, *Sputnik,* p. 219.
11. AWF AS, Box 16, Eisenhower to Gruenther, 1 Feb. 1955.
12. Divine, *Eisenhower and Cold War,* pp. 55–56.
13. Eisenhower, *Mandate,* pp. 463–64.
14. M. B. Ridgway, *Soldier: The Memoirs of Matthew B. Ridgway* (1956), p. 280.
15. Hoopes, *Devil and Dulles,* p. 270.
16. F. R. Dulles, *American Policy Toward Communist China, 1949–1969* (1972), pp. 134–35.
17. AWF DDE DS, Box 9, Eisenhower to Churchill, 25 Jan. 1955.
18. Eden, *Full Circle,* p. 309.
19. AWF AS, Box 16, 8 Feb. 1955.
20. Ferrell, *Diary of Hagerty,* p. 172.
21. AWF DDE DS, Box 9, Eisenhower to Churchill, 25 Jan. 1955.
22. Eden, *Full Circle,* pp. 309–10.
23. AWF AS, Box 16, Eisenhower to Gruenther, 1 Feb. 1955.
24. Ferrell, *Diary of Hagerty,* p. 174.
25. AWF AS, Box 16, Eisenhower to Gruenther, 1 Feb. 1955.
26. AWF DHS, Box 3, 25 Feb. 1955.
27. DP WHMS, 7 Mar. 1955.

28. PPP, 1955, pp. 332–33.
29. Eisenhower, *Mandate,* p. 478.
30. See, for an early example, G. Wills, *Nixon Agonistes* (Boston, 1969), p. 123; and for a later one, Greenstein, *Hidden-Hand Presidency,* p. 69.
31. Divine, *Eisenhower and Cold War,* p. 66.
32. Ambrose, *Eisenhower,* II, p. 245.
33. DP WHMS, 17 Apr. 1955.
34. AWF DDE DS, Box 9, 11 Mar. 1955.
35. BSD, 18 Mar. 1955, p. 1826.
36. Eisenhower, *Mandate,* p. 481.
37. DP WHMS, 4 Apr. 1955.
38. Dulles, *American Policy,* pp. 164–65.
39. PPP, 1955, pp. 428, 425.
40. DP WHMS, 11 Mar. 1955.
41. Hughes, *Ordeal,* p. 208.
42. Ibid., p. 151.
43. AWF DS, Box 2, 26 June 1954.
44. AWF DS, Box 10, 26 Dec. 1960.
45. AWF DHS, Box 2, 23 May 1954.
46. PPP, 1955, p. 676.
47. Divine, *Eisenhower and Cold War,* p. 106.
48. AWF DHS, Box 5, 9 Nov. 1955.
49. PPP, 1955, p. 703.
50. Parmet, *Eisenhower,* p. 404.
51. AWF DHS, Box 14, 11 July 1955.
52. DP TCS, Box 10, 29 July 1955.
53. Eisenhower, *Mandate,* p. 514.
54. H. Macmillan, *Tides of Fortune* (London, 1969), pp. 616–17.
55. Eisenhower, *Mandate,* p. 518.
56. S. Talbott, *Khrushchev Remembers,* II (London, 1974), pp. 397–98.
57. OH, D. D. Eisenhower on J. F. Dulles.
58. C. E. Bohlen, *Witness to History 1929–1969* (1973), p. 384.
59. OH, Eisenhower on Dulles.
60. WHO OSS, Box 3, 22 July 1953.
61. Eisenhower, *Mandate,* p. 519.
62. OH, A. J. Goodpaster, 26 June 1975, p. 86.
63. PPP, 1955, p. 725.
64. Eden, *Full Circle,* p. 310.
65. DP TCS, Box 10, Adams to Dulles, 28 July 1955.
66. PPP, 1955, p. 725.
67. DP TCS, Box 10, 11 Aug. 1955.
68. DP TCS, Box 10, 4 Aug. 1955.
69. AWF DHS, Box 4, 22 Jan. 1956.
70. AWF DHS, Box 4, 23 Jan. 1956.
71. LCAP, Box 16, J. K. Galbraith to J. Alsop, 10 Oct. 1960.
72. J. L. Finkle, *The President Makes a Decision: A Study of Dixon Yates* (Ann Arbor, 1960), p. 159.
73. Donovan, *Eisenhower,* p. 336.
74. PPP, 1955, p. 653.

75. AWF NS, Box 15, Eisenhower to L. Finder, 15 July 1955.
76. Branyan and Larsen, *Eisenhower Administration,* I, p. 431.
77. WHO OSS, Box 3, 1 Apr. 1955.
78. OH, Adams, p. 229.
79. W. H. Chafe and H. Sitkoff, *A History of Our Time* (1983), p. 90.
80. BSD, p. 2004.
81. Washington *Star,* 24 Sept. 1955.
82. Donovan, *Eisenhower,* p. 366.
83. P. Brendon, "For Shame, Gentlemen," *Columbia Journalism Review,* March–April 1984, p. 53.
84. DP WHMS, Dulles to Eisenhower, 11 Oct. 1955.
85. WHO OSS, Box 3, 7 Oct. 1955.
86. Nixon, *Memoirs,* p. 168.
87. AWF DDE DS, Box 9, 13 Mar. 1956.
88. T. Morgan, *FDR* (1985), p. 352.
89. Nixon, *Six Crises,* p. 161.
90. AWF DS, Box 8, 9 Apr. and 13 Mar. 1956.
91. BSD, 10 Sept. 1955, p. 2042.
92. AWF NS, Box 2, Eisenhower to M. Eisenhower, 12 Sept. 1955.
93. AWF DS, Box 8, 11 Jan. and 9 Feb. 1956.
94. AWF NS, Box 18, Eisenhower to Hazlett, 2 Mar. 1956.
95. AWF DDE DS, Box 11, Eisenhower to Hazlett, 15 Aug. 1955.
96. Donovan, *Eisenhower,* p. 405.

Chapter 16: Three Spectaculars

1. Alexander, *Holding the Line,* p. 164.
2. AWF DDE DS, Box 11, 18 Apr. 1956.
3. E. B. Geelhoed, *Charles E. Wilson and Controversy at the Pentagon 1953–1957* (Detroit, 1979), p. 182.
4. AWF DS, Box 8, 29 Mar. 1956.
5. AWF DS, Box 8, 25 Apr. 1956.
6. DP TCS, Box 10, 18 May 1955.
7. WHO OSS CS, Box 3, 9 Mar. 1956.
8. WHO OSS CS, Box 3, 23 Mar. 1956.
9. PPP, 1956, pp. 335–36.
10. WHO OSS CS, Box 3, 23 Mar. 1956.
11. AWF DS, Box 7, 10 July 1956.
12. J. W. Anderson, *Eisenhower, Brownell, and the Congress* (Montgomery, Ala., 1964), p. 46.
13. AWF DS, Box 10, 19 Aug. 1956.
14. I. F. Stone, *The Haunted Fifties* (London, 1963), p. 111.
15. AWF DS, 8 June and 20 July 1956.
16. R. E. Neustadt, *Presidential Power* (1960), p. 98.
17. R. M. Jennings, "Dramatic License in Political Broadcasts," *Journal of Broadcasting* 12 (Summer 1968): 241.
18. *Time,* 6 Jan. 1958.
19. Washington *Post,* 11 Oct. 1956.
20. Augusta *Chronicle,* 11 April 1956.

21. BSD, p. 2223.
22. AWF DS, Box 7, 30 Jan. 1957.
23. DP TCS, Box 11, 7 Dec. 1956.
24. BSD, pp. 2232, 2221.
25. PPP, 1956, p. 625.
26. Richardson, *Presidency of Eisenhower,* p. 92.
27. J. K. Galbraith, *The Affluent Society* (Harmondsworth, 1965 ed.), p. 219.
28. G. E. Meyer, *Egypt and the United States* (Cranbury, N.J., 1980), pp. 80, 161.
29. DP TCS, Box 11, 28 and 29 Nov. 1955.
30. Ferrell, *Eisenhower Diaries,* p. 319.
31. DP WHMS, Box 4, 26 Apr. and 9 May 1956.
32. DP TCS, Box 12, 15 May 1957.
33. K. Love, *Suez: The Twice-Fought War* (1969), pp. 321, 334.
34. DP TCS, Box 11, 7 Sept. 1956.
35. AWF DS, Box 8, 11 Aug. 1956.
36. Eden, *Full Circle,* p. 428.
37. AWF DDE DS, Box 11, 16 Dec. 1955.
38. AWF DDE DS, Box 15, 31 July 1956.
39. Eden, *Full Circle,* p. 437.
40. AWF DHS, Box 5, 2 Aug. 1956.
41. C. L. Cooper, *The Lion's Last Roar: Suez, 1956* (1978), p. 149.
42. AWF DHS, Box 4, 31 Aug. 1956.
43. Eisenhower, *Waging Peace,* p. 664.
44. AWF DHS, Box 4, 31 Aug. 1956.
45. WHO OSS, Box 3, 3 Aug. 1956.
46. *End of Empire: Egypt,* British Channel 4 TV program, 3 June 1985.
47. BSD, 4 Sept. 1956, p. 2239.
48. PPP, 1956, p. 883.
49. DP TCS, Box 11, 7 Sept. 1956.
50. DP WHMS, Box 4, 24 Oct. 1956.
51. DP TCS, Box 11, 28 Oct. 1956.
52. NYT, 4 Nov. 1956.
53. AWF DDE DS, Box 20, 29 Oct. 1956.
54. AWF NS, Box 33, Tedder to Eisenhower, 30 Nov. 1956.
55. DP TCS, Box 11, 30 Oct. 1956.
56. Cooper, *Lion's Last Roar,* p. 166.
57. DP TCS, Box 11, 30 Oct. 1956.
58. Cooper, *Lion's Last Roar,* p. 171.
59. Cf. H. Finer, *Dulles over Suez* (London, 1964), p. 386; Cooper, *Lion's Last Roar,* p. 167.
60. AWF DDE DS, Box 20, 5 Nov. 1956.
61. NYT, 6 Nov. 1956.
62. AWF DDE DS, Box 15, 30 July 1956.
63. Hughes, *Ordeal,* p. 223.
64. AWF DS, Box 8, 6 Nov. 1956.
65. Ibid.
66. AWF DS, Box 8, 7 Nov. 1956.
67. AWF DDE DS, Box 2, 20 Nov. 1956.
68. Hoopes, *Devil and Dulles,* p. 405.

69. Love, *Suez,* p. 630.
70. OH, Eisenhower on Dulles, quoted in Love, *Suez,* p. 387.
71. Cooper, *Lion's Last Roar,* p. 181.
72. DP WHMS, 21 Dec. 1955.
73. Finer, *Dulles over Suez,* p. 446.
74. AWF DDE DS, Box 20, 6 Nov. 1956.
75. Hughes, *Ordeal,* p. 217.
76. Finer, *Dulles over Suez,* p. 374.
77. AWF DDE DS, Box 25, Eisenhower to Gruenther, 2 Nov. 1956.
78. I. McDonald, *The History of the Times,* vol. V, *Struggles in War and Peace, 1939–1966* (London, 1984), p. 268.
79. AWF DDE DS, Box 19, 27 Oct. 1956.
80. Hoopes, *Devil and Dulles,* p. 373.
81. PPP, 1956, p. 1060.
82. DP TCS, Box 11, 30 Oct. 1956.
83. DP WHMS, Box 4, 7 Nov. 1956.
84. PPP, 1956, p. 1072.
85. Eisenhower, *Waging Peace,* p. 88.
86. AWF DHS, Box 6, 9 Nov. 1956.
87. J. B. Martin, *Adlai Stevenson of Illinois* (1976), p. 340.
88. Eisenhower, *Waging Peace,* p. 13.
89. *Time,* 5 Nov. 1956.
90. NYT, 4 Nov. 1956.
91. *Time,* 12 Nov. 1956.
92. AWF AS, Box 17, Eisenhower to Gruenther, 17 Sept. 1956.
93. AWF DDE DS, Box 25, 8 Nov. 1956.
94. Hughes, *Ordeal,* pp. 227–28.

Chapter 17: Winds of Change

1. AWF DS, Box 8, 8 Nov. 1956.
2. OH, W. Aldrich, p. 11.
3. AWF DS, Box 8, 14 Dec. 1956.
4. DP WHMS, Box 4, 3 Dec. 1956.
5. AWF DS, Box 8, 21 Jan. 1957.
6. PPP, 1957, pp. 61–63.
7. AWF DS, Box 5, Eisenhower to Rockefeller, 24 May 1955.
8. WHO LMS, Box 4, 9 May 1957.
9. AWF DS, Box 9, 21 May 1957.
10. AWF DS, Box 5, 25 May 1955.
11. AWF NS, Box 33, H. Wallace to Eisenhower, 26 Nov. 1956.
12. PPP, 1957, pp. 7–8.
13. Eisenhower, *Waging Peace,* p. 178.
14. DP TCS, Box 11, 15, 24, and 25 Feb. 1957.
15. AWF DS, Box 8, 10 Jan. 1957.
16. AWF DDE DS, Box 20, 20 Nov. 1956.
17. H. Macmillan, *Riding the Storm, 1956–1959* (1971), p. 240.
18. AWF DS, Box 8, 10 Jan. 1957.
19. Macmillan, *Riding the Storm,* pp. 242, 213.

20. AWF DS, Box 8, March 1957.
21. Slater, *Ike I Knew*, p. 153.
22. I. F. Stone, *The Haunted Fifties* (London, 1963), p. 207.
23. NYT, 5 May 1957.
24. Perrett, *Dream of Greatness*, p. 554.
25. AWF DS, Box 8, 4 Feb. 1957.
26. Larson, *Eisenhower*, p. 15.
27. Hughes, *Ordeal*, p. 238.
28. NYT, 17 Jan. 1957.
29. PPP, 1957, p. 74.
30. PPP, 1957, p. 100.
31. OH, Goodpaster, 10 Apr. 1982, p. 35.
32. W. H. Chafe and H. Sitkoff, *A History of Our Time* (1983), p. 83.
33. DP TCS, Box 11, 21 May 1957.
34. PPP, 1957, pp. 174–75.
35. PPP, 1957, p. 214.
36. NYT, 31 Mar. 1957.
37. PPP, 1957, p. 343.
38. Eisenhower, *Waging Peace*, p. 146.
39. AWF DS, Box 9, 2 Feb. 1959.
40. D. Kearns, *Lyndon Johnson and the American Dream* (London, 1976), p. 150.
41. PPP, 1957, p. 131.
42. A. Steinberg, *Sam Johnson's Boy* (1968), p. 470.
43. AWF NS, Box 18, Eisenhower to Hazlett, 22 July 1957.
44. PPP, 1957, p. 521.
45. Morrow, *Black Man*, p. 119.
46. AWF DDE DS, Box 26, Eisenhower to R. Woodruff, 6 Aug. 1957.
47. Steinberg, *Sam Johnson's Boy*, p. 474.
48. AWF DDE DS, Box 26, 21 Aug. 1957.
49. Eisenhower, *Waging Peace*, p. 154.
50. NYT, 13 Aug. 1957.
51. PPP, 1957, p. 546.
52. PPP, 1957, pp. 641, 646.
53. *Time*, 16 Sept. 1957.
54. NYT, 20 Oct. 1957.
55. *Time*, 16 Sept. 1957.
56. Ferrell, *Eisenhower Diaries*, p. 347.
57. PPP, 1957, p. 674.
58. PPP, 1957, p. 689.
59. *Time*, 7 Oct. 1957.
60. AWF DS, Box 7, 24 Sept. 1957.
61. PPP, 1957, p. 692.
62. AWF DDE DS, Box 28, 2 Oct. 1957.
63. A. Lewis, *The Second American Revolution* (London, 1966), p. 55.
64. AWF DDE DS, Box 27, 3 Oct. 1957.
65. C. S. King, *My Life with Martin Luther King, Jr.* (London, 1969), pp. 175–76.
66. Ferrell, *Eisenhower Diaries*, p. 319.
67. *Time*, 14 Oct. 1957.
68. *Time*, 28 Oct. 1957.

69. W. E. Leuchtenberg, *A Troubled Feast: American Society since 1945* (Boston, Mass., 1979), p. 108.
70. AWF NS, Box 29, Robinson to Eisenhower, 30 Dec. 1957.
71. NYT, 13 Oct. 1957.
72. *Time,* 7 Oct. 1957.
73. NYT, 1 Oct. 1957.
74. *Time,* 21 Oct. 1957.
75. B. Mooney, *LBJ: An Irreverent Chronicle* (1976), p. 100.
76. *Time,* 28 Oct. 1957.
77. PPP, 1957, pp. 723, 729, 727.
78. *Time,* 28 Oct. 1957.
79. Eisenhower, *Waging Peace,* p. 211.
80. NYT, 13 Oct. 1957.
81. WHO OSS, Box 3, 18 Oct. 1957.
82. *Time,* 28 Oct. 1957.
83. PPP, 1957, p. 793.
84. AWF DDE DS, Box 27, 29 Oct. 1957.
85. WHO OSS CS, Box 3, 24 Jan. 1958.
86. AWF DDE DS, Box 30, 4 Feb. 1958.
87. Manchester, *Glory and Dream,* p. 796.
88. Killian, *Sputnik,* p. 221.
89. AWF DDE DS, Box 28, 6 Nov. 1957.
90. DP WHMS, Box 5, 26 Dec. 1957.
91. AWF DDE DS, Box 28, 6 Nov. 1957.
92. Alexander, *Holding the Line,* p. 213.
93. Killian, *Sputnik,* p. 219.
94. AWF DDE DS, Box 30, 28 Feb. 1958.
95. Eisenhower, *Waging Peace,* p. 207.
96. AWF DDE DS, Box 25, 20 Dec. 1956.
97. AWF DDE DS, Box 45, 20 Jan. 1960.
98. AWF DDE DS, Box 30, 28 Jan. 1958.
99. AWF DS, Box 9, 15 Jan. 1958.
100. Macmillan, *Riding the Storm,* p. 321.
101. Eisenhower, *Waging Peace,* p. 228.
102. DP WHMS, Box 5, 1 Dec. 1957.
103. J. Tebbel and S. M. Watts, *The Press and the Presidency: From George Washington to Ronald Reagan* (1985), p. 475.

Chapter 18: Worst Year

1. *Time,* 3 Mar. 1958.
2. Killian, *Sputnik,* p. 234.
3. *Time,* 13 Jan. 1958.
4. WHO OSS, Box 3, 3 Jan. 1958.
5. AWF DS, Box 9, 12 Mar. 1958.
6. AWF DS, Box 9, 13 Mar. 1958.
7. AWF DHS, Box 6, 7 Mar. 1958.
8. OH, G. V. Allen, p. 128.
9. *Time,* 13 Jan. 1958.

10. AWF DS, Box 7, 10 Oct. 1955.
11. NYT, 15 Jan. 1958.
12. DP WHMS, Box 5, 19 Mar. 1958.
13. PPP, 1958, pp. 265, 262.
14. DP WHMS, Box 5, 12 Aug. 1958.
15. *Time,* 10 Mar. 1958.
16. PPP, 1958, p. 358.
17. Ewald, *Eisenhower,* p. 226.
18. DP WHMS, Box 5, 13 May 1958.
19. AWF DDE DS, Box 35, 14 July 1958.
20. R. Cutler, *No Time for Rest* (Boston, 1966), pp. 363–64.
21. AWF DS, Box 10, 14 July 1958.
22. H. Macmillan, *Riding the Storm, 1956–1959* (1971), p. 513.
23. Eisenhower, *Waging Peace,* p. 273.
24. AWF DDE DS, Box 35, 14 July 1958.
25. AWF DDE DS, Box 35, 15 July 1958.
26. PPP, 1958, pp. 554–55.
27. Eisenhower, *Waging Peace,* p. 266.
28. DP WHMS, Box 8, August 1958.
29. AWF DDE DS, Box 35, 15 July 1958.
30. AWF DDE DS, Box 35, 14 July 1958.
31. C. W. Thayer, *Diplomat* (London, 1960), p. 69.
32. WHO OSS, Box 3, 18 July 1958.
33. Murphy, *Diplomat Among Warriors,* p. 398.
34. AWF DDE DS, Box 35, 14 July 1958.
35. *Time,* 27 Jan. 1958.
36. Hughes, *Ordeal,* p. 194.
37. PPP, 1958, p. 479.
38. NYT, 13 July 1958.
39. AWF DDE DS, Box 35, 14 July 1958.
40. D. Gilmour, *Lebanon: The Fractured Country* (Oxford, 1983), p. 32.
41. D. C. Watt, *Succeeding John Bull,* p. 134.
42. PPP, 1958, p. 479.
43. *Time,* 23 June 1958.
44. AWF DDE DS, Box 35, 7 July 1958.
45. NYT, 13 July 1958.
46. Minneapolis *Morning Tribune*, 13 July 1958.
47. NYT, 13 July 1958.
48. AWF DDE DS, Box 35, 7 July 1958.
49. *Time*, 30 July 1958.
50. AWF DS, Box 10, 4 Sept. 1958.
51. *Time,* 29 Sept. 1958.
52. AWF DS, Box 9, 17 Sept. 1958.
53. Neal, *Eisenhowers,* pp. 396–97.
54. Morrow, *Black Man,* p. 195.
55. AWF DS, Box 10, 2 Feb. 1959.
56. NYT, 22 June 1958.
57. AWF DS, Box 10, 5 Mar. 1959.
58. LCAP, Box 16, J. Alsop to Anthony Head, 22 June 1960.

59. AWF DS, Box 10, 30 July 1959.
60. AWF DS, Box 10, 9–15 Aug. 1959.
61. DP WHMS, Box 7, 12 Aug. 1958.
62. AWF DDE DS, Box 35, 25 Aug. 1958. Ike said that they had been "worth defending" as "outposts" in 1954, having evidently forgotten that even then he had considered them to be of psychological rather than military importance.
63. DP WHMS, Box 7, Dulles to Macmillan, 4 Sept. 1958.
64. PPP, 1958, p. 642.
65. AWF DDE DS, Box 35, 25 Aug. 1958.
66. PPP, 1958, p. 697.
67. Macmillan, *Riding the Storm,* pp. 545–46.
68. AWF NS, Box 12, Milton Eisenhower to Eisenhower, 6 June 1958.
69. DP WHMS, 23 Sept. 1958.
70. Quoted in *Time,* 13 Oct. 1958.
71. Eisenhower, *Waging Peace,* p. 304.
72. *Time,* 29 Sept. 1958.
73. Kistiakowsky, *Scientist,* p. xlvi.
74. *Time,* 24 Nov. 1958.
75. Ambrose, *Eisenhower,* II, pp. 493–94.
76. DP WHMS, Box 7, 29 Sept. 1958.
77. AWF DDE DS, Box 35, Eisenhower to C. S. Jones, 22 Aug. 1958.
78. *Time,* 27 Oct. 1958.
79. PPP, 1958, p. 760.
80. AWF DDE DS, Box 37, 5 Nov. 1958.
81. Quoted by *Time,* 17 Nov. 1958.
82. *Commentary,* November 1958.

Chapter 19: The "New Eisenhower"

1. AWF DDE DS, Box 39, 10 Mar. 1959.
2. WHO OSS, Box 3, 27 Feb. 1959.
3. AWF DDE DS, Box 41, 19 May 1959.
4. AWF DDE DS, Box 39, 9 Mar. 1959.
5. AWF DDE DS, 26 Mar. 1959.
6. J. M. Schick, *The Berlin Crisis* (Philadelphia, 1971), p. 52.
7. AWF DDE DS, Box 42, 9 June 1959.
8. H. Macmillan, *Riding the Storm 1956–1959* (1971), p. 646.
9. Ewald, *Eisenhower,* p. 170.
10. Macmillan, *Riding the Storm,* pp. 645, 649.
11. AWF DDE DS, Box 7, 23 July 1953.
12. AWF DDE DS, Box 41, 4 May 1959.
13. AWF DS, Box 10, 14 and 18 Feb. 1959.
14. *Time,* 27 Apr. 1959.
15. AWF DDE DS, Box 41, 19 May 1959.
16. AWF DDE DS, 26 May 1959.
17. AWF DHS, Box 9, 24 June 1959.
18. AWF DDE DS, Box 39, 26 Mar. 1959.
19. Eisenhower, *Waging Peace,* p. 407.
20. AWF DDE DS, Box 43, 22 July 1959.

21. *Time,* 15 June 1959.
22. Quoted by *Time,* 4 May 1959.
23. AWF DDE DS, Box 43, 22 July 1959.
24. *Time,* 4 May 1959.
25. AWF DDE DS, Box 42, Holmes Alexander of the McNaught Syndicate, 29–30 June 1959.
26. AWF DS, Box 10, 22 July 1959.
27. *Time,* 24 and 17 Aug. 1959.
28. NYT, 16 Aug. 1959.
29. AWF DS, Box 10, 7–15 Aug. 1959.
30. OH, C. Halleck, 26 Apr. 1977, p. 19.
31. *Time,* 20 July 1959.
32. Morrow, *Black Man,* pp. 162–63.
33. AWF DDE DS, Box 39, 3 Feb. 1959.
34. AWF DS, Box 10, 10 Nov. 1958.
35. Eisenhower, *Waging Peace,* p. 432.
36. NYT, 13 Aug. 1959.
37. AWF DS, Box 10, 1 July 1959.
38. NYT, 13 Aug. 1959.
39. PPP, 1959, p. 575.
40. PPP, 1959, p. 593.
41. *Time,* 2 Nov. 1959.
42. *Time,* 16 Nov. 1959.
43. AWF DS, Box 10, 8 and 23 July 1959.
44. NYT, 13 Aug. 1959.
45. PPP, 1959, p. 625.
46. Eisenhower, *Waging Peace,* p. 424.
47. Macmillan, *Riding the Storm,* p. 748.
48. AWF DS, Box 10, 16 Sept. 1959.
49. S. Talbott, *Khrushchev Remembers,* II (London, 1974), p. 407.
50. R. Medvedev, *Khrushchev* (Oxford, 1982), p. 146.
51. AWF DDE DS, Box 43, 5 Aug. 1959.
52. Talbott, *Khrushchev Remembers,* II, p. 376.
53. Kistiakowsky, *Scientist,* p. 86.
54. *Time,* 28 Sept. 1959.
55. Eisenhower, *Waging Peace,* p. 439.
56. Talbott, *Khrushchev Remembers,* II, p. 378.
57. Eisenhower, *Waging Peace,* pp. 432, 438.
58. AWF DS, Box 10, 16 Sept. 1959.
59. *Time,* 28 Sept. 1959.
60. AWF DDE DS, Box 44, 25 Sept. 1959.
61. AWF DDE DS, Box 43, 5 Aug. 1959.
62. Talbott, *Khrushchev Remembers,* II, p. 410.
63. AWF DDE DS, Box 44, 24 Sept. 1959.
64. Kistiakowsky, *Scientist,* p. 91.
65. OH, J. S. D. Eisenhower, 10 Mar. 1972, p. 117.
66. PPP, 1959, p. 700.
67. Talbott, *Khrushchev Remembers,* II, p. 412.
68. PPP, 1959, p. 696.

69. Talbott, *Khrushchev Remembers*, II, pp. 412–13.
70. AWF DDE DS, Box 45, 27 Nov. 1959.
71. Kistiakowsky, *Scientist*, p. 163.
72. AWF DDE DS, Box 45, 1 Dec. 1959.
73. AWF DDE DS, Box 45, 21 Oct. 1959.
74. Kistiakowsky, *Scientist*, p. 158.
75. AWF DS, Box 10, 2 Jan. 1960.
76. AWF DDE DS, Box 45, 27 Nov. 1959.
77. AWF DDE DS, Box 39, 3 Mar. 1959.
78. I.F. Stone, *The Haunted Fifties* (London, 1963), p. 289.
79. AWF DDE DS, Box 45, 6 Nov. 1959.
80. AWF DDE DS, Box 45, 5 Dec. 1959.
81. AWF DHS, Box 10, Eisenhower to Herter, 12 Dec. 1959.
82. *Time*, 21 and 28 Dec. 1959.

Chapter 20: Down from the Summit

1. AWF DS, 11 Jan. 1960.
2. Kistiakowsky, *Scientist*, pp. 213, 219.
3. AWF DDE DS, Box 28, 18 Mar. 1960.
4. PPP, 1960–61, p. 234.
5. Ibid., p. 220.
6. H. Thomas, *Cuba* (1971), pp. 1062, 1211.
7. OH, Gordon Gray, 25 June 1975, p. 27.
8. Ambrose, *Ike's Spies*, p. 295.
9. BSD, 4 Sept. 1956, p. 2239.
10. Kistiakowsky, *Scientist*, p. 331.
11. Kalb in *New York Times Magazine*, 2 Aug. 1981, p. 34.
12. OH, R. Thayer, June 1972, p. 15.
13. M. S. McAuliffe, "Commentary/Eisenhower, the President," *Journal of American History* 68 (December 1981): 626.
14. Ewald, *Eisenhower*, p. 271.
15. OH, G. Gray, p. 26.
16. OH, Goodpaster, 10 Apr. 1982, p. 39.
17. Kalb in *New York Times Magazine*, 2 Aug. 1981, pp. 44, 46.
18. Ambrose, *Eisenhower*, II, pp. 555–56.
19. AWF DHS, Box 10, 23 Apr. 1960.
20. Kistiakowsky, *Scientist*, p. 293.
21. I am grateful to Dr. Jay Winter for supplying me with these figures.
22. AWF DS, Box 10.
23. NYT, 8 May 1960.
24. D. Wise and T. B. Ross, *The U-2 Affair* (London, 1963), p. 54.
25. Lyon, *Eisenhower*, p. 808.
26. OH, Goodpaster, 11 Oct. 1977, p. 80.
27. Ambrose, *Eisenhower*, II, p. 568.
28. G. F. Kennan, *Memoirs* (London, 1972), pp. 185–86.
29. C. de Gaulle, *Memoirs of Hope* (London, 1971), p. 247.
30. NYT, 10 May 1960.
31. London *Times*, 10 May 1960.

32. PPP, 1960–61, p. 403.
33. Lyon, *Eisenhower,* p. 810.
34. NYT, 8 May 1960.
35. J. M. Schick, *The Berlin Crisis* (Philadelphia, 1971), pp. 114–15.
36. *Time,* 30 May 1960.
37. Eisenhower, *Waging Peace,* p. 550.
38. S. Talbott, *Khrushchev Remembers,* II (London, 1974), p. 447.
39. NYT, 12 May 1960.
40. NYT, 11 May 1960.
41. Kistiakowsky, *Scientist,* p. 321.
42. AWF DS, Box 10, 9 May 1960.
43. OH, G. V. Allen, p. 108.
44. T. G. Smith, ed., *Merriman Smith's Book of Presidents* (1972), p. 248.
45. OH, Harrison Salisbury, 6 Oct. 1972, p. 42.
46. H. Macmillan, *Pointing the Way* (London, 1972), pp. 215, 202.
47. *Time,* 30 May 1960.
48. Macmillan, *Pointing the Way,* p. 204.
49. AWF DDE DS, Box 50, 16 May 1960.
50. Macmillan, *Pointing the Way,* p. 205.
51. De Gaulle, *Memoirs,* p. 250.
52. AWF DDE DS, Box 50, 16 May 1960.
53. Manchester, *Glory and Dream,* p. 875.
54. AWF DS, Box 10, 24 May 1960.
55. AWF DDE DS, Box 50, 17 May 1960.
56. AWF DDE DS, Box 49, Eisenhower to W. R. Hearst, 27 May 1960.
57. NYT, 24 July 1960.
58. AWF DDE DS, Box 50, 26 May 1956.
59. *Time,* 30 May 1960.
60. Kistiakowsky, *Scientist,* pp. 374–75.
61. AWF DS, Box 10, 24 May 1960.
62. AWF DDE DS, Box 50, 16 May 1960.
63. Kistiakowsky, *Scientist,* p. 375.
64. De Gaulle, *Memoirs,* p. 243.
65. Hughes, *Ordeal,* p. 307.
66. OH, Salisbury, p. 42.
67. Eisenhower, *Waging Peace,* p. 562.
68. NYT, 15 May 1960.
69. AWF NS, Box 20, 11 June 1960.
70. PPP, 1960–61, p. 653.
71. PPP, 1960–61, p. 658.
72. Nixon, *Six Crises,* p. 327.
73. A. M. Schlesinger, Jr., *A Thousand Days* (London, 1965), p. 114.
74. Kistiakowsky, *Scientist,* p. 402.
75. T. H. White, *The Making of the President, 1960* (London, 1962), p. 200.
76. AWF DS, Box 5, 25 May 1955.
77. AWF DDE DS, Box 54, Nov. 1960.
78. White, *Making of President, 1960,* p. 310.
79. AWF DDE DS, Box 54, 9 Nov. 1960.
80. Slater, *Ike I Knew,* p. 230.

81. AWF DDE DS, Box 54, 10 Nov. 1959.
82. AWF DDE DS, Box 54, 6 Dec. 1959.
83. M. Eisenhower, *President Is Calling,* p. 512.
84. T. C. Sorensen, *Kennedy* (London, 1975), p. 231.
85. AWF DDE DS, Box 54.
86. Governor G. Mennen ("Soapy") Williams of Michigan.
87. AWF DDE DS, Box 54, Eisenhower to R. Anderson, 3 Jan. 1961.
88. Ewald, *Eisenhower,* p. 314.
89. Slater, *Ike I Knew,* p. 244.
90. Post PP AB, Box 2, Eisenhower to Allen Dulles, 23 Aug. 1965.
91. Schlesinger, *Thousand Days,* p. 114.
92. Post PP AGS, Box 11, 19 Jan. 1961.
93. P. Wyden, *Bay of Pigs* (London, 1979), p. 89.
94. Schlesinger, *Thousand Days,* p. 296.
95. AWF DDE DS, Box 54, 16 Dec. 1960.
96. AWF DDE DS, Box 54, 9 Jan. 1961.
97. AWF DDE DS, Box 54, 31 Dec. 1960.
98. AWF DDE DS, Box 54, 9 Jan. 1961.
99. PPP, 1960–61, p. 1038.
100. A. D. Litfin, "Eisenhower on the Military–Industrial Complex: Critique of a Rhetorical Strategy," *Central States Speech Journal,* 25 (1974), p. 201.
101. PPP, 1960–61, pp. 1037, 1039.
102. Lyon, *Eisenhower,* p. 825.
103. Hughes, *Ordeal,* p. 7.
104. A. M. Schlesinger, Jr., *Robert Kennedy and His Times* (London, 1978), p. 386.
105. Eisenhower, *Waging Peace,* p. 618.

Chapter 21: Death of a Statesman

1. AWF DS, Box.
2. WERP, Box 4, Eisenhower to Robinson, 1 July 1961.
3. Lyon, *Eisenhower,* p. 512.
4. Post PP PF, Box 4, Eisenhower to Churchill, 22 Apr. 1961.
5. Lyon, *Eisenhower,* p. 833.
6. *New York Review of Books,* 6 Jan. 1966.
7. NYT, 31 Oct. 1965.
8. NYT, 10 Nov. 1963.
9. P. Burnham, "Eisenhower the Man, Eisenhower the Mystique," *Commonweal,* 27 Dec. 1963, p. 408.
10. NYT, 31 Oct. 1965.
11. Post PP SNF, Box 4, Eisenhower to Nixon, 15 Jan. 1962.
12. Post PP AB, Box 2, Eisenhower to W. Paley, 21 Sept. 1964.
13. A. M. Schlesinger, Jr., *Robert Kennedy and His Times* (London, 1978), p. 386.
14. Post PP AGS, Box 10, 22 Apr. 1961.
15. Post PP AB, Box 2, Eisenhower to A. Dulles, 23 Aug. 1965.
16. Post PP AGS, Box 11, 8 Nov. 1966.
17. AWF DDE DS, Box 54, 28 Nov. 1960.
18. A. M. Schlesinger, Jr., *A Thousand Days* (London, 1965), p. 585.
19. Post PP AB, Box 2, 3 June 1964.

20. NYT, 12 July 1964.
21. Post PP AB, Box 2, Eisenhower to Scranton, August 1964.
22. Ewald, *Eisenhower,* 314.
23. Post PP AB, Box 2, 15 May 1964.
24. New York *Herald Tribune,* 25 May 1964.
25. Lyon, *Eisenhower,* p. 840.
26. Post PP AB, Box 2, 2 July 1964.
27. T. H. White, *The Making of the President, 1964* (1965), p. 70.
28. J. Tebbel and S. M. Watts, *The Press and the Presidency: From George Washington to Ronald Reagan* (1985), p. 476.
29. W. O'Neill, *Coming Apart* (Chicago, 1971), p. 111.
30. White, *Making of President, 1964,* p. 217.
31. O'Neill, *Coming Apart,* p. 111.
32. Neal, *Eisenhowers*, p. 436.
33. Post PP AB, Box 2, 12 May 1965.
34. NYT, 16 July 1964.
35. Post PP AB, Box 2, 3 Aug. 1964.
36. Post PP AB, Box 2, Eisenhower to B. Harlow, 11 Aug. 1964.
37. Post PP AB, Box 2, Eisenhower to Milton Eisenhower, 27 July 1964.
38. Post PP AB, Box 1, Eisenhower to Rockefeller, 19 Oct. 1964.
39. Post PP AB, Box 2, 12 Sept. 1964.
40. White, *Making of President, 1964,* p. 330.
41. Rovere, *Eisenhower Years,* p. 367.
42. Post PP AB, Box 2, Eisenhower to Humphrey, 4 Sept. 1964.
43. R. A. Caro, *The Path to Power* (London, 1983), pp. 156, 454.
44. Post PP AB, Box 2, Hagerty to Eisenhower, 23 Sept. 1964.
45. Post PP AB, Box 2, 14 Dec. 1964.
46. Post PP AB, Box 2, 18 Aug. 1965.
47. Post PP AGS, Box 10, 17 Feb. 1965.
48. Post PP AGS, Box 9, 3 Aug. 1965.
49. Lyon, *Eisenhower,* p. 846.
50. O'Neill, *Coming Apart,* p. 137.
51. Post PP AB, Box 2, Eisenhower to Johnson, 8 Apr. 1965.
52. Post PP AGS, Box 9, 14 Sept. 1965.
53. Post PP AGS, Box 9, 22 June 1966.
54. Post PP AGS, Box 9, 19 Sept. 1966.
55. Post PP AB, Box 3, Congressman Laird to Eisenhower, 24 Aug. 1965.
56. Post PP AB, Box 10, 18 Aug. 1965.
57. Post PP SNF, Box 8, Nixon to Eisenhower, 22 Dec. 1965.
58. Post PP SNF, Box 10, Eisenhower to Freeman Gosden, 18 Aug. 1965.
59. *CBS News Special,* 28 Nov. 1967.
60. Ambrose, *Eisenhower,* II, p. 664.
61. WERP, Box 3, Eisenhower to Robinson, 14 Jan. 1967.
62. Ferrell, *Eisenhower Diaries,* p. 391.
63. A. S. Nevins, *Gettysburg's Five-Star Farmer* (1977), p. 153.
64. Post PP AB, Box 3, 18 Jan. 1967.
65. H. Kissinger, *The White House Years* (Boston, 1979), pp. 431, 452.
66. J. S. D. Eisenhower, *Strictly Personal,* p. 336.
67. OH, J. S. D. Eisenhower, p. 115.

Bibliography

The following is a selection of the most useful books on the life and times of Dwight D. Eisenhower. Those who wish to read further can consult the detailed references in this book or the bibliographies compiled by Peter Lyon and Stephen Ambrose in the works cited below. Robert D. Bohanan's valuable monograph, *Dwight D. Eisenhower: A Selected Bibliography of Periodical and Dissertation Literature* (1981), may be obtained from the Eisenhower Library in Abilene. All the books mentioned below are published in New York unless otherwise indicated.

Acheson, D. *Present at the Creation,* 1969.
Adams, S. *Firsthand Report: The Story of the Eisenhower Administration,* 1961.
Alexander, C. C. *Holding the Line: The Eisenhower Era, 1952–1961.* Bloomington, Ind., 1975.
Ambrose, S. E. *Eisenhower,* 2 vols. 1983–84.
———. *Ike's Spies: Eisenhower and the Espionage Establishment.* 1981.
———. *The Supreme Commander: The War Years of General Dwight D. Eisenhower. 1970.*
Beschloss, M. *Mayday: Eisenhower, Khrushchev and the U-2 Affair.* 1986.
Blumenson, M. *Mark Clark.* London, 1985.
———. *The Patton Papers.* 2 vols. Boston, 1972–74.
Bradley, O., and C. Blair. *A General's Life.* London, 1983.
Brandon, D. *Mamie Doud Eisenhower.* 1954.
Branyan, R. L., and L. H. Larsen. *The Eisenhower Administration 1953–1961.* 2 vols. 1961.
Butcher, H. *My Three Years with Eisenhower.* London, 1946.
Cook, B. W. *The Declassified Eisenhower.* 1981.
Davis, K. S. *Soldier of Democracy: A Biography of Dwight D. Eisenhower.* 1945.
D'Este, C. *Decision in Normandy.* London, 1983.
Divine, R.A. *Eisenhower and the Cold War.* 1981.
Donovan, R. J. *Eisenhower: The Inside Story.* 1956.
Eisenhower, D. D. *At Ease: Stories I Tell to Friends.* 1967.
———. *Crusade in Europe.* 1948.
———. *Letters to Mamie.* Ed. J. S. D. Eisenhower. 1978.
———. *Mandate for Change.* 1963.
———. *The Papers of Dwight David Eisenhower.* Vols. 1–5, ed. A. D. Chandler, Jr., et al.; vols. 6–11, ed. L. Galambos et al. Baltimore, 1970.

————. *Public Papers of the Presidents of the United States: Dwight D. Eisenhower.* Washington, D.C., 1954–62.

————. *Waging Peace.* 1965.

Eisenhower, J. S. D. *Strictly Personal,* 1974.

Eisenhower, M. S. *The President Is Calling.* 1974.

Ewald, W. B., Jr. *Eisenhower the President.* Englewood Cliffs, N.J., 1981.

Ferrell, R. H., ed. *The Diary of James C. Hagerty.* Bloomington, Ind., 1983.

————, ed. *The Eisenhower Diaries.* 1981.

Goldman, E. F. *The Crucial Decade and After.* 1966.

Gray, R. K. *Eighteen Acres Under Glass.* 1962.

Greenstein, F. I. *The Hidden-Hand Presidency.* 1982.

Griffith, R., ed. *Ike's Letters to a Friend.* Lawrence, Ks., 1985.

Gunther, J. *Eisenhower: The Man and the Symbol.* 1952.

Hamilton, N. *Monty: Master of the Battlefield, 1942–1944.* 1983.

Hatch, A. *Red Carpet for Mamie.* 1954.

Hoopes, T. *The Devil and John Foster Dulles.* London, 1974.

Hughes, E. J. *The Ordeal of Power.* 1963.

James, D. C. *The Years of MacArthur,* vol. 1. Boston, 1970.

Killian, J. R. *Sputnik, Scientists, and Eisenhower.* Cambridge, Mass., 1977.

Kistiakowsky, G. B. *A Scientist at the White House.* Cambridge, Mass., 1976.

Kornitzer, B. *The Great American Heritage: The Story of the Five Eisenhower Brothers.* 1955.

Larson, A. *Eisenhower: The President Nobody Knew.* 1968.

Lyon, P. *Eisenhower: Portrait of the Hero.* Boston, 1974.

McCann, K. *America's Man of Destiny.* London, 1952.

Macmillan, H. *War Diaries.* London, 1983.

Manchester, W. *The Glory and the Dream.* London, 1973.

Moch, J. *Rencontres avec Darlan et Eisenhower.* Paris, 1968.

Morrow, E. F. *Black Man in the White House.* 1963.

Murphy, R. *Diplomat Among Warriors.* London, 1964.

Neal, S. *The Eisenhowers: Reluctant Dynasty.* 1978.

Neff, D. *Warriors at Suez: Eisenhower Takes America into the Middle East.* 1981.

Nixon, R. M. *Memoirs.* 1978.

————. *Six Crises.* London, 1962.

Parmet, H. S. *Eisenhower and the American Crusades.* 1972.

Perrett, G. *A Dream of Greatness.* 1979.

Pogue, F. C. *George C. Marshall.* 3 vols. to date, 1966–.

————. *The Supreme Command.* Washington, D.C., 1954.

Reeves, T.C. *The Life and Times of Joe McCarthy.* 1982.

Richardson, E. *The Presidency of Dwight D. Eisenhower.* Lawrence, Ks., 1979.

Rovere, R. H. *The Eisenhower Years.* 1956.

Slater, E. D. *The Ike I Knew.* Privately printed, 1980.

Sulzberger, C. *A Long Row of Candles.* London, 1969.

Summersby, K. *Eisenhower Was My Boss.* 1948.

————. [Morgan]. *Past Forgetting: My Love Affair with Dwight D. Eisenhower.* 1976.

Truman, H. S. *Memoirs.* 2 vols., 1955–56.

Watt, D. C. *Succeeding John Bull.* Cambridge, 1984.

Weigley, R. *Eisenhower's Lieutenants.* Bloomington, Ind., 1981.

Wilmot. C. *Struggle for Europe.* 1952.

Index

478   Index